LANDS AND PEOPLES

1 Africa
Index

2 Asia
Australia
New Zealand
Oceania
Index

3 Europe
Index

4 Europe
Index

5 North America
Index

6 Central and South America
Antarctica
Facts and Figures
Selected Readings
Index

LANDS AND PEOPLES

GROLIER   Danbury, Connecticut

EUROPE

Volume 3

CONTENTS

Europe: An Introduction   1
Europe   5
Alps   299
Austria   308
Belgium   211
Danube River   328
France   150
Germany   239
Ireland   65
Liechtenstein   305
Luxembourg   207
Monaco   204
Netherlands   237
Switzerland   285
United Kingdom   79
  England   97
  Wales   121
  Scotland   131
  Northern Ireland   142

Illustration Credits   330
Index

FLAGS OF EUROPE

IRELAND

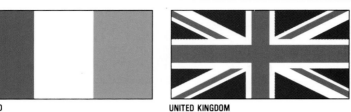

UNITED KINGDOM

FRANCE

MONACO

LUXEMBOURG

BELGIUM

NETHERLANDS

GERMANY

SWITZERLAND

LIECHTENSTEIN

AUSTRIA

This lovely resort on Lake Como, nestled in the Italian Alps, typifies the regal splendor of European scenery.

EUROPE: AN INTRODUCTION

The waning of the Cold War, the collapse of the European Communist regimes, and the introduction of a common currency called the euro in 11 West European countries closed the dramatic and eventful 20th century. The early 1990s were filled with hope for a better world. Now, a more cautious mood has set in.

The ethnic wars in Croatia and then in Bosnia and Herzegovina reminded Europeans of World War II. Thanks to the United States, the fighting stopped in 1995 after agreements were signed by the warring parties in Dayton, Ohio. Soon, however, another armed conflict erupted, this time in the Yugoslav province of Kosovo, a sacred region for Orthodox Serbs but inhabited mostly by Muslim Albanians. Farther east, the dissolution of the Soviet Union and the subsequent disintegration of its once iron-clad dominion over the region precipitated a series of ethnic clashes in Moldova in 1992–93 and later, in 1994 and 2000, a full-scale war in the Russian republic of Chechnya.

Meanwhile, Western Europe has steadfastly pursued the building of a "common European house." The last decade of the century began with the signing of the Treaty of Maastricht in December 1991 and ended with the introduction of a common European currency—the euro—on January 1, 1999. The Maastricht Treaty, establishing a common market of goods, labor, and capital among the 12 countries of the European Union (EU), was followed by the admission of three new members: Sweden, Finland, and Austria. During that same time, most former Communist European countries signed association agreements with the EU and began to prepare for their eventual entry into this organization. At least five are expected to join the EU by 2004.

The countries of Europe now fall into several groups. Fifteen Western states—Germany, France, the United Kingdom, Ireland, the Netherlands, Belgium, Luxembourg, Denmark, Sweden, Finland, Austria, Spain, Portugal, Italy, and Greece—are members of the EU. Twelve of them (not counting the United Kingdom, Sweden, and Denmark) became members of the European Monetary Union (EMU) and on January 1, 2002, replaced their national monies with the new European currency, the euro. Two island countries, Malta and Cyprus, expect to join the EU in 2004. Iceland, Norway, Liechtenstein, and Switzerland belong to the European Free Trade Association (EFTA).

Three Central European countries—Poland, the Czech Republic, and Hungary—have been in the forefront of post-Communist transformation, and are expected to join the European Union shortly after 2000. Two other small nations—Estonia in the Baltics and Slovenia, formerly the northernmost republic of Yugoslavia—will be in the same group.

The next category includes Slovakia, Romania, Bulgaria, Croatia, Macedonia, and Albania. The post-Communist developments in these countries have been much more difficult. In Slovakia, an authoritarian prime minister and his government tried to curb civil rights. In Romania and Bulgaria, economic transformation lagged for several years and gathered speed only in the late 1990s. Croatia has had to repair the damage caused by the war of 1991–92, and the other former Yugoslav republic, Macedonia, was also shaken by ethnic violence in 2001. Albania experienced repeated economic crises and, in 1998, was overwhelmed by waves of Albanian refugees from the Yugoslav province of Kosovo.

Bosnia and Herzegovina is emerging from years of war, and NATO troops are overseeing postwar reconstruction. In 1998, new fighting broke out in the Yugoslav province of Kosovo, and NATO responded by bombing Yugoslavia the following year. Kosovo subsequently became a virtual NATO protectorate. In 2001, the Serbian leader largely blamed for the bloodshed in the region, Slobodan Milošević, was extradited to the International Tribunal at the Hague. Yugoslavia then began a healing process, and changed its name to Serbia and Montenegro.

Compared to the successful Estonia, its two Baltic neighbors, Latvia and Lithuania, are lagging in economic transformation, but in other ways they have drifted far from their Communist past. Of the other former European Soviet republics, Moldova is shockingly poor, albeit peaceful.

Ukraine, slightly larger than France, seemed on the verge of economic collapse in 1993, but then rebounded. The country was united with Russia for centuries, and many people still prefer to speak Russian rather than Ukrainian. Even so, the forging of a separate national identity continues. Meanwhile, the pro-Russian president of Belarus, Alexander Lukaschenko, has turned his country into Europe's sole remaining dictatorship.

Stretching from the Baltic Sea across the whole of North Asia to the Pacific, Russia is in a category of its own. As the heir of a nuclear superpower, the country aspires to a special international status, but its economic performance remains weak. Yet Russia seems to have made a turnaround under President Vladimir Putin, who has initiated a program of thorough modernization. After the terrorist attacks on September 11, 2001, Putin also became a steadfast ally of the United States.

The collapse of Communism is receding into the past, and young people in the former Communist countries have quickly become accustomed to the new freedoms and now cannot imagine a return to the past —despite all the problems and difficulties. Yet not much more than a decade ago, the Communist empire seemed solid as a rock. Underneath, however, it was rotting. The growing internationalization of the world economy—with its computer links, telephones, and satellite communications—made it possible for citizens of the Communist countries to be in touch with the free world. The need for external trade and foreign exchange made opening to the West more and more important, which in turn led to an increasing awareness of the multiple failings of the Communist system. Economic and political pressure within the Soviet Union, combined with Western military steadfastness, finally resulted in an irresistible demand for profound change.

The tasks now facing the European nations are, in the first place, to overcome the Cold War division and to clear up old historic enmities, and also to provide new jobs, reform the social-welfare systems, and curb racial violence. All this will require a great deal of work, but it will be worth it.

Unification of Europe

The union of the nations of Europe is an ancient dream. In 1961, Swiss writer Denis de Rougemont published a book with the evocative title *Vingt-Huit Siècles d'Europe* ("Twenty-eight Centuries of Europe"). In it he quoted hundreds of authors who, in one form or another, raised and defended the idea of a union of European countries. Through the centuries, philosophers, poets, and reformers have urged the nations of Europe to unite and thus end the innumerable wars that set one nation against another. Now, after two world wars and a long Cold War, most European countries finally seem prepared to work together.

As early as the end of World War I, Aristide Briand, then French minister of foreign affairs, presented the idea of a European federation to the League of Nations. The proposal was vague, and the political climate of the time was not propitious. Communism, fascism, and Nazism were opening ever-deepening ideological chasms in Europe, and Briand's attempt had no success.

At the end of World War II in 1945, the dominant idea in the policy-making circles of Western nations was the maintenance of the alliance made with the Soviet Union. The United Nations was created to settle the problems posed by peace. In 1946, however, Winston Churchill declared in two historic speeches that the Soviet Union presented a danger to the free world, and he insisted that the countries of Western Europe unite for their defense and economic recovery.

In 1948, a congress that was to have historic importance met at The Hague. All the movements whose goal was the propagation of a united Europe were represented there. It was no longer a question of noble but vague discussions of a great idea, but rather a question of considering a boldly practical way to realize that idea. In 1949, the Council of Europe and its consultative parliamentary assembly were created. Three years later, in 1952, the Coal and Steel Community was born as the first supranational authority in Europe.

In 1955, at the Messina Conference in Sicily, the idea of a united Europe was sensationally reborn. The six governments whose countries belonged to the Coal and Steel Community—Belgium, France, West Germany, Italy, Luxembourg, and the Netherlands—decided to create among themselves an economic community that would encompass agriculture, industry, transportation, finance, currency, and politics. After years of often passionate and dramatic debate, the treaty concerning this economic revolution was signed in Rome in 1957, and the European Economic Community (EEC)—known as the European Community (EC) from 1967 on—was formed. Three additional countries—the United Kingdom, Ireland, and Denmark—formally joined the original six in 1973. Greece became a full member of the organization in 1981, and Spain and Portugal joined the group in 1986.

In the late 1980s, the EC began to prepare for a common market of goods, labor, and capital among the 12 member countries, which took effect on January 1, 1993. A milestone declaration was signed in December 1991 in Maastricht, the Netherlands, changing the name of the community to the European Union, and pledging to create a single European currency by 1999.

By January 1995, three new members had joined the EU—Austria, Sweden, and Finland. Norway also had been admitted to the EU, but Norwegian voters rejected the membership in November 1994.

Meanwhile, most post-Communist countries signed association agreements with the EU and began discussions about full membership. In early 1996, the Intergovernmental Conference began its sessions to prepare for the admission of new members. It is expected that the first to join, most likely in 2004, will be Poland, the Czech Republic, Hungary, Slovenia, and Estonia.

During the time of the Maastricht Treaty signing, Western Europe seemed excited about the approaching unity, but in the following years the enthusiasm declined somewhat. "Euroskeptics" in various countries could be heard more loudly. The European Union, with its seat in Brussels, is indeed an easy target for criticism. Its maze of regulations and red tape can seem stifling. When the "club" consisted of only a few countries, it was relatively easy to devise rules; but with 15 current members and more to join soon, rule-making has become much more difficult.

Consider the question of languages. Since the EU is an organization of equal partners, there are currently 11 official languages, and all important meetings must be simultaneously interpreted into these languages. In the mid-1990s, the EU employed more than 2,000 interpreters, who had to service more than 10,000 sessions. The written documents—more than 1 million pages annually just for the European Commission, one of the key bodies of the EU—must then be translated. All this is cumbersome and expensive. Yet many believe it is worth the cost because a unified Europe is the best safeguard of peace.

In the mid-1990s, many doubted that the proposed EMU would be introduced as planned, but the deadline was kept. On January 1, 1999, the national currencies of 11 EU members were joined by a new currency called the euro. Two years later, Greece came on with the original 11 EMU members, and on January 1, 2002, the national currencies of those 12 European countries were abolished. The transition went quite smoothly, even though the change was enormous; for instance, nearly 4 million vending machines throughout the continent had to be adapted to accommodate the new monetary unit. It is hoped that the euro will eventually develop into as strong an international currency as the U.S. dollar.

Interlaken, Switzerland, is one of Europe's scenic resorts.

EUROPE

Is Europe a continent? The answer to the question is both yes and no. The textbook definition of a continent is "one of the great divisions of land on the earth," and most continents can be easily identified on a world map or globe. Europe, however, looks like a western extension of the huge Asiatic landmass. It is, in fact, a peninsula that stretches westward from the main body of Eurasia, as the entire landmass is called. Because of Europe's enormous importance in world history, however, it has been considered a separate continent for a very long time.

The people of the ancient Middle East divided the world they knew into three parts. One division was the area in which they lived. They called the land to the east of them Asu—"land of the rising sun." The land to the west was called Ereb—"land of the setting sun." It may be that our names for Europe and Asia come from these ancient words.

Most of Europe's boundaries are clearly marked by the seas and oceans that lap its shores. And the separation from Africa and Asia, except for the Russian part, is a sharp one: the Mediterranean and its open connection with the Black Sea by way of the Dardanelles and the Bosporus.

merfest • Vardo

B A R E N T S
S e a

• Murmansk

alo •

White
Sea

• Archangel

Ural Mts.

NORTH AMERICA

GREENLAND

North | Pole

Arctic
Ocean

Novaya
Zemlya

Atlantic
Ocean

ASIA

EUROPE

mi •

• Syktyvkar

• Kotlas

AFRICA

FINLAND

• Kuopio

Lake
Onega

• Kirov

Perm •

Equator

Lake
Ladoga

• Lahti

Helsinki

Finland

allinn

• Sokol

Izhevsk •

R   U   S   S   I   A

Volga R.

Asia
Europe

TONIA

• St. Petersburg

LATVIA

• Novgorod

• Tver

Nizhni Novgorod

Kazan •

Ufa •

Asia
Europe

• Kuibyshev

HUANIA

rus

• Minsk

★ Moscow

• Roslavl

Ryazan •

• Tula

Saratov •

• Uralsk

KAZAKHSTAN

Ural R.

BELARUS

• Kursk

• Voronezh

Dnieper R.

Aral
Sea

• Lutsk

Kiev ★

• Kharkov

Don R.

• Guryev

UKRAINE

Poltava •

Donets R. • Voroshilovgrad

Volgograd •

UZBEKISTAN

Dniester R.

Dnepropetrovsk •

Garlovka •
• Makeyevka

• Zavetnoye

Astrakhan •

Krivoi Rog •
• Donetsk

MOLDOVA

Zaporozhe •

• Rostov

Caspian

osanı •

Jassy •
Chisinau ★

• Nikolayev

Sea of
Azov

• Stavropol

TURKMENISTAN

OMANIA

Odessa •

asov •

Ploesti •
Galati •

Europe   C a u c a s u s
Asia

• Grozny

Sea

Baku ★

★ Bucharest

• Yalta

40°E

GEORGIA

• Constanta

• Varna

B l a c k   S e a

AZERBAIJAN

ULGARIA

Danube R.

ARMENIA

50°E

Plovdiv •

• Bourgas

Bosporus

• Istanbul

Europe
Asia

avalla •

Dardanelles

T U R K E Y

I R A N

30°E

an Sea

rete

CYPRUS

SYRIA

IRAQ

Fishnets dry in the sun on Mykonos, a Greek island popular with tourists.

Geographers have long debated the location of Europe's eastern boundary, but most now draw the line along the Ural Mountains, the Ural River, and through the Caspian Depression to the Caspian Sea. Russia is thus divided into two parts—European Russia and Asian Russia.

A large number of islands are also part of Europe. They include Spitsbergen and Novaya Zemlya in the north, and Great Britain, Ireland, the Hebrides, Orkney Islands, Shetland Islands, Channel Islands, Isle of Man, Faeroe Islands, and Iceland in the northwest. There are many islands in the Baltic Sea. The Balearic Islands, Corsica, Sardinia, Sicily, Malta, and the Greek islands are in the Mediterranean Sea.

Including the adjacent islands and European Russia, the continent covers roughly 4,200,000 sq. mi. (10,878,000 sq. km.), the second-smallest continent after Australia. Europe's smallness is in dramatic contrast to the gigantic size of Russia, which alone covers 6,591,104 sq. mi. (17,070,959 sq. km.) and stretches from the Baltic Sea to the Bering Strait across almost 180 degrees of longitude, or about half the globe. Peninsulas, bays, islands, and fjords give Europe very irregular coastlines. As a result, the coast is quite long for the total area, about 50,000 mi. (80,500 km.).

The Nations of Europe

Today 44 nations occupy the continent of Europe, a large number for such a small area. The most northerly countries, which are called the Scandinavian nations, are Sweden, Denmark, and Norway. Finland and Iceland are sometimes included in this group, too.

Belgium, the Netherlands, and Luxembourg, which are often grouped as the Benelux nations or the lowland countries, are on the northern edge of Western Europe. France, Ireland, and the United Kingdom are also in Western Europe.

The walled city of San Marino is one of Europe's countless historic landmarks.

Italy occupies its own peninsula in Southern Europe; Spain and Portugal share the Iberian Peninsula in the southwest; and Malta occupies an island in the Mediterranean. Greece, European Turkey, Bulgaria, Albania, and most of Romania are on the Balkan Peninsula in the southeast. This peninsula is also the home of the former Federal Republic of Yugoslavia, which split into five new countries in 1991 and 1992: Slovenia, Croatia, Yugoslavia (consisting of Serbia and Montenegro), Bosnia and Herzegovina, and Macedonia. The nations of Central Europe include Switzerland, Austria, and Germany. Poland, the Czech Republic, Slovakia, and Hungary are emerging from decades of Soviet domination. Seven new republics arose in late 1991 in the European part of the former Soviet Union: the three Baltic states—Estonia, Latvia, and Lithuania—and Ukraine, Belarus, Moldova, and Russia itself. Europe also contains five tiny nations renowned for charming settings and fascinating histories. Vatican City and San Marino are located in Italy; Monaco is on the southern coast of France; Liechtenstein is tucked between Switzerland and Austria; and Andorra is set high in the Pyrenees.

EUROPE AND THE WORLD

Europe's nearness to Asia and Africa and the open sea-lanes to the Americas have made it possible for Europeans to spread ideas that have shaped and influenced the modern world. The voyages of discovery and exploration, religious missionary efforts, and colonization helped disseminate European beliefs, traditions, and languages around the globe. Three other continents—North and South America in the Western hemisphere and Australia—are inhabited largely by descendants of Europeans who speak European languages. Europeans have also greatly influenced the other two continents—Asia and Africa.

INDEX TO EUROPE MAP

Aberdeen C2
Adriatic Sea E3
Aegean Sea F4
Ajaccio D3
Aland Islands E1
Amsterdam D2
Aneto, Pico de D3
Antwerp D2
Archangel H1
Astrakhan H3
Athens F4
Azov, Sea of G3
Baku H3
Balaton, Lake E3
Balearic Islands D4
Baltic Sea E2
Barcelona D3
Barents Sea G1
Bari E3
Basel D3
Belfast C2
Belgrade F3
Beloye, Lake G1
Bergen D1
Berlin E2
Bern D3
Bilbao C3
Birmingham C2
Biscay, Bay of C3
Black Sea G3
Bologna E3
Bonn D2
Bordeaux C3
Bosporus F3
Bothnia, Gulf of F1
Bratislava E3
Bremen D2
Brno E3

Brussels D2
Bucharest F3
Budapest E3
Cagliari D4
Canea F4
Capri E3
Cardiff C2
Caspian Depression ... H3
Caspian Sea H3
Catania E4
Channel Islands C3
Chisinau F3
Chkalov J2
Cluj F3
Cologne E2
Constanta F3
Copenhagen E2
Cork C2
Cracow E2
Crete F4
Cyclades F4
Dardanelles F3
Dnepropetrovsk G3
Donetsk G3
Dresden E2
Dublin C2
Edinburgh C2
Elbrus, Mt. H3
English Channel C2
Etna, Mt. E4
Faeroe Islands C1
Finisterre, Cape C3
Finland, Gulf of F2
Florence E3
Frankfurt D2
Galdhopiggen D1
Gdansk E2

Genoa D3
Gibraltar,
    Strait of C4
Glasgow C2
Goteborg E2
Graz E3
Hague, The D2
Hamburg D2
Hammerfest F1
Hanover D2
Hebrides, Inner C2
Hebrides, Outer C2
Helsinki F1
Ilmen, Lake G2
Ionian Islands F4
Ionian Sea E4
Irish Sea C2
Istanbul F3
Ivanovo H2
Kaliningrad F2
Kattegat E2
Kazan H2
Kerch G3
Kharkov G3
Kiel E2
Kiev G2
Krasnodar G3
Krivoi Rog G3
Kuibyshev J2
Kuibyshev Reservoir .. J2
Kursk G2
Ladoga, Lake G1
Land's End C2
Lapland F1
Le Havre D3
Leipzig E2
Ligurian Sea D3
Linz E3

Lipari Islands E4
Lisbon C4
Liverpool C2
Ljubljana E3
Lodz E2
Lofoten Islands E1
London C2
Lviv F3
Lyons D3
Madrid C3
Majorca D3
Makeyevka G3
Málaga C4
Malar, Lake E2
Malmo E2
Manchester C2
Man, Isle of C2
Marmara, Sea of F3
Marroquí, Point C4
Marseilles D3
Matterhorn D3
Mediterranean Sea ... E4
Milan D3
Minsk F2
Mont Blanc D3
Moscow G2
Munich E3
Murmansk G1
Nantes C3
Naples E3
Negoi Peak F3
Nizhni Novgorod H2
Nordkyn F1
North Sea D2
Norwegian Sea D1
Ochrida, Lake F3
Odessa G3
Olympus F3

Onega, Lake G1
Oporto C3
Orkney Islands C2
Oslo E2
Padua E3
Palermo E4
Palma D4
Paris D3
Patras F4
Peipus, Lake F2
Perm (Molotov) J2
Plovdiv F3
Poltava G3
Poznan E2
Prague E2
Prespa, Lake F3
Pripet Marshes F2
Reykjavik A1
Riga F2
Roca, Cape C4
Rome E3
Rostov G3
Rotterdam D2
Rybinsk Reservoir ... G2
Saimaa, Lake F1
Salonika F3
Saragossa C3
Sarajevo E3
Saratov H2
Sardinia D3
Scutari, Lake E3
Sevastopol G3
Seville C4
Shetland Islands ... C1
Sicily E4
Skagerrak D2
Skopje F3
Sofia F3

Stockholm E2
St. Petersburg G2
Strasbourg D3
Stuttgart D3
St. Vincent, Cape ... C4
Subotica E3
Surtsey B1
Szeged F3
Tallinn F2
Tampere F1
Tirana E3
Toulouse D3
Tours D3
Trieste E3
Tula G2
Turin D3
Turku F1
Tver G2
Tyrrhenian Sea E3
Ufa J2
Valencia C4
Vaner, Lake E2
Varna F3
Vatican City E3
Vatter, Lake E2
Venice E3
Vesuvius E3
Vienna E3
Vilnius F2
Volgograd H3
Vorkuta K1
Voronezh G2
Warsaw F2
White Sea G1
Zagreb E3
Zaporozhe G3
Zhdanov G3
Zurich D3

FACTS AND FIGURES

LOCATION: North central and northeastern hemispheres: **Latitude**—71° 08′ N to 36° N. **Longitude**—66° E to 9° 30′ W.

AREA: Approximately 4,200,000 sq. mi. (10,900,000 sq. km.) with adjacent islands.

POPULATION: 728,000,000 (2002; includes entire population of Russia).

PHYSICAL FEATURES: Highest point—Mount Elbrus (18,481 ft.; 5,633 m.). **Lowest point**—Caspian Sea (depression) (92 ft.; 28 m. below sea level). **Chief rivers**—Volga, Danube, Dnieper, Don, Pechora, Dniester, Rhine, Elbe, Vistula, Loire, Tagus, Neman, Ebro, Oder, Rhone, Neisse, Po, Thames, Seine, Arno, Tiber, Severn.

For several centuries, Europe ruled vast portions of the globe, but its importance was due not only to its military power and technological innovation. Europeans speaking Latin, Greek, French, German, Spanish, Italian, Portuguese, and English carried ideas about life and death, government and religion, art and music, and literature to the rest of the world. Their influence was so great that, to this day, in order to understand almost anything—from such large problems as the turmoil in Asia to smaller and pleasanter ones like the literature of South America—one must first know something of Europe.

Among Europe's most enduring legacies are ideas about how to govern. Ancient Greece gave the world the concept of democracy and of the democratic state. Rome added the idea of just laws stressing obedience to government. England contributed the whole body of English law, based on the theory that the individual's life, liberty, and property must be protected by the government. And from Europe, too, came the patterns for constitutional, or limited, monarchies; representative government; and the notion that government must attend to human rights and hopes. Social legislation and the use of the power of the state to support the individual in his or her drive for economic security came from Europe. Socialism and Communism also were born in Europe.

COUNTRIES OF EUROPE

COUNTRY	AREA (sq. mi.)	(sq. km.)	POPULATION (2002)	CAPITAL
Albania	11,100	28,750	3,100,000	Tirana
Andorra	174	450	100,000	Andorra la Vella
Austria	32,375	83,850	8,100,000	Vienna
Belarus	80,151	207,590	9,900,000	Minsk
Belgium	11,780	30,510	10,300,000	Brussels
Bosnia and Herzegovina	19,781	51,233	3,400,000	Sarajevo
Bulgaria	42,822	110,910	7,800,000	Sofia
Croatia	21,829	56,537	4,300,000	Zagreb
Czech Republic	30,387	78,703	10,300,000	Prague
Denmark	16,639	43,094	5,400,000	Copenhagen
Estonia	17,462	45,226	1,400,000	Tallinn
Finland	130,127	337,030	5,200,000	Helsinki
France	211,208	547,030	59,500,000	Paris
Germany	137,803	356,910	82,400,000	Berlin
Greece	50,942	131,940	11,000,000	Athens
Hungary	35,919	93,030	10,100,000	Budapest
Iceland	39,768	103,000	300,000	Reykjavík
Ireland	27,135	70,280	3,800,000	Dublin
Italy	116,305	301,230	58,100,000	Rome
Latvia	24,938	64,589	2,300,000	Riga
Liechtenstein	62	160	30,000	Vaduz
Lithuania	25,174	65,200	3,500,000	Vilnius
Luxembourg	998	2,585	500,000	Luxembourg
Macedonia	9,781	25,333	2,000,000	Skopje
Malta	124	320	400,000	Valletta
Moldova	13,012	33,700	4,300,000	Kishinev
Monaco	.77	2	30,000	Monaco-Ville
Netherlands	16,036	41,532	16,100,000	Amsterdam
Norway	125,181	324,219	4,500,000	Oslo
Poland	120,726	312,680	38,600,000	Warsaw
Portugal	35,672	92,391	10,400,000	Lisbon
Romania	91,699	237,500	22,400,000	Bucharest
Russia	6,592,772	17,075,200	143,500,000	Moscow
San Marino	23	60	30,000	San Marino
Slovakia	18,859	48,845	5,400,000	Bratislava
Slovenia	7,821	20,256	2,000,000	Ljubljana
Spain	194,884	504,750	41,300,000	Madrid
Sweden	173,730	449,960	8,900,000	Stockholm
Switzerland	15,942	41,290	7,300,000	Bern
Ukraine	233,089	603,700	48,200,000	Kiev
United Kingdom	94,525	244,820	60,200,000	London
Vatican City	.17	.44	900	Vatican City
Yugoslavia (Serbia and Montenegro)	39,517	102,350	10,700,000	Belgrade

Although none of the world's major religions were born in Europe, it was in Europe that Christianity grew and flourished. The Roman Catholic Church inspired Europeans after the decline and fall of imperial Rome. Later, after the Protestant Reformation, other Christian denominations arose in Europe. Disagreements about doctrine led to bitter wars, but they also led dissenters to establish the colonies that ultimately became the United States.

Europe's educational institutions, which were at first mainly religious, grew secular over the centuries. The emphasis on the idea of the dignity and equality of individuals led finally to the concept of universal education. Such ancient universities as Padua, Bologna, Florence, Paris, Oxford, Cambridge, Uppsala, Prague, and Heidelberg sent their scholars and their ideas to every corner of the globe.

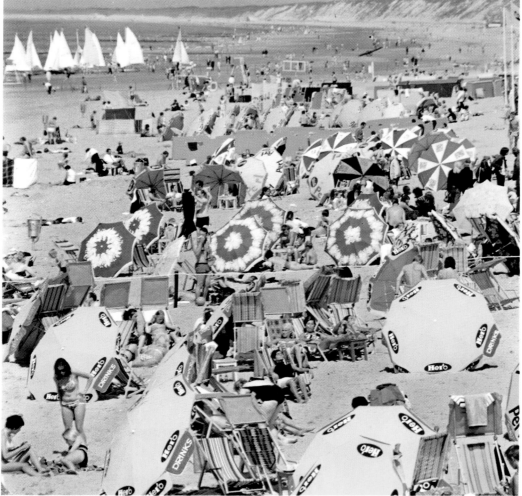

Europe's beaches, such as this one in the Netherlands, draw big summer crowds.

In the arts, as in government, religion, and education, the influence of Europe has been far greater than the continent's small size would lead one to guess. In painting, sculpture, architecture, music, and literature, Europeans blazed trails that are still being explored. Painters everywhere study the work of Europeans who discovered new ways of painting perspective and of showing light and shadow. Techniques for depicting religious scenes, satirical scenes, or simply portraying a human face on wood, stone, and canvas were developed and perfected in Europe. From the most elaborately decorated Gothic cathedral to the most starkly modern office building, European architects developed new ways of using stone and wood, steel and glass to shelter and inspire people.

Such musical forms as the symphony, concerto, sonata, opera, operetta, and ballet originated in Europe. And every educated person is aware that Europe gave the world of literature the essay, the ode, the lyric, and the sonnet. No matter where a person lives, his or her life is enriched by the works of such European giants as Homer, Virgil, Dante, Chaucer, Shakespeare, Milton, Voltaire, Goethe, Tolstoi, and many others.

In such fundamental matters as how to live better with the resources of the continent, Europeans also developed techniques that made life easier. It was probably northern Europeans who first discovered that the soil could be used longer if crops were rotated. This made it possible to settle in one place and establish permanent homes. With permanent communities came the growth of the villages, towns, and cities that became centers of commerce and culture.

The Greeks are usually credited with being the first to inquire scientifically into human life and the environment, seeking rational explanations of such natural phenomena as the seasons of the year and the tides of the sea. The speculations of the ancient Greeks about the nature of the universe led to the beginnings of astronomy, medicine, physics, and psychology. As the centuries passed, more and more Europeans added to our knowledge of this world. It was a European who discovered that the Sun rather than the Earth is the center of our universe. Other European scientists provided the basic knowledge of gravitation, thermodynamics, and the laws governing motion, sound, and light. The list of European contributions is endless, ranging from medical discoveries that lengthen human lives to the discovery of radio waves, which are able to bring people together no matter how far apart they may live. The extraordinary number of contributions made by Europeans to scientific knowledge and the way in which we live can be measured by imagining what the world might be like if the philosophers Aristotle and

A pastry shop tempts a young Frenchman.

Plato, the physicians Hippocrates and Galen, the astronomers Copernicus and Galileo, the scientists Newton, Pasteur, and Einstein, the psychoanalyst Freud, and countless others of their stature had not lived.

A disposition for scientific inquiry and an abundance of natural resources such as coal and iron led to the Industrial Revolution, which began in Europe in the mid-18th century. Machines powered by steam and coal replaced tedious hours of human labor. Industries grew that altered the face of the world completely. Factories were built, and railroads spread their iron tracks across the land. And as the new industries flourished, people had increasingly more leisure time for entertainment and enjoyment of the arts.

Today travelers by the millions visit Europe, seeking the beauty and inspiration of the continent that has in many ways been the cradle of modern civilization. They go to Athens, birthplace of democracy; to Rome, which for so long was the capital of much of Europe and now contains the seat of the Roman Catholic Church; to Paris, a wellspring of history and art; to Vienna, a pivotal city in European events; to Moscow, the capital of Russia; and to London, the still-splendid capital of the vanished Empire and of the living Commonwealth. In smaller cities, there are memories of the past as well. In Prague, one is reminded of the forerunners of the Protestant Reformation, and in Seville, one finds the meeting of two great cultures—the Muslim and the Christian. The distant past of the first Europeans can be evoked at Altamira in northern Spain, where the cave walls are covered with paintings made in prehistoric times, or at Stonehenge in England, where a great circle of stones may represent a primitive astronomical calendar. Closer in time are the medieval walled cities such as Carcassonne in central France, the majesty of Westminster Abbey in London, and the hill towns of Italy.

Visitors crowd the museums—the Louvre in Paris, the Hermitage in St. Petersburg, the Rijksmuseum in Amsterdam, the National Gallery in London, the Prado in Madrid, the Uffizi in Florence—to see masterpieces of world art painted by geniuses of the past. In Denmark, Norway, and Sweden, there are museums recalling the triumphs and conquests of the seafaring Vikings. In Munich's Deutsches Museum, the adventures of science are explored. Hundreds of towns have smaller museums, featuring exhibitions of all kinds, from armor to glassware, cuckoo clocks, butterflies, and 19th-century safety matches.

Just as the human past has been preserved in museums, monuments, and historic buildings, Europeans strive to keep from destroying the natural beauty of the continent. Despite the environmental dangers posed by the steady growth of population and industry, the majestic Alps, the fjords of Norway, the golden beaches of the Black Sea coast, the vast plains of the Ukraine, and the jewel-like lakes of northern Italy

Few Russians can afford to shop at the smart boutiques that have opened in Moscow in recent years.

Most of Europe receives enough precipitation to support agriculture without the need for irrigation. In England (above), the cool, moist climate helps the landscape maintain a lush green color.

still offer their special charms and their recollection of Europe before nations grew crowded for space and fought for preeminence.

The continent has for centuries been the site of numerous conflicts, and indeed, scarcely a corner of Europe has not been witness to bloodshed. The fierce nationalism and religious feuds so prominent in European history still survive, as has been demonstrated in Ireland and in the former Yugoslavia. Mostly, however, the old historic animosities have virtually disappeared. One can now hardly imagine Britain and France, or France and Germany, at war with one another.

THE PEOPLE

Europe, including the European part of Russia, accounts for more than 12 percent of the world's population crowded into about 7 percent of Earth's land area. In addition, the people of Europe are divided into many ethnic groups, which differ in language, culture, and customs. A detailed map of Europe's ethnic groups looks like a crazy quilt. A boundary change often means not only a change in language but in religion as well. Where the Europeans came from and how they diversified into so many nations is a long story that begins in prehistoric times.

Present-day Europe reflects the result of many movements of population. The various groups blended and consolidated finally into national groups and states. Influenced by existing civilizations—Greek, Roman, Byzantine, and later Latin Christian—they became a part of Europe, regionally different, but nevertheless European.

In the story of human development, Asia served as a kind of reservoir from which peoples moved in all directions. What caused those migrations is not yet clear. Perhaps climatic changes, such as long dry periods, caused people to wander. The approach over the Russian plain was wide open, but the complex landforms of Europe then broke the advance into smaller units. Existing populations were destroyed or assimilated. Some of the earlier inhabitants, however, retreated into less hospitable environments. The Basques settled in the northern Pyrenees; the Celtic peoples in Wales, Scotland, and Ireland; and the Britons in the Britanny region of France. In isolated corners, these peoples have preserved their languages and customs.

From the Middle East came the Jews in a steady stream, beginning more than 2,000 years ago. There were never great numbers of them, but they played a significant role in European history. Out of Central Asia arrived waves of migrant raiders, beginning with the Huns in the 4th century A.D., and ending with the Mongols (Tatars) in the 13th. Most of them were stopped militarily or ran out of steam and returned to Asia. The Magyars, who settled on the Danubian Plain in what is present-day Hungary, and the Bulgars, after whom Bulgaria is named, remained to form European nations. In the 14th century came the Ottoman Turks, who twice advanced to the walls of Vienna and controlled the Balkans until the 19th century. Also from Asia, but by way of North Africa, came the Arabs, who overran the Iberian Peninsula in the 8th century A.D. and ruled it until the end of the 15th.

Germanic Migrations. One great migration merits special attention because it has influenced the history of Europe up to the present. This was the westward movement of Germanic tribes of east-central Europe into the weakening Roman Empire in the early centuries after Christ. The Rhine and Danube rivers had been the boundaries of the Roman state. East of that line lived certain Germanic tribes whose independence had been protected by the dense forests of central Europe. When Rome began to weaken in the late 2nd century A.D., those tribes invaded Roman territory. One group, the Lombards, occupied Italy and settled in the north—in present-day Lombardy. Another Germanic tribe, the Goths, occupied Spain; still another Germanic tribe, the Vandals, even moved into Africa; and the Franks took over France, which is named after them. Other tribes such as the Jutes and the Danes crossed over into the British Isles. They were relatively few in number, and in due time were assimilated into the existing population. The Elbe became the eastern boundary of the Germanic people; beyond the river a kind of vacuum was left that was occupied by Slavic peoples.

In the 11th and 12th centuries, when conditions in Western Europe had stabilized, the Germanic peoples reversed their interest and looked east across the Elbe, intending to reclaim that land. They moved into what was then Slavic territory and occupied wide areas—a process that continued up to the last century. Large regions, particularly in present-day Poland and the Czech Republic, were entirely Germanized; in others the rural population was left alone, while the Germans controlled the towns.

Poland was the first important state to obstruct this eastern march, but by the end of the 18th century, Poland was defeated and divided up completely among Prussia (a German state), Austria, and Russia. The Russians were the last obstacle, and some observers regard the German conquest of western and southern Russia in both world wars as part of that historic Germanic drive. But in both wars the Germans were defeated and lost most of the territories they had taken from the Slavs. After World War I, Poland was reborn; after World War II, the Soviet Union was enlarged to the west, and Poland was ceded large tracts of German territory. This resulted in tremendous displacement of ethnic Germans.

The Slavs. The original homeland of the Slavs lay between the Volga and Oder rivers. In the 6th century, Slavic tribes began to migrate, probably in conjunction with the movement of Turkic Avars, and by the end of the 1st millennium, there were three distinct groups of Slavic peoples. The West Slavs, ancestors of modern Czechs, Poles, and Slovaks, settled in north-central Europe. South Slavs, ancestors of Bulgarians, Serbians, Croatians, Macedonians, and Slovenians, became established in the Balkan Peninsula. The largest Slavic group, the East Slavs—the future Russians, Ukrainians, and Belorussians—advanced to the sparsely populated east.

Beginning in the 16th century, the Russians began to try to expand westward into Europe proper. This movement was blocked by a line of countries that were to fall only gradually under Russian control. Before World War I, Russia included Finland, the Baltic states (Estonia, Latvia, Lithuania), the eastern part of Poland, and part of Romania. All this territory was lost at the end of the war. Poland was re-created, as were the Baltic states and Finland, while Romania reclaimed its lost territory. In 1939, however, thanks to an agreement with Nazi Germany, the Soviet Union regained most of these areas, except Finland, which remained a free state. After World War II, Poland acquired part of eastern Germany, while the Soviet Union absorbed part of eastern Poland, formerly held by imperial Russia. The introduction of non-Slavic peoples into the Soviet empire produced strong ethnic and political tensions. This became evident once Soviet central control weakened after 1989, leading to independence movements in the Baltic states and elsewhere.

Language and Religion

The existence of a state is based on the desire of a group of people to be politically independent. That desire is generally influenced by a common background, common customs, and a common language. It seems logical that an ideal state is one in which those principles are realized: one country, one language, and perhaps also one religion. In most of Europe, religion has ceased to be a deciding element, and religious minorities are regarded as equal. There are exceptions, particularly in Ireland and the former Yugoslavia. Northwestern Europe, except for the Irish Republic, is chiefly Protestant; parts of eastern and southeastern Europe are Eastern Orthodox; and the rest of Europe is largely Roman Catholic. Interspersed are areas in the Netherlands, Germany, and Switzerland where Catholics and Protestants are about equally represented. Growing immigrant populations have created Muslim concentrations in many urban areas, straining traditional religious tolerance in some countries.

Language remains one of the chief unifying factors for a state, and a linguistic map of Europe reflects the political units. There are three major language groups—namely, the Germanic, the Romance, and the Slavic, all of them belonging to the large family of Indo-European languages. In addition to these, there are numerous small linguistic groups, such as Basque, which is a separate non–Indo-European language that may be distantly related to the family of Caucasian languages; the three Ural-Altaic languages, Finnish, Estonian, and Hungarian; and the remnants of the Baltic branch of the Indo-European family, Latvian and Lithuanian. Until World War II, many Jewish communities in Central and Eastern Europe spoke Yiddish, predominantly a Germanic language, but with strong elements of Hebrew and Slavic languages.

The Language Structure of Europe

Iceland and the Scandinavian nations—Norway, Sweden, and Denmark—have Germanic languages, related but somewhat different. Finland has its own language (Finnish), but on the coast, Swedish is spoken, and the two languages are both recognized as national. The people of each of the Baltic states—Latvia, Lithuania, and Estonia—speak their own languages. The British speak a Germanic tongue with some Latin influence due to the impact of the Norman invasion of William the Conqueror in the 11th century. However, in northwest Scotland, Gaelic is still spoken, as is Welsh (Cymric) in Wales. Most of the people in Ireland speak English, but both Irish Gaelic and English are accepted as national languages. Germany and the Netherlands speak their own Germanic language. Belgium is bilingual; in the north the Flemings speak Dutch, and in the south the Walloons speak French. Luxembourgers speak a Germanic dialect, but French is the official language. France is a Latin country, but there are some linguistic minorities.

Switzerland is quite special. It has three major language groups as well as a remnant language, Rhaeto-Romanic (Romansh), spoken in the eastern mountains by about 1 percent of the population. About 70 percent of the Swiss people speak a German dialect (German Swiss); 19 percent speak French; and 10 percent speak Italian.

Spain and Portugal speak a Latin language. Basque, a relic of the past, is spoken on both sides of the northern Pyrenees, in Spain as well as in France. The people of Italy speak Italian, a Latin, or Romance, language. Austrians speak German, and the Poles speak Polish, a Slavic language. Czechs and Slovaks speak related Slavic languages, but culturally and historically, they are different, as the Czechs were long under Austrian domination, and the Slovaks under Hungarian. Hungarians speak their own Magyar language brought by invaders from Asia in the late 9th century A.D. Albanian is an Indo-European language, but it stands on its own.

The peoples of the former Yugoslavia speak related South Slavic languages: Slovenian, Croatian, Serbian, and Macedonian. The Greeks speak a modern version of ancient Greek. Bulgarians speak a Slavic language. Romanians speak a greatly changed Latin language that, in spite of many invasions, has been preserved since Roman times.

Russian is spoken not only by Russians but also in most former Soviet republics. Ukrainian and Belorussian are other East Slavic languages. Most people in Moldova speak Romanian.

Gothic cathedrals are soaring monuments to the central role of religion in the lives of medieval Europeans.

WAY OF LIFE

Obviously the vast numbers of people who live in the many countries of Europe lead lives that vary a good deal. What is surprising is that Europeans as different from one another as the English, Poles, Austrians, Greeks, or Italians have so much in common. While living under different types of government, influenced by manifold climatic conditions and landscapes, and speaking various languages, the European is a member of a cultural family that has been influenced by common social and intellectual currents and by much common history.

The day-to-day life of the average man and woman and of schoolchildren in Moscow, London, Budapest, or Stockholm does not differ as much as their lives differ from the day-to-day lives of their own countrymen who live in rural areas. City people lead quite different lives from country people in most countries of the world. City people share many of the same pleasures and same concerns all over Europe.

Folk customs vary widely across Europe. In the Black Forest region of Germany, certain holy days are commemorated by religious processions with marchers wearing traditional costumes.

Most Europeans work or go to school five days a week, but many ambitious young professionals also work on weekends and evenings. Thousands of employees in services, particularly those related to tourism, also work on weekends. In large cities, Europeans suffer the miseries of traffic jams or crowded public transportation during their commutes.

For centuries, European fathers came home for their midday meal. Offices and shops were closed, and that was the time when the family assembled for the main meal. Today that is less and less true, except where the climate, such as in southern Italy, Greece, and Spain, is conducive to a siesta after the noon meal. In the extreme south of Europe, when it is possible, businesses close for two to four hours, and then reopen in the midafternoon and stay open until early evening. In most European countries, however, the workday schedule is like that in North America.

Everywhere in Europe, cities are growing and becoming more crowded as people move—as they are doing all over the world—to the metropolitan centers. Most come, especially the young, because they are bored on the farm or because modern technology has reduced the need for human agricultural labor. They also seek the education, job opportunities, and stimulation offered in the cities. Housing is in short supply in many European cities, especially in eastern Europe.

Most of the cities of Europe are a fascinating combination of old and new. In Lisbon or in Rome, it is still possible for someone living in the shadow of a modern office building to go to a fountain in the square to obtain water. Narrow, cobblestoned streets run between rows of old houses, some of which have been occupied for hundreds of years. Centuries-old churches occupy places of prominence in these old quarters. But European cities are beginning to be filled with modern concrete-and-glass structures, office buildings, and apartments. European cities share with large cities all over the world the plagues of air and water pollution caused by wastes from cars, homes, and industry.

Even in the newest areas of European cities, an old custom has been preserved. Nearly always there is a pleasant café where one may stop and enjoy a drink or snack. You may sit outdoors on the sidewalk surrounding a square, as in Rome or Athens, or you may be inside the café, cozy and snug while it rains outside, as it often does in Dublin, London, or

Europeans are renowned for their fine handicrafts.

Brussels. What you eat or drink may differ. It can be beer or tea in a London pub or tearoom, or a glass of local wine in any of the cities of Europe. And often today, in almost any country, it might be Coca-Cola or Pepsi-Cola, even as far east as Moscow. But whatever the drink, the time spent is time for chatting and discussing literature, movies, or politics, especially among the older generations. The young are more likely to be found in discos, at rock concerts, or in Internet bars.

Europeans share an avid interest in theater and opera. Long ago, strolling players sang, danced, recited poetry, and performed plays. Traveling Punch-and-Judy shows entertained young and old, and so did itinerant trainers and their performing bears or dogs. In many European countries today, opera, symphony, drama, folk dance, and ballet companies are subsidized by the state and are a subject of great national pride. Knowing and responsive audiences greet the Royal Ballet of Denmark, the St. Petersburg and Moscow ballets, the La Scala Opera Company of Milan, the British National Theatre Company, the Swedish Royal Opera, the Vienna Philharmonic, and other renowned ensembles. American movies are popular, especially among young people, but many European countries have flourishing film industries. Italian, French, Swedish, British, Polish, and Czech movies continue to attract large audiences.

Europeans are great sports enthusiasts. In Spain and Portugal, they pack the bullrings to see the bullfights. In Switzerland, skiing is a national pastime. In Russia, thousands of people watch the gymnastic and figure-skating exhibitions. The Dutch in Holland take their skates out to the frozen canals in the winter. The Danes, Swedes, and Norwegians sail in their northern waters. Sometimes there are special national variations of well-known games, such as boccie (Italian bowling) or pelota (Spanish handball). All over Europe, there is intense interest in soccer, whether it is played by schoolchildren or by professional teams. Tennis is also played everywhere. For years, Czechoslovakia had a veritable "tennis factory" that turned out a stream of world champions. Where geography and climate permit, people flock to the beaches—on the Black Sea of Romania, Bulgaria, Ukraine, and Russia; on the Adriatic coasts of Italy and Croatia; and on the Mediterranean of France, Italy, and Spain. In the summer, many central and northern Europeans travel to the warmer beaches of southern Europe, to the islands of the Mediterranean, to Turkey, to the North African coast, or to the Azores in the Atlantic.

Europeans enjoy bicycling and hiking. They often take vacations by hiking through the many lovely forestlands of Europe and camping beside sparkling streams. It may be in tiny Luxembourg, in the Swiss or Austrian Alps, in the French or English countryside, or in almost any country of Europe. In dozens of countries, there are attractive campsites and inexpensive hostels to accommodate these hikers.

Each spring, summer, and autumn, thousands of Europeans go to spas, a tradition that dates from Roman times. Hotels, rest homes, and sanatoriums cater to the people who come to these resorts to bathe in and drink the waters from underground springs, whose mineral properties are supposed to aid in the treatment of some ailments.

In recent years, Europeans have become even greater travelers than in the past. It is not a long trip for anyone, except a resident of the central area of Russia, to get to a foreign land in Europe. In most countries, it is less than an hour by plane. In most areas, frontiers are barely noticed, and people can go quite freely from one country to another. The removal of barriers between Eastern and Western Europe, and the 1992 economic union among Western countries, has made travel even easier. In August, the almost universal European vacation month, it often seems as if all Europeans are on the go—by foot, bicycle, motorbike, train, car, boat, or plane. With their high standards of living, Europeans also make up a large percentage of tourists throughout the world.

The 1992 economic union has also accelerated the movement of workers between countries. Citizens of any European Union (EU) member state now have the right to work in any other member state, a system that has produced migration from countries with high unemployment to those with labor shortages.

These workers, who often remain for a few years and then return home, demonstrate that there are great variations in the prosperity of the different countries of Europe. Switzerland has the highest standard of living (per-capita income) in all of Europe, and one of the highest in the world. Albania has the lowest per-capita income in Europe. In between are countries in many stages of industrial development and opportunity for employment. The highly industrialized countries of Northern Europe not only provide jobs, but also a great variety of social benefits for their citizens, and their high social-welfare benefits have attracted immigrants from many countries, such as Turkey and former African colonies.

The economies of the former Communist countries are being transformed at an unequal rate. Outwardly, many parts of Moscow, Budapest, Warsaw, Prague, and other Central and Eastern European capitals look completely Westernized—with flashy cars, McDonald's restaurants, and luxury stores—but behind this front there linger many remnants of the totalitarian past. The Central European trio—Poland, the Czech Republic, and Hungary—have been in the forefront of changes, but by 2000 they had been overtaken by Slovenia, which now has the highest standard of living of all formerly Communist countries. These four nations—as well as Estonia, in the Baltics—are negotiating their admission to the EU, which is currently envisioned for 2004.

By early 2002, the economic situation began to improve in Balkan countries, such as Bulgaria and Romania, and in certain areas of the former Yugoslavia, which were finally free of conflict. Farther east, economic transformation stalled in Ukraine, Belarus, and Moldova, but picked up speed in Russia, where President Putin's leadership seemed to improve the nation's quality of life.

All across Europe, the differences between rural and city life persist to this day, even though the vast growth in communications—especially the spread of television and the Internet—is lessening this difference. In rural areas, people still live more confined lives that are often centered around their homes and churches. Even remote villages have their cafés or pubs, but in many countries (particularly in southern Europe) these are frequented only by men. Young people, in search of opportunity and excitement, often leave the farms for cities, and the rural population dwindles. Yet thanks to greater efficiency, a shrinking number of farmworkers can feed the growing urban population.

The role of women in society differs greatly from country to country in Europe. In Sweden, women hold many public offices, and there are day-care centers to take care of children while mothers work. In some countries—particularly Spain, Greece, and Portugal—women are still ordinarily found at home. Some European women had to wait a long time for the right to vote: for instance, in France women could not vote until 1945, and in Switzerland, not until 1990.

In the former Communist countries, women were constitutionally recognized as equal and were strongly represented in many professions (for instance, most Soviet doctors were women), but actually very few women had leading positions anywhere. The main reason why most women were employed was economic necessity: one salary failed to provide for essential expenses. In most post-Communist countries, there are very few women in political and public life.

There are some differences in what are regarded as essential rights of citizens in the countries of Europe. In London's famous Hyde Park, any man or woman can bring his or her own box or platform, mount it, and proceed to say whatever he or she pleases about any subject. In Denmark, there is no restriction on the publication of any material, even what Americans might consider outright pornography. However, most citizens must carry national identity cards, and police at times are given greater latitude than might be permitted in the United States.

A great expansion of civic freedoms has occurred in the former Communist countries. Several are now fully comparable to Western democracies, but in most of them some vestiges of totalitarian practices continue. This is not surprising, particularly because such countries as Russia, Romania, and Bulgaria lack strong democratic traditions. The inhabitants of these nations thus have yet to develop an understanding of the personal responsibility that comes with political freedom.

All the countries of Europe have been greatly influenced by the American way of life. Today blue jeans are seen much more often than the embroidered peasant costumes of the past. Radio, films, television, and travel have brought many Americanisms to the most remote parts of Europe. American "fast-food" outlets provide hamburgers, pizza, and fried chicken to their fans in many parts of Europe.

Many intellectuals and also groups of young anarchists and ecologists have criticized the Americanization of Europe, but the United States continues to attract people from all parts of the continent, and American products are popular with the European public. In the 1990s, hundreds of American investors set up firms in Central and Eastern Europe. At the same time, European automobiles, foodstuffs, and many other products found markets in the United States.

The American influence and the rapid industrialization of much of Europe have brought many changes. Education for the technological society, involving vast public-education systems ranging from elementary schools to universities and requiring higher levels of basic education for all citizens, has broken down class barriers. Competition for top jobs in management is intense, and positions more often go to the ablest than in former days, when they might have been inherited or gone to political-party functionaries. The rush to the cities has brought a breakdown in the old family structures and also in the authority of the church. At the beginning of the 21st century, the new information-age economy has further changed the European way of life. And yet, despite ubiquitous computers and the Internet, Europe continues to be a truly magical blend of the old and the new.

THE LAND

A relief map of Europe shows a confusing mass of mountains, plateaus, and lowlands. However, it is possible to bring some order out of the confusion and recognize four major physical regions—the Northwestern Uplands, the Central Lowlands, the Central Uplands, and the alpine mountains.

The Northwestern Uplands

Uplands—rugged mountains, high plateaus, and deep valleys—stretch from Brittany in western France through the British Isles and Scandinavia all the way to the Arctic Ocean. The uplands vary greatly in height from rather low in Brittany to high in Scotland and Norway. These areas have been only thinly settled because the land is generally too rocky and mountainous for farming. The climate can be summed up in one word—"wet." In the northern uplands, moors and bogs are typical. In the far north, snow covers are permanent, and glaciers inch down toward the coast. In fact, during the Ice Age, most of this region was covered by ice. Today the landscape has many glacial features such as U-shaped valleys, lakes, and fjords—arms of the sea that often stretch far inland and are bordered by steep mountains.

Where the uplands are broken up or have a low elevation, living conditions are better. Good examples are central Ireland, which is a saucer-shaped lowland basin with an upland frame; the central valley of Scotland; and the area around Oslo in Norway. But people in the Northwestern Uplands live mainly along the coasts, where the fish-rich oceans offer a better living than does farming the rocky land itself. The land's importance comes from the minerals that are mined there and from the forests, which are an important source of timber.

The Central Lowlands

The Central Lowlands are the most densely settled part of Europe. They extend from the Garonne Valley in southwest France to the Ural Mountains. The lowlands are rather narrow in the west, and then widen to embrace all the space between the Arctic Ocean and the Black Sea. They include northern France, most of Belgium and the Netherlands, southeastern Britain, northern Germany, Denmark, Poland, the Baltic states, Belarus, Ukraine, and practically all of European Russia. The Central Lowlands are perfectly flat in the Netherlands, but elsewhere they are hilly with isolated elevations or long ridges. These ridges are called downs in Britain and *côtes* in France. Around the Baltic Sea, Ice Age glaciers have left their mark with terminal moraines—mounds built up of rock debris carried down by the glacier to the point at which it stopped. After the ice receded, most of the great lowland area became densely forested, but it was cleared by early settlers to make room for growing crops. However, the wetter western part of the Central Lowlands was probably always covered by grass and used for grazing.

Today the Central Lowland region is the home of most Europeans. The largest cities, the densest networks of transportation, and the heaviest concentration of industry are there in Europe's core area. Only a few parts of the region are still uncrowded, perhaps because the soil is poor or the climate too extreme, as in the north, with its short growing season, or the southern part of European Russia, where the climate is very dry.

The Central Uplands

A band of uplands lies between the Central Lowlands and the alpine mountains, and stretches from the Atlantic coast of Spain through France and Germany to Poland. Among the most important of these uplands are the Meseta in Spain, the Massif Central of France, the Ardennes of Belgium, the Vosges of France, the Black Forest of Germany, and the mountain rim around the Bohemian Basin in the Czech Republic. It is a somewhat more hospitable region than the Northwestern Uplands, but many parts are only sparsely inhabited.

The Alpine Mountains

The most dramatic physical features of Southern Europe are the alpine mountains, which stretch from Spain to the Caucasus. These mountains are young as geologists measure time, and there is still some mountain building going on, as demonstrated by the eruption of such active volcanoes as Vesuvius, near Naples, Italy; and Etna, on the Italian island of Sicily; and by disastrous quakes that shake the earth in a band extending eastward from Portugal.

Moving from west to east, the alpine mountains include the Sierra Nevada in Spain; the Pyrenees between Spain and France; the Apennines, which run like a spine down the Italian Peninsula; and such mountainous Mediterranean islands as Corsica, Sardinia, Sicily, and the Balearics. North of the Po River are Europe's most famous mountains, the Alps, which curve in a great arc before dividing into two branches. The Carpathian and Balkan mountains form the northern branch; the Dinaric Alps form the southern branch.

The Caucasus Mountains, between the Black and Caspian seas, are a nearly impenetrable wall separating Europe from the Middle East. Unlike the Caucasus, the low, forested Ural Mountains, which form Europe's eastern border, are easily crossed, so that there is no natural wall separating Europe and Asia.

Over thousands of years, glaciers like this one shaped the European continent.

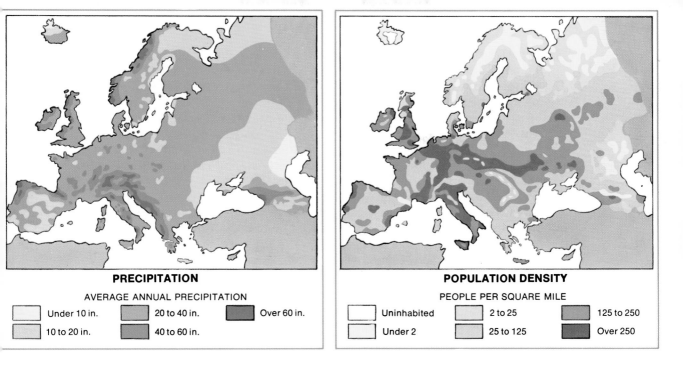

PRECIPITATION

AVERAGE ANNUAL PRECIPITATION

Under 10 in.	20 to 40 in.	Over 60 in.
10 to 20 in.	40 to 60 in.	

POPULATION DENSITY

PEOPLE PER SQUARE MILE

Uninhabited	2 to 25	125 to 250
Under 2	25 to 125	Over 250

The alpine mountain region is quite thinly populated except for some of the larger valleys. The outstanding example is Italy's Po Valley, which is really not a valley at all, but a depression between the Alps and the Apennines, and is one of Europe's most-crowded areas. Other rather densely settled parts of this region are the Swiss Plateau and the Danubian Plain. The narrow coastal plain of the Mediterranean Sea has been densely settled since early in history.

THE CLIMATE OF EUROPE

Climate is the most important factor in the physical environment of humans. It influences their life, their work, and their products. Some geographers believe, for example, that Western civilization was born in the Mediterranean region because the climate was neither extremely hot nor extremely cold, neither too rainy nor too dry. This, they say, made it possible for humans to work efficiently the year round without having to devise special clothing to protect themselves, or special buildings to protect the harvest of grain, which they could grow easily in the mild climate. Humans slowly grew more adept at building and heating their houses and at using tools. They found ways to grow crops in more-extreme climates and then to keep the crops from rotting. All of these developments made it possible for them to settle parts of the continent where the climate was not quite as gentle as in the south. It has been suggested that northwestern Europe's climate, with its cool (but not usually cold) winters and warm (but rarely hot) summers and abundance of precipitation, may be the ideal climate for people to live and work in.

Because Europe is located on a much higher latitude than the United States, Europe's southernmost point has approximately the same latitude as Cape Hatteras, North Carolina, and most of Europe is at the latitude of southern Labrador. The North Atlantic Drift of the Gulf Stream, which washes the coasts of northwestern Europe, causes mild sea air to warm up the winter temperatures.

Europe's three major climatic regions are the Atlantic, which is greatly influenced by the ocean currents; the Continental, which is typical for Central Europe and most of Belarus and Russia; and the Mediterranean in the south.

The Winter Climate

In winter, Atlantic air masses move in from the west, but are blocked in their eastern course by permanent continental air masses. There is, therefore, a great contrast between the climate of the west coast and that of the interior. Relatively warm temperatures are typical for the west coast. The Atlantic air masses also penetrate into the Mediterranean, but the winter storms are less severe, and, about half of the time, the skies are clear. Temperatures around 50° F. (10° C.) make the Mediterranean an attractive place to live and alluring to tourists.

The eastern part of Europe is influenced by the continental high-pressure system. Moscow has a January average of 15° F. (−9° C.). Farther east, toward the Ural Mountains, it grows even colder. Precipitation in the continental-climate zone is rather low, but the snow that does fall does not melt, and the wind piles the snow in drifts.

There is no distinct break between the Atlantic climate and the Continental one. The battle between the two climatic regions shifts constantly. Freezing cold weather at times comes quite close to the west coast. Warm air masses occasionally invade Russia. Even the mild Mediterranean region is at times invaded by cold continental air masses, and snow may fall over Rome and cover the Apennine Mountains in Italy. The Netherlands in northern Europe also experiences climatic variations of the usual pattern. The usual winter weather is cloudy, windy, and rainy, with temperatures close to 40° F. (5° C.) But at times, generally for a short period, the eastern air masses move in; temperatures drop below freezing, ice covers the canals, and the Dutch have wonderful ice festivals and enjoy great skating. There may be snow and a great deal of fog. As a rule, as one goes farther east in Europe, these cold periods become more frequent and last longer.

The Summer Climate

In summer, conditions change. The Atlantic has a cooling influence on the warmer land. The westerly winds are still there, but cyclonic storms are less severe, and the winds are less strong. July averages are still relatively low, in the 60s° F. (10s° C.); even Paris has a July average of only 65° F. (18° C.). The continental high in the east is replaced by a low-pressure area, and Atlantic air masses move into Siberia without obstruction. Temperatures are warmer than in the west—in the low 70s° F. (20s° C.). This is the rainy season for eastern and also central Europe, with storms caused by convection of air that has been heated over land, although the amounts of precipitation are not high. The mountains capture more rain, and have a large range of climatic conditions depending upon their height and orientation in relation to the prevailing winds. During the summer in Switzerland, for instance, it is often cool and wet. In fact, a snowfall in July at an altitude as low as 4,000 ft. (1,220 m.) has been recorded.

Summer climatic conditions in southern Europe are quite different because the subtropical high-pressure zone has moved in. The sky is

The city of Béziers in southern France dates back to Roman times.

generally clear, rain is scarce, and the temperatures are well up in the 70s° F. (20s° C.) and 80s° F. (30s° C.). In the summer, there is a zone of transition between the Mediterranean and the rest of Europe. Northern Italy, for instance, is still warm, but there is also precipitation. Generally, even the warmest European regions seldom experience the high humidity typical of much of the American East Coast.

Each of the three major climatic regions has its good and bad points, but people are able to live and to adjust their lives and economy to them. However, two additional climates are represented in Europe, and both are unfavorable for humans because they are either too dry or too cold. In the dry climates, lack of water prevents the growing of crops except when irrigation is available. This is true of part of the Spanish Meseta, which has a basin shape with a mountain rim that keeps out the moisture-bearing winds. Southeastern European Russia, behind the Carpathian Mountains, is also dry. The other unfavorable climate is one where freezing temperatures are permanent or the growing season too short. These cold climates are found in the high mountains and along the shores of the Arctic Ocean in the so-called tundra belt.

VEGETATION

Tundra and Taiga. The tundra belt, which covers northern Russia and Lapland, takes its name from a Finnish word meaning "barren hill." During most of the year, the soil of the tundra is permanently frozen, and strong winds make it impossible for trees to grow. It is only during the very short Arctic summer that the temperatures rise enough to melt the uppermost layer of the soil.

South of the Arctic tundra belt, there is a zone where evergreens predominate. "Taiga" is the name of this wide belt, which starts in Norway and continues through Sweden, Finland, and Russia all the way to the Pacific. Part of this tremendous forest is still untouched, but the pines and spruces of this zone are Europe's foremost source of lumber.

Mixed Forests and Grasslands. Where the growing season is longer, a mixed forest of beeches, oaks, and pines replaces the taiga. Over the years, a great deal of this mixed forest has been cleared to make room for crops and grassland, but large stands still exist, and the Central Lowlands are far from treeless. Trees line the roads, surround the farmhouses, and often form the border between properties. The English park landscape is famous for its large individual trees set on grassland. Along the Atlantic coast, with its wetness, strong winds, and lack of sunshine, grass replaces the forest. Ireland is known as the Emerald Isle because of its grassy green landscapes, and the Netherlands is known for its beautiful green meadows. On the high Alps, above the line where trees can grow, are the alpine meadows, where beautiful wildflowers are found and cattle graze in summer.

Mediterranean. This zone has special vegetation—plants and trees that are able to withstand the long, warm, and dry summers because

The countryside in southern Spain has typical Mediterranean vegetation.

of their deep roots, thick bark, thorns, or tough leaves. Evergreen oaks, cypresses, cedars, olive trees, and eucalypti are common in the Mediterranean. Where humans have felled the trees in large quantities, the trees have been replaced by a dense mixture of scrub plants called maquis. Maquis flower in spring, but grow brown and lifeless in the summer.

Steppe Vegetation. On the steppes—the level, treeless plains of the lower Danube and southern European Russia—where the climate is dry, grasses thrive. Most grassland is plowed under to provide cropland. In drier areas, such as around the Caspian Sea, saltbushes grow.

ANIMAL LIFE

Wild animals such as the musk ox, ibex, bison, and chamois, which used to be found in large numbers in Europe, must now be protected from hunters and the encroachment of modern life by special laws, game preserves, and even cages in zoos. To see the now-rare European bison, one must travel to the Bialowieza Forest, the national park in eastern Poland. Ibex and chamois—swift-footed alpine animals—can be found in Italy's Gran Paradiso National Park; chamois, lynx, and brown bear are found in a preserve in the High Tatra Mountains.

Some animals still live free, such as the polar bears of Spitsbergen and the wolves and wild boars in eastern Europe. Mouflon, wild sheep with curling horns, roam the hills and mountains of Corsica and Sardinia, off Italy's west coast. Saigas, Europe's only native antelope, live in the dry steppe region between the Volga River and the Ural Mountains.

Rabbit, hare, deer, and fox are still hunted in Europe; but important fur-bearing animals such as mink, ermine, and sable, for which Russia is especially famous, are now carefully raised on fur farms because they were nearly exterminated by trappers.

The birds of Europe have survived better than the mammals, except when they have tempted people by being delicious to eat, as is the case with grouse, wild ducks, larks, and partridges. Other familiar birds such as the cuckoo, skylark, and nightingale are still seen and heard.

Fish such as trout, carp, and the sturgeon of the Caspian Sea—which is caught for its roe (caviar)—are also still plentiful. The pollution in many rivers has eliminated some fish species, but ecological measures have started to reverse some of this damage.

ECONOMY

The Roman historian Tacitus wrote that Central Europe "either bristles with woods or festers with swamps." If he were to revisit the continent today, he would see vast changes in the landscape. Over the centuries, people have slowly cleared the land of the great forests, filled in many of the swamps, and reclaimed land from the sea to make farmland. Bustling industrial cities have replaced most of the forests and swamps.

Food Supply

European farmers have learned to make the most of their not-always-fertile land. The simple tools of the earliest European farmer have been replaced nearly everywhere by modern farm machines and modern farming methods. As early as Roman times, farmers knew the value of enriching the soil with manure, of rotating the land on which crops were

Vines like these in France are the source of Europe's well-known wines.

grown, and of irrigating the dry land. The Romans grew olive and other fruit trees, cultivated grapevines, and carried their agricultural arts to the most distant parts of their empire. Some of the vines growing on the terraced slopes of the Rhine were probably planted by Roman soldiers.

As time passed, villages and towns grew into cities. Once, most of the population lived on the land and grew their own food. Then a slowly increasing number of people began to live in the cities and needed to buy food. As the first large trading cities grew up in northern Italy, southern Germany, and in Flanders (now part of Belgium), and then in England and France, the farms that provided their food had to be changed to meet the new demand. Fields and pastures that had once been shared were enclosed and individually owned. Crop rotation replaced the method of letting a field lie fallow between plantings. Cattle were more carefully selected for breeding, with the result that larger and more-profitable animals were raised. New plants were introduced.

But there were other factors that were beyond the skill or control of Europe's farmers. Uncertain weather could ruin a crop—as is periodically the case with the wheat crop in Ukraine and Russia. A blight of unknown origin could destroy the staple food of a nation, as happened with the potato crop in Ireland in the 19th century. Famine, disease, and desolation were terrible threats that could and did alter the face of Europe. Beginning in the 17th century, another factor had an important effect on Europe's agriculture. The size of the population, which had remained nearly the same since A.D. 1000, slowly began to increase. Between 1750 and 1850, the population of Europe grew from about 140 million to 260 million. By the beginning of World War I in 1914, the population of Europe numbered 400 million. In the British Isles alone, the population grew from about 8 million in the early 18th century to some 21 million a century later. These figures are the beginning of an explanation for the enormous waves of emigration from Europe. The small continent, even with its relatively advanced methods of farming, could not support its population. As many as 40 million Europeans settled in the Americas, Australia, New Zealand, and other parts of the world.

Today, about 30 percent of the total area of Europe is devoted to agriculture, 20 percent to pasture, and a little less than 30 percent to forests. These percentages are quite high compared to other continents, but they tell only a part of the story because they say nothing about yields per acre and total production. In general, yields are high in Europe, but there are great differences between nations. A Dutch farmer produces four times as much per acre as a farmer in Portugal because of differences in climate and methods of farming. In some former Communist countries, particularly in Russia, Ukraine, and Belarus, agriculture is much less developed and agricultural machinery is scarce; in remote villages, farming has changed little since the 19th century.

Except for Britain, Europe is self-sufficient in food production, although some tropical products and fodder for livestock are imported. Part of this self-sufficiency is based on higher yields. Europeans have also seen great changes in their diets. There has been a shift from cereals to meat, fruit, and dairy products. Prosperity has made that shift possible: the Italians eat less pasta, and the French, less bread. The Finns and the Portuguese are also concerned about healthy eating habits, while the Austrians and the Greeks generally stick to their traditional diets.

In 2000 and 2001, bovine spongiform encephalopathy (BSE), or the so-called mad-cow disease—which, in rare cases, may be transmitted from cows to humans and cause a fatal illness—terrified much of Western Europe and led to a significant decline in beef consumption.

The type of food produced is to a large extent based on climate: dairy products come from the wet northwest; cereals (rye and wheat) and sugar beets are grown in the Central Lowlands. Corn is cultivated in the transition zone between the Mediterranean climate and that of central Europe. In the Mediterranean lands, wheat, fruits, and vegetables are raised, partly with the help of irrigation. Other important factors operate despite, rather than because of, climatic conditions. These are the demands of the market and the concentrated production of perishable foods near the areas of greatest population.

In highly developed central and northwestern Europe, very few people earn their living in agriculture; on the average, about 7.6 percent of the population of the European Union countries are farmers. This is less true elsewhere in Europe. In Greece, for instance, farmers represent about 20 percent and, in Poland, approximately 25 percent of all population.

It is not only the land that gives Europe its food; there is also the ocean. The coastal waters of Western Europe abound in fish: herring and cod in the north, sardines and tuna farther south. The former Soviet Union had one of the largest fishing industries in the world, and its annual fish catch was the second largest in the world, after that of Japan. Iceland's economy is based on fishing; its production is one-quarter that of the United States, which has 1,000 times as many people.

Strangely enough, the Mediterranean, which teems with fish, has never become an important fishing ground, primarily due to its warm water. In cold water, fish species appear in schools, and the catch is generally of one or two kinds. In warm water, however, fish do not congregate; the catch is a colorful display of all kinds of fish—interesting, but commercially of little value.

Modern methods of canning, freezing, and preserving have made it possible to enjoy European foods thousands of miles from the continent. English sole, Belgian endive, and wild strawberries from France are welcomed on American tables, while stores have shelves loaded with wines from France, Italy, Germany, Greece, Spain, Portugal, and Hungary. Long white asparagus from France, hams from Poland and Denmark, canned fish from Scandinavia and Portugal, and cheeses from the Netherlands, Switzerland, and Italy are only a sampling of the fine foods that Europe exports to the world.

Industries, Products, and Services

Power Resources. From the time of the waterwheel and the windmill through the Coal Age and the beginning of the use of hydroelectricity, Europe had all the power it needed. When oil became a major source of power, Europe west of Russia was in trouble. Oil is found in many parts of Europe, but generally in small amounts. These amounts were sufficient in preindustrial Europe for such novel experiments as the lighting of some streetlamps in Prague with oil in 1815, but they are insufficient for power industries and vehicles. The Ploesti oil fields in Romania, which were the largest in Europe outside the former Soviet Union, are no longer as important as they once were. Petroleum from the North Sea, discovered in the 1970s, is providing an important supply of this valuable resource for the nations of Western Europe. And an enormous underground reservoir of natural gas was discovered in the northern Netherlands. But the need to import oil and natural gas continues throughout much of Europe—except in Russia, which has the largest crude-oil reserves after the Middle East and Venezuela.

Tankers transport oil from the Middle East and North Africa to the other nations of Europe. Rotterdam, at the outlet of the Rhine River, is the world's greatest oil port. In its huge refineries, crude oil is transformed into its final products. Pipelines carry the oil to the nearby German industrial region. North African oil goes chiefly to Europe's Mediterranean ports, especially Genoa, Italy, and Marseilles, France. Pipelines also cross the Alps to Switzerland and Germany.

Historically, the coal-producing areas in such countries as the former Soviet Union, the United Kingdom, Belgium, France, Germany, and

Poland were the first centers of manufacturing. Coal is not as important a power source as it was in the past, but it is still used in large quantities, and Europe has enough to meet its needs.

The availability of hydroelectricity depends on plenty of running water—if possible, throughout the year—and a difference in elevation because the water must drop rapidly, as over a waterfall, to supply power. This is why power plants are usually built on mountains that have plenty of precipitation, such as those of Scandinavia, the Alps, and the Pyrenees. Norway and Sweden are major producers of hydroelectric power, and could produce more if there were an outlet to less-fortunate countries. However, transferring hydroelectric power over long distances is still a problem.

France, Italy, Switzerland, Austria, and Spain also have a great deal of waterpower. This is especially important in Italy and Switzerland, as both have practically no coal resources. Alpine valleys, especially those in Italy, are carefully utilized; one dam (with a dammed lake) and power plant follows the next one downstream because, in contrast to coal, water can be used over and over again. Hydroelectric power in Russia is based on its rivers, where huge amounts of water compensate for small differences in elevation. Two of the largest hydroelectric dams in the world are on the Volga River in European Russia. In the late 1960s, a huge hydroelectric system was constructed jointly by Romania and Yugoslavia at the historic Iron Gate gorge on the Danube River.

Iceland, the volcanic island off Europe's northwest coast, has a unique power source—hot springs. The Icelandic government uses these hot springs to produce electricity at low cost. The hot springs, once only columns of steam roaring up from mud pits to the amazement of visitors, now pipe heat directly to homes.

Some people consider the power resource of the future to be nuclear energy, which could replace the waning reserves of such traditional sources as coal and oil. But the expansion of the use of nuclear power has slowed because of pressure by various environmental groups and movements, which are concerned about the safety of nuclear-power plants and the disposal of radioactive wastes. In 1986, a major accident at the nuclear-power plant in Chernobyl, Ukraine, which caused the loss of many lives and produced widespread radioactive contamination, reinforced such fears. Chernobyl was shut down in late 2000. At that time, Austrian environmentalists repeatedly blocked the Czech-Austrian border to protest a new Czech nuclear plant at Temelin. Denmark, Norway, Ireland, Portugal, Greece, and Austria currently do not have nuclear-power plants, and Germany plans to close all of its reactors by 2021.

Mineral Resources. Europe west of Russia is not blessed with many minerals. The important exception is iron ore. The combination of coal and iron ore was to a large extent responsible for the Industrial Revolution. Britain, for example, was extremely fortunate in having its coal and iron-ore deposits close to each other. While iron ore is mined in many parts of Europe, there are two areas of outstanding production. Lorraine, an area in eastern France (extending into Luxembourg), is located close to the coal of the Saar Basin in Germany. The other important iron-ore mines are in northern Sweden.

Otherwise, Europe is not an important producer of the major metallic minerals. Copper is mined in some quantities by Finland, Norway,

Sweden, Yugoslavia, and Spain. Germany, Spain, and Sweden produce small quantities of lead ore. Zinc production is slight, and the tin mines in Cornwall, England, which once attracted traders from as far off as the eastern Mediterranean, are now empty. The picture is brighter in alloy metals such as tungsten, which is found in Portugal and Spain, and chromium, mined in what was Yugoslavia. Europe is also quite well supplied with some of the minor minerals: mercury from Spain and Italy, and sulfur from Italy. Bauxite, for aluminum, is also found in adequate quantities. In fact, its name comes from the small town of Les Baux in southern France, where it was first discovered.

Russia has large quantities of nearly every metallic mineral, but much of it is located in the Asian section of the country. In the Ukraine, the nation's production of iron ore, the most important mineral, surpasses that of the United States. The chief source is the Krivoi Rog area west of the bend in the Dnieper River. It is also supplied with bauxite, copper, lead, nickel, molybdenum, and manganese.

Europe's nonmetallic mineral production includes abundant building materials such as stone, clay, sand, gravel, and the world's largest potash deposits. Potash, which is used in fertilizers, exists in such large quantities in eastern Germany that some experts believe it could meet the world's needs for this product for 1,000 years. Salt is mined in some places, extracted from underground brine, and taken from the sea off the Mediterranean coast mainly for use in the chemical industries. Sulfur and magnesite are two other important nonmetallic minerals found in

High-quality European automobiles and farm equipment have found worldwide markets.

European aircraft manufacturers have made steady inroads into what once was a U.S.-dominated industry.

Europe. Even with this seemingly impressive list of resources, Europe must still import minerals for its industries and agriculture.

Manufacturing. Generally, early peoples made their own personal tools, weapons, clothing, pottery, and other articles. Gradually, within a group or a city, experts would specialize in certain types of manufacturing (literally, "production by hand"), either for direct consumption or for sale. During the Middle Ages in Europe, experts in the same branch of manufacturing would join in a kind of union known as a guild to protect their industry. These associations often built beautiful guildhalls, such as those that still stand in Brussels.

The Industrial Revolution, despite its stress on coal and the creation of many new, generally ugly, towns of factories and row houses, did not entirely destroy the former craft specialties. Glasswork in Venice, steel blades in Toledo, watches in Switzerland, blue chinaware in Delft in the Netherlands, lacework in Flanders, and linen in Ireland are examples of such specialties that are still produced. But the main emphasis of the Industrial Revolution was on heavy industries and mass production.

In the 19th century, Europe, with its coal resources and its good transportation, became the world's greatest manufacturing area. Heavy industries developed near the coalfields in Britain, northern France, Belgium, Germany, and Poland. Later, when hydroelectric power was introduced, the already-existing industries of central Sweden and of northern Italy expanded. Large cities attracted factories. Harbors became prime locations for manufacturing industries where imported raw materials were most cheaply available.

The post-World War II development in Europe might have taken a different course had it not been for American help, principally the Marshall Plan of 1948. Moreover, the United States has invested many billions of dollars of private capital in Europe. American know-how and efficiency have also contributed much to Europe's industrial development. But, in the final analysis, it was the Europeans themselves who performed the economic miracle (as it is sometimes called) with their own hard labor, thrift, and intelligence.

Economic Development in the Former Communist Countries. After the Bolshevik revolution in 1917, the need to transform the Soviet state into a top industrial manufacturing power was a constant preoccupation of the Communist regime. Similar emphasis on heavy industries, especially those connected with the military, characterized the development of Soviet satellites in Eastern Europe following World War II. Meanwhile, stores were few and far between and often sparsely stocked.

The political and economic upheavals of recent years laid bare the inherent problems of Communist-managed industrial development. These flaws included complicated red tape that had always discouraged personal initiative, wasted energy, and technological backwardness.

The modernization of huge former Soviet industrial centers—particularly those around Moscow, in the middle Urals, or in the Donets Basin in Ukraine—is an overwhelming task. Many large and inefficient factories have closed or will soon do so. In Central Europe, heavy industry is being scaled down and services are expanding.

The 21st-Century Economy. In addition to the traditional economic mainstays, such as agriculture and industry, Europe, like the United States, is in the process of developing a more service-oriented economy, in which creativity and originality play ever-increasing roles. European leaders are aware that, overall, the continent continues to lag behind the United States in these fields, and are determined to narrow the gap. Several recent meetings of the EU were held to formulate a plan of action for the immediate future.

According to the EU, the goals necessary for Europe to prosper in the 21st century include: greater support for science and research; liberalization of national public-utilities markets; the creation of a public-transportation network across Europe; and the integration of national financial markets into one single market by 2005. The most difficult task facing European nations is the overall modification of social legislation. In contrast to their U.S. counterparts, European citizens have traditionally looked to the state as their sole provider of social benefits. For example, many Europeans enjoy job security, lengthy vacations, and early retirement, thanks to government programs. Any future legislation designed to alter or remove these benefits will likely be met with widespread disapproval.

Tourism. It is impossible to talk about the economy of Europe without mentioning tourism. Most of the traveling is done by Europeans themselves, although Americans, Japanese, and other affluent non-Europeans provide a good percentage. Tourism as it is now is quite different from what it used to be. Until the end of World War II, relatively few people traveled abroad. It was a pastime of the rich living separately in luxury hotels. Now everybody travels, by private automobile as well as by the large buses utilized by travel clubs—those organizations offering their members a selection of various trips for a small monthly payment. The mass of cars leaving Paris on the first of August, the traditional beginning date of French vacations, is almost unbelievable. Many stay in France, generally on the coasts, but others go abroad, including increasing numbers who visit the United States. The warm Mediterranean is a special attraction in summer, and along the Alpine crossings, cars drive or stand bumper to bumper.

Of course, tourism means welcome income for a nation. Spain, for example, can be called a tourist miracle. Until relatively recently, Spain was a forgotten country as far as most tourists were concerned. Roads, except for a few major ones, were bad; and hotels, except in the big cities, were few in number. Then Spain was "discovered," and people poured in across the Pyrenees. Roads were improved; new hotels arose everywhere. The main attraction is the Mediterranean coast: the Costa Brava—"wild coast"—between the Pyrenees and Barcelona, and more recently the Costa del Sol—"coast of the sun"—west of Málaga.

Tourism to and between the former Communist nations is also increasing. The removal of travel restrictions in many countries and the relative bargain prices have attracted visitors to the rich historical and natural treasures of the region. After decades of limited access, tourists are bringing much-needed foreign exchange to the economies that are struggling to shed the Communist ways of doing business.

Transportation

Roads. The impulse for the construction of better roads in Europe came initially from the military. Ancient Rome was the first to build roads for the swift movement of its troops. Napoleon constructed the French road system for similar reasons, and Hitler was responsible for the network of superhighways called *autobahns* in Germany. In later years the development of mass automobile production in Western Europe and the desire to attract tourists became the impetus for building first-class roads. Car tunnels such as the 7.5-mi. (12-km.)-long Mont Blanc Tunnel connecting France and Italy greatly shorten travel time. In Central Europe, the highways are generally narrower, but in relatively good condition. Farther east, the quality of roads declines and there are fewer of them.

The number of cars on the roads has increased rapidly since the end of World War II. Sweden has almost one car for every two inhabitants. In Northern Europe, bicycles are still popular, especially in the Netherlands and Denmark, and bicycle paths are often found on either side of the road. Since the fall of the Iron Curtain, the number of cars in the former Communist countries has mushroomed. In Prague, for instance, there are now twice as many cars as there were in 1989.

Railroads. Railroads started in Europe. In 1804, the world's first steam locomotive pulled a train of cars loaded with coal from a mine in Wales. In 1825, the Stockton and Darlington in England became the first railroad to be opened to the public. Gradually, the European rail network grew into the densest system in the world. In contrast to those in the United States in recent years, European passenger trains have increased in number and speed, and passenger traffic is heavy. Trains are generally comfortable, and many of them are considered luxurious by U.S. standards. With relatively short traveling distances between stations, railroads continue to compete with planes. A vast network of EURO-CITY and INTER-CITY trains now stretches east into the formerly Communist countries. Currently, the fastest train in Europe is the French TGV, which connects Paris and Lyons at a speed of 170 mi. (270 km.) per hour. The

Chunnel, a 31-mi. (50-km.)-long train tunnel under the English Channel, was opened in 1994 after seven years of construction.

Airlines. Europe was the home of the world's first commercial airline, Royal Dutch Airlines (KLM), established in 1919, and aviation has been important since the beginning of the century. Today practically every European country of any size has its own airline. Air France is the world's largest airline in terms of route mileage served. Some European countries, such as Denmark, Norway, and Sweden, have pooled their resources to operate a joint airline (Scandinavian Airlines). Britain and France together built and operate one of the world's two supersonic airliners, the Concorde. (The other is the Tupolev TU-144, an aircraft developed by the former Soviet Union.) Airlines connect all cities of any importance and, of course, connect Europe with all parts of the world. Such European "gateway" airports as Heathrow in London (the busiest airport in Europe), Orly in Paris, and Zurich in Switzerland handle vast amounts of traffic annually. The modernization of Prague's airport has made it a Central European traffic hub.

Waterways. Since ancient times, rivers have been major arteries of transportation. The main international rivers of Europe, the Rhine and the Danube, have played a part throughout history. The Rhine was used by the Romans, who also controlled its outlet. The Normans sailed up the rivers to plunder the commercial cities along their courses. In modern times, both the Rhine and the Danube are under international supervision. Of the two, the Danube is longer and connects more countries, but the Rhine is the more important economically. The Danube flows away from the main European markets and empties into the somewhat isolated Black Sea. The Rhine, however, serves Europe's most industrialized area; the port at its mouth at Rotterdam handles more freight than any other in the world. Rhine barges, under their own power or pulled by tugboats, go all the way to Basel, Switzerland. A narrow old canal connecting the Rhine with the Danube (and thus the North and the Black seas) has been replaced by a new shipping canal that opened in 1992.

Most rivers in the Central Lowlands, such as the Elbe and Oder in Germany and the Seine and Loire in France, are connected by a complicated maze of canals, which had their period of glory before the arrival of the railroads. England also had its own network of canals, now somewhat forgotten. It is still possible to cross most of Europe by small boat, going from the North Sea to the Mediterranean Sea, ending in Marseilles by way of a mountain boat tunnel.

Large shipping canals have been constructed in modern times. The New Waterway, the artificial outlet of the Rhine, looks more like a river than a canal and is lined for 16 mi. (26 km.) by harbor basins, which are part of the Rotterdam harbor complex, called Europoort by the Dutch. The Germans constructed the Kiel Canal as part of the trade route between the North Sea and the Baltic. Manchester, England, has its shipping canal to the Irish Sea. Antwerp, Belgium, has a canal joining it to the Rhine so that it can share in the Rhine trade. Romania recently completed a new shipping canal connecting the Danube River, near its mouth, with the Black Sea.

Being primarily lowlands, Russia is a country of large rivers. Except for those toward the Arctic, whose outlets are blocked by ice most of the year, these have long been major routes of transportation. The Volga, the

Its setting, history, and art make Venice a popular goal for tourists.

The Grenadier Guards at Windsor Castle represent the pageantry in English life.

longest river in Europe, is for Russia what the Rhine is for Germany, a river of folklore and historic significance as well as great economic importance.

The largest waterway is, of course, the ocean, and harbors are the contacts between continent and ocean. Europe has a great variety of coasts, some favorable, some unfavorable for shipping. In old times a port was adequate if it could serve ships of up to a few hundred tons; now there are supertankers of 300,000 tons. Some of the most important European ports are London and Liverpool in Britain, Rotterdam in the Netherlands, Antwerp in Belgium, Hamburg and Bremen in Germany, Le Havre and Marseilles in France, Genoa and Naples in Italy, Gdańsk and Szczecin in Poland, and Odessa in Ukraine.

Megalopolis

Since the Industrial Revolution, people have flocked into towns, where jobs are readily available. In capital cities, the government is usually the largest employer. Most Europeans are thus town or city dwellers. In Britain, for instance, 80 percent of the population lives in urban districts. More than 30 European cities have passed the 1 million mark, and many others are quite close to that number. The European successor states of the former Soviet Union have eight cities with more than a million inhabitants, led by Moscow. These statistics are often given for urban agglomerates. Generally, the old city core loses part of its population to the suburbs, where life is more pleasant.

For still-larger urban concentrations, the word "megalopolis" has been coined. It signifies a gigantic urbanized area, but it does not have to be continuous, and open spaces (greenbelts) may occur. In the United States, the word describes the coastal zone from Portland, Maine, to Washington, D.C. In Europe, a megalopolis is developing comprising northern France, central Belgium, the western Netherlands, and the lower Rhine region of Germany; its population may exceed 40 million.

Europe's Economic Future

With the economic integration of 1992 and the planned admission of former Communist countries into the European Union, Europe is turning into an economic giant, but it has to solve two major problems that have plagued the wealthy West European countries for quite some time: high unemployment and an overburdened social-security system. By the turn of the millennium, it became clear that the traditional European ways—paying high taxes, receiving extensive benefits, staying in one job and one location for an entire life—will have to be modified and complemented by more American-style flexibility and mobility. Several countries, especially in Scandinavia, have already jumped on the bandwagon of the information-age economy. The new European currency, the euro, replaced the national currencies of 12 countries on January 1, 2002. By that time, some of the former Communist nations had also begun to reap the benefits of their transformation from rigid, government-controlled economies into a free-market system.

HISTORY

The Europe of the earliest settlers was an uninviting place. Vast glaciers still covered much of the land. The climate was unpleasant—cold and damp. The vegetation was probably of the tundra type that is still found in the most northerly parts of the continent. The inhabitants of Europe during the Paleolithic period (Old Stone Age) did little to change the appearance of the land. These first Europeans lived as nomads—hunting animals, catching fish, and gathering food. Their skills were extremely limited, and the tools they made of bone, stone, and flint were rough and unpolished.

As the glaciers retreated, the climate gradually became more moderate, and the vegetation of Europe began to resemble that of the continent today. Waves of invaders, mainly from the east, brought new ideas and techniques that slowly altered the way of life of the first Europeans. The culture of Southwest Asia is believed to have entered Europe by way of three routes—the Aegean Sea, the Morava-Vardar River gap to the plains of the Danube, or the Bosporus to the lower Danube. Among the most enduring contributions of these invaders were language, tools, and the knowledge of how to live as settled farmers. Indo-European—the ancestor of all the modern European languages except Estonian, Finnish, Hungarian, and Basque—may have come with the invaders.

The knowledge of farming that developed in India, Mesopotamia, and Egypt spread slowly into Europe. It led to the establishment of permanent communities that shared their tools for farming and pooled their resources for mutual defense. A gradually increasing knowledge of the continent's resources—ranging from the tin of Cornwall to the copper of Austria—made it possible to make better tools for farming and defense. Animals, including horses, were domesticated. Wheeled carts and ships were built. Routes for trade in such commodities as amber, which was highly prized for jewelry, began to spread across the continent—the forerunners of today's network of rails and highways.

THE CLASSICAL CIVILIZATIONS

The combination of a rather mild climate and the nearness of the more highly developed cultures of the East acted as a stimulus to the first great European civilizations, which grew up on the northeastern edge of the Mediterranean Sea. From about 1600 to 1400 B.C., the Minoan civilization of the island of Crete dominated the Aegean. The Minoans, whose name may have come from Minos, a legendary priest-king who ruled over them, were a community of farmers, seafarers, traders, and artisans. Their culture is known for its emphasis on good taste and elegance. The houses of the wealthier citizens often were five stories tall and had terraces and individual wells.

The Civilization of Ancient Greece

The Minoans' development was first paralleled and then surpassed by the Mycenaeans, whose life centered around the city of Mycenae on the mainland of Greece from about 1600 to 1200 B.C. An elaborate government ruled over a community whose organization and variety are indicated in its preserved tax records and occupation census, where jobs are listed ranging from longshoreman to bath attendant. Although plentiful gold ornaments suggest that the Mycenaeans were as luxury-loving as the Minoans, they had a disposition to wage war. Their most famous conflict, under the leadership of their king, Agamemnon, was the 10-year-long Trojan War. This, the first recorded war in European history, is known to us through the first great European literary work, Homer's

Delos, one of the Cyclades Islands, offers evidence of the glories that were Greece.

epic the *Iliad,* which was composed several centuries after the Trojan War ended.

In the years between 1200 and 750 B.C., the older cultures of Crete and Mycenae disappeared, and successive waves of Dorian invaders from the north took over the Greek Peninsula and the nearby islands. Refugees from the Dorian invaders found a home in Athens, where the ancient cultures were preserved. In the upheaval caused by the invaders, only the smallest political units survived—the city-states, whose governments (whether they were tyrannies, aristocracies, or later, democracies) exerted a profound influence on all European political development. Despite the division into hundreds of political units, the Greeks were united by their language, their alphabet, and the beginnings of a political philosophy. Each adult male was responsible to his city, and the city in its turn was responsible for protecting the citizen by law and by arms.

Wine, olives, and wool were the chief products and the basis of Greek trade. But constant wars and a shortage of land plagued the Greeks, who did not know how to rotate crops, and thus often had large tracts of land lying fallow. As the population became too large for the land to support, Greek colonists settled in Ionia (the coast of Asia Minor) and in regions as distant as the Black Sea coast, Sicily, Massilia (Marseilles), and Tarraco (Tarragona, Spain). The seeds of modern European ideas based on Greek thought swept into Europe with the Greek traders who followed the Rhone River north to trade in Gaul (most of modern France and western Germany) and perhaps even in Cornwall and Ireland.

During the 5th century B.C., the Athenians and the Spartans turned back the Persians who threatened to occupy their lands. The defeat of the Persians in 480 B.C. marks the beginning of the most glorious, if brief, moments in human history—the Golden Age of Greece, when art, literature, and government reached heights that have scarcely been equaled since. Then the rivalry between the cities of Sparta and Athens led to the Peloponnesian Wars, which marked the close of the Golden Age and the defeat of Athens as a great power. But during the century that followed, some of the greatest Greek thinkers of all time lived. They included Socrates, his student Plato, and Plato's student Aristotle.

Aristotle, whose ideas were to dominate science for centuries, was himself the teacher of Alexander the Great, a man of action rather than reflection. Yet it is through him that so much Greek thought spread around the world and has come down to us. In 336 B.C., Alexander began a program of conquest that swept over Greece and across the Middle East to India and included all the lands along the eastern Mediterranean. In the city of Alexandria, which Alexander founded in Egypt, Greek ideas continued to be studied long after Alexander's vast empire had been divided.

The Rise and Fall of Rome

After Alexander's death in 323 B.C., the center of political power moved slowly westward to the Italian Peninsula, especially the city of Rome. Rome began as a city that was a sort of transition point between the culture of the Greek cities of the south and the Etruscan domains of the north. Rome gradually dominated the entire peninsula. It eliminated the threat of a rival imperial power, Carthage, in the course of the long Punic Wars (264–164 B.C.), and thus added the Carthaginian territories of Sicily, Spain, and parts of North Africa to its own growing empire. Threats from Macedonia and Greece were met by armed intervention, and soon Rome held outposts along the eastern coast of the Adriatic Sea. By A.D. 14 the Roman Empire had grown to include all the lands to the north as far as the Rhine and Danube rivers. In this way the civilization of the Mediterranean world become a part of the fabric of European life.

The ruins of the Roman Forum bear testimony to the grandeur of Europe's ancient civilizations.

Medieval castles were built of stone and surrounded by water-filled moats, to ward off attackers.

A highly centralized government, Rome was administered first as a monarchy, then as a republic, a military government, and finally, beginning in 27 B.C., as an empire. For some two centuries, from 30 B.C. to A.D. 193, Rome ruled its widespread empire in relative peace. Greco-Roman ideals, the Latin language, and an effective network of roads combined with a large standing army to unite people as different from each other as the Belgians, Iberians, and Britons. Art, literature, and philosophy flourished. Sciences grew more accurate. For the bureaucrats and land-holders, life was fairly easy and comfortable. For the dispossessed—peasants, slaves, and the unemployed—life was often harsh and difficult.

The most important religion that developed in the late Roman Empire was Christianity, which gradually replaced the cults of pagan gods. Groups of Christians grew larger in spite of persecution, and in A.D. 380, Christianity was proclaimed the state religion. Increasing numbers of Roman government officials became Christian bishops.

The First Barbarian Invasions

Barbarians had been pressing in on Rome's territory since the 3rd century A.D. To fend off invasions, Emperor Diocletian (A.D. 284–305) decided to divide the empire into an eastern and a western half so that it could be administered and defended more easily, and he shared power with a co-emperor. Although in A.D. 324, Constantine became sole emperor and the two halves were united, the empire was split again when Emperor Theodosius died in 395.

The richer Eastern Empire, Greek in culture, ultimately developed its own form of Christianity that came to be known as Eastern Orthodoxy. The poor western division, initially less cultivated because of continued fighting with barbarians, followed a different form of worship under Roman bishops, using Latin. Thus the faith branched out on two separate paths, although the final split between the East and western Roman Catholicism did not take place until 1054.

Pressing in on this divided state from the west and the south were Germanic tribesmen. Some joined the Roman army, others were enslaved, and still others became farmers. But they were never fully absorbed into Roman life, and as the need for land grew, they turned to conquest. In 410, the Goths attacked, looted, and burned the city of Rome. The city that for eight centuries had represented order and civilization worldwide had fallen.

By the end of the 5th century A.D., the Roman Empire in the west was ended, although the eastern half, centered at Constantinople (now Istanbul), continued to exist until the mid-15th century. The dream of reviving the huge, united Roman Empire lingered on for a long time in European civilization, and the title of "Roman Emperor" was also revived, in various forms, at later dates.

THE EARLY MIDDLE AGES

Historians writing in the 18th century viewed the history of Europe as the steady progress of humanity to the high point marked by the cultivated society of their own time. The period of the barbarian invasions, with its restless movement of populations, chronic warfare, and neglect of classical learning, seemed to the 18th-century mind to be the "Dark Ages." The six centuries following the Dark Ages are often called the Middle Ages. Generally the Middle Ages covers the era of European history from approximately the 8th to the 14th centuries. These years witnessed the last of the barbarian invasions, the triumph of Christianity as a unifying force, the clearing and settlement of forest and fringe lands, and the establishment of nearly all the towns and cities of Europe.

The peopling of Europe was almost completed by the beginning of the Middle Ages. The Bulgars settled in the state that bears their name. Hungary dates its founding to the establishment of the Magyar Empire in 896. During the previous century, Arabs had conquered Spain and threatened to overrun southwestern France.

The *Völkerwanderung*—as the movement of the Germanic tribes is called—left a lasting mark on Europe. They destroyed the Roman Empire in the west. In its place came the scattered kingdoms of the Ostrogoths in the lower Danube, northern Italy, and southern Gaul; the Franks' occupation of France, parts of Germany, Belgium, and the Netherlands; and the occupation of the lowlands of Britain by the Angles, Saxons, and Jutes.

Church and State

In a remarkably short period, the Christian faith spread across Europe. The political unity that Rome had provided was replaced by the Church, whose faith and whose language—Latin—shaped a new spiritual unity. The Church gave Europe a standard of values, a system of governing, and a link with the achievements of the classical past. The

Vatican City, an independent state surrounded by Rome, is the headquarters of the Roman Catholic Church.

kings of the new political units and the bishops of the Roman Church often worked together—the kings gaining power as they spread the gospel in the name of the Church to the remaining areas of paganism. In the monasteries, to which devout men retreated to worship and to study, a new band of teachers was born.

From the Irish monasteries, monks went to preach the faith to the Franks. In 597 Pope Gregory sent an Italian missionary, who later became St. Augustine of Canterbury, to England to convert the king and his subjects. In 716 a Benedictine monk named Boniface set out from England to ally the eastern Frankish Church with the popes. His success was capped by the elevation of Pepin as king of the Franks "by the grace of God" by the pope in 751. Not only had the kingship been made sacred and hereditary, but the indebted king could now be called upon to defend the Papal States that had grown up in central Italy. The king, for his part, could call upon the Church for support. The first powerful alliance between the temporal and spiritual world had been made. Such alliances were to be important for centuries to come.

By the time Pepin's son Charlemagne came to the Frankish throne in 768, everyday life in Western Europe was regaining the stability it had lost in invasions and wars. New lands were opened for cultivation, and improved farming methods were developed. Industry and trade also grew. Charlemagne added another element to this changing scene—a revival of the ideal of a politically united Europe. In the course of many campaigns, Charlemagne's Frankish armies drove the Avars out of Hungary, the Lombards out of the Papal States, set up the east march (or border) that formed the basis of the Austrian state, took Barcelona from the Muslims, and unified western Germany.

In A.D. 800, Charlemagne was named Roman emperor by the pope. Charlemagne established a strictly organized government, revived education, and sponsored the arts. After the death of Charlemagne in 814, his empire was divided and subdivided much as Alexander the Great's had been. The enfeebled successor states became easy prey to the seafaring warriors of Scandinavia—the Vikings.

The Vikings

"From the wrath of the Norsemen, O Lord, deliver us!" was perhaps the most common prayer heard in the 9th century. It reflected the terror of the population of Western Europe at the repeated attacks of Viking seamen from Scandinavia. They attacked towns as distant from their homeland as Cádiz in Spain and Pisa in Italy.

No one is quite sure what caused the sudden explosion of these seafarers from their coastal homes in Scandinavia. It may have been over-population or a hunger for wealth and power that drove them out of their homeland in their superbly built, oar-driven longships. The ancestors of the modern Danes, Norwegians, and Swedes followed different courses of plunder and trade. Danish Vikings took their ships to the nearby coasts of continental Europe and to the British Isles. By the middle of the 9th century, they had settled forces along the mouth of the Thames, the Loire, and the Seine. From these bases, they were able to send out fleets to besiege London, Paris, and other prosperous cities. Gradually, however, the invaders settled down. The name of Normandy in France, for example, reflects its settlement by the Norse.

Norwegian and Swedish Vikings ambitiously sailed farther from their bases in Scandinavia. The Norwegians occupied Ireland for about two centuries, and also succeeded in colonizing the Faeroes, Hebrides, and Orkney Islands, Iceland, and Greenland; in about the year 1000, they reached North America. The adventurous Swedish Vikings followed still another course of conquest and trade. They penetrated northern Russia, and then sailed south along the Volga and the Dnieper rivers. From their trading settlements at Nizhny Novgorod and Kiev, they took furs, amber, and slaves to trade with the inhabitants of the then-remote and wealthy cities of the Middle East. The unusual goods—such as silver, spices, and brocades—that they brought back provided the Swedish Vikings with the basis of a flourishing trade with the merchants of England, France, and Germany.

The years of the Viking conquests, which lasted from about A.D. 800 to 1000, had significant results for Europe. One of the most important results was that these fearless sailors traveled the seas of northern Europe. They opened up new routes of trade that rivaled and then eclipsed the local trade of the Mediterranean Basin. The Swedish Vikings, by becoming the rulers of their territories, helped establish the first Russian state. Russia may even have taken its name (Rus') from *ruotsi* (rowers), the Finnish word for the Viking invaders. Finally, the threat posed by the Viking raiders to the scattered and disunited governments of the continent led to the formation of institutions that were better equipped to deal with the realities of war and peace.

Feudalism

Europe at the time of the Viking raids was broken up into hundreds of poorly fortified communities. The basic political units were villages clustered around the castle of the local lord or the abbey of the monks.

Both the abbey and the castle served as fortresses when necessary. "Men of prayer, men of war, and men of work," as the 9th-century King Alfred the Great of England called them, made up the three large divisions of early medieval society.

The disasters caused by repeated invasions led to the growth of the feudal system. The system was based generally on an exchange of land for protection in time of need. Feudalism was based on the overlord's granting land—a fief—to a vassal. In exchange for his fief, the vassal would swear homage to his overlord. This meant that a vassal could be called upon to provide a certain number of knights to serve in the lord's army. The size of a man's landholding and the number of knights that he commanded determined his rank. Unfree peasants, called serfs, who actually farmed the land made up the broad base of the social structure. Over them, in order up to the overlord, were the squires, knights, and the nobles. The trained warriors provided by this system; improvements in weapons, armor, and the use of cavalry; and the growth of heavily fortified towns and cities helped bring some stability to the continent.

The feudal system prevailed in most of Europe until the 14th century, by which time the greatest and most powerful overlords had transformed themselves into hereditary monarchs. By the end of the 16th century, serfdom, too, had disappeared from Western Europe, although in central and Eastern Europe, it was not abolished until the 19th century. Traces of the feudal structure also remained in some areas such as parts of Italy, Germany, and Russia into the 19th century. In other parts of Europe, hereditary kings and standing armies provided a more effective response to the threat of war and served to protect the rapidly growing commerce of the cities.

THE LATE MIDDLE AGES

The end of the invasions and the organization of Europe into stable units of government, beginning in the 11th century, were heralds of

Cardiff Castle in Wales is a typical medieval fortress.

modern times. From England to Russia and from Norway to Italy, the forerunners of modern nations were evolving. The Church, under the guidance of outstanding popes, embarked on a series of reforms to strengthen and purify itself. In the arts the growing prosperity of the times was reflected in the building of magnificent and richly decorated churches. Education in schools and newly founded universities was extended to the laity as well as the clergy.

The increased productivity of the farms, which was based in part on crop rotation and technological improvements such as heavier plows pulled by draft animals, began to provide a surplus of food that freed some farmworkers to join the tradesmen in nearby villages. As the economy grew, villages became towns, and towns expanded into cities. Paris, Rouen, Hamburg, Cologne, Prague, Venice, Genoa, Florence, and Pisa became centers of trade.

The woolen textiles of Flanders, the metals of Bohemia, the wines of France, the swords of Toledo, and the leather of Córdoba were traded at markets and fairs all over Europe. The increasing wealth of the city merchants gave them enough political power to form a new middle class that had the independence to accept or reject the rule of an overlord. A new ideal of freedom and dignity for every man was striking at the foundations of the rigid feudal system.

Outside Influences on Europe

The many factors that shaped the relative peace and prosperity of Europe from the 11th to the 13th century freed Europeans to look beyond their own territories. The once-powerful empire formed by the Muslims was losing its unity, and the centuries-long reconquest of Spain by Christian warriors was under way. In the east was the Byzantine, or Eastern Roman, Empire. Constantinople, the capital, was the seat of a powerful, cultured Christian empire separated from the west because it was Greek in its traditions and because its church leaders refused to acknowledge the supremacy of the Roman Catholic pope. Beginning in about the year 1000, however, the Byzantine Empire started its decline. It was threatened by the Muslim Turks in the east and by the rising power of such city-states as Venice.

When the Roman Catholic popes rallied Western Europeans to recapture the Holy Land from the Muslims, Crusaders easily cut across Byzantine territory (1097–99, 1147–48), and in 1204 they turned on Christian Constantinople itself, capturing and sacking it. The Byzantine court returned to Constantinople in 1261, but the territory it ruled until it was finally overthrown by the Turks in 1453 was a collection of virtually independent states rather than a united empire.

One branch of the Orthodox Christian community survived far to the north of Constantinople in the disunited and troubled Russian principalities. But the life of these scattered Russian ministates was repeatedly threatened by nomadic invaders from the east. In the early 13th century, Mongols from Asia reduced almost all of Russia to the status of a tribute-paying state. The collection of the tribute to the Mongols' Golden Horde was the job of the grand dukes of Moscow, who thus slowly grew in power and prestige. By the end of the 15th century, Ivan III of Moscow was powerful enough to stop sending the tribute, an important step in shaping Russia's future as a major nation.

The Crusades

In the west the power of the popes continued to grow—a fact that was reflected in their successful control of the Holy Roman emperors and of the dramatic response from all Europe to the call to free the Holy Land from the "infidel" Muslims. Thousands sought that end in nine separate Crusades between the 11th and 14th centuries. Although the Crusaders succeeded in freeing Jerusalem for only about 100 years, these warrior pilgrimages had important repercussions in Europe. Since most of the Crusaders took the land route to the Holy Land, they passed through Constantinople, which was still the most cultured and important city in Europe. The influence of Byzantine culture on the relatively unlettered Crusaders was profound. The contact with the Muslims had the important effect of renewing the bonds between Europeans and the civilization of their Greek ancestors, whose learning had been preserved by Mohammed's followers.

The Crusades had other significant consequences for Europe. The money needed to outfit and transport the Crusaders was circulated in coins made of precious metals. Where money was not immediately available, forms of credit were devised—the forerunners of modern banking. The taste of new, exotic goods that was stimulated by the Crusaders' discoveries in the Middle East helped to stimulate trade and growth of the merchant class.

The mixture of nationalities represented in each Crusade reflected both a united Christendom and the birth of national awareness. Men from hundreds of isolated localities in Europe, unified only by their religion, met and fought side by side in the Crusades. Unavoidably, a sense of national differences arose and provided a powerful impetus to the development and support of centralized monarchies.

In England, a strongly centralized government was formed in the 11th century by William the Conqueror. When the barons forced King John to grant the Magna Carta—Great Charter—in 1215, an important step had been taken in the evolution of England's unique form of constitutional monarchy. France was united under the reign of Saint Louis (1226–70), and solidified its position on the continent in the Hundred Years' War (1337–1461), which ended England's claim to the French throne. In Scandinavia, Russia, Austria, and Hungary, monarchies were also well established by the end of the Middle Ages. By 1492, the Spanish had succeeded in driving the Muslims out of their land and forming a central government. Elsewhere in Europe, less centralization was still the rule. Germany and Italy remained divided into a number of small separate states until the 19th century.

Renaissance and Exploration

Two important movements mark the close of the Middle Ages in Europe and the beginning of modern times. They were the Renaissance (as the rebirth of interest in classical civilizations is called) and the great explorations of European seamen.

The Renaissance, which started in the prosperous commercial cities of northern Italy in the 14th century, had spread across Europe by the 16th century. The Renaissance is set apart from the Middle Ages because people actually changed their way of looking at the world. Such outside influences as the Crusades combined with the growth of the European

Wealth from trade and exploration helped to develop the Netherlands.

economy to make people more curious about themselves, their lives in this world, and the universe as a whole. The period was marked by an effort to revive classical ideals and forms. There was a widespread revival of interest in the writings of ancient philosophers and poets, as the Italian poet Dante's *Divine Comedy* demonstrates. There were also remarkable developments in art. Purely religious art, which had flourished throughout the Middle Ages, was replaced by realistic portrayals of everyday events and people. The development of linear perspective, which makes a two-dimensional picture seem to have three dimensions, is considered one of the major contributions of Renaissance artists. Such creative giants as Leonardo da Vinci, Michelangelo, Machiavelli, Shakespeare, Rabelais, Montaigne, and Erasmus provided new perspectives on every phase of human life. Through the variety of their achievements, these men earned fame as "universal men"—the ideal of all Renaissance people because it represented the highest achievement possible on this Earth.

Just as the Renaissance opened up new perspectives in art and thought, so the great voyages of exploration revolutionized knowledge of Earth. Sailing under the flags of the major merchant kingdoms of the continent, such explorers as Christopher Columbus (1451–1506), Vasco da Gama (1469?–1524), and Ferdinand Magellan (1480?–1521) opened up the world's sea-lanes and revealed the existence of the Americas as well as new routes to Africa and Asia. The wealth of Africa, Asia, and the Americas first poured into Portugal and Spain. When the English, Dutch, and French expanded their influence overseas, they built up even larger and more durable empires. The development of powerful navies that could control the sea-lanes provided the basis of power for the great colonizing nations until the 20th century.

THE BIRTH OF MODERN EUROPE

The growing prosperity and spiritual unity of Europe was shattered at the beginning of the 16th century. In 1517 a German priest, Martin Luther, launched a protest movement against what he felt were abuses by the Roman Catholic Church. Neither the pope nor the Holy Roman emperor was able to contain the Protestant movement. Emperor Charles V, who also ruled as the king of Spain, was preoccupied protecting his own far-flung possessions. The Church itself was at first too entangled in local politics to concern itself with Luther's heresy. By the time the pope and the emperor were free to act, Luther's Protestant followers numbered in the thousands. The Counter Reformation launched by the papacy and supported by the Habsburg Holy Roman emperor reformed and reorganized the Church and succeeded in retaining most of its followers in southern and central Europe.

Yet national ambitions and religious beliefs continued to fan the flames of war. Throughout the closing years of the 16th century, civil wars raged in France, ending only when Henry of Navarre abandoned his Protestantism to become King Henry IV. However, he gave a wide degree of freedom to the Protestants in his kingdom. Spain's provinces in the Netherlands gained what amounted to independence in the early 17th century and divided along religious lines—a fact that is reflected today in the existence of predominantly Catholic Belgium and the largely Protestant Netherlands. The civil war that raged in England between 1642 and 1648 involved Protestant sects, but was caused by questions about Parliament's power as well. By 1689 the issue was resolved in favor of the Anglican Church and the supremacy of Parliament.

The most terrible religious wars of the 17th century were caused by the Habsburg emperors' efforts to suppress Protestantism in Bohemia (now part of the Czech Republic) and Germany, and ultimately involved Sweden, Denmark, and France. The Thirty Years' War (1618–48), as it is known, resulted in the worst devastation Germany was to experience until World War II. The German states remained divided between the Roman Catholic and Protestant faiths. Politically, a union of the German states was delayed by the religious issues. The powerful, united monarchy of France became the leading European state.

By the middle of the 17th century, the religious quarrels were largely settled, and the interests awakened by the Renaissance could be pursued again. The work of such scientists and philosophers as Sir Isaac Newton, René Descartes, Baruch Spinoza, and John Locke seemed to show that humans and their universe were subject to natural laws that could be observed, measured, and predicted. If, indeed, the world was based on these orderly, clockwork principles, it meant that people and their institutions could be improved by using reason. History itself was seen as a staircase on which humankind was rising to higher levels.

Throughout the 18th century in Europe and America, educated people explored the philosophic, scientific, economic, political, and religious consequences of these theories. The result was an intellectual revolution. Humans, whom religion had portrayed as helpless victims of uncontrollable forces, were transformed into rational creatures capable of guiding and improving their own destinies. Such ideas fitted the views of the prosperous, self-made middle class perfectly, but threatened the very existence of organized religion and absolute monarchy. The political theorists of the 18th century first thought that the most appropriate form of government would be "enlightened despotism"; that is, government based on the rule of an intelligent monarch who could impose and enforce reforms. Such monarchs as Catherine II of Russia, Joseph II of Austria, and Friedrich (Frederick) II of Prussia seemed to embody the virtues of the enlightened despot. In France, with its absolute monarch, and in the American colonies, ruled by a distant king, the ideas of the Enlightenment were the seeds of revolution.

Two Revolutions

From the end of the religious wars in the mid 17th-century until 1789, France was a flourishing but troubled nation. The middle class increasingly disliked the absolute rule of its kings, who claimed to rule by "divine right." Prosperous merchants hoping for a voice in government were unhappy to hear the legendary remark of King Louis XIV, "L'état c'est moi [I am the state]." The revolution that began in France in 1789 was based on the "enlightened" hope that the government could be reorganized to serve all French citizens equally. The results were less clear-cut than the philosophers had hoped, and various groups came into conflict over what was the best route for France to follow.

Politically, one of the obvious achievements of the revolution was the overthrow of the monarchy and an end of the feudal tradition in France. The middle class achieved a central role in national life, as it would all over Europe in the course of the next century. The triumph of "Liberty, Equality, and Fraternity" was not reflected, however, in the realm of government, which was taken over by General Napoleon Bonaparte in 1799 after years of chaos. Through internal reforms and brilliantly executed military maneuvers, Bonaparte made France the leading power

Versailles, a French palace, symbolized royal power and prestige.

The National Museum of Natural History, in Paris.

in Europe. Napoleon's decision to invade Russia, however, proved disastrous. Napoleon's final downfall came at the Battle of Waterloo in 1815. Yet France's dramatic rise to immense power under Napoleon left its mark on the subsequent history of Europe.

An entirely different kind of revolution stemming from the Enlightenment began in the middle years of the 18th century. The Industrial Revolution, as it is called, replaced manpower with the power of machines. Harnessing the resources of the earth began the period of change that would literally alter the face of the globe and the life of people everywhere. Where wind- and waterpower had once been the chief substitutes for individual labor, there emerged a host of machines using coal as a power source. The revolution began in England, where James Watt's steam engine (invented in 1769) was followed by such devices as the flying shuttle, spinning jenny, and power loom for use in large-scale textile production. The work of thousands of skilled individuals was replaced in a matter of years by the work of machines. A similar change followed in the mining of coal, the manufacture of machinery, and the processing of metals. Green landscapes were replaced by clusters of factories and houses for industrial workers. Canals, roads, and later railways and steam-driven ships provided new links between mines and factories, factories and consumers, and finally between nations.

In the course of the 19th and 20th centuries, the Industrial Revolution created more far-reaching changes in Europe than any other event in its history. The leaders of the Enlightenment surely would have considered the Industrial Revolution a sign of progress. Thousands and thousands of people were made more nearly equal by the provision of standard goods for all who could afford them. A surplus of food became available. Advances in medicine helped eliminate diseases that had destroyed entire generations, and advances in housing and education provided obvious benefits.

Yet some observers soon began to point out that industrialization was a mixed blessing. The beauties of the countryside were blotted out by factories and squalid houses. The long hours of routine factory work proved to be dull and dispiriting, and craftsmanship and a worker's pride in a job well done were lost. The relationship between a factory worker and his or her employer was often less stable than the one that had existed between a farmer and his lord. If business was bad, workers were laid off and left to survive as best they could. And so, along with liberalism—the political, social, and economic philosophy of the capitalist middle class—there developed the theory of socialism, which attracted many members of the working classes. The most important proponent of economic equality and justice was the German philosopher Karl Marx (1818–83), who developed a vision of "classless society," or Communism.

Meanwhile, the extension of European power outside the continent, which had begun 1,000 years earlier with the Vikings, reached its height in the last years of the 19th century. At that time, several nations of Europe constituted what amounted to a world superpower, directly controlling dozens of countries around the globe.

Many European cities have sidewalk cafés or coffee shops where pedestrians can relax and enjoy refreshments.

Paris' Arc de Triomphe, the world's largest triumphal arch, was built as a memorial to Napoleon's victories.

The 20th Century

In 1900, European leaders were still for the most part hereditary kings and emperors. France alone among the major European nations was a republic. When the German states were finally united in 1871, the new nation was organized as an empire, and it surged to a leading position on the continent, threatened only by its powerful rivals, England and France. German fears of encirclement by its enemies, and its enemies' fears of German preeminence, led to World War I (1914–18), which was much more brutal than all previous European military conflicts. For the first time, the new destructive instruments of airpower, tanks, submarines, and chemical weapons were used. Germany and Austria-Hungary were eventually defeated by the Allies—France, England, and the United States—but at a tremendous cost: 10 million people killed and 20 million wounded. It seemed impossible that people would ever seek war as a solution again. Indeed, contemporaries called the conflagration "the war to end all wars." The subsequent establishment of the League of Nations and the Versailles peace treaties seemed to ensure a peaceful future for both the old and the newly established European states.

In place of the vast Austro-Hungarian Empire, which had ruled much of Central Europe, there now appeared Poland, Czechoslovakia, Hungary, Yugoslavia, and the small Austrian Republic. Russia, which had been convulsed by revolution in the closing years of the war, emerged as the Communist Union of Soviet Socialist Republics—a massive counterbalance to the nations of Western and Central Europe. Germany itself became a republic and was forbidden by treaties to manufacture weapons; in addition, it was required to pay enormous reparations to the Allies.

The rebuilding of a new Europe out of the rubble of the war, however, was soon undermined by inflation in the 1920s and by the worldwide Depression of the 1930s. Millions of people became unemployed and impoverished. Labor unrest then led to the rise of fascism in Italy, under Benito Mussolini, and to Nazism in Germany, under Adolf Hitler. The stage was set for World War II.

This conflict, which started in 1939 and soon involved countries from three other continents, seemed to herald the final destruction of European civilization. It is estimated that there were almost 15 million military deaths and probably an equal number among civilians. Millions of Jews, as well as members of other ethnic groups targeted by the Nazis and their allies, were exterminated in Hitler's concentration camps. These dreadful events added a new horror to warfare—genocide, the murder of an entire people. But the tide turned against Hitler when, like Napoleon before him, he attacked the Soviet Union. A war fought on two fronts—one in the west against the growing underground resistance aided by Allied bombings, the other in a long battle against the Soviets in the east—finally overwhelmed the Nazi war machine in 1945.

This time, Europe's economic recovery was remarkably swift, particularly in the western half, which allied itself with the United States. But even in Eastern Europe, increasingly dominated by the Soviet Union, the scars of war soon disappeared. Most of the remaining European colonies in Asia, Africa, and Central America gained their independence after World War II.

The United States and the Soviet Union were both founding members of the United Nations in 1945. But soon after the war ended, the

The Palais des Nations in Geneva, Switzerland, is the European headquarters of the United Nations.

The Berlin Wall long symbolized the opposing philosophies of the Communist East and the democratic West.

Soviets' determination to extend their political and economic control throughout Eastern Europe fractured the wartime alliance and launched the Cold War. Its symbol, the "Iron Curtain," was a heavily fortified barrier constructed by Communist regimes, not only to exclude Western people, goods, and ideas, but also to keep their own populations from fleeing. Where it passed through the divided city of Berlin, the barrier was actually a solid wall of masonry. Two different political, religious, social, and cultural systems developed on the opposing sides of the Iron Curtain. Free-market capitalism and liberal democracy flourished on the Western side of the boundary, while Marxist-Communist regimes in the East attempted to exercise central control over all aspects of the lives of their people. The tension and hostility between the two parts of Europe produced two military alliances: the North Atlantic Treaty Organization (NATO), established in 1949 and including the United States, and the Warsaw Pact, established in 1955 and headed by the Soviet Union.

And so in the late 1940s, Europe became a continent divided and remained so for the next four decades. The center of world power shifted outside Europe to the two nuclear superpowers, the United States and the Soviet Union.

In 1949, the Council of Europe was founded in Strasbourg, France, as part of a cooperative effort at reconstruction. Other cooperative organizations followed, and the large Western European nations thus became closely intertwined. In 1957, six countries formed the European Economic Community (or Common Market), the precursor of the future European Union.

The United States played a crucial role in Western European development: it provided massive economic aid in the form of the Marshall Plan, which helped Germany and other nations to rebuild their bombed cities, repair damaged roads and bridges, and revitalize industry. The United States also protected Western Europe by maintaining its military bases there, mainly in Germany, but in other countries as well. As the leading member of NATO and the Organization for Economic Cooperation and Development (OECD), the United States became much more involved in European affairs than ever before. Western Europeans occasionally resented certain American policies or actions, but a generally positive attitude prevailed, and the peoples of the two Atlantic outposts of democracy became great friends.

On the other side of the Iron Curtain, the Euro-Asian Soviet Union ruled with an iron hand. In contrast to Western Europe, the "satellite" Eastern European countries were kept under Soviet domination by force. Whenever citizens in those countries showed the slightest disobedience to Moscow, they were severely punished. In 1953, Soviet troops suppressed a workers' demonstration in East Germany. In 1956, the Soviet army brutally crushed a Hungarian uprising, killing thousands. And in 1968, half a million Warsaw Pact soldiers invaded Czechoslovakia to put an end to the liberalization policies known as the Prague Spring. Ironically, this was the only military operation of the Soviet-dominated Warsaw Pact.

The Soviet Union also bound its satellites in an economic alliance known as COMECON (Council for Mutual Economic Assistance), set up in 1949. In contrast to Western European economic organizations, which supported regional cooperation, COMECON's primary purpose was to serve the interests of the Soviet Union. Many Eastern European countries felt that they were being exploited by their "Big Brother." The only advantage of COMECON for them was the supply of inexpensive Soviet oil.

Contemporary architecture in Europe has assumed a distinctly abstract form.

CONTEMPORARY EUROPE

In March 1985, the last of the old guard of Soviet Communist leaders died; he was replaced by a representative of the new generation, Mikhail Gorbachev. He tried to reform the Soviet system, but it was like trying to square a circle. Only Gorbachev's "new thinking" in foreign policy proved to be a success, because it led to the end of the Cold War.

In 1989, Communist leaders in Poland, Hungary, East Germany, Bulgaria, and Czechoslovakia stepped down with astonishing but impressive restraint. Only in Romania was the change a violent one. In 1990, East Germany and West Germany were united after the fall of the Berlin Wall, and early the following year, Albania held its first-ever free elections. The turbulent breakup of Yugoslavia also began. And then, on December 25, 1991, an era came to an end, as the red Soviet flag—with its distinctive hammer and sickle—was lowered to signify the dissolution of the Communist superpower.

The earthquake that completely rearranged the former Communist world came at the same time that Western Europe was under the spell of the "spirit of Maastricht." The name of this small Dutch town came to embody the Western European unification effort. In December 1991, 12 member countries of the European Community signed a treaty at Maastricht, renaming their organization the European Union and pledging to coordinate their economic, social, and foreign policies, and to create a single European currency before the end of the century.

In the years following these historic events, new challenges have appeared. Before 1990, many imagined that once the Communist regime was toppled, a rosy capitalist and democratic future would lie ahead. In reality, the transformation was far more arduous. Even though Communism as a system is gone, many of its characteristics still survive. In several countries, corruption has increased dramatically. The worst developments occurred in the former Yugoslavia and in the Russian republic of Chechnya, where armed conflicts and ethnic disputes killed hundreds of thousands of people or destroyed their homes.

Meanwhile, Western Europe has concentrated on the Economic Monetary Union (EMU), which was put in place on January 1, 1999, and on conducting extensive negotiations with several countries that want to join the European Union. The EU countries have also begun talks on setting up their own defense system and not to rely solely on NATO.

In the beginning of the 21st century, Europe is becoming more unified—with many transnational institutions and corporations complementing national governments and companies—and, at the same time, decentralized, with hundreds of new regional centers, sister cities across the continent, and border communities in which people of different languages and history organize communal events. Yet one major problem seems to be emerging—the handling of the ever-increasing numbers of immigrants from poorer regions of the world. Many governments have already made their immigration laws more restrictive. Despite this development, the younger generation of Europeans has largely discarded old nationalistic rivalries, and feels comfortable moving from country to country. More Europeans have come to understand that they must combine old traditions with new flexibility in order to help realize their continent's full potential.

JOSEPH F. ZACEK, State University of New York at Albany

Ireland is truly an "emerald isle."

IRELAND

The island of Ireland, a land of great natural beauty, forms the western boundary of the Eurasian landmass. Its most remarkable natural feature is its greenness, which has given it the title of the Emerald Isle.

Ireland has had a long and often tragic history. For over 700 years the people struggled against oppression, famine, and disease. Despite these hardships, the Irish have made great contributions to the world, including an extraordinary wealth of great literature. So many Irish have emigrated that today, about 70 million people worldwide claim Irish ancestry, including 40 million in the United States alone. Good times came in the 1990s, when Ireland was dubbed the "Celtic Tiger" for its spectacular economic growth. At the turn of the millennium, many Irish said that their country jumped from the 19th century right into the 21st.

THE LAND

Ireland resembles a saucer, with a fertile central plain and a rim of hills and low mountains. The most famous of the mountain ranges are the Macgillycuddy's Reeks, where Ireland's highest peak, Carrantuohill,

Peat being cut in County Donegal for use as fuel.

rises 3,400 feet (1,040 meters) above sea level. Everywhere the Irish coast is broken by indentations. The west coast is a place of wild grandeur, with sheer cliffs broken by mysterious coves and inlets.

Central Ireland is a region of meadows, bogs, lakes, and many twisting, turning rivers. Peat covers much of the surface of the island. These peat bogs are a mixture of mosses, heather, and other materials that, because of special soil and climatic conditions, have become compressed and carbonized over the centuries. The peat is cut and dried to be used as fuel in homes and in industry. As the bogs are cleared, the land is being made usable for planting. About one fourth of Ireland is cultivated and one fourth is occupied by peat bogs, marshes, mountains, and lakes. The rest is meadowland, where the world-famous Irish horses and cattle graze.

Rivers and Lakes. Running through the island is the great Shannon River, the longest river in the British Isles. For over 200 miles (320 km.), the Shannon serenely winds its way through the beautiful Irish countryside, widening out at places to form spectacular lakes, such as Lough Allen, Lough Ree, and Lough Derg.

Climate. Ireland is so far north that one would expect severe winters. In fact, the weather is relatively mild all year long. The North Atlantic Drift brings the warm waters of the Gulf Stream to the coast of Northern

IRELAND

Europe. At the same time, because of the westerly Atlantic winds, it brings the rainfall that with the mild weather makes Ireland so intensely green. In the west as much as 80 in. (200 cm.) of rain falls in a year, while in the east it may be only 30 in. (80 cm.).

THE PEOPLE

The Irish are a people of predominantly Celtic stock, who were for many centuries under English rule. In 1922, 26 largely Catholic counties became independent of Britain, while the mainly Protestant northeastern counties secured a parliament of their own, subject to the Parliament of the United Kingdom of Great Britain and Northern Ireland.

John Millington Synge (1871–1909), an Irish playwright, said, "It's in a lonesome place, you do have to be talking with someone...." And the Irish do indeed love to talk—at any time, to anyone, anywhere. Words flow melodiously, rivers of words full of wit and color. But Irish wit, humor, and warmth are mixed with a sense of fatalism and a deep reverence for religion. The Irish constitution separates church and state, but recognizes the "special position" of the Roman Catholic Church. The strength of traditional religious feelings was evident in a long legislative battle over divorce, which was legalized only in 1995—but dissolving a marriage is still much more difficult in Ireland than elsewhere.

A pub—public house—is a popular meeting place in Ireland.

As in many countries where the Industrial Revolution came late, there is a great difference in the way families in rural Ireland and those in the industrial centers live. However, everywhere in Ireland family life is close, and there is great devotion to parents. In rural Ireland particularly, the pub is the man's social club, where he may have his glass of black stout, the famous Irish beer, and enjoy the company of his neighbors. Thanks to the "economic miracle" of the 1990s, however, even traditional Irish ways are changing and the talk in local pubs now often revolves around investment opportunities and stock-exchange news.

The Irish are passionate sports enthusiasts. Traditionally they have always hunted and fished. They love horses, and horse racing is a great national sport. The Irish Derby is one of the world's most famous races, and betting on the National Sweepstakes, run for the benefit of the Irish hospitals, is virtually a national industry.

Among the most popular sports is the ancient game of hurling. It is a type of field hockey played with a curved ash stick and a small leather ball by two teams of 15 players, who need great strength, skill, and timing. Gaelic football (a combination of soccer and rugby), soccer, rugby, golf, bowling, and sailing are all very popular.

Céad míle fáilte ("a hundred thousand welcomes") is the traditional Irish greeting, and the Irish are renowned for their hospitality. A visitor will be urged to come for a drink or a meal.

Dublin University (Trinity College), is a world-famous institution of higher learning.

Language and Learning

Irish (or Gaelic), one of the oldest languages in Europe, was the speech of the Celts in Ireland. Its use began to decline early in the 1800s. When the Irish government was set up in 1922, strenuous efforts were made to revive Irish. The teaching of Irish was made compulsory in all schools, and it became the language of instruction in the teachers' colleges. In the Irish Constitution of 1937, Irish was declared the "first official language" of Ireland, English the second. Recently, the drive to revive Irish has been quite successful, and the difficult language is recognized as one of the official languages of the European Union (EU).

Education is free and compulsory for all children between the ages of 6 and 15. Since the 1970s, the Irish government has invested heavily in education, and today, many more children continue their studies beyond the secondary level. This policy has translated into the current flourishing economy. There are four universities—Dublin University (which is also called Trinity College); the National University, with colleges in Dublin, Maynooth (Kildare), Cork, and Galway; Dublin City University; and the University of Limerick. Dublin has two fine schools of technology, where architects and engineers are trained. And in Dublin and Cork there are well-known schools of music and art. The National Museum of Ireland is located in Dublin as is the National Gallery of Ireland. The James Joyce Museum has relics of the world-famous author.

Irish Literature

Long before any school existed in Ireland, there was a great native oral tradition. The earliest known literature of Ireland dates from the 8th and 9th centuries when the poet-singers, or bards, recited the romances, or sagas, of their heroes. The Ulster Cycle relates the story of the great hero Cuchulain. The collection of tales known as the Fenian Cycle deals with the exploits of Finn Mac Cool and his band of warriors, the Fianna. Poets enjoyed the patronage of kings in the old Gaelic society. They wrote court poems honoring their kings, but also recorded history and dealt with law and medicine. During the troubled years of war, the songs of Ireland became sad songs. The poets, forbidden to sing openly of their love for Ireland, addressed instead a mythical queen, Cathleen Ní Houlihan, one of the poetic names for Ireland.

Some poetry is still written in Irish in the new Ireland, but it is writing in English that has made Irish literature famous throughout the world. Jonathan Swift, Dean of St. Patrick's Cathedral during the first half of the 18th century, was the first of a long line of what have been called Anglo-Irish writers. *Gulliver's Travels* is read today as a delightful fantasy, but it was written, as were many of Swift's works, as a bitter satire on English rule in Ireland, as well as on humanity in general. Other great Irish literary figures of the 18th century wrote and lived in England. They included Oliver Goldsmith, the poet, novelist, and playwright; Edmund Burke, the political philosopher; Richard Brinsley Sheridan, the dramatist; and Richard Steele, the essayist. Possibly the best-known 19th-century Irish writer was the poet, novelist, and playwright Oscar Wilde.

The 20th century has come to be known as the period of the Irish literary renaissance. The fight for independence aroused interest in the Irish past, and ancient sagas were revived. Ireland's greatest modern poet, William Butler Yeats, was inspired by the old tales and stirred by the heroism of the struggle for independence. Together with Lady Augusta Gregory, Yeats in 1897 helped found the Irish National Theatre in Dublin. It is famous throughout the world as the Abbey Theatre, the home of the Abbey Players. Yeats influenced John Synge to return from abroad to write in his native Ireland. Synge's ability to record the poetry of peasant speech and to write about the poor honestly and beautifully is best illustrated by his play *The Playboy of the Western World*. Another famous playwright, Sean O'Casey, also wrote for the Abbey Theatre.

Ireland's best-known dramatist, George Bernard Shaw, lived and wrote in England. *Candida, Arms and the Man, Caesar and Cleopatra, Man and Superman, Major Barbara, Pygmalion,* and other plays are about contemporary social problems and sparkle with Irish wit and satire.

The writer who is often called the greatest literary figure of this century, James Joyce, also lived and wrote abroad, but his work was about his native Ireland. *Ulysses,* his most famous novel, is about a day in Dublin, June 16, 1904. Joyce vividly records everything that his three main characters did, thought, and felt during that day and night.

Wherever books are read, 20th-century Irish writers are well-known. Liam O'Flaherty, Sean O'Faolain, Frank O'Connor, Samuel Beckett, and Brendan Behan are just some of these world-renowned Irish authors. More recently, Frank McCourt, a 66-year-old teacher who had never before written a book, gained immense popularity with his memoir of Irish childhood, *Angela's Ashes*, which won a Pulitzer Prize in 1997.

Finely crafted Waterford crystal is one of Ireland's best known exports.

ECONOMY

There have been many changes in modern Ireland, with industry displacing agriculture as the most important source of income. Although some two-fifths of the population is rural, less than 10 percent of the labor force works in agriculture. The high rainfall and the moderate temperature make Ireland one of the finest grass-growing countries in the world. As a result most of the land is devoted to pasture. Cattle and milk account for about 85 percent of all agricultural production. Sheep, pigs, and the famous Irish horses are also very important. The principal field crops are barley, oats, potatoes, wheat, and sugar beets.

The government has done much to promote progressive farming, to develop better strains of livestock, and to increase the average size of farms by programs of land reform. There are large horse farms, cattle ranches, and dairy farms. A substantial portion of Ireland's industry has been related to processing agricultural products into food, drink, and leather. New industries based on the processing of imported raw materials include oil refining, shipbuilding, and the manufacture of clothing, textiles, chemicals, and machinery.

Traditional Irish exports are well-known. Waterford crystal has been admired for years. Irish whiskey, beer, oatmeal, and hams are sold in many countries, as are clothing and other products.

For much of the 20th century, Ireland's greatest preoccupation was industrial development, with the goal of catching up with more-advanced European countries, raising the standard of living, employing the young people, and stemming the flow of emigration.

A new chapter in Ireland's history opened in 1973, when Ireland, together with Great Britain and Denmark, joined the European Economic Community, known then as the Common Market. The membership in this expanding organization—which was renamed the European Union in 1991—enabled Ireland to build up and improve its communication networks and extend economic ties with other countries. At the same time, Irish leaders began to support education, realizing that the greatest asset of the nation is its youth. In a sense, Ireland is a very young country, with more than half of its population under the age of 25. The third important factor in recent developments was the increasing emphasis placed on the newest high-tech economy.

In the first years of the 21st century, Ireland is a confident, robust country, with the highest economic growth rate in Europe (more than 9 percent), practically no unemployment, and a steady flow of foreign investors. Dublin has become established as one of the financial centers of Europe, and the city's building boom has been unable to keep pace with the ever-increasing demand for office space. The exuberant Irish now point out with pride that their living standards have even surpassed those of Great Britain.

DUBLIN, IRELAND'S CAPITAL CITY

Dublin, the heart of Ireland, is set on a wide, sandy bay on the Irish Sea. In the distance you can see the heather-covered slopes of the hills of Wicklow. An old city, Dublin was first mentioned by the Alexandrian geographer Ptolemy in A.D. 140. It is a city where much of Ireland's history has taken place, and many of its buildings bear the scars of battle. Some of the finest buildings, such as the Customs House and the Four Courts Buildings, were destroyed in the fighting of the 1920s but have been restored.

The museums are filled with treasures of the past. In Trinity College is the great Book of Kells, the 340-page hand-illuminated Celtic manuscript of four books of the New Testament. Beautifully painted and inscribed by 9th-century monks, it is considered by many to be the most beautiful manuscript in existence. The old parliament house (now the Bank of Ireland), the Abbey Theatre, famous churches, elegant Georgian town houses, and great parks and gardens grace the city. Phoenix Park, with its racecourse and famous zoo, is one of the world's largest and finest enclosed public parks. Dublin was a city of great elegance in

O'Connell Street, Dublin's main thoroughfare, is named for a 19th-century Irish patriot.

The colorful horse show is an annual event in Dublin.

the 18th century and at one time was considered to be second only to London. After the Act of Union in 1800, when the old Dublin parliament ceased to exist, the city gradually fell into decay. Many of the magnificent Georgian houses became tenements, and the glow and glamour of life began to fade away. Since Dublin became a seat of government again in 1922, it has indeed expanded in a new way. It has now become a thriving industrial complex, with all that this involves in factories, supermarkets, and office blocks. However, a shadow of the old elegance still haunts such streets and squares as Harcourt Street, Merrion Square, and St. Stephen's Green.

Other Cities of Ireland

In the south is **Cork**, the Republic of Ireland's second city. It has less than one-fourth the people of Dublin, but it, too, played a large role in the fighting of the 1920's. The oldest part of the city is ringed by the two channels of the Lee River. The loveliness of Cork is heightened by the palms, azaleas, and bamboo that flourish there and by the hills that form the backdrop for the old streets. Near Cork is the legendary Blarney Castle, where the visitor must bend over backwards to reach the fabled Blarney Stone and thus acquire the power of eloquence.

Westward from Cork is **Killarney**, known for hundreds of years as one of the grandest areas of natural beauty to be found anywhere. Killarney, where "the long light shakes across the lakes and the wild cataract leaps in glory," is only one of the magnificent stops in the Ring of Kerry, a 110-mile (175 km.) circle that encompasses lakes with mysterious islands, mountains with crashing cataracts, silent forests, sleepy valleys, and mountain passes—as well as historic abbeys and castles.

A quay on the Lee River in Cork, Ireland's second largest city.

Near Shannon, in the southwest of Ireland, is **Limerick**, once noted for its lacemaking. It is also another center of great natural beauty. Nearby are barren hills with strange Arctic and Mediterranean flowers existing side by side. And on the coast are the spectacular Cliffs of Moher, rising 700 feet (210 m.) and extending along the pounding Atlantic Ocean.

Galway, in Ireland's west, is another ancient town with winding streets, old houses, and broad quays. Near Galway are interesting archeological remains and many strange subterranean streams under the grassy limestone plain.

In the southeast is **Waterford**, an old port, famous for its glassware, and **Wexford**, where the Opera Festival brings visitors each autumn to hear rarely performed works.

HISTORY

Earliest Inhabitants. Hunters and fishermen, whose name and race we do not know, came to Ireland about 6000 B.C., but they left little trace of their existence. After 3000 B.C., during the late Stone Age, farming was introduced, and the people of this era left behind tombs constructed with stones so huge that legend says they were built by giants.

The Irish-speaking Celts may have appeared in Ireland about the middle of the 4th century B.C. They came from the continent, conquered the primitive tribes on the island, and established a complex civilization. There were seven small tribal kingdoms, where each king ruled surrounded by lawmakers, soldiers, poets, and musicians. The high king, the Ard Rí, whose seat was at Tara in the kingdom of County Meath, ruled over all the kings. Every third year he presided over the Feis of Tara, a great assembly for law, music, games, and literary contests. This

The formal gardens at Powerscourt, an old estate in County Wicklow.

highly developed society continued uninterrupted for 1,000 years, because Ireland, on the edge of Europe, escaped Roman invasion.

The Golden Age. Christianity came to Ireland in A.D. 432, with the coming of Saint Patrick. Patrick was a slave in Ireland who escaped, may have studied for the priesthood on the continent, and returned to Ireland as a bishop. The people were rapidly converted to Christianity, and Ireland became renowned for its great monastic schools. Students came from all over Europe to the monasteries, such as Clonard and Clonmacnoise. During a time when civilized Europe was falling to invaders from north and east, Ireland became the haven for ecclesiastical learning. This time has become known as the golden age in Ireland. After the decline of Rome, the Irish were among the first European peoples to produce a literature in their native language, Irish.

These days ended when the Vikings, sailors from northern Europe, raided the undefended monasteries during the 9th and 10th centuries. They established settlements on the Irish coast and at Dublin, Cork, Waterford, Limerick, and other places, and remained in control for many years. Their power was finally broken in A.D. 1014, at the battle of Clontarf, near Dublin. The High King Brian Boru defeated the Danes in this battle, but was slain at the moment of victory. No high king of similar strength succeeded him. The divided country was no match for the Norman knights who came to Ireland in 1170. The Normans then submitted to the English king, Henry II.

English Rule. For 750 years Gaelic chieftains attempted to carry on their struggle against the English, but gradually the English rulers tightened their grip. In 1366 the repressive Statutes of Kilkenny were passed to keep the English and Irish apart. It became illegal for the English to intermarry with the Irish or for anyone to speak Irish, to use Irish dress or customs, or to employ Irish musicians or storytellers.

Henry VIII (1491–1547) was the first English monarch to add "King of Ireland" to his title. He began the policy of trying to impose the Protestant Reformation upon the Irish. Succeeding English rulers continued to deprive the Irish of their lands. Queen Mary "planted" two midland counties with English settlers. Queen Elizabeth I took land in southwest Ireland and gave it to Sir Walter Raleigh (1552?–1618), who brought the potato to Ireland.

The Irish resisted strongly, and there were many bloody encounters, but their fate was determined for hundreds of years by their defeat at the battle of Kinsale in 1601. Oliver Cromwell (1599–1658), the Puritan leader of England, cruelly crushed all remnants of Irish resistance. His army laid waste much of the country and massacred thousands of people. Many soldiers were exiled to France and Spain, and many men and women to the West Indies and Virginia. Cromwell filled the country with English settlers. In 11 years the Irish population was reduced to less than half the number it had been when Cromwell came to Ireland. Three quarters of all Irish land passed to Protestant landlords, many of them living abroad. But the only English plantation that was ultimately successful was the plantation of Ulster, established after the battle of Kinsale.

At the end of the 17th century Ireland was the scene of the struggle between William III (William of Orange), a Protestant, and James II, a Catholic, for the British Crown. William was the victor at the battle of the Boyne in 1690. Because the Irish Catholics had opposed William, the English Parliament passed the Penal Laws of 1695, which assumed that every Catholic was an enemy of England. Irish Catholics were forbidden to vote, to hold office, or to retain military, civil, legal, or teaching positions. Catholic schools were abolished. More land was confiscated, and no Irish Catholic was allowed to own a horse of any value. The Penal Laws, which reduced the Irish to terrible poverty, were finally repealed in 1829, but even greater hardship was in store for Ireland.

The Famine.   The most terrible times in these long, unhappy years for Ireland started in 1845. A famine, which lasted 4 years, was caused by a fungus that attacked the potato crop and thus wiped out the basic food supply. It would be hard to exaggerate the suffering of the Irish during these years. Even before the famine, people often went hungry between the end of the old potato crop and the time when the new plants were ready. Most of the farmers were tenants who farmed tiny plots owned by absentee landlords. The famine made it difficult and even impossible for farmers to pay their rent, so the crop failure caused people to lose not only their source of food but also their homes. Landlords evicted tenants and often burned their homes to clear the land for pasture, since they found it more profitable to use the land for grazing cattle grown for export. Thousands of men, women, and children, dressed in rags, roamed the muddy roads during the chill, rainy weather looking for food and shelter. Often they lived in ditches. An epidemic added to the horror. At least 1,000,000 Irish died of starvation and disease. Another 1,000,000 emigrated to North America. These emigrants traveled in poor cargo ships, which have become known as coffin ships because so many people died en route.

Home Rule. The spirit of independence in Ireland had been aroused by the French and American revolutions. A rebellion in 1798 was put down, and in 1800, Ireland and Britain were united by the Act of Union. In the 19th century, Daniel O'Connell and Charles Stewart Parnell became leaders of the Home Rule movement. Through O'Connell's efforts, the Penal Laws were repealed and Catholics were admitted to Parliament. Both leaders, however, failed to gain home rule for Ireland.

During World War I, many Irish joined the British army to fight against Germany, but others joined the Irish Volunteers. This group was the military arm of a political party, Sinn Fein ("ourselves alone"), which was formed in 1904. The Volunteers and the Citizen Army attempted to capture Dublin on Easter Monday, 1916. They called themselves the Irish Republican Army (IRA) and raised their green, white, and orange flag over the Dublin Post Office. After about a week, they had to surrender to the British. Many of their leaders were executed.

Until 1921, a bitter guerrilla war raged in Ireland. The IRA fought no pitched battles, but they were very successful in quick raids and harassment. The British acts of reprisal were harsh. King George V intervened, and a settlement was worked out whereby 26 of the 32 counties of Ireland became a self-governing free state in the British Commonwealth. Six counties of the northern province of Ulster remained a part of the United Kingdom. Even though the treaty was accepted by Dáil Éireann (the House of Representatives), no immediate peace followed. Eamon de Valera led the forces opposed to the treaty, and a civil war started. In 1923, peace was restored with the defeat of those opposing the treaty.

In 1926, de Valera founded a new party, the Fianna Fáil (Warriors of Destiny). When the Fianna Fáil and de Valera came to power in 1932, they abolished the oath of allegiance to the British Crown and other restrictive clauses of the peace treaty. In 1937, a new constitution was adopted. It declared Ireland to be a sovereign, independent, democratic state. The following year, Britain gave up its naval bases in Ireland. During World War II, Ireland remained neutral. In 1948, the Irish government announced that "the description of the State shall be the Republic of Ireland," and thus modern Ireland was born.

GOVERNMENT

The head of state is the president, elected for a term of seven years by all citizens over 18. He or she may serve two terms. In December 1990, Ireland's first woman president, Mary Robinson, took office. She was succeeded in 1997 by Mary McAleese, Ireland's first president from Northern Ireland. The Oireachtas (parliament) consists of two houses. Dáil Éireann has 166 members elected by proportional representation, which guarantees representation of every substantial minority. Seanad Éireann (Senate) has 66 members. The actual head of the government is the *taoiseach* (prime minister), who is nominated by Dáil Éireann and appointed by the president. For most of modern Ireland's history, the Fianna Fáil (the Republican Party) has been in power. From December 1994, the country was ruled by a coalition of three center-left parties. In June 1997 and in May 2002, Fianna Fáil again won the elections. Its leader, Bertie Ahern, is the prime minister. In 1997, Sinn Fein for the first time was represented in the parliament by one deputy. After the 2002 elections, the party's deputies numbered five.

Dublin is Ireland's chief port, handling more than half of the nation's seaborne trade.

Modern Ireland

A new political generation came to power in the early 1960s. It faced the future with new self-confidence and new demands for industrial and social reforms. Changes within the Catholic Church, a freer press, television, and the growth of industries, city life, and tourism helped to create a more progressive attitude.

The new leaders turned against the old self-imposed isolation of Ireland. They started to play a major role in the United Nations, particularly in the UN Special Committee on Peacekeeping Operations. In 1973, Ireland also joined the precursor of the European Union (EU), then known as the European Economic Community, or Common Market, and increasingly took advantage of the vast "Euroland" markets. This was the beginning of spectacular growth and the "Irish miracle" of the 1990s. Government support of education and emphasis on the new high-tech economy turned Ireland from one of Europe's poorest countries into one of the most affluent. The country is blossoming and its young people are no longer emigrating, confident instead that the future belongs to them.

The reunification of the northern and southern parts of the island has been controversial for many years. A major step toward resolving this crisis was a peace agreement that was overwhelmingly approved in a popular vote in May 1998. Three interconnected government bodies were created to handle, respectively, issues within Northern Ireland itself; between Northern Ireland and Ireland; and between Ireland and Britain. The agreement also called for a referendum on amending the constitution to end the country's claim to Northern Ireland. In October 2001, in a move that was clearly influenced by the September 11 terrorist attacks on the United States, the IRA began to surrender its arms.

THOMAS FITZGERALD, Department of Education, Dublin, Ireland

The British monarch, head of the state of the United Kingdom, resides in Buckingham Palace (above), in London.

UNITED KINGDOM

Today, you can reach the United Kingdom from North America in a matter of hours, flying over the wide Atlantic. Or you can arrive from the European continent in minutes, traveling either across or under the English Channel. But for thousands of years, thanks to a surrounding moat of deep water, these green isles remained isolated from the rest of the world.

Today, the United Kingdom stands out as one of the most densely populated nations on Earth. Yet it remains, for the most part, a lush and fertile land. Outside the bustle of its great cities, the landscape gently unfurls along tree-lined country lanes, past tidy gardens and carefully mowed pastures, until one reaches the windswept moors of the lonely highlands.

It is often said of the United Kingdom that it is "in Europe but not of it." But this long-standing sense of isolation may be near an end, as the United Kingdom merges its market with that of the European Union (EU) in the coming years. What will remain is a nation that has played a colossal role in world history. Indeed, over the past 300 years, the kings and queens of this land have at one time or another reigned over nearly one-third of the world's surface. Although the 20th century saw the dismantling of the once-vast British Empire, the people of the United Kingdom still play a leading role in the realms of technology, science, culture, and world economy.

Much of the United Kingdom retains its rural character. The mild climate and frequent rainfall combine to help the grassy countryside keep its intensely green color throughout much of the year.

One Nation, Many Names

It is easy to get confused when trying to sort out the many terms applied to this country and the four separate "kingdoms" it encompasses. The name United Kingdom is short for the United Kingdom of Great Britain and Northern Ireland. Located off the northwestern coast of the European mainland, the United Kingdom occupies Great Britain—the largest island in Europe—the northern tip of the neighboring island of Ireland, and a surrounding fringe of small islets.

The main island of Great Britain, in turn, can be divided into the ancient kingdoms of England, Scotland, and Wales. These kingdoms united in the early 18th century, with Ireland joining their union in 1801. When the majority of Ireland declared its independence in 1921, the six counties of Northern Ireland opted to remain part of the United Kingdom. Despite centuries as a united nation, the four kingdoms—England, Scotland, Wales, and Northern Ireland—proudly retain their distinct cultures and languages, although English is now the common language of government and business.

THE LAND

The United Kingdom of Great Britain and Northern Ireland stands on the eastern edge of the North Atlantic Ocean, separated from the European mainland by the English Channel. France comes within 20 mi. (32 km.) of the United Kingdom at the Channel's narrowest point—the Strait of Dover. The North Sea breaks against the United Kingdom's northeastern shore. The Irish Sea and Atlantic Ocean wash against the west. The United Kingdom shares a land border with the Republic of Ireland.

With a physical area of about 94,500 sq. mi. (244,755 sq. km.), the United Kingdom is comparable in size to the state of Oregon. England makes up roughly 53 percent of the country in area, as it spans the south-

The mountains of Scotland, long denuded of their trees, now sustain great expanses of heather (right) and other hardy plants.

eastern half of Great Britain. Stretching north from England, Scotland makes up another 32 percent. West of England, Wales covers about 9 percent, and across the Irish Sea, Northern Ireland makes up 6 percent.

In addition to Ireland and the main island of Great Britain, the United Kingdom encompasses thousands of tiny offshore islands and islets. Clockwise from due north, the largest include the Orkney Islands and the Shetland Islands, north of Scotland; in the English Channel; the Isle of Wight and the Channel Islands; the Isles of Scilly, off England's southwestern coast; Anglesey and the Isle of Man, in the Irish Sea; and the Hebrides, off Scotland's west coast.

The United Kingdom encompasses a wide variety of landforms, which fall into two broad geographic regions: the lowlands and the highlands. An imaginary diagonal line divides the two from southwest to northeast, like a shoulder belt across the main island of Great Britain.

One of the first glimpses of the United Kingdom seen by visitors from the European continent is the fabled White Cliffs of Dover (below), a dramatic chalk formation along the English Channel coast.

United Kingdom
of Great Britain &
Northern Ireland

The Lowlands

The southeastern lowland zone consists of a vast plain with a gently rolling surface, most of which remains less than 500 ft. (150 m.) above sea level. The flattest and lowest part of this region rises up from the English Channel to surround two broad inlets: the mouth of the Thames River and, to the north, the bay known as The Wash. Over the past millennium, farmers have filled in the swamps and marshes of this coastal plain. But in places, it dips below sea level, notably in the area known as the Fens—the United Kingdom's lowest point, at −13 ft. (−4 m.).

West of the coastal plain, the land rises slightly to form the Midland Plain. Chains of hills and ridges run across this region. They include the Cotswold and Chiltern Hills and the North and South Downs. But few of these elevated regions reach more than 1,000 ft. (300 m.) above sea level, and the typically gentle character of the land prevails.

The west coast of Great Britain and Northern Ireland likewise contains lowland areas. They include England's Cheshire Plain and the broad, almost circular valley surrounding Northern Ireland's Lough Neagh, the largest lake in the United Kingdom.

The Highlands

To the west and north, the island of Great Britain rises up into a region of rocky hills and low, eroded mountains spaced by stony plains and valleys. This rugged region, often called the "rough country," extends into Northern Ireland, on the other side of the narrow North Channel. The United Kingdom's most prominent mountains include the Pennine Chain of northern England; the Cambrian Mountains of Wales; the Southern Uplands, Grampian Hills, and Northern Highlands of Scotland; and Northern Ireland's Sperrin Mountains. At 4,406 ft. (1,343 m.), Ben Nevis, in the Grampians, is the country's highest peak.

The jagged coastline of the United Kingdom—some 7,720 mi. (12,420 km.) long—forms many dramatic inlets and bays. Rocky cliffs typify the western coasts, especially in the north where the highlands drop down to the sea. The gentler southern and eastern coasts form long expanses of sandy and pebbly beaches, as well as glistening chalk cliffs, the best known being the White Cliffs of Dover.

Rivers and lakes abound throughout the United Kingdom. The longest, the Thames and the Severn, each run approximately 200 mi. (320 km.). The Thames rises in the Cotswold Hills, flows east across England, through London, and empties into the North Sea. The Severn rises in east-central Wales; flows northeast, east, and then south; and empties into the Bristol Channel in southwestern England. Other rivers of importance include the Mersey, which enters the Irish Sea at Liverpool; the River Clyde, which empties into the Atlantic; and the Welland, Humber, Trent, Tees, and Tyne, all of which empty into the North Sea. Northern Ireland's most important rivers include the Lagan, Bann, and Foyle. Long used for shipping and hydroelectricity, none of these great waterways flow wild. Most link to each other and smaller rivers by elaborate networks of canals.

Outside of Ireland's Loch Neagh, most of the United Kingdom's major lakes occur in northern Great Britain. They include Scotland's Loch Lomond and the 15 large lakes of northwestern England's famous Lake District.

Climate

The surrounding ocean gives the United Kingdom a mild maritime climate marked by cool summers and mild winters. It enjoys warmer weather than Canada's east coast (at the same latitude), thanks to the Gulf Stream, which flows north across the Atlantic to deliver warm water from the Caribbean. Daily temperatures in the United Kingdom seldom rise above 75° F. (24° C.) or dip below 23° F. (−5° C.). Precipitation falls every month, if not every week and, in some areas, every few days.

FACTS AND FIGURES

OFFICIAL NAME: United Kingdom of Great Britain and Northern Ireland.

NATIONALITY: British.

CAPITAL: London.

LOCATION: Off the western coast of Europe. **Boundaries**—North Atlantic Ocean, North Sea, English Channel, St. George's Channel, Irish Sea, Ireland.

AREA: 94,525 sq. mi. (244,820 sq. km.).

PHYSICAL FEATURES: Highest point—Ben Nevis (4,406 ft.; 1,343 m.), in Scotland. **Lowest point**—Fenland (13 ft., or 4 m., below sea level), in England. **Chief rivers**—Thames, Severn, Wye, Dee, Clyde, Forth, Bann. **Major lakes**—Lough Neagh, Lough Erne, Loch Lomond, Loch Ness, Windermere, Bala.

POPULATION: 60,200,000 (2002, annual growth rate 0.1%).

MAJOR LANGUAGES: English, Welsh, Gaelic.

MAJOR RELIGIONS: Anglican, Roman Catholic, other Protestant denominations, Muslim, Hindu, Jewish.

GOVERNMENT: Constitutional monarchy. **Head of state**—queen or king. **Head of government**—prime minister. **Legislature**—bicameral Parliament.

CHIEF CITIES: London, Birmingham, Belfast, Glasgow, Leeds, Sheffield, Liverpool, Bradford, Manchester, Edinburgh.

ECONOMY: Chief minerals—coal, oil, gas, sands and gravels. **Chief agricultural products**—grains, vegetables, cattle, sheep, poultry, fish. **Industries and products**—finished metals (steel), processed foods, textiles, chemicals. **Chief exports**—fuels, manufactured goods, foods. **Chief imports**—manufactured goods, machinery, foods, fuel.

MONETARY UNIT: 1 British pound = 100 pence.

NATIONAL HOLIDAY: Queen's Birthday, celebrated second Saturday in June.

■ THE ISLE OF MAN

The green and hilly Isle of Man rises out of the Irish Sea midway between England, Ireland, Scotland, and Wales. Its ancient kingdom escaped notice when the Romans and Normans swept over the rest of the British Isles. Then, as today, the Manx people lived free. Indeed, their ancient parliament—known as Tynwald—is the world's oldest, providing more than 1,000 years of unbroken democratic rule.

Today, this green, hilly island, about 33 mi. (53 km.) long and 13 mi. (21 km.) wide, is a beloved tourist spot, renowned for its beautiful beaches, peaceful woods, and wildlife sanctuaries. (Forty percent of the island remains uninhabited.) Thanks to the Isle of Man's mild climate, subtropical plants thrive in its many gardens, flower nurseries, and fruit orchards. The capital city of Douglas is also an international banking center.

The Isle of Man holds the distinction of being home to the tailless Manx cat.

In recent years, the Manx people (approximately 74,000 in 2002) have invested great energy in reviving their ancient culture, including the nearly extinct Manx language—a form of Gaelic. The popular heritage trail, known as the "Story of Mann," includes dozens of museums, medieval castles, and other historic sites.

Like the Channel Islands, the Isle of Man ranks as a "crown dependency." The island shares with the United Kingdom many services, such as postal and telephone systems. The Isle of Man government recognizes the British monarch as its ceremonial head of state, and awards him or her the title "Lord of Mann." The Isle of Man is also the home of the Manx cat, a tailless breed that arose several hundred years ago from a mutation in the island's isolated cat population.

The United Kingdom's climate, like its topography, varies considerably from one end to the other. In general, the southeastern lowlands enjoy sunnier, drier, and warmer weather than the cooler, wetter, and windier highlands of the north and west coasts. The northwestern mountains receive the most rain and snow, an average of 100 in. (2,540 mm.) per year. The southeast receives the least precipitation, about 26 in. (660 mm.) per year. A typical day in the United Kingdom sees a mixture of sun and clouds.

Plant Life

Dense forests of oaks and birches once covered virtually all of Great Britain and Ireland up to an elevation of about 1,000 ft. (300 m.). Very little remains of this native forest. That the United Kingdom retains a wooded appearance owes primarily to the many trees planted alongside farms and country lanes and in parks and pastures. The largest woods include the historic forests of Sherwood, Dean, New, and Kielder.

Great expanses of treeless moors cover much of the country's highlands. Grasses and mosses grow on the wetter moors. Heather carpets the drier areas. Centuries ago, this country's many famous wildflowers became favorites of gardeners worldwide. Among the most familiar and loved: bluebells, buttercups, daisies, lavender, poppies, and roses.

Animal Life

Thousands of years of hunting and urban development have eliminated the majority of the United Kingdom's native mammals. Its bears, wolves, beavers, and wild boars are all long extinct. Species that survive in small numbers include foxes, otters, red squirrels, and badgers. Red and roe deer thrive in some forests and highland areas. Introduced mammals include rabbit, black rats, and mink.

The United Kingdom's location at the center of several migratory routes makes it a bird-watcher's paradise, with more than 200 species in residence at least part of the year. The most common year-round birds include robins, blackbirds, starlings, crows, and various kinds of woodpeckers, wrens, and tits. Large flocks of ducks, geese, and other waterbirds spend the winter in estuaries and wetlands along the coast.

Five native species of frogs and toads survive. While Ireland has no snakes, the island of Great Britain has three species, one of which (the adder) is poisonous. Cod, haddock, whitings, herring, soles, and mackerel abound offshore. Freshwater fish include salmon and trout.

Wealth of the Land

The United Kingdom remains rich in energy resources such as coalfields (some of the largest in the world), large offshore deposits of natural gas and petroleum, and abundant waterpower. Mineral deposits include small amounts of tin, iron, kaolinite (china clay), sands, and gravels.

Throughout the English countryside, quaint, fastidiously maintained villages are tucked away in lush little pockets formed by slow-moving brooks, gently sloping hills, and well-manicured pathways.

THE PEOPLE

The citizens of the United Kingdom classify themselves in terms of their native regions. Accordingly, the English make up about 83 percent of the population; Scots, 9 percent; Welsh, 5 percent; and Irish, 3 percent. Some apply the term "British" to all these groups. But technically, the British include only residents of Great Britain—namely, English, Scots, and Welsh. Similarly, the term Irish describes both residents of Northern Ireland and of the independent Republic of Ireland.

Historically, the people of Ireland, Scotland, Wales, and the English district of Cornwall (the "Cornish") trace their ancestry to the Celtic people who settled on these islands thousands of years ago. Most English trace to later invaders from the European mainland—primarily the Germanic tribes known as the Angles and Saxons. Although centuries of intermarriage have blended their characteristics, people of Anglo-Saxon descent are apt to be tall, blond, and blue-eyed. Those of primarily Celtic ancestry are more likely to be shorter, with dark or red hair.

Since the Middle Ages, smaller waves of refugees have broadened the land's diversity of people. They have included French Protestants in the 1600s, African sailors in the 1700s, and European Jews in the late 1800s and early 1900s. Over the past 50 years, the United Kingdom has welcomed millions of immigrants from distant countries once part of the vast British Empire, most especially India, Pakistan, and the various islands of the British West Indies. These "new Britons," their children, and their grandchildren now make up about 5 percent of the population.

Sherwood Forest (left), best known to Americans for its Robin Hood connection, is one of the largest wooded areas in the United Kingdom. Other parts of the country are dominated by moors, the bleak setting for a number of classic 19th-century novels.

THE CHANNEL ISLANDS

Castles, cows, and crabs stand among the best-known features of the Channel Islands, a crown dependency that lies closer to France than to the United Kingdom. The islands take their name from their location, the English Channel, which separates the United Kingdom from the rest of mainland Europe. They became a part of medieval Great Britain when their ruler, William the Conqueror of Normandy, captured the English crown in 1066.

The four principal islands of this dependency are Jersey (45 sq. mi.; 117 sq. km.), Guernsey (24 sq. mi.; 62 sq. km.), Alderney (3 sq. mi.; 8 sq. km.), and Sark (2 sq. mi.; 5 sq. km.). Associated with them is a scattering of much smaller islands, most of them uninhabited. Each of the four main islands, together with its surrounding islets, has its own independent government. As "crown dependencies," the Channel Islands all rely on the United Kingdom for their defense, as well as for certain shared services such as mail and telephone. Many residents come from French families that have lived on the islands for hundreds of years. Over the past 50 years, a newer, largely English population has arrived, drawn to the dependency's exceptionally low taxes.

Far sunnier than the nearby island of Great Britain, the Channel Islands draw throngs of visitors to their magnificent beaches and resort hotels each year. Just offshore, scores of small fishing boats add to the picturesque scene. Crab and lobster are the local specialty.

Most familiar of all, however, may be the distinctive cows originally bred on these islands centuries ago and now found on dairy farms throughout the world. Jerseys and Guernseys still graze the meadows of the islands whose names they bear. In many cases, they do so in the shadow of medieval castles. Among the most famous of the island's many citadels are Castle Cornet, a 13th-century stronghold that looms over St. Peter Port, the capital of Guernsey, and Elizabeth Castle, a 16th-century fort on an island in St. Aubin's Bay, in Jersey. One can also see more-recently built fortifications, left throughout the islands by the German troops that occupied them during World War II.

Local dialects and accents abound. Some Scots and Irish still speak their regional forms of Gaelic—the ancient language of the Celts. Another Celtic language—Welsh—can still be heard throughout Wales, most especially in its northern and western communities.

Religion continues to be a defining characteristic of certain population groups. In Northern Ireland, bitter political conflict continues between the Roman Catholic "nationalists," who strive to join the Irish Republic, and the Protestant "unionists," who want to remain within the United Kingdom. Overall, the majority of the United Kingdom's population does not regularly attend religious services, although most (37 million) consider themselves Christians. Other distinct religious groups include Muslims (1 million), Sikhs (400,000), Hindus (350,000), and Jews (350,000).

The people of the United Kingdom live primarily in cities. Indeed, theirs is the third-most densely populated nation in Europe (after the tiny nations of Netherlands and Belgium). England remains the most densely populated part of the country, by far, with some 900 people per sq. mi. (350 per sq. km.). Scotland, by contrast, remains the most sparsely populated, with a roomier 160 residents per sq. mi. (60 per sq. km.). Wales and Northern Ireland fall in between, with 350 and 300 people per sq. mi. (135 and 115 per sq. km.), respectively.

The United Kingdom has welcomed thousands of immigrants from all over the world. Many have come from colonies and territories that once belonged to the United Kingdom's far-flung empire.

EDUCATION AND ARTS

Many of the United Kingdom's most prestigious schools date back to the Middle Ages. They include some of the world's first—and still finest—universities. This country's populace stands among the most highly educated in the world, with a literacy rate exceeding 99 percent.

Law requires children in the United Kingdom to start school by age 5. National tests administered at ages 7, 11, and 14 assess student progress and help group children by academic ability. At age 16, students can quit school altogether, pursue job-related studies at a vocational or technical institute, or continue their academic studies to prepare, or "prep," for entrance to a university. The most prestigious of the country's prep schools are the private boarding schools of Eton, Harrow, and Winchester.

Oxford and Cambridge stand out as the foremost universities. Another 30 colleges and universities operate in England and Wales, eight in Scotland, and two in Northern Ireland. Adults can also take courses and earn degrees through the publicly funded "Open University," which offers courses via the Internet, videos, and public-radio and -television programs.

British and Irish writers have dominated world literature for hundreds of years, beginning with Geoffrey Chaucer (ca. 1340–1400), the greatest of England's medieval poets. He is best remembered for his *Canterbury Tales*. The English Renaissance of the late 16th and early 17th centuries introduced the world to such unsurpassed writers as the dramatist Christopher Marlowe, the poet John Donne, and of course, William Shakespeare—still widely regarded as the greatest playwright in human history. A legion of influential and enduring writers followed over the next 300 years. Among the most famous of the 19th century: Jane Austen, Charles Dickens, Sir Walter Scott, the Brontë sisters, George Eliot (a pseudonym for Mary Ann Evans), Robert Louis Stevenson, Robert Browning, and Alfred Tennyson. Dominating the early 20th century were Rudyard Kipling, James Joyce, Virginia Woolf, and Dylan Thomas.

The United Kingdom has remained a world center for dramatic arts, with more than 300 theater companies—half of these in London. The world-famous Royal Shakespeare Company continues to perform in London as well as in Shakespeare's hometown of Stratford-upon-Avon. Not surprisingly, this small country also produces a large percentage of the world's leading actors of English-language stage and film. Today's most acclaimed include Dame Judi Dench, Glenda Jackson, Vanessa Redgrave, Kenneth Branagh, and Emma Thompson.

English, Scottish, Welsh, and Irish music have likewise played to a world audience for hundreds of years, beginning with their medieval church music. In modern times, the United Kingdom has

Canterbury Tales by Geoffrey Chaucer helped establish English as a literary language.

produced many great orchestral composers, including Ralph Vaughan Williams, Henry Purcell, and Benjamin Britten. The country's music scene exploded in the 1960s, with the unrivaled worldwide success of dozens of rock groups—most especially the Beatles and the Rolling Stones. Some British rock musicians (Elton John, Paul McCartney, Sting, and others) have influenced popular music for decades, while younger groups such as Oasis have risen to world fame.

Elton John has been a prominent and influential figure in popular music for decades.

ECONOMY

Although no longer the world's leading economic power, the United Kingdom remains a center of world trade and finance. Approximately 70 percent of the nation's workers hold service jobs in such professions as banking, law, medical services, sales, clerical work, and office management. The country's international-banking, insurance, and financial-investment industries remain among the world's largest and most sophisticated. More recently, the telecommunications industry has gained national prominence, with many new companies offering services such as Internet, mobile communications, and cable television, in addition to traditional phone service. The United Kingdom also has one of the world's largest publishing industries, with scores of book-publishing houses and nearly 10,000 local and regional newspapers and periodicals.

About 25 percent of U.K. workers are employed in mining, manufacturing, and related industries. Oil production on the North Sea has replaced coal mining as a major industry over the past half century. Other important manufactured products include computers, automobiles, communications equipment, and electronics. Scotland in particular has recently become a major computer producer in its so-called "Silicon Glen," between Glasgow and Edinburgh. In Northern Ireland, the production of whiskey, textiles, and clothing remains as important as it has been for centuries. Farming, fishing, and forestry employ another 2 to 3 percent of U.K. workers.

The United Kingdom stands out among European nations as having one of the highest percentages of women in its labor force. In all, nearly two-thirds of women between the ages of 15 and 65 work for wages in the United Kingdom. They account for nearly half the nation's full-time workers and more than three-quarters of its part-timers.

In recent decades, the United Kingdom has also seen a dramatic rise in self-employment. Some 3 million workers, or nearly 12 percent of the

■ THE DEPENDENCIES

While the United Kingdom's larger dominions eagerly sought their independence, more than a dozen small islands and the European territory of Gibraltar have chosen to remain within its protection. Those closest to home—the Channel Islands and the Isle of Man—retain an especially close relationship to the United Kingdom as "crown dependencies" (see separate sidebars). In the 1980s, the other 13 dependencies became known as the United Kingdom Overseas Territories. Except for Gibraltar and the

British Indian Ocean Territory, which consists of the six main island groups—some 2,300 islands—of the Chagos Archipelago. Gibraltar, on the southeast coast of Spain, forms a 2.25-sq.-mi. (5.8-sq.-km.) peninsula jutting into the Mediterranean Sea.

These scattered territories—the last remnants of the far-flung British Empire—have a combined population of about 185,000. Each has its own government. None send a representative to the U.K. Parliament. But all depend on the United Kingdom for military defense, international relations, and administrative and economic support.

As can be expected given their locations, these islands tend to be richest in natural beauty, and depend largely on tourism for income. Until recently, many also served as international havens for drug smuggling and money laundering. In exchange for clamping down on these unlawful activities, in 1998, the United Kingdom granted full British citizenship to the inhabitants of its territories. U.K. citizenship gives the people of the territories the right to vote, and to work anywhere in the United Kingdom.

For the most part, the United Kingdom's loose control of its remaining territories has been peaceful. Nonetheless, the country has proved its willingness to shed blood in their defense. In April 1982, after Argentine troops seized the Falkland Islands, the United Kingdom engaged in two months of intense fighting, with a loss of more than 250 British and 950 Argentine soldiers. Gibraltar has proved to be another source of continuing conflict, in this case with Spain. The United Kingdom has vowed not to abandon the territory so long as Gibraltar's citizens strongly support their ties to the British Crown.

The Rock of Gibraltar stands strategically at the mouth of the Mediterranean Sea.

United Kingdom's claim to Antarctic land, they consist of small tropical and semitropical islands.

They include the Pitcairn Islands, in the South Pacific; the Falkland Islands, South Georgia and the South Sandwich Islands, and St. Helena and its associated islands, in the South Atlantic; Anguilla, Bermuda, British Virgin Islands, Cayman Islands, Montserrat, and Turks and Caicos Islands, in the Caribbean; and the

The Royal Liver Building (above, on the banks of the River Mersey) is a dominant feature in the skyline of Liverpool, one of the United Kingdom's leading industrial centers and an important port on the Irish Sea.

workforce, now work for themselves. Overall, unemployment in the United Kingdom has remained moderate since the 1980s. The beginning of the 21st century saw an unemployment rate of around 7 percent. However, this rate continues to vary considerably between regions—with eastern England tending to have the lowest rates, and Northern Ireland the highest.

HISTORY

Over the past 2,000 years, many emperors, monarchs, and armies have tried to unite the ancient kingdoms of these two great islands. The unification of Northern Ireland and the rest of the United Kingdom continues to provoke bitter conflict. The mergers of England, Wales, and Scotland, on the other hand, were eased by royal marriages and family ties in centuries past.

In 1485, Henry VII—member of the Welsh Tudor family—ascended to the English throne. This eased the first merger of kingdoms, between England and Wales. Their union became official in 1536. More than a century later, Elizabeth I chose James I of Scotland as her successor. This led to the union of the Scottish and English crowns in 1603 and, in 1707, to the unification of the whole of Great Britain as a single country.

Compared to these largely peaceful mergers, British rule of Ireland consisted of nearly 1,000 years of bloody conflict. The defeat of the rebellion of 1798 led to Ireland and Britain's official union in 1800, and the official creation of the United Kingdom of Great Britain and Ireland.

The Empires

Between the 16th and 19th centuries, Britain had also amassed and partially lost a vast empire with claims to much of North America and the Caribbean islands. The American Revolution of 1775 to 1783 freed the 13 colonies that became the United States of America. To the north, the provinces and territories of Canada remained part of the British Empire until 1867, when Parliament peacefully recognized Canada's independence. Like

■ HADRIAN'S WALL

Nearly 2,000 years ago, the vast Roman Empire reached as far north as Great Britain. But the mighty Roman legions never entirely conquered the island. So-called "barbarians" remained in the remote mountains and rocky hills of what is now Scotland. If the barbarians could not be defeated, the Roman emperor Hadrian decided, they could at least be walled off. And so, at Hadrian's order, in 122 A.D., Roman soldiers and their slaves built a fortified barricade across the narrowest point of northern England, between the River Tyne, on the east coast, and Solway Firth, on the west. Running for 73 mi. (117 km.), the wall formed a barrier 8 to 10 ft. (2.4 to 3 m.) thick and 15 ft. (4.6 m.) high, with gated towers every Roman mile (about 5,000 ft.; 1,500 m.). A moat flanked the northern, or "barbarian," side of the wall. A military road ran the length of its southern, "civilized" face.

Today, large intact sections of the wall still stand, along with several adjoining stone garrisons that were used to house Roman soldiers. Archaeologists continue to excavate, study, and repair Hadrian's Wall, which was designated a World Heritage Site in 1987. Special events each summer include Roman dramas, festivals, and battle re-creations. Visitors can also walk sections of the wall and visit the Roman Army Museum to experience a taste of Roman life on the northern frontier some 2,000 years ago.

The well-preserved ruins of Hadrian's Wall (above) can still be seen in the north of England. The wall marks the northernmost extent of the Roman Empire, which 2,000 years ago controlled much of what is now the United Kingdom.

many former colonies, Canada chose to keep its ceremonial ties to the British monarchy. Meanwhile, in 1833, Parliament abolished slavery. A decade later, it abolished child labor in Britain's coal mines.

Despite the loss of its North American territories, the United Kingdom remained Europe's foremost power throughout the 19th century, with an unrivaled navy that ruled the world seas. In large part, the nation's strength stemmed from the wealth generated by its nearly century-long Industrial Revolution (1750–1830). Moreover, peace in Europe allowed the United Kingdom to focus its attention on remoter parts of the world. The nation began amassing a second, even larger empire made up of the many trading posts, plantations, and coal mines around the globe. These included vast colonies surrounding the Indian Ocean and extending into Southeast Asia and across Oceania.

The monarchy retains a powerful symbolic role in the United Kingdom. Much pageantry surrounds important state occasions such as the opening of Parliament (above), presided over by the reigning sovereign.

In 1875, Prime Minister Benjamin Disraeli wisely bought control of the Suez Canal Company. In doing so, the United Kingdom gained almost exclusive power over one of the world's most important sea routes, and quicker access to its colonies in the Pacific and Indian Oceans.

In 1876, Britain's Queen Victoria had herself proclaimed "Empress of India," marking the official creation of the "British Empire." At its peak, in 1914, this second empire encompassed about one-fifth of the globe's land surface and one-quarter of its population. At that time, it could be truthfully said: "The Sun never sets on the British Empire." The era of the British Empire also spread the use of the English language and the United Kingdom's unique brand of technology, commerce, and parliamentary democracy throughout the world. British colonies, in turn, fueled the United Kingdom's extraordinary economic growth and leadership in world affairs.

From Empire to Commonwealth

The United Kingdom played the leading role in the "Allied" fight against Germany during World War I (1914–18). During this time, the United Kingdom drew heavily on the materials and fighting men of its dominions around the world.

The years immediately after World War I brought the beginning of the end of the British Empire. In 1922, continuing violent rebellion in Ireland led to a compromise: the majority of Ireland became an independent republic. Only the largely pro-British, Protestant population of its northern six counties chose to stay within the newly renamed United Kingdom of Great Britain and *Northern* Ireland. In 1928, women won the right to vote.

In 1931, the United Kingdom officially dissolved the British Empire, with an invitation to most of its former dominions to become free and equal

In London, the new millennium featured, among other things, the inauguration of the London Eye, the world's largest Ferris wheel, which has now become a permanent addition to the capital city's skyline.

partners within the new "Commonwealth of Nations." It retained control, however, over India. Another 16 former colonies chose to remain closely tied to the United Kingdom, as dependencies (see sidebar, page 90).

During World War II (1939–45), the United Kingdom, together with the United States and the Soviet Union, was one of the three great Allied powers that defeated Germany. But the war took a terrible toll on Britain, whose cities were subjected to heavy bombing by the German air force.

The Postwar Kingdom

After World War II, the United Kingdom joined with the United States and several European countries to form the North Atlantic Treaty Organization (NATO), for the continued defense of Europe. At the same time, the country refocused the energy once directed into empire building into improving conditions at home. Most importantly, perhaps, it established an extensive health-and-welfare system to provide low-cost or free medical care for all of its residents, in addition to old-age pensions, unemployment benefits, and financial assistance for the poor.

In 1947, the United Kingdom let go of its possession of the Indian subcontinent, which split into the largely Muslim nation of Pakistan and the largely Hindu country of India.

The 1950s and 1960s brought a renewed flowering of the arts throughout the United Kingdom—with the work of many composers, musicians, filmmakers, television producers, and actors and actresses gaining world fame. By contrast, the 1970s brought economic recession and the resumption of violence tied to the continuing "Troubles" in Northern Ireland. The ongoing hostility between unionists and nationalists there precipitated terrorist attacks in England, especially in London. On a positive note, in 1973, the United Kingdom threw off more than 1,000 years of isolation from mainland Europe and joined the European Community—the intergovernmental organization now known as the European Union (EU). Nonetheless, the decade culminated in the "winter of discontent" of 1978–79, when a wave of labor strikes nearly crippled the United Kingdom's economy.

Continuing dissatisfaction with a weak economy led to the defeat of the Labour Party by the Conservatives in 1979. The Conservatives chose as their leader Margaret Thatcher, making her the United Kingdom's first female prime minister. The Thatcher government's sweeping overhaul of the economy included a dramatic reduction in income taxes and the privatization of many unprofitable, state-owned companies such as British Steel, British Airways, and British Telecom. Thatcher's popularity declined in 1990, in part over her creation of a widely hated "poll tax" charged equally to all residents regardless of their income or wealth. The Conservative Party continued to control Parliament under the leadership of Prime Minister John Major, until the Labour Party swept the 1997 general elections.

Under moderate Labour Party leader Tony Blair, the United Kingdom has entered the 21st century with stronger military and diplomatic ties with the United States and stronger economic ties with the countries of the EU. The degree to which the United Kingdom will merge its economy with Europe's remains a controversial issue for the country.

A handshake in 2002 between British Prime Minister Tony Blair (left) and U.S. President George W. Bush once again re-affirms the "special relationship" between the United Kingdom and the United States.

Under Blair's leadership, the United Kingdom has been deeply involved in peace negotiations both at home and abroad. Among the most important for the nation have been talks aimed at bringing an end to the nationalist-unionist violence in Northern Ireland. In 1998, eight parties representing the communities of Northern Ireland signed the Belfast Agreement (Good Friday Agreement), with the political support and active encouragement of world leaders including U.S. President Bill Clinton. The agreement allowed people living in Northern Ireland to choose citizenship in the United Kingdom, Republic of Ireland, or both. But it did not determine the ultimate fate of Northern Ireland.

In March 1999, the air forces of the United Kingdom and the United States led a NATO attack on the government forces of Serbia, in southeast Europe, to stop atrocities against the country's Kosovar Albanians, who were seeking independence. In 2001, the United Kingdom rallied behind the United States in the wake of the terrorist attacks on New York City's World Trade Center and the Pentagon in Arlington, Virginia. In the following months, troops from the United Kingdom fought alongside those from the United States in Afghanistan, helping to topple the Taliban government that had harbored the terrorist organizations behind the attacks. In late 2001 and early 2002, U.K. troops returned to Afghanistan to lead a multinational peacekeeping force there.

GOVERNMENT

The government of the United Kingdom is a constitutional monarchy. This means that a monarch stands as the ceremonial head of state, but he or she is forbidden to become involved in politics. The king or queen of England "rules" as monarch for the entire United Kingdom (as well as for certain other countries once part of the British Empire). He or she inherits this position through an established line of succession.

The United Kingdom's system of parliamentary democracy stands out as one of its greatest contributions to the world at large. The beginnings of parliamentary democracy trace to the Middle Ages and the tribal councils that advised the early Saxon kings and queens. In the 13th century, these councils evolved into the House of Lords (members of noble families) and the House of Commons (landowners and wealthy businessmen of the lower classes), which together came to be known as Parliament.

Today, all real political power lies with the democratically elected members of the House of Commons. Each of the United Kingdom's approximately 650 local "constituencies" sends one representative. The members of the House of Commons then choose the nation's executive officers, including a prime minister. In practice, the prime minister and most of his or her cabinet ministers come from whichever political party has the most elected members in Parliament. If no single political party has a clear majority, two or more parties may combine forces to form a "coalition government." New elections may be called whenever the prime minister loses the support of the majority of members, or at least every five years. The House of Commons passes laws, makes decisions regarding taxes, and controls how the government spends its money.

Today, the United Kingdom's main political groups include the Labour and Conservative Parties. One or the other held the majority of seats in the House of Commons for most of the 20th century. Other parties include Liberal Democrats and the locally important Scottish Nationals, Welsh Nationalists, and Ulster Unionists (Northern Ireland).

The United Kingdom's Parliament still contains the once-powerful House of Lords. Its members include hereditary peers (who inherit their membership by right of their nobility), life peers (appointed for life based on their accomplishments), certain bishops and archbishops of the Anglican Church, and 10 senior judges, or "law lords." The law lords perform the judicial duties of this house, which is the United Kingdom's top court of law—much like the Supreme Court of the United States.

The other lords retain only the power to review and debate laws being considered by the House of Commons. However, they generally do not delay legislation, because any interference with the democratically elected government draws strong public protest. In 1999, Prime Minister Tony Blair dramatically reduced the number of hereditary lords, from more than 700 to about 90, and removed their right to bequeath their seats to their heirs.

In another historic change, in 1999, Scotland formed its own independent parliament, and Wales formed its own government assembly. Each now handles its own government affairs. Northern Ireland had its own parliament until 1972, when political conflict and violence between Protestant unionists and Roman Catholic nationalists forced the central government to assume direct control. The United Kingdom lacks a written constitution. Instead, it bases its laws largely on the body of "traditional rights" established over the past 700 years.

London's Trafalgar Square (above) is one of England's world-famous landmarks.

ENGLAND

Perhaps nowhere else in the world has so much history been packed onto so little land. Indeed, if England were a U.S. state, it would rank 29th in area, behind Florida, Arkansas, and Alabama. Yet few places hold a more dominant position in world civilization than Shakespeare's "blessed plot" and the poet William Blake's "green and pleasant land."

England takes its name from the barbarian Angles, a Germanic people who, together with the Saxons, conquered it in the 5th century. Over the course of the next 1,400 years, this ancient kingdom, with its scores of rivalrous kings and queens, would develop into a world power that ultimately controlled a global empire beyond compare. By the late 20th century, most of its dominions had gained their independence. Nevertheless, England itself remains the principal political division of the United Kingdom of Great Britain and Northern Ireland.

THE LAND

England spans the southern and eastern two-thirds of the island of Great Britain, which stands off the northwest coast of mainland Europe. Its land area totals 50,352 sq. mi. (130,412 sq. km.), and it shares borders with Wales, to the west, and Scotland, to the north. Its shores are washed by the North Sea on the north and east, the English Channel on the south, and the Irish Sea on the west.

England's deeply indented coastline, like that of all Great Britain, may be its most distinctive physical characteristic. Indeed, its many protected bays and inlets helped make England the world's premier naval power for nearly half a millennium. The high tides of the North Sea, in particular, have carved great estuaries and harbors around the mouths of England's easterly flowing rivers. Stunningly white chalk cliffs rise up to form England's southern coast, along the English Channel. Darker, rockier cliffs dominate its west coast on the Irish Sea. These western cliffs extend inland into a highland region of rugged hills and mountains. To the west and south, the landscape drops in elevation and flattens to form a much larger lowland region of coastal plains. Regardless of where you travel in England, you are always within 100 mi. (160 km.) of the sea.

Highland England

The chain of mountains known as the Pennines forms the backbone of England's highland region, extending down from its northern border with

Scotland. The Pennines contain England's highest point—Scaffel Pike (3,209 ft.; 978 m. above sea level). Their western slopes hold the country's renowned Lake District, arguably England's most beautiful natural region. The Lake District lies within a 35-sq.-mi. (91-sq.-km.) national park famous for its spectacular waterfalls, mountain lakes, and dramatic

England is a country of great scenic beauty. Lakes and waterfalls (left) abound in the remote areas of the northern counties. The milder climate in the south of England is especially conducive to agriculture (below).

U-shaped valleys. The area's largest lakes include Windermere, Ullswater, Bassenthwaite, Derwent Water, and Coniston Water.

Lowland England

Dropping down out of the northeastern high country, rolling plain typifies most of central and eastern England. The hillier central region, or "Midlands," contains deep veins of coal and an abundance of flowing water. These two natural energy sources led to the industrialization of the Midlands in the 18th century. Over the next 200 years, the smokestacks of factories and foundries darkened the Midlands' skies and coated the landscape with soot. Owing to this phenomenon, the area came to be known as the "Black

Half-timber architecture and flower-lined walkways add a special charm to many houses in the English countryside (top). Much different are the dark cliffs and rocky beaches of Cornwall (above), in the southwest.

Country." In recent decades, a dramatic reduction in air pollution has removed the blackness from the skies, if not the name.

To the east of the Midlands, the land drops low and flat to form the marshy coastal plain of eastern England. Over the past 1,000 years, farmers have drained and filled this region's native swamps. A particularly large area of reclaimed farmland, the Fens, extends along the Ouse River and contains some of England's best agricultural land. Sinking as low as 13 ft. (4 m.) below sea level in places, the Fens form England's lowest point. North of the Fens, smaller areas of filled-in marsh stretch alongside the Humber River, as

During a spell of sunny, warm weather, people flock to the outdoor cafés that have cropped up in many cities, or perhaps take a stroll through Portobello Market (bottom), London's antique-shop district.

they do along the Thames just south of London.

South of the Midlands, the land rises slightly to form many small chains of chalk hills and cliffs that eventually drop to the sea along the English Channel. The largest of these chains include the Cotswold and Chiltern Hills, north of the River Thames, and the North and South Downs, south of it. The chalk cliffs rise again offshore to form the dramatic Isle of Wight, its chalky uplands cut by an abundance of rivers.

To the west, England's southern coast forms a broad finger of land that separates the English Channel from the Irish Sea. Generally referred to as the West Country, this peninsula consists of a granite plateau some 1,700 ft. (500 m.) high. Most notably, it contains Dartmoor, a region of moors, peat bogs, and dwarf forests that make up England's largest wilderness area. The West Country culminates at Land's End, where granite cliffs stand more than 60 ft. (20 m.) above the water. The 140 tiny Isles of Scilly lie to the west-southwest, about 25 mi. (40 km.) offshore.

Climate

Thanks to warm waters and winds flowing across the Atlantic from the Caribbean, England enjoys a remarkably mild climate for its high latitude (the same as Canada's chilly Labrador). In general, temperatures below freezing or above 80° F. (26° C.) are cause for headlines. Yet England's weather is infamous for its changeability. Regardless of season, a typical day will see clouds, rain, and sunshine chase each other across the sky. So while it is true that more than half the days of the year are overcast in England, most days likewise enjoy periods of sunshine.

In general, English winters see occasional frost and snow, thick fog, and plenty of rain. Average daytime temperatures range from 43° F. (6° C.) in January to 70° F. (21° C.) in August. Summer highs occasionally rise to heat-wave levels, with high humidity. Temperatures vary somewhat between

FACTS AND FIGURES

OFFICIAL NAME: England.

NATIONALITY: English.

CAPITAL: London.

LOCATION: Southern and eastern parts of the island of Great Britain. **Boundaries**—Scotland, North Sea, English Channel, Wales, Irish Sea.

AREA: 50,352 sq. mi. (130,412 sq. km.).

PHYSICAL FEATURES: Highest point—Scaffel Pike (3,209 ft.; 978 m.). **Lowest point**—the Fens (13 ft. or 4 m. below sea level). **Chief rivers**—Thames, Severn, Mersey, Trent, Yorkshire, Ouse, Tyne. **Major lakes**—Windermere, Coniston Water, Derwent Water.

POPULATION: 50,015,800 (2002).

MAJOR LANGUAGE: English.

MAJOR RELIGIONS: Protestant (especially Anglican), Roman Catholic, Muslim, Sikh, Hindu, Jewish.

CHIEF CITIES: London, Birmingham, Liverpool, Manchester, Sheffield, Bristol.

ECONOMY: Chief minerals—natural gas, petroleum, coal, iron, clay, chalk. **Industries**—steel, machine tools, automated equipment, ships, aircraft, motor vehicles and parts, electronics and communications equipment, metals, chemicals. **Chief agricultural products**—cereals, oilseed, potatoes, vegetables, cattle, sheep, poultry, fish. **Chief exports**—manufactured goods, fuels, chemicals, food and beverages. **Chief imports**—manufactured goods, machinery, fuels, foods.

ENGLAND

regions. Warm summers and mild winters typify the southwest. The southeast experiences warm summers and colder winters, while the north of England has cool summers and the coldest winters. Precipitation varies more widely, with the sunnier east coast receiving less than 25 in. (635 mm.) in a typical year. By contrast, the southwest receives 40 to 60 in. (1,000 to 1,500 mm.) annually, and the northwest Lake District more than twice that, with an average of 130 in. (3,300 mm.) of rain and snow each year.

Wildlife

In prehistoric times, thick forests of oak, beech, and yew covered England below an elevation of about 1,000 ft. (300 m.). Several thousand years of farming have largely cleared the English landscape, making England one of the least forested areas in all of Europe. (Only Ireland and the Netherlands have less.) Woodlands still cover about 8 percent of the land, but they consist mainly of conifers introduced from other parts of the world. The early Romans introduced another nonnative plant—the spiny shrub known as gorse. It now grows throughout England, most thickly along roadsides and other disturbed areas. An abundance of native wildflowers carpets England's meadows and brightens its woods. Some of the most common include bluebells, buttercups, daisies, scarlet pimpernel, lords-and-ladies, monkshood, and rockrose. Heather and moss cover the moors of the northern and southwest mountains.

Centuries ago, hunters and farmers wiped out England's large, native mammals, including its wolves, bears, wild cattle, and boars. Native species of deer, foxes, hare, and badgers remain. Even more common is the rabbit, introduced long ago from mainland Europe.

For more than 900 years, all British coronations have taken place in Westminster Abbey (above).

England enjoys a great abundance of bird life thanks to its many estuaries and its position along major migratory routes. Among the most common are sparrows, blackbirds, tits, wrens, crows, pigeons, starlings, and thrushes. Reptiles, never particularly abundant in England, have become downright rare. Those that survive include the "common" lizard, poisonous adder, the grass snake, and the slowworm (a legless lizard). England's native amphibians include several kinds of newts, salamanders, frogs, and toads. Trout, salmon, carp, pike, and eels populate its streams and lakes.

Mineral Wealth

England's Midlands and North Region contain some of the world's deepest and richest coalfields. Five centuries of intensive mining have all but depleted the coal veins nearest the surface. England also lays claim to vast offshore deposits of petroleum and natural gas in the North Sea. Northwestern England has substantial deposits of iron and lead. The southwest holds tin and kaolinite (china clay). Other parts of England contain large deposits of limestone, salt, dolomite, and gypsum.

THE PEOPLE

Only archaeological evidence remains of England's first occupants—Stone Age and Bronze Age people who hunted and later farmed the land thousands of years ago. Most modern-day English trace their ancestry to a mixture of early Celtic invaders and later waves of Romans, Germanic Anglo-Saxons, Danes, and Normans (from Normandy, on the coast of France). Despite centuries of intermarriage, the physical characteristics of these historic peoples show through in different regions of England. The darker features and shorter stature of the Celts, for instance, remain most common in the extreme northwest of England and in the southwestern county of Cornwall. The lighter features of Anglo-Saxon, Dane, and Norman heritage dominate the rest of England, most especially its eastern lowlands.

Since the 17th century, small groups of political refugees have broadened England's ethnic diversity. They included French Protestants in the 1600s, African sailors in the 1700s, and European Jews in the late 1800s and early 1900s. The 1960s and 1970s brought larger waves of immigrants from nations of the former British Empire, most especially India, Pakistan, and various African and Caribbean states. With their distinct physical features, languages, religions, and customs, these new groups have changed English culture in a way not seen since the Norman invasions of the Middle Ages. Today, they make up about 5 percent of England's population.

Outside Buckingham Palace, the royal residence in London, the changing of the guard (left) is conducted at regular intervals—and always with great pageantry.

Approximately 25 million English citizens consider themselves "Anglican." That is, they belong to the Church of England, although they may not regularly attend religious services. Adherents of Roman Catholicism account for another 7 million. Non-Anglican Protestants total about 1.5 million, and the number of English Muslims recently passed the 1 million mark. Other major religious groups include Sikhs, Hindus, and Jews.

Although a great gap remains between the rich and poor in England, the population as a whole enjoys nearly full employment and considerable government support in the form of free to low-cost medical care, financial support for the needy, and old-age pensions. Just over half own their own homes, which tend to be smaller than those in the United States, owing to England's dense population and limited land area.

As a whole, the people of England share a tremendous pride in their history. The most obvious aspect of this pride is their continued celebration of the English monarchy and its pageantry. Along these lines, the English continue to observe some of the ceremonial aspects of nobility and peerage, which date back to the Middle Ages. A person born to a noble family, for example, may be properly addressed as duke, duchess, earl, countess, baron, or baroness, as the case may be. The English monarch bestows the honor of knighthood each year to recognize individuals of professional distinction and great public service. Men and women so named are then properly addressed as "Sir" or "Dame." Famous recent examples include Dame Judi Dench, honored for her acting career, and Sir Paul McCartney, knighted for his music.

ARTS AND EDUCATION

As a whole, the English tend to be a highly educated people, with a literacy rate near 100 percent. All able children ages 5 to 16 attend school. About 90 percent attend publicly funded schools. The other 10 percent attend private schools, most of them run by churches or synagogues. The most prestigious of England's private schools date back to the Middle Ages. They include the boarding schools of Eton, Harrow, and Winchester.

It is not as common in England as in the United States for students to follow graduation from secondary school with university attendance. Instead, approximately half of graduating students pursue job-related studies at one of 300 or so vocational colleges, polytechnics, or institutes of art, business, agriculture, or education.

The arts flourish in England. In London, a command performance at the Royal Opera Houses (above) sets a formal tone.

Until 1846, England had only two universities, both dating back to the 13th century. The oldest universities in Britain, Cambridge and Oxford, or "Oxbridge," remain among the world's most prestigious (see the sidebar on page 105). Today, English students pursuing a degree can choose among nearly 40 universities.

Perhaps reflecting its highly literate population, England abounds with local and national museums (hundreds) and libraries (tens of thousands). The largest can be found in London, and include the British Library, British Museum, National Gallery, Tate Gallery, and the Victoria and Albert Museum.

Above all, English culture has long benefited from the richness of the English language itself. Its diverse blend of Latin, Celtic, Germanic, Norse, and French vocabulary reflects the waves of conquering invaders that have ruled this land over the past two millennia. Indeed, word for word, the English language stands out as the world's largest. Over the centuries, English writers have taken full advantage of its great tapestry to produce the greatest body of literature ever written. English literature developed continuously over the course of 15 centuries, beginning with the epic Anglo-Saxon poem *Beowulf* (8th century), continuing through Chaucer's *Canterbury Tales* (1380s) and Shakespeare's unsurpassed plays and sonnets (1592-1616), and on to the 19th- and 20th-century novels of Jane Austen, Charles Dickens, Charlotte Brontë, Thomas Hardy, Robert Louis Stevenson, Rudyard Kipling, James Joyce, D.H. Lawrence, and Virginia Woolf.

SPORTS

When the duke of Wellington defeated Napoléon at Waterloo in 1815, he is said to have quipped that the great battle "was won on the playing fields of Eton." True or not, the comment reflects the overriding importance of intensely competitive sports in English life—and not only in the school yard. The bat-and-ball game known as cricket remains England's traditional "national" game, and its popularity swells to a fever pitch around the Test Matches and World Cup.

In recent years, however, cricket has been overshadowed by the growing popularity of rugby and football (soccer). At times in recent years, the fervor among English football fans at international matches has spun into violence, giving them a bad reputation throughout Europe.

Other popular sports revolve around England's long-standing love of horses. Polo, brought to England from India, has many fans, especially among the wealthy. Members of the royal family remain among its many

OXFORD AND CAMBRIDGE

The oldest universities in the English-speaking world, Oxford and Cambridge still reign as the crown jewels of higher education in England. To be "Oxbridge"—that is, to graduate from one of these two institutions—is to stand among an academic elite respected throughout the world.

The University of Oxford, located 55 mi. (89 km.) up the River Thames from London, dates to the 1100s, when European scholars began settling there and giving lectures. By the 1300s, it had become the Western world's preeminent university. Over the centuries, Oxford became known primarily for classical and law studies. Its graduates, or "members," have included such statesmen as William Penn, the founder of Pennsylvania; James Oglethorpe, the founder of Georgia; and President Bill Clinton, who attended (but did not graduate) on a Rhodes scholarship for international students. Today, the spires, turrets, and towers of the university's 36 colleges still give the town of Oxford the look of a medieval fairy tale.

The University of Cambridge, founded a century later, stands some 50 mi. (80 km.) due north of London, on the banks of the River Cam. Like Oxford, Cambridge consists of many centuries-old colleges spread throughout a tree-lined town that retains the feel of a medieval village. Over its history, Cambridge has distinguished itself as a world leader in mathematics and natural sciences, and has produced more than 60 Nobel Prize winners in these fields. Its most famous graduates include the "father" of modern physics, Sir Isaac Newton, and naturalist and evolutionary scientist Charles Darwin.

Since medieval times, these two schools have enjoyed a lively competition. The most famous of their "varsity matches" is the annual rowing-team race held on the upper Thames. Nearly a

A degree earned at Cambridge (above) or Oxford, among the world's leading universities, imparts great prestige to its conferee.

quarter of a million spectators line the riverbank to watch the contest—one of the most popular televised sporting events in England, with some 400 million viewers worldwide.

More recently, controversy has centered on charges that these elite schools discriminate against minorities and the "lower-class" poor. Critics point out, for example, that while England has become ethnically diverse, 85 percent of Oxbridge students still come from England's "wealthy and white" upper class. In 2000, such criticism spurred the government to pass laws requiring universities to show they were taking steps to combat racial prejudice.

players. Horse racing, with legalized betting, is a leading spectator sport. Controversy swirls around the enduring sport of foxhunting, which the poet Oscar Wilde described as "the unspeakable in full pursuit of the uneatable." Less competitive, though equally popular, are the English pastimes of bird-watching, hiking, and trout fishing.

The Thames, England's most important river, provides London access to the sea. Upstream from London, the Thames assumes a more recreational nature, with crew teams taking to the river in regular competitions.

CITIES

London, with a population of 7.2 million, has been England's largest city, main port, and center of business and government for more than 1,000 years (see sidebar on pages 110 and 111). It is also home to the Houses of Parliament, the seat of government for the whole of the United Kingdom, as well as Buckingham Palace and Westminster Abbey.

Birmingham, with a population just over 1 million, ranks as England's second-largest city. It dominates the highly industrialized Midlands region, about 120 mi. (190 km.) northwest of London. One of the world's major manufacturing centers in its own right, Birmingham also serves as a commercial and financial center for the industrial towns that surround it.

The history of Birmingham's modern industries traces back to the Middle Ages, when miners discovered substantial deposits of coal and iron nearby. England's 18th-century Industrial Revolution started in large part there. Since then, Birmingham has been linked by human-made canals to all of England's major ports.

Today, Birmingham is home to five major universities. Its art galleries and museums include the new Birmingham Museum of Science and Discovery, which celebrates the city's long history of technology, including the invention of the steam engine by Birmingham resident, or "Brummie," James Watt. Other cultural attractions include the city's botanical gardens, opera, royal ballet, and its world-famous symphony orchestra. In recent decades, dramatic reductions in air and water pollution have fostered Birmingham's tourism industry, which draws visitors primarily for shopping, especially in the city's historic jewelry district.

Leeds, on the banks of the Aire River, is England's third-largest city (population 731,000) and the commercial and industrial center for the northern part of the country. The city's most important industries include the manufacture of clothing, electric equipment, and paper products. Its major art galleries and museums date back to the 19th century, when canals and railways first linked Leeds with the rest of the country and made it an important distribution hub. The city is the home of the highly respected Uni-

The English are great sports enthusiasts. Cricket (bottom) is played by English schoolboys of all ages and backgrounds. Polo, by contrast, is an expensive sport by and large reserved for the wealthy; notable participants include Prince William (at left, in photo at right). Grass courts and regal trappings help make the annual tennis tournament at Wimbledon (below) the most prestigious in the sport.

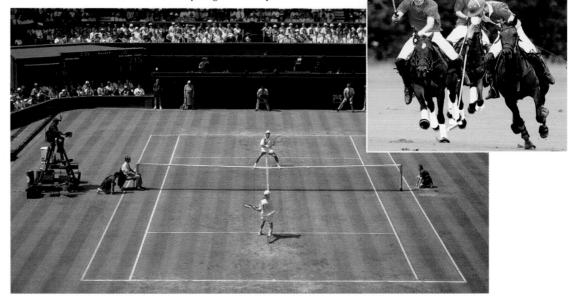

versity of Leeds, established in 1904, and the more recent Leeds Metropolitan University (1992).

Sheffield, 35 mi. (56 km.) south of Leeds at the foot of the Pennine Mountains, ranks as England's fourth-largest city (population 531,000). It, too, serves as an important manufacturing center. Steelmaking has been the city's major industry for hundreds of years. Indeed, it was here that English inventor Sir Henry Bessemer developed the modern steelmaking processes that revolutionized the industry in the 1850s. Sheffield remains world famous for its fine stainless-steel cutlery. Its centuries-old brass and iron foundries remain important as well.

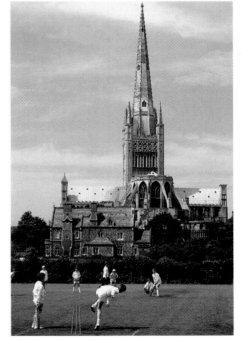

Sheffield's many historic buildings include the 15th-century Cathedral Church of St. Peter and St. Paul and the 15th-century Bishops' House, now a museum. Many other historic buildings were lost when Sheffield suffered heavy German bombing during World War II. It has since been rebuilt into a highly modern city. It is home to the University of Sheffield and Sheffield Hallam University.

Liverpool, best known perhaps as the home of the phenomenally successful Beatles rock group, serves as England's second-busiest seaport and fifth-most-populous city (population 456,000). Located in northwestern En-

To many people, Liverpool is known primarily as home to the Beatles (above), the influential 1960s rock group.

gland, it stands on the banks of the Mersey River, near the river's mouth on the Irish Sea. Liverpool's seaport activities include the import and export of materials and the ferrying of people and vehicles between England and Ireland. Liverpool's industries include pharmaceuticals, electronic equipment, and the refining of sugar and flour. Major auto factories operate just outside its city limits. As English cities go, Liverpool is relatively new, having remained an insignificant hamlet until the late 17th century. Like Sheffield and London, Liverpool sustained heavy bombing during World War II and has since been largely rebuilt. The city boasts a symphony orchestra, many theaters and music halls, two universities, and several scientific-research institutes.

Manchester, 30 mi. (50 km.) inland from Liverpool, serves as the commercial, financial, educational, and cultural center of northwestern England. The city itself is home to nearly 440,000 people, making it England's sixth-largest city. But its greater metropolitan area encompasses more than 7 million. Like Birmingham, Manchester shares a claim to being a birthplace of the 18th-century Industrial Revolution. There, James Hargreaves invented the "spinning jenny" that revolutionized cloth making and helped make Manchester the world textile center it remains today. The Manchester Ship Canal, completed in 1894, made Manchester a major inland port by linking it to the Mersey River and the Irish Sea.

Manchester, renowned for the scientific research conducted at its four universities and at its National Computing Centre, is the home of more than 20 winners of Nobel Prizes. Many of their accomplishments can be seen at the popular 7.5-acre (3-ha.) Museum of Science and Industry. Other local attractions include the 600-year-old Manchester Cathedral, and Sportcity, a colossal sports complex and academy built for the XVII Commonwealth Games, held there in 2002. Manchester is also the headquarters of the *Guardian*, one of the world's most widely read and respected newspapers for more than a century.

Newcastle, on the Tyne River in the northeast, stands out as perhaps the most Victorian of England's major cities. A military outpost in Roman times, this ancient city rose to great wealth first in the Elizabethan age, as a major coal exporter, and again in the 19th century, as an industrial center. During the late 19th and early 20th centuries, the city showed off its wealth with the building of many grand Victorian mansions, churches, and office buildings. The city, England's seventh largest (population 282,000), takes its name from its Norman castle, built there in 1080.

ECONOMY

As the United Kingdom's largest and most populous region, England drives the larger nation's economy. For more than 500 years, England, especially London, has reigned as a world center for international banking and

Piccadilly Circus (above) is one of London's busiest traffic junctures. Five major thoroughfares radiate from the giant intersection, including fashionable shopping areas and London's theater district.

finance. For nearly as long, England has been a leader in the manufacture of steel and textiles. Automobile and aircraft manufacturing became another major industry in the 20th century. Rich in fuel resources, England powered its early industries with waterpower and the coal dug from its Midlands and northern regions. In the second half of the 20th century, rich offshore deposits of petroleum and natural gas took coal's place as England's most important energy source.

The 1970s and 1980s saw the loss of many manufacturing jobs throughout England, as companies moved their factories overseas to take advantage of cheaper labor and materials. Today, manufacturing accounts for just 20 percent of the English economy. But factories in England's Midlands region continue to produce large amounts of finished metals, vehicles, aircraft, synthetic fibers, and electronics equipment. The Greater Manchester region remains known for its cotton and synthetic textiles, coal, and chemical industries. To the northwest, West Yorkshire County is England's main textile center. In the far northeast, Tyne and Wear County has active coal mines and major steel, chemical, and shipbuilding industries. London is England's busiest port, followed by Liverpool, on the Irish Sea, and Southampton, on the English Channel.

Tourism continues to grow in economic importance in most regions. In recent years, the Internet has enabled local communities to better market their many castles, cathedrals, museums, musical venues, and other attractions to the world.

During the 1990s, English agriculture suffered from livestock epidemics of "mad cow" disease (bovine spongiform encephalopathy) and foot-and-mouth infection. Containing their spread required the slaughter of much livestock. Most farms survived the crisis with government assistance.

Helping to offset the loss of traditional factory and farm work in England has been the emergence of the information-technology industry.

LONDON

Think of any other of the world's great cities, and one or two images may spring to mind: the skyline of New York City, the Champs Élysées of Paris, the Sydney Opera House. But think of London, and you may come up with enough images to fill a mental album: London Bridge, Big Ben, Buckingham Palace, the Tower of London, red double-decker buses circling

a fortress wall when they rebuilt it in 120 A.D. After the Romans abandoned England in the 5th century, Celts, Saxons, Danes, and Normans fought over it in succession. London prospered in the 12th and 13th centuries, when the city's monarchs and archbishops filled it with magnificent palaces, towers, and cathedrals, and rebuilt the London Bridge out of stone.

London reached a new level of importance during the reign of Queen Elizabeth I (1558–1603). From London's docks, Elizabeth sent out a navy to defeat the Spanish Armada, and explorers to chart a world empire. From her London court, Elizabeth also fostered a great flowering of the arts.

By the conclusion of the Elizabethan Age, London had grown into a crowded city of narrow, twisting streets. The Great Fire of 1666 consumed much of the city. The famed architect Sir Christopher Wren oversaw its reconstruction and the addition of St. Paul's

On a typical day, London's major avenues are congested with taxicabs and other vehicles—not to mention thousands of pedestrians.

Piccadilly Circus, St. Paul's Cathedral, perhaps even Shakespeare's Globe Theatre, newly rebuilt on the banks of the storied River Thames.

An ancient yet modern city, London has reigned as England's center of power, culture, and commerce for nearly 2,000 years. For good reason, this famed metropolis is also the most written-about city in world literature, featured in everything from nursery rhymes to classic novels, medieval poetry to modern movie scripts. Simply put, London remains one of the most interesting places on Earth.

London through the Ages. In 43 A.D., the conquering Romans built a bridge across the River Thames, fixing the position of London—then *Londinium*—for the ages. The Celtic queen Boudicca ordered London destroyed 28 years later. The Romans wisely encircled the city with

Cathedral. The 1700s brought the building of elegant mansions, and the 1800s saw the spread of London's industrial suburbs, with docks and shipping operations stretching for miles downriver. Nineteenth-century London also enjoyed great social reforms, including the establishment of an unarmed police force, known affectionately as the "bobbies." In 1890, London opened the world's first electric underground railway.

Destruction again rained on London during World War II, when German bombs and rockets destroyed much of the city, killing thousands. In the following years, skyscrapers sprang up from the rubble. In 1968, the often-rebuilt London Bridge "fell down" once again. More accurately, it was torn down and shipped, stone for stone, to Arizona (as a tourist attraction), before being rebuilt out of concrete to handle modern traffic.

Among the most dramatic changes in recent decades, great reductions in air pollution have largely lifted the dark fogs that had shrouded London's skies for centuries.

21st-Century London. Today, London's importance centers on its being the capital of the United Kingdom and an international financial hub. These activities take place primarily in "the City," meaning the 1 sq. mi. (2.6 sq. km.) of land that is London's ancient heart. Fewer than 5,000 people live in this district. But nearly half a million arrive to work there each weekday, many on the subway.

Greater London, by contrast, encompasses approximately 610 sq. mi. (1,580 sq. km.), extending about 15 mi. (24 km.) in every direction from Charing Cross, the city's traditional center. A population of 7.2 million makes Greater London Europe's most populous city. Its residents live in various well-known sections such as Westminster, Kensington, Chelsea, and Paddington, many of which began as separate villages centuries ago. Until recently, each of the city's 30-odd sections had its own mayor and a decidedly confusing body of municipal laws. Hoping to streamline their government, the residents of Greater London recently decided to elect a single mayor and 25-member assembly to handle citywide affairs. In addition, a ceremonial "Lord Mayor" reigns over the inner City, but wields no real power.

London has always been a town of immigrants. But up until the 20th century, its arrivals came primarily from other parts of the United Kingdom. Then, in the early 1900s, Jewish refugees arrived from Europe, and Asian workers from China. The decades following World War II brought larger influxes from all corners of the former British Empire—most especially India, Pakistan, and the Caribbean. Most recently, immigrants from Hong Kong, Somalia, and Ethiopia have further broadened the city's diversity. Many of London's newer immigrants tend to live in ethnic neighborhoods that specialize in particular trades, such as the Bangladeshi garment industry of London's East End.

London abounds with educational and cultural institutions. Today, the University of London ranks as the United Kingdom's largest. London's many schools of fine arts include the Royal Academy of Arts, the Royal Academy of Dramatic Art, the Royal College of Music, and the Royal Ballet School. London museums of international importance include the National Gallery, the

A familiar image of London might well feature a double-decker bus driving past Big Ben and the Parliament buildings.

British Museum, the Tate Gallery, and the Victoria and Albert Museum. London is also home to four world-class orchestras, the Royal Ballet, and the Royal Opera. More than 100 theaters stage performances in the city, the most elaborate in London's famous West End. Still, the simple pleasures of London's many wooded parks rank among the city's host of pleasant pastimes. The most famous—Kensington Gardens—is the legendary home of the original Peter Pan.

Many of London's commuters rely on the Underground, the city's subway system, to travel to and from work.

Telecommunications firms and Internet companies now employ a growing percentage of England's workforce, from highly trained "IT" managers and electrical engineers to the many people who answer telephones at service call centers.

In recent years, the U.K. government has invested heavily in the growth of new industries through England's nine regional-development agencies. These agencies financially support scientific research at area universities, technology institutes, and private research centers. Among the major success stories of this program has been the tremendous growth of England's bio-pharmaceutical industry. The regional-development agencies also continue the challenging work of revitalizing the aging centers of England's many centuries-old industrial cities.

HISTORY

The archaeological remains of England's prehistoric inhabitants (Neanderthals and Cro-Magnons) show that they hunted reindeer there during the last Ice Age, around 11,000 B.C. At that time, the present-day island of Great Britain was connected to the European mainland, splitting off about 8,500 years ago. By 3500 B.C., a farming people called the Iberians, or Long Skulls, had crossed over from southwestern Europe. Several hundred years later, the Bronze Age "Beaker" people arrived from the same region. Named for their pottery drinking vessels, the Beaker people left behind huge and mysterious stone monuments such as Stonehenge, near the present-day town of Salisbury, in southern England.

By 1500 B.C., the Iron Age Celts of mainland Europe swept over England, conquering and absorbing its more primitive peoples into their own society. The Celts cleared vast swaths of forest with their iron axes, cultivated the heavy soil with their iron plows, and mined the land's tin, which they traded in places as far away as Greece. The Celts gave this land its first kings and queens, who ruled Celtic society

England's communications industries utilize state-of-the-art technology to meet the demands of the densely concentrated population.

along with the high priests known as Druids. The Celts also developed an intricate, curvilinear art form, one of the glories of Western civilization.

Roman Conquest

In 55 B.C., the Roman general and statesman Julius Caesar arrived to briefly battle with the Celts over the land he called *Brittonum.* A decade later, under Emperor Claudius, the Romans began their conquest in earnest. Claudius established the fortified city of Londinium (now London), on the River Thames, 40 mi. (64 km.) from its mouth on the North Sea. The Romans took over most of the island of Great Britain. In doing so, they drove the Celts into the highlands of northern England and Scotland, but not without fierce resistance. In 60 A.D., the forces of the Celtic queen Boudicca burned the Romans' Londinium to the ground. By 122 A.D., the legions of Emperor Hadrian completed the Roman conquest of England and walled off the raiding "barbarians" on the north side of the 73-mi. (117-km.)-long fortification known as Hadrian's Wall. (See sidebar in the article UNITED KINGDOM on page 92.)

During their prolonged stay, the Romans dotted the landscape with luxurious villas, resorts such as Aquae Sulis (now Bath), and fortified towns, many of them with names ending in "cester" or "caster." Most important, perhaps, the Romans built the network of roads that would become the basis for England's transportation system. They also imposed Christianity in place of the Druids' form of nature worship. Yet for the most part, Britain remained little more than a military outpost—the northernmost corner of the vast Roman Empire. Moreover, keeping Britain's rebellious natives in check required the presence of a full one-tenth of the Roman Army. Consequently, the Romans abandoned Londinium and the rest of Britain when troubles struck closer to home around 400 A.D.

Angle-land

Before the end of the 5th century (the 400s), the tall, fair-haired tribes known as Angles, Saxons, and Jutes had swept over from mainland Europe. Their raiding parties traveled along Britain's Roman-built roads, slaughter-

SAY AGAIN?

Winston Churchill, Britain's wartime prime minister, was born to an English father and an American mother. He once quipped that England and the United States are two countries "separated by a common language." Here are some examples of what he had in mind.

ENGLISH SAY	AMERICANS SAY
biscuits	cookies
bonnet (of a car)	hood
boot (of a car)	trunk
caravan	truck trailer
car park	parking lot
chemist	pharmacist
chips	french fries
dressing gown	bathrobe
flat	apartment
holiday	vacation
lift	elevator
lorry	truck
mack, or mackintosh	raincoat
mum	mom, or mother
pavement	sidewalk
petrol	gasoline
post	mail
solicitor	lawyer
vacuum flask	thermos

■ STONEHENGE

The massive monoliths of Stonehenge, on the windswept Salisbury Plain of southern England, remain one of the world's enduring mysteries. From as early as 1066 A.D., historians have been speculating who might have built this gigantic stone structure and why. Medieval writers called it *Staneges*, from the Anglo-Saxon expression meaning "hanging stones." Early on, researchers noticed that Stonehenge's prehistoric builders had oriented the structure such that its entryway pointed east to the spot on the horizon where the Sun rises on the summer solstice—the longest day of the year. Other stone markers within the structure appear to direct the viewer to the Sun's location at the winter solstice and to its position during predictable eclipses.

Early theories about the who and why of Stonehenge centered around the Druids, Celtic priests who spread their unique form of nature religion across Great Britain beginning in 1500 B.C. Researchers now know that, while the Druids may have worshiped at Stonehenge, they clearly did not build it. In fact, Stonehenge predates their arrival in England by more than 1,000 years. Indeed, radiocarbon dating shows that the oldest sections of the monument date to around 2900 B.C.—older than the pyramids.

Of special interest are the herculean efforts that the monument's makers invested in quarrying, carving, and hauling its colossal stones from as far away as the Atlantic coast of Wales. Presumably, they transported the 25- to 50-ton blocks first in rafts over sea and river, and then on rollers across the countryside. Researchers estimate that it took at least 50 men to haul the blocks up the steepest slopes, then raise them upright with ropes and levers, and crown them with a continuous circle of stone caps.

Visitors to Stonehenge can no longer enter its inner circle of stones, but must view the site from a distance. Nonetheless, each summer solstice, "New Age" Druids try to sneak or push their way past the monument's guards to re-create an imagined pagan festival.

The arrangement and purpose of the monoliths of Stonehenge (below) continue to mystify scholars and archaeologists.

ing or enslaving those they encountered. Many Romanized Celts fled west into Cornwall and Wales and, across the Irish Sea, to Ireland. From this period comes the English legend of King Arthur, based on a Celtic British king who fought bravely against the Saxon invaders.

The Anglo-Saxons introduced feudalism to their newly established kingdom of Anglia, or "Angle-land." In this form of government, the ruling king or queen granted land and power to an upper class of lords and ladies,

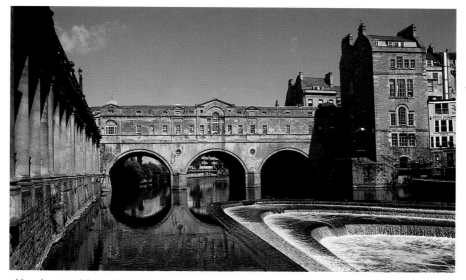

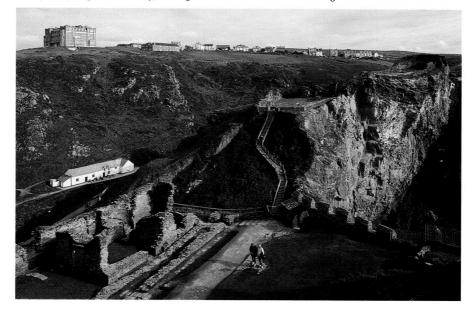

Although many of the notable buildings in contemporary Bath (above) date to the 18th century, the city itself was founded by the ancient Romans, who created public baths that exploited the healing properties ascribed to local mineral springs. Tintagel Castle (now in ruins, below), in Cornwall, is reputed to be the birthplace of the legendary King Arthur, an important figure in literature from the Middle Ages.

who in turn granted land to knights in return for their military service. Members of the peasant class worked the land of their masters for a portion of the food they raised. Over the next century, the Anglo-Saxons established the seven kingdoms of Kent, Sussex, Essex, Wessex, Northumbria, Mercia, and East Anglia. Christianity returned to England in the 6th century, with emissaries from Rome and Celtic Christian monks from Ireland and Scotland.

In the 9th century, England's often-warring kingdoms united to meet an outside threat. Danish Vikings had been raiding England's coastal settlements for decades. In 865, they invaded in force. King Alfred of Wessex led the decade-long resistance. He created the first English navy and, in 878, recaptured London and pushed the Danes out of his southwestern kingdom.

SHAKESPEARE LIVES!

For all its famous sons and daughters, England perhaps takes it greatest pride in the Elizabethan poet and dramatist William Shakespeare. Sixteenth-century Londoners considered the works of "the Bard" merely "entertaining" when they were first performed in the city's Globe Theatre in the 1590s. But over the centuries, Shakespeare's creations would rise to a height of global popularity and acclaim that remains unsurpassed in world history. Indeed, so many editions and translations of Shakespeare's 36 plays and 154 sonnets have been published over the past 400 years that no bibliography can come close to providing a complete and definitive list.

The traditional heart of "Shakespeare country" can be found in Stratford-upon-Avon, the village of the Bard's birth and a popular tourist destination. But nowhere else can one see more Shakespeare *performed* than in London, where a day does not go by without at least one play—usually several—being staged. Summer, in particular, brings scores of outdoor performances of *Midsummer Night's Dream*, *Taming of the Shrew*, *Twelfth Night*, and other favorites.

Best of all for Shakespeare fans has been the recent opening of the faithfully reconstructed, open-air Globe Theatre, just 200 yd. (180 m.) from where the original Globe stood on the south bank of the Thames. Surrounding the recreated theater is an education center, library, and exhibition hall featuring the world's largest collection of Shakespearean artifacts.

William Shakespeare (above) is universally acknowledged as the greatest playwright in the English language. His home (left), in Stratford-upon-Avon, is a popular tourist attraction.

In 886, a peace treaty signed by Alfred awarded the northeast of England (the Danelaw) to the Danish, and the southwest to Alfred.

Remembered as Alfred the Great, the king of Wessex established a strong government with written laws. He also established schools and promoted reading—a skill previously restricted to the clergy. Alfred's son and grandson recaptured the Danelaw and united the whole of England under one kingdom for the first time. A century of peace followed. But in the 11th century, a mightier Danish army and navy made England part of Denmark.

England bounced back and forth between warring Danish and Wessex kings until 1066, when William the Conqueror, duke of Normandy (on the French coast), a distant relative of Alfred the Great, invaded the country.

Norman England

As a Norman, William I introduced new laws, customs, and the French language to England. French became the language of royalty, while the "common people" still spoke "Old English," or Anglo-Saxon. Over the years, Anglo-Saxon and Norman French would meld to produce the foundations of modern English.

William gave most Saxon land to his French lords and taxed the English people heavily. In 1086, the completion of the *Domesday Book*, England's first census, enabled tax collectors to do their work more efficiently. Over the years, William and his successors—his sons William II and later Henry I—strengthened the English monarchy and extended its power to include parts of Ireland.

In the 12th and 13th centuries, the English monarchy came into conflict, first with the powerful bishops of the English church and then with its own nobles. The first struggle culminated in 1170, with the murder of Saint Thomas Becket, the archbishop of Canterbury. The second resulted in the document that would become the foundation of democracy in England and, through it, much of the world.

Magna Carta

When King Richard I, the Lion-Hearted, died in 1199, his brother King John tried to extend royal power and frequently placed himself above the law. In 1215, a group of barons—supported by powerful London merchants and the new archbishop of Canterbury—forced John to sign an agreement by which he admitted his wrongdoing and vowed to respect English Law. Known as the Great Charter, or *Magna Carta* in Latin, the document required the monarch to gain his nobles' consent before levying any new taxes. It also gave them the right to trial by a jury of their peers. In time, these rights would come to apply to all of England's people.

England prospered over the following century. Sheep raising for meat and wool became an important industry, merchants grew wealthy, and London became a major world trading center. England's church likewise grew rich. With this wealth, the church built impressive cathedrals

The Magna Carta, signed in 1215 by King John (above), forms the foundation of English law.

across the country and developed Oxford and Cambridge into two of the world's first major universities (see sidebar on page 105). Powerful craft guilds called ministries controlled their particular professions, including the assignment of apprentices to the "masters" from whom they would learn their trade.

Between 1277 and 1284, King Edward I conquered much of Wales. He appointed his eldest son Prince of Wales, a title that has since been held by the English monarch's oldest son. In 1295, the king's council of advisers became the English Parliament. Over the next century, Parliament would form two levels—with barons and bishops in the House of Lords, and the representatives of towns and counties in the House of Commons.

Opposition, plotting, and murder supplanted one king after another, leading to the reign of Edward III, who launched the Hundred Years' War with France in 1337, with the hopes of enriching his royal coffers. Over the course of this century-long war, English replaced French as the language of

THE ENGLISH MONARCHY

The English monarchy traces back more than 1,200 years to King Egbert, the first to unite England under one ruler. Almost-absolute authority mixed with rivalry, intrigue, and murder typified the first eight centuries of English monar-

reigned since 1952. Occasionally, the English bestow an honorific on a monarch for a special deed, trait, or failing. Aethelred the Unready, Alfred the Great, and Richard the Lion-Hearted stand out as memorable examples.

Queen Elizabeth II (center) heads the royal family, which includes (from left): her grandsons Prince Harry and Prince William; her son and heir, Prince Charles; her husband, Prince Philip; her second son, Prince Andrew; and his two daughters.

chy—until Parliament assumed all real power with the beheading of King Charles I in 1649.

Succession to the English crown has long been hereditary. Specifically, the eldest son assumes the throne when the ruling king or queen dies. Should the monarch lack sons, the eldest daughter becomes queen. At various times through history, the throne has passed to a new royal family, or "house," owing to conquest, civil war, or the lack of a suitable heir.

By tradition, English royals go by their first name only, with a number indicating their order, if needed. Queen Elizabeth I, for example, ruled during Renaissance times. Elizabeth II has

A monarch's children automatically become princes and princesses. If the reigning monarch is a king, his wife becomes queen. If the reigning monarch is a queen, her husband is simply referred to as "royal consort." The queen may award him additional titles, from duke to prince, but never "king." The mother of a ruling king or queen becomes the "Queen Mother."

The English have long debated whether the monarchy should be abolished. But polls show that the institution remains very popular today. The show of grief that followed the death of Princess Diana in 1997 suggests that many outside the country share that sentiment.

the nobles, Geoffrey Chaucer produced the first great poetry in the English language, and the Black Death (the bubonic plague) killed one in three of England's people. All the while, various branches of the royal family continued to vie for the English throne. The peak of conflict came with the civil

England's Protestant tradition dates to the reign of Henry VIII in the 16th century. Under his daughter, Elizabeth I, England became a major player in the age of exploration and sowed the first seeds of empire.

war called the Wars of the Roses, after the emblems of the two battling sides. In 1485, Henry Tudor killed King Richard III, to become King Henry VII and finally bring peace to the land.

Under the Tudor kings, England flourished, and its growing fleet of merchant ships expanded their reach and opened new markets for English goods. In 1497, John Cabot explored the northeastern coast of North America as far south as Delaware, claiming the land for England.

In 1534, the pope refused to grant Henry VIII a divorce from his first wife, Catherine of Aragon. In order to marry Anne Boleyn, Henry had himself appointed the head of the new Church of England, or Anglican Church.

Although he married six times—divorcing and beheading various wives in his quest to have a son—Henry had only one. When that son, Edward, died in his youth, Henry's Catholic daughter from his first marriage became queen. When Mary died, her half-sister Elizabeth rose to the throne and became one of the most powerful and influential monarchs England—and possibly the world—had ever known.

The Elizabethan Age

Under Elizabeth's command, the English Navy defeated the Spanish Armada in 1588 and entered a period of unparalleled prosperity. Explorers such as Francis Drake and Sir Martin Frobisher sailed on voyages of discovery that led to the expansion of the first British Empire. Wealth and security brought a flowering of the arts under Elizabeth's active encouragement. This was the age of Shakespeare and his contemporaries—the playwright Christopher Marlowe, the writer Ben Jonson, and the poet-adventurer Sir Walter Raleigh. Elizabeth never married. She raised her nephew James Stuart, heir to the Scottish throne, to be her successor. And so, in 1603, James VI of Scotland became James I of England, uniting the Scottish and English crowns. However, it would take another century of civil war to officially unite Scotland with the English realms.

The Stuarts and Civil War

A scholarly king, James is best remembered for authorizing a new translation of the Bible in 1611. The "King James Version" would exert an enormous influence on English literary style for centuries. But James neglected his navy and his country's economy. The people also chafed under the king's control of the church and his appointment of bishops.

The conflict came to a head during the reign of James' son Charles, who refused to consult Parliament and demanded taxes without its permission. Harsh measures led to a Scottish rebellion in 1640, and in 1642, civil

The Royal Pavilion (above), at Brighton, is noted for its Asian architectural style—a reflection of the foreign ideas and concepts that flooded England during the time when the British Empire reached it greatest extent.

war broke out between parliamentary forces led by Oliver Cromwell and Charles' Catholic supporters. On Charles' defeat in 1649, Parliament had him beheaded for treason. Cromwell ruled England until 1658. In 1660, Charles' son was recalled from exile and restored the monarchy.

When Charles II died in 1685, his brother, James II, became king and tried to forcibly convert England to Catholicism. Parliament again raised an army. It sent James II into exile with the help of William of Orange, prince of the Netherlands—who had married James II's Protestant daughter Mary. Mary and William assumed the throne, and Parliament passed the Bill of Rights. The bill firmly limited any monarch's power and established the democratic rule of England through the elected members of Parliament. With the last Scottish rebellion put to rest, the Scottish and English Parliaments ratified the Act of Union in 1707. England, Scotland, and Wales had become one nation: the United Kingdom of Great Britain.

[For later history, see the article UNITED KINGDOM.]

GOVERNMENT

For purposes of providing local services and government, England is divided into 46 unitary authorities, 34 counties (or "shires"), and Greater London. The counties, in turn, are subdivided into some 240 districts. Counties generally provide such services as education, transportation, fire protection, and libraries. Districts control local planning, highways, building inspections, and health services. Unitary authorities provide both. Residents elect council members to preside over each level of local government. In districts large enough to be called cities or boroughs, the council chairperson serves as the mayor.

As part of the United Kingdom, England is also divided into "constituencies," each of which elects one member to represent it in Parliament's House of Commons (the national legislature). For more on the workings of the national government, see the article UNITED KINGDOM.

On a broad peninsula along the west-central coast of Great Britain sits Wales, a region of great scenic beauty, where the ruggedness of the mountains is offset by rivers, lakes, and lushly green farmland.

WALES

The Land of Castles. The Land of Poetry. The Land of Song. The ancient principality of Wales has been called all of these things. It is also an evergreen land of moor and mountain, where thundering waterfalls and rivers carve rocky chasms and steep valleys as they tumble their way to the sea. Signs with the cryptic greeting *Croeso i Gymru* ("Welcome to Wales") hail visitors crossing Offa's Dyke, the centuries-old ditch-and-mound barrier that separates ancient Wales from the younger kingdom of England, to the east. Although virtually everyone in Wales speaks English, schoolchildren also learn Welsh, or *Cymraeg*, Europe's oldest surviving language.

THE LAND

One of the four main administrative divisions of the United Kingdom, Wales stands on the island of Great Britain, where it occupies a broad western peninsula jutting out into the Irish Sea. On the east, it shares a land border with England. About 135 mi. (217 km.) from north to south, and varying between 36 and 96 mi. (58 and 154 km.) from east to west, Wales totals

Many of Wales' powerful rivers are now important producers of hydroelectricity. The enormous reservoirs behind the dams were originally built to provide drinking water for nearby areas of England.

8,016 sq. mi. (20,761 sq. km.). It includes the island of Anglesey, separated from the mainland by the 1,000-ft. (300-m.)-wide Menai Strait.

The vast Cardigan Bay and many smaller inlets indent the Welsh coast, which extends some 750 mi. (1,200 km.)—from the estuaries of the Dee River, in the north, and to the Severn River, in the south. The shoreline alternates between sandy beaches, low-lying estuaries, and high, rocky cliffs.

Mountains and powerful rivers dominate the countryside. The largest range—the Cambrian Mountains—forms a north-to-south backbone, rising to an average elevation of 1,500 ft. (460 m.). Other ranges include the Snowdonia Mountains in the north, with the highest peak in Wales— Snowdon (3,560 feet; 1,085 m.). On the eastern fringe of Snowdonia lies Llyn Tegid, or Bala Lake, the largest natural body of water in Wales.

West of Snowdonia, the Lleyn Peninsula points a hooked finger into the Irish Sea. North of Snowdonia lies the flat and fertile island of Anglesey. Since medieval times, the Welsh have called the island *Mam Cymru*, or "Mother of Wales," because its fields once fed much of the populace.

The peaks of the rugged Brecon Beacons tower above south Wales, their slopes carved by powerful rivers such as the Usk, Neath, and Tawe. The rivers slow and broaden when they reach the southern coastal plain— Wales' only extensive lowland. In the plain's southeast corner, Wales' longest rivers—the Severn (180 mi.; 290 km.) and Wye (130 mi.; 210 km.)— empty into the Bristol Channel.

Although Wales accounts for just 9 percent of the landmass of the United Kingdom, its spectacular landscape boasts three of its 10 national parks. These preserves encompass much of Snowdonia, the Brecon Beacons, and the unspoiled beaches of the Pembrokeshire coast. In addition, Wales has five regions that have been designated "Areas of Outstanding Natural Beauty"—the Wye Valley, Gower Peninsula, Lleyn Peninsula, the island of Anglesey, and the Clwydian Range.

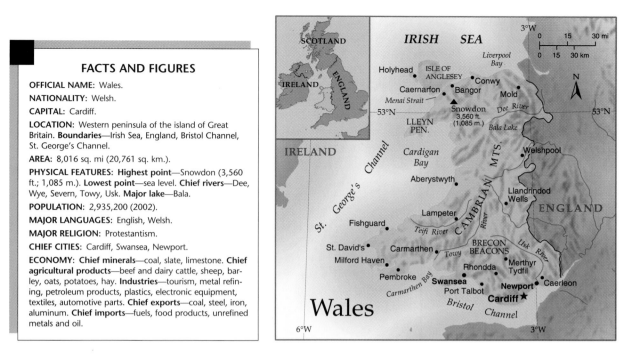

Climate

Like other highland regions of the British Isles, Wales receives abundant rain. Annual precipitation averages 50 in. (1,300 mm.) overall. This amount varies considerably, from as little as 30 in. (760 mm.) on the south coast to 100 in. (2,500 mm.) in the northern mountains.

The Welsh mountains block the cold east winds from reaching the southern plains and western valleys. The resulting weather is so mild that one needs little more than a raincoat and sweater in winter. Typical of Wales is Aberystwyth, on the west coast, where daily high temperatures average 44° F. (7° C.) in January and 64° F. (18° C.) in July.

Plant and Animal Life

Lush grassland covers much of Wales. This is now true even in southeastern Wales, where the open scars of former coal mines have largely returned to their natural green state. Forests cover about 12 percent of Wales, consisting primarily of replanted trees, although some oak, ash, . and native conifer stands survive in the mountains. At high elevations, trees give way to hardy shrubs, coarse grasses, and alpine flowers.

The pine marten and the polecat, long extinct in England, are still found in Wales. Wales also boasts an abundance

Agriculture in Wales centers mainly on livestock. The rich pastureland supports a thriving dairy industry.

of foxes, otters, badgers, water voles, and bats. Seals bask on Welsh beaches and rocky coves. Amphibians include several kinds of newts, the common frog, and common toad. Conservationists have introduced the rare sand lizard to a number of wildlife preserves. Welsh rivers and streams and the coastal waters hold an abundance of fish.

Birds of the Welsh seashore include puffins, herons, swans, geese, cormorants, gannets, and several kinds of ducks. Garden birds include the European robin, yellowhammer, nuthatch, and several kinds of finches and tits. The countryside supports many birds of prey, including the peregrine falcon, red kite, sparrow hawk, and several kinds of owl.

Natural Resources

The thundering rivers of the countryside provide Wales with an abundance of hydroelectric power, and Welsh reservoirs supply the English cities of Birmingham and Liverpool with water. South Wales remains rich in coal deposits, although most mines have closed. Other natural resources include slate, limestone, and limited amounts of copper, gold, manganese, lead, uranium, and zinc. Fertile soil for farming occurs along the southern coastal plain and on the island of Anglesey.

THE PEOPLE

The Welsh trace their heritage in part to Great Britain's first people—the Stone Age tribes known as Iberians. Some 3,000 years ago, a group known as the Brythonic Celts arrived and intermarried with the native Iberians. (Historians use the name Brythonic to distinguish these tribes from the Gaelic Celts of Scotland and Ireland.) The resulting people called themselves *y Cymry*, meaning "compatriots." Then, 1,000 years later, the invading Saxons would call the local population *wealas*, or Welsh, meaning "foreigners." Today, most Welsh descend from a mixture of Welsh, Anglo-Saxon, Norse, and French ancestors. Nearly a quarter of the people can speak Welsh, or *Cymraeg*, as well as English.

Other ethnicities make up less than 2 percent of the population, or about 40,000 people. They include the descendants of immigrant workers from all over Britain and Ireland, and notably Italy, who arrived in the 19th and early 20th centuries, and those of European Jewish refugees who came during World War II. In recent years, Wales has received a trickle of the larger stream of immigrants from Asia and Africa arriving in neighboring England.

The majority of the Welsh consider themselves Protestant, and belong to either the Church of England in Wales (Anglican) or the nonconformist chapels, an umbrella term for a group of other Protestant denominations. Well over half of the Welsh population lives in the south, particularly in the area around the former coal-shipping ports of Cardiff and Swansea.

The Welsh take great pride in their heritage. Traditional costumes are usually reserved for special holidays.

EISTEDDFOD

The largest and oldest celebration of Welsh culture, the National Eisteddfod traces back to 1176. In that year, the Welsh Lord Rhys sponsored the first "competition of the bards" at his castle in Cardigan. He invited poets and musicians from throughout Wales and awarded a "chair" at the Lord's Table to the principality's best. The tradition prevails at the modern-day National Eisteddfod, revived in 1880 and now held annually.

Today, the National Eisteddfod stands out as one of the largest cultural festivals in the world.

Entrants compete in a variety of artistic categories, including poetry, song, instrumental music, drama, and arts and crafts. Competitors for the traditional "bardic chair" must compose an *awdl*, or traditional Welsh ode. In addition, many towns and schools in Wales hold local eisteddfods throughout the year.

The Welsh are renowned for their beautiful voices, both singing and speaking. Each year, the National Eisteddfod, one of the world's largest cultural festivals, draws some 6,000 competitors and more than 170,000 attendees.

THE ARTS

As a group, the Welsh remain passionate about their ancient culture. At its heart is the melodious Welsh language—*Cymraeg*—which took shape in the 6th century from a mixture of Brythonic Celtic and Latin. The language flourished for many centuries until the Act of Union between England and Wales, in 1536, resulted in laws that forbade the use of Welsh. Yet, despite this, by the early 19th century, about 70 percent of the population spoke *only* Welsh. The Industrial Revolution that followed, with its influx of English-speaking workers, caused a significant decline in the language. In the 20th century, the work of Plaid Cymru (the Welsh political party) and the Welsh Language Society led to the Welsh Language Acts of 1967 and 1993, which secured the official use of Welsh in courts of law and its mandatory teaching in schools.

Intertwined with the Welsh language is a strong tradition of poetry that likewise dates to the 6th century. Then as today, the most important cultural festival was the *eisteddfod*—a gathering of poets, musicians, and artists for friendly competition (see sidebar above). Nearly as old is the Welsh tradition of choral singing, which dates to the 12th century. Many towns still hold an annual *Cymanfa Ganu*, or hymn-singing festival.

Among the most important of historic Welsh writings is the famous epic poem *Y Gododdin*, by Aneirin, the 6th-century poet, which describes a brave but unsuccessful battle with the invading Saxons. The mid-20th cen-

Wales produced Dylan Thomas, one of the best-known poets of the 20th century. A sculpture of Thomas is set prominently in Swansea, his birthplace.

tury brought a renaissance in Welsh literature, with novelists and poets writing both in English and in Welsh. Most famous of all was Dylan Thomas, widely known for his powerful poetry readings over BBC (British Broadcasting Corporation) radio. Thomas' most familiar works include "Do Not Go Gentle into That Good Night" and the radio sketch "A Child's Christmas in Wales."

Education. Welsh children must attend school from ages 5 to 16. Most continue their education at either a vocational institute or a secondary school that prepares them to enter a university. The University of Wales has several colleges, including a medical school, with the oldest campuses in Cardiff, Swansea, Lampeter, Aberystwyth, and Bangor. The study of the Welsh language begins in the earliest grades.

CITIES

Cardiff, the Welsh capital, stands at the mouth of the Taff River on the Bristol Channel. With a population of 328,000, it is Wales' largest city and its cultural and financial center. During the 19th century, Cardiff reigned as the "energy capital of the world," being the main seaport for the export of Welsh coal. The city flourished until World War II, when bombing raids caused its near-total destruction. Cardiff rebuilt itself as a modern city in the mid-20th century, and despite the decline of the coal industry, became a major business center. It remains an important international port for the export of industrial and agricultural products.

One of the few survivors of the war bombings is the small but magnificent Cardiff Castle, at the city's center. Romans built the wall surrounding the castle in the 1st century A.D.; Norman conquerors built the castle in the 11th century. In the 19th century, the wealthy third marquess of Bute restored the castle in a flamboyant medieval style. Cardiff is also home to Wales' renowned National Museum &

Cardiff Castle, in the Welsh capital city, dates to about 1090. Below the castle are the remains of a Roman fort built more than 1,000 years earlier.

LLANFAIRPWLLGWYNGYLLGOGERYCHWYRNDROBWLLLLANTYSILIOGOGOGOCH
THE CHURCH OF MARY IN THE HOLLOW OF THE WHITE HAZEL NEAR THE FIERCE WHIRLPOOL AND THE CHURCH OF TYSILIO BY THE RED CAVE

The teaching of the Welsh language is required in all schools in Wales, and both Welsh and English appear on street signs (right). In the case above, a single Welsh word is expressing a concept that requires a dozen or more English words to describe.

Gallery, the Welsh National Opera, and several universities. The city's renovated waterfront boasts several new architectural masterpieces, including the Welsh Assembly Building, the Millennium Stadium (an international sports complex), and the Wales Millennium Centre, an impressive new venue for the performing arts slated to open in 2004.

Swansea, Wales' second-largest city (population 235,000), stands about 40 mi. (65 km.) west of Cardiff, at the mouth of the Tawe River. The city is best known as the birthplace of Dylan Thomas, and the poet's life and writings are celebrated with an annual festival each autumn. The Dylan Thomas Trail leads visitors past landmarks associated with the 20th-century bard's writings, including his birthplace in the city's Uplands neighborhood.

Swansea has a long history as a trading center and seaport, dating back some 2,000 years. Like Cardiff, Swansea endured heavy bombing during World War II, and suffered great damage. The city rebuilt its destroyed docks into a modern marina lined with storefronts and luxury homes. Swansea's Maritime and Industrial Museum tells the story of the city's growth and transformation. Swansea's modern industries include the manufacture of steel, auto parts, and petrochemicals. Swansea borders the scenic Gower Peninsula to the west and, to the east, the "Waterfall Country" of the lush vales of Afan and Neath.

Newport, Wales' third-largest city (population 150,000), is its gateway to neighboring England. Newport stands on the banks where the Usk River empties into the Severn Estuary. The Severn Bridge links Newport to England, on the estuary's southeast bank. The town's original name, *Casnewydd-ar-Wysg*—New Castle on the Usk—dates back some 2,000 years to its origins as a Celtic settlement. The Normans built a castle here in the 12th century, but only its ruins remain. Today, Newport continues to be a major seaport, exporting iron and steel processed at local plants.

■ OFFA'S DYKE

"A certain vigorous king called Offa . . . had a great dyke built between Wales and Mercia from sea to sea." So reads the 9th-century account of the great mound-and-ditch barrier that extended for nearly 130 mi. (209 km.) from the Dee estuary on the Irish Sea to the Wye River on the Bristol Channel. Much of Offa's Dyke remains today, running close to the official border dividing England and Wales.

As originally constructed around 785 A.D., Offa's Dyke measured 88 ft. (27 m.) wide and 26 ft. (8 m.) tall from ditch bottom to bank top, making it one of the most remarkable structures in Great Britain. Although longer than Hadrian's Wall (see page 92), Offa's Dyke served less as a military barrier than a border marking. According to legend, the English cut off the ears of any Welshman found east of the dike, and the Welsh hanged any Englishman found west of it. In any case, this giant earthwork remains a physical symbol of the cultural differences that continue to distinguish the Welsh from the English.

ECONOMY

Mining is an important part of the Welsh economy. Although most coalfields have closed, those that remain produce 10 percent of the United Kingdom's coal exports. Other mining products include limestone and slate.

Agriculture, especially livestock, remains important as well. Sheep, beef cattle, and dairy herds graze over more than half the Welsh countryside. Crops include barley, oats, potatoes, and hay. Government reforestation programs continue to increase the amount of timber available for logging. The Bristol Channel supports a fishing industry.

In the late 1980s, Japanese and U.S. investment helped boost the Welsh economy. By the mid-1990s, Wales had become the largest European center for the manufacture of Japanese products. Today, the most important manufactured products include steel, tin, aluminum, refined-petroleum products, textiles, and automotive parts.

Wales has witnessed a tremendous growth of its tourism industry. Especially popular is the principality's concentration of castles, the legacy of centuries of medieval conquest by Norman and English kings. The land's scenic beauty—from its sandy beaches to its rugged mountains—attracts even more visitors each year.

HISTORY

Stone Age Iberians lived in this land during the last Ice Age, some 4,000 to 5,000 years ago. Archaeological artifacts such as polished ax heads and giant stone monuments suggest that the Iberians reached a high level of craftsmanship and civilization.

Around 3,000 years ago, Celtic tribes entered the region and intermarried with its native peoples. Their descendants became the Welsh people— or *y Cymry*, as they called themselves. The Welsh beat back the invading Romans in 55 B.C., with archers on chariots and mounted cavalry. The Romans returned in 75 A.D. and established forts in southern Wales.

In 61 A.D., the Brythonic queen Boudicca rebelled. Her army sacked Roman towns and camps as far away as London. The Romans responded by attacking the Welsh island of Anglesey—the capital of the Celts' Druid reli-

Caerphilly Castle (above), dating to 1271, is among the earliest of a number of castles built by the English to keep the defeated Welsh in check. Today, the castle is especially noted for its double-wall design.

gion. The Romans razed Anglesey, executed its Druid priests, and destroyed their great literature and records. During this time, Christianity came to Wales from Ireland, via Romanized monks who established a string of monasteries across the land.

When the Romans abandoned Wales in the early 5th century, they left behind many Latin words, which enriched the budding Welsh language. In the centuries that followed, Germanic and Scandinavian tribes invaded the land. From this period comes the legend of King Arthur, based on a Welsh king who resisted the barbarian invaders.

Wales had become a distinct country by the 8th century, when England's King Offa of Mercia built his famous dike separating the political entities of England and Wales (see sidebar, page 128). In the next century, King *Rhodri Mawr*, or Roderick the Great, and his sons united the Welsh tribes and kept Viking raiders at bay. In the 10th century, their family produced *Hywel Dda*, or Howel the Good. Hywel forged the tribal customs of Wales into a system of written laws and oversaw a great flowering of the arts, especially poetry.

In 1066, the Norman king William conquered England and encouraged his western earls to extend their territories into Wales. As they did so, they built castles across the countryside. The Welsh and Normans battled for more than 200 years, until King Edward I of England defeated Llywelyn ap Gruffudd in 1267. Edward divided Wales into counties under the rule of his earls, who built still more castles and rings of fortresses.

Still, Wales remained rebellious, with new princes wresting large regions from English control. The Welsh princes patronized the country's bards, or poets, and many wrote their own poetry and songs as well.

In 1301, Edward I gave his newborn son the title Prince of Wales and allowed him to be raised as a Welsh-speaking prince. This "peace offering" helped usher in a peaceful century during which Wales became a prosperous center for textile and cattle. (It also began the tradition of conferring the title Prince of Wales upon the male heir-apparent to the British throne.)

Peace ended with a rebellion led by a Welsh prince—*Owain Glyndwr*, or Owen Glendower. Glyndwr's war of independence ended in defeat in 1416. Presumably, Glyndwr died in hiding, but his body was never found. Legend holds that Glyndwr will return when his country needs him.

In 1485, when Henry Tudor ascended the English throne as King Henry VII, he fulfilled an old Welsh prophecy that a Welshman would someday rule Great Britain. In 1536, Henry VIII and the English Parliament incorporated Wales with the Act of Union. The act gave the Welsh people the right to elect their own representatives to Parliament. However, an accompanying act replaced traditional Welsh laws with English ones and forbade the use of the Welsh language in government business. In 1588, Queen Elizabeth I authorized a popular Welsh translation of the Bible, which helped save the language from extinction.

The 1700s brought the rise of the nonconformist chapels, which gave the Welsh many leaders. In 1811, the Welsh Anglican Church broke away from the Church of England, sparking a new sense of independence.

The Industrial Revolution of the 1800s shifted Wales from an agricultural economy to one based on coal. Farm villages emptied as workers flocked to the coalfields and foundries of southern Wales. By the end of the 19th century, more than half the population lived in a small section of south Wales. Thousands more left for North America, Australia, and New Zealand.

Meanwhile, Welsh nationalism grew and gave rise to Plaid Cymru, the Welsh political party, founded in 1925. In 1966, Gwynfor Evans, the party's president, was elected as the first member of Parliament to represent Plaid Cymru in London, paving the way for future Plaid members to represent Welsh interests in the British Parliament. In 1979, the Welsh people rejected a proposal to return, or "devolve," control of many national-government powers to a Welsh Assembly. Not coincidentally, the voters defeated the proposal by a margin of four to one—the proportion of English to Welsh speakers at the time. Over the following years, the teaching of Welsh to schoolchildren greatly increased the proportion of native speakers. In 1997, just over half of voters approved a new referendum to create the National Assembly for Wales.

GOVERNMENT

Welsh voters elect representatives to both Parliament, in London, and the recently established National Assembly for Wales, or *Cynulliad Cenedlaethol i Gymru*, in Cardiff. Laws passed by Parliament still apply to Wales, and the assembly lacks the power to collect taxes. It spends the money allotted to it by Parliament, and controls many public services such as health care, housing, education, environmental protection, and policies regarding the use of the Welsh language.

The 60 elected members of the National Assembly for Wales choose a first minister, usually a member of the political party with the most elected members. The first minister, in turn, appoints a cabinet.

In 1996, Wales replaced its many shires, boroughs, and districts with 22 unitary authorities. The residents of each authority elect representatives to manage local services such as libraries, parks, fire and rescue departments, and waste disposal.

People everywhere associate bagpipes and tartans with Scotland and its distinctive culture.

SCOTLAND

Scotland is a rugged and romantic land more crowded with history and scenic beauty than with people. It boasts the United Kingdom's highest mountains, most rugged coastline, and the vast majority of its lakes and islands. By contrast, urban areas take up a mere 3 percent of the landscape.

The hardy Scots people, although officially "British" for more than two centuries, remain proud of their distinct culture, dialect, and large degree of government independence. Their pride has ample basis, as their tiny kingdom has produced some of the world's greatest writers, inventors, philosophers, scientists, and political leaders, as well as some of its most romantic heroes and heroines.

THE LAND

About the size of South Carolina, Scotland encompasses the northern third of the island of Great Britain, and includes nearly 800 islands, the majority smaller than 3 sq. mi. (8 sq. km.). It faces the Atlantic Ocean to the north and west, and the North Sea to the east. To the south, Scotland shares a land border of approximately 100 mi. (161 km.) with England. The Scottish mainland stretches for about 285 mi. (460 km.) from north to south and 24 to 150 mi. (39 to 241 km.) from east to west—encompassing a total land area of 30,167 sq. mi. (78,133 sq. km.).

The sparsely populated Scottish countryside is home to many more sheep than people. As is the rule throughout the United Kingdom, motorists in Scotland drive on the left side of the road.

Scotland's highly irregular coastline extends for a remarkable 2,300 mi. (3,700 km.). The sea encroaches in deeply penetrating inlets called *sea lochs*, as well as broad river estuaries called *firths*. Inland, an abundance of short, powerful rivers and long glacial lakes, or *lochs*, crisscross the landscape. Scotland's longest river, the Tay, flows 120 mi. (193 km.). Its largest lake, Loch Lomond (28 sq. mi.; 73 sq. km.), is also the largest in Great Britain. In addition, Scotland boasts Britain's tallest mountain (Ben Nevis, at 4,406 ft.; 1,343 m.), highest waterfall (Eas a Chual, at 660 ft.; 201 m.), and deepest lake (Loch Morar, at 1,017 ft.; 310 m.).

The landscape of Scotland varies tremendously among its three geographic regions: the northern Highlands, central Lowlands, and southern Uplands. Their differences in topography and vegetation trace to their underlying geology, with hard igneous rock underlying the rugged Highlands, and softer sandstone and conglomerate (mixed rock) forming the gentler Lowlands and Uplands.

The Highlands. The most rugged region of Great Britain, the Highlands dominate the northern two-thirds of Scotland, including most of its islands. World-famous for their lonely grandeur, the Highlands consist of parallel mountain chains divided by steep valleys. A huge natural depression—Glen More—cuts across the middle of the Highlands from coast to coast, dividing them into northwestern and southeastern halves. The great chain of lakes that runs through Glen More includes Loch Ness, famous for its legendary "sea monster." In 1847, Scottish engineers linked the lakes to create the 60-mi. (97 km.)-long Caledonian Canal.

On one side of Glen More rise the heavily eroded peaks of the northwest Highlands, most of which rise between 2,000 and 3,000 ft. (600 and 900 m.) above sea level. Sparkling lochs, stone-covered fields, and short, powerful streams typify the landscape. On the northwest coast, the mountains abruptly fall to the sea along sea lochs bordered by high cliffs. The longest sea lochs extend some 40 mi. (64 km.) inland from the open ocean.

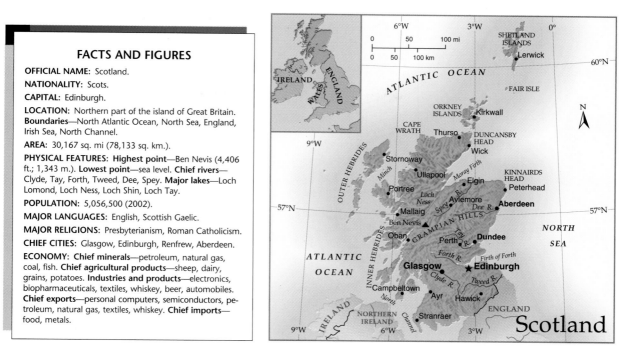

FACTS AND FIGURES

OFFICIAL NAME: Scotland.

NATIONALITY: Scots.

CAPITAL: Edinburgh.

LOCATION: Northern part of the island of Great Britain. **Boundaries**—North Atlantic Ocean, North Sea, England, Irish Sea, North Channel.

AREA: 30,167 sq. mi (78,133 sq. km.).

PHYSICAL FEATURES: Highest point—Ben Nevis (4,406 ft.; 1,343 m.). **Lowest point**—sea level. **Chief rivers**—Clyde, Tay, Forth, Tweed, Dee, Spey. **Major lakes**—Loch Lomond, Loch Ness, Loch Shin, Loch Tay.

POPULATION: 5,056,500 (2002).

MAJOR LANGUAGES: English, Scottish Gaelic.

MAJOR RELIGIONS: Presbyterianism, Roman Catholicism.

CHIEF CITIES: Glasgow, Edinburgh, Renfrew, Aberdeen.

ECONOMY: Chief minerals—petroleum, natural gas, coal, fish. **Chief agricultural products**—sheep, dairy, grains, potatoes. **Industries and products**—electronics, biopharmaceuticals, textiles, whiskey, beer, automobiles. **Chief exports**—personal computers, semiconductors, petroleum, natural gas, textiles, whiskey. **Chief imports**—food, metals.

Southeast of Glen More rise the dramatic Grampian Hills, with four peaks exceeding 4,000 ft. (1,200 m.), and approximately 500 peaks more than 3,000 ft. (900 m.). The Grampians are the Highlands of tourist brochures—with cloud-covered mountaintops, salmon-filled rivers, and sweeping, heather-covered vistas.

Central Lowlands. South of the Highlands, the broad central Lowlands form Scotland's narrow waist. "Low" only in comparison to the mountains on either side, this region encompasses many small chains of hills running along river valleys. The Lowlands' numerous waterways include Scotland's longest and most important rivers—the Tay, Clyde, and Forth. Here, too, are Scotland's largest fertile plains—the Strathmore Valley, in the northeast, and the Lothian region, in the southeast. The Lowlands extend along the fringe of Scotland's southeast coast all the way to its border with England.

Southern Uplands. Southwest of the Lowlands, the landscape rises again, but gently. The grassy hills, wooded valleys, and gentle streams of the southern Uplands figure prominently in the writings of many great Scottish poets and novelists. Several Upland peaks rise above 2,000 ft. (600 m.), with the highest being Mount Merrick (2,768 ft.; 844 m.).

The Scottish Isles. Scotland's hundreds of islands and islets tend to be as

Mysterious monoliths dot the landscape of the Orkneys, a group of islands to the north of the Scottish mainland.

EDINBURGH AND ITS CASTLE

The menacing yet intriguing Edinburgh Castle stands guard over Scotland's capital from atop Castle Rock. Bordered on three sides by sheer cliffs, this black volcanic crag has served as a fortress since prehistoric times. Scotland's King David II began building the present-day castle in 1356. Impossible to approach except from the front, the castle has only twice been captured in combat—each time by Scots vanquishing English "interlopers" holed up within.

Today, Edinburgh Castle's One O'clock Gun continues to boom out each day, startling many unsuspecting tourists below. The castle is most famous for its annual Military Tattoo, a colossal display of Scottish music and marching bands that features scores of pipe-and-drum corps from

Edinburgh Castle (above) stands regally amid Scotland's capital city, and magnificently backdrops the renowned Military Tattoo (below), the highlight of Edinburgh's summer festivals.

around the world. Some 200,000 visitors attend the Tattoo each year, and nearly 100 million watch it on television. Following the Tattoo each year are Edinburgh's summer arts festivals, a three-week "carnival of culture" long considered one of Europe's best.

Leading away from Edinburgh Castle is the Royal Mile, a thoroughfare of historic houses, churches, museums, and fashionable boutiques that makes its way to Holyrood Castle, the former residence of Mary, Queen of Scots, and beyond it, to the new Scottish Parliament Building. Nearby stands the University of Edinburgh, founded in 1585 and world famous for its schools of medicine and law.

In addition to being Scotland's center of government and culture, Edinburgh reigns as a major European financial center, with offices for scores of international banks, insurers, and stockbrokerages. Its other major industries include publishing, paper production, whiskey distillation, electronics, food products, and chemicals.

hilly and rugged as the Highlands of which they are part. The largest group—the Hebrides—stand off the west coast. Numbering more than 500, only 100 are inhabited. The widely scattered Inner Hebrides lie just offshore, stretching from the large Isle of Skye in the north to Islay in the south. The rockier Outer Hebrides rise up some 30 mi. (48 km.) offshore, and stand close enough to each other to be dubbed "Long Island." Still farther west, in the open Atlantic, cluster the small group of islets known as St. Kilda.

Due north of the Scottish mainland, the treacherous waters around the Orkney Islands have long been infamous for their racing tides and rock reefs. Although for the most part treeless, the largest of the 70 Orkneys boast some of the most fertile soil in Scotland. Their main islands surround Scapa Flow, a sheltered anchorage and age-old naval base. Farther north, past bleak little Fair Isle, stand the 100 islands and islets of the Shetlands, famous for their small, powerful ponies. Relatively few islands stand off Scotland's smoother east coast. Lighthouses warn North Sea sailors away from the small but dangerous exceptions.

Climate. The north-flowing Gulf Stream gives Scotland an unusually mild climate for its northern latitude. Still, winters tend to be cold, with average temperatures ranging from 37° to 41° F. (3° to 5° C.) in January. Cool summer temperatures average from 55° to 59° F. (13° to 15° C.) in July. The northwestern Highlands, snowcapped in winter, receive more than 100 in. (2,540 mm.) of precipitation per year. Rainfall decreases to the east, where coastal areas average just 35 in. (890 mm.) per year.

Plant and Animal Life. Small, hardy plants such as heather, moss, fern, and grass typify the Scottish landscape. Trees cover 15 to 20 percent of the land, with a few large forests in the southeastern Highlands. They consist primarily of conifers such as native fir, pine, and larch, with a scattering of native oak. At high elevations, conifers give way to mountain willow and other alpine species.

Scotland's only surviving large mammals are roe deer and red deer, the red being abundant in the Highlands. Smaller mammals include the pine marten, hare, otter, ermine, and rabbit. Scotland's native wildcat is an ancestor to the domestic cat. Far more abundant are Scotland's many game birds, including several species of grouse, ptarmigan, blackcock, duck, and goose. Its raptors include the kite, osprey, and golden eagle. Scottish rivers and lakes support thriving populations of salmon and trout. Cod, haddock, herring, and many kinds of shellfish live in its coastal waters. On windless summer days, swarms of tiny biting insects called midges can make life miserable for people and animals alike.

Natural Resources. At the bottom of the North Sea is found Scotland's most valuable natural resource—large deposits of oil and natural gas. The Scottish mainland contains significant deposits of coal and smaller deposits of zinc. Scotland's many rivers power Great Britain's largest hydroelectric-generating stations. The kingdom's limited acreage of fertile soil lies in the Orkneys and central Lowlands.

THE PEOPLE

The vast majority of the Scottish population trace their ancestry to an age-old mixture of European tribes who arrived between the prehistoric Stone Age and medieval times. These include Scotland's early Picts and Celts, followed by invading Scandinavians, Anglo-Saxons, and Normans. Centuries of intermarriage have blurred the ethnic distinctions of these different groups. Nevertheless, the inhabitants of the remote northern Highlands continue to preserve their region's long-standing Celtic traditions and Gaelic language, just as the people of the Shetland Islands retain a more Scandinavian culture. Those of the Hebrides celebrate their own mixture of Gaelic and Scandinavian customs.

Ethnic minorities make up less than 2 percent of the Scottish population and live primarily in urban areas. They include approximately 30,000

Abbotsford House, the home of poet and novelist Sir Walter Scott, is a popular tourist attraction.

people of Pakistani or Bangladeshi descent and 15,000 Chinese. People of Indian, African, and Jewish descent each number about 10,000.

Most Christian Scots belong either to the Church of Scotland, which is Presbyterian, or to the Scottish Episcopal Church. Glasgow and Edinburgh have large enough populations of Muslims, Jews, and Hindus to support their own mosques, synagogues, and temples.

Up until the 1980s, Scotland suffered from centuries of population loss through emigration to Canada, the United States, Australia, and New Zealand, as well as neighboring England. New opportunities in Scotland's growing high-tech industries have helped reverse this trend in recent years.

Language. The Scots people speak one or both of two distinctive languages. Virtually everyone speaks English—but it is not the English of England or North America. Indeed, the thick "burr" of some regional Scots dialects can sound incomprehensible to outsiders. Some common features include the trilled "r" sound, the pronunciation of the long "o" sound as "ai" (as in "stane" for "stone"), and pronouncing "oo" as "ui" ("buik" for "book"). Scots English derives from a northern dialect of Middle English (the English of medieval times).

A growing number of Scots also speak Gaelic—the language of Scotland's ancient Celtic people. Gaelic remained the primary language of Scotland until the 16th century, after which it gradually disappeared outside the remotest Highlands. In the 1980s, fewer than 1,000 people spoke it exclusively. Since that time, a renaissance of interest has increased Scotland's Gaelic speakers to nearly 100,000, although virtually all of them also speak English. Even less known to the outside world is Lallans, or "Lowland Scots," a Germanic-English language spoken by Scottish aristocracy from the 14th to 18th centuries and still used in modern Scottish poetry. Lallan words that remain in Scots speech include *aye* for yes, *wee* for little, and *bonnie* for pretty.

ARTS AND EDUCATION

Scots take great pride in their distinctive culture, especially their rich history of poetry, prose, song, and dance. Each August, Edinburgh's International Festival of Music and Drama draws hundreds of thousands of visitors from the United Kingdom and abroad, making it one of the world's premier cultural events. Equally popular are the scores of clan gatherings and Highland Games that take place throughout the year (see sidebar, page 139). The Scottish Arts Council supports the country's widely acclaimed national orchestra, opera, and ballet companies.

Scotland has been producing great writers since the 14th century, when John Barbour composed the epic poem *The Bruce* (celebrating a victorious Scottish king). Its national hero—the 18th-century poet Robert Burns—wrote primarily in the Lallans dialect and authored such enduring lyrics as "Auld Lang Syne." The writings of the 18th-century Scottish philosopher David Hume continue to be widely studied throughout the world, especially his ideas about superstition and religion.

The Scots' great tradition of learning produced some of Europe's first universities in the 15th and 16th centuries. Today, they number eight, remain renowned in medicine and engineering, and have become recently famous for research in biotechnology.

On the grade-school level, Scotland's education system is distinct from that in the rest of the United Kingdom. Free education starts in nursery school (age 3) and continues through secondary school (age 18). All children must attend school from at least ages 5 to 16. Local educators and parents largely determine their school's curriculum, or learning goals, so there can be great variation from one school to the next: some, for instance, emphasize Gaelic language, while others include religious studies.

CITIES

Although urban areas cover just 3 percent of Scotland, they are home to nearly two-thirds of the population. The vast majority live in the central

Glasgow has shed its image as a gritty industrial center and emerged as a prosperous, cosmopolitan city.

Whiskey remains an important export. The distillery above, in Edradour, holds the distinction of being the smallest in all of Scotland.

Lowlands that extend between Glasgow and Edinburgh, Scotland's two largest cities.

Glasgow, on the Clyde River in the western Lowlands, has long been Scotland's major seaport, industrial powerhouse, and largest city (population 620,000). After the collapse of its heavy industries 50 years ago, Glasgow went from being one of the world's most beautiful and wealthiest cities to one of its most depressed. In recent decades, the city has transformed itself once again, replacing its crumbling docks and abandoned warehouses with cultural institutions, beautiful parks, and stylish restaurants and shops. Today, its principal industries include tourism and electronics, especially the manufacture of personal computers. The University of Glasgow is renowned for its medical and veterinary schools.

Edinburgh (pronounced edin-burrah), due east of Glasgow on the North Sea coast, reigns as Scotland's capital and second-largest city, with a population of about 450,000 (see the sidebar on page 134).

Aberdeen, 130 mi. (210 km.) north of Edinburgh, ranks as Scotland's third-largest city, with a population of about 200,000. Tourists know Aberdeen as the gateway to the renowned "Castle Trail" of the Deeside Valley. The trail's many spectacular castles include Balmoral, the summer home of the British royal family. In the 1970s, the discovery of oil and gas off Aberdeen's coast transformed the city into a petroleum-industry service center. Aberdeen's other industries include fishing, granite quarrying, and the manufacture of chemicals, machinery, textiles, and paper.

Dundee, Scotland's fourth-largest city (population 150,000), stands at the mouth of the Tay River, midway between Aberdeen and Edinburgh. Second only to Glasgow in economic importance, its diversity of industries include petroleum shipping, publishing, printing, and the manufacture of textiles, rope, carpet, plastic, processed food, and light machinery.

ECONOMY

Manufacturing continues to employ more than 300,000 Scottish workers, almost one-third of the kingdom's workforce. Scotland's major manufacturing industries include not only traditional products such as textiles and whiskey, but also state-of-the-art electronics products. Scotland has more recently emerged as Europe's leading maker of personal computers and has earned similar renown in the world of biotechnology. Scottish biotech researchers have succeeded in a variety of areas, from developing therapies for cancer and heart disease to producing medicinal human proteins in the milk of transgenic livestock.

■ HIGHLAND GAMES

Legend has it that Celtic chieftains started the Highland Games more than 2,000 years ago to find the strongest men for warriors, the fastest runners for messengers, and the best musicians and dancers for entertainment. Today's events still feature such age-old traditions as tossing the caber, a 17-ft. (5-m.) pole, and the shot, a 16- or 22-lb. (7.26- or 10-kg.) steel ball.

Nonathletic competitions include Scottish dancing, bagpipe playing, and the recitation of Gaelic epic poems. Highland Games take place throughout the summer in scores of Scottish towns, as well as in several Scottish communities in the United States and Canada. The Scottish Games Association registers all world records set during the competitions.

Traditional dancing (above), costumes, and athletic contests add to the festive atmosphere of the Highland Games.

Tourism ranks as the second-most-important segment of the Scottish economy, employing about 195,000 people, or nearly 10 percent of the workforce. The production and transport of oil and natural gas from the deposits under the North Sea employ another 100,000 workers. Nearly as many work in Scotland's finance industry, the sixth largest in Europe. Yet another 100,000 work in Scotland's "creative industries," which include such fields as architecture, advertising, publishing, film, music, and other artistic and cultural activities.

Agricultural land encompasses about 20 percent of Scotland, although it employs an ever-decreasing proportion of the population. Sheep and cattle graze over the majority of this land. Of age-old importance, Scotland's leading crops include barley, oats, wheat, and potatoes.

HISTORY

Scotland's earliest Stone Age hunters and gatherers arrived some 10,000 years ago, but left few traces. Celtic tribes came during the Iron Age, around 2,700 years ago. They lived in organized communities within hill forts encircled by stone walls.

Around 80 A.D., the Roman legions occupying England penetrated into Scotland, but they failed to conquer the tribes they called the Caledonians. Around 120 A.D., the Romans built Hadrian's Wall across northern England to mark

Mary, Queen of Scots, one of the best-known women in Scottish history, was executed by her cousin, Queen Elizabeth I of England.

In 1999, Scotland inaugurated its first Parliament since 1707. The Parliament will oversee the internal affairs of Scotland, and regulate the taxation of the Scottish people.

the northern boundary of their empire. This line of defense signaled the end to Roman efforts to conquer Scotland.

Over the next 500 years, four groups settled across Scotland. The Picts, a group of mysterious origins, occupied the central and eastern Highlands. The Scots, a Gaelic-speaking tribe from Ireland, spread through west-central Scotland, establishing the kingdom of Dalriada. In the southwest, British Celts related to the Welsh created the kingdom of Strathclyde. In the southeast, Angles and Saxons established Northumbria.

Around 845, the Gaelic chieftain Kenneth MacAlpin rallied the Picts and Scots to fight a common threat—Viking raiders attacking the coast. Their united kingdom spread across central Scotland and would eventually expand to include Strathclyde and part of Northumbria. The following centuries saw a series of murdered and murderous Scottish kings, including MacBeth (of Shakespearean fame), who in 1040 killed King Duncan, to reign 17 years before being killed by Duncan's son, Malcolm III. Under Malcolm and his English wife, Scotland established strong links with England. Over the next century, the Scots gradually expelled the Norse Vikings from the mainland, leaving them only the Orkney and Shetland Islands.

In 1296, Scottish unity crumbled for lack of a strong king, and England's King Edward I seized power. The next year, Sir William Wallace (of *Braveheart* fame) became Scotland's first national hero when his forces briefly drove the English out of Scotland and invaded northern England. In 1306, the next great Scottish hero—Robert the Bruce—led a successful revolution to become King Robert I.

Despite on-and-off fighting with England, the 15th century brought a flowering of the arts and sciences in Scotland. The Scots founded the first of their great universities—at St. Andrews (1411) and Glasgow (1451). In the 16th century, the Presbyterian preacher John Knox launched Scotland's Reformation. It would be the start of centuries of violent conflict between Scotland's Presbyterians, Episcopalians, and Catholics.

The Catholic Mary Stuart (Mary, Queen of Scots), numbered among the Reformation's first victims. Forced to give up her throne in 1567, she fled to England. There, she was imprisoned and later executed for plotting to overthrow Queen Elizabeth I. Elizabeth chose Mary's son, James, as her heir to the English throne. On Elizabeth's death in 1603, he became king of both countries (as James VI of Scotland and James I of England).

Although united under a single crown, Scotland and England remained separate states for another century. The Scottish Presbyterians fiercely resisted the efforts of King Charles I to impose his religious preferences on the Scottish people. In 1642, when the English Parliament tried to overthrow Charles, the Scots first fought against the king, then switched sides and fought for him when he agreed to their religious demands. The English parliamentary forces defeated and executed Charles in 1649, and religious conflict continued in Scotland for another 50 years.

True unification between Scotland and England finally came with the overthrow of Charles' Catholic son—King James II—in favor of his Protestant daughter Queen Mary II and her husband, William of Orange. They allowed the Scots to have their Presbyterian Church. In return, the Scottish Parliament agreed to the Act of Union, which combined the English and Scottish governments and created the United Kingdom of Great Britain.

One more failed attempt at independence followed—an uprising of Catholic "Jacobites" who wanted the Catholic Stuart family on the throne. In 1745, the legendarily "bonnie" (handsome) Prince Charlie (Charles Edward) led the Jacobites in an unsuccessful invasion to seize Scotland and England for his father. Defeated, Charles escaped only when the Jacobite heroine Flora Macdonald smuggled him aboard a ship for France, dressed as her maid.

During the late 18th and early 19th centuries, Highland land barons evicted hundreds of thousands of family farmers in order to graze sheep on their land. Many immigrated to North America. Others went to work in Lowland factories, becoming part of the great Industrial Revolution started by Scottish inventors such as James Watt, creator of the steam engine. Manufacturing industries brought new wealth to Scotland, followed by a serious depression after World War II.

Scotland's profitable petroleum industry sprang to life in the 1970s, following the discovery of oil and gas in the North Sea. A new nationalist movement likewise dawned in the 1970s. A vote on "Home Rule" failed in 1979, but gained new support in the 1990s. In 1997, the Scots voted by a 79-percent margin to restore their own Parliament and reclaim many of the powers and responsibilities that had been transferred to the British Parliament nearly 300 years earlier. Meanwhile, in 1996, Scottish researchers electrified the world with "Dolly," the first mammal cloned from an adult cell.

GOVERNMENT

The restoration of the Scottish Parliament involved a great transfer of power from the British Parliament in London. In 1999, the Scottish Parliament formally took over responsibility for the region's health services, education, economic development, arts, and environmental protection. The Scots also gave their new Parliament the power to raise or lower their British income taxes. The British Parliament retained authority over defense, foreign affairs, and overall economic and monetary policies. Scottish voters elect representatives to both parliaments. In the Scottish Parliament, the political party or party coalition holding the most seats chooses a first minister (comparable to the prime minister in the British Parliament).

The Scots also retain a legal system separate from the rest of the United Kingdom. It derives from a combination of ancient Roman law and the customs of Scotland's medieval feudal system. Scottish lawmakers have recently decided that parts of this system need modernizing. Scottish land rights, for instance, give ownership of most private land to a few noble families whose claims trace to medieval times. Anyone who purchases property from one of these land barons does not own it outright, but technically becomes the baron's "vassal."

Northern Ireland's troubled cities seem far from the romantic ruins of one of its seaside castles.

NORTHERN IRELAND

The world knows Northern Ireland as a troubled but achingly beautiful land. Year-round rain cloaks its landscape in the emerald green long associated with all things Irish. Northern Ireland's six counties once belonged to the ancient Irish province of Ulster. When the rest of Ireland declared its independence in 1921, the majority of Northern Ireland's people were of Scots-English descent. They chose to keep their province within the United Kingdom. Since that time, the traditionally Irish segment of Northern Ireland's population has steadily grown. When it becomes a majority, as is expected in coming years, reunification with the Republic of Ireland is likely. Meanwhile, the people of Northern Ireland remain bitterly—and sometimes violently—divided.

THE LAND

Northern Ireland occupies the northeastern corner of the island of Ireland. Approximately the size of Connecticut, Northern Ireland covers about 5,452 sq. mi. (14,121 sq. km.), and includes Rathlin Island and several smaller islets in the Irish Sea. The Irish Sea's North Channel flows along Northern Ireland's eastern and northern shores. The Republic of Ireland shares its land border on the south and west.

Despite its modest size, Northern Ireland encompasses a variety of landscapes, from rugged mountains to gentle valleys, sandy beaches to vast marshlands. The United Kingdom has designated approximately two-thirds of Northern Ireland's coast and its wooded Glens of Antrim as protected "Areas of Outstanding Natural Beauty." The famous Giant's Causeway, on the province's north-facing coast, consists of some 40,000 basalt columns, the broken tops of which form "stepping-stones" leading into the sea (see sidebar, page 146).

A ring of mountains and hills surrounds Northern Ireland's central lowland plain. The Antrim Mountains stretch along the northeast coast. The Sperrin Mountains stand in the west, and in the southeast, the Mourne Mountains rise to nearly 3,000 ft. (900 m.) at Slieve Donard, the province's highest peak. At their center lies Lough Neagh, its area of 153 sq. mi. (396 sq. km.) making it the largest lake in the United Kingdom. Other ribbonlike glacier lakes stand in the southwest, including the upper and lower halves of Lough Erne. Major ocean inlets include Lough Foyle, on the north coast; Belfast Lough, on the east coast; and, to the south, Strangford Lough. Countless mountain streams empty into Northern Ireland's three major rivers—the Foyle, Bann, and Lagan. The Bann, which rises in the Mourne Mountains, flows in two directions. Its "upper" half drains inland to Lough Neagh, while its "lower" half flows north to the sea.

Climate. Northern Ireland enjoys year-round mild weather, with cool winters and comfortable summers. Temperatures average 40° F. (4° C.) in January and 59° F. (15° C.) in July. Humid ocean winds deliver an abundance of rain, averaging more than 45 in. (1,140 mm.) in the hills and mountains and around 30 in. (760 mm.) on the plains.

Plant and Animal Life. Northern Ireland's generally flat terrain and central depression slow water drainage, creating vast areas of wet grassland, peat bog, and marsh. Like all of Ireland, the north lost most of its tree cover to logging in the 17th century. Reforestation programs continue to expand its isolated woodlands of native oak, ash, rowan, alder, birch, and hawthorn. A distinctive Irish orchid (*Spiranthes stricta*) grows in the valley of the River Bann.

The isolation of Ireland from mainland Europe and its glaciation during the last Ice Age have limited its variety of animals. The viviparous lizard and the leatherback sea turtle are its only reptiles (There are no snakes in Ireland.) The common frog and smooth newt are its only amphibians. Native mammals include the fox, badger, otter, Irish hare, stoat, pine marten, wood mouse, red deer, and pygmy shrew. Many kinds of whales and dolphins pass through the waters off the Irish coast. Distinctive birds include the jay, coal tit, and dipper. An abundance of freshwater fish inhabit the numerous streams and rivers.

In Belfast, the Grand Opera House (below, left) stands on Great Victoria Street, a main thoroughfare.

THE PEOPLE

Upwards of 99 percent of Northern Ireland's population descends from a mixture of the Celtic, Anglo-Saxon, Scandinavian, and Norman tribes that settled Great Britain and Ireland more than 1,000 years ago. Despite this ethnic uniformity, the country's population remains deeply divided between those who identify themselves as Roman Catholic Irish and those who trace their ancestry to Protestant Scots and English who settled there in the 16th and 17th centuries. In the past century, this division has been less about religion than about opposing desires for the future of Northern Ireland. Most Protestant Scots-English—also known as Loyalists or Unionists—favor remaining part of the United Kingdom. Most Catholic Irish—also known as Nationalists or Republicans—want Northern Ireland to become part of the Irish Republic.

At the time of Northern Ireland's creation in 1921, Protestants made up more than 60 percent of the population, and Catholics made up about 33 percent. Since that time, the Catholic segment of the population has increased to more than 40 percent, and the Protestant has decreased to just over half. Catholics are expected to eventually be the majority.

Ethnic minorities make up less than 1 percent of the population. They include about 4,000 Asian-speaking people and about 1,500 each from India, Pakistan, Africa, and Arab-speaking countries. Irish Travellers, formerly known as "gypsies," likewise number about 1,500.

Despite a birthrate higher than that of the rest of the United Kingdom, Northern Ireland's population grows slowly—owing to continued emigration to Great Britain, the Republic of Ireland, North America, Australia, and New Zealand.

English is Northern Ireland's official language. An estimated 100,000 residents also speak the Scots-Gaelic dialect known as "Ulster Scots," and about 80,000 speak Irish Gaelic. Some Travellers still speak the mysterious language known as Shelta.

FACTS AND FIGURES

OFFICIAL NAME: Northern Ireland.

NATIONALITY: Northern Irish.

CAPITAL: Belfast.

LOCATION: Northeastern corner of the island of Ireland. **Boundaries**—Atlantic Ocean, North Channel, Irish Sea, Republic of Ireland.

AREA: 5,452 sq. mi (14,121 sq. km.).

PHYSICAL FEATURES: Highest point—Slieve Donard (2,796 ft.; 852 m.). **Lowest point**—sea level. **Chief rivers**—Bann, Lagan, Foyle, Blackwater. **Major lakes**—Lough Neagh, Lough Erne.

POPULATION: 1,744,500 (2002).

MAJOR LANGUAGES: English, Gaelic.

MAJOR RELIGIONS: Presbyterianism, Anglicanism, Roman Catholicism, Methodism.

CHIEF CITIES: Londonderry, Belfast.

ECONOMY: Chief minerals—clay, limestone. **Chief agricultural products**—livestock, barley, potatoes, wheat. **Industries and products**—textiles, ships, aircraft, clothing, processed food and beverages, electronics. **Chief exports**—textiles, ships. **Chief imports**—petroleum, raw materials, produce.

In Belfast, it is not unusual for workers from nearby offices to regularly patronize the same restaurant for lunch. At night, local residents prevail.

ARTS AND EDUCATION

Northern Ireland's vibrant folk arts run along two separate veins: Scottish and Irish. They include traditional storytelling, singing, and dancing to the tune of age-old instruments such as the fiddle, flute, fife, hand drums, and bagpipes. Political parades remain a noisy summer tradition, with Protestant bands parading in mid-July to celebrate Orange Day (see the History section), and smaller numbers of Catholics parading in August.

Northern Ireland shares in the great tradition of Irish literature that extends back to its ancient Celtic myths, especially the 100 tales of the Ulster Cycle, which describe the heroes of northern regions of Ireland from the 2nd century B.C. to the 4th century A.D. In 1995, native poet Seamus Heaney won the Nobel Prize in Literature. National cultural institutions include Opera Northern Ireland, the Belfast Philharmonic Society (a leading choral group), and the Ulster Orchestra.

Education. Northern Ireland provides free schooling for children ages 4 to 18, with all children required to attend until at least age 16. Like its population, Northern Ireland's school system tends to be divided along Catholic and Protestant lines. In recent years, local education boards and parents have been working together to establish an increasing number of "integrated schools" attended by children of both communities. Also growing is the number of "Irish-medium" schools that conduct all of their classes in Irish Gaelic. Northern Ireland has two universities: Queen's University, in Belfast; and the University of Ulster, with campuses in Belfast, Coleraine, Jordanstown, and Londonderry.

CITIES

Nearly half of Northern Ireland's population lives in small towns and rural areas. The rest of the people live in or around the two large cities that dominate the province.

Belfast, Northern Ireland's capital and largest city, has a population of about 255,000 (2002 estimate), reduced considerably from its peak of 445,000 in 1951. Much of the population loss traces to the political violence and tight security measures that have made life there exceedingly difficult for decades. British soldiers patrol Belfast, but in much smaller numbers than before. Occasional violence still erupts between Republicans and Loyalists, but their warring militias have largely laid down their weapons. Grim reminders of the turmoil are the walls that still divide traditionally Catholic and Protestant neighborhoods; gone, though, are the laws prohibiting Catholics from living in particular areas.

This beautiful city stands on a half circle of hills and cliffs surrounding the mouth of Lagan River, where it flows into Belfast Lough and

GIANT'S CAUSEWAY

Some 40,000 towering columns make up the strange geologic formation known as the Giant's Causeway, on the beautiful Antrim coast of northern Northern Ireland. Ranging up to 20 ft. (6 m.) tall and 20 in. (50 cm.) wide, the mostly hexagon-shaped columns seem to form a gigantic staircase that tumbles down to the sea.

Geologists say that this unusual promontory formed some 60 million years ago, when a lava flow reached the ocean and cooled so quickly that it cracked into a geometric pattern. The ancients of Ireland knew better, of course. Their legends tell of the great Ulster giant Finn MacCool, who fell in love with a giantess across the Irish Sea, on the island of Staffa. Finn built the causeway to reach her—although a rival giant later tore it up in a decidedly violent fit of jealousy.

Today, the Giant's Causeway remains one of Northern Ireland's most popular tourist attrac-

tions. Its visitor center pays equal attention to the heroic exploits of Finn (he also created Lough Neagh when he scooped up a handful of mud to throw at his rival) and the less-fanciful theories of modern geologists.

Along the north-facing coast of Northern Ireland stands Giant's Causeway, a bed of basalt columns formed by rapidly cooling lava as it entered the sea.

the Irish Sea. Belfast's harbor has long reigned as one of the shipbuilding capitals of the world—the birthplace of many grand ocean liners, including the ill-fated *Titanic*. The docks of Belfast remain the source of the city's wealth, pride, and personality. Belfast is also the center of Northern Ireland's linen industry.

Belfast's harborside and riverbanks boast many new luxury hotels, conference centers, and apartment buildings. Restaurants and theaters line the city's lively "Golden Mile," which extends from its Grand Opera House to its university district. On the city's eastern outskirts stands Stormont, the meeting place for the Northern Ireland Assembly.

Londonderry, or "Derry," with a population of about 84,000 (2002 estimate), stands 95 mi. (153 km.) northwest of Belfast, straddling the River Foyle, near the head of Lough Foyle. Its history traces to the founding of the Derry monastery in the 6th century; English settlers added the prefix "London" in the early 17th century. Like Belfast, Londonderry grew into a major shipbuilding and textile-making center in the 18th century. And like Belfast, it endured political violence in the 1970s and 1980s. The heart of the city remains within a set of ancient, unbroken walls, famous for withstanding two major 17th-century attacks.

Northern Ireland's other sizable towns all stand within 30 mi. (48 km.) of Belfast. In order of size, they include **Newtownabbey** (population 59,300), **Bangor** (population 58,500), and **Lisburn** (population 44,600).

ECONOMY

Small family farms cover about two-thirds of Northern Ireland. Most produce fodder for livestock, especially dairy cows. Barley and potatoes grow on much of the rest. Local fishing fleets harvest herring and whitings in the Irish Sea, and salmon, trout, and pollan in freshwater lakes.

Northern Ireland's long-standing industries include shipbuilding, aircraft manufacturing, and the making of textiles and rope. These industries declined substantially during the second half of the 20th century, causing widespread unemployment and emigration. In recent years, Northern Ireland's economy has become increasingly focused on information technology and on services such as computer programming, financial investment, and tourism. So the overall number of jobs has grown, despite the decline in manufacturing. The United Kingdom and the European Union continue to send considerable financial aid to Northern Ireland to help spur its economic growth.

HISTORY

Archaeologists have found evidence that, some 9,000 years ago, Stone Age people lived in what is now Northern Ireland. Around 2,750 years ago, Celtic tribes arrived with their Druid religion and Iron Age tools and weapons. Missionaries introduced Christianity to Ireland about 1,600 years ago. The most famous of these—Saint Patrick—established missions across Northern Ireland. Scandinavian Vikings seized control of Ireland in 840; the Irish expelled them in 1041. When England's Henry

Northern Ireland has a thriving market for consumer goods. Many of the province's rural residents visit malls and shopping centers in the cities to buy new clothes and other items.

II invaded in the 1100s, he left most of what is now Northern Ireland, then known as "Ulster," to the Irish.

The seeds of disunion between Ulster and the rest of Ireland were sown in the early 1600s. For centuries, the great Irish clans of O'Neill and O'Donnell ruled the north, while England controlled the rest of the island. Then, in 1601, O'Neill and O'Donnell marched south to join an invading Spanish army. Defeated, the two Irish princes left for Europe with most of their supporters. The English government then "planted" the princes' abandoned Ulster with English and Scots settlers.

The trio of Belfast girls above heads to school, seemingly oblivious to the turbulence and violence that surround them.

Some 50 years later, the native Irish rose up in rebellion against England's Protestant King William of Orange and supported the return of the exiled Catholic king James II. The two kings and their powerful armies fought their war in Ireland. Its famous battles included James' unsuccessful Siege of Derry in 1689, which lasted 105 days and killed thousands. The next year, William defeated James at the Battle of the Boyne. Each July 12, Northern Ireland's Loyalist "Orangemen" still celebrate the victory with rowdy political parades.

Following an unsuccessful Irish rebellion in 1800, an Act of Union disbanded Ireland's Parliament and created the United Kingdom of Great Britain and Ireland. From the 19th into the 20th century, Ireland's predominantly Catholic population supported its independence. But the Protestant Loyalist majority in the north opposed the formation of an Irish state, in which they would be rendered a small minority. In 1912, the Loyalists organized armed volunteers in opposition to independence. With Ireland on the brink of civil war, the British government decided to exclude Ulster from the negotiations for a free Ireland.

World War I postponed all progress toward independence until 1920, when the Home Rule Bill created separate parliaments for Ulster and southern Ireland. The Irish Nationalists rejected this agreement, because it did not grant them full independence. The next year, they negotiated the creation of the Irish Free State in the south, leaving the pro-British north as a province of the United Kingdom.

Protestant Loyalists took immediate and complete control of Northern Ireland's government. They passed laws that excluded Catholics from positions of power, prevented them from moving to traditionally Protestant neighborhoods, and denied them access to favorable jobs. By the late 1960s, this had led to a Catholic civil-rights movement. The movement's initially peaceful demonstrations provoked attacks from Loyalist militia groups. British troops arrived to maintain order in 1969.

But hostilities increased when the Nationalists launched their own militia—the Irish Republican Army (IRA). The "Troubles" had begun.

In 1972, the British government suspended Northern Ireland's Parliament and imposed direct British rule. In the following years, the spiral of violence included IRA terrorist attacks against targets in England as well as Northern Ireland. The most infamous included "Bloody Friday": July 21, 1972, when IRA bombs in Belfast killed nine people. (IRA warnings had cleared most areas of people before the bombs went off.)

In 1985 and again in 1995, the governments of the United Kingdom and the Irish Republic pledged to cooperate in finding a peaceful resolution to the conflict. Secret negotiations lead to a cease-fire between the IRA and Loyalist militias in 1994, but renewed attacks broke the peace.

In 1997, former U.S. Senator George Mitchell led fresh peace negotiations. For the first time, these included representatives from all of Northern Ireland's political factions, as well as the governments of the United Kingdom and the Irish Republic. United States President Bill Clinton lent critical support to the negotiations. The resulting Good Friday Agreement of April 1998 recognized the importance of eliminating weapons from all militias. It also set in place a power-sharing government that would represent all of Northern Ireland's citizens and guarantee free access to jobs and housing. The agreement gave every Northern Irish citizen the option of claiming Irish or British citizenship, or both. It also entitled the majority to choose whether Northern Ireland would remain part of the United Kingdom or become part of the Irish Republic in the future. Later that year, the Nobel committee awarded its prestigious Peace Prize to the agreement's chief architects—the Unionist leader David Trimble and the Nationalist leader John Hume.

But the Troubles had not yet ended. In August 1998, a breakaway militia group calling itself the Real IRA set off a bomb in the town of Omagh. The explosion killed 29 people—marking the single worst atrocity since the start of the Troubles in 1969. Over the course of more than 30 years, the death toll from the violence has exceeded 3,600 people, including more than 1,230 Catholic civilians, nearly 700 Protestant civilians, more than 500 militia members, and 1,000 British soldiers and Irish police. Today, Northern Ireland teeters on the edge of an uneasy peace. Outright warfare has stopped. But the militias have yet to finish laying down their weapons, and sporadic gang violence and rioting continue. In October 2002, the British once again imposed direct rule over Northern Ireland.

GOVERNMENT

Since December 1999, a restored Northern Ireland Assembly and its executive committee have taken control of responsibilities such as education, employment, health and safety, environmental protection, and economic development. However, Britain's secretary of state for Northern Ireland controls the region's security forces and criminal-justice system, and the British Parliament retains power over foreign affairs and national security. Parliament also continues to send soldiers to Northern Ireland to maintain the uneasy peace between Loyalists and Nationalists.

The Northern Irish elect representatives to both their own Assembly and the British Parliament. Local governments consist of 26 local authorities. The residents of each authority elect a governing council, and each council chooses a mayor or borough executive.

In the heart of Paris, Notre Dame Cathedral rises above the Île de la Cité, an island in the Seine River.

FRANCE

It has been said that "everyone has two homes—his own and France." For centuries, France has been a wellspring of inspiration in art, music, and literature. For centuries, France has been a fountainhead for many of the world's great ideas. The language of the country is still a second language for many cultivated people everywhere.

In France, taste and elegance are in the air, and simply being there is an exhilarating experience. It is a dynamic country where much of Europe's intellectual and artistic pace is set. As a modern industrial nation with a young population, France is also a country whose people are creating valuable new traditions to add to the glorious old ones.

THE LAND

France, which is the largest nation in Western Europe, has an area of approximately 211,000 sq. mi. (546,490 sq. km.). It borders on Spain in the south, Italy and Switzerland in the east, and Germany, Luxembourg, and Belgium in the northeast. These land frontiers are partially formed by Europe's greatest river, the Rhine, and by several of Europe's

Chamonix, near the foot of Mont Blanc, is one of France's top winter resorts.

great mountain ranges—the Pyrenees, the Alps, and the Jura. In the French Alps in the east there are soaring, snowcapped peaks, including Mont Blanc, at 15,781 feet (4,810 meters). Mont Blanc is the highest in Western Europe.

But about half of France's total border is formed by coastline, with the Mediterranean on the southeast and the Atlantic and the English Channel (La Manche, or "the sleeve," to the French) on the west and northwest.

Climate

Within these boundaries France has a variety of climates. On the shores of the Mediterranean, for example, and in much of southern France, summers are hot and dry. Although winters in the south are extremely mild, cold winds from the Pyrenees and the Alps sweep down across the flatter plains below. One of these winds, the mistral of the Rhone delta, reaches speeds near hurricane force, blowing for 3 or 4 days in a row. Many trees in this region have been permanently bent by the power of the mistral, and the wind is also said to have a psychological effect on the people exposed to it.

In the Alps and the nearby Jura, the mountain peaks are snow-covered all year round. On France's Atlantic coastline, on the other hand,

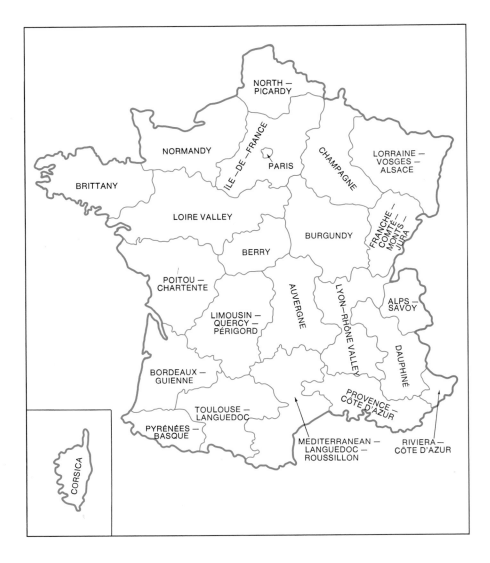

from Hendaye in the south to Dunkirk in the north, winds from the sea carry abundant rainfall to the land. The warm waters of the Gulf Stream also bring generally mild temperatures to this part of France. In the interior, away from both coasts and mountains, the climate is less moderate, but temperatures rarely reach great extremes of hot or cold.

Rivers and Canals

The rivers of France form a vast network that fans out across the land, tying different regions and cities together. The Seine, the country's longest navigable river, flows northwest from eastern France through the great capital city of Paris and empties into the Channel at Le Havre. The Loire—often considered France's most beautiful river—begins farther south, flows northwest to Orléans, and turns west to empty into the Atlantic at Saint-Nazaire. The Garonne, which rises in the Pyrenees, flows northwest past the now industrial city of Toulouse and through the Bordeaux wine country. Where it empties into the Atlantic, the river is called the Gironde.

The Rhone flows southwest from Lake Geneva in Switzerland. South

FRANCE

FACTS AND FIGURES

OFFICIAL NAME: French Republic.

NATIONALITY: French.

CAPITAL: Paris.

LOCATION: Western Europe. **Boundaries**—English Channel, Belgium, Luxembourg, Germany, Switzerland, Italy, Monaco, Mediterranean Sea, Spain, Andorra, Bay of Biscay.

AREA: 211,208 sq. mi. (547,030 sq. km.).

PHYSICAL FEATURES: Highest point—Mont Blanc (15,805 ft.; 4,807 m.). **Lowest point**—sea level. **Chief rivers**—Seine, Loire, Garonne, Rhone, Rhine. **Major lake**—Geneva.

POPULATION: 59,500,000 (2002; annual growth 0.4%).

MAJOR LANGUAGE: French.

MAJOR RELIGIONS: Roman Catholicism, Protestantism, Islam, Judaism.

GOVERNMENT: Republic. **Head of state**—president. **Head of government**—prime minister. **Legislature**—bicameral Parliament.

CHIEF CITIES: Paris, Marseilles, Lyons, Toulouse, Nice, Nantes, Strasbourg.

ECONOMY: Chief minerals—iron ore, coal, bauxite, potash, zinc. **Chief agricultural products**—beef, cereals, sugar beets, potatoes, wine grapes. **Industries and products**—steel, machinery, textiles, chemicals, food processing, metallurgy, aircraft, motor vehicles, wine, tourism. **Chief exports**—machinery and transportation equipment, foodstuffs, agricultural products, iron and steel products, textiles and clothing, chemicals, wine. **Chief imports**—crude petroleum, machinery and equipment, chemicals, iron and steel products, agricultural products.

MONETARY UNIT: 1 euro = 100 cents.

NATIONAL HOLIDAY: July 14 (Bastille Day).

Barge traffic on the Seine—a vital part of France's network of waterways.

of the Burgundy wine-growing region it is joined by its major tributaries, the Saône and the Isère. The Rhone branches out into a wide delta as it nears the Mediterranean. Just before it reaches its delta, the river flows past the town of Avignon. There is a modern bridge over the Rhone at Avignon today, but the ruins of the bridge that gave its name to the song *Sur le Pont d'Avignon* ("On the Bridge at Avignon") can still be seen. Children all over France enjoy singing the ancient song and dancing the circle dance that is associated with it.

Some 3,000 mi. (4,800 km.) of canals link the major French rivers to one another and to the great rivers of Europe. This extensive network carries many of the products of French agriculture and industry. The wheat and grain of the northwest can be taken south to Marseilles for export by river and canal. The iron ore of Lorraine may be exported from the great Channel ports of Le Havre and Cherbourg after a trip on the inland waterways. The steel manufactured in Dunkirk and used in the shipyards of Saint-Nazaire is shipped largely by canal, too.

ECONOMY

After World War II, France began a 30-year-period of almost steady growth, and today it has one of the most diversified and healthy economies in Europe. Unlike the nation's economy of 50 years ago, the majority of citizens no longer work in the fields of industry or agriculture; 70 percent of the labor force is now employed in the service sector.

Sheep graze near a village in the Pyrenees, the mountain range that forms a natural border with Spain.

Agriculture

Since land in France has always been extremely costly, the traditional French farm was small and family owned. Each farm had its dairy cow, a flock of chickens, and a few pigs. These small farms are gradually disappearing, however, as modern farming methods become more and more prevalent. As a result, French farm output as a whole is increasing. At the same time, the number of people working in agriculture has decreased to just 4 percent of the labor force, compared to 9 percent as recently as the mid-1980s.

France now produces more foodstuffs than any other single European Union country. It supplies all of its own wheat and exports the surplus. Barley, oats, and many different kinds of vegetables are also raised. French orchards yield an abundance of fruit, from the apples of Normandy and oranges of the Mediterranean area to the cherries, apricots, and tiny, yellow-green mirabelle plums of Lorraine.

Livestock production is increasing steadily. Nearly half of all French livestock is cattle, although sheep, poultry, horses, pigs, and goats are also raised. The dairy herds of Normandy produce the rich milk and cream that are important ingredients in so many delicious French dishes. Much of the dairy yield is also used to make the almost endless variety of French cheeses. Today, France's Limousin and snowy-white Charolais steers, known for their tender meat, have made the country a leader in European beef production.

Cognac, a well-known French product, is aged and blended in wooden casks.

But the best-known product, and one of France's most important agricultural exports, is wine. Wine has been produced in France since Roman times and perhaps earlier. There is hardly a region of France that does not have its vineyards. Ranging in color from pale rose to deep ruby, from golden amber to almost clear white, the wines of France are considered by many to be the finest in the world. There are the rosés of Provence and Anjou, the reds of the Rhone, and the whites of the Loire and Alsace. The sparkling wines of the Champagne region are the only ones in the world legally entitled to use the name. Some of the wines of the Cognac and Armagnac regions are distilled into fine brandies. The great red wines of Bordeaux and Burgundy are justly renowned around the world, though often they may come from holdings only a few acres in size.

Besides the important well-known vineyards, such as Rothschild and Romanée-Conti, there are local wines and everyday wines (*vins ordinaires*), which are rarely exported. Many small farms have their own prized vines, producing just enough for family and friends.

In some parts of France, after picking time, farmers still trudge up the slopes to prune their weathered, gnarled vines with old-fashioned long-handled knives, as they did in the time of Saint Vincent, long ago. According to an old Burgundian legend it was this saint who first taught that severely pruned vines yield more grapes. It takes year-round, unremitting toil to grow the grapes that keep France in the forefront of the world's wine producers.

Industry and the Economy

France also has the sources of energy for modern industry. At the beginning of the Industrial Revolution in the early 19th century, France was handicapped by not having abundant supplies of coal and iron. France's scattered coal deposits never yielded enough to meet the nation's needs. The principal French iron deposits in Lorraine and near the Saar were long regarded as worthless because of their high phosphorus content. France lost these regions to Germany at the end of the Franco-Prussian War in 1871—just when the British were finding out how to make this kind of ore industrially useful.

After World War I, Lorraine was returned to France. Steel production is booming today. French mills turn out steel for agricultural machinery, railroad track, aircraft and aircraft engines, trains, and ships. French steel goes into the finely engineered cars that roll off the assembly lines of Renault and Peugeot-Citroën, making France the fourth largest automobile producer in the world. In addition, France is one of the world's leading steel exporters. Since the end of World War II, the French government has made concentrated efforts to modernize mineral production in Lorraine. France today leads Western Europe in the extraction of iron ore, and much of that ore comes from Lorraine. In addition, the per-capita daily production of a coal miner in the Lorraine fields is among the highest in Europe.

France has an abundance of hydroelectricity from damming its many swift-flowing rivers. The rivers have also been responsible for the growth of the French textile industries. Lyons, on the Rhone, was known as early as the 15th century for its fine silks. Today the whole Rhone Valley area is the home of mills that turn out excellent synthetic fabrics, many of them first developed for *haute couture,* or high fashion, designers of Paris. Rouen, on the Seine, also has a thriving synthetics industry, and cotton and woolen fabrics are made in north and northeast France. France has a large-scale oil-refining industry based on imported crude oil from North Africa and the Middle East.

Beyond these energy sources, France has harnessed the seas off Brittany to build the world's first tidal power station on the Rance River near Dinan. At Odeillo, in the Pyrenees, an enormous experimental solar-power station uses the Sun's rays to produce energy. The uranium deposits of central France are used to fuel nuclear reactors that run huge power generators. France has the highest number of nuclear plants in Europe, and about three-quarters of its electricity needs are supplied by this source.

France is also well supplied with the "light metals"—such as aluminum—that are so important in the world's economy today, especially in the transportation industries. Aluminum ore, or bauxite, was named for Les Baux, the town in southern France where it was first discovered and mined in the 19th century.

France is also proud of the many luxury industries for which it has always been known. A label bearing the words "Imported from France" is still a sign of quality and ensures sales in many other countries. French clay is made into the delicate, artistically decorated porcelain of Sèvres and Limoges. Equally famous is the fine hand-cut crystal of Baccarat and St. Louis.

Paris is the traditional center of France's most important luxury industries. There, exquisite jewelry, fine handbags, and beautifully made shoes are produced—often by small manufacturers with worldwide reputations. Paris is also—to the delight of fashion-conscious people around the world—the home of *haute couture*. This industry makes an important contribution to the French economy and also to France's fame as a country where styles are set. The great names in this field, such as Dior, Chanel, Givenchy, and Yves Saint-Laurent, have been joined by those of numerous younger designers.

Until the 1980s, the French economy was characterized by extensive government intervention, but since then, a gradual but substantial change has been taking place, with the privatization of many large corporations, especially in the field of telecommunications. There is now more competition and more flexibility, even though the government is still committed to preserve the basic elements of a welfare state, with generous unemployment and retirement benefits, long vacations, and a virtually cost-free public health-care system.

In the late 1990s, as the use of the Internet began to spread, young entrepreneurs were starting new Web-based companies by the hundreds. Although many have since failed, France has firmly established itself as a force in the postindustrial information age.

CITIES

All of the cities of France take great pride in their contributions to the nation's past and in their work toward its future. There is hardly a city in France that has not carefully preserved—and often restored—some monuments and relics of French history. The cities are equally proud, however, of their huge power plants and automated factories.

Reminders of the past are kept alive and cherished in modern France.

Marseilles, France's chief port, lies on the Mediterranean.

Because they reflect so much of the country's beauty and diversity, France's cities have been described as the jewels in a crown. Of all the jewels, **Paris** has always been the largest and most dazzling. In the 19th century, the American author Oliver Wendell Holmes wrote, "Good Americans, when they die, go to Paris." For many people, Paris remains their idea of heaven. Other cities are compared to it and are called "the Paris of the North" or "the Paris of the South." There are songs about it in every language, and almost everywhere in the world its name evokes an image of gaiety, elegance, and beauty.

Over the years, the city's atmosphere has made it a magnet for artists and intellectuals from all countries. All of them were drawn to Paris by its freedom, and all of them drew something special from being there. They also helped to give Paris its reputation as *la ville lumière,* the City of Light. (See article on PARIS, which follows.)

Marseilles, on the Mediterranean, is the chief port of France. It is also the country's oldest city and has always been its gateway to the East. Since ancient times, both the goods and culture of Africa, the Middle East, and Asia have entered France at Marseilles' docks.

Almost everything in Marseilles' life has to do with the sea, from the colorful, cheerfully noisy fishmarket to the hilltop church of Notre Dame de la Garde, patron saint of the city's fishing fleet. From the liveliest street, La Canebière, it is only a few steps to the old port. There, dozens of restaurants offer the Marseilles specialty called bouillabaisse—a spicy, delicious fish stew—and a fine view of all the bustle of the busy harbor.

Marseilles is an ideal starting point for trips to the Riviera resorts—Cannes, Juan-les-Pins, Antibes, and Nice—strung out along the Mediterranean shore. Also nearby are the lovely hill towns of Provence and Languedoc, such as Aix-en-Provence, Arles, Avignon, Nîmes, Orange, and Carcassonne. In many of them, ancient theaters and buildings still stand, relics of Roman times.

Some 170 miles (270 km.) north of Marseilles is **Lyons**. Located where the Rhone and Saône rivers meet, it is an important port and

Fresh fish from the Mediterranean tempts shoppers in Nice.

The wide-bodied Airbus aircraft are assembled in Toulouse, the center of the French aerospace industry.

communications center. The traditional blue-collar heart of France and home to its silk manufacturing and chemical industries, Lyons has been going through a brisk renewal in the 1990s. It is now the seat of one branch of the prestigious École Normale Supérieur and headquarters of Interpol, the international police. The city is also famous for its foods, especially the enormous variety of *saucisses* and *saucissons* (sausages). One of Lyons' *superchefs*, Paul Bocuse, has recently opened franchises as far away as Florida and Japan.

Strasbourg. This city, the capital of Alsace, is France's port on Europe's most important river, the Rhine. The city has long been a crossroads of commerce and industry. The best-known local food product is the fine goose-liver spread called pâté de foie gras. In recent decades, Strasbourg has also become an important scientific and medical center: it has three universities with 50,000 students, and is home to the world-respected Research Institute for Cancer of the Digestive System (IRCAD).

Strasbourg was not always French, however. Until 1681, and again between 1871 and 1919, it was a German city, and much of its culture is still German today. In 1949, Strasbourg became truly international when it was made headquarters of the Council of Europe, which works toward European unity. The European Parliament was set up in Strasbourg in 1958 and the European Court of Human Rights in 1960.

Toulouse. North of the Pyrenees sits the historical capital of the south-

Carcassonne, a medieval stronghold, perches on a hill in southwestern France.

west and a center of the French aircraft industry. There, the huge Sud-Aviation engineers developed the Concorde, the huge supersonic airliner built jointly by France and Great Britain. The city has also made a contribution to French cuisine with its cassoulet—a succulent stew of goose meat, sausage, pork, and beans. By 2000, Toulouse had blossomed into a high-tech center, with a workforce that drew upon 115,000 students from its three universities. Other important French cities include Bordeaux, a major industrial city and port as well as a wine center; and Lille, the industrial center of the north.

PLACES OF INTEREST

The French landscape is extremely varied, from the harsh, windswept coasts of Brittany, facing the Atlantic, to the palm-lined promenades of Nice and Cannes on the Mediterranean. Each region has some striking features and characteristic beauty to catch the eye. But France is equally rich in the works of man, and Frenchmen and visitors alike can see the whole panorama of history spread out across the land.

In the foothills of the Alps there are towns with steep stair-step streets, such as Briançon. Still crowned with ancient fortifications, Briançon is one of the highest walled cities in Western Europe. Carcassonne, in southwest France near the Pyrenees, is the best preserved. Restoration of the medieval town, with its towers and crenelated walls, was begun in the 19th century under the direction of France's leading architect, Eugène Viollet-le-Duc. The restoration has been so exact that today a visit to Carcassonne makes it seem as if time did not exist—as if the 12th century had come to life again, side by side with the 20th.

About 400 miles (640 km.) to the east are the rolling, vine-clad hills of the Champagne region, near the Marne River valley. This pleasant area, home of the most famous wine of France, also has military cemeteries of both world wars, silent witnesses of past battles. Rheims, the largest city in the Champagne region, has one of the most beautiful cathedrals in France. The cathedral was the site of the coronations of 24 kings of France.

In the south, near the resorts of the Riviera (the Côte d'Azur, or "azure coast," to the French), is dry, windswept Provence. Here gnarled olive trees are silhouetted against bright blue skies, and small houses with characteristic orange tile roofs cluster against the hillsides. It is easy

The spires of Mont-Saint-Michel pierce the sky above France's Channel coast.

A marina at Calais, an ancient city near the narrowest stretch of water separating England and France.

to see why this region has always been such a favorite with artists, both French and foreign.

On the Channel, in the north, there are the dunes of Dunkirk beach and the great ports of Le Havre and Cherbourg. Many of the smaller towns along this stretch of coastline are fishing villages, for France has always used the sea as a source of food as well as a highway of trade. The French fishing fleet was completely modernized after World War II. It still sails from the Channel ports of Boulogne and Dieppe, bringing in huge catches of cod, herring, and sardines from the Atlantic. The icy waters off the rocky coast of Brittany yield lobsters, crabs, and oysters said to be the best in the world. Every year, the tiny Breton village of Locmariaquer celebrates the beginning of the oyster season with a festival in which all the residents—and many visitors—take part.

Down the Channel coast past Cherbourg stands the towering Abbey of Mont-Saint-Michel. Built on a spur of land that becomes an island at high tide, the Abbey has been one of the unique beauties of France for more than 10 centuries. Still farther south along the Atlantic coast, there is more evidence of France's history as a maritime power. Brest is an important Atlantic port, and Saint-Nazaire is the site of the country's largest shipyards, where many of its great transatlantic liners were built.

Pilgrims flock to the grotto at Lourdes where, in 1858, a peasant girl had visions of the Virgin Mary.

In the extreme south, close to the Spanish border, is the town of Biarritz. In the mid-19th century, drawn by the mild climate and the peaceful atmosphere, European royalty began to vacation there. Today Biarritz, with its beautiful beaches, elegant hotels and shops, and busy casinos, is one of the most famous resorts in the world.

Some 80 miles (130 km.) inland to the east lies the small city of Lourdes. There, in 1858, a young girl named Bernadette Soubirous said she had visions of the Virgin Mary. This story and the waters of Lourdes' springs—said to have miraculous healing powers—have made the town the goal of religious pilgrimages ever since. Hundreds of thousands come to Lourdes annually to worship at its basilica and to be cured by its waters.

Amid the wheatfields and flat plains of north central France—the Paris basin—is the town of Chartres. Chartres' massive Gothic cathedral, with its beautiful stained-glass windows, is one of the great achievements of the Middle Ages.

Even closer to Paris are two vast structures built to reflect the power and splendor of the French kings. The palace of Fontainebleau was begun during the reign of Francis I in the 16th century, and every succeeding king added to it. The Forest of Fontainebleau—some 40,000 acres (16,154

The Hall of Mirrors in the palace of Versailles is where the Treaty of Versailles was signed in 1919.

The palace of Fontainebleau is another monument to France's royal past.

ha.) of unspoiled woodland—is under government protection. It is still popular with artists, as it was in the 19th century when Jean Baptiste Camille Corot and Jean François Millet painted there.

To the northwest of Fontainebleau lies Versailles, the royal palace of King Louis XIV. With its Hall of Mirrors, sweeping staircases, and lovely formal gardens, the palace of Versailles is a reminder of the days when France was the political center of Europe. Every spring and summer *son et lumière* ("sound and light") performances are held at Versailles, with the voices of great French actors evoking the palace's past.

Hundreds of miles to the south, past some of the principal agricultural and industrial areas of France, contrasts still abound. Near Périgueux are the Lascaux Caves, whose walls and ceilings are covered with paintings of animals dating from prehistoric times. The caves were closed to visitors in 1963 because a fungus was destroying the paintings, but a partial replica, Lascaux II, was opened in 1983.

In Avignon, on the banks of the Rhone in southeastern France, there is a 14th-century palace, built to accommodate a number of French popes who, at that time, reigned at Avignon instead of Rome.

The island of Corsica, in the Mediterranean Sea off the coast of Italy southwest of Livorno, has been part of France since the 18th century. Once known as a bandit hideout, the mountainous island's chief claim to fame is as the birthplace of Napoleon. The Bonaparte family home may still be seen in Ajaccio, Corsica's capital and an important port. The city has another museum dedicated to Napoleon, and there are streets and squares named for him as well. Visitors can also enjoy the excellent beaches near Ajaccio and elsewhere on the island.

In late 2001, after years of friction with Corsican nationalists, the French parliament approved a bill giving the island more autonomy.

The castle and vineyards in Châteauneuf-du-Pape, near Avignon.

Boats line the harbor at St.-Tropez, a fashionable Mediterranean resort on the French Riviera.

Under the hot Mediterranean sun of the southeast is the town of Grasse. Nearby, fields of roses, violets, and mimosa form a patchwork of color to delight the eye. The flowers' lovely fragrance is captured in essential oils produced in Grasse, "the perfume capital of the world."

To the west, several miles past Marseilles, is the deep-water oil port of Fos. There, mostly in the 1970s, the French erected a gigantic, ambitious complex of modern harbor facilities and industrial plants, producing steel, plastics, and other commodities, in part on filled-in swamplands. This is close to the Rhone delta area known as the Camargue, whose marshes and lagoons have long been a bird and wildlife sanctuary. Herds of small horses still roam the region, while nearby, "cowboys" tend huge *manades,* or droves, of black cattle. Every spring and autumn, the tiny Camargue town of Saintes-Maries de-la-Mer, at the mouth of the Rhone, celebrates a religious festival that dates back many centuries. The ceremonies include the blessing of the cattle, which are driven into the sea to receive a kind of baptism. Side by side with these ancient traditions, however, industries and extensive land reclamation projects have begun to bring the Camargue into the 21st century.

Environment Planning

The French people would be deeply upset if industrialization and progress spoiled their land. So government and industry have joined in trying to preserve the natural beauty of the country and the heritage of

Ronchamp chapel, by Le Corbusier (C. E. Jeanneret), France's top modern architect.

the past while promoting the large-scale use of France's resources. Wherever possible, an official policy of *aménagement du territoire* ("environment planning") retains the best features of the countryside as the demands of production are met. The effects of this policy can be seen all over France—in the construction of a modern superhighway system; restoration of a Roman amphitheater or an ancient church; new industrial development; widespread reforestation projects; and the transformation of desolate, mosquito-infested wastelands, such as along the extreme western shore of the Mediterranean, into up-to-date resorts.

THE PEOPLE

Concern with making money, and then more money, in order to buy the conveniences and luxuries of modern life, has brought great change to the lives of most Frenchmen. More people are working than ever before in France. In the cities the traditional leisurely midday meal is disappearing. Offices, shops, and factories are discovering the greater efficiency of a short lunch hour in company lunchrooms. In almost all lines of work emphasis now falls on ever-increasing output. Thus the "typical" Frenchman produces more, earns more, and buys more consumer goods than his counterpart of only a generation ago. He gains in creature comforts and ease of life. What he loses to some extent is his sense of personal uniqueness, or individuality.

Some say that France has been Americanized. This is because the

United States is a world symbol of the technological society and its consumer products. The so-called Americanization of France has its critics who fear that "assembly-line life" will erase the pleasures of the more graceful and leisurely (but less productive) old French style. What will happen, they ask, to taste, elegance, and the cultivation of the good things in life—to revel in the smell of a freshly picked apple, a peaceful stroll by the river, or just happy hours of conversation in a local café?

Critics of Americanization and globalization—*la mondialisation* in French—are still being heard, but a new mood has swept the country recently. The trends are unmistakable: flexibility, multiculturalism, individual entrepreneurship, openness to change, and dynamism.

One problem yet to be solved is the huge size of the public sector, which employs one in four French citizens. The public employees held a number of crippling strikes in the early and mid 1990s in order to preserve their generous fringe benefits. Large protests were also organized in late 1999, when the government decreed a mandatory 35-hour workweek for companies with more than 20 employees, in order to lower unemployment. Among the young high-tech generation, the standing joke is "I love the 35 hours so much I do it twice a week."

Changing Population

Since the 1940s and the wartime German occupation, the French population has been growing at a rapid rate. Approximately 27 percent—more than 15 million people—are under the age of 20. France is also becoming a multiethnic society, with about 14 million citizens having an immigrant parent or grandparent. Most of these immigrants came from Muslim Arab or African countries, former French colonies, and Islam has thus become for all intents and purposes the second religion of France, with 4 million to 5 million adherents.

Today's young people of France are better educated than their parents and less bound to tradition. According to a 2000 survey by the World Health Organization, France has the best health care system in the world. Half of the girls born today will live up to the age of 100. The booming economy of the late 1990s has resulted in a great deal of purchasing power in the hands of young adults. These are buyers who want to enjoy what they can get now, who are confident of tomorrow, and whose tastes show a willingness to experiment, to sample the new, and to use up and replace goods. This is a startling contrast to the traditional French attitude of making what one has last as long as possible.

The people of France, the country's greatest resource, have always been a mélange (mixture). The reasons for this are not hard to find. First, France has no really formidable natural frontiers—even the Pyrenees and the Alps have passes through them—so it was always accessible by land. The extensive coasts, washed by the Channel, the Atlantic, and the Mediterranean, and marked by the mouths of navigable rivers such as the Seine, the Loire, the Gironde, and the Rhône, have made the land accessible by water, too.

First there were cave dwellers, and then explorers and traders—notably Phoenicians and Greeks from the eastern Mediterranean—some of whom stayed and settled. Over the years came Celts, Romans, Teutons (such as the Germanic Franks), Norsemen, Saracen North Africans, and Jews. All of these groups contributed significantly to the French of today. More recently the many elements in the modern French nation have come to include descendants of the Senegalese, Congolese, Indo-Chinese, and other African and Asian peoples, as well as Germans, Russians, Poles, Italians, Spaniards, and others.

The French are tolerant of differences of all kinds. This is not to say that the French are wholly without prejudice, but in general they do not systematically exclude whole groups. There has always been fairly continuous assimilation of newcomers. Thus, to be French is not so much to claim any certain ancestry as it is to "feel" French.

Education

One of the strongest influences in the making of the French is education. Today the French schools are playing a vital role in the transformation of France into a modern society. In the past the cultural heritage was transmitted only to a small elite of each generation. Now, all French children have the chance to discover and develop their abilities and aptitudes. As the result of a series of reforms, two major changes have taken place in education. First, there is a variety of courses, allowing all students a wide choice of the professional and technical careers necessary in today's world. Then, parents and schools work together so that a program may be chosen that best suits the unique needs and abilities of each child.

School is compulsory for children between the ages of 6 and 16. There are both government-run and private *écoles maternelles,* or nursery schools, some taking children as young as 2. In the eighth grade if pupils want to prepare for the traditional "classic" higher education, they begin to study Latin and sometimes Greek. There are also other programs, including those with the study of two modern foreign languages. Or they may go into general education combined with vocational training.

Those students who do go to the 3-year academic high school, or lycée, have a variety of majors to choose from—literature, social sciences, mathematics, pure and applied science, and an important recent addition, industrial technology, reflecting the new needs of the economy. At the end of the three years, the students take stiff examinations for their baccalaureat (or "bac") degree.

At the university level, too, important changes have taken place. In the wake of the student protests of 1968, most of the larger universities were subdivided into smaller units to make them more responsive to the students' needs. Students and teaching staff were given a role in their administration, and instead of central control of budgets and curricula by the ministry of education, the reorganized multidisciplinary universities were made into autonomous institutions. Again, more science and technology courses have been added. Although such curricula are fairly new in French education, the students who choose them are nevertheless following an old and honorable French tradition. Many important advances in science and medicine were made by French people or others who had made France their home.

Recreation

Young people in France today take their education as seriously as their parents take their jobs and professions. But the French are nevertheless aware that "all work and no play makes Jacques a dull boy." Popular pleasures and innumerable pastimes abound, and there is something for every taste.

In many households, television fills a large amount of leisure time. There are several commercial networks, and American programs are common. This wave of American culture has provoked a good deal of opposition from those who feel French culture is being submerged. In a further infiltration of American entertainment, in 1992 a huge European Disney theme-park complex was opened near Paris. Popular music, from folk to hard rock, is popular, often with the characteristically French themes of love and its joys and sadness.

A singer has really arrived when he or she performs at the Olympia, long Paris's best-known music hall. There, *chanteurs* and *chanteuses* set records for coming back year after year to sing to their adoring fans. In-person appearances in the provinces, too, are now a regular part of the French entertainment scene. With state subsidies for the arts, theaters have multiplied so that almost every French city has a thriving popular theater, even down to tiny houses seating 50 people at most. But wherever the theater and whatever the play, prices are low and theaters are

Visitors to the Eiffel Tower must pay the admission fee in euros. Indeed, the euro is now used to conduct all transactions of money in France; the franc, the country's former unit of currency, is no longer used.

packed. This, too, is in keeping with the old French tradition of universal interest in the arts.

French Food

Another universal French interest is food, for good eating has always been one of the favorite pastimes of the French people. In caves near the hill town of Roquefort in south-central France, a tangy, blue-veined cheese is cured. Roquefort, made of sheep's milk, is a gourmet treat around the world, as are Brie, Camembert, Port Salut, and Coulommiers. Over 400 different cheeses are produced in France, and they are only one indication of the French love of fine food.

Le bon goût ("good taste") is as important when it comes to food as it is in every aspect of life in France. It is not unusual to see a butcher or grocer arranging wares with all the care an artist might devote to a still life painting, and French housewives take pride in preparing even the simplest meal well. From the smallest bistro to the most elegant restaurant, dining is a pleasure in France. Every meal offers foods with a distinctly French flavor. For breakfast, there are flaky croissants, brioches, crisp *petits pains,* and other rolls to enjoy with jams and a piping hot cup of café au lait. Other meals present such delights as *soupe à l'oignon* (onion soup), served bubbling hot with cheese on top; *escargots bourguinonne* (snails prepared with garlic and herbs); or *pot-au-feu,* a savory stew; all of them accompanied by enough long, crusty loaves of bread to enjoy the last of the sauce or gravy. Countless varieties of fluffy omelets are consumed daily in France, and *bifteck et pommes frites* (steak and french fried potatoes) are enormously popular. For dessert, there are literally hundreds of different patisseries to choose from. Or the lucky visitor might select a *mousse au chocolat,* a *crème caramel,* or simply end the meal with a *glace* (ice cream).

In the *grand luxe* restaurants of France, especially those of Paris, sparkling crystal, dazzling white linens, and silverware placed "just so" form a backdrop for the best of *gastronomie* (fine eating). There a chateaubriand or a soufflé is prepared to order and served with elegant precision and even drama. One seemingly simple dish may take the combined efforts of six chefs to produce. French food is a joy the visitor can share with the French, and it is also an art form that is admired and imitated everywhere.

Sports

In July 1998, the French team won the World Cup in soccer, the first time ever, and the entire country went wild in celebrations. The rejoicing was repeated in 2000, when the French won the gold in the all-European soccer championship, and brought home 39 medals from the Sydney Olympics.

Physical education is compulsory in schools and universities. Swimming pools, stadiums, and gyms are available to everyone. The two most popular team sports are soccer and basketball. Among individual sports, skiing leads the field. Geography and climate have blessed France with snowy slopes, especially in the Alps and nearby Jura Mountains. Clustered in valleys or nestled at the foot of snowy peaks such as Mont Blanc are dozens of winter resorts, including Mégève, Chamonix, and Albertville—site of the 1992 Winter Olympics. Many smaller ski towns such as Courchevel, Font-Romeu near Prades, and Barcelonnette are

Skiers enjoy the slopes at Montgenèvre, near the Italian border.

Saint-Malo is one of the most popular Channel resorts in France.

The Vingt-Quatres Heures of Le Mans thrills Frenchmen and foreigners alike.

rapidly gaining popularity. Almost any Frenchman can learn to ski today, for there are frequent excursions to low-cost resorts. In winter whole school classes move to ski areas, and skiing is added to regular studies during these *classes de neige* ("snow classes").

Other popular sports are judo, sailing, and water-skiing. *La chasse* ("hunting") is a passion for many Frenchmen, reflecting their love for *gibier* ("game")—from partridge to wild boar—on the table. The rivers and streams of France provide excellent fishing—another well-loved recreation.

In every season there is something for everyone in France, but August is still when most Frenchmen enjoy their *vacances* ("vacation"). The average Frenchman has little taste for wandering to exotic corners of the world. Even in this age of great mobility, he is likely to find true contentment in a return from the city in which he lives to the small corner of France where he feels his roots are. Many Frenchmen still show this love of the land by taking camping trips or annual family excursions simply to "breathe the country air." Nevertheless, more and more young people are traveling today. Many low-cost vacation groups have been set up—some with their own resorts—not only in France but all over Europe and North Africa.

Another great French love is automobiles. This fascination with cars is evident in the excitement generated by the great annual race, the grueling Vingt-Quatres Heures ("24 hours") of Le Mans in western France. Each spring sees hundreds of thousands of Frenchmen crowding the route of the classic in western France and cheering wildly for their favorite drivers. International bicycle races, such as the 3,000-mile (4,800 km.) Tour de France, are equally popular with Frenchmen, and their mud-splattered winners become heroes all over Europe.

But in spite of the increasing interest in sports and popular entertainment, the serious culture of France still plays a real part in the lives of its people. To many people, both Frenchmen and foreigners, the very essence of France is its richness in the arts of the past and present.

Medieval illuminated manuscript from "Le Livre de la Chasse" ("Book of the Hunt") by Gaston Phoebus. The Cloisters, Metropolitan Museum of Art, New York City.

The Fine Arts

Playwright Jean Giraudoux's statement *Sans style rien ne vit et rien ne survit: tout est dans le style* ("Nothing can live or survive without style: style is everything") is particularly true of the fine arts in France—a country that has always cherished and promoted great artistic works. One of the oldest surviving examples of the artistic spirit among remote, primitive ancestors of the French is found on the walls and ceilings of the Lascaux Caves, in southwestern France. These graceful paintings of animals were discovered during World War II, and scientists estimate that they are over 20,000 years old.

The art of medieval France, from tapestries, illuminated manuscripts, and stained glass to altarpieces and sculpture, was largely done for the Church. But the most important art works were actually the churches themselves. In the 12th century, French builders began to develop the Gothic style. With its graceful pointed arches and slender spires pointing toward heaven, Gothic architecture gradually spread all over Europe.

In the 16th and 17th centuries, French Renaissance architects were influenced by styles from Italy. One of them, Francois Mansart (the mansard roof is named for him), used Italian ideas to form his own style. French Renaissance painters were also strongly influenced by Italian works. Seventeenth-century artists were often inspired by the classics and painted subjects from the Bible and Greek and Roman mythology.

By 1700, France had become the most powerful nation in Europe, and the court of King Louis XIV, who died in 1715, had become the artistic as well as the political center of the world. As the 18th century went on, French styles in painting and architecture became more ornate and decorative, and were imitated all over Europe.

At the end of the 18th century, along with the political revolution, a kind of revolution took place in French art. Painters became increasingly experimental and adventuresome. The Romantic painters of the mid-19th century took an interest in the vivid colors and swirling action of such exotic lands as North Africa.

In the mid-1800s, Jean Baptiste Camille Corot was the leading nature painter. His sun-drenched landscapes and lakes surrounded by silvery birches show his great love for the French countryside. Edouard Manet was another artist of the time who believed in painting from life.

The leading French artists of the late 19th and early 20th centuries are known as the impressionists. They painted from life, but not with photographic realism; instead they tried to capture on canvas the subtle effects of changing light. The key names of this movement include Claude Monet, Auguste Renoir, Edgar Degas, and Camille Pissarro. The latter influenced the unique Paul Gauguin, who is known for the paintings he completed during stays in Tahiti and Martinique.

One great French influence on 20th-century art was Paul Cézanne, the leading post-impressionist. Cézanne's interest in shape and structure was the beginning of a great change in world art. By the 1920s, Georges Braque and the Spaniard Pablo Picasso (a resident of France) helped to develop cubism, in which various planes of an object or person are shown at once and things are reduced to their essential shapes. Until the beginning of World War II, France continued to be an international crossroads of artists and the birthplace of such new artistic trends and schools as expressionism, surrealism, and abstract painting.

Centuries of Great Literature

From the days of the medieval singers who traveled from town to town or knightly court to knightly court, France has made major contributions to world literature. Many of the significant trends in Western poetry and prose originated or developed in France.

The literature of 16th-century France includes the fullest expression of the Renaissance (the word itself, meaning "rebirth," is French). All of the spirit of discovery and the joy in human abilities characteristic of the period were reflected in the works of French writers such as François Rabelais and Michel de Montaigne. But less than 100 years later, partially as a reaction to the exuberant Renaissance style, French literature changed again. The 17th-century playwrights, especially Pierre Corneille and Jean Racine, emphasized a return to older traditions. Using stories from classical mythology and ancient history, they imposed rigid limits of subject, time, and place on their work. They described the struggle of human emotions against reason and order. Their contemporary Molière (Jean Baptiste Poquelin) made fun of everyday life. Many of their plays are still performed by the world-famous Comédie-Française, the oldest of the French national theaters.

In *A Discourse on Method* (1637), René Descartes, mathematician, scientist, and philosopher, expressed the feeling of the age that man was fundamentally a thinking—and questioning—creature. Belief in man as a reasoning being was central to the classicism of the age, which sought order, form, and style in every human expression. It was natural, therefore, that the French language should come under scrutiny. In 1635, the Académie Française was established to guide the development of the language and to insure its purity. It serves largely the same purpose today.

By the early 18th century, French writers had turned to observation of the quality of human life—especially in the areas of politics and social criticism. They began to question the nature of government and the proper relationship of kings to those they ruled. As a group they were known as *les philosophes,* or "the philosophers," and they expressed the principles of *liberté, egalité, fraternité* ("liberty, equality, fraternity") that culminated in the French Revolution in 1789.

A kind of revolution swept through French literature, too, and by the 1830s, feeling and imagination had become the key themes in French writing. The novels and poems of 19th-century France are vivid examples of this new Romantic spirit. A leading novelist of this movement was Victor Hugo, whose masterpiece *Les Miserables* continues to enjoy a high level of popularity even today. Another well-known Romantic author was Alexandre Dumas, whose novel *The Three Musketeers*, still enchants readers. Two other major writers of this period, Honoré de Balzac and Stendhal, depicted French society more realistically. Somewhat later, Emile Zola shocked readers with his harsh, naturalistic tales dealing with the French working class.

In the mid-19th century, Charles Baudelaire, in his poems *The Flowers of Evil,* used the French language to create word pictures. The symbolist poets who followed Baudelaire also used words to suggest intense feelings and ideas, rather than to make simple statements.

Marcel Proust's *Remembrance of Things Past,* a multi-volume portrait of an era, began to appear in 1913. It exerted a great influence on later 20th-century writers in France and all over the world.

Twelve French writers of the 20th century received the Nobel Prize for Literature. Before World War II, major names included Louis Aragon, André Gide, François Mauriac, and André Malraux. In the second half of the century, novelists Albert Camus and Jean-Paul Sartre formulated the basic principles of a new philosophical school called existentialism.

Book publishing is still a major industry in France today, and the French public reads avidly. The annual announcements of winners of the important literary competitions (such as the Prix Goncourt and the Prix Femina) are awaited by some as eagerly as soccer fans await the results of a major match.

Music

French contributions in the realm of music—from the songs of the medieval troubadours, to the precise, courtly measures of Jean-Baptiste Lully, to the sometimes dissonant scores of today's composers—have long been well known.

Much of the music of medieval France was church music, often based on the Gregorian chant. An important composer of secular music during this period was Josquin des Prez, whose melodies became known all over Europe in the late Middle Ages.

As secular music developed, 15th- and 16th-century French composers wrote battle songs and music based on sounds of nature. In the 16th and 17th centuries, as royal power grew, the courts at Paris and Versailles became musical centers. Composers of the period wrote music for court theatricals and ballets, as well as individual pieces. Music was supported—and even produced—by the kings; King Louis XIII himself was a composer.

But possibly most often played are the rich, rolling works of the 19th century, especially the symphonies of Hector Berlioz and the Belgian César Franck, and the piano compositions of the Pole Frédéric Chopin. Equally popular are the colorful, romantic French operas; perhaps the best known are Charles Gounod's *Faust* and *Roméo et Juliette* and Georges Bizet's *Carmen*.

In the late 19th century, at about the same time that painters were developing Impressionism, music, too, took a new turn. After Claude Debussy and Maurice Ravel, the first musical "impressionists," came the musical "cubists" Erik Satie and Francis Poulenc. Their compositions were often as startling to their audiences as a Picasso or Braque painting was to its viewers. Two major avant-garde composers of the 20th century were Olivier Messiaen and Pierre Boulez.

French Film

No view of French life and culture would be complete without noting French achievements in cinema. From the very earliest examples of this art form, French contributions have been among the most significant. In the 1950s, the young directors of the "New Wave" made film even more an art for its own sake. A major director of this school was François Truffaut, but others also gained international recognition, including Jean Renoir, Jacques Tati, Jean-Luc Godard, Éric Rohmer, and Louis Malle. France has also been the birthplace of many movie stars, such as Catherine Deneuve and Gérard Dépardieu, who are well known throughout the world.

HISTORY

By 51 B.C., Roman legions under Julius Caesar had conquered much of the land called Gaul—an area that includes all of present-day France as well as Belgium and Switzerland. Though Greek and Phoenician traders had settled on the Mediterranean coast centuries before, Caesar's victory marked the beginning of more than 5 centuries of outside rule.

Under the Romans, cities (including Lyons, Nîmes, and Arles) were built, and a communications network—roads, bridges, and aqueducts—was set up to serve them. Some of the bridges, such as the Pont du Gard in Languedoc, are still used today. In many parts of France modern highways lie above the ancient Roman roads. Roman civilization came with conquest, and in culture and language Gaul gradually became a Latin country.

In the 3rd century A.D., Gaul experienced the first invasions across its eastern boundaries by wandering Germanic tribes. Over the next 2 centuries more and more of these invaders—notably Franks, Burgundians, and Visigoths—swept into Gaul. Rome no longer had the strength to push them back. So in some cases the invaders settled down and set up their own areas of control side by side with lands that remained under nominal Roman rule. Toward the end of the 5th century, the Franks decisively defeated the last remnants of Roman power and gained control of most of Gaul. By 500 a Frankish kingdom under King Clovis had accepted Christianity. The kings who followed Clovis had to fight off new invaders. In 732 the Franks defeated a Muslim army that had

The Pont du Gard, near Nîmes, was used to carry water for more than 1,000 years.

crossed the Pyrenees from Spain. By 800, when Charlemagne was crowned Holy Roman Emperor by the Pope, the Franks had extended the borders of their kingdom to include parts of present-day Austria, Germany, Italy, and Yugoslavia. Under Charlemagne (Charles the Great), the Holy Roman Empire grew even larger. Charlemagne set up schools, gave France a code of laws, and strengthened the emperor's authority.

After Charlemagne's death, however, central power declined, and his kingdom was divided among his grandsons. The western part became Francia, the nucleus of today's France. The king's authority grew very weak in the second half of the 9th century, and disastrous raids by Vikings weakened it even more.

The Middle Ages

In 987 Hugh Capet was elected king of France by the nobles. Slowly, with the support of merchants and the growing middle class in the cities, the Capetians strengthened the monarchy. By the 13th century the king of France had become the most powerful ruler in Europe. French agriculture flourished. Guilds in the towns and cities turned out quality products. Foreign trade increased. French universities attracted scholars from all over Europe. In every way France became a European center of styles and ideas.

During the later Middle Ages serious conflict arose between the king of France, Philip IV, and the Church. In 1305 a Frenchman was elected Pope Clement V. He had the papal palace moved to Avignon, in south-

The Château of Chenonceaux is one of the loveliest in the Loire Valley.

ern France; and, for some 70 years, the popes were almost puppets of the French Crown. In 1378, the papacy returned to Rome. (Even today, a wine grown in the Avignon area is called Châteauneuf-du-Pape, or "the Pope's new chateau.")

The Hundred Years War

In 1066 William, the Duke of Normandy—a large region in northern France—became king of England. From that time on, English kings held sizable lands in France. Almost 300 years after William conquered England, Edward III even laid claim to the French throne. In 1337 Edward invaded France. Although hostilities actually lasted longer than a century, the conflict came to be known as the Hundred Years War. The English won many victories—notably Crécy, Poitiers, and Agincourt—but they were never able to seize and hold the throne of France. In the 1420's Joan of Arc, a young farm girl, appeared at the French court. She said

Orléans. In 1429, Joan of Arc led in lifting the English siege of the city.

God had commanded her to lead the French armies and to have the Dauphin—the rightful heir to the throne—crowned at Rheims. Joan's leadership helped to turn the tide. Although she was betrayed and burned at the stake, her courage so inspired the French that they were finally able to drive the invaders out. In 1429 the Dauphin was crowned King Charles VII, and by 1450 the French had recaptured most of their land. When the war ended, the French Crown was far stronger and the land of France more unified than before.

Religious Strife

In the 16th century the Reformation, based on the ideas of Martin Luther, swept France. Many noblemen and even some members of the royal family became Huguenots, as the French Protestants were called. There were violent clashes as King and Church tried to wipe out the Huguenots. France was divided into factions, and civil war broke out. In 1572, by royal order, thousands of Huguenots were massacred in Paris and other French cities.

Henry IV

Stability returned in 1598, when King Henry IV, who had been converted from Protestantism to Catholicism, issued the Edict of Nantes. This allowed the Huguenots some religious freedom.

Under Henry agriculture was encouraged, and the French economy was reformed. As France regained its prosperity, there was an increase in trade. French ships ranged far from home in search of new sources of wealth. In this way France began to acquire colonies in the New World.

But 12 years after the Edict of Nantes, Henri IV was assassinated. His queen, Marie de Médicis, became regent for their young son, Louis XIII. There was division and dissent among the nobility, and, once more, there was conflict between Huguenots and Catholics. Royal power was weakened.

Richelieu and the Sun King

Cardinal Richelieu began his rise to power under Marie de Médicis in 1614. He eventually became Louis XIII's chief minister, with nearly absolute control over all aspects of French government. For almost 20 years he worked not only to restore royal power but to make France the strongest state in Europe.

Richelieu crushed all opposition inside France, including the Huguenots and the nobility. He levied high taxes, especially on peasants and city merchants. He encouraged foreign trade and expanded the French Empire in North America, the Caribbean, and elsewhere.

In foreign policy Richelieu opposed the powerful Habsburg monarchies of Austria and Spain. The Cardinal allied France with the Habsburgs' enemies in the Thirty Years War. His work set the stage for the absolute monarchy of Louis XIV.

Louis came to the throne as a child, in 1643. For the first 18 years of his 72-year reign, his chief minister, Cardinal Mazarin, continued Richelieu's policies. Opposition within France, which had flared into the open under a child-king, was again suppressed and France's position abroad was consolidated. When Louis XIV began to rule for himself, he was the strongest king in Europe. In 1685 he revoked the Edict of Nantes, and the Huguenots either fled or suffered gross indignities and even death if they refused to convert. Louis involved France in costly wars with Spain, the Netherlands, and England but actually gained little for his country. He summed up his theory that he was God's representative on earth (and responsible to no one) with the words, *"l'état c'est moi* [I am the state]." Everything Louis did was a reflection of the centralized power of *le roi soleil,* "the sun king."

In the early 18th century, Louis XV succeeded his great-grandfather as king. Royal power seemed as strong as ever, but below the surface trouble was developing. France was defeated by England in the Seven Years War and lost much of its territory in North America. By 1774, when Louis XVI became king, dissatisfaction with social, political, and economic conditions, along with the growth of an able, educated middle class, had created an inflammable situation. Protests, riots, and dissent grew into a revolution that swept away the old regime. Crown, Church, and privilege were destroyed.

The French Revolution

French aid to the American colonies in their revolt against England strained finances past the breaking point. To raise money, the King in 1789 called a meeting of the Estates-General (representatives of the clergy, the nobility, and the middle class) for the first time in over 175 years. After an unauthorized meeting in the Jeu de Paume—or royal indoor tennis court—some representatives, mostly middle-class deputies, banded together in a national assembly and vowed to write a constitution for France. Shortly after, on July 14, 1789, a Parisian mob stormed the Bastille, an ancient prison that symbolized all the oppressions of the old regime. Next, in August, the assembly issued the Declaration of the Rights of Man. The revolution had begun.

The revolution rapidly grew increasingly violent. France was declared a republic in September, 1792; and Louis XVI and his queen, Marie Antoinette, were beheaded a few months later. Radical leaders, such as Maximilien Robespierre, took over. A reign of terror swept the country as these men tried to exterminate all enemies of the Revolution.

Meanwhile France was also engaged in foreign war. Fear of the revolutionary events in France had spread all over Europe. Every crowned monarch felt gravely threatened by what had happened to Louis XVI. Thus France, from 1793 onward, found itself at war with five major powers, including England.

The war continued even after 1795, when the Reign of Terror ended and the Revolution became more moderate. For the next 4 years France was governed by the Directory, a five-man executive board. But internal dissent continued, and the government became increasingly dependent on army support.

Napoleon Bonaparte

In 1799 Napoleon Bonaparte, a young Corsican general who had won brilliant victories for France, took control. He eliminated all opposition and set up the Consulate, a committee of three. As First Consul, Napoleon made all the decisions. France began to enjoy stability, although freedom had been lost.

Napoleon believed that he was the repository of the people's will. He had a legal code drawn up for France. (The Code Napoléon, as it came to be known, is still the foundation of French law and of the laws in many areas that were once under French influence.) In 1801 he signed the Concordat, making peace with the Pope and gaining Church support. He reformed the educational system and set up a professional civil service for which people were chosen on the basis of ability. Napoleon's armies continued their victories in Europe, carrying French ideas far beyond French borders. In 1804, Napoleon crowned himself emperor of France. Gradually extending his empire, Napoleon defeated most of France's enemies—Austria, Prussia, Russia, and Italy. Finally only England remained free of French control, thanks to its sea power. The armies of the French Empire had redrawn the map of Europe.

In 1812 Napoleon decided to crush what remained of Russia's strength. He led the Grande Armée—over 600,000 men—in the invasion. After several great victories, the French occupied Moscow, which had been abandoned and set on fire. The Russians retreated constantly, destroying all supplies as they went. Finally Napoleon ordered the long march back to France. But the snows and bitter cold of the Russian winter soon set in, and Russian soldiers harassed the retreating French. Only about one sixth of the glorious army survived to return home. The empty victory had turned to defeat.

Now Napoleon's enemies—and even some of his allies—joined to defeat him. In 1814 he was forced to abdicate and was exiled from France. Under Louis XVIII (Louis XVI's brother), France became a constitutional monarchy. In March, 1815, however, Napoleon decided he had enough support to seize power again. He left the Mediterranean island of Elba and returned to France; Louis XVIII fled. Napoleon was emperor of France once more, but only for 100 days.

What began in Russia in 1812 ended on the battlefield at Waterloo, not far from Brussels, Belgium, in 1815. In June a multi-national army, led by the English Duke of Wellington and the Prussian Field Marshal Gebhard von Blücher, defeated Napoleon for the last time. He was exiled once more, this time to St. Helena, a tiny island in the South Atlantic.

Two Revolutions—1830 and 1848

Louis XVIII was restored to the French throne. For 15 years he and his successor, Charles X, ruled France. Both acted more and more as if the revolution had never taken place. The vote was restricted, parliamentary power reduced, and the press strictly censored. The Church played an increasingly important role in controlling education. The early 19th century brought the Industrial Revolution to France, as it did to the other nations of Europe. More and more Frenchmen were drawn to the cities in search of jobs and a better life. At the same time, the middle class grew larger—and wealthier. These Frenchmen were resentful of the government's policies.

In July, 1830, the King dissolved the parliament, reduced the vote still further, and destroyed what little remained of a free press. Strikes and riots broke out in Paris, and Charles was forced to abdicate. This revolution gave France a revised constitution and brought Louis Philippe, the Duke of Orléans, to the throne.

At first, Louis Philippe seemed satisfied to rule as a constitutional king. Industrialization continued. Cities grew larger, especially in the textile centers of the north and the mining areas of the east. The government did almost nothing to improve conditions for the workers or to help the unemployed. There was dissatisfaction with foreign policy as well.

By 1848 liberals had joined discontented workers in a campaign to draw attention to their demands. Strikes were widespread. In February, demonstrations and riots in Paris led to clashes between royal troops and the rioters. A new revolution seemed underway. Louis Philippe abdicated and went into exile. France was a republic again. The provisional government of the Second Republic called for a constitutional convention and made attempts to help the workers. But a majority of conservatives were elected to the convention. In June the Paris workers revolted against their rule and were put down by the Army.

Napoleon III and the Second Empire

Elections were held under the new Constitution of 1848, and Louis Napoleon (a nephew of Napoleon I) was chosen president of the Second Republic. By 1851 he had decided to follow in his uncle's footsteps. Because the Constitution allowed him only one term, he arrested his opponents, dissolved the National Assembly, and called for a national vote to make France an empire once more. He was crowned Napoleon III in December, 1852.

Napoleon III's main aim was to make France the most powerful nation in Europe. He had Baron Georges Haussmann, a leading city planner and administrator, redesign much of Paris as a modern capital city. Napoleon III encouraged the expansion of industry and communications, especially railroads. After an agreement with the Egyptian Government, French engineers, led by Ferdinand de Lesseps, dug the Suez Canal, gaining a foothold for France in the Middle East.

Napoleon III's ambitions also involved military glory. In 1854 he led France into the Crimean War against Russia, which had been trying to win an outlet on the Mediterranean. Five years later he supported the Italians in their fight for liberation from Austrian control, and France annexed the Italian territories of Nice and Savoy. He tried to extend French influence to the New World by putting the Austrian archduke Maximilian in charge of a Mexican "empire." (The venture failed, however, and Maximilian was executed by a Mexican firing squad.)

The Franco-Prussian War.   But France was in a period of economic decline, and Napoleon III's wars were costly. Opposition to his policies grew steadily. There was also a threat from outside. The north German kingdom of Prussia had grown powerful under the leadership of Chancellor Otto von Bismarck. In July, 1870, Bismarck created a situation in which France was forced to declare war. Within 3 months Napoleon's armies had been defeated, he had been captured, and Paris was under siege. Prussia's peace terms were harsh—France lost most of Alsace and Lorraine and had to pay 5,000,000,000 francs to Germany. The Second Empire had been destroyed.

The Third Republic

Upon learning of Napoleon III's defeat and capture, the citizens of Paris had revolted and proclaimed France a republic once again. After the peace treaty of 1871, much internal unrest continued. When the elected National Assembly decided to meet in Versailles, site of the royal palace, Parisian workers and liberals, fearing a return to monarchy, set up their own revolutionary government—the Commune. For more than 2 months they tried to win national support, but the Commune was finally crushed by Versailles' troops under Marshal Patrice de MacMahon.

The Third Republic quickly paid the war indemnity to Germany and put France on the road to economic recovery. Industrial and agricultural output increased. Shipping and trade expanded. France gained colonies in Africa, including Morocco and Tunisia, and in Indochina (now Laos, Cambodia, and Vietnam). By the late 1880's the Third Republic had weathered many storms. There had been dissent from disappointed royalists and from newly born socialist groups and labor unions, some of which drew inspiration from the history of the Paris Commune.

The Dreyfus Case. In 1894 a young Jewish army captain, Alfred Dreyfus, was accused of selling military secrets to Germany. He was court-martialed, convicted, and sent to Devils Island—the French prison colony off the coast of South America. His family attempted to prove his innocence and gained the support of men like novelist Emile Zola and journalist and political leader Georges Clemenceau. In 1906 Dreyfus was completely cleared.

The Dreyfus Case was more than an injustice against one man. It was a national upheaval, and it became a focus for many of the political and social questions of the day. The division between the conservative forces of the Church, Army, and monarchists and the liberals was intensified. As a result of the Dreyfus Case, by the early 20th century the Army's influence in government had been largely destroyed, and the monarchists were also no longer politically effective. In 1905 the Concordat with the Catholic Church was repealed, and Church and State were completely separated. But little was done to improve working conditions in France. There were constant strikes and protests. Liberals, led by Clemenceau, tried but failed to put through reforms, including old-age pensions, workmen's compensation, and an income-tax bill.

World War I. In 1907 France signed the Triple Entente with England and Russia, each pledging its support should the others be attacked. Italy and the Austro-Hungarian Dual Monarchy joined Germany, which had grown more powerful since 1870, in the Triple Alliance. By 1914 almost every nation in Europe had entered one alliance or another, and when war broke out in July, it involved all of Europe.

The French fought the German invaders bravely, using every resource at their command. Nevertheless they were pushed back, and the Germans drew closer and closer to Paris. At one critical moment even Paris taxicabs were rushing reinforcements and supplies to the defending troops. The French capital was saved. On the western front, a stalemate gradually developed. By 1915 France had lost almost 800,000 men, although neither side had gained much ground. As the war continued, the French had some military successes. But again, the cost was enormous. In 1916, during the defense of Verdun alone, there were some 500,000 casualties.

The United States entered the war in 1917. Before the end of 1918 a combined French, British, and American army was able to push the Germans out of France.

Between the Wars

In 1919, by the Treaty of Versailles, France regained Alsace and Lorraine, with their rich mineral resources. The German coalfields in the Saar Valley were ceded to France for 15 years. Germany was disarmed and had to pay billions in damages. But over 1,300,000 Frenchmen had died in the war, and France had been devastated. French agriculture had been ruined and its factories destroyed. Shipping and trade were at a standstill.

The work of rebuilding the economy was begun. Industry and agriculture were modernized, and prosperity began to return. At the beginning of the 1930s France had a thriving economy, and the franc was stable. But during 1931, the worldwide Depression hit France. Thousands were out of work, and there were renewed strikes and demonstrations. In this situation no single party could maintain control for long, and within 5 years there were 14 cabinets. In spite of intensive efforts to stabilize the country, the divisions within France grew deeper.

Perhaps most important, a re-armed Germany under the leadership of Adolf Hitler again presented a threat to peace in Europe. In September, 1939, when Hitler's armies marched into Poland, France and England came to the support of their ally. Soon all of Europe was at war once again.

World War II

The Maginot Line, which the French had built along the border with Germany, proved useless when the Germans chose to strike at France from the Low Countries. France fell in June, 1940. Marshal Pétain, a World War I hero, signed an armistice with Germany. Most of northern and central France, including Paris, was under German occupation. In southern, unoccupied France a new government was set up, based in the resort town of Vichy. Led by Pétain and Pierre Laval, the Vichy government worked with Nazi Germany.

But most of the French did not collaborate, and internal resistance movements sprang up. Their efforts ranged from work slowdowns and sabotage to the guerrilla tactics of the fighters known as the Maquis. There was resistance outside of France as well. In 1940, the French general Charles de Gaulle escaped to England, where he issued a call to continue the fight. He put himself at the head of the Free French movement, which worked with the Allies against Germany. Later de Gaulle was recognized as a leader of a French provisional government organized in liberated North Africa. (The Vichy forces in Tunisia, Morocco, and Algeria had surrendered almost immediately.) In retaliation, the German Army occupied all of France, and the country became part of Hitler's Festung Europa ("fortress Europe").

On D-Day—June 6, 1944—the Allied counteroffensive began. American and British forces landed on the beaches of Normandy and began fighting their way inland. Allied planes struck from the air, and the German defeat was underway. By late August, Paris was liberated. General de Gaulle led a triumphal march down the Champs-Elysées, and within a few months, all of France was free.

De Gaulle had become a worldwide symbol of French resistance, and for over a year after his return to France he was a virtual dictator by acclamation. In the fall of 1945 an elected constitutional convention

The old port of Honfleur, in Normandy, is near the D-Day invasion sites.

named him provisional premier-president of the new Fourth Republic. In January, 1946, however, de Gaulle resigned because he felt the constitution that had been drafted did not provide enough power for the president. Nine months later, in spite of de Gaulle's opposition, a new constitution was finally adopted. France returned to regular political life for the first time since 1940. But once again there were so many factions and so much party rivalry that the resulting coalition governments could not stay in power long.

Postwar France

Because of the desperate political situation, French recovery from the war was slow at first. Prices rose, the franc was unstable, and there was serious inflation. Strikes were the order of the day, and the Communist Party gained strength as discontent grew.

By 1949, however, the situation had improved. Under a plan designed by economist Jean Monnet, and with Marshall Plan aid from the United States, French industry was rebuilt and modernized. Coal and steel production in Lorraine increased, and gradually all French industrial production reached or surpassed its prewar strength. French agricultural output expanded too, as farming methods became more modern. The French merchant marine was soon carrying French exports all around the world once more. With prosperity, tourism grew in importance.

After the war, many European leaders felt greater economic recovery and strength could come through cooperation and union. In the 1950s, the French statesman Robert Schuman took the lead in proposing that the countries of Western Europe pool basic resources. This led to the six-nation Coal and Steel Community. Soon thereafter came the European Economic Community (EEC), or Common Market. France both contributed greatly to and gained much economic strength from these European developments. Many French leaders believed that genuine European unity—political as well as economic—might eventually follow.

Although the French economy grew stronger, politics remained shaky. There was also trouble in the French colonies. Indochina had revolted at the end of World War II, and nine years later the French Army still had not been able to regain control. In North Africa, too, France was faced with multiplying difficulties—especially in Algeria. A drive for independence began there in the 1950s, but the *colons* (French-Algerians, many of whom had never lived in France) and the army were equally determined that Algeria remain French. Tunisia and Morocco were also demanding independence.

In 1954, under the leadership of Socialist prime minister Pierre Mendès-France, the nation relinquished its control of Indochina. The French government also granted more autonomy to Tunisia and introduced reforms in Morocco. In Europe, France continued to participate in the North Atlantic Treaty Organization (NATO), of which it had been a founding member. But the Algerian situation, which had become a full-scale revolution and civil war, could not be resolved. By 1958, the question had so divided France that effective government was at an end.

De Gaulle and the Fifth Republic. In May 1958, faced with an uprising in Algiers, the National Assembly called General de Gaulle to power. His condition for accepting leadership again was the adoption of a new constitution, with strengthened powers for the executive branch, as well as economic and social reforms. The constitution was accepted by approximately 80 percent of French voters.

De Gaulle's Fifth Republic began in June 1958. By 1962, the Algerian conflict was settled, and Algeria gained independence. The new constitution had also created the French Community—an association of France and its former colonies. De Gaulle was president of the Fifth Republic for 11 years. He believed that France should be the leader of Europe and therefore he withdrew France from NATO military affairs in 1966.

Dissatisfaction with de Gaulle's policies culminated in the student protests of 1968. The next year, his proposals for further constitutional reform were rejected and he resigned. His successors, Georges Pompidou and Valéry Giscard d'Estaing, governed France along conservative lines until François Mitterand, a Socialist, was elected in 1981. He nationalized some banks and industries, and made history in 1991 by naming France's first woman prime minister, Edith Cresson.

The growing discontent with the Socialists led to the victory of the conservative Jacques Chirac in the 1995 presidential election. Two years later, however, the conservatives suffered a defeat in parliamentary elections and Chirac was forced to name a socialist prime minister, Lionel Jospin. This awkward arrangement—a president of one party sharing power with a prime minister of another party—was called "cohabitation."

In 2001, the French people voted to shorten the presidential term of office from seven years to five. In spring 2002, the country experienced a political earthquake when, in a surprising showing, the ultraconservative candidate, Jean-Marie Le Pen, placed second during the first round of the presidential elections. Le Pen, who is notoriously anti-Semitic and favors a policy of strict limits on immigration, upstaged the candidate of the left, Lionel Jospin. In the second round, the shocked French electorate then chose Jacques Chirac, even though many voters were strongly opposed to him because of his alleged involvement in a number of financial scandals and charges of corruption. One month after the presidential election, in June 2002, the nation's political right was also victorious in the parliamentary elections.

French Overseas Departments and Territories

France once controlled a vast empire. Today it retains only a few holdings. Its four Overseas Departments include French Guiana in South America (see Volume 6), Guadeloupe and Martinique in the Caribbean (see Volume 5), and Réunion in the Indian Ocean (see Volume 1). The two Overseas Territorial Collectivities are the island of Mayotte in the Comoros (see Volume 1) and the islands of Saint Pierre and Miquelon near Newfoundland (see Volume 5).

The French Overseas Territories are the South Pacific island groups of French Polynesia, New Caledonia, and Wallis and Futuna Islands (see the article OCEANIA in Volume 2). France also claims territories on and near Antarctica, and administered the New Hebrides group jointly with the United Kingdom until it became the independent nation of Vanuatu in 1980 (see Volume 2).

Soon after the French Community was established in 1958, 12 of the African colonies became independent. For some years, economic, cultural, and defense ties were maintained among the member nations through the Community. But eventually, the African nations forged links directly among themselves and with France, and the Community ceased to exist. France's last African colony, the Afar-Issa Territory (now Djibouti), became independent in 1977. France's involvement with its former colonies has been much reduced in recent years.

The Future

In spite of changing governments, economic progress, and new and different ways of life, the essential nature of France remains unchanged. Not long ago, a prominent French citizen said, "France is not only a land, a people, and a state, it is also a spirit." On many occasions, this *esprit* has brought France to the peak of European power. It also has helped France to rise from total defeat to new life. France is a nation that brings to the future of Europe and the world a heritage of intellectual and cultural leadership and a belief in the power of human intelligence.

JEAN JOUGHIN, The American University

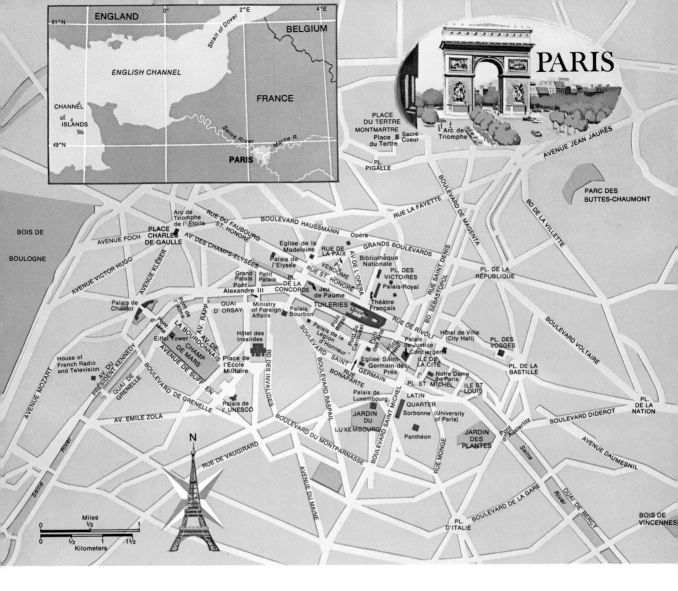

Paris

In 16th-century France, conflict between Huguenots (French Protestants) and Roman Catholics erupted into full-scale civil war. Prince Henry of Navarre, a Huguenot, was recognized as the heir to the French throne in 1589, but he had to fight to gain his kingdom. He had brilliant military successes—up to a point, for Paris refused to submit. Without Paris Henry knew he could never win the country, so in 1593 he took the only course left and gave up his Protestant faith. According to tradition, he said, "*Paris vaut bien une messe* [Paris is well worth a mass]." Within a year he was crowned King Henry IV of France.

Almost 350 years later, during World War II, a very different kind of European leader also recognized the great symbolic value of the French capital. Adolf Hitler had given orders to General Dietrich von Choltitz—his commander in German-occupied Paris—to mine many of the city's great buildings. If the Allies took Paris, the general was to light the fuses. As the Allies reached the suburbs, the time had come. But even after a personal call from Hitler in Berlin during which the Nazi leader demanded, "Is Paris burning?" the mines were not set off. Von Choltitz said later that he could not take on the responsibility of destroying a city that was such a vital part of the heritage, not only of Frenchmen, but of people everywhere.

PARIS AND ITS RIVER

What has often been called the most beautiful city in the world began about 2,000 years ago as Lutetia Parisiorum ("Lutetia of the Parisii"). Then it was a tiny community on an island in the Seine River in northwestern France. Its people, the Parisii, lived by fishing and trading. After Roman legions conquered Gaul in the 1st century B.C., the town began to expand, mainly onto the left bank of the Seine. Today Paris has more than 2 million inhabitants, and covers an area of some 41 sq. mi. (106 sq. km.) on either side of the Île de la Cité ("island of the city"), where it began.

Location on a river with access to the sea was always important to the growth of Paris. It was a trading center in its early days, and today various canals have made it a major inland port. Goods from many countries are loaded and unloaded at its docks. Barges from all over Western Europe pass under its bridges and can be seen tied up below the embankments.

The Seine is also one of the beauties of Paris, and in this role, too, it is central to the life of the city—so much so that it is easy to understand why one old song describes the river as "a lover whose beloved is Paris." Parisians and visitors alike enjoy quiet walks along its quays and embankments. Fishermen can still be seen at many locations along the Seine, though their catches are usually so small that they are thrown back. Another Seine attraction is the *bouquinistes'* stalls, found mainly along the Left Bank quays. These large stalls, filled with old books and prints, offer many happy hours of another kind of "fishing" to the stroller.

As the Seine curves through Paris, it divides the city into two sections. The Rive Droite, or Right Bank, lies north of the river, and the Rive Gauche, or Left Bank, lies to the south. A trip on the river in a *bateau mouche* (sight-seeing boat) under its *ponts* (bridges) and past many of the city's great buildings on either bank is an ideal—and restful —way for the visitor to get a feeling for the many cities that are Paris.

Île de la Cité and Île Saint-Louis. On the Île de la Cité stands the majestic Cathedral of Notre Dame, begun in the 12th century. On clear days, its soaring spires and arching buttresses cast their reflections in the rippling waters below. The sculptures on the portals of the cathedral are considered among the world's finest examples of Gothic art. The cathedral tower offers an excellent view of Paris, as well as a close-up look at the gargoyles. These grotesque stone monsters, whose fantastic horned and beaked heads are popular symbols of Paris on postcards and posters, were added to the cathedral during a 19th-century restoration.

Also on the Île de la Cité is Sainte-Chapelle, built for King Louis IX of France (Saint Louis). The 13th-century building—which actually houses two chapels—is known for its beautiful stained-glass windows,

The glowing stained-glass windows of Sainte-Chapelle—a building that is a masterpiece of Gothic architecture and one of the great beauties of Paris.

The Pont Neuf spans both arms of the Seine at the tip of the Île de la Cité.

depicting scenes from the Bible, and for its richly decorated interior. Its graceful, gilded pillars and arches form a lovely contrast to the red and blue walls and ceilings, embellished with gold fleurs-de-lis (the royal symbol of France).

Near Sainte-Chapelle is the massive Conciergerie, a building that witnessed a grim period in French history. A visit to its cells still summons up reminders of the French Revolution and of those who were imprisoned there before going to the guillotine.

Across from the Ile de la Cité is the Ile Saint-Louis. With its 17th-century mansions and quiet courtyards, it is a peaceful place in the middle of Paris, and a walk around the island is like a journey back in time.

The oldest bridge in Paris crosses the Seine near the western end of the Ile de la Cité. It is one of the many contradictions that make up Paris that the bridge is still called Pont Neuf ("new bridge"), though it was completed in 1604. Below the bridge, on the very tip of the Ile de la Cité, is the small Square du Vert Galant. Named for King Henry IV (who was called the evergreen gallant because of his lifelong interest in women), this tiny park with its sheltering trees is one of the most charming—and romantic—spots in Paris.

THE RIGHT BANK

Downstream, the next bridge across the Seine is the Pont des Arts, and on the right bank of the river are the vast buildings of the Louvre, one of the world's greatest art museums. Originally a royal palace, its halls and rooms contain countless masterpieces. The Louvre is grander than ever after a 15-year, $1.7 billion renovation completed in 1998, featuring a stunning glass pyramid designed by I.M. Pei. Among its treasures are the ancient Greek *Vénus de Milo* and *Winged Victory*; Leonardo da Vinci's *Mona Lisa*; and James McNeill Whistler's *Arrangement in Gray and Black* (better known as "Whistler's Mother").

The Louvre's impressionist and postimpressionist collections, once housed in the Jeu de Paume, former site of the royal tennis courts, are now impressively displayed in the new Musée D'Orsay, a glittering, renovated former railway station. Found there are the splendid paintings of Edouard Manet, Claude Monet, Paul Cézanne, and Paul Gauguin.

The Tuileries is a formal park, with bright flowerbeds and ancient shade trees, and it makes a lovely oasis amid the city's bustle. Parisians and visitors alike enjoy strolling there, often stopping for a drink or a snack. For children, the gardens offer pony rides, miniature carousels, and other activities. Toy boats can be rented; seen against Paris' blue skies, their white and scarlet sails echo the colors of the French flag.

A few steps from the Tuileries is the Place de la Concorde. This great square, with its fountains and statues representing eight French cities, is one of the most beautiful in the world. It also has some of the world's most notorious traffic jams, which even the Paris police have difficulty unsnarling. In 1793, during the French Revolution, the guillotine was set up in the square. Louis XVI and his queen, Marie Antoinette, were only two of its many victims.

The Place de la Concorde faces the broad, tree-lined and café-lined Avenue des Champs-Elysées, which stretches 1.25 mi. (2 km.) to the Place Charles de Gaulle, with the Arc de Triomphe at its center. This structure, the world's largest triumphal arch, was begun in 1806 as a memorial to Napoleonic victories. In its shadow an eternal light burns over the tomb of the French Unknown Soldier. Though there is an elevator, many visitors seem to prefer climbing the dark, 164-foot (50 meters) winding staircase to the roof. The view from the top of the arch is excellent, and it also explains the former name of the place, l'Étoile, because 12 wide avenues radiate from it like the points of a star. (*Étoile* means "star.")

Every Bastille Day (July 14) the tricolor is seen all along the Champs-Élysées, and a brilliant military parade is held there. Tanks bearing the names of great French generals and victories thunder down the avenue, followed by field artillery and *pompiers* (fire engines). The horsemen of the Garde Républicaine ride by, their spurs jingling and their golden helmets flashing in the sun.

The streets branching off the Champs-Élysées are lined by many of the elegant hotels, restaurants, and theaters for which Paris is known. Many of the houses of *haute couture* ("high fashion") that have made Paris a world fashion center are located there as well. In the 19th century, an Englishman named Charles Frederick Worth opened a dressmaking shop on the Rue de la Paix. When Empress Eugénie (wife of Napoleon III) began to patronize Worth, a Worth gown—and soon a Paris gown—became a symbol of style, elegance, and luxury. Fashion became an important Paris industry. Today, for many women a trip to Paris would be incomplete without a stop at the fashion houses of Dior, Chanel, Givenchy, St. Laurent, or any one of at least a dozen others.

Paris' most elegant street, however, is the Rue du Faubourg-St. Honoré, which starts near the Place Vendôme. Site of the Élysée Palace, home of French presidents, the street is best-known for its shopping. Both

The magnificent fountains in the Place de la Concorde are copies of those at St. Peter's Square in Rome.

Bastille Day. Jet smoke trails paint the tricolor across the Paris sky.

sides are lined with shops offering a dazzling array of fine goods to tempt the shopper and collector. From the graceful symmetry of the Place Vendôme, with its column built from cannons captured in the Napoleonic victory at the battle of Austerlitz (1805), it is only a short walk to the Madeleine. This massive church, designed like a Roman temple, was built as a "temple of glory" for Napoleon and his armies. To the east, down the Boulevard de la Madeleine, is another landmark, the Opéra. The ornate, 19th-century building has long been a magnet for music lovers from all over the world.

Nearby are the Grands Boulevards—a series of wide avenues that run roughly from the Place de la Concorde to the Place de la Bastille. The avenues include the Boulevard de la Madeleine, the Boulevard des Capucines, and the Boulevard des Italiens. These streets, too, are known for their cafés, restaurants, movie houses, theaters, and shops. Two of the largest department stores in Paris—the Galeries Lafayette and Au Printemps—are located on the Boulevard Haussmann. This avenue was named for Baron Georges Haussmann, who was appointed prefect of the Seine by Napoleon III in 1853. Under Haussmann's direction many of Paris' streets were widened to relieve traffic congestion, and new connecting avenues were laid out. The city was divided into 20 arrondissements for more efficient administration. Haussmann is also remembered for his modernization of the Paris sewers, and even today a trip through the *égouts* in a boat is one of the most curious ways a visitor can get to know Paris. A memorable scene in Victor Hugo's 19th-century novel *Les Misérables* involves a chase through their dank depths. The sewers also carry the city's telephone and telegraph cables as well as the complex network of the *pneumatiques*—tubes through which letters, in metal containers, are transmitted rapidly by compressed air.

South of the Grands Boulevards is another Paris attraction. At the Comédie-Française, the French national theater, the works of great classic

The Champs-Élysées, Paris's finest avenue, is lined with busy cafés, shops, hotels, and theaters.

playwrights are produced. The spot also has other associations, for Joan of Arc was wounded here in 1429, during the Hundred Years War.

At the eastern end of the Grands Boulevards, near the very old section of Paris called the Marais, is the Place de la Bastille. Nothing remains there of the ancient royal prison—symbol of the oppressive power of the French monarchy—that was attacked on July 14, 1789, signalling the beginning of the French Revolution. Only a column commemorating the 1830 and 1848 revolutions marks the spot today.

Also near the Grands Boulevards is the Forum des Halles, a modern leisure complex of glass and concrete, containing shops, cafés, restaurants, and movie houses. The Forum was opened in 1979. For eight centuries the site had been occupied by Les Halles, the central meat, fish, and produce market that the 19th-century author Emile Zola called *le ventre de Paris* ("the belly of Paris"). No longer able to handle the vast volume of goods, the ancient market was moved to the suburbs in 1969, and two years later its old iron pavilions, dating from the mid-19th century, were torn down.

Close by the new Forum, on Rue St. Martin, stands the ultra-modern Georges Pompidou National Center of Art and Culture, named after the second president of the Fifth Republic. When it opened in 1977, its architecture, with its visible plumbing and electrical pipes, transparent escalators and elevators, and prominent structural beams, was a shock to many conservative tastes. The building houses the National Museum of Modern Art, an industrial design center, a large public library, research facilities, and a children's workshop. Besides the attractions of its excellent collections and temporary exhibits, the Beaubourg Center, as it is generally known, has already become a focal point where street artists, musicians, and mimes ply their trades to throngs of *les vrai Parisiens* ("true Parisians") and tourists alike.

Les Halles' new location covers some 1,540 acres (623 hectares) at Rungis near Orly Airport, south of the city. Orly is among the world's busiest international airports. With its modern facilities, shops, restaurants, and hotels, it has been described as a self-sufficient city. North of Paris, at Roissy, is the new Charles de Gaulle Airport. Larger than Orly, it is in the same category in terms of air traffic. Closer to Paris is the city's domestic airport, Le Bourget.

THE LEFT BANK

For many visitors to Paris, the essence of the city is still found on the left bank of the Seine. Since the 13th century, when the Sorbonne (now part of the Universities of Paris) was founded there, the Left Bank has traditionally been the students' section of the city. The area was also called the Latin Quarter because Latin was the universal language of learning in the Middle Ages.

Much of the life of the Latin Quarter centers around the wide Boulevard Saint Michel, known affectionately as the Boul' Mich. Its many cafés are popular with students, who often meet there to discuss their work. Just off the Boul' Mich is the Palais du Luxembourg, built in the 17th century for Marie de Médicis, widow of Henry IV. The Jardin du Luxembourg (Luxembourg Garden), with its lake, terraces, and flowerbeds, is also a favorite spot for students.

Another focus of Left-Bank activity is the Boulevard Saint-Germain, which intersects the Boul' Mich. The boulevard takes its name from the oldest church in Paris, Saint-Germain-des-Prés, begun in the 10th century. The church contains the tombstones of several famous Frenchmen, including the 17th-century philosopher René Descartes. Near the church, there is a bust by Pablo Picasso dedicated to the 20th-century poet Guillaume Apollinaire.

At the cafés and brasseries in the area the visitor can have an espresso or *une fine* (one of France's excellent brandies) while he enjoys all the activity and bustle going on around him. The narrow streets of the Left Bank are also fun for the visitor, for they are a shopper's delight, abounding with antique shops, bookstores, and art galleries. Every year, too, there are more and more of the tiny boutiques that sell inexpensive young fashions that bear the unmistakable stamp of Paris.

One of the city's best-known sights is the Panthéon, atop the hill of Saint Genevieve. Begun during the reign of King Louis XV, the building was to be dedicated to Genevieve, the patron saint of Paris. However, after its completion in 1789, the revolutionary government decided to turn the building into a *panthéon,* from the ancient Greek word for "a temple of all the gods." Great Frenchmen—the "gods" of their time—were buried there, from the politician Mirabeau to the philosophers Voltaire and Jean Jacques Rousseau. In the 19th century, the authors Victor Hugo and Emile Zola, and the teacher Louis Braille, who developed a method by which the blind can read and write, were interred in the Panthéon.

Another Left-Bank landmark is the Hôtel des Invalides, founded by Louis XIV in the 17th century as a home for disabled soldiers. Today it houses one of the world's largest military museums. But the building is best-known as the final resting place of the last remains of Napoleon, brought back from the South Atlantic island of St. Helena and placed there in 1840. Many people still visit the tomb of the man who brought France both glory and disaster, and who played such a central role in the history of the world.

The huge complex also includes two churches, one with a chapel dedicated to Napoleon. On sunny days, the Invalides' gilded dome, with its tall spire piercing the sky, is one of the most striking sights in Paris. The best view is from the right bank of the Seine, across the broad Pont Alexandre III, built in 1900.

The Métro

No one can truly say he or she knows Paris without having traveled on the Métro (short for Métropolitain). The Paris subway system was opened in 1900, and today its total length is well over 100 mi. (160 km.). The Métro is one of the most efficient subways in the world. Its stations are clean and brightly lit, and have easy-to-follow maps that make it simple—even for foreigners—to reach any destination. At the Louvre station, reproductions of paintings adorn the walls and replicas of famous sculptures stand in niches along the platforms. The high-tech line, number 14, between Madeleine and the new National Library, was opened in 1998; it is fully automated and runs without an engineer.

Montmartre

One favorite trip for Parisians and visitors alike is out to Sacré-Coeur—the Basilica of the Sacred Heart—high on the Butte de Montmartre (Montmartre hill) in northern Paris. At a centrally located Right-Bank station, such as the one at Concorde, the Métro rider buys a ticket for the Porte de la Chapelle line. (Like most Métro lines, it is named for its last stop, one of the ancient gates of Paris.) He gets off at the Abbesses stop, in Montmartre. Near the pleasant, tree-lined Place des Abbesses, a funicular climbs the hill to the lower terraces of Sacré-Coeur.

The white domes of this church have been a symbol of Paris since 1914. After the overwhelming French defeat in the Franco-Prussian War (1870–71), French Catholics started a national fund for a church of the Sacred Heart. The church was to be a symbol of French hope and a new beginning. Some 50 years—and 40 million francs—later, the huge building was consecrated. Statues of Saint Louis (King Louis IX) and Joan of Arc stand on the upper terrace, above a steep flight of steps leading to the entrance of the Basilica. Sacré-Coeur's steeple contains the Savoyarde, a 19-ton bell that is one of the largest and deepest-sounding in the world.

But there is more to Montmartre than Sacré-Coeur. The community on the hill is one of the oldest and most picturesque sections of Paris, and since the mid-19th century, it has been the home of countless artists and painters. One of the best-known was Maurice Utrillo, whose charming paintings of Montmartre's ancient, winding streets, usually with the domes of Sacré-Coeur in the background, captured the atmosphere of the area for people everywhere. Perhaps because of all the artists who lived—and still live—in Montmartre, it is also known for its night life. The cafés around the Place du Tertre are crowded every evening, as are

The whole panorama of Paris can be seen from the terraces of Sacré-Coeur.

the nearby nightclubs and dance halls of the Place Pigalle. The Moulin de la Galette, formerly a windmill, is one of these.

The Two Bois

Visitors can also ride the Métro out to the two *bois* ("woods") of Paris—the Bois de Boulogne in the west and the Bois de Vincennes in the southeast. The Bois de Boulogne, with its ancient trees, was a favorite spot for walks *à la campagne* ("in the country") as long ago as the 17th century. By the mid-19th century, Paris had grown outward until it reached the edge of the Bois. In 1852, Napoleon III gave the forest to the city. Because Napoleon admired everything English, Baron Haussmann based his designs for the Bois on London's Hyde Park. Shady paths wind through the trees and around the Bois' two lakes, where rowboats can be rented. Paris families often spend Sundays in the Bois, enjoying a picnic they have brought along. There are also several outdoor restaurants in the Bois, and nothing could be more pleasant than a peaceful lunch outdoors, watching the ever-changing patterns of the sunlight through the leaves and finishing the last of the wine. The Bois de Boulogne also contains an amusement park, a zoo, and the two Paris racetracks, Longchamp and Auteuil.

Some 9 mi. (15 km.) across Paris to the southeast is the Bois de Vincennes, with its 14th-century castle. Among those who died in the castle dungeons was King Henry V of England, in 1422. The Bois de Vincennes is also the home of the Paris Zoo, where most of the animals live in large enclosures that resemble their natural environments.

The Suburbs of Paris

Surrounding the city on all sides are its many suburbs. In the northern suburbs, industrial equipment and chemicals are produced. Farther west, along the Seine, are the Citroën and Renault plants—the two largest automobile manufacturers in France. The huge Euro Disneyland complex, opened in 1992, is located in Marne-la-Vallée, about 20 mi. (32 km.) to the west of the city proper. Most French movies are made in the southern suburbs of Boulogne-Billancourt and Joinville-le-Pont. Paris is constantly expanding, and each year finds new housing developments—and often whole new towns—growing up farther and farther away from the city center.

CITY OF LIGHT

The great capital is the center of France in every way. It is the country's biggest city. All major French roads begin or end there. It is the center of the French railway network, and some 1 million travelers use its *gares,* or stations, daily. It has the largest airport and is the focus of one of the biggest industrial complexes in the country. It is also the seat of government, from which the country is run. In all these ways, Paris can be compared to a huge, powerful magnet.

But the most fitting description of Paris is still as *la ville lumière,* the City of Light, for the capital is also like a great lamp, whose rays reach far beyond the city's boundaries. The decisions made in Paris, and the ideas born there, affect all of France. The city is the intellectual center of France —and, by extension, of much of Europe. Most of the 18,500 books published in France annually come from Paris, and many of them are written there as well. The country's most important newspapers, such as *France-Soir, Le Figaro,* and *Le Monde,* and its leading magazines, such as *Paris Match* and *L'Express,* are published there. It is the home of the French radio and television industry.

Because it is a city of ideas, with an atmosphere of freedom of thought, many international organizations have made Paris their headquarters. One of these, UNESCO (United Nations Educational, Scientific, and Cultural Organization), has added something special to the city. Besides its unusual architecture (it is shaped like a three-pointed star), the UNESCO building has paintings by Picasso and Rufino Tamayo, a contemporary Mexican artist; sculptures by Henry Moore of England and mobiles by Alexander Calder of the United States; and outdoor murals done in enamel by the Spaniards Joan Miró and Josep Artigas.

Across the Seine, past the level green fields of the Champ de Mars, and past the Eiffel Tower, is the Palais de Chaillot. Today the palace houses several museums, and in the years after World War II, some of the first meetings of the United Nations were held there.

The Eiffel Tower in Paris, erected in 1889 from more than 12,000 wrought-iron parts, is 1,056 ft. tall.

The Eiffel Tower

The Eiffel Tower was designed by the French engineer Alexandre Gustave Eiffel for the Paris Universal Exhibition of 1889. Originally considered an ugly blot on the city's landscape, the tower was almost torn down several times, but it eventually became the city's best-loved landmark. On clear days the view from the top extends more than 42 mi. (67 km.) over the many cities that are Paris—the Paris of some 2.5 million tourists per year, with its hotels, fine restaurants, and museums; and the Paris of some 2 million Parisians, as rich and varied as life itself. Traditionally, just before sunset is the best time to visit the tower. Then, for the people who love it, the City of Light takes on a special glow. A 16th-century Parisian, the essayist Michel de Montaigne, proclaimed that he was a Frenchman only because of the great city, which he called "the glory of France and one of the greatest ornaments of the world."

Reviewed by RÉGINALD DE WARREN, Counselor
Embassy of France to the United States, Washington, D.C.

Monaco, a principality on the Mediterranean, draws thousands of tourists to its famous beaches and casino.

MONACO

Monaco is the playground for the elite of Europe and home to the Grand Prix auto race, the Monte Carlo casino, and a celebrity royal family.

LAND AND PEOPLE

Monaco, surrounded on three sides by France, occupies only 0.7 sq. mi. (1.9 sq. km.)—about half of the area of New York City's Central Park. The land forms a natural amphitheater as it slopes from rocky cliffs to the country's 3-mi. (5 km.)-long coastline—the Côte d'Azur, or "azure coast." The principality enjoys about 300 sunny days a year.

About 85 percent of residents are noncitizens, mostly French and Italian. Roman Catholicism is the official religion, and the veneration of Saint Devote, a 4th-century woman martyr, is the most popular religious tradition. Education is compulsory for ages 6 through 16.

WAY OF LIFE

The capital, **Monaco-Ville,** is on a rocky promontory, more than 200 ft. (60 m.) above sea level. There, in addition to the castle, is the world-famous Oceanographic Museum, founded by Prince Albert I, the great-grandfather of the present prince. A fine scientist, Prince Albert

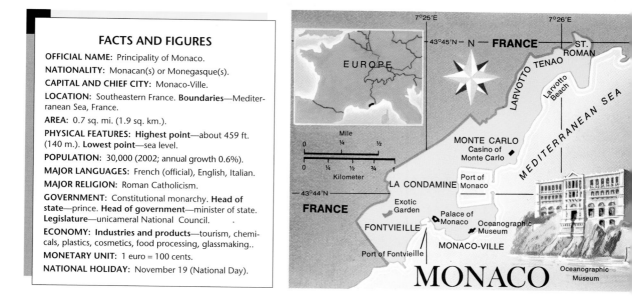

started Monaco on its way to becoming a center for modern oceanographic research. Albert also began the Exotic Gardens, which grow on the slopes of a rocky cliff. The gardens contain one of the world's finest collections of subtropical and semidesert flora.

This little country offers a great variety of sporting and cultural events. There is the Monaco Grand Prix, an annual event in which some of the world's greatest automobile racers speed through the hilly, winding city streets. The opera house, which is a part of the Grand Casino building, was the scene of the original presentations by the famed Ballets Russes de Monte Carlo of some of the masterpieces produced by the great choreographer Sergei Diaghilev. It was also the site of the first productions of a number of world-renowned operas.

Monaco is the site of an imaginative urban-renewal program. In 1964, the railroad that ran through Monaco was rerouted underground. The entire seafront area was rebuilt, and an area of 1,000,000 sq. ft. (93,000

The Monte Carlo Casino, off-limits to the native Monegasques, provides three percent of Monaco's revenue.

square meters) of land was reclaimed from the sea by filling in the shore-line with soil from nearby French hillsides and with rock from the 2-mi. (3-km.) underground tunnel that was blasted out of a hillside to accommodate the railroad. A new highway was constructed, and new hotels, apartments, and restaurants were built. The program continued with a larger reclaimed area beyond the rock, which provided additional industrial sites and more land for high-rise luxury hotels. They house visitors who come to this miniature nation where, as Colette, the famous French novelist, said, the "frontiers are only flowers."

ECONOMY

The economic life of Monaco is based on the same ingenuity that has kept the country independent all these years. This is a state that has no national debt, very limited income taxes, and no taxes on inheritances.

What is the basis for the fiscal magic? Profits from tourists who flock here to enjoy the unfailingly delightful weather are most important. For most of the year, the streets of Monaco are filled with foreigners, and the sparkling waters of the harbor are full of pleasure craft flying flags from countries all over the world. The government also profits from the sale of tobacco, and from sales, customs, and business taxes.

A large amount of revenue comes from the sale of postage stamps. Ever since Monaco's first stamps were issued in 1860, collectors have prized the many artistic series illustrating the principality's famous landmarks and its major activities.

At one time, Monte Carlo's glittering casino accounted for three-quarters of Monaco's revenue, but it is now much less. Despite limited space, the principality has a prosperous industrial community in the section called Fontvielle, near the western boundary. There, cosmetics, perfumes, elegant clothing, jewelry, fine art books, chocolates, and small precision instruments are produced. The bustling business section around the port is called La Condamine.

HISTORY AND GOVERNMENT

The coat of arms of the Grimaldi Family, showing two monks with raised swords, commemorates the capture of the fortress. In 1297, François ("the Malicious") Grimaldi, a member of a powerful family that had been exiled from Genoa, Italy, came to the gate of the town disguised as a monk and begged admittance. An armed band entered with him and conquered the town. Since then Monaco has belonged to the Grimaldis, except for a few brief periods; one of them was from 1793 until 1814, when Monaco was annexed to France.

Since the early 20th century, Monaco has been a constitutional monarchy. If the reigning prince should die without a male heir, the principality would be incorporated into France. For a while the people in Monaco worried that this might happen, but in 1956, the prince, Rainier III, married Grace Kelly, a popular American actress. Three children were born: Princess Caroline, Prince Albert (heir apparent), and Princess Stephanie. In 1982, Princess Grace died in a tragic auto accident. In 1999, Prince Rainier celebrated the 50th anniversary of his reign. The constitution of 1962 provides for an elected 18-member National Council, which shares both legislative and executive power with the prince.

M.A. PALMARO and PAUL CHOISIT, Consulat General de Monaco, New York

Picturesque Esch-sur-Sûre, in Luxembourg's Ardennes region, dates from the Middle Ages.

LUXEMBOURG

To the tourist's first glance, the Grand Duchy of Luxembourg appears a fairy-tale kingdom. Beautiful towns and more than 120 medieval castles dot a romantic landscape of forested hills and rocky gorges. The capital, Luxembourg city, is an ancient fortress with great battlements and tunnels known as the Casemates. Yet the tiny country, about the size of Rhode Island, is very much of the modern world. One of the leading steel producers of Europe, Luxembourg has become a communications center and more recently a banking and insurance center.

THE LAND

Wedged between Belgium, France, and Germany, Luxembourg possesses two distinct geographic regions. In the north is the upland of the Ardennes; its most spectacular section is called Petite Suisse, meaning Little Switzerland. Mountainous and heavily wooded, with dramatic ravines and twisting rivers, it holds much game, including partridge and wild boar.

A smaller section in the south is the Bon Pays, or Good Land. Although not especially fertile, the land produces good crops of potatoes, oats, rye, wheat, corn, and roses. Some dairy products are exported. The southwest tip of the duchy contains a rich supply of iron ore and sufficient limestone (used in steel mills) to make the nation a steel-producing power.

Luxembourg city, the capital, is headquarters of the Grand Duchy's sizable steel industry.

The Our, Sûre, and Moselle rivers mark the long border with Germany on the east. Many other streams drain the Ardennes; the capital is located on the Alzette, which rises in France. For generations, Luxembourg has relied on its excellent railroad system for commercial shipping. Canalization of the Moselle in the 1960s connected the duchy to the waterways of the Rhine system and brought construction of a port at Mertert. The climate is mild, without great heat or severe cold, although the average winter temperature is below freezing. Rain falls often; in the Ardennes region, snow accumulates in the winter.

Vianden, a town near Germany, stands beneath one of many medieval castles found in Luxembourg.

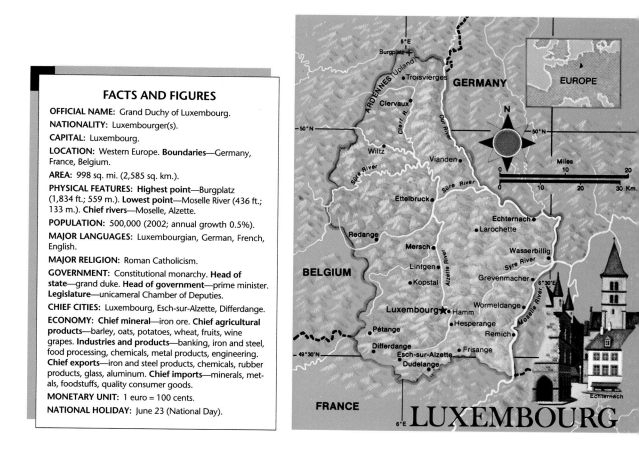

THE PEOPLE

A Luxembourg saying proclaims: "We wish to remain what we are." The motto reflects the Luxembourgers' confidence in their way of life and desire for independence. Their native dialect of German known as Luxembourgian (Letzeburgisch) is the first official language of the country. German is the chief language of the press and of the primary schools. All children also learn French from the first grade on, and soon add English. French predominates in secondary schools, the civil service, and parliament. Most Luxembourgers are thus trilingual or even quatrilingual. There are several agricultural institutes and one university, but most students seeking higher education must go abroad to study.

Everywhere in the strongly Roman Catholic nation there is a sense of stability. The people like hiking, fishing, hunting, movies, and eating their famous good foods. These range from the white wines of the Moselle region to sausages, pâtés, wild game, and fresh trout.

A large majority of the population resides in the south, nearly 20 percent in the capital. The population growth rate is low. Demand for additional labor in times of peak steel production is met by numbers of guest workers, especially from Italy and Portugal.

THE ECONOMY

For all its greenery, Luxembourg is highly industrialized, with considerable prosperity and high per-capita income. Agriculture involves only 2.5 percent of the population and makes up roughly 1 percent of the gross domestic product (GDP).

At one time, the iron and steel industry represented up to four-fifths of the total value of exports, but by the early 21st century, the duchy's economic strength depended mostly on financial services and the activities of various intra-European political organizations. In 2000, Luxembourg had the world's highest density of personal computers: 73 machines for every 100 persons.

The service sector of the economy employs about 83 percent of the duchy's work force. The greatest growth has taken place in banking and insurance. Luxembourg's central location in Europe, multilingual staff, political stability, and laws protecting secrecy of accounts and records lure foreign banks and money to Luxembourg. It is now the seventh largest financial center in the world, where more than 250 banks have set up their offices. The chief financial institution of the European Union, the European Investment Bank, is located in the capital. International insurance companies are also clustered in the duchy.

Although the European Parliament meets in Strasbourg, France, its Secretariat is located in Luxembourg, as are the European Court of Justice, the Court of Auditors, and the offices of numerous European Union (EU) commissions. Powerful Radio Luxembourg, a commercial station, is the duchy's single largest taxpayer.

HISTORY AND GOVERNMENT

It was in A.D. 963 that Siegfried, Count of the Ardennes, acquired by barter the site of a Roman fortress overlooking the Alzette. Lucilinburhunc—or "little fort," as the Celts called it—grew as Siegfried's dynasty became established until it was the "Gibraltar of the North." In 1815, after centuries of both independence and domination by various states, Luxembourg was declared a grand duchy by the Great Powers. Portions of the duchy joined with the Belgians in their revolt against the Netherlands. The current borders were set by treaty in 1839.

A crisis over the possible sale of Luxembourg to France led the powers in 1867 to declare and guarantee the duchy's neutrality. After German invasions in 1914 and 1940, the duchy abandoned neutrality in 1949 and joined the North Atlantic Treaty Organization (NATO).

Luxembourg supports European integration. It became part of the Belgian-Netherlands-Luxembourg (Benelux) Economic Union in 1948, and the European Economic Community (now the EU) in 1957. The duchy maintains only a small army.

The Grand Duchy of Luxembourg is a constitutional monarchy. The succession rules for the House of Nassau-Weilburg brought the separation of Luxembourg from the Dutch throne in 1890. Under the Constitution of 1868 and its amendments, the grand duke serves as head of state, while the parliamentary government is led by the prime minister. In October 2000, the reigning grand duke abdicated in favor of his son, Henri. The ministerial Council of Government is responsible to the elected Chamber of Deputies, consisting of 60 members. An advisory Council of State is appointed by the grand duke for life. Among the other advisory bodies is the Social and Economic Council, a committee that evaluates all of the duchy's projects and proposals. Elections generally lead to coalition governments formed alternately by two of the following parties: the Christian Social Party, the Socialist Workers' Party, and the Democratic Party.

JONATHAN E. HELMREICH, Allegheny College

Bruges, now mainly noted for its lovely canals and bridges, was a leading commercial city in the Middle Ages.

BELGIUM

The greatest distance between two points in Belgium is just 175 miles (280 kilometers). Yet this small country, only slightly larger than the state of Maryland, hosts great cultural and economic diversity; and its history reflects much of the history of Western Europe.

The northern portion of the country, somewhat more than half, is known as Flanders. This is the home of the Flemings, who speak a variety of Dutch. The southern region is Wallonia, and its French-speaking people are called Walloons. Differences between these groups have grown ever sharper since Belgium gained independence from the United Netherlands in 1830. In recent years those differences have forced the government into a form of federalism. The country has three primary subdivisions: Flanders, with about 7 percent of the population; Wallonia, with a third of the population; and bilingual Brussels, the capital and home for about 10 percent of the citizens. The Flemings and Walloons each have their separate cultural communities, as does a small group of German-speaking Belgians in the east.

Despite, or perhaps because of, its own nationality differences, Belgium is a leader in international cooperation. The European Union, the North Atlantic Treaty Organization (NATO), the Belgian-Netherlands-Luxembourg Economic Union (Benelux), and other international agencies have offices in or near Brussels. So, too, do many international businesses and banks. For many Europeans, Brussels has actually become a symbol of the new unifying Europe. Long famous for castles, refined art, music and ballet, and culinary delights, Belgium was also a leader in the 19th-century industrialization of the continent. Modern shipping communications, financial activities, and machinery and chemical production today augment the traditional income derived from textiles, specialized agriculture, tourism, glass manufacture, and the declining coal, iron, and steel industries. The mix of ancient culture, pleasant modern living, dynamic trade, international cooperation, and the challenge of accommodation of linguistic differences give Belgium political significance and cultural and economic excitement much greater than its size.

THE LAND

Belgium is a country of lowlands and low plateaus that rise gently from sea level along the North Sea coast to a high point at Botrange, located in the extreme east near the German border. Geographically, Belgium may be divided into three land areas. To the north there is a 42-mi. (67-km.) coast on the North Sea. This area of wide beaches and dunes, where fashionable and popular seaside resorts are located, stretches south to a low plain of rich farmland drained by canals and protected by dikes. Polders, land long ago reclaimed from the salt marshes and protected by dikes, add close to 200 sq. mi. (520 sq. km.) of fertile grazing areas. These blend with another low, sandy, marshy region to the east known as the Campine.

Central Belgium is the most populous area and the site of Brussels and other important cities. Higher than the coastal region, it has rolling fields and rich soil. The coal seams and iron ore deposits of the Borinage sector in its south nourished the early development of Belgium's steel industry; their exhaustion has brought severe unemployment.

South and east of the Meuse River is a higher plateau that reaches its greatest height at Botrange (2,283 ft.; 696 m.) in the Ardennes. The woods and hills of the Ardennes, although providing lovely landscapes and good hiking and hunting, are not sufficient to block invasion. The lack of natural boundaries has greatly affected Belgium's history. Despite the elevation of the Ardennes, the altitude of the country as a whole is just over 525 ft. (160 m.); the eastern third averages only 60 ft. (18 m.) above sea level. No wonder that Belgium, like the Netherlands, is called a Low Country.

Belgium's Rivers

Rivers contributed to Belgium's early success as a trading center and to its continuing prosperity in the transshipment trade. The two largest, the Scheldt (or Schelde) and the Meuse, rise in France, flow through Belgium to the Netherlands, and empty into the North Sea. These rivers

FACTS AND FIGURES

OFFICIAL NAME: Kingdom of Belgium.

NATIONALITY: Belgian(s).

CAPITAL: Brussels.

LOCATION: Northwestern Europe. **Boundaries**—North Sea, Netherlands, Germany, Luxembourg, France.

AREA: 11,780 sq. mi. (30,510 sq. km.).

PHYSICAL FEATURES: Highest point—Signal de Botrange (2,277 ft.; 694 m.). **Lowest point**—sea level. **Chief rivers**—Scheldt, Meuse, Lys.

POPULATION: 10,300,000 (2002; annual growth 0.12%).

MAJOR LANGUAGES: Flemish (Dutch), French, German.

MAJOR RELIGIONS: Roman Catholicism, Protestantism.

GOVERNMENT: Constitutional hereditary monarchy. **Head of state**—king. **Head of government**—prime minister. **Legislature**—bicameral Parliament.

CHIEF CITIES: Brussels, Antwerp, Ghent, Liège.

ECONOMY: Chief minerals—coal, natural gas. **Chief agricultural products**—sugar beets, fresh vegetables. **Industries and products**—engineering and metal products, processed food and beverages, chemicals, motor vehicle assembly, basic metals, textiles. **Chief exports**—iron, steel, automobiles, petroleum products, diamonds. **Chief imports**—fuels, foodstuffs, chemicals, grains.

MONETARY UNIT: 1 euro = 100 cents.

NATIONAL HOLIDAY: July 21 (National Day).

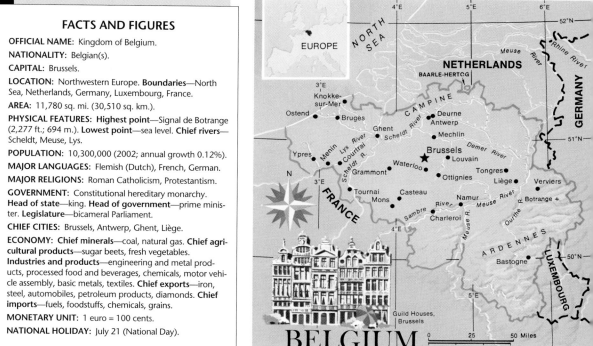

have been linked by canals to the Rhine and other waterways. The great harbor of Antwerp, located well inland on the Scheldt, is an important port of entry to the continent for goods from Britain and has prompted that nation's solicitude for Belgian independence.

The North Sea affects Belgium's climate, as the proximity of the warm Gulf Stream keeps winter from being too harsh; snowfall, except in the Ardennes, is usually light. Winds from the sea keep summers cool and bring frequent clouds and showers. There may be flashes of bright sun each day, but rain falls some 150 to 200 days each year.

THE PEOPLE

The region we now call Belgium was probably first settled by tribes of Celts. Julius Caesar and later Romans conquered much of the area. They so established their influence in the southern portion of Belgium that, even though tribes from across the Rhine later conquered Gaul, the Latinized tongue of Wallonia was not replaced by the Germanic speech of the Frankish invaders.

The Flemings and the Walloons

The line of linguistic demarcation separating the Flemings and Walloons originally ran from near Boulogne in France to Cologne in Germany. Along the coast it has shifted north and now coincides with the French-Belgian border; inland, it has moved south. Traditional stereotypes picture the Fleming as unemotional and the Walloon as excitable. The Fleming has been historically more active in the life of the Roman Catholic Church; the Walloon attends Mass less regularly. Protestant and Jewish congregations in either region are not numerous. Flanders has a markedly higher birthrate than that of Wallonia. Historically,

Flemings have tended to prefer closer ties to Britain, while the Walloons have looked to France for support.

Many old distinctions between Fleming and Walloon, especially those concerning style of life, are increasingly less valid in modern Belgian society because they were based on economic status differences that are rapidly disappearing. In the years after the nation's founding, Walloons dominated government, commerce, and the professions. Dutch-speaking citizens were tried in courts conducted entirely in French, and Walloons considered Flemish a language spoken only by the working class. Flemings served primarily as laborers and developed a simple way of life. This included cooking based on stews, sausage, potatoes, and beans that is praised and practiced today for its nourishment and flavor. In 1898 the Dutch language won equality with French as the legal language of the country and its laws. Money and postage stamps were printed in Dutch and French.

Expansion of the right to vote gave Flemings a greater voice in politics in the period between the world wars. Better organized and angry over social and economic inequities, the Flemings pressed their demands. In 1921 the linguistic regions were officially separated. The government drew an imaginary line along the traditional language boundary from the western border near Menin to the eastern border east of Tongres. North of the line was decreed to be Dutch-speaking; south, French-speaking. The capital region of Brussels became a bilingual region, though at present it is more than 20 miles (32 kilometers) north of the linguistic border. The city center is still predominantly French, but the working class is Flemish (or increasingly consists of foreigners such as Turks and Indians), and many suburbs are Flemish speaking. The University of Ghent was changed to a Flemish-speaking institution. Laws of 1932 and 1935 decreed that government offices, courts, schools, and business were to be conducted only in the language of the area. A child in a state school must be taught in Dutch north of the line and in French south of the line. In Brussels, children study in either French or Dutch, according to whichever language is used in the home.

In the late 1960's, a bitter dispute centering around the University of Louvain caused the fall of the government. Louvain, the world's largest Catholic university, was founded in 1425. Situated just inside the Flemish border, it continued to teach in French but introduced a Dutch section. This did not satisfy the Flemings. Riots and strikes led to a parliamentary decision to divide the ancient university and to build a new French section just inside Walloon territory.

In 1980 the Belgian parliament passed a law establishing regional assemblies in Dutch-speaking Flanders and French-speaking Wallonia. These bodies control local matters such as culture, health, roads, and urban projects. Although intermarriage and national economic and defense concerns tie the linguistic groups together, their rivalry remains strong. It continues to cause the fall of government cabinets, most of which are carefully balanced coalitions among representatives of the two linguistic groups as well as among political parties. Such was the case in 1987, when the elected mayor of a commune in the Flemish zone that contained numerous French-speaking residents refused to conduct official business in Dutch, although familiar with the tongue. The issue became one of national proportion and brought the prime minister's resignation. The politician agreed in 1989 not to run again, permitting the issue to fade from prominence.

The Belgian Way of Life

The Belgians are hard workers, with little respect for idleness. They are politically aware, and illiteracy is almost unknown. In the many small cafés at which they gather with their friends after working hours, they will discuss politics and movies and read the particular newspaper that matches their political views. Circles of acquaintances may be large, but intimate friendships are limited, usually formed in childhood years and maintained throughout life. Belgians are very attached to their neighborhoods, homes, and well-tended vegetable gardens; rather than move, they prefer to commute some distance to work on their well-run network of railways and trolley cars.

The Belgians are especially fond of music and sports. Symphonies, piano and violin competitions, noon musicales, opera, choral ensembles, driving rock and jazz, and village brass bands are all part of the musical scene. Professional bicyclists and soccer teams are cheered. At the local level, there are organized clubs for bicyclists, motorcyclists, soccer, chess, and the like. A favorite lunchtime break is a game of *boules* (a form of lawn bowling). Festivals based on history, legend, and religion are widely enjoyed and involve many participants. Some, such as the procession of the Holy Blood in Bruges, the march of the Gilles at Binch, the Procession of Giants at Ath, *Ommegang* at Brussels, *Lumeçon* at Mons, and numerous carnivals before or at mid-Lent have become tourist attractions. In good weather, the Belgians love to walk and picnic in parks, such as the Soignes Forest outside Brussels, or camp in the Ardennes. During other parts of the year, they may seek vacations and sunny weather in Italy or Spain.

Belgians eat well; their cooking is world-famous. Fresh fish is available everywhere—mussels, shrimp, oysters, sole, turbot, trout, and eels. There are specialties, such as Flemish *waterzooï,* a rich soup made with vegetables and chicken; Ardennes ham; specially grown grapes, strawberries, and endive; eels in green garlic sauce; and an incredible array of sausages and pâtés. Traditional mainstays include beefsteak, mussels, and french fried potatoes, and *carbonnade flamande* (a beef stew cooked in beer). More beer per capita is consumed in Belgium than in any other country; more than 300 varieties are brewed. Desserts may include fruit tarts; delicate pancakes called *crepes,* filled with jelly; *cramique,* a raisin bread; *pain d'épices,* a type of gingerbread; or many other delightful pastries and cakes.

CITIES

Within Europe, Belgium is second only to the Netherlands in population density. Many quiet towns dot the countryside. It is in the great cities of Belgium, however, that is found the mix of history, well-developed culture, and modern industrialization, technology, and commerce that identifies the country today.

Brussels. In the heart of Brussels stands the Grand' Place, one of the great municipal squares of the world. Just blocks from its Gothic stone towers, skyscraper hotels soar and European Union agencies and the Royal Library are housed in modern concrete architecture. To the west, neon

Imposing Gothic buildings dominate the Grand' Place, the center of Brussels' commercial district.

lights shine on lengthy streets of restaurants, department stores, and movie theaters. To the east stand art museums, holding the ancient treasures of Breughel and Van Eyck and the modern work of Ensor and Magritte; beyond lie the park and the stately royal palace. No visitor to Brussels should miss the Grand' Place, with its 15th-century city hall and old guild houses that were once the headquarters of the butchers, brewers, tailors, painters, and other artisans. Today these buildings, preserved in their original splendor, contain shops, restaurants, and municipal offices.

Brussels is such a busy city that it seems always under construction. Laborers from Turkey, Spain, Italy, India, and Algeria work alongside Belgian construction workers. The city is also filled with foreigners living in Brussels on assignment from their governments or their companies to work in the many European agencies and international businesses that have made Brussels their headquarters. Just outside Brussels is the seat of the North Atlantic Treaty Organization (NATO). At Casteau, near Mons, about 30 miles (50 kilometers) from Brussels, is the home of SHAPE (Supreme Headquarters Allied Powers Europe).

Antwerp, located 55 miles (90 kilometers) up the Scheldt River from the North Sea, has been a wealthy city for centuries because of its great port. It has a famous cathedral and wonderful museums, including the home the painter Peter Paul Rubens designed for himself. Antwerp is the center of the new industrial development in Flanders.

The third largest city of Belgium is **Ghent**. Long the heart of the Flemish textile trade, it is rich in art and historic treasures. So too is **Bruges**. In ancient times that city, busy with trade and textile manufacture, was larger than London. Today the people of Bruges live quietly along the city's peaceful canals. Nuns still dwell in the ancient abbeys, and chimes still sound from the many belfries. Visitors take motorboat rides along the canals, ducking their heads under some of the dozens of old bridges, and visit the many impressive, well-preserved buildings. There is the Hospital of St. John with its Memling gallery and dispensary active since the 12th century. There are the church of Notre Dame and the Gruuthuuse, a 15th-century merchant's palace that was used for women who had retreated from the world. To visit this museum city is to go far back in history.

Liège, in the east, an important modern industrial center, always has been the cultural focal point of French-speaking Belgium. Once again, modern industries may be found close by the ancient palace of the prince-bishops of Liège.

Many other cities of Belgium reveal this mixture of the modern with the ancient. Near Liège are the picturesque towns on the Meuse River and in the Ardennes forest. On the coast of Belgium are the seaside resorts of Knokke-sur-Mer and Ostend. Elsewhere are the cathedral town of Tournai, the university town of Louvain, and the old church center of

Antwerp, Belgium's largest city, is site of the Steen, a medieval castle that houses the National Museum.

Mechlin. Everywhere that one travels in Belgium, there are fine roads, a delightful place to lunch, an old chateau, monastery, abbey, or museum to visit, and modern industries nearby.

THE ECONOMY
Farms and Farming

Both at home and abroad, Belgium is known as an industrial nation, yet agriculture has always played an important part in the life of the country. By hard work, intensive cultivation, and use of scientific methods, the Belgians obtain high yields from their farms. Some foodstuffs, especially grains and citrus fruits, must nevertheless be imported.

Almost 50 percent of the land is under agriculture but is tilled by only about two percent of the total work force; nevertheless, the farms are among the smallest in Europe. Key products are livestock and dairy goods, poultry, sugar beets, and flax. Specialized farms and nurseries export Belgian endive (a salad delicacy) and shrubs and flowers such as begonias, azaleas, and orchids grown in the glass hothouses in the region between Brussels and Ghent. Belgian grapes, berries, and carrots, often grown in greenhouses, are found preserved or fresh in gourmet food shops in many countries.

Cattle graze beneath the memorial commemorating Napoleon's final defeat at Waterloo in 1815.

In Ghent, the ornate guildhalls that line the Lys River figured prominently in the city's history.

Trade and Manufacturing

Slightly more than a quarter of Belgium's working population is employed in industry. Many of these industries had their beginnings centuries ago. During the Middle Ages, Flanders, with its lace and tapestry makers and cloth weavers, was the textile center of Europe. Today's thriving textile industry is still centered in such old cities as Ghent, Tournai, and Courtrai, which produce cottons, linens, and synthetic fibers, and in Verviers, which manufactures woolens. Bruges, Brussels, and Malines (Mechlin) laces are famous. Liège still produces armaments and glassware, products for which it has been famous since the 16th century. Antwerp continues to be, as it has been for hundreds of years, a world center for diamond cutting and trade.

Coal was mined in Belgium in Roman times. Many of the early mines of the Sambre and Meuse valleys were depleted and have now closed. The steel mills located in regions about Liège and Charleroi, so important a few decades ago, must rely on imported ore and sometimes coal. This is expensive; the mills themselves are becoming outdated; and international competition is stiff. Some plants have been forced to close, creating unemployment and political unrest in Wallonia.

Meanwhile, newer coal mines and industries have been developed in Flanders. Since World War II, multinational chemical and electronic firms have established factories in Flanders. Their arrival was stimulated by growing demand for plastics and petrochemical products, nourished by the proximity of the sea terminals of Antwerp and Rotterdam and attracted by the legendary working capacity of the Flemish laborer. The rise of employment, property values, and prosperity in Flanders and the coincidental decline of Wallonia have given the Flemings more leverage in national economic and political issues.

Traditionally, Belgium has maintained an open, free-trade economy. It has imported materials such as cotton, electronic components, zinc, copper, and lead, processing them with skilled workmanship. After their value has been increased, the goods have in turn been exported as valuable products. Some 63 percent of Belgium's gross domestic product is exported annually.

Shipping, Transport, and Banking

Belgium is also active in the transshipment industry. Lying at the heart of one of the world's most industrialized regions, Belgium is near the Ruhr region of Germany; Paris; and London. Its ports and well-developed canal, rail, and superhighway systems enable it to profit in the task of moving goods into and out of the European continent. Antwerp is the principal container-handling port of western Europe, and major

Fishing boats line the harbor of Ostend, Belgium's most important fishing port.

renovations have been made in the harbor at Zeebrugge to draw trade away from Rotterdam. All this commerce has stimulated the banking industry. In the early 2000s, almost three-quarters of the working population was employed in services and in the transportation industry. For decades, Belgium has been a leader in international agreements, from the Benelux treaties in the late 1940s to the European Monetary Union in 1999. The introduction of the euro, which first replaced the Belgian franc in banking—and then, on January 1, 2002, in retail and other cash dealings—is expected to make all intra-European financial transactions easier and less costly.

Recent Economic Developments

Belgium endured hard times in the final two decades of the 20th century, mostly because of a decline in the steel industry. In 1982, the government had to devalue the Belgian franc to enhance the country's ability to sell goods abroad. Austerity measures were introduced in the mid-1980s to reduce the government deficit.

Since Belgium has relatively few natural resources, its economy is heavily dependent on foreign trade. Its most important trading partners are fellow members of the European Union (EU), so Belgium's economic performance is directly tied to those of its EU partners.

Ironically, the increasing internal Belgian disunity, between Flemish-speaking north and French-speaking Wallonia in the south, presents a striking contrast to the trend toward European integration. The two main ethnic regions of the country differ not only in language and religion, but also in economic attitudes. While the people of Flanders are generally more entrepreneurial and pro-business, industrial Wallonia has a more socialist outlook, with strong trade unions. Unemployment is much higher in the latter. In 2001, the most recent reorganization of the state gave additional autonomy to the two main regions of the country, making them, economically, virtually independent.

In late 2001, Sabena, Belgium's national airline and one of the nation's few unifying economic symbols, declared bankruptcy. It was the second major European national airline—after Switzerland's Swissair—to be grounded in the wake of the September 11, 2001, terrorist attacks on the United States. The airline's collapse triggered the nation's most-serious social and economic crisis of recent times. Massive layoffs followed, not only of Sabena employees, but also those of numerous firms that provided parts and supplies to the airline.

GOVERNMENT

The House of Representatives is the dominant body in the national legislature, and is directly elected by universal suffrage under a system of proportional representation. A portion of the Senate is elected by the regional councils, some by fellow senators, and the largest group by direct vote. The Belgian judiciary is modeled after the French system. The highest court, the Court of Cassation, is led by a chief justice appointed by the king. Courts do not examine the constitutionality of laws.

A special group consisting of senior statesmen, the Council of State, gives advisory opinions on legislation and in times of crisis. Each of the major political parties (Social Christian, Socialist, Liberal) has Flemish and Walloon wings, which sometimes act almost as independent parties.

The Justus Lipsius Council Building in Brussels contains the offices of the European Union.

There are more extreme nationalist Flemish and Walloon parties and growing ecology parties, plus a small Communist party and a few revolutionary cells of Communist Combattants. Movement toward further federalism in Belgium is blocked by an inability to reach agreement regarding the place of Brussels in a federated state.

HISTORY

Belgium's history is shaped by its valuable location and commerce coveted by aggressive neighboring states, by its limited military strength, and by internal linguistic and religious differences. After the decline of Roman rule, the territories of modern-day Belgium became part of Charlemagne's realm. In the feudal period following the disintegration of that empire, Belgium was split among many hereditary princes, bishops, and other local rulers. It was a period of prosperity, the flowering of the trade guilds, and the development of a wealthy, educated middle class. In the 15th century, a series of pacts, noble marriages, and wars brought Belgium under the control of the dukes of Burgundy. Belgium subsequently passed under the rule of Spain (1517–1715), Austria (1715–94), France (1794–1815), and the United Netherlands (1815–30).

King William I of the Netherlands treated the Belgians as second-class citizens, forcing them to assume responsibility for the large Dutch national debt and to pay unpopular taxes. He did not grant them equal representation by population in the national governing body. However, he did ensure freedom of religion, a policy opposed by Belgian Catholic conservatives who wished to keep Dutch Calvinism out of the country.

The king's actions forged an alliance of Belgium's Catholic and liberal factions that earlier had fought each other. On August 15, 1830, stimulated by news of revolt in Paris and by the performance in Brussels of an opera filled with appeals to liberty (Auber's *The Mute from Portici*), the people of Brussels looted the homes of the Netherlands ministers. The revolt spread and caused a meeting of representatives of the great powers in London. The French were sympathetic to the Belgians, while the British did not wish Antwerp to fall into the hands of France. In December 1830, the powers agreed on the separation of Belgium from the Netherlands. William I of the Netherlands objected and invaded Belgium. Despite opposition from the Netherlands, with the aid of French and British armies, Belgian independence was assured. In 1839 the European powers guaranteed Belgium's independence and perpetual neutrality.

Growth of the Nation

The Belgians chose as their king Prince Leopold of Saxe-Coburg-Gotha (reigned 1831–65), the uncle of Queen Victoria of England; he soon chose as his consort the daughter of French King Louis-Philippe. He negotiated well with the powers on behalf of Belgium and encouraged industrialization and development of trade. At the time, a republic was unacceptable to the great powers, still perturbed by the French Revolution of 1789, and to a majority of the populace. A constitutional monarchy was constructed that, while technically making the king the source of executive authority, gave most governmental control to the Council of Ministers. The council, headed by a prime minister, was responsible to the two parliamentary chambers: the Senate and the House of Representatives.

Leopold I and his son Leopold II (reigned 1865–1909) exerted considerable influence on the course of government. They also became deeply involved in colonial activities. Acting on his own as a private citizen, Leopold II founded in 1876 the International African Association, which in turn became the huge Congo Free State, ruled by Leopold. It was eventually taken over by Belgium as a colony in 1908. In subsequent decades the immensely rich province would become an important source of copper and uranium, as well as rubber. Of tremendous significance to the Belgian economy, its separation from Belgium in 1960 as the independent state of Zaïre (now the Democratic Republic of Congo) caused much political and economic stress in Belgium.

The Two World Wars

Despite its status as a neutral, Belgium was invaded by Germany in 1914. Under the leadership of King Albert (reigned 1909–34), the Belgian army fought throughout World War I, even though most of Belgium was occupied. Following the war, the Belgians abandoned neutrality, signed a military accord with France, and struggled to rebuild their economy. The linguistic controversy became more bitter. In 1936, King Leopold III (reigned 1934–51), in an effort to gain the support of both factions in strengthening the army to face the threat of Hitler's Germany, declared Belgium once again neutral. This course did not deter a German invasion on May 10, 1940.

After the surrender of the Belgian army, the king chose to remain in his country rather than follow his cabinet into exile in London during World War II. The German occupation of Belgium was particularly harsh. Following liberation by the Allies in 1944, a controversy arose over whether Leopold should remain king (he was accused of being pro-German). In 1950, a plebiscite was held that approved his rule by a small majority. Still, within a year, continuing demonstrations brought about Leopold's abdication in favor of his son, Baudouin I.

Modern Belgium

Women were granted the right to vote in 1948. The "school war," which since the 19th century had pitted the Catholic party first against the Liberals and then against the Socialists, was finally resolved 10 years later. Compromise settled the percentage of costs of church schools that would be paid by national taxes, upheld freedom of curriculum, and barred political propaganda from the classroom.

Continuing attempts to adjust the linguistic border provoked bitter parliamentary debate. As measures of reform, the constitution was amended in 1970 and 1980 to create a more centralized system of government. The country was divided into the three regions: Flanders, Wallonia, and Brussels. Flemish, Walloon, French-speaking, and German-speaking community assemblies and executives for regional and cultural affairs were created. In February 1993, Parliament voted to once again amend the constitution, creating a federal state of Belgium.

Since then, Belgium has been headed by King Albert II, who succeeded his childless brother Baudouin. The Belgian royal family remains extremely popular, uniting what has become an often discordant country. In October 2001, Belgians welcomed with great excitement the birth of Princess Elisabeth, second in line to ascend the throne after her father, Crown Prince Philippe.

International Cooperation

The experience of World War II convinced Belgian leaders of the importance of international cooperation. Belgium, linked in economic union with Luxembourg since 1921, joined with the Netherlands to form the Benelux Economic Union in 1948, with the goal of eliminating tariffs and economic barriers among these nations. In the 1950s, the Benelux countries joined in establishing the European Economic Community, which has since gained importance, and became the EU in 1991. It now has 15 members, and up to 10 new nations, mostly former Communist countries, are slated to join. In 2001, as Belgium took over the rotating presidency of the EU, a crucial debate about the future character of the enlarged organization began.

JONATHAN E. HELMREICH, Allegheny College

Amsterdam, the Netherlands' capital and largest city, is called "Venice of the North" for its miles of canals.

NETHERLANDS

A famous story about the Netherlands is the tale of a boy who saved his country one stormy night by keeping his finger in a crack in a dike until help finally came. Like tulips and windmills and wooden shoes, the story is part of the mythology and charm of the Netherlands. And like most myths, it is based on reality but is not the whole picture. Today, the Netherlands is much more than a country of charming traditions. This small nation, with a high standard of living, has a modern, complex economy.

Few people outside its boundaries call the Netherlands by its formal name. Instead they speak of Holland, after its most populous and wealthy region, because it was Holland that led in the creation of the modern country. Inhabitants are rarely referred to as Hollanders or Netherlanders; almost always they are called the Dutch. Yet the Netherlands is an accurate name, for it means "the low lands," and this is the lowest country in the world, with more than two-fifths of its land below sea level. It is also the most densely populated, with more than 1,000 people per square mile (385 per square kilometer). A visitor, however, is struck by the way the Dutch manage to preserve a sense of space. Even where the towns are only a few miles apart, the land between is cultivated or used as parks.

Tourists continue to be charmed by the quaintness of the Old Holland of myth. Windmills with a distinctive shape dot the landscape, giving the country its most characteristic feature. Old buildings display their stepped gables. Farmers still wear wooden shoes with distinctive up-turned toes as they work the muddy soil. Canals cut their way through every city, where often buildings must be built on pilings sunk deep through the boggy land to the underlying hard ground. But this is not a country that lives off the tourist trade; it is a land of advanced industry and commerce as well as an agriculture whose efficiency is the envy of the world. If this were not so, the Dutch would not have achieved one of the highest standards of living in the world.

THE LAND

The Netherlands takes in almost the entire delta formed by three great rivers—the Lower Rhine, the Meuse, and the Scheldt—that flow together on its territory, dividing into numerous arms. The Rhine changes its name to the Waal as it leaves Germany and forms several tributaries before it empties into the North Sea. The Meuse is known in Dutch as the Maas and the Scheldt as the Schelde. These rivers link the Netherlands to its neighbors, Germany to the east and Belgium to the south. To the west and north the Netherlands borders on the North Sea. The Netherlands enjoys a moderate climate with abundant precipitation.

The unique landscape of the Netherlands is visible to visitors from abroad landing at Amsterdam Airport. As they look to the edges of the airfield, they will often see canal boats passing by on waterways considerably higher than the level of the airfield. Visitors will see, too, signs

The Eastern Scheldt Sea Barrier and other dams and dikes protect the low-lying reclaimed land from floods.

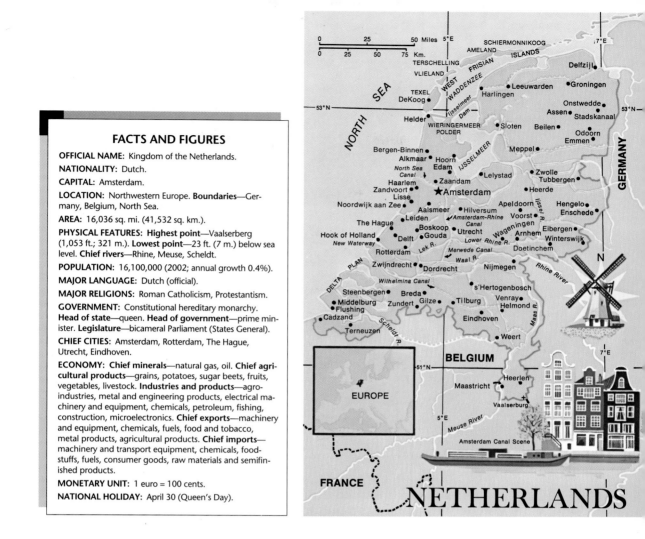

calling the airport "Schiphol," which means "Ship Hole" in Dutch. The two observations are linked: The land where the airport was constructed lies at the bottom of what was until the 19th century a very large lake. Like more than two-fifths of the country, this territory is reclaimed land below the level of the sea. The Dutch even have a special name for such land, "polder."

Pushing Back the Sea

In ancient times almost all the countryside west of the city of Utrecht was marshland, separated from the sea by a rim of dunes. People lived precariously on the dunes and on artificial mounds, called "terpen," built up from the bogs. They herded livestock, grew some grain, and fished. During times of high water, they drove their livestock up the terpen, and there both humans and animals stayed until the floodwaters receded.

In the 13th century, windmills came into use to pump the water out of land enclosed by dikes. At first, grain was grown on the new land, but it was discovered to be more productive as pastureland, and, ever since, dairy farming has been a major agricultural pursuit. Milk, butter, and cheese are produced for the constantly increasing population of the Low

Uniformed porters of the Cheese Carriers Guild add to the pageantry of the traditional cheese market days.

Countries and are exported to the outside world. In the 20th century the Dutch have employed the more powerful tools that became available—engines and pumps—to reclaim land from the sea. A 20-mile (32-kilometer)-long dike was built across the Zuider Zee from the tip of North Holland to Friesland, turning that sea into a fresh-water lake called the IJsselmeer (Ijssel Lake). Then, one by one, huge polders were constructed. The salt in the soil was leached by years of rain, and then modern farms were established and new cities built.

In February 1953, the dikes along the North Sea coast in Zeeland and southernmost Holland collapsed during a fierce winter storm, accompanied by high tides. The sea raced inland, killing about 1,800 people and destroying more than 70,000 homes. To prevent a recurrence of the disaster, the country embarked on a project called the Delta Works. All the outlets to the sea except the southernmost, the West Scheldt, and the northernmost, the Maas, would be controlled by dams with gates that could be closed in case of high water. The last dam was completed in 1987. In 1993, the Dutch began a radical plan to let in the sea. The constant need for drainage has led to immense land sinkage in some reclaimed areas. The Dutch hope to return about 600,000 acres to the sea.

Polders have given the Dutch landscape its distinctive look. The land is flat, divided into long, narrow strips by drainage ditches; there is little need for fences. The thousands of windmills that once drove the pumps are now chiefly ornamental, replaced by nearly invisible electrical pumps. The eastern part of the country is generally above sea level, with drainage canals less frequent. But everywhere canals are used for transport of goods. The landscape changes only in the extreme southeast, in Limburg province, where there is hill country above the valley of the Maas River.

Natural Resources. The natural resources below ground are limited. The coal mines in Limburg, with their veins largely depleted, have been closed. Today, the country's principal fuel is natural gas taken from an immense field in the northern province of Groningen. There are also large underground supplies of rock salt, which is used in the chemical industry. The supply of pure water for home consumption and industrial use is a persistent problem. The flat countryside does not permit the construction of large reservoirs, and the volume of rain water that can be retained in underground sand beds is limited. The principal source is water from the rivers, but removal of pollution is difficult and costly.

THE PEOPLE

A large majority of the Dutch are a Germanic people, and they have been clearly distinguished from Germans only since the 16th century. The name "Dutch," in fact, is the same word as the German's name for themselves, *Deutsch*. The country has long been open to immigrants seeking refuge from oppression or merely a better livelihood. These included many thousands from the Southern Netherlands (modern Belgium) in the 16th century, Jews from Portugal and Spain in the 16th and 17th centuries and from eastern Europe in the 19th century, and Germans from Westphalia and the Rhineland. The most recent are Turks and Moroccans who came as "guest workers" after World War II, and Indonesians and Surinamese from former Dutch colonies.

The Netherlandish Language

The language spoken by the Dutch is the same as the Flemish spoken in northern and western Belgium, with small differences in vocabulary and pronunciation; both the Dutch and Flemings call it *Nederlands*, "Netherlandish," because their common country was called the "Low Countries" until the 16th century. Modern Dutch speech throughout the country is based on the usage of Holland, although local dialects continue to be spoken, especially in the countryside. Dutch grammar is much like that of German, but simpler. Many words are taken from French and in recent times from English. Frisian, the native tongue in Friesland, in the north, is a distinct language, closer to English than Dutch; all Frisians also speak Dutch. Knowledge of foreign tongues is widespread; English is a second language for almost everyone, and German and French are widely spoken. Dutch schoolchildren start learning foreign languages at an early age. The sorry other side of this relationship is that Dutch is known by few foreigners, and few works of Dutch literature are translated into foreign languages.

The Dutch Way of Life

The Dutch spirit has tended to be realistic, sober, and concerned with ethical questions. Although the outward look of the Dutch pattern of life has lost virtually all of its obvious differences from those of its neighbors, Dutch society has retained important characteristics of its own. This is despite the ease with which the Dutch absorb other cultures.

A wide variety of groups that rose out of the turbulent religious and ideological conflicts of the 16th and 17th centuries have continued separate although parallel lives. Virtually all social activities were until recently conducted within associations based on religious or ideological identity: sports clubs, insurance companies, labor unions, agricultural communes, and political parties. These "pillars," as they are called, are weakening, but the ideal of the "melting pot" is far from universally accepted. The Dutch have on the whole stressed mutual tolerance of differences rather than making efforts to reduce or even eliminate them. Yet neighborliness, which may sometimes become prying interference, is emphasized over privacy.

This "pillar" system is maintained in the educational structure. All schools, public and private (which usually means church-affiliated), from kindergartens to universities, have equal right to financial support by the national government, which in turn closely supervises curriculum and administration. Elementary and secondary education have undergone considerable and frequent revision in recent years; and the universities, 12 in number, have been in turmoil due to government-imposed reforms. Among these are reorganization of programs and efforts to reduce expenditures, especially those limiting state aid to individual students and the number of years students may remain in school.

Most of the Dutch live in cities, which in the western part of the country have grown to the extent that today they merge into each other. Yet the Dutch retain a great love for life in the open—picnicking and playing in the parks, heathlands, and woodlands, which are carefully preserved. Modern homes, whether private houses or in apartment buildings, have large windows to let the sun pour in. The Dutch are famous for the cleanliness of their surroundings. Housewives for centuries have kept their homes—and the sidewalks in front of them—scrupulously clean, to the surprised admiration of visitors from less meticulous lands.

THE ECONOMY

The central fact in Dutch economic life is that the country cannot live in isolation but must draw its livelihood from intense participation in international commerce, both within Europe and outside. The Dutch for centuries have earned their living from agriculture, commerce, shipping, fishing, and industry. All continue to play a role, but the contribution of each to the nation's prosperity has changed immensely in the last century.

Dutch farmers have declined in number and now represent only a small percentage of the population. Their share in national income has also fallen, but the average income of individual farmers has risen. Dutch agriculture is one of the most efficient in the entire world; machinery and chemicals are employed intensively. Indeed, the large amounts of fertilizer put into the soils and the nearness of the fields to canals and rivers have caused severe water pollution, but the Dutch are addressing the problem with their customary efficiency.

Relatively little of the farm land is used for growing grains, which can be imported more cheaply. Dutch dairy farming, the most widespread agricultural activity, has become world famous; most of the milk produced is used for making cheese, of which the Gouda and Edam

Brilliant fields of flowers are cultivated in the Netherlands. Tulip bulbs are an especially important export.

varieties are best known. The Netherlands exports more cheese than any other country in the world. It is also the world's largest producer and exporter of flowers and bulbs, many of which are shipped by air freight across the oceans. The tulip fields near Haarlem attract huge crowds of tourists every spring to see field upon field of massed, exquisitely colored flowers. Less dramatic but hardly less valuable are the hothouses in the district called Westland, between Rotterdam and the sea, which grow fresh fruit and vegetables under glass the year round. These hothouse products are an important Dutch export.

For centuries the Dutch have also "tilled the sea" by fishing. More than 500 years ago they invented the pickling of fish at sea, so that in the days before refrigeration, their ships could venture far beyond the North Sea to the open ocean. Sole and herring are the principal varieties caught, although eels, caught in inland waterways, are a favorite delicacy. In recent years, when European commercial fishing has been controlled by decisions of the European Economic Community designed to preserve stocks from overfishing, the Dutch fishing industry has complained that it was given too small a quota.

Shipping and trade have long been the core of Dutch prosperity. Holland's location at the mouth of great rivers on the western shore of Europe put it at the crossroads of coastal trade between Southern and Northern Europe and riverborne trade to the continent's heartland. During the 17th century, Amsterdam was the storehouse of Europe, exchanging the grain and naval stores (pine products, especially tar) of the North for the wines, olive oil, and other luxury products of the South. After other countries, in particular England and France, began to trade directly with these lands and with their overseas possessions, Dutch trade with Germany increased in importance. A complex network of canal and river traffic moves goods to and from Dutch ports. Rotterdam is now the

Rotterdam is the world's largest port. The entire city was rebuilt after being gutted during World War II.

largest port in the world, although most of the goods that it handles are transshipped. Its facilities for storing and refining petroleum are the biggest in Europe.

The most important shift has been toward manufacturing. Once a relatively unimportant economic activity serving the needs of commerce and shipping, it has risen since the late 19th century to become the leading producer of wealth in the country. The first large manufacturing industry was textiles in the late 18th and 19th centuries; but, faced with competition, especially from Asia, most textile factories have closed.

Steel mills were built at the beginning of the 20th century at the mouth of the North Sea Canal, meeting most of the country's need for steel. Most spectacular has been the rise of the electronics and electrical-appliances industry, with the Philips company based at Eindhoven one of the most powerful in the world. Other Dutch companies of worldwide importance include the Akzo chemical company, the Royal Dutch-Shell petroleum company, and the Royal Netherlands Airline company (KLM).

Dutch bankers and insurance and financial brokers have long been important factors in international finance. During and after the American Revolution, loans from Dutch bankers helped to keep the new republic afloat. The modern business of life and commercial insurance was in large part the creation of Dutch firms. The Dutch are also very active in overseas investment. Amsterdam traditionally has been a center for the diamond trade. Although it has lost a large part of the business to Israel, diamond cutting and trading remain an important industry in Holland.

Since World War II, the Dutch have taken the lead in economic-integration activities in Europe, including the formation of the Benelux customs union with Belgium and Luxembourg and the foundation of the European Economic Community (EEC) in 1958, which grew and gained in importance during the following decades. In 1991, it was renamed the

European Union (EU). The surprising victory of the nation's political right during the spring 2002 parliamentary elections is expected to lead to a more cautious attitude toward further enlargement of the EU.

CITIES

Amsterdam. Founded in the 13th century on the Amstel River, the city got its original name, Amstelledamme, when the river was dammed. From its beginning, as wooden houses clustered in narrow streets, the city grew in size and importance to the point of having serious traffic problems. To ease these difficulties, a series of concentric canals was dug—the beginning of Amsterdam's modern network of canals. There are about 60 of them, crossed by more than 550 bridges, and they have made the city a composite of some 90 islands.

Among the city's highlights is the Rijksmuseum (National Museum), which is renowned for its extensive collection of paintings by great Dutch artists. The Stedelijk Museum contains an outstanding collection of modern paintings, including the works of Vincent van Gogh and the works of such 20th-century Dutch painters as Piet Mondrian, Kees van Dongen, and Karel Appel. Amsterdam's rich heritage from the past includes the Schreierstoren (weeper's tower), where 17th- and 18th-century travelers to the New World took leave of their relatives. It also is the site of the artist Rembrandt's house, which has been restored as a museum. Amsterdam is the home of the Concertgebouw, a leading symphony orchestra.

Amsterdam remains a world leader in the production of diamonds for jewelry and industrial purposes. The city's industrial complex ranks first in the nation. The port of Amsterdam, linked to international waters by the North Sea Canal, is one of the most modern in Europe. The city is the home base of KLM (Koninklijke Luchtvaart Maatschappij, or Royal Dutch Airlines) and the site of Schiphol International Airport, one of the largest duty-free airports in the world. All these combine to make Amsterdam a focus of international trade and travel.

Rotterdam and The Hague. In a square in the center of Rotterdam, there stands a statue of a human figure with its arms raised despairingly and questioningly toward the sky. The statue represents the destruction of Rotterdam by German bombs in May 1940. Although the port was further damaged later in World War II, Rotterdam has not only managed to recover, but has far surpassed its former position. A huge extension called Europoort was added after the war, and today Rotterdam is the world's largest port. The city's location on an arm of the Rhine has earned it the name Gateway to Europe. Tugs and river barges take goods upstream to the countries of Europe, while others bring the products of European industry and agriculture downstream for export to the world. An exciting view of the port can be seen from the top-floor restaurant of the tall tower called Euromast, where one can also view the attractive modern buildings and museums of rebuilt Rotterdam. The city's subway—the first in the Netherlands—opened in 1968.

The Hague (known in Dutch as 's Gravenhage or Den Haag) is the third-largest city in the Netherlands. While Amsterdam is the capital, The Hague is the seat of government—where Parliament meets and where the country is run—and of foreign embassies. Various international peace conferences have been held in The Hague, and in 1921, the Permanent Court of Arbitration (International Court of Justice), or World Court (associated first with the League of Nations and now with the United Nations) was established there. Three of the royal palaces are in The Hague and nearby Scheveningen.

GOVERNMENT
The Monarch

The Netherlands is a constitutional monarchy in structure and a democracy in practice. The head of state is a monarch (a queen for the past century) who succeeds according to the hereditary principle of primogeniture in the royal House of Orange-Nassau. Under the most recent constitutional revision, there is no preference for males over females. The monarch, who embodies the national sovereignty, is a symbol of national unity above political parties. The power of the state rests in the parliament, called by the historic name of States General, and the cabinet, composed of the premier and ministers who head government departments. Laws and decrees are issued in the name of the monarch, who in theory has all authority and is not answerable to parliament; but legislation must also be signed by a minister, who is responsible to it. Members of the cabinet do not serve in parliament; if they have seats in it, they must resign them. Even though the monarch theoretically has unlimited power, it would be unheard of for her to refuse to sign a duly approved piece of legislation. The sovereignty of the queen is therefore a useful constitutional fiction. In practice, the monarch uses her position above parties to facilitate the formation of a new cabinet after an election or when a cabinet resigns. With other members of the royal family, the queen performs a host of ceremonial functions and represents a unifying force in Dutch society.

The States General

The premier and ministers come before the houses of parliament to present bills for their approval and to explain and defend their political conduct. The States General is composed of two houses, the First Chamber, or senate, and the Second Chamber, or lower house. In the event of conflict with the senate over a bill, the approval of the Second Chamber is sufficient for the measure to become law. This arrangement reflects their respective electorates: The Second Chamber is elected directly by the people, the First Chamber by the Provincial States, which are the legislatures of the various provinces.

All adult citizens take part in parliamentary elections. In local elections, immigrants with established residence also have a vote. In elections for the Second Chamber, there is a nationwide system of proportional representation, which assures that the 150 seats in the chamber are distributed precisely according to the popular vote. Both major and most minor parties have a voice in parliament. Because no individual party in modern times has won a majority, cabinets are always coalitions. Until the spring of 2002, the Dutch political situation was quite stable, with three major parties representing the center of the political spectrum. Their position was suddenly shaken by the emergence of a new right-wing radical group, called Lijst Pim Fortuyn after its charismatic leader and founder. In a shocking development, Pim Fortuyn was assassinated two weeks before the elections. Nevertheless, his party came in second, signifying the increasingly conservative attitudes of Dutch voters.

How the Country Is Governed

The government of the Netherlands is unitary; that is, all power radiates from the center, and local governments derive all their powers from the national government. Although Amsterdam is called the capital (*hoofdstad*, "head city") in recognition of its size and preeminence, the seat of government is The Hague. There the States General meet in two ancient buildings together called the *Binnenhof* (Inner Court), which is also the popular name for the central government.

There are 12 provinces; all but one have the names of historic provinces, but their boundaries have been redrawn in modern times. The Provincial States, each headed by a royal commissioner, are allowed a considerable degree of self-government. The entire country is divided into local self-governing communities called *gemeenten* ("communes"), which vary in size from an entire city like Amsterdam to an assemblage of villages. They are headed by a mayor (*burgemeester*), named by the central government, and a board of aldermen, locally chosen.

Two outlying dependencies in the Caribbean are the Netherlands Antilles (which consists of two groups of islands: Curaçao and Bonaire, off the coast of Venezuela, and, to the northeast, St. Eustatius, Saba, and the southern third of St. Martin) and the island of Aruba. These self-governing dependencies remain integral parts of the Netherlands.

Legal System. The legal system of the Netherlands is a mixture of Roman and the Napoleonic Code, which was instituted during the reign of King Louis of Holland (1806–10), as modified by almost two centuries of legislation. Judges hear minor cases singly and form tribunals for major cases. The rights of defendants are scrupulously observed. Prison sentences are relatively short.

HISTORY

The Netherlands as a separate nation and state dates back no further than the late 16th century. Until then, it and Belgium were part of a loose unit called the Low Countries. In ancient times, the area was peopled by Germanic and Celtic tribes called the Belgae, the Batavi, and the Frisians. In the 1st century B.C., they were conquered by the Romans under Julius Caesar, with the exception of those Frisians who lived on the farthest northwest coast. During the Middle Ages, the northern Low Countries became part of the Holy Roman Empire (Germany), while some of the southerly provinces were under French rule. The province of Holland gradually rose to importance for its shipping and fishing activities.

Between the late 14th and early 16th centuries, all the Low Countries passed by inheritance and conquest under the rule of the French dukes of Burgundy. Their wealth enabled the duchy to establish its virtual independence from both the Holy Roman Empire and France. The chance for full separate existence was lost, however, when the dukes married first into the Habsburg family, whose members eventually ruled both the Holy Roman Empire and Spain. Charles V, who was born at Ghent in 1500, became Holy Roman emperor and king of Spain. When he abdicated in 1556, he divided his dominions between his brother, Ferdinand, who received the empire as his share, and his son Philip II, who received Spain and the Low Countries.

Philip's attempt to suppress Protestant heresies in the Low Countries and to rule them in the same absolutist way he governed in Spain led to riots in 1566 and a revolt in 1568, which were led by a great nobleman, William of Orange. After the rebels seized the little port of Brielle in Holland in 1572, they gained control of most of the northern Low Countries. William's most important supporters were the Calvinists, the most militant of the Protestant denominations. The rebellion spread to the southern provinces four years later but failed to maintain itself there. The northern provinces declared their independence of Philip II in 1581, becoming a new nation, the Dutch Republic.

The Dutch Republic

The republic, despite its tiny size, became one of the great powers of Europe in the 17th century. During most of the republic era, a member of the House of Orange led the country—but with the title of Stadholder rather than King. After 80 years, Spain acknowledged Dutch independence in the Peace of Westphalia (1648). The Dutch successfully defended their freedom in wars against both England and France, their former allies against Spain. Overseas they established colonies in the Americas and the East Indies. At home they created a haven for personal and religious freedom unmatched anywhere in Europe, although Calvinism remained the official church and increased its numbers to become almost a majority of the population. Dutch wealth expanded fabulously, providing the resources for a Golden Age. Dutch art, especially painting, reached the heights of achievement, with Rembrandt van Rijn only the most famous of dozens of great artists.

In the 18th century, the republic, exhausted by its immense military efforts, slipped well behind the rising power of England and France. It was, however, the first country to give full diplomatic recognition to the new United States of America in 1782.

The Evolution of the Monarchy

Between 1795 and 1813 the country was under French domination, first as the Batavian Republic (1795–1806), then as the Kingdom of Holland (1806–10) under Napoleon's brother Louis, and finally incorporated into the French Empire (1810–13). In this period political institutions were totally reorganized. The federal system of the republic was replaced by a unitary state, which was continued when French rule was thrown off in 1813, and a monarchy, still under the House of Orange, was instituted under King William I.

William shared his powers to a limited extent with a parliament (States General) but ruled with generally enlightened policies directed in particular to economic rehabilitation of a country badly hurt by a quarter century of war and occupation. He abdicated in 1840 after failing to prevent Belgium, which had been united with the northern Netherlands by the Congress of Vienna (1815), from winning its independence (1830–39). His son, William II, frightened by the revolutionary movements elsewhere in Europe in 1848, conceded full constitutional government as proposed by Johan Rudolf Thorbecke, who was the father of the modern Dutch system of government.

The Netherlands in the 20th Century

The next century brought full democracy to the Netherlands. The most difficult question was the school system, where dissident Protes-

An oil painting by Jacob van Ruisdael captures the essence of the 17th-century Dutch countryside.

tants and Roman Catholics sought state support for their private schools. This issue was not settled until a compromise, called the "Pacification," was worked out in 1917. By it, public financing of all schools was granted and universal suffrage was introduced. The Netherlands had effectively withdrawn from any major part in foreign affairs after Belgian independence, accepting a neutral status that was maintained until invasion by Nazi Germany in May 1940.

The cabinet, Queen Wilhelmina, and the rest of the royal family escaped to London, where a government in exile contributed to the Allied war effort. There was great suffering in the country, especially in the last winter of 1944–45, before liberation by Allied forces in 1945. Dutch Jews, who had lived in the country for centuries in safety, were hunted down by the Nazis and shipped to death camps; only about one in ten survived.

Peace brought freedom and the restoration of democratic, parliamentary government. Wilhelmina resumed her throne, and the first task was rebuilding the shattered economy. In 1948, Wilhelmina abdicated in favor of her daughter Juliana. For the next 15 years management, labor, and government collaborated. Strikes were avoided, and full use was made of American Marshall Plan aid. The policy of neutrality, which had not kept the country out of the war, was abandoned. The Netherlands enthusiastically joined the alliance of Western democratic states embodied in the North Atlantic Treaty Organization (NATO). It was unable, however, to retain its hold upon the Netherlands East Indies, which

Parliament buildings in The Hague. Although not the capital, The Hague is the seat of the Dutch government.

declared their independence as Indonesia; there was much bitterness against U.S. support for the Indonesian cause. The system of religious-ideological "pillars" was maintained and strengthened.

The 1960s brought significant changes. The discovery of natural gas provided new revenue, which was put to use in instituting a welfare system that included not only insurance for the aged, the disabled, and the unemployed, but also lavish support for education and culture. The public sector soon expanded to take in more than half of the gross national income. In the 1980s and early 1990s, the strain upon the export-dependent Dutch industry persuaded the coalition cabinet of Premier Ruud Lubbers to cut welfare expenditures. This policy was continued by Lubbers' successor, Willem Kok, who was prime minister from 1994 to 2002. In May 2002, the Christian Democrats won the elections and united with the radical Lijst Pim Fortuyn party. The new coalition government is expected to make further cuts in social programs.

The end of the Cold War and the dissolution of the Soviet Union in the early 1990s reduced domestic tensions over the nation's role in foreign policy. In the 1990s, Dutch industry prepared for the increased competition expected with the planned economic and political unification of the European Union (EU) nations. The Netherlands was particularly concerned about its place in the new Europe, since it was one of the smaller, less powerful countries. Nevertheless, in 1992, the Dutch cemented their commitment to the EU by signing and ratifying the Maastricht Treaty. In January 2002, the Netherlands was one of the 12 countries that replaced its currency with the euro.

HERBERT H. ROWEN, Rutgers University

Germany's importance on the world stage has not diminished the country's unique folk culture—even if the wearing of lederhosen (above) and other traditional costumes is now mostly limited to special occasions.

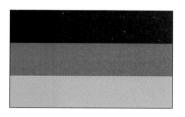

GERMANY

For 45 years, the dividing line between West and East in Europe ran through Germany. The line was real: an 858-mi. (1,381-km.) border strip of barricades, barbed wire, and minefields. On one side of the border lay the Federal Republic of Germany, usually known as West Germany, a prosperous and democratic nation. On the other side was the German Democratic Republic, known as East Germany. Throughout the decades of the Cold War, East Germany was a harsh Communist dictatorship.

The artificial division of Germany at the end of World War II separated families and divided people with the same culture and history. In 1989 and 1990, this division came to an end. First, in the fall of 1989, the barrier between the two countries was dismantled. The political union followed on October 3, 1990. The speed of this bloodless revolution made it one of the most astounding events in recent European history.

The excitement of those days is almost forgotten, and in many ways Germany continues to be divided, even though the Berlin Wall—a structure

FACTS AND FIGURES

OFFICIAL NAME: Federal Republic of Germany.

NATIONALITY: German(s).

CAPITAL: Berlin.

LOCATION: Central Europe. **Boundaries**—Baltic Sea, Poland, Czech Republic, Austria, Switzerland, France, Luxembourg, Belgium, Netherlands, North Sea, Denmark.

AREA: 137,803 sq. mi. (356,910 sq. km.).

PHYSICAL FEATURES: Highest point—Zugspitze (9,721 ft.; 2,963 m.). **Lowest point**—sea level. **Chief rivers**—Rhine, Elbe, Weser, Oder-Neisse, Danube, Main.

POPULATION: 82,400,000 (2002; annual growth –0.1%).

MAJOR LANGUAGE: German.

MAJOR RELIGIONS: Protestantism, Roman Catholicism.

GOVERNMENT: Federal republic. **Head of state**—president. **Head of government**—chancellor. **Legislature**—bicameral chamber.

CHIEF CITIES: Berlin, Bonn, Cologne, Dresden, Essen, Frankfurt, Hamburg, Leipzig, Munich.

ECONOMY: Chief minerals—iron, coal, lignite, potash, uranium, copper. **Chief agricultural products**—rye, wheat, barley, potatoes. **Industries and products**—iron and steel products, coal, cement, chemicals, machinery, shipbuilding, motor vehicles. **Chief exports**—machinery, vehicles, chemicals, metals and manufactures, foodstuffs, textiles. **Chief imports**—machinery, vehicles, chemicals, foodstuffs, textiles, metals.

MONETARY UNIT: 1 euro = 100 cents.

NATIONAL HOLIDAY: October 3 (German Unity Day).

that separated East and West Berlin for 28 years—is gone. Viewed from the longer perspective, however, the turbulent 1990s have strengthened Germany, and the five new northeastern states have been transformed almost beyond recognition.

At the beginning of the third millennium, Germany is the wealthiest country in Europe and, after Russia, the most populous. It is an ever more active and responsible member of the international community. German soldiers were involved in the Persian Gulf War and in the Balkan peace missions, and in late 2001, Germany joined the worldwide antiterrorism campaign by sending 3,900 troops to Afghanistan to assist the United States.

THE LAND

Germany lies in the heart of Europe—south of the Scandinavian countries, west of the Slavic ones, and north and east of the Romance nations. It is a country that has varied greatly in size during the long existence of the German people.

Germany can be divided into three principal regions—the northern lowlands, the central highlands, and the southern alpine region, south of the Danube River. The northern region extends between the North and Baltic Seas: the border is a zigzag line stretching from Cologne in the central west through Düsseldorf, Dortmund, Paderborn, Osnabrück, Hannover, and Magdeburg,

Germany is renowned for its autobahn system—the network of expressways that interconnects the cities.

Germany

to Wittenberg in the east. The geography consists of a mostly flat plain, dotted with marshes and lakes. Fertile soil lies near the coast and in the river valleys. Much of the region is sandy heathlands used for both sheep grazing and agriculture. The largest of these areas, lying between the cities of Hamburg and Hannover, is the Lüneburger Heide, a 55-mi. (88-km.) stretch of purple heather, golden gorse, and juniper trees.

Between the plain and the highlands lies a transitional belt known for the richness of its soil. It starts in the region around Cologne in the west and continues toward the east to the cities of Halle, Leipzig, and Dresden. From the early Middle Ages on, this area, which has long been one of the most densely populated regions of Europe, has been heavily traveled.

The central highlands offer a diversity of landscapes between the upper regions, with their rich stands of timber, and the lower slopes and valleys, where numerous crops are grown. The Harz Mountains, the best-known range in the highlands, straddle the line that for 40 years formed the border between the two parts of Germany. These mountains have peaks that

Resorts along the Baltic Sea (above) draw great numbers of summer vacationers to their fine beaches.

exceed 3,000 ft. (914 m.) in altitude. In the western part of the country, the highlands form a series of plateaus into which the rivers, especially the Rhine, have cut steep gorges of great beauty. This area contains forests, fields, vineyards, and mountains. To the east lies the Thuringian Forest, the site of many health spas. On the border with the Czech Republic are the Erzgebirge Mountains ("ore mountains"), which are named for the variety of minerals found there, including uranium ore.

No clear demarcation exists between the central highlands and the alpine areas of the extreme south. In the southwest is the Black Forest Range, named for the dark spruces and firs that line its slopes. These mountains, the home of the cuckoo clock and the background for many fairy tales, are a favorite vacation spot. The Danube River originates in these heights, and flows eastward for about 400 mi. (644 km.) across southern Germany. (See the article DANUBE RIVER on page 326.)

The Bavarian Alps are an extension of a minor range of the Alps. On the border with Austria rises the highest peak in Germany, the Zugspitze (9,721 ft. or 2,963 m.). The snow-covered peaks and many lakes make the Bavarian Alps a favorite resort area.

Climate. A damp maritime climate prevails along the North Sea and Baltic coasts, but farther inland and toward the south, the pattern becomes more typically continental. The average January temperature is between 21° and 34° F. (-6° and 1° C.), depending on the location. In July, the corresponding averages are 61° and 68° F. (16° and 20° C.). On the high plateaus, winter temperatures may be lower, and in parts of the Rhine Valley, the summers are sometimes a little warmer than the average.

Rain falls in all seasons, but generally more precipitation occurs in the summer. Precipitation is heaviest in the south, where most of it falls as snow, which attracts winter-sports enthusiasts. The northern lowlands and the central highlands receive more rain than snow.

Rivers, Canals, and Lakes. Germany has a number of navigable rivers and an extensive system of canals. The best-known river is the Rhine. Although it originates in Switzerland and empties into the North Sea in Dutch territory, the Rhine is generally thought of as a German river. This important waterway, together with its tributaries, carries more traffic than any other river system in Europe. (See the sidebar on page 244.)

The Weser, Elbe, and Oder Rivers drain the northern plain. The Weser empties into the North Sea after flowing past Bremen and its port of Bremerhaven. The Elbe, which rises in the Czech Republic, flows northwest through the country, past Dresden and Magdeburg, to empty into the North Sea at Hamburg. Between 1949 and 1990, the lower reaches of the Elbe formed the border between the two Germanys. This river's chief tributaries are the Saale and the Havel. The Spree, which runs through Berlin, merges into the Havel. In 2002, torrential rains caused the worst flooding in 100 years in Dresden and other cities along the Elbe River.

The Oder also originates in the Czech Republic and, with its tributary the Neisse, forms most of Germany's eastern border with Poland.

A network of canals crisscrosses the country, connecting the various German rivers. The longest is the Mittelland Canal, which enables travelers to cross the whole length of northern Germany entirely by water. The Kiel Canal, farther north, connects the North Sea to the Baltic. More paying ships pass through the Kiel than through any other canal in the world. A canal between the Main River and the Danube in the south provides a convenient link for ships traveling from the North Sea to the Black Sea.

In the south lies Lake Constance, Germany's largest lake, and part of the course of the Rhine. Its surface is 210 sq. mi. (544 sq. km.), and it is more than 46 mi. (74 km.) long. The lake is shared by three countries: Germany in the north, Switzerland in the southwest, and Austria in the south.

The visitor's facility atop the Zugspitze, Germany's highest peak, affords magnificent views of the Alps.

■ RHINE RIVER

The snowy peak of Six Madun soars 10,000 ft. (3,000 m.) into the sky over southern Switzerland. From Lake Toma, more than halfway up the mountain, and from Paradies Glacier, two streams flow east. Near the town of Reichenau, they unite to form the Rhine—the great river that, in its 820-mi. (1,319-km.) jour-

ney, links not only the six countries touched by its waters, but, because of its economic importance, every country in Europe.

At Bregenz, Austria, the river enters the lovely Lake Constance. The lake, enormously popular with tourists, acts as a natural control for the Rhine by slowing its tumbling, rushing flow. After it leaves the lake, below Schaffhausen, Switzerland, the Rhine plunges over a 65-ft. (20-

From the deck of a Rhine riverboat, passengers are treated to a highly picturesque succession of vineyard-covered hillsides and quaint medieval villages. Above, a tourist riverboat plies its way by Bacharach in the gorge between Mainz and Koblenz.

The deep Lake Chiem, the largest in Bavaria, is one of the most beautiful lakes in the country.

The northeastern part of Germany contains a number of lakes, the largest of which is Lake Müritz, covering about 44 sq. mi. (114 sq. km.). Many other small lakes have been created behind dams.

Natural Resources. Germany's most important resource is coal. Bituminous coal is found in the Ruhr—a highly industrialized area that covers about 2,000 sq. mi. (5,180 sq. km.) in the western part of the country. The Ruhr is the center of the German iron and steel industries. Essen, Dortmund, and the Rhine port city of Duisburg owe much of their industrial power to the nearness of the seemingly inexhaustible supply of coal. Rich seams of coal are also found near the city of Aachen and in the Saarland.

m.) drop to form a spectacular waterfall that is sometimes called the European Niagara.

Basel, Switzerland, is the first major city on the Rhine. From there, the river flows north to form the border between France and Germany. Still flowing north, the river then enters Strasbourg, a crossroads of French commerce and industry. Canals reach out from its port to connect the Rhine with the larger French rivers. About 50 mi. (80 km.) downstream from Strasbourg, the Rhine enters Germany in the Black Forest.

Past Wiesbaden, flowing west through a region called the Rheingau, the Rhine becomes the romantic river of legends. Golden vineyards cling to the steeply sloped riverbanks, and ruined castles perch on hilltops and on islands in midstream. The river then turns north again, toward Koblenz. The dangerous whirlpools and narrows of this part of the river inspired the legend of the Lorelei, a lovely maiden sitting atop a rock and singing so beautifully that she lured sailors to their doom. She was immortalized in a poem by the German poet Heinrich Heine. The golden treasure of the Nibelungs—a legendary family of German mythology and of Richard Wagner's Ring operas—is said to be buried at the foot of Lorelei's rock.

At Koblenz, where it meets its longest tributary, the Moselle River, the Rhine leaves the land

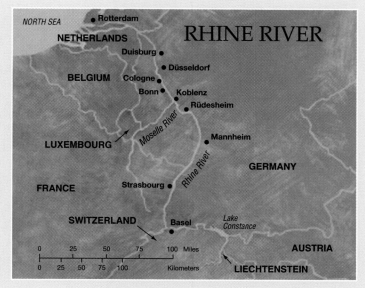

of legends. Soon it reaches Bonn, the birthplace of Ludwig van Beethoven and the capital of West Germany until 1991. Farther downriver at Cologne, the towering twin spires of the city's great Gothic cathedral dominate the landscape. Now broad and placid, the Rhine then enters the industrial Ruhr region, with its coal mines and iron foundries, blast furnaces and steel mills.

When the Rhine leaves the Ruhr, it turns west and crosses the Netherlands border near Emmerich. In this low, flat country, the river branches out into a vast delta. The last arm of the river is a 16-mi. (26-km.) human-made passage called the Nieuwe Waterweg (New Waterway), which extends from Rotterdam to the North Sea.

Lignite, or brown coal, is mined chiefly in the central highlands. Before the unification of East and West Germany, lignite represented the backbone of East German heavy industry. This coal is of lower quality than bituminous coal, and its use has caused significant air and water pollution in the southern part of the former East Germany. Most of these plants have been closed.

Although crude-oil deposits have been found in the Lüneburger Heide and around Schleswig-Holstein, as well as offshore in the North Sea, they are not sufficient for domestic needs. Some iron ore, lead, zinc, and copper are also mined. Potash salts are used as fertilizers: Germany is one of the world's largest suppliers of this substance. Germany also has reserves of rock salt and kaolin, which is used in the famous Dresden china; kaolin is produced chiefly at nearby Meissen.

Millions of Germans are employed in heavy industry. The country remains a leading producer of steel (above).

THE PEOPLE

The people known as Germans are really a mixture of three principal and several minor ethnic stocks. In the early years of the Christian era, tribes of Teutonic origin mingled with Celtic peoples in various parts of what is now known as Germany. In Roman times, a Mediterranean strain was added to the Celtic-Teutonic stock. Further migrations brought in people of Baltic and Slavic origins, and repeated invasions through the centuries contributed still more variety to the mixture.

Roughly speaking, the western and southern regions are mostly Celtic and Mediterranean in composition, the central parts largely Celtic and Teutonic, and the eastern part Teutonic and Slavic. These generalizations, however, have become less true in recent times, and it is difficult today to identify or separate the diverse elements that make up the German people.

The five new northeastern states—which until 1990 constituted East Germany—are much less densely populated than the western 10. Visitors often remark that the former East Germany looks in many ways like Germany before World War II. Communist Germany was a country of small towns and hamlets: only 15 cities had populations of more than 100,000. In fact, the population declined over the years. Immediately after World War II, many people moved to the Western zones, prompting the construction of the wall through Berlin to stop the flow. Later years saw a low birthrate that was insufficient to sustain the population. East Germany imported thousands of foreign workers to supplement its labor force, mostly from Vietnam and other developing nations. After unification, many of these people were repatriated.

The former West Germany is one of the most densely populated regions in Europe. Over the years, the employment needs of the booming economy have attracted nearly 4 million foreign workers, many of them from Turkey and southern Europe. Due to the wave of refugees in recent years, about 7 million foreigners lived in Germany in 2000. These immigration rates are comparable to those experienced by the United States in the early 20th century. As with other developed coun-

Flower headbands and bouquets help make the day special for some German girls in Eckental.

Most Germans belong to Christian denominations. The Lutheran Church, founded in Germany in the 16th century, still counts among its members a majority of Germans. Many North Americans also adhere to Lutheranism.

tries, however, Germany is becoming increasingly inhospitable, and by the late 1990s, the majority of applications for asylum were rejected.

A small Danish minority lives in the north. Dependents of U.S. military troops, foreign students enrolled at German universities, and businesspeople from other countries contribute to the cosmopolitan character of major German cities.

For several years after unification, Germany continued to host thousands of foreign armed forces. By late August 1994, however, all of the 370,000 former Soviet troops stationed in East Germany had left for their native countries. In a gesture of goodwill, Germany contributed financially to their relocation. The combined U.S., British, and French forces still in Germany numbered about 150,000 in the late 1990s. By September 1994, all foreign troops had left Berlin.

Religion. Protestantism arose in Germany, and the dividing line between Catholic and Protestant Europe cuts through the country. Until unification, the West German population was almost equally divided between these two major denominations, but, with the addition of five new northeastern states, the balance has shifted in favor of Protestants. Bavaria has the highest percentage of Catholics.

Despite the official policy in postwar East Germany of creating a state without religion, churches remained an important aspect of life and became centers for the nonofficial peace movement; they were also the major organizers of the wave of demonstrations that swept away the Communist regime in the fall of 1989.

Education. Because the Germans have traditionally placed a great emphasis on education, they have a well-developed educational system. School is compulsory from the age of 6 to the age of 18. For the first four years, all children attend a basic primary school. At this point, students take examinations that decide their future education. Those who continue in primary school may then attend school part-time while they also work and learn a trade. Students who go on to attend the six-year intermediate schools are usually trained for a business career. They must learn one foreign language, as well as mathematics, science, and business skills.

A student who passes the examination for secondary school, called *Gymnasium,* continues his or her education for nine more years. A *Gymnasium* stresses classical or modern languages or mathematics and science. At the age of 19, *Gymnasium* students must take another examination to qualify for the university.

German was the international language of central Europe for several hundred years, and was long the leading scientific language. Today, the overwhelming majority of young people are bilingual, speaking German as well as English fluently.

Germany's Young People. Many young people, particularly in the former West Germany, no longer fit into a truly national mold. Quite a few consider themselves Europeans rather than simply Germans. Having been exposed to European and world affairs through travel, television, and other media, they are often more curious than their parents, and more open to liberal influences than were past generations.

On the other hand, the influx of immigrants from the East in the past few years has led to a wave of racial violence, perpetrated in par-

Young people in Germany pursue many of the same pastimes as their North American counterparts. Like anywhere else, school provides an important social outlet (above), a place where students of roughly the same age meet and form friendships (top) that can last a lifetime. Vocational schools (right) prepare students for engineering colleges.

Traditional costumes, folk dances, and special music add an air of excitement to an annual festival held in Dinkelsbühl—one of a number of German communities with a well-preserved medieval city center.

ticular by young people belonging to neo-Nazi and skinhead groups. Many of these incidents took place in the former East Germany, most often in cities along the Polish-German border. There have been thousands of attacks on foreign workers and refugees.

Way of Life. The neo-Nazis and skinheads represent only a tiny extremist minority. Historically, Germans have been stereotyped as formal, punctual, hardworking, and officious, and while all these qualities exist to some extent, there is also a lighter side to the German character. In fact, Germans are quite similar to Americans: they take great joy in all kinds of celebrations. The Bavarian Oktoberfest, which is held every September into October, is a well-known tourist attraction. Even in the staid former East Germany, the annual Shrovetide carnival is marked by dances in the streets, masked balls, and processions.

Since World War II, Germany has also become a tourist superpower: prior to unification, West Germans could be found in every corner of the world, and East Germans were the most numerous tourists in Czechoslovakia, Hungary, and Bulgaria. Recently, Germans have traveled even more.

German women were traditionally focused on the three "K's"—*Kinder, Küche, und Kirche* (children, kitchen, and church)—but these times have changed. About 56 percent of German women now work in paying jobs, 30 percent of the seats in the parliament are held by women, the world's first female bishop (Protestant) was a German woman, a woman presides over Germany's Constitutional Court, and one-third of all new German firms are led by women. In 2000, the conservative Christian Democratic Union (CDU), which had been headed by Helmut Kohl for 25 years, elected a woman, Angela Merkel, to its chairmanship.

Food. Germans love to eat, and they take pride in their reputation as excellent cooks. Each section of the country has its specialty. In Bavaria, it is the delicious dumpling known as the *Knödel,* in all its infinite varieties. In Hamburg, every kind of fish and seafood is served, including *Seezunge* ("sole"), prawns, and the popular eel soup. Westphalia has its dark-brown pumpernickel, and its tender ham is a delicacy.

Germany is the land of the *Wurst* ("sausage"), and many different kinds are produced. Berliners are especially fond of the fat pork *Bockwurst. Leberwurst* ("liver sausage"), *Blutwurst* ("blood sausage"), *Knackwurst* (the name comes from the popping sound made by the first bite), and *Bratwurst* ("fried pork sausage") are but a few others. The frankfurter is the most famous German sausage, but though it is known by that name around the world, in Germany—and even in Frankfurt—it is called *ein Wiener Würstchen,* or "a Vienna sausage"! Among the best-known German contributions to international menus are *Sauerbraten,* a tasty pot roast in a sauce, and the almost endless varieties of potato salad (*Kartoffelsalat*).

German cuisine includes almost innumerable varieties of sausage, or *Wurst* (above), including the frankfurter.

One of the most traditional of German meals is still the Christmas dinner. The meal takes days to prepare, and includes Christmas fruit bread, or *Stollen,* and a wide variety of beautiful cookies. On this happiest of all German holidays, crisply roasted goose is traditionally served.

And of course, Germany is known for its beer. Brewing is a 1,000-year-old tradition, and some 6,000 varieties are produced today. Many are as popular in New York and Tokyo as they are in Germany.

Sports. Germans have always been sports-minded. Hiking and camping through the lovely countryside and mountain forests are ever popular. Skiing and other winter sports attract people of all ages. Lovely seaside resorts such as Travemünde on the Baltic Sea; the North Sea surf; or the pools in almost every town offer many opportunities for swimming. Sailing, handball, tennis, and horseback riding are also popular. About one-third of all young Germans are members of sports clubs.

Germany boasts a variety of spectator sports. When international soccer matches are played, fans crowd the stadiums and the streets. Six-day bicycle races and automobile racing are particularly popular.

The former East Germany was a veritable sports machine, famous for its many Olympic successes: in the 1988 Summer Olympics, for instance, East Germans won 102 medals. These achievements now appear in a somewhat different light: since reunification, investigations have proved that the performance of many East German athletes was enhanced by illegal steroids. The connection of leading sports figures to the East German secret police has cast further shadows on the athletic establishment.

The Germans are great sports enthusiasts, and huge fans of soccer (top left). German skiers rank among the world's best—and most daring (top right). For amateurs, windsurfing (above) has become increasingly popular. Cycling competitions (right) draw participants of all ages and abilities.

Cultural Life. Germans are great readers and theatergoers. Books of all sorts sell extremely well. The works of post–World War II authors—such as Günter Grass (Nobel Prize winner in 1999), Uwe Johnson, Gisela Elsner, and Heinrich Böll (who won the Nobel Prize in 1972)—are especially popular. Wolf Biermann, Reiner Kunze, and Manfred Bieler began their writing careers in the former East Germany, but then moved to the West, finding enthusiastic audiences. Among the younger generation, Thomas Brussig has gained great popularity with his book *Heroes Like Us*, published in 1994. It is a humorous satire, partly reminiscent of Philip Roth's work, but at the same time a mocking denunciation of the East German police state.

Opera, music, and dance are flourishing, and so are museums. More than 30 million people attend the theater every year. Most theaters are maintained by the federal, state, and city governments, but many private ones exist as well. Both classical and contemporary works draw large audiences. In the 1960s, the controversial plays of Rolf Hochhuth aroused much comment in Germany. The leading playwright of absurd drama was Wolfgang Hildesheimer, and Peter Weiss wrote plays containing bitter social criticism.

Günter Grass (above), a prolific German author, artist, and activist, won the 1999 Nobel Prize for Literature.

Music is often subsidized by state and city governments. Countless music festivals are held throughout the country each year.

Very popular among modern music ensembles is the Kraftwerk group, which combines pop with experimental synthesized music. During the 1990s, Berlin became the largest showcase of "techno" music during its Love Parade festival each June. This gathering, begun in Berlin in 1989 shortly before the fall of the Berlin Wall has grown explosively and, in 2000, was attended by more than 1 million fans.

East and West Germans. Throughout the postwar period of divided Germany, the people on the two sides of the Iron Curtain had a complex and often ambivalent relationship with each other. On the one hand were the bonds: the division of Germany cut through many families. For about a decade after 1961, there was almost no individual human contact between the two parts of the country. In the 1970s, it became possible for West Germans to visit their relatives in the East, and in the 1980s, even some East Germans, especially the older ones, could visit their kin in the West.

There were also grudges and arrogance. As West Germans became more affluent and cosmopolitan, they tended to look down on their East German compatriots, who in turn often envied the luxuries and freedoms available in the West. West German television was viewed in virtually all of East Germany, and its impact seriously contributed to the undermining of the Communist system: no other people in the Communist world were able to compare, on a daily basis, their own substandard surroundings and daily frustrations to the situation of their neighbors, who had the same cultural heritage but lived under a different system.

When the Berlin Wall opened, West Germans welcomed their liberated neighbors with great generosity. Since then, however, it has become obvious that unification alone will not make all Germans economically and socially equal. Many former East Germans now feel like second-class citizens (their wages are less than two-thirds of the wages in the West), while former West Germans complain that 40 years of Communism have greatly undermined the work ethic of "Easterners"—or "Ossies," as they are derogatorily called.

CULTURAL HERITAGE

A unified Germany is a relatively modern development. Before 1990, the German people had lived under one government for only 74 years, from 1871 to 1945; but throughout the centuries of their long history, they were held together by the bond of their culture and common language. These links made the Cold War division into two Germanys seem artificial and unnatural to Germans on both sides of the Iron Curtain.

Language and Literature

German is a member of the Indo-European family of languages. From its origins thousands of years ago along the coasts of the Baltic and North

Seas, it gradually spread southward and westward as the Germanic tribes moved into new lands. One of the strongest influences on the developing language was Latin, and many German words still show clearly traceable Latin origins.

By the 9th century A.D., many different regional dialects had developed, but no single German language yet existed. Martin Luther's translation of the Bible in the 16th century and the use of movable type—an invention of the German Johannes Gutenberg—helped create standard written German.

Modern German is an inflected language, with changing endings of verbs and nouns. It also has three genders—mas-

Participants dance on top of a waste container in front of the Brandenburg Gate during Berlin's Love Parade, the world's biggest "techno" festival.

culine, feminine, and neuter—plus other complicated grammatical rules. All of this makes German a difficult language to master, especially for those whose mother tongue is English, which is structurally simpler. Many common words in English and German, however, share the same roots.

Myths, sagas, and folklore, passed on by word of mouth during the wanderings of the early Germanic tribes, are part of the German literary heritage today. The earliest literature was written in Latin by the monks. Anonymous authors collected and recounted various old themes in the *Nibelungenlied* ("Song of the Nibelungs"), which tells of battle, bravery, treason, and revenge. It has become a national epic.

From the 17th century on, German writers produced many works of literature that, in the words of Johann Wolfgang von Goethe, "like all good things, belong to the whole world." Goethe, born in Frankfurt am Main in 1749, is considered to be Germany's greatest writer. From his lyric poetry, to his novel *The Sorrows of Young Werther,* to his masterpiece *Faust,* his ideas have continued to inspire people everywhere.

The 18th century was also the time of playwright-critic Gotthold Lessing, whose *Nathan the Wise* was a plea for religious tolerance. At this time, too, Friedrich von Schiller helped to carry German literature to international attention. In such plays as *Die Räuber* ("The Robbers"), he showed his concern for the individual's place in society. Such 18th- and 19th-century German philosophers as Immanuel Kant and Georg Wilhelm Friedrich Hegel have had a global influence on moral thinking.

Children of all nationalities are familiar with the collection of fairy tales compiled by Jacob and Wilhelm Grimm in the early 1800s. In the 19th century, Heinrich Heine's verse included *Die Lorelei,* which told the story of the beautiful Rhine maiden whose singing lured sailors to their death.

Two 19th-century philosophers who had a tremendous impact on 20th-century thought were Friedrich Nietzsche and Karl Marx. Nietzsche's idea of a moral superman found a distorted echo in Hitler's theory that every

Germany has a proud artistic tradition. *The Self-Portrait of Albrecht Dürer* (below left) and *Temptation of Saint Anthony* (above center, by Matthias Grünewald), were both painted around 1500. At far left, Karl Blechen's *Mill Valley near Amalfi* has elements of romanticism, while *People on the Street* (right) by Ernest Ludwig Kirchner is a masterpiece of expressionism.

German was an *Übermensch* ("superman"). Marx's *Communist Manifesto,* written with Friedrich Engels, and his monumental *Das Kapital* became the foundations of Communism.

A major figure of early 20th-century German literature was Nobel Prize winner Thomas Mann, the author of such enduring novels as *Buddenbrooks* and *The Magic Mountain.* In 1933, Mann left Germany and went into self-imposed exile in Switzerland and then the United States.

True intellectual life in Germany ceased under Hitler. On the evening of May 10, 1933, torchlight parades in Berlin and several other cities ended with the burning of thousands of books, many written by authors of international repute. Art, music, and literature all eventually came under Nazi control. Ultimately, Heine's prediction came true—"Where books are burned, people are burned in the end."

The Arts

All Germans share a rich heritage of the great contributions made by their countrymen to music, literature, and art. Early German art often expressed Christian themes in ivory carvings and illuminated manuscripts. The strong religious character of the art also found an outlet in the stark and emotional Gothic sculpture of the 13th and 14th centuries.

In the years between 1500 and 1550, several artists were active who later became known for their outstanding use of color, line, and detail. Albrecht Dürer was a fine painter, but it was the masterly use of line and design in his woodcuts and engravings that made him a major artist. Matthias Grünewald used color superbly in his greatest achievement, the *Isenheim Altarpiece,* now in a museum in Colmar, France. Part of this magnificent masterwork portrays a realistic Crucifixion. Hans Holbein the Younger is noted for his superb portraits—among the best known is that of King Henry VIII of England, for whom he was court painter. Lucas Cranach the Elder brought freshness and charm to his mythological and court paintings, as well as to his portraits of the leaders of the Reformation.

In the 17th and 18th centuries, when baroque and rococo architecture flourished in Europe, many richly decorated churches and castles were erected. Some charming buildings of this period have been preserved or restored. The Pilgrimage Church of the Wies, located in an alpine meadow near Steingaden in southern Bavaria, is one of the loveliest examples of German rococo architecture.

In the late 19th and early 20th centuries, all the arts adopted a modern and simpler style. In her lithographs and etchings, Käthe Kollwitz portrayed the emotions of working people. The German love of color was seen in the *Blaue Reiter* (Blue Rider) group, in which artists such as Franz Marc moved German expressionism toward abstract art. In the same period, Ernst Barlach's sculptures in bronze and wood captured the suffering of the common man.

At the Bauhaus, an art school established in Weimar in 1919, new ideas for industry, architecture, and crafts were generated that influence industrial design to the present day. Architects such as Walter Gropius and Ludwig Mies van der Rohe were great innovators in their field.

Music. The German people have always loved music. It is not surprising, then, that over the centuries, German composers have contributed a great deal of superb music—symphonies, concerti, chamber music, and opera—to the world. The clergy, nobility, and common people contributed to early German music. From the church came the musical reading of Latin texts, called Gregorian chants after the

German architectural ideas have had worldwide impact. Ludwig Mies van der Rohe, a prominent architect, designed buildings (top) and furniture (middle) that still retain a contemporary look. The Bauhaus Museum in Berlin (right) was designed by Walter Gropius.

6th-century Pope Gregory I, who was one of the first to collect them. The minnesingers were knights and lyric poets of the 12th and 13th centuries who traveled from court to court singing their poems of love and nature. The Meistersinger, who believed that the art of music could be learned like a trade, flourished from the 14th to the early 17th century. The music of the Meistersinger and a great wealth of *Volkslieder,* or "folk songs," originated from the common people. With the Protestant Reformation, church music was introduced to people as hymns.

To recite the names of German composers is to read much of the repertory of orchestras around the world. In the early part of the 18th century, baroque music reached its height in the works of Johann Sebastian Bach. He composed the world's greatest organ music as well as incomparable cantatas, fugues, and concerti. A contemporary, George Frideric Handel, who composed much of his wide range of work in England, is perhaps best loved for his oratorio the *Messiah.*

Probably the greatest of all German composers was Ludwig van Beethoven, who began his immortal work at the end of the 18th century. His nine symphonies and five piano concerti are among the world's most moving music. Beethoven's chamber music and his opera, *Fidelio,* are also part of his great legacy.

In the 19th century, Robert Schumann composed melodious piano music and symphonies. He is also known for the warmth and charm of his *Lieder* ("songs"). Felix Mendelssohn finished his first mature work, the overture to *A Midsummer*

Ludwig von Beethoven's house (left), in Bonn, has been preserved as a museum. Each year, huge crowds come to the Bayreuth Festival to attend operas (below) composed by Richard Wagner.

KING LUDWIG AND HIS CASTLES

King Louis, or Ludwig, II of Bavaria, known during his life as the Mad King, personified the romantic spirit of the 19th century. He was born in 1845 near Munich, the elder son of Bavarian King Maximilian II, and was well educated in the classics. For 22 years, Ludwig was king of Bavaria, ascending the throne when he was just 18. Yet from a very early age, he showed a tendency to eccentricity. Gradually, Ludwig retired from politics and devoted himself to his private artistic projects. He was officially declared insane at the age of 41, and ended his life, either by accident or by suicide, shortly thereafter.

When he was just 15, Ludwig first heard the music of Richard Wagner, recognized his talent, and soon became the composer's most important patron. Ludwig identified himself with legendary heroes of Wagner's *Nibelungen* saga, and was instrumental in setting up the famous festival in Bayreuth that to this day features Wagner's operas.

In addition to playing a crucial role in the promotion of Wagner's music, Ludwig also left a mark as a builder of extravagant castles. He began to construct the first, Neuschwanstein, in 1869, as a tribute to his beloved Wagner. The fairy-tale turreted castle is perched atop a rock ledge near Füssen in the Bavarian Alps, southwest of Munich near the border with Austria, and is decorated with themes from the operas *Lohengrin*, *Parsifal*, and *Tannhaüser*. It is a most eccentric palace, with interior styles ranging from Byzantine through Romanesque to Gothic. Although it was never fully completed, Neuschwanstein is now a major Bavarian tourist attraction.

In 1870, Ludwig embarked on his second project, the Linderhof Castle, which was patterned after the Petit Trianon palace of the French King Louis XVI. Of Ludwig's three castles, Linderhof was the only one to be finished (in

1879), and in fact became the king's favorite residence. It is mostly in rococo style, and features the famous Venus Grotto from the opening scene of Wagner's *Tannhäuser*.

The most magnificent project, the Castle Herrenchiemsee, was intended as a full-scale

Glorious Neuschwanstein stands in the Bavarian Alps, testimony to the artistic inclinations of King Ludwig II. The structure is said to have inspired the design of the Sleeping Beauty castles at the Disney theme parks.

copy of the Versailles Palace in France. It was conceived as a tribute to the French royal dynasty of Bourbon, and, a monument to the idea of absolute monarchy. The founding stone was laid in 1878, but by Ludwig's death in 1886, the palace was only partially finished. The king spent just 16 days there.

THE BLACK FOREST

The Black Forest—or *Schwarzwald* in German—lies in the state of Baden-Württemberg in southwestern Germany. This largest continuous forested region in the country extends roughly in a south-north direction along the right (eastern) bank of the Rhine River, which forms the boundary with France in that stretch. The name Black Forest derives from the dark-colored firs that grow in the higher elevations. The highest peak, Feldberg, rises to 4,898 ft. (1,493 m.).

The enchanting scenery, even though slightly sinister in places, includes idyllic valleys, many with natural lakes. The north is more densely forested than the south, predominantly with oaks and beeches. Unfortunately, acid rain and air pollution have damaged many trees in recent decades. The southern part is more agricultural, with pastureland, fruit orchards, and vineyards. An important source of income has traditionally been the timber industry. At present, the Black Forest also belongs to the prime tourist areas of Germany, with dozens of resorts and spas around the picturesque lakes.

Throughout Europe and North America, the most famous product of the Black Forest could well be the cuckoo clock. Clock making has been popular in the area since the 17th century, and it was in 1738 that the first cuckoo clock made its appearance. It was handcrafted by Franz Anton Ketterer, who lived in the small village of Schönwald, near Triberg. To imitate the cuckoo's call, he used two small bellows. Within a very short time, the production of cuckoo clocks became the main winter occupation of the Black Forest's residents—for long months, they were snowed-in and had plenty of time to

Cuckoo clocks, a product closely associated with the Black Forest, provide outstanding examples of the excellence of German craftsmanship.

learn how to put the clocks together and decorate them with handcarvings. Each spring, the clock peddlers set on their journeys to European towns and cities, where the cuckoo clocks became a desired luxury. By early 19th century, the number of clock makers and clock peddlers reached into the hundreds and, in 1850, a clock-making school was founded in Furtwangen.

Since then, the cuckoo-clock industry has developed and branched out, and the production today is thoroughly modernized. Many kinds of cuckoo clocks are available, but the traditional type with a cuckoo behind a small door is still decorated with handmade wood carvings. The large ones are quite expensive.

Night's Dream, at the age of 17. Many of his later compositions, such as the Italian Symphony, are still worldwide favorites. Johannes Brahms produced beautifully clear, lyric symphonies, as well as chamber music and *Lieder.* Richard Wagner brought a new dimension to German opera with his theory of the *Gesamtkunstwerk* ("total work of art"). Wagner was interested in every aspect of the opera, from the subject to the set design. In such operas as *Die Meistersinger von Nürnberg* ("The Mastersingers of Nuremberg") and *Der Ring des Nibelungen* ("The Ring of the Nibelungs"), he used old German themes as the stories. In the Bavarian town of Bayreuth, a *Festspielhaus* ("festival theater") was built especially for Wagner. Today, the Wagner festival is held annually from late July until late August in Bayreuth.

Another composer of the period, Richard Strauss, carried German music into the 20th century. Strauss also used old German folk themes. In one of his many tone poems, he used the music to describe the merry pranks of a popular folk hero, the rascal Till Eulenspiegel. Strauss' other compositions include the operas *Electra* and *Ariadne auf Naxos.*

In the 20th century, composer Paul Hindemith created new harmonies. German conductors such as Bruno Walter and Otto Klemperer, and composers such as Hans Werner Henze and Karlheinz Stockhausen, gained worldwide recognition. Kurt Masur, who rose to prominence in East Germany, was music director of the New York Philharmonic from 1991 until his retirement in 2002.

ECONOMY

At the end of World War II, the German economy was almost completely ruined. The excessive demands of the Nazi war machine had drained the resources of the country, and air raids had devastated the cities and industries. In addition, the Allies dismantled many of the remaining industrial plants for reparations. The nation's economic life came to a halt. In rebuilding their economies, the two parts of postwar Germany took widely divergent paths, leading to very different results.

East Germany

Although the devastation of the war was about the same in the East and the West, important differences in the East slowed its recovery. The German Democratic Republic had none of the magnificent resources of West Germany's Ruhr district; it had few resources to work with except farmland, potash, and brown coal. It also suffered from massive dismantling of its industrial plants by the Soviet Union in reparation for the losses the U.S.S.R. had incurred at German hands during the war. There was no Marshall Plan to aid the economy, as there was in West Germany. The country faced the future with crippled industries, insufficient agricultural output to feed its people, and nothing to trade for raw materials.

Nationalization of the economy on the Soviet model resulted in a large-scale flight to the West of the skilled labor force: 2.5 million people left East Germany in the first 12 years of its existence. Not until the erection of the Berlin Wall in 1961 was the mass emigration effectively halted.

In comparison with other Communist states, however, East Germany was relatively prosperous and was even hailed as a showcase of socialism. It established international recognition for its optical equipment, but most of its other products were significantly inferior by Western standards. Automobiles (including the troublesome little Trabants, which were the butt of many jokes because their bodies were made of hard plastic rather than metal), pharmaceutical drugs, household appliances, toys, and musical instruments were exported to Eastern Europe, Asia, and Africa. East Germany also produced plastics, petrochemicals, textiles, and fertilizers. East German industry was tied closely to the Soviet Union by a 2,500-mi. (4,023-km.)-long oil pipeline.

The farmlands in East Germany were historically parts of large estates rather than the small, owner-worked strips that were the rule in the West.

When the Soviet Union occupied this area, a radical program of land redistribution was begun. The small farms established by this program, however, were not as productive as had been hoped, and so they were gradually collectivized. It took until 1960 before collectivization was completed.

West Germany

Unlike East Germany, which was slow to recover, West Germany soon after the war experienced an economic comeback of such magnitude that it was called a *Wirtschaftswunder,* an "economic miracle." Much of that miracle was due to the help given West Germany under the European Recovery Program. From 1948 to 1952, the Marshall Plan—as the program was called—poured no less than $3.5 billion into the country.

The money received was wisely used. Investments in modern machinery and the complete retooling of industrial plants enabled West German industry to manufacture products efficiently and inexpensively enough to compete in the world market.

A combination of many factors brought prosperity beyond anything Germany had ever experienced. The Federal Republic had no military expenditures during the early postwar years. (After it became a member of the North Atlantic Treaty Organization—known as NATO—in 1955, Allied troops remained at their stations as West Germany developed its defense forces.) Moreover, in a country where 20 percent of the dwellings were completely destroyed or heavily damaged by the end of the war, the need for new housing was enormous. Capital from an increasingly healthy economy spurred the rebuilding effort. All kinds of consumer goods were in demand and provided an excellent market for industry. Manufactured products were exported throughout the world and further contributed to the "economic miracle." By the mid-1950s, virtual full employment prevailed.

After the first impetus, a general expansion of world trade began. Because of German production and marketing skills, the country's export volume doubled, redoubled, and more than doubled again. West Germany's charter membership in the European Economic Community in 1958 helped to increase prosperity.

In the postwar years, Germany emerged as an important automaker, with Volkswagen, BMW, and other manufacturers producing enormously popular cars.

Industry

The heart of Germany's industrial might is still centered in the state of North Rhine–Westphalia, whose coal mines, steel plants, and huge industrial concerns employ about 3 million workers. The coal supply of the Ruhr keeps the blast furnaces and rolling mills turning out steel. As a result, Germany is one of the world's largest producers of steel.

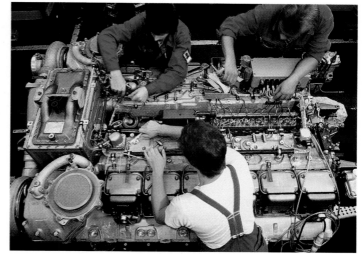

A highly skilled team of mechanics assembles a marine diesel engine at one of Germany's giant shipbuilding plants.

Düsseldorf, the capital of North Rhine–Westphalia, is home to many of Germany's metalworking plants. The city owes its growth to its location on the Rhine and to its rail connections to the Ruhr.

Other sources of income for Germany include chemical and textile industries, particularly in the field of synthetics. German optical and precision instruments, fine cameras, and watches are sold in every major city. Electronic equipment, television sets, radios, and musical instruments are all part of the stream of German products. Imaginatively designed and intricately decorated toys have long charmed children all over the world.

Germany has experienced an uninterrupted rise in exports of heavy machinery, machine tools, electrical equipment, and chemical products. Another leading export is automobiles. From Volkswagen to Mercedes-Benz, German cars are popular the world over.

The former East Germany went through an unprecedented industrial collapse just after unification. Of more than 3 million people employed in industry, about 2 million lost their jobs. Thanks to huge investments from the West (about $70 billion each year), the economy is slowly improving, but it is estimated that it will take 20 to 30 years to bring the former socialist "showcase" to the level of its Western relative. Indeed, by 2000, eastern Germany was peppered with gleaming shopping malls and high-tech factories, and its telephone system was the most sophisticated in the world—but productivity remained at 60 percent of the western level, and unemployment exceeded 17 percent, compared to 8 percent in the West.

Agriculture and Fishing

For many years, Germans have been moving away from the country and farming and into the cities and industry. Today, less than 3 percent of the population is engaged in agriculture, forestry, or fishing. Most of the farms are small—about 22 acres (9 ha.) on the average—and are worked by their owners.

Germans are productive farmers. Crop rotation, the proper use of fertilizers, and modern machinery have helped to increase productivity. The most important crops are wheat, barley, potatoes, and sugar beets. Dairy farming and the raising of livestock—cattle, pigs, sheep, horses, and chickens—are responsible for a large part of agricultural income.

The growing of grapes and the accompanying industry of wine making, although a small part of the national economy, are part of a heritage that dates back to Roman days. The fine Riesling wines come from vineyards along the banks of the Rhine.

A thriving fishing industry is centered around the North Sea ports. Bremerhaven is one of the busiest fishing ports of Europe. Many fishermen travel to faraway grounds in the North Atlantic or even in the Arctic Ocean in search of seafood. Herring makes up the bulk of the catch, but cod, sole, and flounder are also caught in some quantities.

Services

Similarly to all other highly developed countries, Germany has seen a profound change in the structure of its economy during the past decades. At the beginning of the 21st century, only one-third of the working population was employed in industry, and almost two-thirds earned their living in trade, transportation, government agencies, or services.

Germans love to travel, and the country is home to Europe's largest travel agencies. In 2001, about 76 million Germans (out of a population of 83 million) traveled abroad, and 38 million foreigners visited Germany from other countries. The flourishing tourism industry is closely linked to the abundance of information on the Internet.

Germany is the leading member of the European Monetary Union (EMU), and, in 2002, the German mark was replaced by the euro.

The Welfare State

Although the cost of reunification has been much higher than projected, workers in the western part of Germany continue to enjoy a better life than

German agriculture is highly efficient. Its vineyards (right) produce wines of worldwide renown. In mountainous areas, sheep (below) and other domestic animals graze in the high meadows.

Germany's offshore waters provide a livelihood for a small number of fishermen (above), although quite a few more seek the bigger catches to be had in the rich North Atlantic and Arctic fishing grounds.

workers anywhere else. Their average workweek is only 37.5 hours, they have an annual vacation of six weeks, and they often retire at the age of 60. They have comprehensive health care and generous pensions. When their children want to study at a college or university, they do not have to worry about high tuition costs.

Germany is a very comfortable and efficient place to live. Intercity trains are equipped with onboard computers that show travelers how many minutes until the next stop. Public transportation is well developed, and many cities boast "pedestrian only" zones. Germany employs prudent environmental policies that discourage unnecessary waste.

As in most other developed countries, however, the population is growing older as people live longer and fewer children are born. In 2000, there were two Germans of working age for every retiree; by 2035, there will be only one. Although the government has been grappling with this issue for quite some time, it has not found an easy solution. Increased immigration would be one way to address this imbalance, but many people in Germany, including politicians, think that immigration is currently too high. In fact, immigration is becoming one of the largest public issues in the early 2000s. Many politicians argue that non-European newcomers from Asia and Africa are increasing the burden on the welfare system, because, unlike in the United States, they are entitled, immediately after arriving, to a wide range of social benefits.

Germany: Today and Tomorrow

In the second half of the 1990s, many Germans felt dissatisfied and even talked about a looming crisis. Part of this mood was clearly connected with unfulfilled expectations about the unification process, expectations that ran high after the Berlin Wall was dismantled. In 1989, Chancellor Kohl promised West Germans that no tax increases would be needed to pay for reunification. He was unable to keep that promise, and the actual costs— about $70 billion each year—were covered by the so-called "solidarity tax"

Germany no longer has an ethnically homogenous population. On nearly any Berlin sidewalk (above), the diversity of the crowds testifies to Germany's appeal to immigrants from distant continents.

that West Germans were required to pay. Only in 1997 was this surcharge decreased, from 7.5 to 5 percent.

Continuing unemployment, which reached an all-time postwar high of 12.6 percent in January 1998, and stifling bureaucratic regulations have contributed to the discontent. In some German states, a new business needs approval of up to 90 government agencies before it can open. The regulations also affect services, which have traditionally been a German weak point. For example, each state strictly enforces shopping hours, and most stores are closed Saturday afternoons and Sundays.

By the turn of the millennium, however, the mood seems to be changing. Social security, so valued by older generations (Germans were seldom laid off, and few companies went bankrupt), does not seem to worry younger Germans, who increasingly turn to Anglo-American models—more individual responsibility coupled with greater risks, yet greater chances for success. The country is fascinated by young entrepreneurs—*die Jungen Unternehmer*—and their success stories. Some of these young people have made their fortunes in the former East Germany. A majority of old enterprises there were dismantled and new facilities built from scratch, which enabled young managers and owners to be more flexible and innovative. The new Opel automobile factory built near the town of Eisenach in 1992, for example, is one of the most efficient car plants in the world.

Meanwhile, the government is trying to boost the information-age economy. In the late 1990s, German universities increased their capacity for information-technology (IT) students from 13,000 to 40,000, and in the spring of 2000, the government issued temporary work permits for 20,000 IT specialists from other countries to help fill open jobs in this sector. All this bodes well for the future.

CITIES

German cities are both rooted in the past and thoroughly up-to-date. At the end of World War II, most of them lay in ruins, but they have all been restored and renovated and are sparkling with life.

Sections of many cities were reduced to rubble at the end of World War II. In their determination to restore the old, medieval parts of cities, known as the *Altstadt,* the Germans sometimes duplicated well-remembered streets down to the last cobblestone. This has caused many traffic jams, as cars from modern four-lane highways are funneled into narrow replicas of streets laid out centuries ago. Skyscrapers, housing developments, and modern factories can also be found alongside much older buildings, and crenellated castles sometimes hover over newly built supermarkets. Huge metropolises have sprung up around the cities of Essen, Hamburg, and Munich. In the former East Germany, on the other hand, the growth of large cities at the cost of smaller towns and villages was slower than in West Germany.

Berlin, the largest German city and its capital since 1991, is treated in a sidebar beginning on page 280. Other major cities include:

Hamburg. Germany's second-largest city after Berlin, Hamburg is a busy, cosmopolitan port with an English influence. Shipyards, docks, and wharves line both shores of the Elbe River as it flows toward the North Sea.

One of the leading seaports in all of Europe, Hamburg has many faces. A skyscraper rises in the center of the new university complex. Hagenbecks Tierpark is at once a park and a zoo. In the Planten und Blumen botanical garden, the displays of flowers, the open-air theater, the children's playgrounds, and the restaurants on the lake make the area a pleasure park for all.

The Inner Alster and the Outer Alster, two lakes in the heart of the city, provide a delightful setting for

In Bremen (above) and many other German cities, the central districts have been transformed into pedestrian-only zones.

the office buildings and homes that rim their shores.

Lübeck. Northeast of Hamburg, on the Trave River near the Baltic, is the small city of Lübeck. Residents still take pride in their city's fame as "queen of the Hanseatic League"—the medieval association that controlled shipping as far away as Norway and the Netherlands. The steeply gabled salt warehouses date from the 14th and 15th centuries. Lübeck's best-known product is marzipan, an almond paste often shaped into fanciful forms. Marzipan confections have gained worldwide popularity.

Potsdam. Just southwest of Berlin is Potsdam, where the palace of Prussia's King Frederick II (Frederick the Great) is located. He was a lover of

Hamburg is Germany's second-largest city and one of the leading ports in Europe. Its location—68 miles inland on the Elbe River—offers ships protection from unpredictable North Sea weather.

all things French, and he named his castle *Sans Souci* ("Carefree"). This 18th-century monarch invited many of Europe's intellectuals to visit and exchange ideas with him. In the palace are the rooms used by the French writer Voltaire when he was Frederick's guest. The building is now a popular museum and tourist attraction. The Potsdam Conference at the end of World War II was held in the city.

Düsseldorf. This port on the Rhine is the business center for the Ruhr industries. The city is the capital of the richest state in Germany, North Rhine–Westphalia. Completely rebuilt after the war, Düsseldorf boasts modern buildings, lovely parks, and several museums—including two art museums, an economics museum, and a Goethe collection. Its huge convention facilities can accommodate thousands of people, making Düsseldorf a much-sought-after site for many important business meetings and international trade conferences.

Cologne. The Rhine River city of Cologne (Köln am Rhein) is famous for its Gothic cathedral, begun in 1248 but not finished until 1880, and for its university, dating from 1388, the second oldest in Germany (after Heidelberg). In the 18th century, an Italian chemist named a new product for the city—*Kölnisch Wasser*, or "eau de Cologne."

Cologne is a major industrial city, and a business and cultural center for the surrounding region. It is also an important communication hub, with a large airport and river port.

Stuttgart. This important industrial city and railroad junction is the capital of the state of Baden-Württemberg. It is also a publishing center and

Lübeck's salt warehouses (above) look much as they did 500 years ago. Today, Lübeck is perhaps best known for its marzipan, a popular almond-based confection.

is home to art and music academies, a famous ballet company, and the New State Gallery. The city dates to the 10th century, but it began to grow only after the Napoleonic Wars in the early 19th century. It was heavily damaged during World War II and had to be almost completely rebuilt from scratch.

Bonn. In 1949, when the Federal Republic of Germany was formed, the quiet university city of Bonn was chosen as the capital. It sits on the Rhine River, about 15 mi. (24 km.) south of Cologne. Many new buildings, including the *Bundeshaus,* or parliament, were erected to house the government. During the 1990s, the government was transferred to Berlin, and a number of United Nations (UN) agencies and other international organizations moved to Bonn.

It was in Bonn in 1770 that composer Ludwig van Beethoven was born. His birthplace is preserved as a museum, and a music festival is held there every two years.

Aachen. West of Cologne and Bonn, near the Belgian border, is the famous city of Aachen. A health resort since Roman times, it was the capital of the 9th-century Holy Roman Emperor Charlemagne, who built his palace there. The 14th-century town hall was erected on the ruins of that

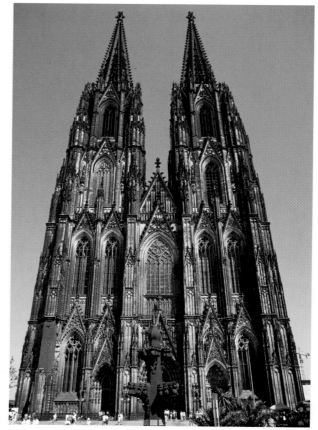

Cologne Cathedral (right), Germany's best-known example of Gothic architecture, took more than 600 years to build.

palace. Winding streets and ancient red-brick houses surround the octagonal cathedral (Dom), begun during the emperor's reign and containing his tomb.

Leipzig. After East Berlin, Leipzig was the largest city in East Germany. About 90 mi. (145 km.) southwest of the capital, it has been an important trading center since the early Middle Ages. The Leipzig Fair, a showplace for merchants' goods, has been a tradition for more than 800 years. Today, this international exhibit takes place twice a year. Leipzig is also a center of publishing.

The great composer Johann Sebastian Bach, who died in Leipzig in 1750, is buried in the Thomaskirche (Church of St. Thomas) in Leipzig. Bach, the greatest member of a famous musical family, was the director of music at the church. Richard Wagner was born there in 1813.

Dresden. Another important city located in the former East Germany is Dresden, which had been the capital of the medieval and Renaissance duchy of Saxony. During World War II, Dresden, 65 mi. (105 km.) southeast of Leipzig, was the most heavily bombed city of Germany. In February 1945, more than 700 British planes, followed by American aircraft, rained fire, destruction, and death on Dresden. Firestorms raged for almost two weeks. According to most accounts, about 135,000 people were killed, including many refugees, prisoners of war, and slave laborers from Eastern Europe. More than 70 historic buildings were completely destroyed, and hundreds of thousands of people were left homeless. One of the most vivid portrayals of this event is in Kurt Vonnegut's anti-war novel *Slaughterhouse Five* (1969), which was also made into a movie.

Many of Dresden's famous buildings were restored according to the detailed paintings of the Venetian painter Bernardo Bellotto (Canaletto the Younger), who worked in Dresden in the 18th century. The most famous restoration is the Zwinger. This building contains such well-known paintings as the *Sistine Madonna* by the Italian artist Raphael.

After World War II, Dresden became a busy industrial city. The delicate Dresden china that is its best-known product, however, is made in the town of Meissen, about 15 mi. (24 km.) away. The nearby deposits of kaolin have been used since the 17th century for the manufacture of china.

Weimar. In the wooded hills some 55 mi. (89 km.) southwest of Leipzig is the peaceful town of Weimar. Germany's greatest literary figure, Johann Wolfgang von Goethe, lived and worked there for a good part of his life. He died in Weimar in 1832. In the Goethe Haus today, visitors can see the desk at which he wrote his masterpiece, *Faust.* Germans come here each year to pay tribute to this great writer. It was in this town, after World War I, that the constitution for the short-lived Weimar Republic was written.

Frankfurt. On the Main River in west-central Germany is the old city of Frankfurt (the full name is Frankfurt am Main, to distinguish the city from

Frankfurt an der Oder, near the German-Polish border). Although relatively small (only the fifth-largest city in Germany), Frankfurt is a busy, modern city, with one of the largest airports in Europe. It has been an important banking center since the Middle Ages; five of Germany's largest banks are headquartered there. It is also home to machinery, leather, and chemical industries. About 30 percent of Frankfurt's residents are foreigners.

Its cathedral, begun in the 13th century, and the ancient Römer (the *Rathaus,* or city hall) are

Meissen (left) is world famous for the beautiful hand-painted porcelain produced there. Many of the structures in the principal town square of Frankfurt (below) epitomize the half-timber style of construction.

Heidelberg's Old Town is sandwiched between the Neckar River and the hills that lead up to the ruins of the city's castle (background), a 13th-century structure featuring Gothic turrets and Renaissance-style walls.

only two of the many restored buildings in Frankfurt's *Altstadt* ("old city"). The birthplace of Frankfurt's most famous son, Goethe, with the original furnishings, draws many visitors.

Heidelberg. South of Frankfurt, nestled in the Neckar Valley, is the town of Heidelberg, with its 13th-century castle and its world-renowned university. The university, the oldest in Germany, was founded in 1386. Much has been written about student life in Heidelberg, with emphasis on dueling. Members of the *Burschenschaften* (fraternities) proudly displayed facial scars as proof of valor. Dueling was forbidden by the Allies after World War II. But traditions die hard, and some dueling, though legally outlawed, may still be going on to this day.

Munich. Munich, the capital of the state of Bavaria, is the fastest-growing city in Germany. The charm and vigorous pace of this south German metropolis, the fine Ludwig-Maximilian University, and the high wages paid by its many factories have made it a magnet for newcomers every year.

This fascinating city has much to offer, and it no longer bears the scars of war. Almost every building was damaged by air raids in World War II. The Frauenkirche (Cathedral of Our Lady), whose copper-domed spires are the city's landmark, has been restored. The Alte Pinakothek, one of Europe's great museums, is in perfect condition. The National Theater and the charming Cuvillies Theater have also been rebuilt.

Munich's outdoor pleasures include the botanical and zoological gardens and the many fine walks in the Englischer Garten.

The joyous side of Munich's life starts with the pre-Lenten carnival, the Fasching, with parades, floats, and masked balls. In March and May, there are beer festivals, with extra-strong beer on tap. For hundreds of years,

MUNICH AND THE OKTOBERFEST

Munich is an important south German city on the Isar River. A major ford existed in this location in Roman times, and then a settlement called Munichen (from the German word for "monk") was established by members of the Benedictine order from a nearby abbey. The official founding of Munich took place in 1158, when a duke of Saxony built the first bridge across the river, and the town was granted market rights. By the end of the Middle Ages, Munich was a busy trading crossroads, and during the 19th century, it became a center of music and theater. Unfortunately, the city is also closely connected with the darkest chapter in German history: it was the birthplace of the Nazi Party in 1920, and the place of the ill-fated Munich Pact of September 1938, a prologue to World War II.

This connection is slowly receding into the past, and the name of Munich is now associated mostly with the world's largest festival and open-air fair, the Oktoberfest, a celebration that takes place each September and October. The feast lasts 16 days and attracts millions of visitors from many countries. Huge tents are set up, in which people listen to bands, sing, drink beer from special 1-liter (2-pint) glass mugs, and eat white sausage (*Weisswurst*), a Munich specialty, pig's knuckles (*Schweinshaxen*), and roasted fish pieces on spits (*Stecklersfisch*).

The Oktoberfest dates from 1810, when the wedding of Crown Prince Ludwig of Bavaria (later King Ludwig I) was celebrated by festivities lasting for five days. They included parades, music, eating and drinking, and a final horse race. The next year, an agricultural festival was added in which horses and oxen were awarded prizes. Soon carousels and swings were brought in, and the tradition of huge beer tents began. In 1881, the world's biggest chicken rotisserie opened on the grounds.

During the first half of the 20th century, because of political upheavals and wars, Germans had few incentives to engage in merriment. In 1950, however, the tradition of Oktoberfest was renewed by the mayor of Munich, and the festival has grown more and more popular ever since. Only breweries from Munich are permitted to sell their beer at this occasion. Recent Oktoberfests have each year welcomed about 6 million visitors who drank almost that many liters of beer.

Tourists flock to Munich each year for the Oktoberfest, the city's annual beer festival. The celebration begins in late September and lasts 16 days, always concluding on the first Sunday of October.

Munich has maintained a reputation for its fine beers. The many *Bierstuben, Biergarten, Bierhallen,* and *Bierkellern* (beer rooms, beer gardens, beer halls, and beer cellars) serve every variety.

But the greatest festivities take place during the Oktoberfest, a 16-day holiday that begins at the end of September. Huge tents, amusement parks, yodelers, bands, folk dancers, mountains of food, and rivers of beer are all features of this Bavarian festival. (See the sidebar on page 271.)

Nuremberg. About 95 mi. (153 km.) north of Munich is the city of Nuremberg, home of the 16th-century artist Albrecht Dürer. Much of the medieval part of this town has been restored, including the Dürer Haus, the 14th-century Schöner Brunnen ("beautiful fountain"), and the lovely Gothic Frauenkirche (Church of Our Lady). Nuremberg has long been the center of the German toy industry. Each December, the Christkindlmarkt (Christmas fair), featuring handmade tree ornaments and glittering Nuremberg tree angels with gold-foil wings, is held there, as it has been for many years.

But Nuremberg's past has its dark side, too, particularly in the era preceding and during World War II. The city was the scene of the massive torchlight parades of the Nazi Party. The infamous Nuremberg Laws of 1935 deprived the Jews of their civil rights. And at the conclusion of the Nazi era, the war-crimes trials took place there.

HISTORY

It was only in 1871 that the first political unification of Germany was completed and a centralized government was formed. In this respect, Germany is one of the newer nations of Europe. Although there was no Germany until the 19th century, the history of the people goes far back in time. Germans were first mentioned in recorded history by the Romans, when they extended their conquests northward from Italy in the 1st century B.C.

In A.D. 9, Germanic tribes were victorious against the Roman legions in a battle in the Teutoburg Forest beyond the Rhine River. From then on, the Romans were content to remain behind their protective ramparts on the lower Rhine and upper Danube Rivers. They founded cities and brought Roman civilization to the nearby tribes. Vestiges of their presence can still be seen in towns along the Rhine.

In the 4th century A.D., barbarian tribes from the north and the east began to attack the Romans. The Roman Empire started to collapse, and Germanic tribes from beyond the Rhine-Danube border poured into western Europe. Some became Christians as they mingled with the Romans and adopted Roman customs. Smaller groups merged, and gradually some tribes—such as the Alemanni, the Saxons, and the Franks—became more powerful than others.

The Holy Roman Empire (First Reich)

The Frankish tribes carved out a kingdom in Gaul (present-day France) and on both sides of the Rhine. The greatest of the Frankish kings was Charlemagne, whom both the Germans and the French claim as their own. As he pushed eastward from the Rhine to the Elbe, Charlemagne brought Christianity to the warlike Saxons. In Rome, in A.D. 800, he was crowned by Pope Leo III and proclaimed "Emperor of the Romans." From his capital at Aachen, Charlemagne ruled the territories known as the First Reich.

With the death of Charlemagne, the empire began to fall apart. In 843, the Treaty of Verdun divided the empire among Charlemagne's three grandsons. One grandson took the German lands to the east, one took the western part (later France), and another took the center (later the Low Countries and parts of France and Italy).

Within the east Frankish kingdom, five great tribal duchies developed—Franconia, Swabia, Bavaria, Saxony, and Lorraine. Each was a powerful force within the kingdom, and the dukes ruled their lands almost as if they were independent kingdoms. Even within the duchies, lesser nobles—counts, bishops, and margraves—often fought for independence from the dukes who reigned over them.

In the 10th century, Otto, the duke of Saxony, grew strong enough to command unity. Because he repulsed the Hungarian invaders in A.D. 955, he was hailed as the savior of Christendom. Otto, too, was crowned in Rome as ruler of a revived Holy Roman Empire that was to last until the early 19th century. Succeeding emperors had to struggle to hold the empire together, gradually losing much of their power at home. And the German nobles grew increasingly more unwilling to give up power to an emperor.

The boundaries of the empire grew too narrow to contain the German people. From the 10th century onward, there was a steady migration eastward in search of new land. By the 13th century, Germans were firmly established in lands to the east that would later form the nucleus of the kingdom of Prussia. At the same time, there was a growth of trade, shipping, and industry. Some cities became strong enough to be free from the rule of princes or dukes.

In the west of the country, not far from the border with Luxembourg, stands Trier, one of the most ancient cities in Germany and the site of the country's best-preserved Roman ruins (above).

Other free cities, such as Bremen and Lübeck, banded together to protect their trade and shipping. This association was called the Hanseatic League, and it became the most powerful force in the North and Baltic Seas.

The great unifying force in the divided country was the Roman Catholic Church. But in 1517, Martin Luther, a Roman Catholic priest, became the leader of a movement that would further divide the land. Martin Luther believed that forgiveness was a free gift from God, and not something to be purchased from the church in a document known as an indulgence. His 95 Theses on the subject of indulgences began the Protestant movement in Germany. Bitter religious strife ensued between Catholics and Protestants. Most of the south Germans and their rulers continued to worship as Roman Catholics. In the north, many of the princes and their followers accepted Protestant teachings and were anxious to have a Protestant king. Religious dissension touched off the Thirty Years' War, which involved many other countries, but was fought mainly on German soil. The Peace of Westphalia, which ended the war in 1648, paved the way for religious toleration. But Germany was a wasteland; its commerce was in ruins. One tiny Bavarian town, Oberammergau, still commemorates its deliverance from a terrible plague in 1633. Every 10 years, the inhabitants enact Christ's last days on Earth. Visitors come from all over the world to see the Oberammergau Passion Play, performed to fulfill a pledge made during the Thirty Years' War.

At the end of the war, there were more than 300 separate units of government. The Germanys, as they were often called, were actually a collection of petty principalities under the Holy Roman Emperor.

The Rise of Prussia

With the return of peace in the 17th century, the various rulers tried to restore some prosperity. The most successful was Frederick William I of Brandenburg, who took over the duchy of Prussia. He devoted his reign to the task of building military might in his small state. His son took the title of Frederick II, king of Prussia, in 1740, and became known as Frederick the Great. Under the rule of the Hohenzollern dynasty (Hohenzollern was the family name of the Prussian kings), Prussia turned into a European power of consequence. To extend his control, Frederick the Great seized the province of Silesia in 1741, and in 1772, he joined with Austria and Russia in the first partition of Poland.

The Hohenzollern princes were schooled in stern discipline. All-important virtues were absolute obedience, hard work, and frugality, among others. As Prussia struggled to achieve power and success, it also glorified patriotism and militarism. These Prussian traditions exerted a profound influence on later German history, when Prussia became the primary center of German nationalism.

At the beginning of the 19th century, Napoléon I of France annexed much of Germany. He swept away scores of ancient ministates in a series of reorganizations and reforms. Napoléon refused to recognize the title of Holy Roman emperor, and thus crushed forever the remains of the medieval empire.

Frederick the Great (above) and other rulers of the 18th-century Hohenzollern dynasty had a profound impact on German history.

Prussia, too, had been defeated by Napoléon. In a few years, however, it was Prussia that rallied the German states to rise against the French. In a "war of liberation," German armies pushed Napoléon back across the Rhine in October 1813.

The Rise of Modern Germany

The peace settlement reached at the Congress of Vienna in 1815 made Prussia even stronger by giving it the Rhineland, with the seemingly inexhaustible coal deposits of the Ruhr. At the same time, the congress further consolidated the country.

Democratic stirrings in the following generation led to the revolutions of 1848. In sections of Germany, as well as the rest of Europe, a struggle for political, economic, and social changes took place. The strong spirit of German nationalism found expression in a constitution drawn up in Frankfurt.

The constitution called for a federal state of Germany, with a constitutional monarchy headed by the king of Prussia. The king of Prussia rejected the constitution, and, even among the reformers, there was disagreement. Many Germans left for the United States when all revolt was crushed.

German unity under Prussian leadership was achieved a generation later by Otto von Bismarck. Bismarck, known as the Iron Chancellor, was a brilliant statesman and an advocate of autocratic Prussian power. He was ready to wage war to achieve German unification. In quick succession, he guided Prussia to military victories over Denmark (1864) and Austria (1866). In 1867, he organized the North German Confederation, which united German states north of the Main River.

In 1870, Bismarck maneuvered the French into the Franco-Prussian War. A victorious Prussia pressed harsh terms on France and took most of the provinces of Alsace and Lorraine as well as huge reparations. During this period, the south German states joined Bismarck's confederation. In 1871, at the palace of the kings of France in Versailles, William I of Prussia was declared the emperor of a Germany united as the Second Reich. The military character of the assemblage was symbolic of the part the army would play in the German Empire.

The German Empire and World War I

A united nation had now been created in the heart of Europe. Berlin was the capital of the new Germany, as it had been for Prussia. The new state was a constitutional monarchy, but Chancellor Bismarck kept an iron grip on the country. From 1871 to 1918, the people were officially called "German subjects" rather than citizens.

This was a time of great prosperity for the new nation. Germany became a leading industrial power. Arts and sciences flourished. Theaters, opera houses, and concert halls sprang up throughout the country. Universities were built, and, because of their excellence, they attracted scholars from all over the world. Germany, seeking its "place in the Sun," built up a colonial empire in Africa and in the Pacific.

Some Germans, however, seeing their country hemmed in at the center of Europe, spoke of a fear of encirclement by its enemies. The young Emperor William II, who had ascended the throne in 1888, wanted to run the empire in his own way, and in 1890, he dismissed Bismarck.

The brief period of peace and prosperity that Germany enjoyed beginning with unification was consumed in the fires of World War I. In 1914, after Archduke Francis Ferdinand, the heir to the Austrian throne, was assassinated by a Serbian student, Austria made impossible demands on the Serbian government. Germany backed Austria in these demands. In World War I, Germany and Austria faced Britain, France, and Russia. By the time the United States entered the war in 1917, the conflict had taken a terrible toll on the battlefield and was beginning to cause much suffering on the home front in Germany. In 1918, the military leadership sued for peace. The kaiser (emperor) was forced to abdicate.

The Weimar Republic

In 1919, a democratic republic was proclaimed. Because the national assembly met in Weimar to write a constitution, the new government became known as the Weimar Republic. The new state started under difficult handicaps as it tried to meet the terms of a severe peace treaty.

At the same palace in Versailles where the German Empire had been declared in 1871, a German delegation received the terms of peace. The Treaty of Versailles of 1919 returned Alsace and Lorraine to France and stripped Germany of its colonies. New boundaries were drawn for Germany that took away border areas that had large non-German populations. Germany was not allowed to own or manufacture tanks or military planes. The armed forces were to be held down to 100,000 troops. A huge amount of money was to be paid in reparations.

The Germans found it difficult to accept these terms, and even more difficult to make a recovery. Inflation destroyed the buying power of Germany's currency, the mark. At one point in the early 1920s, a U.S. dollar could buy billions of paper marks. Life savings were wiped out, and people had to carry their salaries home in suitcases, only to find that the money could scarcely buy a loaf of bread.

But many Germans refused to acknowledge that Germany had been defeated on the battlefield. The Weimar Republic became identified with the loss of the war, the humiliation of the Versailles Treaty, and the hunger and inflation of the postwar years. By the late 1920s, however, a stabilized currency had halted the devastating inflation.

A worldwide depression, triggered by the U.S. stock-market crash of 1929, shook Germany just when some stability had been achieved. Millions of Germans lost their jobs. By the winter of 1932, more than 6 million people were unemployed. Breadlines formed in all of the cities.

The economic crisis opened the door for Adolf Hitler. He was the leader of the Nationalsozialistische Deutsche Arbeiterpartei (National Socialist German Workers' Party). The Nazis, as they were generally called, promised a rebirth of German greatness. Despite the violence of their tactics, their appeals to national pride attracted thousands to their ranks.

Hitler was a passionate and hypnotic speaker. His promises to restore prosperity and to regain Germany's lost territories won him many followers. His vicious attacks on the Jews gained support from those who were happy to find a scapegoat for the country's woes.

The Third Reich

In January 1933, although the National Socialists had not obtained a majority in free elections, aging President Paul von Hindenburg was persuaded to appoint Adolf Hitler as chancellor of Germany. Hitler was given dictatorial powers by an act of the Reichstag and became *führer* ("leader") of the Third Reich. Hitler established a totalitarian and utterly ruthless dictatorship. He outlawed all other political parties, as well as the trade unions, and turned the press and radio into instruments of Nazi propaganda. Opponents of the regime were imprisoned and often murdered. The 600,000 German Jews were deprived of citizenship by the Nuremberg Laws of 1935, and those who could not emigrate faced unbelievable horrors.

But many Germans were eager to identify with Hitler and Nazism because the man and his movement seemed to be restoring Germany to its prewar glory. Youth camps and public-works projects helped to relieve unemployment. Rearmament, too, provided new jobs, as Hitler openly disregarded the Versailles Treaty ban on German arms.

In March 1936, Hitler ordered his soldiers into the demilitarized Rhineland. At this point, he probably could have been stopped. But France and Britain, unable to agree on what to do, looked the other way. In

Germany played a pivotal role in the events of the early 20th century. World War I caused great suffering and ultimately led to the end of monarchy with the abdication of Kaiser Wilhelm II (left, on horseback). Adolf Hitler (right) and the Nazi Party led Germany into World War II. Much of Germany lay in ruins by the end of the war.

October of the same year, Benito Mussolini, the Italian dictator, and Hitler formed an alliance, often called the Rome-Berlin Axis. Later, Japan joined Germany in the Anti-Comintern Pact, supposedly aimed against the spread of Communism. Italy became the third member in 1937.

Encouraged by the ease with which he had taken the Rhineland in 1936, Hitler went on to annex Austria in March 1938. Half a year later, at a conference in Munich, Britain and France agreed to Hitler's "last demand"—the Sudetenland. This was an area of Czechoslovakia that had a large German-speaking population. The Munich Pact, which became a symbol of appeasement (a policy of trying to pacify an aggressor), lasted only six months. In March 1939, Hitler broke his pledge and seized all of Czechoslovakia. It was the last of his bloodless conquests.

In August 1939, the leaders of Nazi Germany and of the Soviet Union astounded the world by signing a nonaggression pact. Secure in the knowledge that they would not have to wage a war on two fronts, Nazi troops advanced into Poland on September 1. Britain and France, honoring treaty commitments to Poland, declared war on Germany, and World War II began. The following year, in a *Blitzkrieg* ("lightning war"), Germany overran Denmark, Norway, the Low Countries, and France. The German *Luftwaffe* (air force) bombed Britain mercilessly, but the Royal Air Force saved it from invasion.

When Hitler turned on his Russian ally and invaded the Soviet Union in June 1941, he was the master of most of Europe. He had gained control of the Balkans, but the battle for Yugoslavia and Greece had delayed his timetable for entering and conquering the Soviet Union. This had disastrous consequences because Hitler's armies would now be confronted, not only by the Soviet Army, but by the brutal winter in the U.S.S.R.

On December 7, 1941, Japan, Germany's ally, attacked Pearl Harbor, and the United States entered the war. The U.S.'s productive capacity, the fortitude of the Soviets, the vastness of the Soviet front, and the wrath of the peoples under the Nazi heel were to spell doom for Hitler. The tide turned

THE HOLOCAUST

World War II, the cataclysmic event of the 20th century that cost 45 million people their lives, is remembered in different ways by the countries involved in the war. In the former Soviet Union, for example, the period is commemorated as the Great Patriotic War, in which the gallant Red Army crushed the Nazi enemy. In Western Europe, countless books and movies celebrate the heroic feats of Resistance fighters. In the United States, World War II stories revolve around Pearl Harbor, D-Day, the Battle of the Bulge, and the struggle in the Pacific.

For the Jewish people around the world, World War II is remembered as the *Holocaust*. This Greek word, which until the 1950s was translated and used literally to mean "burnt sacrifice," now generally refers to the systematic massacre of about 6 million Jews during the Nazi period. This dark chapter of Germany's history is also described as *genocide,* a term adopted by the United Nations to describe policies that deliberately result in the extermination of a large national or ethnic or religious group.

The "Final Solution," a code name for the total annihilation of European Jewry, was formalized by Nazi leaders in a protocol signed in 1942. The persecution of Jews, however, began immediately after the accession of Hitler to power in 1933, and it gained in intensity in 1935, with the passage of the Nuremberg Laws depriving German Jews of many basic freedoms. The first concentration camps were set up before the beginning of World War II, and after the war started, many more camps were established in the conquered territories, especially in Poland.

Some of the camps later became extermination centers, in which inmates—mostly Jews—

At the site of the former concentration camp in Dachau, barbed wire still stands, grimly suggestive of the horrors that occurred within.

were killed in specially designed gas chambers. In Auschwitz, 1.5 million people perished. Thousands of other Jews died in pogroms; one of the worst atrocities was the slaughtering of almost 34,000 Ukrainian Jews at the Babi Yar ravine near Kiev.

Over the years, some publicists have argued that the figure of 6 million is exaggerated, but these numbers were first given by Nazi leaders themselves, at the Nuremberg Trials, and later were confirmed in hundreds of studies.

when the Soviets held firm at the Battle of Stalingrad in 1942. Thereafter, the Soviets kept sweeping westward toward Germany.

While the Nazi armies were engaged in battle, other Nazis killed and tortured countless men, women, and children in special camps set up in Germany and in conquered territories, particularly in Poland. Although the Jews were by far the worst sufferers, millions of other victims were confined under atrocious conditions. Extermination centers, prisoner-of-war camps, and concentration camps held people of almost every European nationality, as well as many Germans who had protested against the regime or were suspected of anti-Nazi feelings. The iron grip of the German security forces (known by the feared initials "SS") made any protest difficult and dangerous. Yet resistance—even at the penalty of death—became widespread, tied up large German forces, and ultimately sabotaged the Nazi war machine.

As the Allies opened new theaters of war and counterattacked on all fronts, Germany's military triumphs were slowed. Battles in North Africa and Italy, and then the brilliantly executed Allied D-Day invasion of Normandy on June 6, 1944, began to push back the German armies. The Red Army advanced westward from battlefields deep within the Soviet Union. Allied air raids reduced many German cities to rubble.

A group of German conspirators tried to assassinate Hitler on July 20, 1944. Hitler escaped, and crushed the uprising in a wave of blood and terror that took thousands of lives. But the end was drawing near. By March 1945, Allied troops had crossed the Rhine and were marching into Germany. As the Russian troops entered Berlin from the east, Adolf Hitler committed suicide. On May 7, 1945, the German high command surrendered unconditionally. The Nazi era—the Third Reich—lasted only 12 years instead of the 1,000 that Hitler had predicted.

Oddly, two of Hitler's major objectives, German unity and the end of communism, have only recently become reality, decades after his death. The irony, of course, is that neither of these developments bears any resemblance to his plans, and they actually refute everything for which he stood. The unification of Germany and the collapse of the Communist regimes in Europe and in the Soviet Union are both evidence of the economic and moral strength of the forces that defeated Hitler. Liberal democracy and freedom of expression are the goals of today's movements.

In one major respect, Hitler's legacy is the opposite of his ambitions. The *Holocaust* (see the box on the facing page), as his campaign to exterminate the European Jews is now called, culminated not only in the creation of the first Jewish state in 2,000 years, but also in the growing awareness of the role that the Jewish people have played in European civilization.

Germany's Rebirth—The Years After World War II

Armies of the United States, Britain, France, and the Soviet Union occupied Germany during the final phase of the war. Germany was divided into four zones: American, British, French, and Soviet. In the same fashion, Berlin was divided into four sectors.

At the Potsdam Conference in 1945, the United States, Britain, and the Soviet Union discussed denazification, demilitarization, and the reeducation of Germany. No peace treaty was drafted, but territorial adjustments were made. Part of East Prussia was given to the Soviet Union. Poland received all of Germany east of the Oder and Neisse Rivers. The removal of Germans from Poland, Czechoslovakia, and Hungary resulted in a movement of about 10 million people, most of whom went to the Western zones.

East Germany

When the Soviet Union took over its zone in Germany, it set up a Communist system. Walter Ulbricht, who had been a German Communist leader before Hitler came to power, became the head of the government.

In June 1948, the Soviets imposed a travel ban through East Germany to West Berlin—the so-called Berlin Blockade—which in fact denied the

■ BERLIN

For Germans, Berlin will always be special—not only because it was the first capital of unified Germany in 1871 and a dynamic metropolis in the 1920s, but also because it was the site of the famous Berlin airlift of 1948–49 and of the infamous Wall, a tragic division between two worlds. In 1998, Berlin resumed its role as the capital of the newly united Germany.

The city covers an area of 342 sq. mi. (886 sq. km.) and has a population of about 3.5 million, making it the fourth-most-populous city in Europe (after Moscow, London, and St. Petersburg). The Spree River connects Berlin with the Elbe River and through it with the North Sea.

Seven hundred years ago, Berlin was a small fishing village. In the 15th century, the Hohenzollern rulers of Brandenburg made it their capital. The Thirty Years' War in the 17th century ravaged Berlin, but during the following century, it was revived and became the capital of the Prussian kingdom. During this period, the famous avenue of Unter den Linden was laid out. By 1871, when it became the capital of the newly united German Empire, Berlin had a population of 800,000.

BERLIN BETWEEN THE WARS

Spared damage in World War I, Berlin in the 1920s was known as one of the most glittering and stimulating capitals in the world. Writers, artists, musicians, and filmmakers found the new air of freedom and a prevailing spirit of "anything goes" in the city inspiring. Playwright Bertolt Brecht and composer Kurt Weill collaborated in the writing of *Die Dreigroschenoper* (*The Threepenny Opera*).

The 1972 movie musical *Cabaret* vividly captured the spirit of Berlin in the early 1930s. It was still a free, vibrant city then, but the clouds of Nazism were already gathering. When Adolf Hitler came to power, all intellectual life in Berlin was crushed.

A CITY DIVIDED

During World War II, Berlin was subjected to intense bombing. The city was captured by Soviet forces on May 2, 1945, two days after

Adolf Hitler killed himself. The former metropolis lay in ruins. In July, the United States, the Soviet Union, France, and Great Britain took over the administration of the city. In 1948, the Western powers united their sectors into a single unit. A few months later, the Soviet Union declared that the four-power administration of the city had

Select slabs of the Berlin Wall are preserved to commemorate the structure that for nearly 30 years split the city into a free western half and a totalitarian eastern half.

ceased to exist, and imposed a blockade around the combined Western sector. From June 1948 to May 1949, however, a magnificently orchestrated airlift by U.S., British, and French planes brought food, fuel, and other necessities to the beleaguered city. The final division of the city was completed in August 1961, when East Germans built a heavily fortified wall across the city.

West Berlin. Because of Cold War tensions, West Berlin was in the peculiar situation of being a city-state without a country. People young and old found it difficult to live there, surrounded by a wall and isolated within a sometimes-hostile Communist country. Nevertheless, postwar rebuilding went ahead.

Notable new buildings included the Philharmonic Hall, ultramodern in design and acoustics, and the glass-walled National Gallery, designed by Ludwig Mies van der Rohe, the great contemporary architect. The Kurfürstendamm, or Ku-damm, was one of West Berlin's busiest streets. With its showrooms, offices, elegant shops, cafés, theaters, and nightclubs, the area was bustling both day and night.

The Free University was founded in 1948 to replace the old University of Berlin that lay in the Soviet sector. Abundant parklands within the city were especially dear to West Berliners during the isolation of the Cold War. A favorite excursion was a day trip to the chain of lakes in the Wannsee area to the southwest.

East Berlin. The city was made the capital of the German Democratic Republic. Until the removal of the Berlin Wall in 1989, any foreigner wishing to go from West Berlin to East Berlin had to pass through an entry point nicknamed "Checkpoint Charlie."

In contrast to West Berlin, East Berlin was a drab place of new, uninteresting buildings, constructed in the heavy Stalinist style. At night, there were few of the bright neon lights and little of the excitement, energy, and bustle that characterized West Berlin. The historic *Unter den Linden* boulevard lost most of its sparkle. Yet the city remained a cultural center. East Berlin's most famous theater company was the Berliner Ensemble, founded by Bertolt Brecht in 1948, and managed by his wife for 22 years. The best-known museums were the Pergamon, with its fine collection of Greek sculpture, and the Egyptian Museum, with the 3,000-year-old bust of Egypt's Queen Nefertiti.

THE CAPITAL AGAIN

Since the dismantling of the Berlin Wall, the city has experienced an injection of energy and dynamic change. It has become a major cultural center and a favorite place for international conferences. A festival called Love Parade attracts huge crowds each June.

In 1991, the German Parliament agreed that Berlin should again become the capital of the united country. The historic Potsdamer Platz has turned into an immense construction site. When it is completed, it will be the largest square in Europe.

Berlin's government area is comparable in size to the Washington Mall. In 1999, the German

Berlin is once again the capital of a united Germany. The German Parliament holds its sessions in the Reichstag building (below). Some of Berlin's structures, including the World Time Clock (above), are noted for their decidedly futuristic design.

Parliament had its first sessions in the newly opened Reichstag Building; two years later, the chancellor moved into his new headquarters. The transfer of the capital from Bonn to Berlin is symbolic of a deeper transformation of Germany—from a nation immersed in the past into a nation looking to the future.

city most of its necessities. For nearly a year, all supplies to West Berlin were brought in by a smoothly organized airlift. It was after the failure of the blockade and the establishment of the Federal Republic of Germany in May 1949 that the German Democratic Republic was officially proclaimed.

There was a revolt of construction workers, industrial workers, and other East Berliners in June 1953. Soviet tanks put down the revolt, killing 40 people. After this event, the government improved economic conditions. Despite these improvements, however, many skilled workers and professionals continued leaving for the West. To stop the flow, East Germany in 1961 built a wall separating East and West Berlin.

In the 1970s, after Erich Honecker replaced Walter Ulbricht as head of the party in East Germany, and Willy Brandt became chancellor of West Germany, the two Germanys entered a period of rapprochement. They signed a treaty allowing closer ties in 1972, which led to increased contacts and visits between relatives. Yet East Germany remained a Communist police state and an ally of the Soviet Union. Even when Mikhail Gorbachev began to liberalize the Soviet system after 1985, it seemed that East Germany would remain rigidly Communist for decades to come.

Everything changed in 1989, when tens of thousands of East Germans migrated west through openings in the Iron Curtain provided by Hungary and Czechoslovakia. Meanwhile, rapidly swelling demonstrations in dozens of East German cities brought the Communist government down. On November 9, 1989, the Berlin Wall was opened, and a new chapter in German history began.

West Germany

The United States, Britain, and France combined their zones, and in 1949, the Federal Republic of Germany (or West Germany) was established.

A pair of young bicyclists (left) rides alongside concrete panels and abandoned watchtowers, seemingly unaware that for many years, these structures effectively separated East Germany from the West. Since the end of World War II, U.S. troops (below) have been stationed in Germany.

Under Konrad Adenauer, elected federal chancellor in 1949, the Federal Republic of Germany joined a number of important international organizations. It made valuable contributions to the Council of Europe, the North Atlantic Treaty Organization (NATO), and the European Economic Community (EEC).

Willy Brandt, the Social Democratic Party leader, became the federal chancellor in 1969. He advocated the "Eastern policy," which had as its goal the improvement of relations with the Communist countries. A West German–U.S.S.R. nonaggression pact in 1970, in which the Oder-Neisse line as the border of East Germany and Poland was accepted, was the first success of this policy. In 1971, the United States, the Soviet Union, France, and Britain reached an accord that eased access to West Berlin, and Willy Brandt was awarded the Nobel Peace Prize. In the next year, a treaty normalizing relations between the two Germanys was signed, and in 1973, both countries joined the United Nations. Brandt's successor, Social Democrat Helmut Schmidt, continued to develop economic and political ties with Eastern Europe and the Soviet Union.

Frankfurt is one of many modern German cities that has had great success combining the contemporary with the classic.

United Again

The closing page of the postwar chapter of German history began in May 1989, when Hungary dismantled the barbed wire on its border with Austria. During the summer, some East Germans vacationing in Hungary took advantage of this opening to cross into Austria and then West Germany. Hundreds grew into tens of thousands. Street protests and demonstrations in many East German cities added pressure until the Communist Party ousted Council Chairman Erich Honecker. In November, the entire cabinet resigned, to be followed by most of the Politburo. Honecker and other former Communist leaders were arrested on corruption charges, and the government was forced to agree to hold multiparty elections.

The first free elections in East Germany were held in March 1990, resulting in an overwhelming mandate for reunification with West Germany. A coalition government was formed with a free parliament, and negotiations on the mechanism of reunification began almost immediately. The talks were held in consultation with France, Britain, the United States, and the Soviet Union, since these four countries still technically exercised authority as the occupying powers of World War II.

By mid-1990, reunification had already become a fact in many areas. In July 1990, the two Germanys adopted one currency—the West German *deutsche mark*. On October 3, 1990, the two Germanys merged into one state, and the first all-German elections since 1937 took place in December.

The chief architect of German unification was Christian Democrat Helmut Kohl—the German chancellor from 1983 to 1998—who was the longest-ruling German leader since Bismarck. Even before he reached the age of 20, shortly after World War II, he became convinced that the only way to prevent another war was to unite the continent. And the first step toward that unity was improved relations between France and Germany, the traditional European enemies. Kohl's goal of a united, democratic, and peaceful Germany at the heart of a united, democratic, and peaceful Europe remains key to the continent's future.

In early 1998, unemployment reached an all-time high of nearly 13 percent, which, coupled with an increasing disillusionment over the unification, led to the defeat of Christian Democrats in September by the Social Democratic Party. Kohl was replaced as chancellor by Gerhard Schröder. The following year, Kohl became embroiled in a financial scandal and was forced to step down from the chairmanship of the party. He was replaced by Angela Merkel, who grew up in East Germany. She is another sign of a new Germany—the first woman to head a major political party in the country.

GOVERNMENT

Shortly before the two Germanys were unified, East Germany reestablished five historic states, which replaced the 15 counties into which the country had been divided since 1952. The new states were Mecklenburg–West Pomerania, Brandenburg, Saxony-Anhalt, Saxony, and Thuringia. Following unification, these states then gained the same status as the 10 states that had constituted West Germany under the Basic Law of 1949, which functions as a constitution. These 10 *Länder* ("states") are Schleswig-Holstein, Bremen, Hamburg, Lower Saxony, North Rhine–Westphalia, Hesse, Rhineland–Palatinate, Saarland, Baden–Württemberg, and Bavaria. The Basic Law stipulated that any part of pre–World War II Germany could be admitted as a new state, providing the mechanism for reunification. Unified Berlin became the 16th German state.

The highest authority in the republic is the bicameral federal parliament. The larger and more powerful of the two houses, the *Bundestag* (Federal Diet), has 656 members popularly elected for four-year terms. The other chamber is the *Bundesrat* (Federal Council), whose 69 members are elected by the state governments. The head of state is the federal president, elected for a five-year term by a special assembly made up of the *Bundestag* and an equal number of delegates chosen by the state legislatures. The president, however, has no actual power—presidential functions are purely formal and ceremonial. Real executive power is wielded by the chancellor, or head of government, who is chosen by a majority of the *Bundestag*. The *Bundestag* can at any time, by a simple majority, vote a chancellor out of office. Each state (*Land*) has its own legislature and government.

Political Parties. The two major political parties are the Christian Democratic Union (CDU) and the Social Democratic Party (SPD). The Bavarian Christian Social Union (CSU) has been allied with the CDU since the late 1940s. A small Free Democratic Party (FDP) has alternately allied itself with the CDU/CSU and with the SPD. The environmentalist Green Party, which in 1983 gained representation in the *Bundestag*, won nearly 7 percent of the vote in the 1998 elections. The former dominant party in East Germany renamed itself the Party of Democratic Socialism.

PAUL FREEDMAN, *The Journal of Commerce*

Grindelwald is just one of countless Swiss "picture-book" towns.

SWITZERLAND

Since the 19th century, when tourism first became widespread, the Alps have been the most important part of the world's image of Switzerland. This picture of the country is usually completed by small wooden chalets clinging to sheer hillsides, meadows blanketed by brilliantly colorful wildflowers, and pastures dotted with contented cows and agile goats. Yodeling cowherds can still be encountered in the mountains, and the Swiss also continue to be famous as cheesemakers, chocolatiers, and watchmakers.

To a great degree the Swiss themselves contributed to this image—most notably the author Johanna Spyri. Her novel *Heidi,* the tale of a little orphan who finds a happy life with her grandfather in the Swiss Alps, has been loved by children around the world since 1881.

But Switzerland is more than mere quaintness surrounded by some of the highest and most beautiful peaks in Europe. It is one of the most advanced industrial nations in the world, and it also ranks among the world's oldest democracies. The country is an international financial center, and Geneva, the third-largest city, has been the seat of many international agencies and organizations for the past century.

THE LAND

This small, landlocked country is bounded on the west by France; on the north by Germany; on the east by Austria and tiny Liechtenstein; and on the south and southeast by Italy. Although Switzerland often seems to be all mountains, within its area of almost 16,000 square miles (41,000 square kilometers) it possesses a wide variety of geographical features. In the northwest the soft folds of the Jura Mountains, lined with lush green meadows, form part of the border with France. To the south and southeast the land soars upward to form Switzerland's landmark, the Alps—a majestic company of wild and lofty rocks, snowy peaks, deep gorges, and vast glaciers grouped around the Saint Gotthard and the Bernese Alps. The Swiss Alps reach their highest altitude at 15,203 feet (4,634 meters) in the Dufourspitze of the Monte Rosa group, near the border with Italy. Over 50 Swiss peaks rise higher than 12,000 feet (3,600 meters)—among them the piercing Matterhorn, the towering Finsteraarhorn, the treacherous Eiger, and the dazzling Jungfrau. (An article on the ALPS appears in this volume.)

Still farther south the Alps descend in steep shelves, finally sloping down to one of the most surprising facets of Switzerland—Ticino. Gone is the looming majesty of gleaming peaks. In Ticino, an almost Mediterranean breeze from Italy stirs the oleanders and the palms, and small stone houses painted in pastel tones offer a friendly welcome.

Between the Alps and the Jura lies the central plateau. About two thirds of the Swiss people make their homes in this peaceful region, with its gently rolling hills and pleasant valleys. It is a rich agricultural area, and it is also where most of Switzerland's cities are located.

Rivers and Lakes

The Alps form a vast watershed, and, not unjustly, Switzerland has been called Europe's mother of rivers. The meltwaters of mountain snows and glaciers drain into the sources of two of the continent's great rivers—the Rhine and the Rhone. Two other major rivers that start in the Alps are the Ticino, which joins the Po in Italy, and the Inn, which joins the Danube on the Austro-German border. After carving their way through the rocks of their birthplace, sometimes cascading downward as sparkling waterfalls, all of them flow peacefully toward the seacoasts of Europe, hundreds of miles away.

Another distinctive feature of the Swiss landscape is its approximately 1,500 lakes, ranging from small, icy, crystal-clear ones high in the Alps to larger, more placid ones—Geneva, Lucerne, Zurich, Neuchâtel, Constance, Lugano, and Maggiore—at lower elevations, with cities and resorts on their shores.

Climate

Switzerland's climate is strongly influenced by its Alps. Though temperatures vary with altitude, in most parts of the country winters are cold and summers warm. In the higher mountains winter comes early, with the first snows often falling before the end of October. Most of the peaks above 9,000 feet (2,700 meters) are snow-covered all year round, and, while this contributes to much of the country's beauty, it also presents a grave danger—the avalanche. In the spring, alpine winds melt and loosen huge masses of snow. As the snow hurtles down the

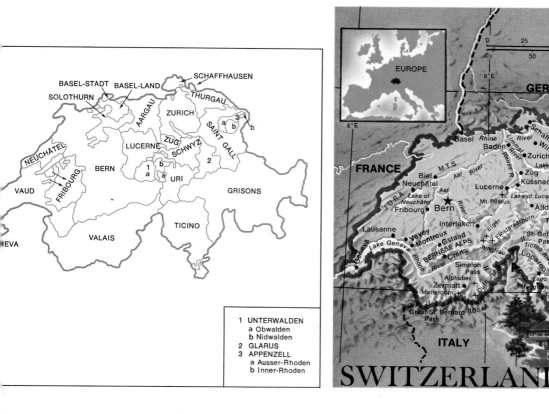

SWITZERLAND

FACTS AND FIGURES

OFFICIAL NAME: Swiss Confederation.

NATIONALITY: Swiss.

CAPITAL: Bern.

LOCATION: Central Europe. **Boundaries**—Germany, Austria, Italy, France.

AREA: 15,942 sq. mi. (41,290 sq. km.).

PHYSICAL FEATURES: Highest point—Dufourspitze (15,204 ft.; 4,634 m.). **Lowest point**—shore of Lago Maggiore (636 ft.; 194 m.). **Chief rivers**—Rhine, Rhone, Ticino, Inn, Aar. **Major lakes**—Geneva, Zurich, Constance, Neuchâtel, Lucerne, Lugano, Maggiore.

POPULATION: 7,300,000 (2002; annual growth 0.2%).

MAJOR LANGUAGES: German, French, Italian.

MAJOR RELIGIONS: Roman Catholicism, Protestantism.

GOVERNMENT: Federal republic. **Head of state and government**—president. **Legislature**—bicameral Federal Assembly.

CHIEF CITIES: Zurich, Basel, Geneva, Bern, Lausanne.

ECONOMY: Chief mineral—salt. **Chief agricultural products**—grains, fruits, vegetables, meat, eggs. **Industries and products**—machinery, chemicals, watches, textiles, precision instruments. **Chief exports**—machinery, chemicals, metals, watches, agricultural products. **Chief imports**—machinery, agricultural products, chemicals, vehicles, metals, textiles.

MONETARY UNIT: 1 Swiss franc = 100 centimes.

NATIONAL HOLIDAY: August 1 (Anniversary of the Founding of the Swiss Confederation).

mountainside it gains momentum and sometimes buries everything in its path—trees, animals, houses, and even whole villages.

But in some parts of Switzerland, the mountains also offer protection. The climate in the central plateau is moderate, without great extremes of temperature; and in Ticino, on the southern slopes of the Alps, summers are hot and winters mild.

ECONOMY

Legend has it that in the 17th century an Englishman traveling in Switzerland asked a blacksmith to repair his watch. The blacksmith studied the complicated mechanism, repaired it—and also made a copy, thus starting the Swiss watchmaking tradition. Fine watches soon became one of the country's best-known products. About 25 million watches and clocks are produced for export each year.

With almost no mineral resources of its own, except salt, Switzerland must import the raw materials for industry. But the Swiss have harnessed many of their rivers, using them as "white coal" to produce hydroelectric power for factories and mills. The Swiss metal and machine industry manufactures turbines, diesel engines, locomotives, precision tools, and scientific instruments, and accounts for almost half of total exports.

Switzerland's second-most-important industry is centered in Basel, where some of the world's largest chemical and drug companies have their headquarters. Besides medicines and vitamins, this industry produces plastics, inks, and dyes. While many of these are exported, the dyes are also used in turning out high-quality Swiss textiles. The old Swiss tradition of fine craftsmanship continues, too, in book production and printing.

Switzerland's banking system is the third most important in the world. The secrecy of individual bank accounts attracted rich depositors, but because this anonymity was sometimes abused, banking laws were amended in 1991 to eliminate most of the anonymous accounts as of September 1992.

Agriculture

Although Switzerland is one of the most highly industrialized nations in Europe, agriculture remains a vital part of its economy. Only about one-quarter of the country's area can be farmed, so Switzerland depends heavily on imported foods. On the most fertile land—most of it in the central plateau—wheat and other grains, potatoes, sugar beets, and a variety of vegetables are raised. In the central plateau, too, and in Ticino there are orchards where apples, pears, cherries, and apricots are grown. Known for their size and flavor, these fruits are used to make preserves and fiery brandies. Grapes were introduced by the Romans, and today several cantons produce fine wines.

But it is the pastures that are associated with the country's most important agricultural products. On the high—sometimes incredibly high—Alpine meadows, sheep, goats, and cows graze. Their rich milk is made into butter, cream, and cheese. Switzerland produces over 100,000 tons of cheese a year, mostly the Emmentaler generally thought of as Swiss cheese. But there are many others, including Gruyère, Sbrinz, Bagnes, and Appenzeller (named for the canton in which it is made). The cheeses are Swiss precision products, scrupulously tested for shape, color, flavor, butterfat and water content, and number and size of holes. The same care is used in the preparation of the chocolate and chocolate products that delight "sweet teeth" around the world.

Tourism

Beauty is the basic resource for another major Swiss industry—tourism. Switzerland has an incredible variety of attractions.

The internationally renowned resorts—such as Davos, Gstaad, Zermatt, Interlaken, and Saint Moritz (site of two Winter Olympics)—offer the sports lover the world's finest skiing, skating, and bobsledding. There are many smaller but equally popular spots, including Pontresina,

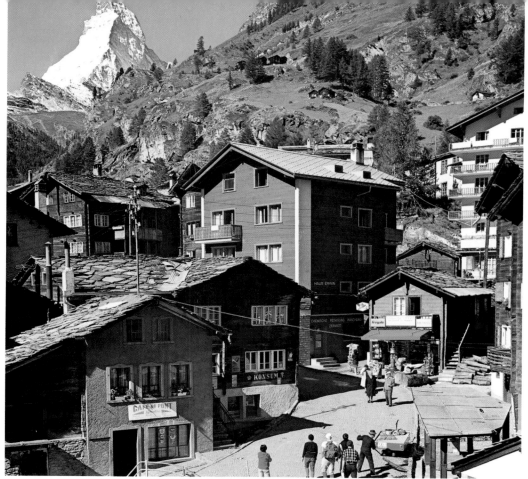

The resort town of Zermatt. In the background is the Matterhorn.

Crans, Arosa, and Chur. All of them are year-round resorts, and in summer there is mountain climbing for experienced or novice climbers and hikes into the foothills of the Alps. Hikers may be rewarded by a glimpse of the surefooted ibex (mountain goat) leaping from crag to crag, or they may come upon edelweiss or other alpine flowers. At countless lakes there is swimming, boating, fishing, and simply peaceful relaxation. Switzerland's huge number of hospitable resorts and inns (more than 7,000) has led to its being called a nation of hotelkeepers.

An excellent railway system, good roads, bridges, cable cars, funiculars, and ski lifts serve the country. Long ago the mountains presented much more of an obstacle than they do today. Now, often in cooperation with neighboring countries, automobile and railroad tunnels have been built through even the highest passes, such as the Simplon, Saint Gotthard, and the Great Saint Bernard. The last is near the monastery once famous for sending out St. Bernard dogs to rescue lost travelers.

A steep decline in air travel and tourism following the September 11, 2001, terrorist attacks on the United States proved devastating for the nation's major airline, Swissair, which had been in financial trouble since earlier that year. The company declared bankruptcy that October.

THE PEOPLE

Unité par diversité ("unity through diversity") is the motto of the Swiss people. Switzerland is a country where loyalty to a hometown or canton is often as strong as—and more immediate than—national feeling. Swiss diversity is emphasized by its four languages. The largest number of people (about 65 percent, mostly in the northern and eastern cantons) speak German, and smaller groups speak French (mostly in the west) and Italian (in or near Ticino). A fourth national language is ancient Romansh, a Latin language. There are also many regional dialects and variations based on each of these.

Way of Life

Every child must attend school up to the age of 16, and there is no illiteracy. Over 100,000 young people, including foreign students, study at institutes of higher learning, which include seven universities.

Numerous Swiss have made their mark in literature, theater, music, arts, and science. Carl Spitteler and the German-born Hermann Hesse won Nobel prizes for literature; the best known contemporary author is probably the playwright Friedrich Dürrenmatt. Paul Klee was a famous painter and Le Corbusier a leading European architect. Naturalized citizen Albert Einstein developed his theory of relativity while working in Bern. Other important 20th-century personalities include psychiatrist Carl Jung, psychologist Jean Piaget, and theologian Karl Barth.

In many areas, skiing is a necessity rather than a sport. Other popular activities, according to the season, are skating, swimming, sailing, camping, and, of course, mountain climbing.

The Swiss is essentially a family man, whose home is his sanctuary. The care of the home, however, is mainly the woman's realm. Swiss homes are kept spotlessly clean, and at the entrance little squares of felt may be parked, on which family and visitors obediently skate across the immaculate mirrors of the floors.

It has been said that Switzerland has "food barriers" as clearly defined as its language lines. Much of German-speaking Switzerland has a marked preference for sausages and flour foods; in the French-speaking areas, steaks, *pommes frites,* and omelets are popular; and in Italian-speaking Ticino savory pasta dishes are served.

Nevertheless, there is a typical Swiss cuisine. It comes generally from areas where cheese was victorious over pork and beef, and its best-known dishes are *raclette* and Fondue. More than meals, they are ceremonies performed at the table.

For *raclette,* a 3-month-old loaf of Bagnes cheese is cut in half and brought close to an open fire to melt slowly. Then it is scraped onto a plate, spiced with pepper, and accompanied by pickled onions and sour gherkins for taste contrast. Small, boiled potatoes are usually served with *raclette,* and fresh plates of melted cheese replace empty ones.

Even more of a ritual surrounds Fondue, a bubbling mixture of grated Gruyère and Emmentaler cheeses, garlic, wine, and kirsch (clear, powerful cherry brandy). It is prepared in an earthenware pot over a small spirit stove on the table. Each guest, armed with a long fork, dips small chunks of bread into the fondue. He tries not to lose any bread in the pot, for if he does he must traditionally pay a forfeit—a bottle of wine, or a kiss for his hostess and the other women at the table.

Other Swiss specialities include delicious *rösti,* crusty cakes of crisply fried potatoes; and Grisons beef (or *Bündnerfleisch*), thin slices of meat dried in the open air, cooked by the sun.

Bears—the emblem of Bern, Switzerland's capital, and the source of its name.

CITIES

In many other countries, industrialization has meant a top-heavy growth of huge metropolises. Swiss cities, however, are relatively small. The five largest—Zurich, Basel, Geneva, Bern, and Lausanne—had fewer than one million inhabitants all together in 1992.

Bern

Bern, the federal capital of Switzerland, was founded in the 12th century on the Aar River, a tributary of the Rhine. In its course from south to north, the river ate a steep-sided U-shaped bed in the area's rocky soil, creating a small, high peninsula. It was only natural that a fortress was built in this dominating position, and equally natural that the fortress later grew into a thriving town.

Today Bern, although not large, is a busy, modern city, yet it still retains many reminders of the past. The sidewalks of its narrow streets, lined with heavy solid houses, are often covered by arcades. There are innumerable lovely fountains, graced by statues of historical or mythological figures. In the center of Bern stands its Gothic cathedral, which dates from the 15th century. Nearby is the city hall, which is also over 500 years old.

Bern's ancient university, founded in 1528, is one of the oldest in Switzerland, and there are also many professional schools and colleges. The Fine Arts Museum has a large collection of works by Swiss and foreign artists. It also houses the Klee Foundation, honoring the painter Paul Klee.

As the seat of government since 1848, Bern is the site of the Swiss Parliament, as well as of the Supreme Federal Tribunal and the National Library and State Archives.

The Limmat River flows through Zurich, the largest city and center of the banking industry in Switzerland.

But not all of Bern centers on Swiss official life. There are many beautiful parks and many spots offering dazzling views of the alpine peaks to the southwest. Bern's 16th-century Clock Tower puts on spectacular hourly performances with its mechanical clowns, puppets, roosters, and dancing bears. Bern's Bear Pit is another well-known attraction. Visitors spend hours watching and feeding the bears, whose favorite treat is bottled soda pop.

Zurich

Zurich is Switzerland's largest city. Located in the northern part of the country on Lake Zurich, by the 18th century Zurich was already an active international market, especially for silk. It has expanded this reputation by becoming the center of Swiss business and banking and a main attraction for tourists.

In addition to silk and other textiles, Zurich's industries include paper manufacturing, printing, and machine tool works. But no sooty factory chimneys soil the face of Zurich, which embraces the northern end of the Lake of Zurich. And business has not suffocated culture—the city's modern architecture has had full respect for the winding lanes, narrow houses, and ancient churches of the Old Town. The latest stock market quotations are posted side by side with announcements of Zurich's Theater Company or Art Museum.

The Federal Institute of Technology is located in Zurich, as well as one of the country's seven universities. Zurich's Pestalozzianum is named for Johann Heinrich Pestalozzi, the Swiss whose theories revolutionized the field of education in the 18th century.

Visitors can enjoy the elegant shops and cafés along the Bahnhofstrasse ("railroad station street"), Zurich's main street, and leisurely walks along the Limmat, watching the ducks and swans that paddle there. They can take a funicular up to the wooded Dolder Hills, where one of Europe's largest swimming pools provides artificial waves—the only waves in Switzerland. And, if they come in April, when winter releases its grip on the country, they can take part in Zurich's Sechseläuten ("six o'clock bells") festival. The cathedral bells signal the beginning of this ancient expression of joy. There is a colorful, costumed parade culminating in the burning of the Böog—a symbolic snowman stuffed with firecrackers.

Basel

Only 57 miles (92 kilometers) west of Zurich, on a sweeping bend of the Rhine, is Basel. Basel is Switzerland's second largest city. Its location on the river where three countries—Switzerland, Germany, and France—meet has long made Basel a crossroads of trade. The Rhine gives Switzerland its outlet to the sea, and on both banks of the river Basel has some of the most modern port facilities in the world. Many of the exports and imports so vital to the Swiss economy enter and leave the country at Basel's docks, including the products of the city's chemical, pharmaceutical, and dye works, textile mills, and breweries. Every spring Basel holds the Swiss Industries Fair—a trade show for manufactured goods from all over Europe.

Basel is also proud of being an intellectual town, with an excellent Art Museum and a famous university. In the 16th century, the Dutch philosopher Erasmus and the Flemish-Belgian anatomist Vesalius taught there. Some 200 years later, the university's professors included the Bernoullis, a Swiss family of scientists who made many important discoveries in mathematics and physics.

Today, though Basel is a thriving, modern city, in its beautiful patrician houses, fountains, and narrow streets it has also preserved the slow contemplative pace of the past.

Geneva

Geneva is located at the southern tip of Lake Geneva near the border with France. It is often considered Switzerland's most French city and its road signs, which all seem to point toward Paris, underline this idea. (Only on one road can one proceed into the rest of Switzerland, via Lausanne.) Many of Geneva's streets have a Parisian flavor, with hundreds of jewelry shops and stores selling other luxury goods.

But although Geneva seems French, it is actually even more international in character. Since the 19th century, when a Swiss businessman, Jean Henri Dunant, helped to found the International Red Cross there, the city has been the home of countless international organizations. Overlooking the lake is the Palace of Nations, built in the 1930's to house the League of Nations. Today, the vast, beautiful building is the European headquarters of the United Nations. Geneva is also the seat of the International Labor Organization, the European Commission for Nuclear Research, and almost 200 more international organizations. In addition, the city hosts many congresses and conferences.

A Genevan landmark is the 426-foot (130 m.) Jet d'Eau—one of the tallest fountains in the world. Among the other attractions of the well-planned city are many parks, an opera house, dozens of art galleries, and several museums. Geneva is the home, too, of one of the world's leading symphonies, the Orchestre de la Suisse Romande. The annual Bol d'Or (Gold Cup) yacht race is a popular sailing competition.

Geneva is European headquarters of the United Nations and a center for international diplomacy. Switzerland, because of its strict neutrality, did not join the UN until 2002.

The University of Geneva, founded in 1559, includes the International Interpreters School and a school of education named for Jean Jacques Rousseau, the 18th-century philosopher whose ideas helped set the stage for the French Revolution. Rousseau was a Genevan, but artists and thinkers from other countries also found the city a magnet—among them the French philosopher Voltaire, the English historian Edward Gibbon, and the English poets Lord Byron and Percy Bysshe Shelley.

Atop the highest hill in Geneva's Old Town is its cathedral, and near the university stands the towering Reformation Monument. Both recall Geneva in the 16th century, when men like John Calvin, Guillaume Farel, John Knox, and Théodore de Bèze made the city a hub of European Protestantism. The school of theology at the university still remains the world center for Calvinist studies. Under Calvin's strict rule, daily life in Geneva was austere. He would hardly recognize—and perhaps not approve of—the busy, cosmopolitan city it has become today.

Lausanne

Some 40 mi. (64 km.) east of Geneva, also on the shores of the lake, is Lausanne. Its university and innumerable private schools and colleges have given Lausanne its reputation as an educator of Swiss and foreign youth. The presence of these students lends Lausanne a lightheartedness far beyond that of other Swiss communities. Lausanne's setting, too, endows it with a special, happy charm. Built on steep hills clustered high above the lake, it is a multilevel city. Among the hills, crowned by the cathedral, is La Cité, the center of old Lausanne; and bustling Place St. François, heart of the city's business district. Nearby, from the 2,100-ft. (640-m.) Signal, there is a fine view of the city, the lake, and the distant mountains. Below, among the flower-bordered promenades of Lausanne's Ouchy lakefront section, are hotels, restaurants, and cafés. From there, visitors can take steamers to other lakeside towns.

A favorite excursion is to **Montreux,** long a popular resort. Near the town, on a rock in the lake, stands the ancient Castle of Chillon. In 1816 Lord Byron based his poem "The Prisoner of Chillon" on events that took place there during the Reformation. Another pleasant trip is to **Vevey,** a charming town between two mountains. Vevey is known for its lovely beaches, and for its wine festivals, held every 25 years. It is also famous as the place where milk chocolate was invented in 1878, and it is still the headquarters of Nestlé, one of the largest chocolate companies in the world.

Other Cities

Located almost in the center of the country, on the Vierwaldstätersee (Lake of Lucerne, or Lake of the Four Forest Cantons) and the Reuss River, is **Lucerne.** It is a bustling modern town, yet there are still many signs of other times around every corner. The covered wooden bridge over the Reuss has painted panels depicting important events in the town's—and Switzerland's—history. Funiculars run up the city's hills, and about 15 miles (24 kilometers) away, Mount Pilatus boasts the steepest cog railway in the world. Lucerne has several excellent libraries and museums, and in August and September the city holds its music festival, featuring performances by leading orchestras and soloists from around the world.

Time dawdles in the Jura Mountains, some 30 miles (48 kilometers) west of Lucerne. At their feet lies the pearly mirror of the Lake of Neuchâtel, with the city of the same name on its western shore. **Neuchâtel** is a peaceful town, proud of its university and its active intellectual life. It is the site of the Swiss Laboratory for Watchmaking Research and of the Neuchâtel Observatory—both signs of the city's leadership in watchmaking. The people of Neuchâtel are renowned for their special esprit (spirit) and politeness.

Other major Swiss cities include Winterthur, near Zurich, with important metalworking industries; and Saint Gall, near the Lake of Constance in northeastern Switzerland, a textile center known especially for the fine lace produced there. The largest cities—Zurich, Basel, Geneva, Bern, and Lausanne—contain a third of the Swiss population.

HISTORY

The English humorist Sir Max Beerbohm wrote, "Switzerland has had but one hero, William Tell, and he is a myth." To this day, no one knows whether Switzerland's national hero really existed or not (though there are statues of him in almost every Swiss town). Nevertheless, he symbolizes the proud independence and love of liberty that characterize the Swiss people.

Roman and German Switzerland

The recorded history of Switzerland begins in the 1st century B.C., with Julius Caesar. On a plaque in Geneva today there is an excerpt from Book I of his *Commentaries*. He boasts of his victory over the Allobroges, who occupied the Geneva region; and over the Helvetii and Rhaeti, who lived in the area enclosed by the Rhine, the Alps, and the Jura.

Roman control of what is now Switzerland lasted some 300 years. Throughout most of this time, the Roman garrisons existed peacefully

One of Lucerne's main landmarks is the ancient wooden bridge on the Reuss.

side by side with the area's Celtic population. Fortifications were built in various places along the Rhine, which was considered the northern frontier. In the mid 3rd century, however, Alemanni, a German tribe, using military roads built by the Romans to defend their empire, overran the region. About two centuries later Burgundians from what is now France invaded from the west and took over the region of the Lake of Geneva. It is because of these two invasions that today's Swiss speak several languages.

In the early 6th century, the Franks struck from the east and overthrew the Alemanni, the Burgundians, and the Rhaeti—making Switzerland part of the Frankish kingdom. Under King Clovis, Christianity was introduced into the area. In 843, after some three centuries of unity under the Franks, the kingdom was divided among the grandsons of the great ruler Charlemagne.

Switzerland was reunited in 1032 under the Holy Roman Empire, which also included much of western and central Europe. However, unity within the empire offered no insurance against internal conflict, and Swiss peasants became involved in power struggles between landowners. By the end of the 13th century, the Austrian Habsburgs grew powerful in the area. One focus of trouble was central Switzerland, around the Lake of Lucerne.

Independent Switzerland

On August 1, 1291—partly according to history and partly to tradition—men from Uri, Schwyz, and Unterwalden met on the Rütli meadow above the Lake of Lucerne. They swore a solemn oath forming a perpetual alliance to support each other and to fight foreign invaders.

In this way they founded the Swiss Confederation, which has lasted until today.

William Tell. It was the circumstances of the Rütli pact that gave birth to the story of William Tell. According to the best-known version (made popular by the 18th-century German playwright Friedrich Schiller), Tell refused to bow in homage to a hat placed in the market square of the town of Altdorf. The hat belonged to Gessler, the Habsburg governor of Uri, Schwyz, and Unterwalden. Tell was brought before Gessler and condemned to shoot an apple off his son's head. An experienced marksman, he split the apple with the first of two arrows. With the second, he stated boldly, he would have shot Gessler if his son had been harmed. The furious governor ordered that Tell be cast into irons. However, Tell escaped shortly afterwards and ambushed and killed Gessler near Küssnacht. He then became one of the leaders of the fight for independence.

Gradually the confederation expanded. More and more towns and cantons (as the Swiss states are called) joined. But the alliance was threatened from the outside, especially by the Habsburgs, and war followed. Though they were often far outnumbered, in a series of battles—Morgarten, Näfels, Sempach, and Dornach—in the 14th and 15th centuries, the confederation defeated the Habsburgs. The Swiss dissolved their allegiance to the Holy Roman Empire. They also gained a reputation for military prowess, and their soldiers were soon in demand all over Europe. (The Swiss Guard that serves in the Vatican today dates from this period.)

But in 1515, in a battle against the French at Marignano (now Melegnano, Italy), the Swiss forces were crushed and thousands of lives were lost. The defeat helped lead the Swiss to adopt the policy of neutrality they still follow today.

The Reformation

The 16th century also taught Switzerland its religious lesson. In Zurich, Neuchâtel, and Geneva, men like Ulrich Zwingli, Guillaume Farel, and John Calvin preached for sweeping reforms of the Roman Catholic Church. As the Reformation spread, there was much conflict between Catholic and reformist cantons. After the battle of Kappel am Albis in 1531, where Zwingli was killed and the reformists defeated, came the wise—and typically Swiss—decision that each canton should choose the religion it pleased. (Legend has it that this kind of peaceful coexistence had already been put into practice on the battlefield. The two opposing armies, one short of bread, the other of milk, agreed to cook a milk soup together. The Catholics provided the milk while the Protestants contributed the bread, and the soup was cooked and eaten with unanimity from one pot.)

From 1648, when Switzerland's independence was confirmed, until the end of the 18th century, Switzerland enjoyed peace and prosperity. Yet however neutral they were, not even the Swiss could avoid Napoleon when he began to change the face of Europe. In 1798 he transformed the country into a centralized, French-style republic, which lasted about four years. In 1802, at bayonet point, he reasserted his control over Switzerland. At the Congress of Vienna (1815) after Napoleon's final defeat, Swiss neutrality was officially recognized.

Modern Switzerland

With the return of peace, the Swiss soon realized that they needed some central authority. In 1848, the 22 cantons then comprising the confederation (a 23rd canton was added in 1978) accepted a new constitution, which transformed the confederation into a federal state modeled on the United States. Modern Switzerland was thus born, proclaiming a policy of lasting neutrality. During both world wars, Switzerland fortified its frontiers, aided refugees—and remained neutral.

Neutrality did not always mean freedom from involvement in wartime events, however. In the 1990s, the Swiss government was accused of selling arms to Nazi Germany during World War II, thus possibly prolonging the war. At the same time, family members of people killed during the Holocaust filed lawsuits against Swiss banks, charging that the banks were illegally keeping money, jewelry, and other assets deposited by Holocaust victims before and during the war. After much wrangling and litigation, and threatened by sanctions, several banks agreed in August 1998 to a $1.25 billion settlement. The Swiss government did not contribute to this payment.

As the union among European nations approached, Switzerland held fast to its independence, joining just the European Economic Area (EEA), set up to link countries outside the European Economic Community (EEC), precursor of the European Union (EU). EEA, however, began to wane, and in 2000, long-lasting opposition to joining the EU finally eroded: 67 percent of Swiss voters backed seven bilateral agreements with the EU dismantling various barriers.

GOVERNMENT

Switzerland's seven-member Federal Council has executive power and also acts as the cabinet. Each minister serves as president for a one-year term. In 1999, the office was held by Ruth Dreifuss, the first female and also the first Jewish president in Swiss history. In the two-chamber parliament—the Federal Assembly—the National Council directly represents the people, while the Council of States represents the cantons.

But the real foundation of Swiss democracy is the local commune, in which every citizen takes an active interest. In 1971, a constitutional amendment was passed granting Swiss women the right to vote in federal elections, and in 1981, an amendment provided equality under the law for women. In 1990, Swiss women finally won the right to vote in all cantons.

Two institutions—referendum and initiative—help the Swiss to influence their country's policies. A law adopted by the Federal Assembly goes into effect only if, during a 90-day period, no petition is made against it. But if at least 30,000 citizens petition for referendum, the people themselves decide whether to accept or reject the law. By initiative, on the other hand, the people—with at least 50,000 signatures—can propose a new law or request revision or rejection of an old one.

In 1989, a referendum was held on the question of whether to abolish Switzerland's armed forces, retaining only a militia for domestic emergencies. In a large turnout, voters soundly rejected the proposal. In March 2002, during an important referendum, the Swiss voted to abandon their long-standing tradition of isolationism and, by a narrow margin, approved the government's proposal to join the United Nations (UN).

DOROTHEA SPADA-BALLUFF, Editor in Chief, *Abitare* (International Edition)

Mountaineers have been challenged by the Alps for centuries.

ALPS

The majestic Alps are Europe's most important physical feature—a 680-mi.- (1,100-km.)-long chain of mountains with snowcapped peaks, narrow valleys, deep blue lakes, immense glaciers, cascading waterfalls, and icy streams. Nestled here and there in the Alps are romantic castles, lovely chalets, quaint old villages with flower-bedecked houses leaning over crooked streets, and some of the world's most popular resorts.

Covering an area of about 80,000 sq. mi. (210,000 sq. km.), the Alps extend in an arc from the Mediterranean coast between France and Italy, through Switzerland, Germany, and Austria, and then along the Adriatic coast of Slovenia, Croatia, and Yugoslavia to Albania. The high, sharp peaks of the Alps show that the mountains are young in geological time. Geologists believe that the Alps were still being formed 70 million years ago. The highest of all the Alps, and the tallest mountain in Western Europe, is Mont Blanc (15,781 ft.; 4,810 m.). Other skyscraping alpine peaks are the Dufourspitze in the Monte Rosa group, which reaches 15,203 ft. (4,634 m.), the Matterhorn (14,701 ft.; 4,481 m.), and the Jungfrau (13,653 ft.; 4,161 m.).

Although a great deal is known about the history of the Alps, no

The Matterhorn looms over a tiny alpine village.

one is quite sure how they got their name. Some authorities believe the source of the name is the Celtic *alp,* meaning "height." Others believe that the correct root is the Latin *albus,* meaning "white." Both words describe the snow-topped mountain chain that looks so formidable but has in fact been a home for men since prehistoric times and a route for travelers, traders, and armies for as long as human records have been kept.

Living in the Alps

It has never been easy to live in the Alps because the climate is not always gentle and there is a shortage of good farmland. Besides, there is often the threat of an avalanche hurtling down the slopes, sealing roads shut, and burying entire villages. We can guess that the people who chose to live in the mountains did so because the mountains provided a natural shelter from the wars and revolutions that regularly disturbed the life of men in the flat, less fortresslike parts of Europe. In time, the alpine people came to be known for their fierce love of liberty.

Many of the alpine people make their living as dairy farmers. During the short summer season, flocks are taken to the high pastures (also called alps) to fatten on the sweet grass. In winter, men and their cattle return to their homes and villages. It is the time when such old crafts as wood carving and weaving flourish.

Life is a little gentler on the southern slopes of the Alps, where the

Skiers cross a slope of Mont Blanc, Western Europe's highest peak.

climate is somewhat milder. The lower mountain slopes are covered with grapevines, and in the valleys corn is grown. There are even orange and lemon groves on the shores of Lake Garda in Italy.

On both sides of the Alps farming is now less important as a source of income than it used to be. The "white coal" of the rushing rivers is being harnessed to provide hydroelectricity for chemical manufacturing, textile production, and metal processing. However, the leading alpine industry today is tourism.

Traveling in the Alps

Until the middle of the 18th century the Alps did not attract tourists. The mountains were something to be crossed as easily as possible or to be looked at with awe from some safe, low level. In the old days the trip across the Alps was extremely difficult and uncomfortable. A horse-drawn carriage rumbling and bumping over the packed dirt road on the Mont Cenis pass, for example, had to be disassembled and carried over the steepest part of the route. The passengers were carried over that part of the road in chairs.

In spite of such hazards, the mountains eventually came to be thought of as a vital part of a young man's education. If the Grand Tour of Europe's leading cities taught him fine manners, then the mountains existed to inspire him with a taste for natural beauty. Later, poets and artists came to the Alps to capture in words and oils the beauty of alpenglow (the reddish light of sunrise and sunset on the mountains),

Farms nestle in the valleys near Switzerland's snowcapped Jungfrau.

the great glaciers like the 16-square-mile (41 sq. km.) Mer de Glace ("sea of ice") on the northern slope of Mont Blanc, and the distant, cloud-wrapped peaks.

Sometimes one of these visitors would express a wish to climb one of the distant peaks, but he was quickly discouraged by tales of fire-breathing dragons that lurked in the ice crevices, sudden death-dealing avalanches, and the treacherously changeable weather at the higher altitudes.

In 1760 a wealthy Genevan, Horace Bénédict de Saussure, tried to put an end to such talk by offering a reward to the first man to climb Mont Blanc. One year passed, then another and another. Men tried to scale the mountain and failed. It was not until 1786 that Michel Paccard and Jacques Balmat succeeded in making the climb. The news of their triumph electrified Europe. English children played a game called "The Ascent of Mont Blanc," which included all the possible pitfalls of the climb. Their fathers and uncles set off for the continent and a try at the Alps. One by one the mountains were climbed. On July 14, 1865,

This ice tunnel is inside the Rhone Glacier in south central Switzerland.

Gstaad, Switzerland, is one of the many ski resorts that abound in the Alps.

the last great challenge that remained—the stony spire of the Matterhorn—was conquered by Edward Whymper and his team of climbers.

Mountaineers still find a challenge in the Alps. Athletes also find the mountains ideal for sports such as skiing, ice skating, and bobsledding. The Winter Olympics have been held in the Alps nine times since the games were begun at Chamonix, France, in 1924. In the summer the mountains are perfect for hiking or for swimming and waterskiing on one of the deep lakes like Constance, Lucerne, or Geneva.

It is becoming easier every year to travel through and across the Alps. There are cableways and cog railways up many of the peaks and superb highways over many passes. The Simplon Pass has the world's longest railroad tunnel—12.3 miles (19.8 kilometers) long. The tunnel cut through Mont Blanc and the Arlberg tunnel in Austria are among the world's longest automobile tunnels. Switzerland is also planning to build two more railway tunnels that will run through the base of the Alps. The tunnels will be used by both freight and high-speed passenger trains. Germany, Austria, and Italy are considering drilling a railway tunnel under the Brenner Pass, and in France, there are plans for a tunnel through the Mont Cenis massif.

Although engineers constantly find new ways to make it easier to travel through and across the Alps, the beauty of the mountains remains unchanged. The mountain air is clear and exhilarating; the scenery is always superb and always peaceful.

Reviewed by SWISS ALPINE CLUB

The Lake of Lucerne, at the foot of Mount Pilatus, is one of the loveliest alpine lakes.

Prince's castle in Vaduz, Liechtenstein's capital.

LIECHTENSTEIN

Tucked into the valley of the Rhine, between Switzerland on the west and Austria on the east, is the tiny principality of Liechtenstein. With its snowy peaks, its meadows covered with wildflowers in summer, its rushing streams, and its crystal-clear lakes, Liechtenstein might almost be a miniature Switzerland. And yet this tiny country has its own history and its own character and customs.

THE LAND

The agricultural and industrial part of Liechtenstein lies to the west in the fertile Rhine Valley, where the river forms a natural boundary with Switzerland. Most of Liechtenstein's towns, including Vaduz, the capital and seat of government, also lie in this area. To the north are Schaan, a resort that is Liechtenstein's only stop on an international railroad line; Bendern; and Schellenberg. To the south are Triesen and Balzers, whose Gutenberg Castle has been overlooking the Rhine since the Middle Ages. All these villages seem like stage sets for operettas. Their small houses have flower-covered wooden balconies, and there are neatly kept orchards and gardens and picturesque inns that are often hundreds of years old.

The eastern part of Liechtenstein, which borders on Austria, is an area of mountain scenery and green pastures dotted with wooden chalets and small white chapels. There are also shady forests that abound with game. This part of the country is a botanist's paradise, too. In springtime the deep-blue shimmer of gentians—Liechtenstein's national flower—spreads over the higher slopes, and in summer, alpine roses paint the mountainsides a glowing red. Many kinds of wild orchids can be found in Liechtenstein. The landscape has inspired many of Liechtenstein's ancient legends, such as the story of the *Wildmannli* ("little wild men"), the shy dwarfs who leave their mountain caves at night to do chores for the sleeping villagers. There is also the tale of three heartless sisters transformed by an angry god into three craggy mountains. Located in the extreme southeast, near Switzerland and Austria, the "Three Sisters" include the Naafkopf, one of Liechtenstein's highest peaks.

HISTORY

Liechtenstein's true history also reads like a collection of legends. In 15 B.C. the area called Rhaetia, which included parts of present-day Switzerland and Germany as well as Liechtenstein, became part of the Roman Empire. In succeeding centuries the Rhaeti had to defend themselves against Germanic invaders and Huns. In A.D. 536, Rhaetia fell to the Franks, eventually becoming part of Charlemagne's kingdom and the Holy Roman Empire. In 1699 Johann Adam von Liechtenstein, an Austrian prince, bought the Barony of Schellenberg in the Rhine Valley and, in 1712, the county of Vaduz. In 1719 the area was consolidated by Holy Roman Emperor Charles VI, who declared it the Principality of Liechtenstein. It remained part of the Holy Roman Empire until 1806.

From 1806 to 1815 Liechtenstein was a member of the Confederation of the Rhine set up by Napoleon I. After Napoleon's final defeat in 1815, the principality became a free and independent state, which has never been conquered since. According to Liechtenstein tradition, there was an attempted invasion in 1939, when Germany sent a well-armed battalion to Liechtenstein. The invaders were met by Liechtenstein's 10-man police force and 9 Boy Scouts, mustered up at the last minute by a Vaduz priest. At this sight, and probably because they considered the country too insignificant, the Germans abandoned the idea of the invasion.

Liechtenstein is still ruled by the hereditary princes of the House of Liechtenstein. Prince Franz Joseph II died in 1989 after reigning for 51 years. His son, Prince Hans Adam, who took over executive authority in 1984, assumed his father's title.

THE PEOPLE

Liechtenstein has a population of about 30,000. They are hard-working and outgoing, with a welcome for friends and strangers alike. Until about 1945 most Liechtensteiners earned their livings as farmers. Though today Liechtenstein's major source of income is industry, some 8 percent of the people still follow the traditional way of life. They raise corn, wheat, and potatoes, and they tend their herds of Brown Swiss dairy cows, whose bells echo across the valleys as they graze the mountain pastures. On the lower slopes of the Rhine Valley, Liechtenstein's carefully tended vineyards have been producing excellent wine

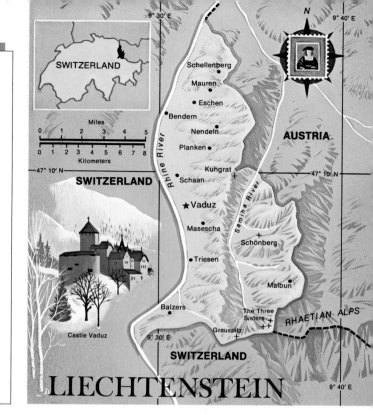

grapes since Roman times. For the farmer or the factory worker in Liechtenstein, good conversation over a glass of Vaduzer (a rosé wine) is still a favorite pastime.

In the 1950s, hydroelectric plants were built in the Samina and Lavena valleys, harnessing the rivers' power for homes and industry. Today Liechtenstein's factories produce chemicals, machine parts, optical instruments, and computer components, as well as the more traditional textiles, sausage skins, and dentures. Liechtenstein's most famous product, however, is its stamps, which have been an important source of income since 1912. Collectors all over the world prize Liechtenstein's stamps for their vivid colors and beautiful designs. Tourism is increasing in importance, and every year more and more people from all over the world come to Liechtenstein to enjoy the beauty of its landscape and the warmth of its hospitality.

Vaduz, Liechtenstein's tiny, bustling capital, lies in a valley surrounded by towering mountains. The city was founded in the Middle Ages. It is especially noteworthy for the great art collection, owned by the royal family, which can be seen by natives and tourists alike.

GOVERNMENT

The Principality of Liechtenstein is a constitutional monarchy, whose government is based on the Constitution of 1921. The legislative body is the 25-seat Landtag, which is elected for four years. The head of government is the prime minister, who leads the five-member cabinet and is appointed by the reigning prince from among the members of the majority party in the Landtag. All legislation must be approved by the prince. In 1984, women were finally given the right to vote. Liechtenstein became a full member of the United Nations in September 1990.

A country church spire soars in an Austrian Alpine valley.

AUSTRIA

Where the Danube River leaves the hills and turns south into the Great Hungarian Plain, north meets south and east meets west in Europe. As a result, Austria's great role in history has been as a frontier post— the protector and defender of Western civilization against the invading tribes that time and again threatened to overrun the whole of Europe.

The Romans used the Danube as their line of defense against the wild tribes of the north. In the 8th century, Charlemagne, emperor of the Franks, a Germanic tribe, designated the region we now call Austria as the Ostmark—the "east march," or boundary. He made it his bulwark against threatened invasions by the Huns and Vandals from the east. In the 10th century, a German emperor made the region into a duchy, whose purpose was to protect his empire from invasion by the Magyars moving in from the southeast. This small frontier duchy was named Ostarichi—"east kingdom"—and it is from this word that Austria's modern German name, Österreich, comes.

Until Yugoslavia dissolved in a bloody civil war in the early 1990s, neutral Austria had served as a buffer land. Its borders touch on seven nations—Germany, Switzerland, Italy, Liechtenstein, the Czech Republic, Slovakia, and Hungary—as well as Slovenia, of the former Yugoslavia.

Vienna's Volksgarten ("people's garden") and Hofburg (Imperial Palace).

The three eastern nations were part of the vast empire ruled by Austria's Habsburg emperors from 1278 to 1918. At its greatest extent the empire stretched from the borders of Poland in the northeast to the Adriatic Sea in the south. The empire included all of the Czech Republic, Slovakia, and Hungary, as well as large parts of present-day Italy, Slovenia, Croatia, Romania, and Poland. Then, at the end of World War I, the empire was erased from the map of Europe. The much smaller Austrian republic took its place. But, like the lilting waltz music for which Austria is famous, the melody of the old empire lingers on.

THE AUSTRIAN PEOPLE

There is, of course, far more to the legacy of Austria's past than its glittering mementos of the emperors, or even the splendor of the art they inspired and supported. The Austrian Empire united under one flag some 50 million people, speaking more than a dozen different languages. A glance through the current Vienna telephone book is like a tour of the old empire, for it is filled with German, Czech, Hungarian, Polish, Slovenian, and Croatian names. The empire, in spite of the shortcomings that finally overwhelmed it, was a step on the road toward a united Europe.

Language and Religion

No matter where they came from, the people who have made their home in Austria are united by their language and their religion.

German, the official language of Austria, is spoken by about 98 percent of the population. Slovenes, Croatians, and Hungarians make up the small linguistic minorities, but German is their second language. Like the language of Germany, Austrian German evolved from Old German to the High German—*Hoch Deutsch*—that is spoken today. But if you learned German in school, you might be a little surprised to hear Austrian German spoken, for it incorporates words from French, Italian, Latin, and English in a seemingly carefree fashion. The gentle, witty, and melodic dialect of Vienna, almost another language in itself, perfectly reflects the character of the inhabitants of this worldly, fun-loving city.

About 90 percent of the Austrian people are Roman Catholics—another legacy of the Roman Catholic House of Habsburg. The only sizable Protestant communities are in Burgenland and Vorarlberg—the easternmost and westernmost federal provinces of Austria—where the Catholic Counter-Reformation did not succeed in suppressing the Protestants. In fact, it was not until the late 18th century that Protestants were granted toleration in Austria. And until the late 1930s the Roman Catholic Church in Austria exerted an important influence on politics. Since World War II the church has not been involved in government, although some Catholic lay organizations still take an active interest in public affairs. The number of Jews in Austria dropped from about 185,000 before the war to a little more than 11,000 when the war ended.

Education

Ever since Empress Maria Theresa ruled Austria, in the 18th century, elementary education has been compulsory. All children must attend school until they are 15 years old. Students planning to attend a university go to a preparatory school called a Gymnasium. At the end of Gymnasium a student takes a final examination called a *Matura,* which he or she must pass in order to be admitted to one of Austria's four universities. The oldest of the Austrian universities, Vienna, was founded in 1365. The other universities are at Salzburg, Innsbruck, and Graz. Besides the usual university studies, a student may attend one of the special academies devoted to music, art, applied arts, or acting. There are also technical, commercial, and industrial schools.

Food

The Austrians, who have made a fine art of cooking, love good food. They have, in the course of their history, taken what they liked best from the vast variety that the cuisine of the empire offered and created a unique style of cooking from that great and colorful selection.

Austria and especially Vienna are names to reckon with in international gourmet circles. A number of Austrian recipes, such as Wiener schnitzel (breaded veal cutlet), have become world-famous. When you are offered the same dish in Italy as *cotoletto milanese,* you should remember that Milan was once part of the empire.

Cakes, creams, and pastries are produced in infinite, mouth-watering variety in Austria. The larger cities are dotted with *Konditoreien*—"pastry shops"—which can only be entered when one throws all thoughts of dieting to the wind. The many coffee shops also serve all sorts of delicious pastries, from the simple crescent-shaped vanilla cookie called *Kipferl* or briochelike *Golatschen* to elaborate cream-filled cakes.

AUSTRIA

Perhaps the best-known of all Viennese cakes is Sacher torte. Sacher torte is named after a Viennese hotel and restaurant. Although it may seem to some to be no more than a delicious iced chocolate cake with a bit of apricot jam, the real recipe is a well-guarded secret, and lawsuits have been filed by the Sacher family for the misuse of the name and title.

Austrians often congregate in fashionable coffeehouses, where friends can socialize over a fresh cup of coffee and a favorite pastry. Vienna has been home to such cafés since coffee was introduced to Austria in the 17th century.

A highway across the Grossglockner, Austria's highest peak.

THE LAND

The land the tourist discovers is best described in one word—mountainous. Almost three fourths of Austria is covered by the Alps. It is only north and northeast of the Danube River that the land begins to roll more gently as it nears the Great Hungarian Plain, across which invaders from the east swarmed into Europe thousands of years ago. The Alps dominate all the rest of Austria, reaching their highest point in the Grossglockner ("great bell").

Climate. In the mountains the climate is marked by heavy snowfalls in winter and almost daily rain in summer. Northern Austria has a milder climate than the mountains, with rainy winters and cool, moist summers. Eastern Austria has a more typical continental climate, with hot, relatively dry summers and cold winters.

Austria's Nine Provinces

Austria's nine provinces—Vorarlberg, Tyrol, Salzburg, Upper Austria, Carinthia, Styria, Burgenland, Lower Austria, and the city of Vienna—are governed as a federal republic. Most governmental authority is in the hands of the federal government, which is parliamentary in form. At the head of the republic there is a president, but real power is represented by the office of the federal chancellor, who is appointed by the president and leads the government. However, welfare and local administration are directed by the provincial governments. Each of Austria's provinces is like a mini-nation, with its own unique attractions, customs, and traditions.

Vorarlberg, the westernmost of Austria's provinces, has an exquisite setting between the towering, snowcapped Silvretta Group of the Alps and the Lake of Constance. Bregenz, the provincial capital, rises from the edge of the lake and is known for its beautiful setting and its annual music festival. The best-known products of the province are embroidered goods.

Once part of the Roman province of Rhaetia, Vorarlberg was added to the Hapsburg crownlands in stages between the 14th and 16th centuries.

Tyrol, which is also in western Austria, has been called the Land in the Mountains because of its spectacular alpine setting. A mecca for tourists and sportsmen, the Tyrol is still crowded with visible reminders of times gone by. The capital city is Innsbruck ("bridge on the Inn"), which was settled in the 5th century B.C., grew during the Roman occupation, and reached its economic height as a trading center during the Middle Ages. In 1964 and 1976 Innsbruck was the site of the winter Olympics, and it is a popular year-round center for visitors from all over the world. In villages all over the Tyrol one can still find people proudly wearing their attractive national costumes, performing folk dances, or simply enjoying the music of a brass band or the tune of a yodeler. Of the province's many products salt, which is mined near Solbad Hall, is one of the most abundant.

Salzburg and its capital city, which is also called Salzburg ("salt city"), offer the typical variety of Austrian attractions—spectacular mountain scenery, the legacies of a long history, and every kind of cultural event. Located in west central Austria, the province was occupied by the Celts and then the Romans, and from the Middle Ages until the

A medieval fortress rises above the Salzach River at Salzburg.

Seefeld, near Innsbruck, is one of the many winter resorts in the Tyrol province.

18th century it was governed by archbishops. It became part of Austria only in the early 19th century. The city of Salzburg, which was the birthplace of Wolfgang Amadeus Mozart, has a Mozart Museum, a Mozarteum music academy, and the Salzburg Festival as memorials to its great 18th-century son. The province also boasts Europe's highest waterfall, near Krimml; Europe's largest ice grottoes; and spectacular salt mines.

Carinthia in southern Austria once included parts of Italy and the former Yugoslavia. With the signing of the World War I peace treaty in 1919, Carinthia's borders shrank, but the province still attracts visitors by the thousands to exquisite alpine lake resorts. The province's industries —metals, lumber, and farm products—play an important part in the Austrian economy. Here, as everywhere in Austria, the past lives on in the present. There is the Hochosterwitz—a fortress-castle with 14 towered gates—and the handsome Romanesque cathedral at Gurk. Carinthia also is the site of the excavated remains of the largest Celtic city that has been uncovered in Central Europe.

Styria, which is known as the most forested province in Austria, is noted for its location in the scenic, mineral-rich eastern Alps. Styria's Erzberg—"ore mountain"—contains the world's largest open-face iron mine. Here, as elsewhere in Austria, the landscape is dotted with hotels and inns, castles and spas. Graz, capital of Styria, is Austria's second largest city and a center of industry, transportation, and culture. Among its most notable landmarks are the Schlossberg, with its ancient clock tower, the Johanneum Museum, which has a great collection of medieval art, the opera house, the Gothic cathedral, and Eggenberg Castle, which houses the world's largest collection of medieval weapons and armor.

Upper Austria, in northern Austria, lies between the Bohemian Forest and the Dachstein peak at the point where the eastern Alps begin to slope gently downward into rolling hills. The region, which was made a duchy in the 12th century, is known for such resorts as Bad Ischl, which was once a favorite vacation spot for European royalty. Here Anton Bruckner and Franz Lehár composed some of their best-known works. The province's industries are clustered around the capital city of Linz, which is known to dessert-lovers as the birthplace of Linzer torte—a delicious lattice-topped cake that is made of nuts, spices, and fruit jam.

Burgenland forms a unique part of the Austrian landscape because the rolling foothills of the Alps flatten out into the plain that separates the Alps and eastern Europe. The large Neusiedler Lake, which lies partly in Austria and partly in Hungary, is in a wine-grape-growing region. Elsewhere in Burgenland nomadic tribes from the east left their mark, and ancient fortress-castles still stand as silent sentinels guarding the land against possible invaders. Today the gentle landscape is better-known for its contribution to Austrian agriculture. Thatch-roofed houses, high-booted, costumed Burgenlanders, gypsies, and storks nesting on chimney tops add their color and charm to the province that was the home of Joseph Haydn, the famous 18th-century composer.

Lower Austria, the largest of Austria's nine provinces, lies astride the Danube and surrounds Vienna. There are tiny typical riverside villages and great castles that once sheltered robber barons. The old monasteries of Klosterneuburg, Melk, Göttweig, and Maria Langegg are counted among the province's most fascinating attractions. Perhaps the most famous single landmark of the region is Dürnstein, in the beautiful Wachau region of the Danube. It was here in 1193 that Richard the Lion-Hearted was imprisoned on his return from the Third Crusade to the Holy Land. Blondel, Richard's troubadour and faithful servant, traveled up and down the land in search of his master, singing melancholy songs in the hope that he would be heard and answered. According to the old tale, Richard heard his minstrel from the prison window, and Blondel hastened to ransom his king, who was released and allowed to return to England.

VIENNA

Vienna, Austria's ninth province, is the nation's capital city and one of the great cities of Europe. As home to about a quarter of the entire Austrian population and as the center for a large part of Austria's industries, it is indisputably the heart of the nation. Located strategically at the edge of the foothills called the Vienna Woods and on the Danube, Vienna has played a major role in the country's history since it was first settled about 2,000 years ago by the Celts. When the Romans occupied what they called the *municipium* of Vindobona, they made it into the strongest military fortress on their eastern boundary. The 2nd century Roman Emperor and state philosopher Marcus Aurelius died in Vindobona.

From Roman times until quite recently the city grew up along the

These buildings were the first public housing in Europe.

banks of the Danube River. The river's course has been changed, and today it is the Danube Canal and not the Danube proper that runs through the city. The city, however, has changed very little since Emperor Franz Joseph I ordered the medieval walls removed in 1857. In place of the walls there runs a wide circular boulevard, which on one side is referred to simply as the Ringstrasse and on the other side, where it borders the Danube Canal, as the Kai. This makes Vienna an easy city to explore, for the fashionable Inner City is more or less identical with the old city. Along the tree-lined Ring are some of the handsomest buildings in Vienna—the Rathaus (City Hall), the Burgtheater, the university, and the city's two great museums—the museum of art and the museum of natural history. Nearby is the vast palace called the Hofburg, with its treasures. Farther along the Ring is the State Opera house.

In the very center of the Inner City stands the beautiful Gothic cathedral of Saint Stephen, whose slender spire dominates Vienna. The cathedral, like all the churches of Austria, has been added to in the course of the centuries. Like those of many other architectural monuments, many of its valuable ancient murals and structural elements have been replaced by whatever was modern at the time. Indeed, the elaborate 18th-century baroque style of architecture has almost everywhere obliterated the former facades and interiors, which gives the impression that the city was founded in the 18th century. Walking through the streets makes you realize, however, that for Vienna 18th-century baroque is not just a style of architecture. It is a style of life!

A visit to Vienna, the capital and chief city of both imperial and republican Austria, can be a nostalgic journey into the past. There is scarcely a corner of the ancient city that does not evoke a memory. A grapevine planted by Roman legionnaires is still growing in the heart of the city. Throughout Vienna there are handsome reminders of the centuries when the city was an imperial capital. The Habsburg winter palace, the Hofburg, which is now open to the public, contains the twin symbols of Austria's power—the imperial crown of Austria and the crown of the Holy Roman Empire. In the state dining room, the table is still lavishly set with the imperial gold service, just as if the emperor and his court were about to come in for dinner. The imperial jewels are on display in another part of the Hofburg. Elsewhere in the city—in museums, stately homes, and churches—the countless facets of the imperial life may be seen. They range from marble memorials to such curiosities as the car in which Archduke Franz Ferdinand was shot to death at Sarajevo in 1914, signaling the beginning of World War I.

Yet there has always been another Vienna too—a little removed from splendid victories and great festivities. It is the Vienna of the people —the merchants, the winegrowers, the clerks, and the apprentices. They have always lived in the shadow of great events. The wars, the plague, the sieges did not make them into a morose, melancholy lot, but rather the contrary. A happy-go-lucky people, full of humorous pranks, they always have made fun of their own misfortunes. Over a glass of wine they discuss politics to forget their everyday troubles. The untranslatable word *Gemütlichkeit* is uniquely fitted to the Austrians, who try to create an atmosphere of comfortable happiness in a place where living is never too fast, never too noisy, never too strenuous and, above all, never too serious.

The Arts

In this setting, which gave a sense of tranquillity even when swords were clanging all around, great music has been born. The irresistible charm of the city on the Danube, surrounded by wooded hills and vineyards, was a powerful inspiration to musicians from all over the world to settle there. First we must mention the greatest—Wolfgang Amadeus Mozart, Joseph Haydn, Ludwig van Beethoven, Franz Schubert, and Anton Bruckner. Then there are the lighthearted geniuses—the two Johann Strausses, Karl Michael Ziehrer, and Franz Lehár—and the moderns, of whom the best-known are Gustav Mahler and Anton von Webern. Grand opera and operetta provided music for everyone in a city where everyone was musical. And the memory of these great men survives in more than their music. Countless streets and lanes are named after them, as well as some airplanes of the Austrian Airlines. The Royal Academy of Music still attracts pupils from all over the world, and every young singer or musician knows that the concerts given in Vienna are a must in his career.

Once a year the great Vienna opera house opens its doors to society people from all over the world, when the famous opera ball takes place. It is the greatest fashion show of the year, and the bejewelled ladies and the gentlemen dressed in black and white, dancing the Grand Polonaise under the brilliant light of the chandeliers, bring back a memory of past glory.

The great city also attracted great minds—the annals of the Vienna medical school include the names of Albert Billroth, the great surgeon;

Ignaz Semmelweis, who discovered the cause of puerperal (childbirth) fever; and Sigmund Freud, the founder of psychoanalysis. The Royal Academy of Art drew people like Egon Schiele, Gustav Klimt, and Oskar Kokoschka; and the University of Vienna sent its professors to teach all over the world.

Vienna has a number of fine theaters. The most famous is still the Burgtheater, which was founded during Maria Theresa's reign. It now stands opposite the City Hall on the Ring, and its beautifully elaborate loggia is sometimes opened on warm spring evenings to let theatergoers catch a breath of air. After being destroyed during World War II, the theater was restored to its original splendor, and is considered among the best in the German-speaking countries. The works of foremost Austrian authors and playwrights, such as Franz Grillparzer, Hugo von Hofmannsthal, and Stephan Zweig, remain fixtures in the theater's repertoire.

However urgent it was after the war to rebuild Austria's industries, the Viennese knew that there were some things more worth rebuilding. These were the landmarks—Saint Stephen's Cathedral and the State Opera. The former—a part of the city for eight centuries—had been almost completely burned out in the last days of the war, and stood as a haunting empty shell reminding the people of past horrors. The latter, even more badly damaged, was a different symbol altogether—for it stood for Austria's name as a center of music and culture the whole world round. To rebuild it not only was the wish of every Austrian, but it was a signpost of the future—a solemn promise never to give up what generations of music lovers had admired and respected. And so, even before industries were rebuilt, the Viennese repaired their cathedral and their opera house, and made both even more beautiful than before.

Not only is Vienna full of beautiful reminders of the past, but the city also boasts impressive examples of modern architecture, such as the buildings designed by controversial artist and architect Friedrich Hundertwasser—who eschewed straight lines and symmetry in his work; his buildings were often endowed with irregularly spaced windows and uneven flooring.

ECONOMY

Austria cherishes its abundant natural resources with the same intelligent care that it has lavished on its cultural and historical landmarks. Mountains are still well-forested, the result of centuries of careful management. The forests also help to protect the high-perched farms from landslides, avalanches, and the slower damage of erosion.

Many swift-flowing, glacier-fed streams and rivers rise in the mountains, providing the country with one of its most valuable resources— water for hydroelectricity, the "white coal" of Austria. There are hydroelectric stations on the Inn, Enns, and Salzach Rivers, all of which are tributaries of the Danube. The Danube, navigable for its entire length through Austria, is the country's most important river.

In addition to its scenery, its power resources, and its forests, Austria has a wealth of minerals. It is one of the world's leading producers of high-grade graphite. The country also has vast deposits of minerals used in modern industry. Coal is mined in Styria and Upper Austria. The most important iron-ore mines are located in Styria's Erzberg region. Other important resources include oil, copper, lead, zinc, and antimony.

Farm workers bring in the hay harvest in the Salzach Valley.

In 1978, Austrians rejected nuclear power during an official referendum, and since 2000, have adamantly protested the opening of a nuclear reactor at Temelin, in the neighboring Czech Republic.

Less than one-fifth of the land can be used for farming in this mountainous nation, but the Alpine slopes provide excellent pastureland. Most farms are small, and many are perched on steep hills and mountain slopes. Only slightly more than 2 percent of the labor force works in agriculture, but careful use of the land and the efforts of hard-working farmers make Austria nearly self-sufficient in food production. Meat, milk, butter, and cheese are the most important foodstuffs.

Austria's industries manufacture a wide variety of goods, including iron and steel products, chemicals, and such consumer items as textiles. Ancient traditions of craftsmanship are still evident in such Austrian handiwork as blown and cut glass, leather goods, pottery and ceramics, wrought iron, jewelry, and lace. Most of these goods continue to be handmade by artisans who served three to four years as apprentices before being recognized as journeymen and, finally, as master craftsmen.

Like all other developed European countries, Austria has entered the postindustrial age; most of its people—more than two-thirds of the nation's labor force—now work in the service sector. In January 2002, the country replaced its traditional currency, the shilling, with the euro.

Hallstatt in Upper Austria, the site of an Iron Age settlement.

HISTORY

The journey into Austria's past begins in the early Iron Age at Hallstatt in Upper Austria. Here careful excavation of ancient burial grounds has revealed the existence of a flourishing community that mined and traded salt. When the Celts moved into Austria about the 3rd century B.C., they took over the thriving salt trade in such towns as Hallstatt and Salzburg and extended their kingdom of Noricum until it included most of Upper Austria, Salzburg, West Styria, and Carinthia.

There is evidence that the Romans had penetrated the region we call Austria by about 100 B.C. By A.D. 10 they had established themselves as the sole rulers of the region they named Pannonia. The Romans were as interested in exploiting the trade of the area as they were in protecting their eastern frontier. The Danube River gave the Romans an east–west trade link. The most important north–south trade route was the so-called Amber Road, which extended from Jutland in Denmark in the north, across western Austria, south to Rome. Traders from the north carried whale tusks and amber (used for jewelry), which they traded for swords, pitchers, and, of course, salt.

For several hundred years the Romans were able to fight off the repeated attempts at invasions by barbarians from the north and east. During this period of relative peacefulness the Romans established the city of

Vindobona (Vienna), and brought their language and later the Christian religion to the region.

But from about A.D. 400 onward, the weakened Roman Empire could no longer successfully defend Pannonia. By the end of the 5th century the country lay open to attack by wave after wave of barbarian invaders—Huns, Slavs, Avars, and Magyars from the east; Teutons from the north; and Bajuvars from the west. It was not until the time of Charlemagne in the 8th century that the region knew stable government again. It lasted for only about a century.

In the year 976 Otto II, the Holy Roman Emperor, gave part of Austria to Leopold of Babenberg to rule as a duchy. The gift was perhaps a little less generous than it seems, for Otto II wanted to protect his eastern frontier from further invasions, and it became the Babenbergs' duty to keep the Magyars (Hungarians) at bay.

The Babenbergs set Austria on the road to steady growth in trade and prosperity. The eastern border of the duchy was never quiet, but it managed somehow to survive all attacks. After nearly 300 years of continuous rule, the last of the Babenbergs died in 1246 in a battle with the Magyars, their fiercest enemies. The Babenbergs had not only erected mighty fortresses to defend their duchy, but also built beautiful monasteries, such as the ones at Melk, Klosterneuburg, Heiligenkreuz, and Admont—splendid stone mementos of their deep religious faith. Christianity had come to the land in the 4th century when Emperor Constantine made it the state religion of Rome. Throughout the centuries that followed, the dukes, kings, and later the emperors of Austria took as their foremost duty the defense of Roman Catholicism against the heathens, the Muslims, and later the Protestant reformers.

Austria Under the Habsburgs

When the last duke of Babenberg died, Austria fell into the hands of King Ottokar II of Bohemia (now part of Czechoslovakia). The German Emperor, seeing the southeastern border of his territory threatened, quickly sent a relief army to Austria. The army, under the leadership of Rudolf of Habsburg, defeated Ottokar in 1278.

This event marked the beginning of Habsburg rule over Austria. It was to last for 640 years, until 1918. Under the Habsburgs, Austria became renowned as a center of music, art, and architecture. The Habsburgs developed another new and singular talent, which made their empire grow and grow until in the 16th century Emperor Charles V could say of his empire that the sun never set on it. This talent was based on a simple, strategic plan for marriages of the Habsburg children and grandchildren, which made duchies and kingdoms fall into Austria's lap like ripe apples.

The first Habsburg to put this strategy into practice was Frederick III, who ruled in the 15th century. He realized that this was a far better way to enlarge the empire than by bloody wars. The following verse should have been inscribed on his crest: *Bella gerant alii, Tu felix Austria nube* ("Let others wage war, You, happy Austria, marry"). Frederick's son Maximilian I added the Duchy of Burgundy (now part of France) and the Netherlands to the empire through his first marriage, to Maria of Burgundy. His grandson Philip made Spain and its colonies a Habsburg possession by marrying Juana of Castile and Aragon (Spain). Frederick

III's great-grandchildren married the heirs to the thrones of Bohemia and Hungary, unions that formed the core of the empire until 1918.

When Charles V came to the throne in the 16th century, Austria reached the height of its power. Charles inherited the Austrian lands and the right of succession to the thrones of Bohemia, Hungary, Burgundy, the Spanish Empire, the Netherlands, Sardinia, Sicily, and Naples. Charles V goes down in history as the great defender of Catholicism, and his strongest enemy, the one he never defeated, was Protestantism. Under Charles' direction, Martin Luther was excommunicated by the Diet of Worms in 1521.

The forces of Catholic Austria were pitted against the Protestants in the Thirty Years' War. During the long war Austria lost holdings in Germany and suffered a terrible loss of manpower. However, in 1620 at the battle of White Mountain, Austria re-asserted its control of Bohemia and Moravia (now part of Czechoslovakia). As its territory grew, the imperial bureaucracy became more strict. At one point the police even told each class of society what clothes to wear and what food to eat.

The Austrian Empire continued to be threatened from the outside. In 1683, 150 years after an unsuccessful attempt to take Vienna, the Turks were again at the city's gates. In a century of warfare the Turkish Army had overrun Asia Minor and the Balkan Peninsula, and the Turks were determined to take over the rest of Europe as well. A force of 300,000 Turks stood at the gates of Vienna to wipe Austria from the face of

Vienna's landmarks include the stately Burgtheater (foreground) and the Gothic-style St. Stephen's cathedral, whose majestic spire rises in the distance.

Schönbrunn, one of the magnificent Habsburg palaces, in Vienna.

the earth. Although the city seemed lost, it never gave up hope. For 2 months the Viennese starved and prayed. Deliverance came suddenly and unexpectedly when the armies of the Polish king, John III Sobieski, and Charles, Duke of Lorraine, swooped down from the wooded hills in a brilliantly timed surprise attack and destroyed the Turkish force. The leader of the Turks, Kara Mustafa, was beheaded by the sultan after what was left of the army fled wildly back across the Hungarian Plain.

All that the Turks left behind—the tents, the jewelry, and the arms—is preserved in Vienna's museums. The most coveted pieces of loot, however, were some sacks of coffee beans from which the Turks made a sweet black liquid that was an immediate success in Vienna. Soon coffee-houses sprang up all over the country. According to legend the delicious little cookies called vanilla *Kipferl* also date to the defeat of the Turks. Viennese housewives eager to celebrate their freedom from the Muslim threat shaped the dough like a crescent moon—the Turkish symbol.

When the Emperor Charles VI died in 1740, the male line of the Habsburgs came to an end, and with Maria Theresa, the first empress of Austria, another brilliant chapter of Austrian history began. Although most of her reign was a desperate fight to assert herself against such aggressive enemies as the Prussian emperor Frederick the Great, she managed not only to hold her own, but to make Austria, and above all Vienna, into the center of the European world. Indeed, she was a woman of extraordinary qualities, who somehow managed to look after the affairs of the state and to raise a large family with her husband, Franz Stefan of Lorraine. Her statue still stands majestically between Vienna's two great museums of art and natural history. The Empress, surrounded by her finest counselors, seems to look at the royal castle as if to say, "All this is mine." It was in Maria Theresa's time that the arts blossomed, when Mozart played to Her Imperial Majesty in Schönbrunn Palace, and the most significant baroque palaces and churches were built. Maria Theresa gave her imperial residence all the splendor of a great capital—a splendor that can still be felt today.

The Habsburg marriage policy, however, proved disastrous with Maria Theresa's daughter, Marie Antoinette, who married the French king Louis XVI and had to share with him the terrible death under the guillotine during the French Revolution. It was impossible in those days to liquidate any one ruling dynasty without in some way offending the House of Habsburg. And when Napoleon Bonaparte, a child of the French Revolution, tried to legalize his self-imposed imperial crown, he chose to marry the Habsburg princess Marie Louise. This, however, did not stop him from twice attacking and overrunning Austria. But at the end of this epoch, during which nearly the whole of Europe was laid waste, it was Austria that played the leading role in uniting Europe. In 1815, emperors, kings, princes, and dukes met at the Congress of Vienna to negotiate a peace. Their success can be measured by the fact that Europe's peace lasted for almost 100 years.

The statesmen of the 19th century were all agreed on one point: if Austria had not existed, one would have had to invent it. It was not like any other country. It did not consist of different nations, but of different peoples. It had a dozen different peoples—Austrians lived with Czechs and Slovaks, Poles with Italians, Croatians with Slovenes, Ukrainians with Bosnians and Germans—all united under one crown, the crown of the Habsburgs.

What is today an unfulfilled ambition, a unified European territory without customs or frontiers, was a reality in Hapsburg Austria. Thus, Austria was way ahead of its time. Yet it was, simultaneously, lagging far behind. In an empire of this size, appropriate reforms could perhaps have prevented the rise of a new and fearful age—the age of nationalism. Nationalism was the scourge of the 19th century, and Franz Joseph, the next-to-last Habsburg emperor, did not or would not understand that nationalism would finally destroy his empire. His reforms were too few and came too late. In 1867, for example, Hungary was granted almost equal status with Austria in the Austro-Hungarian Dual Monarchy. But this was only one small step when many great steps were needed.

The End of the Empire

When the heir to the Habsburg throne, Franz Ferdinand, was murdered in Sarajevo (Yugoslavia) in July 1914 by Gavrilo Princip, a Serbian nationalist, Franz Joseph saw only one way to save the honor of the Crown—war. When the Serbs refused to surrender the assassin, Austria's army marched toward Belgrade.

This not only was the death warrant of the monarchy, but also set off the chain reaction of war declarations that led to World War I. The whole of Europe took up arms, and even America came out of its isolation and joined England, France, and Russia to battle the Central Powers led by Austria and Germany. It was not until Germany and Austria were completely defeated in 1918 that an armistice was declared. The peace treaty left Austria with scarcely more than the little province that had long ago been given to the dukes of Babenberg. The crown lands were made into the independent republics of Czechoslovakia, Poland, Hungary, and Yugoslavia. Romania and Italy took shares of what was left of the empire. Of the approximately 50 million people who lived in the Austro-Hungarian Empire, only 6.5 million were left as Austrian citizens.

The last Habsburg, Charles, who was crowned in 1916 in Hungary, made a feeble attempt to draw Austria out of the war, only to find himself humiliated by Germany and misunderstood by the other allies. When Austria became a republic, he left the country. His son, Otto Habsburg, gave up his claim to the throne in 1961.

The Austrian Republic

The Austrian Republic got off to a shaky start, since the nation's economy had suffered the double blow of war and the loss of imperial markets. Unemployment, hunger, and inflation plagued the small nation. By 1922, however, the country began to get back on its feet. A new constitution was passed, and economic prospects improved.

Unfortunately, just as Austria was regaining its stability, the world experienced a severe economic depression, which in Europe led to the rise of fascism and Nazism. The Nazi leader, Adolf Hitler, was born in Austria, but after several unhappy years in Vienna, he adopted Germany as his homeland. In the 1930s, the Austrian Nazi party grew rapidly, which facilitated the annexation of Austria by Hitler's troops in 1938. For the next seven years, the country was part of the German Reich.

In 1945, at the end of World War II, Austria was occupied by American, British, Soviet, and French forces. The four big powers, although divided on many other issues, soon agreed that Austria should not come under the influence of any one of them, but instead remain neutral. In 1955, all foreign troops left, and the country was on its own.

During the following decades, Austria offered a haven and temporary shelter to thousands of refugees from Hungary in 1956, Czechoslovakia in 1968, and Poland in the 1980s. It also became a transfer point for Soviet Jews emigrating to Israel from the 1970s on.

The bitter legacy of the Nazi era was raised when former UN Secretary-General Kurt Waldheim was elected president in 1986. During his campaign, it was revealed that in World War II he was an officer with an army group that committed brutalities against Yugoslav partisans and arranged mass deportations of Greek Jews to death camps. As a result, Austria was isolated diplomatically until 1992, when Waldheim was succeeded by Thomas Klestil. Klestil was reelected by a landslide in April 1998. Meanwhile, in 1994, Austria joined the European Union (EU). In February 2000, another problem arose when the ultra-right-wing Freedom Party joined the government. The EU, in turn, froze all political contacts with Austria, but the sanctions were lifted within a year.

Government. Austria is a federal republic made up of nine provinces. The head of state is the president, who is elected for six years. The president appoints the chancellor, who serves as the head of government, usually from among the members of the majority party in the legislature. The legislature is composed of the Nationalrat (National Council), elected for four years directly by the people, and the Bundesrat (Federal Council), elected by the provincial legislatures.

HUGO PORTISCH, Chief Commentator, Austrian Television Corporation

DANUBE RIVER

Donau in Germany and Austria; *Dunaj* in Slovakia; *Duna* in Hungary; *Dunav* in Croatia, Yugoslavia, and Bulgaria; *Dunârea* in Romania; and *Dunai* in Russia and Ukraine—all are names for a river as varied and colorful as the countries on its banks—the Danube. Though it is often thought to be exclusively Austrian, or even Viennese, the Danube begins in Germany. It ends in the Black Sea, after wandering, winding, flowing, and sometimes hurtling 1,750 mi. (2,800 km.) through ten very different countries.

THE RIVER BEGINS

Near a castle in Donaueschingen, in Germany's Black Forest, there is a wishing well where tourists like to throw coins. This is the Donauquelle—"Danube spring"—and when its waters meet two local streams that rise in the Alps, the Danube is formed. The Danube flows gently northeast through this part of western Germany, gradually gaining in strength. By the time the river reaches Ulm, it is wide and deep enough for small boats to begin the trip downstream. Heavier craft must start at the ancient city of Regensburg, the northernmost point on the Danube. In the 2nd century A.D., Regensburg—called Castra Regina by the Romans—was a military camp and part of Rome's northern defense lines against invading barbarian tribes.

Even this early in its journey, the river is light brown, because it has already begun to pick up some of the silt that will eventually be deposited in the delta at the Black Sea.

At Passau the Danube enters Austria. Here the steamers of the Donaudampfschiffahrtsgesellschaft—"Danube steamship country"—start their trips downriver, passing Russian, Romanian, and Yugoslavian barges being towed upstream. This section of the river is full of contrasts, at once as new as tomorrow and as old as many yesterdays. The Romans called this part of the river Danubius, and they threw coins into its dangerous whirlpools to calm the river god. The Romans also started the vineyards here that are still the source of fragrant Austrian wines.

On this stretch of the river, there are four great hydroelectric dams, converting the river's energy into power for industries and homes. The dams—Kachlet, Jochenstein, Aschach, and Ybbs-Persenbeug—are symbols of everything new on the Danube. The river next flows through the Wachau region, with its many abbeys and castles, including Dürnstein, where Richard the Lion-Hearted was imprisoned on his way home from the Third Crusade.

FOUR CAPITALS ON THE DANUBE

Before reaching Vienna, the first of the four great cities on the Danube, the river flows past the Wiener Wald ("Vienna woods")—the inspiration for a waltz by the Austrian composer Johann Strauss, Jr. In spite of Strauss' most famous waltz, "The Beautiful Blue Danube," the river is truly blue only on the clearest days, when it reflects the sky.

Once the capital of the vast Austro-Hungarian Empire, Vienna today is still an important international city. It is also still a city of whipped cream, pastries, and beautiful music, as it was in the time of Mozart and Beethoven. Each year, from May to September, cruise ships take passengers downriver from Vienna to the Black Sea. And there are the much faster hydrofoils, appropriately called *Raketen* ("rockets") because they can make the trip to Budapest in less than five hours.

About 40 mi. (64 km.) east of Vienna lies Bratislava, the capital of the newly independent Slovakia. It is a 1,000-year-old city, which served as the capital of Hapsburg Hungary from 1526 to 1784 (at that time it was known by its German name, Pressburg). Bratislava is the gateway to the picturesque Carpathian Mountains.

The Danube, now running due south, divides Hungary's capital city, Budapest, into two parts—Buda, the old section, and Pest, the newer, more commercial section. From Budapest, the river continues south through the Great Hungarian Plain to Mohács, on the border with Yugoslavia. In 1526, about 28,000 Hungarians were slaughtered by 300,000 Turks at this place, giving the Ottoman Empire control of central and southern Hungary for almost 200 years.

The Danube at Ulm, Germany, where the river first becomes navigable for small craft.

Belgrade, Yugoslavia, is the fourth of the capitals on the Danube. Although it is a modern, Western-looking city, it still shows much of the influence of the East. The Kalemegdan, an old Turkish fortress on a bluff high over the Danube, is a reminder of the days when everything to the south and east could be controlled from here, and the Danube Valley rang with marching songs. According to an old saying, whoever was the master of Belgrade was the master of the entire Balkan Peninsula, and the city was destroyed over and over again as various armies fought to take it.

WITH THE DANUBE TO THE SEA

After it leaves Belgrade, the river suddenly becomes narrower and deeper. Only the best pilots can take ships safely through the treacherous currents and eddies of the Kazán Defile, whose name means "boiling cauldron" in Yugoslavia. Farther on, this same forbidding gorge is called the Iron Gate. No one knows when the name was first used, but the reason for it is clear—it seems as if the mountains will refuse to let the water through. Romania and Yugoslavia built a huge power dam here, and when the project was completed, in the early 1970s, a large lake was created in part of the gorge. Several villages were submerged and a monastery had to be moved to higher ground.

As if tired from its struggle with the Iron Gate, the Danube flows on placidly toward the Black Sea. Bucharest, Romania's capital, is only 40 mi. (64 km.) to the north, but the fishermen, shepherds, and buffalo who live along this part of the river make a 20th-century city seem many light-years away.

In Vienna, the Danube flows by the Donaupark Center, where many U.N. agencies are housed.

The Danube River, as it flows through Budapest, the capital of Hungary, on its course toward the Black Sea.

As the river slows down, so does the pace of life on its banks. Galați, Romania's main Danube port, is the last large city on the river as it approaches the delta. Near Tulcea, Romania, the Danube branches out into three main channels—the Kiliya, the Sulina, and the St. George—and hundreds of smaller ones. The Sulina channel has been deepened to allow ships access to the Black Sea, but many of the smaller channels are hardly wide enough to permit rowboats to pass through them.

The Danube Delta

The 1,000-sq.-mi. (2,600-sq.-km.) area between the Kiliya channel on the north and the St. George on the south is the vast Danube Delta, which is growing constantly as the river adds sediment. The delta is one of the largest bird sanctuaries in the world. There are ducks, geese, pelicans, and swans; herons, egrets, kingfishers, and cormorants; and hoopoes, spoonbills, ibis, and storks. Migratory birds from far and near spend the winter in the quiet delta region. The few people who live on the delta live from it, catching fish and gathering water chestnuts. Although parts of the delta were damaged by a reclamation scheme begun in the 1980s, these areas are now being restored by the Danube Delta Biosphere Reserve, created by the Romanian government in 1991.

So when the Danube finally reaches the sea, it has become many small streams instead of one great river. The waters that have been described by the gypsies as "the dustless road," which have formed a highway for trade and travelers and for countless armies as well, flow peacefully into the Black Sea.

Reviewed by THOMAS NOWOTNY
Austrian Information Service, New York

ILLUSTRATION CREDITS

1 © Hubertus Kanus/Shostal/SuperStock
5 Swiss National Tourist Office
8 Ric Ergenbright/Lenstour Photo Service
9 G. Barone/Monkmeyer Press Photo Service
14 A. & S. Faddegon
15 Carl Purcell
16 © Sovfoto/Eastfoto
17 © Tony Craddock/Science Photo Library/Photo Researchers
21 © Steve Vidler/Leo deWys Inc.
22 Joan Brown
23 © Eastcott-Momatiuk/Woodfin Camp
28 Carl Purcell
31 Editorial Photocolor Archives, N.Y.
32 Luis Villota
34 Marc Riboud/Magnum Photos
38 © P. Vauthey/Sygma
39 © F. Lochon/Gamma-Liaison
43 Gaetano Barone/Monkmeyer Press Photo Service; Erich Hartmann/Magnum Photos
46 Srdjan Maljkovic
47 Charles Shapp
48 © Frederick Ayer/Photo Researchers
50 © Giansanti/Sygma
52 David Stemple/Monkmeyer Press Photo Service
55 A. & S. Faddegon
57 Eric Ergenbright/Lenstour Photo Service
58 Allan A. Philiba
59 © Porterfield-Chickering/Photo Researchers
60 Editorial Photocolor Archives, N.Y.
61 © Vance Henry/Taurus Photos
62 © Summer Productions/Taurus Photos
63 © Bernard Pierre Wolff/Photo Researchers
65 Michael A. Vaccaro
66 Irish Tourist Board
67 Mulvey-Crump Associates, Inc.
68 Irish Tourist Board
69 Irish Tourist Board
71 © Ned Haines/Photo Researchers
72 © Thomas Braise/The Stock Market
73 Irish Tourist Board
74 Editorial Photocolor Archives, N.Y.
75 Irish Tourist Board
78 Irish Tourist Board
79 Photographers Consortium/eStock
80 © Dave G. Houser/Houserstock
81 © Spencer Grant/Photo Researchers; © John Heseltine/Science Photo Library/Photo Researchers
84 © Alex Hutzelsider/AP/Wide World Photos
85 © Brian Yarvin/Photo Researchers
86 Both photos: © Churchill & Klehr/Danita Delimont, Agent
88 © B. Gibbs/TRIP/Viesti Associates
89 Hulton/Archive by Getty Images; © Hussein Malla/AP/Wide World Photos
90 © Robert Frerck/Woodfin Camp
91 © S. Samuels/TRIP/Viesti Associates
92 © Walter Bibikow/Viesti Associates
93 © Kieran Doherty/AP/Wide World Photos
94 © Nik Wheeler/Danita Delimont, Agent
95 © Susan Walsh/AP/Wide World Photos
97 © Simon Harris/eStock
98 © Simon Fraser/Science Photo Library/Photo Researchers; © Dave G. Houser/Houserstock
99 Superstock; © Dave G. Houser/Houserstock
100 © Charles Graham/eStock; © Jan Butchofsky-Houser/Houserstock
102 Picture Finders Ltd./eStock
103 © Rex A. Butcher/Stone/Getty Images
104 © John Stillwell/AP/Wide World Photos
105 © Steve Vidler/eStock
106 © Chris Cole/Stone/Getty Images
107 © Anthony Harvey/Newsmakers/Getty Images; © Nik Wheeler/Danita Delimont, Agent; © Mike Yamashita/Woodfin Camp
108 AP/Wide World Photos
109 © Jan Butchofsky-Houser/Houserstock
110 © Steve Bly/Houserstock
111 Picture Finders Ltd./eStock
112 © Lawrence Migdale/Photo Researchers; © Tipp Howell/V.C.L./Taxi/Getty Images
114 © Rafael Macia/Photo Researchers
115 © Rex A. Butcher/Bruce Coleman Inc.; © Walter Bibikow/Viesti Associates
116 Stock Montage/Superstock;
117 © Bill Bachmann/Network Aspen Superstock
118 © Chris Helgrin/AP/Wide World Photos
119 © Dagli Orti/Palazzo Barberini Rome/The Art Archive; Hatfield House, England/AKG Berlin/Photo Researchers
120 Photographers Library LTD/eStock
121 © John Lawrence/Stone/Getty Images
122 © V. Greaves/TRIP/Viesti Associates
123 © Dave G. Houser/Houserstock
124 © Jan Butchofsky-Houser/Houserstock
125 Frantisek Staud
126 © Bryn Thomas/Lonely Planet Images; © Jan Butchofsky-Houser/Houserstock
127 © M. Lee/TRIP/Viesti Associates; © Bryn Thomas/Lonely Planet Images
129 © Churchill & Klehr/Danita Delimont, Agent
131 © Steve Vidler/SuperStock
132 © Dave G. Houser/Houserstock
133 © Andrea Pistolesi/Image Bank/Getty Images
134 © Bill Terry/Viesti Associates; SuperStock
136 SuperStock
137 © Bill Bachmann/Index Stock
138 © Catherine Karnow/Woodfin Camp
139 SuperStock; National Portrait Gallery, London/SuperStock
140 © David Cheskin/AP/Wide World Photos
142 © Richard Cummins/Viesti Associates
143 © Rafael Macia/Photo Researchers
145 © Oliver Strewe/Lonely Planet Images
146 © Eitan Simanor/Bruce Coleman Inc.
147 © Danilo G. Donadoni/Bruce Coleman Inc.
148 © Hugh Thomas/BWP Media/Newsmakers/Getty Images
150 © The Stock Market
151 Leffteroff/World Films Enterprise
154 F. & N. Schwitter Library
155 © Israel Talby/Woodfin Camp
156 Sabine Weiss/Rapho Guillumette Pictures
158 Victor Englebert
159 Jerry Frank
160 Jacques Jangoux
161 © J. C. Francolon/Gamma-Liaison
162 Monkmeyer Press Photo Service
163 Monkmeyer Press Photo Service
164 © K. Benser/Leo deWys Inc.
165 © M. L. Nolan/Taurus Photos
166 © Allyn Z. Baum/Monkmeyer Press; Editorial Photocolor Archives, N.Y.
167 Victor Englebert
168 © John Sims/Click-Chicago
169 Leon Deller/Monkmeyer Press Photo Service
172 © Remy de la Mauviniere/AP/Wide World Photos
174 Editorial Photocolor Archives, N.Y.; Victor Englebert
175 Willis Wood
176 Cloisters Collection Metropolitan Museum of Art/Robert S. Crandall Associates
180 Victor Englebert
181 Allan A. Philiba
182 Ric Ergenbright/Lenstour Photo Service
189 Victor Englebert
192 Mulvey-Crump Associates, Inc.
194 Art Reference Bureau; Susan Heimann
196 © Tibor Bognar/The Stock Market
197 Susan Heimann
198 © Jean-Paul Nacivet/Leo deWys Inc.
201 Skip Ascheim
203 © Luis Villota/The Stock Market
204 © Tibor Bognar/The Stock Market
205 © Marvin Newman/The Image Bank
207 © J. P. Conrardy/Taurus Photos
208 Consulate General of Luxembourg
211 Jerry Frank
216 Jerry Frank
217 Editorial Photocolor Archives, N.Y.
218 Jacques Jangoux
219 Leo deWys, Inc.
220 Leo deWys, Inc.
222 © Francois Lenoir/AP/Wide World Photos
225 © Vance Henry/Taurus Photos
226 © Graham/Sygma
228 © Steve Vidler/Leo deWys Inc.
231 © R. van der Hilst/Gamma-Liaison
232 © Tom McHugh/Photo Researchers
237 Rijksmuseum, Amsterdam
238 © Howard Millard
239 Superstock
240 Superstock
242 © Walter Mayr/Focus/Woodfin Camp
243 © Ric Ergenbright/Danita Delimont, Agent
244 © Wolfgang Kaehler
246 Maximilian Stock Ltd./Science Photo Library/Photo Researchers; © Roland and Karen Muschenetz/Danita Delimont, Agent
247 © Dave Bartruff/Danita Delimont, Agent
248 © David Peevers/Danita Delimont, Agent; © Ulrike Welsch MCMXCIV/Photo Researchers; © Trygve Bolstad/Panos Pictures
249 © Dave G. Houser/Houserstock
250 © Dave Bartruff/Danita Delimont, Agent
251 © Martin Meissner/AP/Wide World Photos; Viesti Associates; © Diether Endlicher/AP/Wide World Photos; © Alessandro della Valle/KEYSTONE/AP/Wide World Photos
252 © Louis Monier/Liaison/Getty Images
253 © Sven Kaestner/AP/Wide World Photos
254 Museum der Bildenden Kunste, Leipzig/A.K.G., Berlin/Superstock; Giraudon/Art Resource, NY; © Erich Lessing/Art Resource, NY; Giraudon/Art Resource, NY
255 © Erich Lessing/Art Resource, NY; Art Resource, NY; © Andrea Schulte-Peevers/Lonely Planet Images
256 © Steve Vidler/eStock; © Frank Boxler/AP/Wide World Photos
257 © Bob Krist/eStock
258 © Holger Stamme/OKAPIA/Photo Researchers
260 ZEFA Gmbh/eStock
261 © Michael Rosenfeld/Stone/Getty Images
262 © Ionas Kaltenbach/Lonely Planet Images; © Michael J. O'Brien/Panos Pictures
263 © Wolfgang Kaehler
264 © Stuart Cohen/The Image Works
265 © Danilo G. Donadoni/Bruce Coleman Inc.
266 © Joachim Messerschmidt/eStock
267 © Dave Bartruff/Danita Delimont, Agent; © Wolfgang Kaehler
268 © Maria Ueda/eStock
269 © Wolfgang Kaehler; Picture Finders Ltd./eStock
270 Bruce Coleman Inc.
271 Superstock
273 © David Peevers/Danita Delimont, Agent
274 © Margot Granitsas/The Image Works
277 AP/Wide World Photos; Courtesy, Staats Bibliothek, Berlin
278 © Stefano Amantini/Atlantide/Bruce Coleman Inc.
280 © Jan Bauer/AP/Wide World Photos
281 © Wolfgang Kaehler; Pictor International/Pictor International, Ltd./PictureQuest
282 © Diether Endlicher/AP/Wide World Photos; U.S. Air Force photo by Staff Sgt. Justin D. Pyle
283 © Steve Vidler/eStock
285 Swiss National Tourist Office
289 Alan Band Associates
291 Editorial Photocolor Archives, N.Y.
292 © Porterfield-Chickering/Photo Researchers
294 © Blaine Harrington/The Stock Market
296 Herbert Fristedt
299 Editorial Photocolor Archives, N.Y.
300 Ric Ergenbright/Lenstour Photo Service
301 Editorial Photocolor Archives, N.Y.
302 Charles Shapp
303 Alan Band Associates; Swiss National Tourist Office
304 Ric Ergenbright/Lenstour Photo Service
305 Editorial Photocolor Archives, N.Y.
307 Frank Schwarz/Lee Ames Studio
308 Ric Ergenbright/Lenstour Photo Service
309 Henry L. Kurtz
312 Ric Ergenbright/Lenstour Photo Service
313 Ric Ergenbright/Lenstour Photo Service
314 Austrian National Tourist Office
316 Ernst Z. Rothkopf
319 Ric Ergenbright/Lenstour Photo Service
320 Ric Ergenbright/Lenstour Photo Service
322 © Michel Hetier
323 Grolier Photo Library
326 Wesley McKeown
327 Fred J. Maroon/Lufthansa Airlines
328 © Harry Redl/Black Star
329 Dankwart von Knobloch/Lenstour Photo Service

Cover photos: Neuschwanstein Castle: IFA/Bruce Coleman Inc.; windmills: © Steve Vidler/Superstock; bagpiper: © Steve Vidler/Superstock

HOW TO USE THE INDEX

In this index, the headings of all entries are in boldface type. Headings which are titles of articles are in all capital letters. The headings, including those of more than one word, are alphabetized letter by letter, as in a dictionary.

> **NEW ENGLAND**
> **Newfoundland**
> **Northeast Passage**
> **NORTHERN IRELAND**
> **Northmen**

Names of persons are listed under the surname, followed by the first name. When there are two or more persons with the same surname, the names are listed alphabetically according to the first name.

> **Smith, Adam**
> **Smith, Ian Douglas**
> **Smith, Joseph**

Rulers of the same name are listed alphabetically by country. Roman numerals are listed numerically under each individual country.

> **Charles I** (king of England)
> **Charles II** (king of England)
> **Charles VII** (king of France)
> **Charles V** (Holy Roman emperor)
> **Charles II** (king of Spain)
> **Charles IV** (king of Spain)

Names of mountains and lakes are inverted.

> **Chad, Lake**
> **Erie, Lake**
> **Everest, Mount**
> **McKinley, Mount**

But when "Mount," "Lake," or "Fort" is used in the name of a place or town, it is entered directly.

> **Fort Smith** (Arkansas)
> **Fort Worth** (Texas)
> **Lake Placid** (resort town, New York)
> **Mount Desert Isle** (Maine)

Inverted headings are alphabetized up to the comma. If the headings are identical up to the comma, alphabetization is determined by the word or words following the comma.

> **Paris, Treaty of**
> **Paris Commune**
> **Victoria, Lake**
> **Victoria Falls**

Mac and Mc are entered as Mac and Mc, and are listed in their alphabetical positions.

> **Mackenzie, Sir Alexander**
> **MacMahon, Patrice de**
> **Mboya, Tom**
> **McKinley, Mount**

In place names, "St." is interfiled with "Saint."

> **St. George** (Bermuda)
> **Saint Lawrence, Gulf of**
> **St. Louis** (Missouri)

Names of saints are entered under the personal name when the saint is better known by that name; otherwise they are entered under the surname.

> **Paul, Saint**
> **Xavier, Saint Francis**

Life dates are given for personal names when needed to differentiate between two persons of the same name.

> **Augustine, Saint** (died 604; 1st
>   archbishop of Canterbury)
> **Augustine, Saint** (354-430; church father)

Matter in parentheses is disregarded in alphabetizing, except when used to distinguish identical headings.

> **New Amsterdam** (Dutch settlement in
>   America, now New York City)
> **New Amsterdam** (Guyana)
> **Pearl Harbor**
> **Pearl River** (Mississippi)
> **Pearl (ZHU) River** (China)

Cross-references are of two kinds, See and See also. Both refer to Index entries.

See references are from an alternative heading of a subject to the ones under which the subject is indexed.

> **American Indians** see Indians of
>   Central and South America;
>   Indians of North America
> **Bolshevik Revolution** see Russian Revolution and Civil War

See also references refer to headings under which additional or related matter can be found.

> **Antilles**
>   *see also* Greater Antilles; Lesser Antilles
> **CANADA**
>   *see also* names of provinces, territories,
>   cities

· · · A · · ·

Aachen (Germany) **3:**244, 267–68
Aalto, Alvar (Finnish architect) **4:**59
Aar River (Switzerland) **3:**291
Abacha, Sani (Nigerian political leader) **1:**229
Abadan (Iran)
 illus. **2:**160
Abbai (river, Ethiopia) *see* Blue Nile
Abbas I (shah of Persia) **2:**163
Abbasid Caliphate (Arab dynasty) **1:**119; **2:**95, 154
Abbey Theatre (Dublin, Ireland) **3:**70
Abbotsford (British Columbia) **5:**131
Abbotsford House (Scotland)
 illus. **3:**136
Abdallah, Ahmed (president of Comoros) **1:**384
Abd-er-Rahman III (caliph of Córdoba) **4:**113
Abdul Hamid II (Ottoman sultan) **2:**65
Abdullah (crown prince of Saudi Arabia) **2:**127
Abdullah II (king of Jordan) **2:**121
Abdullah Hassan, Mohammad (Somali leader) **1:**304
Abdullah ibn Hussein (emir and king of Jordan) **2:**121
Abdul Rahman, Tengku (prime minister of Malaysia) **2:**308
Abéché (Chad) **1:**240, 243
Abenaki (Indians of North America) **5:**95, 99
Abengourou (Ivory Coast) **1:**185
Aberdare Mountains (Kenya) **1:**307
Aberdeen (Scotland) **3:**138
Aberystwyth (Wales) **3:**123
Abidjan (Ivory Coast) **1:**185, 187, 188
 illus. **1:**186
Abiola, Moshood (Nigerian political leader) **1:**229
Abkhazia (region, republic of Georgia) **2:**80, 85
Abkhazians (Asian people) **2:**80, 82
Abomey (Benin) **1:**210, 212
Abomey (early African kingdom) *see* Ardra
Aborigines, Australian **2:**478, 479, 493, 498, 500–501, 502
 arts and culture **2:**497
 Jervis Bay Territory **2:**514, 515
 New South Wales **2:**511, 512
 Northern Territory **2:**533, 535
 Queensland **2:**506, 508
 religion **2:**499
 South Australia **2:**522, 523
 Tasmania **2:**529, 531
 traditions renewed **2:**495, 496
 Uluru **2:**534
 Victoria **2:**517–18, 519, 520
 Western Australia **2:**526, 527
 illus. **2:**493, 518, 522
Abortion **2:**436; **4:**89, 163
Abraham (father of the Jews) **2:**49, 111, 125, 187
Abraham, Plains of (Quebec) **5:**97
Abreu, Casimiro de (Brazilian poet) **6:**180
Abruzzi (region, Italy) **4:**126
Absalon (Danish bishop) **4:**17
Absaroka Range (Wyoming) **5:**315
Abubakar, Abdulsalam (Nigerian political leader) **1:**229
Abu Dhabi (United Arab Emirates) **2:**138, 139
Abuja (capital, Nigeria) **1:**217
Abuladze, T. J. (Georgian film director) **2:**83

Abu Simbel (Egyptian temple) **1:**39, 111
Abyssinia *see* Ethiopia
Académie Française **3:**178
Acadia (Acadie) (early French name for Nova Scotia) **5:**80, 93
Acadia National Park (Maine)
 illus. **5:**182
Acadians (original French settlers in Acadia) **5:**29, 78, 80, 84, 85, 88, 93 *see also* Cajuns
 illus. **5:**85
Acajutla (El Salvador) **6:**43–44
Acapulco (Mexico) **5:**30, 412, 416
 illus. **5:**364, 368, 416
Acatenango (volcano, Guatemala) **6:**31
Accra (capital, Ghana) **1:**196–97
 illus. **1:**196
Aceh (Indonesia) **2:**326
Achaemenid (Persian dynasty) **2:**153, 162, 192
Acheampong, Ignatius (Ghanaian government leader) **1:**204
Acholi (African people) **1:**319, 323
Acid rain **5:**71
Aconcagua (highest peak in the Andes) **6:**2, 101, 266, 281, 345
 illus. **6:**282
Aconcagua River (Chile) **6:**313
Acosta, Tomás de (Spanish colonial governor) **6:**68
Acre (Israel) **2:**109
Acre (state, Brazil) **6:**241
Acropolis (Athens) **4:**196
Actopan (Hidalgo, Mexico) **5:**406
Acts of Union
 England and Ireland (1800) **3:**73, 77, 148
 England and Scotland (1707) **3:**120, 141
 Wales and England (1536) **3:**125, 130
Adamkus, Valdas (Lithuanian president) **4:**304
Adamstown (Pitcairn Island) **2:**563
Adana (Turkey) **2:**46, 63
 illus.
  textile factory **2:**64
Addis Ababa (capital, Ethiopia) **1:**36, 282, 285, 286, 292
 Organization of African Unity **1:**6
Adelaide (capital, South Australia, Australia) **2:**523
Adelaide Festival of Arts (Australia)
 illus. **2:**522
Adélie penguins **6:**327
 illus. **6:**328
Aden (Yemen) **2:**132, 133, 135
 illus. **2:**132
Aden, Gulf of **2:**130
Adena culture (Native American people) **5:**272
Adenauer, Konrad (German statesman) **3:**283
Adige River (Italy) **4:**128–29
Adirondack Mountains (North America) **5:**4, 201, 202, 204
Adirondack State Park (New York) **5:**204
 illus. **5:**204
Adja (African people) **1:**212
Adoula, Cyrille (Congolese leader) **1:**269
Adowa (Adwa), Battle of (1896) **1:**288; **4:**159
Adriatic Sea **3:**47; **4:**271
 Italy **4:**125, 128, 129, 147
Ady, Endre (Hungarian poet) **4:**240
Adzharia (region, republic of Georgia) **2:**82, 84
Aegean civilization **3:**45–46
Aegean islands (Greece) **4:**187, 189–92
Aegean Sea (Turkey–Greece) **2:**57; **4:**187, 188
Aeneas (legendary Trojan prince) **4:**164
Aeolian Islands *see* Lipari Islands

Aetna, Mount *see* Etna, Mount
Afadjato, Mount (Ghana) **1:**195
Afar (Danakil) (African people) **1:**37, 298, 299
Afar (language) **1:**295
Afar-Issa Territory *see* Djibouti
Afewerki, Issayas (president of Eritrea) **1:**296
AFGHANISTAN **2:**27, 29, 174–79
 Iranian troops at border **2:**164
 refugees from **2:**31
 religious strife **2:**170, 342
 Soviet invasion **4:**323
 United Kingdom **3:**95
 United States **1:**308
 illus. **2:**29
  desert **2:**176
  flag **2:**viii
  Khybur Pass **2:**176
  marketplace **2:**177
  site of destroyed Buddhist statue **2:**179
 map(s) **2:**175
Afghans (Asian people) **2:**163, 175
Afonso I (king of Portugal) **4:**75
AFRICA 1:1–64 *see also* names of countries
 AIDS **1:**319
 apartheid **1:**58–59
 Canary Islands **1:**32–33
 Congo River **1:**42–43
 First World War of **1:**270
 Jamaica, people and culture in **5:**474, 475
 Niger River **1:**50–51
 Nile River **1:**38–39
 Réunion **1:**46–47
 Sahara **1:**24–25
 illus.
  bazaar **1:**35
  cattle **1:**54
  flags of the countries **1:**xxii–xxiv
  irrigation **1:**63
  library **1:**28
  medical clinic **1:**26
  nomads **1:**62
  open-air classroom **1:**29
  Roman Catholic priest **1:**37
  savannas **1:**18
  storytelling **1:**15
  tourism **1:**64
  traditional and modern contrasts **1:**60
  witch doctor **1:**13
 map(s) **1:**7, 21
  African kingdoms, early **1:**14
  population **1:**17
  precipitation **1:**17
 table(s)
  area and population **6:**344
  continental extremes **6:**345
  countries **1:**8–9
  great mountain peaks **6:**348
African Americans *see* Black Americans
African kingdoms, early 1:11, 15, 162, 268
 Aksum **1:**288, 296
 Angola **1:**346
 Ashanti **1:**201, 202
 Baguirmi **1:**244
 Benin **1:**210, 214, 226
 Bornu **1:**225, 244
 Buganda **1:**318, 322
 Cush **1:**33, 127, 130
 Egypt **1:**117–18
 Ghana **1:**140, 157, 169, 201
 Ife **1:**226
 Kanem **1:**244

Kongo **1:**43, 260
Mali **1:**140–41, 157
Monomotapa **1:**361–62
Mossi **1:**190, 192
Niger **1:**148
Oyo **1:**226
Sahel **1:**142
Songhai **1:**140
Tekrur **1:**157–58
Wadai **1:**244
map(s) **1:**14
African National Congress 1:394, 405, 406
African Union 1:3, 6
headquarters in Addis Ababa **1:**36
Afrifa, Akwasi (Ghanaian leader) **1:**204
Afrikaans (language) **1:**45, 349, 399, 401
Afrikaners (South Africans of Dutch descent)
1:45, 399, 401, 406
Zimbabwe **1:**358
Agabama Falls (Cuba) **5:**442
Agadès (Niger) **1:**145
Agadir (Morocco) **1:**72
Agadja (king of Dahomey) **1:**214
Agalega Islands (dependencies of Mauritius)
1:379
Agamemnon (king of Mycenae) **3:**45; **4:**199
Agassiz, Lake (ancient glacial lake) **5:**114
Agave (plant) *see* Maguey
Agboville (Ivory Coast) **1:**185
Age of— *see* the main element of the term
Agincourt, Battle of (1415) **3:**182
Aglipayan (Philippine church) **2:**335
Agordat (Eritrea) **1:**294
Agra (India) **2:**172, 215, 216
Agriculture *see* Farms; articles on individual
continents and countries
Agrigento (Sicily) **4:**129
Agua (volcano, Guatemala) **6:**31
illus. **6:**32
Agua Caliente (Costa Rica) **6:**64
Aguán River (Honduras) **6:**35
Aguascalientes (capital, Aguascalientes state,
Mexico) **5:**404
AGUASCALIENTES (state, Mexico) **5:**404
Ahaggar (Hoggar) Mountains (Algeria) **1:**25, 76
illus. **1:**77
Ahémé, Lake (Benin) **1:**211
Ahern, Bertie (prime minister of Ireland) **3:**77
Ahidjo, Ahmadou (president of Cameroon)
1:234
Ahmadabad (India) **2:**203
Ahmadism (religion) **2:**184
Ahmed ibn-Tulun (founder of Muslim Tulunid
dynasty, Egypt) **1:**119
Ahmet Zogu *see* Zog I
Ahmose I (Egyptian king) **1:**117
Aidid, Mohammed Farah (Somalian warlord)
1:305
AIDS (disease)
Africa **1:**26, 63, 319; **1:**354; **1:**400
Asia **2:**37
Haiti **5:**467
illus. **1:**319
Ailinglapalap Atoll (Marshall Islands) **2:**575
Ainu (Asian people) **2:**16, 443, 444
illus. **2:**17, 444
Air conditioning 5:222, 241
Air France (airline) **3:**42
Aïr Massif (region, Niger) **1:**144, 148
Airplanes *see* Aviation
Aitmatov, Chingiz (Kyrgyz writer) **2:**355
Aix-en-Provence (France) **3:**160

Aizo (African people) **1:**212
Ajaccio (capital, Corsica) **3:**167
Ajamis (Bahraini people) **2:**141
Ajanta Temples (India) **2:**216
Ajman (United Arab Emirates) **2:**138
Akan (language) **1:**201
Akanyaru River (Rwanda) **1:**324
Akayev, Askar (president of Kyrgyzstan) **2:**355
Akhal Teke (horse) **2:**357
Akhdar, Gebel el (mountain, Libya) **1:**94
Akhdar, Jabal (region, Oman) **2:**136
Akhenaten (Amenhotep IV) (Egyptian king)
1:118
Akhetaton (ancient city, Egypt) **1:**118
Akhmadulina, Bella (Soviet poet) **4:**314
Akihito (emperor of Japan) **2:**443
Akjoujt (Mauritania)
illus. **1:**134
Akkadian Empire (Mesopotamia) **2:**48, 153
Akmola (Aqmola) *see* Astana
Akosombo (Ghana) **1:**200
Akposo (African people) **1:**206
Akron (Ohio) **5:**273
Aksum (early African kingdom) **1:**130, 288, 296
illus. **1:**289
ALABAMA 5:7, **242–44**
map(s) **5:**243
Alabama (Indians of North America) **5:**253
Alabama River (Alabama) **5:**242
Alacaluf (Indians of South America) **6:**305
Alagoas (state, Brazil) **6:**182
Al Aiún (capital, Western Sahara) **1:**132
Alameda Central (park, Mexico City) **5:**411
Alamo, Battle of the (1836) **5:**252, 383
Alamo, The (San Antonio, Texas)
illus. **5:**252
Alarcón, Abel (Bolivian writer) **6:**237
Alarcón, Fabián (president of Ecuador) **6:**205
ALASKA 5:50, 51, 157, 158, **348–50**
earthquake of 1964 **5:**335
Inuit **5:**58
illus.
fjords **5:**334
fur seals **5:**348
Kodiak Island fishing industry **5:**41
Mount McKinley **5:**349
oil pipeline **5:**24, 350
Unalaska Island **5:**348
map(s) **5:**349
Alaska Highway (Canada–U.S.) **5:**147, 350
Alaska Range (North America) **5:**8, 349
Alaungpaya (Burman king) **2:**271
Álava (Basque province of Spain) **4:**88, 107–8
Alawites (branch of Islam) **2:**91, 92
Al-Azhar Mosque (Cairo, Egypt) **1:**115, 119
Al-Azhar University (Cairo, Egypt) **1:**108–9
Albán, Mount (Mexico) *see* Monte Albán
Alban Hills (outside Rome, Italy) **4:**170, 178
ALBANIA 3:2, 25, 64; **4:**163, **268–73**
illus.
children in run-down area **4:**273
flag **4:**v
Gjirokastër **4:**269
Tirana **4:**268
map(s) **4:**270
Albania (ancient region) **2:**88–89
Albanians (people)
Kosovo **4:**276, 277, 278, 281
Macedonia **4:**291, 292
Albano, Lake (Italy) **4:**128
Albany (capital, New York) **5:**205

Albemarle Island (Galápagos Islands) *see* Isabela Island
Albemarle Sound (North Carolina) **5:**229
Albert (English prince consort) **1:**322
Albert (heir apparent, Monaco) **3:**206
Albert, Lake (central Africa) **1:**19, 38, 262, 316, 317
Albert I (king of Belgium) **3:**223
Albert II (king of Belgium) **3:**224
Albert I (prince of Monaco) **3:**204–5
ALBERTA (province, Canada) **5:**112, 113, **122–27; 5:**143
map(s) **5:**124
Albert Nile (section of Nile River) **1:**38, 317
Albertville (France) **3:**173
Albuquerque (New Mexico) **5:**322
Alcan Highway *see* Alaska Highway
Alcazar, The (castle, Segovia, Spain) **4:**99, 101
illus. **4:**101
Alcázar de Colón (palace, Dominican Republic)
5:455
illus. **5:**453
Alcoholic beverages *see also* Beer; Wine
Bermuda during Prohibition **5:**33
Chile **6:**309
maguey plant **5:**359, 378
Peru **6:**212
Saudi ban on use of alcohol **2:**125
Soviet-era social problems **4:**323
tequila **5:**402
whiskey traders in Canadian history **5:**126
illus.
cognac production **3:**156
Irish pub **3:**68
Scotch-whiskey distillery **3:**138
Alderney (island, Channel Islands) **3:**87
Alegría, Ciro (Peruvian writer) **6:**215
Aleijadinho (Brazilian sculptor) **6:**181
Alemán, Miguel (president of Mexico) **5:**388
Alemán Lacayo, José Arnoldo (president of
Nicaragua) **6:**60
Alemanni (Germanic tribe) **3:**272, 296
Aleppo (Syria) **2:**47, 91, 93, 94–95
Alessandri Rodríguez, Jorge (president of
Chile) **6:**321–22
Alesund (Norway) **4:**33
Aleutian Islands (North America) **5:**157, 348, 350
Aleuts (Alaskan people) **5:**349, 350
Alexander, William (founder of Nova Scotia)
5:90, 93
Alexander I (king of Greece) **4:**208
Alexander III (king of Macedonia) *see* Alexander the Great
Alexander VI (pope) **4:**114; **6:**82
Alexander I (czar of Russia) **4:**56, 59, 300, 321
Alexander II (czar of Russia) **4:**56, 59, 321
Alexander III (czar of Russia) **4:**321
Alexander I (king of Yugoslavia) **4:**280
Alexander I Land (Antarctic) **6:**331
Alexander the Great (king of Macedonia)
2:174; **4:**203–4, 291
Afghanistan **2:**178
Alexandria (Egypt) **1:**115, 119
Asia, South **2:**171
Cyprus **2:**72
Greek thought spread through ancient world
3:47
India invaded by **2:**192, 214
Iraq **2:**153
Middle East **2:**49, 162

Alexander the Great (cont.)
name carved on cliff in Lebanon **2:**97
Syria **2:**94
Turkey **2:**56
Alexandria (Egypt) **1:**115, 116, 119; **3:**47; **4:**113
illus. **1:**115
Alexandria (Virginia) **5:**225
Alexei II (Russian Patriarch) **4:**310
Alfaro, Eloy (Ecuadorian general) **6:**205
Alföld (central plain of Hungary) **4:**236
Alfonsín, Raúl (president of Argentina) **6:**301
Alfonso VI (king of Castile) **4:**98, 113
Alfonso I (king of Portugal) *see* Afonso I
Alfonso XII (king of Spain) **4:**116
Alfonso XIII (king of Spain) **4:**98, 116
Alfred P. Murrah Federal Building (Oklahoma City) **5:**307
Alfred the Great (English king) **3:**52, 115–16
Algarve (province, Portugal) **4:**67, 72
ALGERIA 1:34, 75–84
France, history of **3:**190
Sahara **1:**24, 133
illus.
Ahaggar plateau **1:**77
Algiers **1:**75
Djemila **1:**83
flag **1:**xxii
Ghardaia **1:**78
growing oranges **1:**81
Muslims praying **1:**80
oasis **1:**77
petroleum industry **1:**82
women **1:**79
map(s) **1:**76
Algiers (capital, Algeria) **1:**75, 76–77, 80, 84, 97
illus. **1:**75
Algoman Mountains (North America) **5:**4
Algonquian (Indians of North America) **5:**101, 164, 183, 185, 191, 196, 197, 199, 218
Algonquian (North American Indian language group) **5:**95, 221, 292
Algonquin (Indians of North America) **5:**99; **5:**105; **5:**111, 187, 202, 205, 227
Alhambra, The (palace, Granada, Spain) **4:**113
illus. **4:**79, 112
Al Hanish al Kabar (island, Red Sea) **2:**130
Ali, Muhammad (American boxer) **5:**261
Alianza Popular Revolucionaria Americana (APRA) (Peruvian organization) **6:**227
Alicante (Spain) **4:**109
Alice Springs (Northern Territory, Australia) **2:**485, 534
illus. **2:**535
Ali-Sabieh (Djibouti) **1:**298
Aliyev, Heydar (president of Azerbaijan) **2:**89
Al-Jahrah (Kuwait) **2:**144
Al-Khor (Qatar) **2:**142
Allah (Arabic name for God of Islam) **1:**108
Allegheny Front (region, U.S.) **5:**6, 258
Allegheny Mountains (U.S.) **5:**156, 199, 211
Allegheny Plateau (North America) **5:**156, 258, 271
Allegheny River (Pennsylvania) **5:**212, 213
Allen, Lough (lake in Ireland) **3:**66
Allende Gossens, Salvador (president of Chile) **6:**318, 320, 322
illus. **6:**320
Allentown (Pennsylvania) **5:**213
Alliance for Progress **6:**86, 113, 261
Allied Powers (during the two world wars) **3:**60, 61, 259

Alligators
illus. **5:**163
Allobroges (people) **3:**295
All Souls' Day (November 2) **5:**367; **6:**199, 213
illus.
Mexico **5:**367
Almagro, Diego de (Spanish conquistador) **6:**224, 240, 320
Almaty (Kazakhstan) **2:**348; **4:**309
Almería (province, Spain) **4:**110
Almería (Spain) **4:**109
Almirante (Panama) **6:**77
Almoravids (Berber dynasty) **1:**73–74, 139
Aloha State (nickname for Hawaii) **5:**351
Alpacas 6:87
illus. **6:**206
Alphabet *see* Writing
ALPS (mountains, Europe) **3:**28–29, 32, 37, 299–304
Austria **3:**312
Bavarian Alps **3:**242
Italy **4:**125–26, 128, 132–33
Slovenia **4:**282
Switzerland **3:**286, 289
illus.
Bavarian Alps **3:257**
Grossglockner **3:**312
Gstaad (Switzerland) **3:**303
ice tunnel **3:**303
Italy **4:**126
Jungfrau **3:**302
Lake Como **3:**1
Matterhorn **3:**300
mountain climbing **3:**299
skiing **3:**301
Switzerland **3:**285
Zugspitze **3:**243
Alps, Southern (New Zealand) *see* Southern Alps
Al Qaeda *see* Qaeda, al
Alsace and Lorraine (France) **3:**161, 186, 188, 275, 276 *see also* Lorraine
Altai (mountain system, Asia) **2:**10
Altaic languages 2:28, 59
Altamira Caves (Spain) **3:**16; **4:**110
Altan Khan (Mongolian chieftain) **2:**387
Altdorf (Switzerland) **3:**297
Althing (Iceland's parliament) **4:**5
Altiplano (plateau, South America) **6:**230–31, 233, 236
Altitude sickness 6:212
Alto Adige (region, Italy) *see* South Tyrol
Alto Perú (Spanish viceroyalty) **6:**240
Altyn Tagh (mountains, Asia) **2:**10
Alur (African people) **1:**319
Alvarado, Pedro de (Spanish conquistador) **5:**380; **5:**404; **6:**27, 32, 48
Alvares Cabral, Pedro *see* Cabral, Pedro Alvares
Álvaro Obregón (Tabasco, Mexico) *see* Frontera
Alwa (early African kingdom) **1:**130
Alytus (Lithuania) **4:**302
Alzette River (Luxembourg) **3:**208
Amalienborg (Copenhagen, Denmark) **4:**19
illus. **4:**19
Amaral, Tarsila do (Brazilian artist) **6:**182
Amazonas (state, Brazil) **6:**187
Amazonia (river basin of the Amazon) **6:**168
illus. **6:**87

Amazon River (South America) **6:**3, 86, 168–69, 173, 174, 209
Brazil's *selva* **6:**171
Iquitos (Peru) **6:**218
oil-exploration controversy **6:**201
Venezuela's Guayana region **6:**134
illus. **6:**169
Peruvian houses on stilts **6:**218
map(s) **6:**168
table(s)
longest rivers of the world **6:**346
Ambato (Ecuador) **6:**196, 199
Ambeno (East Timor enclave in West Timor) **2:**327
Amber Road (Roman trade route) **3:**320
Ambodirafia (Madagascar)
illus. **1:**371
Amboinese (people) **2:**318
Ambon (Amboina) (island, Indonesia) **2:**315, 323
Amenemhet III (Egyptian king) **1:**117
Amenhotep I (Egyptian king) **1:**117
Amenhotep IV *see* Akhenaten
America *see* Central America; North America; South America
American Colonization Society 1:182
American Indian Movement (AIM) 5:299
American Indians *see* Indians of Central and South America; Indians of North America
American Revolution *see* Revolutionary War
American River (California) **5:**346
American Samoa 2:601, 602–3
illus. **2:**602
Americans living abroad 5:412
America's Breadbasket (Iowa) **5:**293
America's Cup (yacht race) **2:**547
Americo-Liberians 1:178, 180, 183
Amerindians *see* Indians of Central and South America; Indians of North America
Amhara (African people) **1:**285
Amharic language 1:36, 285
Amin, Idi (political leader of Uganda) **1:**36, 320, 323
illus. **1:**323
Amish (branch of Mennonite Church) **5:**212, 216
illus. **5:**211
Amman (capital, Jordan) **2:**47, 118, 119
illus. **2:**116
Ammon (ancient kingdom in the Middle East) **2:**120
Amon-Re, Temple of (Karnak, Egypt) **1:**111
Ampurdán (region, Spain) **4:**90
Amritsar (India)
illus. **2:**218
Amstel River (the Netherlands) **3:**233
Amsterdam (capital, Netherlands) **3:**231, 232, 233, 235
airport is below sea level **3:**226–27
illus. **3:**225
Amu Darya (river, Asia) **2:**175, 347, 350, 352, 356
Amundsen, Roald (Norwegian explorer) **4:**32; **6:**332
Amur River (Russia–China) **4:**308
table(s)
longest rivers of the world **6:**346
Ana (African people) **1:**206
Anadolu (Turkey) *see* Asia Minor
Anáhuac Plateau (region, Mexico) **5:**404
Anaiza (people) **2:**145
Anangu (aboriginal tribe, Australia) **2:**534

Anansi (character in Creole folklore) **6**:21, 156
Anasazi (Indians of North America) **5**:309, 320, 322, 324, 325, 329
Anatolia *see* Asia Minor
Anatolian Plateau (region, Turkey) **2**:58
Anawratha (Burman king) **2**:270
Ancestor worship
  Asia, East **2**:372
  Bantu **1**:358
  Burkina Faso **1**:190
  China **2**:388
  Ghana **1**:199
  Japan's Ainu **2**:444
  Korea **2**:437
  Madagascar **1**:373
  Melanesia **2**:585
  Nigeria **1**:223–24
  Papua New Guinea **2**:589
  Senegal **1**:156
  Sierra Leone **1**:174
  Uganda **1**:320
Ancha, Sierra (mountains, Arizona) **5**:327
Anchorage (Alaska) **5**:350
Anchovies (fish) **6**:221
Ancient civilizations
  African cities, early **1**:30, 32–33
  American Indians **5**:20–25
  Andes Mountains **6**:100
  Asia, South **2**:171–72
  Asia, wonders of **2**:11–15, 21–22
  Central America **6**:14
  China **2**:14–16, 377
  Egypt *see* Egypt, ancient
  Etruscan **4**:134
  Greece *see* Greece, ancient
  Hittites **2**:56
  Inca Empire **6**:90, 239
  Indus Valley **2**:12–14, 170, 180, 190–91, 213
  Mexico **5**:374–79
  Minoan civilization on Crete **4**:192, 201
  Persia **2**:155, 160, 162
  Rome *see* Rome, ancient
  Tigris-Euphrates Valley **2**:11–12, 50–51
Ancohuma (mountain, Bolivia) **6**:231
Ancón, Treaty of (1883) **6**:227
Andacollo (Chile) **6**:306
Andalusia (region, Spain) **4**:87, 110
  illus. **4**:87
Andaman Sea (Indian Ocean) **2**:266
  table(s)
    major seas of the world **6**:347
Andean Common Market 6:115
Andean Pact (Latin American association) **6**:115
Andersen, Hans Christian (Danish author) **4**:16
Anderson, Laurie (American artist)
  illus. **5**:49
Andes (mountains of South America) **6**:2, 86, 89, 100–101
  Aconcagua, highest peak **6**:266
  Amazon River **6**:168
  Argentina **6**:280–81
  Chile **6**:313, 316
  Colombia **6**:116
  Ecuador **6**:193–94
  mineral deposits **6**:88
  mules and llamas **6**:87
  Peru **6**:206, 207–8, 211–12
  Venezuela **6**:132–33, 139
  illus. **6**:101, 282
    Peru **6**:206, 208
    Torres del Paine **6**:316

  waterfall **6**:303
  map(s) **6**:101
Andes, Army of the (1817) **6**:298, 321
ANDORRA 4:119–22
  illus. **4**:120
  flag **4**:v
  map(s) **4**:121
Andorra la Vella (capital, Andorra) **4**:122
  illus. **4**:120
Andrade, Mário de (Brazilian poet) **6**:112
Andrew (English prince)
  illus. **3**:118
Andrew (hurricane, 1992) **5**:241
Andrianampoinimerina (king of the Merina on Madagascar) **1**:377
Andros, Sir Edmund (English colonial governor) **5**:197
Androscoggin River (Maine) **5**:183
Andros Island (Bahamas) **5**:424
Aneirin (Welsh poet) **3**:125
Angarsk (Russia) **2**:343
Ang Duong (Cambodian king) **2**:291
Angel, Jimmy (American aviator) **6**:134
Angel Falls (Venezuela) **6**:134
  illus. **6**:134
Angkor (Khmer kingdom) **2**:286
Angkor Wat (temple complex, Cambodia) **2**:21–22, 290, 291
  illus. **2**:286
Angles (Germanic people) **3**:49, 86, 97, 113, 140
Anglesey (Mona, Mother of Wales) (island, Wales) **3**:81, 122, 128, 129
Anglican Church *see* England, Church of
Anglo-Afghan Wars (1839–1842, 1878, 1919) **2**:174, 178
Anglo-Boer War (1899–1902) **1**:404
Anglo-Burmese wars (1800's) **2**:271
Anglo-Chinese War (1839–1842) *see* Opium War
Anglo-Irish (English-Irish people) **3**:70
Anglo-Maori Wars (1860–1872) **2**:553
Anglo-Nepali War (1814–1815) **2**:233
Anglos (Southwest U.S. name for whites of European ancestry) **5**:252, 322
Anglo-Saxons (European people) **3**:86, 102, 115
ANGOLA 1:48, **341–46**
  Cabinda **1**:344
  Congo, Democratic Republic of **1**:270
  Portugal **4**:77
  illus.
    diamond mine **1**:345
    flag **1**:xxiv
    refugees **1**:341
    vendors at train stop **1**:343
  map(s) **1**:342
Angora (Turkey) *see* Ankara
Angostura (Venezuela) *see* Ciudad Bolívar
Angostura, Congress of 6:138
Angostura bitters 5:485
Angostura Bridge (Orinoco River) **6**:147
Anguilla (Caribbean island) **3**:90; **5**:495, 496
  map(s) **5**:429
Animal life *see also* Game reserves and parks
  Alaska **5**:349
  Antarctica **6**:327–29
  Antarctic fossils **6**:329–30
  Arctic **5**:59–60
  Australia **2**:476–77, 487, 489–90, 505, 515
  Belarus **4**:342
  Bhutan **2**:234

  Botswana **1**:353
  Brazil **6**:172, 173
  California **5**:343
  Cameroon **1**:232
  Canada **5**:72–73
  Central African Republic **1**:246–47
  Central and South America **6**:7, 9, 86
  China **2**:381
  Colombia **6**:118
  Congo, Democratic Republic of **1**:263
  Danube Delta **3**:329
  Ethiopia **1**:284
  Europe **3**:33
  Everglades **5**:240
  Florida **5**:238
  Fundy, Bay of **5**:79
  Galápagos Islands **6**:192, 202–3
  Himalayas **2**:167
  India **2**:200–201
  Indonesia's Wallace Line **2**:315–17
  Ivory Coast **1**:185
  Liberia **1**:179
  Madagascar **1**:50, 369
  Mountain States **5**:309
  New Zealand **2**:542
  Northern Territory (Australia) **2**:533
  Pakistan **2**:182
  Paraguay **6**:243
  Pine Barrens (New Jersey) **5**:208
  Poland **4**:213
  Romania **4**:249–50
  Rwanda **1**:324–25
  Solomon Islands **2**:591–92
  Sri Lanka **2**:246
  Venezuela **6**:134
  Victoria (Australia) **2**:515
  Western Australia's sea life **2**:525–26
  illus.
    Africa **1**:40–41
    Central America **6**:10
    South America **6**:89
Animas, Sierra de las (mountains, Uruguay) **6**:259
Animism (spirit worship)
  Angola **1**:344
  Asia, East **2**:372
  Asia, Southeast **2**:261
  Benin **1**:213
  Cambodia **2**:289
  Cameroon **1**:233
  Congo **1**:258
  Ghana **1**:199
  India **2**:210
  Japan's Ainu **2**:444
  Kenya **1**:312
  Lamaism **2**:169
  Malaysia **2**:306
  Myanmar **2**:268
  Papua New Guinea **2**:589
  Rwanda **1**:325
  Sierra Leone **1**:173
  Suriname **6**:157
  Tanzania **1**:335
  Togo **1**:207
  Uganda **1**:320
  Vietnam **2**:295
Anjou (region, France) **3**:156
Anjouan (island, Comoros) **1**:48, 383, 384
Anjou dynasty (French rulers in Hungary) **4**:245
Ankara (capital, Turkey) **2**:46, 58, 60, 63
  illus. **2**:61, 62
Ankobra River (Ghana) **1**:195

Ankole (kingdom in Africa) **1:**38, 322
Ankrah, Joseph A. (Ghanaian leader) **1:**204
Ann, Cape (Massachusetts) **5:**188
Annaba (Algeria) **1:**75, 77
An Najaf (Iraq) **2:**149
Annamese (Annamites) (Asian people) *see* Vietnamese
Annamese (Annamite) Cordillera (mountains, Indochina) **2:**281, 294
Annapolis (capital, Maryland) **5:**218, 219
  illus. **5:**35
  U.S. Naval Academy **5:**217
Annapolis Royal (Nova Scotia) **5:**79, 93
Annapolis Valley (region, Nova Scotia) **5:**93
Anne of Green Gables **house** (Prince Edward Island)
  illus. **5:**87
Annobón (island, Equatorial Guinea) *see* Pagalu
Annunciation Cathedral (Moscow, Russia) **4:**327
Ansariyah, Jebel (mountains, Syria) **2:**90, 91
Antaimoro (people) **1:**372
Antananarivo (capital, Madagascar) **1:**371, 373, 374
  illus. **1:**369, 373
Antandroy (people) **1:**373
ANTARCTICA 6:324–38
  Australia's research stations **2:**488
  contrasted with Arctic **5:**55, 57
  environmental studies **6:**336
  fossil hunting **6:**330
  territorial rights **6:**334
  illus. **6:**324, 331
    icebreakers **6:**335
    penguins **6:**328
    scientific research **6:**337
    sled-dog teams **6:**333
    tourism **6:**338
  map(s) **6:**326
  table(s)
    area **6:**344
    continental extremes **6:**345
    great mountain peaks **6:**348
Antarctic Peninsula 6:331, 336
Antarctic Treaty (1959) **6:**324, 334, 335–37
Antelope 6:316
Antelope Island (Utah) **5:**326
Antequera y Castro, José (Paraguayan leader) **6:**249
Anthony, Kenny (prime minister of St. Lucia) **5:**490
Antibes (France) **3:**160
Anti-Comintern Pact (1936) **3:**277
Anticosti Island (Quebec) **5:**5, 99
Antigonish Highland Games 5:92
Antigua (Guatemala) **6:**31
  illus. **6:**32
ANTIGUA AND BARBUDA 5:427, 438, **493–94**
  illus. **5:**493
    flag **5:**vi
  map(s) **5:**494
Anti-Lebanon (mountains, Syria–Lebanon) **2:**90, 91, 97
Antilles (islands, West Indies) **5:**426–40 *see also* Greater Antilles; Lesser Antilles
  Netherlands Antilles **3:**235
Antimony 2:383
Antioch (Turkey)
  illus.
    painting of 1516 battle **2:**65
Antioquia (region, Colombia) **6:**120
Anti-Semitism 4:309

Antofogasta (Chile) **6:**312
Antonescu, Ion (Romanian general) **4:**256
Antony, Mark (Roman general) **1:**38
Antrim Mountains (Northern Ireland) **3:**143
Antsiranana (Diégo-Suarez) (Madagascar) **1:**371
Antwerp (Belgium) **3:**42, 213, 216–17, 219, 220, 223
  illus. **3:**217
Anuradhapura (Sri Lanka) **2:**248
  illus. **2:**247
Anuta (Solomon Islands) **2:**592
Anyi-Baule (African people) **1:**186
ANZAC (Australian and New Zealand Army Corps) **2:**554
ANZUS Treaty 2:502, 554
Ao (China) *see* Zengzhou
Aorangi (mountain, New Zealand) *see* Cook, Mount
Aoun, Michel (prime minister of Lebanon) **2:**103
Aozou Strip (Chad) **1:**44, 243, 244
  Libyan claims **1:**100
  illus. **1:**243
Apache (Indians of North America) **5:**164, 253, 309, 319, 320, 321, 322, 328, 329
  Mexico **5:**393
Apalachee (Indians of North America) **5:**165, 222, 238
Aparecida, Our Lady of (patron saint of São Paulo, Brazil) **6:**178
Apartheid (segregation policy in South African history) **1:**45, 58–59, 394, 400, 404–5
  South Africa differed from rest of Africa **1:**31
Apennines (mountains, Italy) **3:**28; **4:**126, 128
  Apuane Alps marble quarries **4:**132–33
Apia (capital, Western Samoa) **2:**607
Apo, Mount (Philippines) **2:**332
Apollinaire, Guillaume (French poet) **3:**199
Appalachia (region, U.S.) **5:**156, 257
Appalachian Mountains (North America) **5:**5–7, 153–54, 156
  Canada **5:**40, 67, 69, 77, 81, 90
  forests **5:**16
  Great Lakes States **5:**271
  Ice Ages **5:**12, 269
  Middle Atlantic States **5:**199, 202, 208, 211, 218
  New England **5:**179
  Quebec **5:**99
  South-Central States **5:**256, 257, 258, 260, 263
  Southern States **5:**220, 224, 227, 233, 242
  illus. **5:**8
    Blue Ridge Parkway **5:**157
    Cumberland Gap **5:**256
    West Virginia **5:**258
Appalachian Ridge and Valley (North America) **5:**258
Appalachian Trail 5:233
  illus. **5:**156
Appenzell (canton, Switzerland) **3:**288
Appian Way (Rome, Italy) **4:**172
Appleton (Wisconsin) **5:**286
APRA (Peruvian organization) *see* Alianza Popular Revolucionaria Americana
Apuane Alps (mountains, Italy) **4:**132–33
Apure River (Venezuela) **6:**144, 146
Apuseni (mountains, Romania) **4:**249
Aqaba (Jordan) **2:**116, 118, 119
Aqmola (Akmola) *see* Astana
Aquaculture 5:86

Aqueducts
  Rome, ancient **4:**165
  Segovia (Spain) **4:**101, 111
  Turkey **2:**61
  illus. **3:**180; **4:**111
Aquidneck Island (Rhode Island) **5:**192, 193, 194
Aquinas, Saint Thomas (Italian philosopher) **4:**144
Aquincum (capital, Pannonia, region of Roman Empire) **4:**242
Aquino, Benigno (Philippine political leader) **2:**340
Aquino, Corazon (president of Philippines) **2:**337, 338, 340
  illus. **2:**339
Arabia (Arabian Peninsula) (southwestern Asia) **2:**126–27
Arabian Desert (Egypt) **1:**112
Arabian Gulf *see* Persian Gulf
Arabian Peninsula *see* Arabia
Arabian Sea 2:165
  Indus River **2:**170
Arabic (language and script) **2:**28, 44
  Africa **1:**15, 109, 136
  Persian influenced by **2:**157, 159–60
Arabi Pasha, Ahmed (Egyptian leader) **1:**121
Arab-Israeli wars (1948, 1956, 1967, 1973–1974) **2:**32, 47, 52, 104–5, 113–15
  Egypt **1:**113, 122
  Egyptian-Israeli peace treaty **1:**123
  Jordan **2:**116, 121
  Lebanon **2:**102–3
  Suez Canal **1:**121
  Syria **2:**93
Arab League 1:122, 123
Arabs (Semitic peoples) **1:**239; **2:**44
  Arabs in Israel **2:**54, 105, 106–7, 108, 109, 113
  Asia, Southwest **2:**45, 51, 55, 91
  Europe **3:**18, 49
  Georgia (republic) **2:**84
  India **2:**215
  Italian cuisine, influences on **4:**136
  Kenya **1:**312
  Libya **1:**97, 99
  Madagascar, influence on **1:**372
  North Africa **1:**13, 32, 86, 91–92, 132
  Palestine **2:**114–15
  Somalia **1:**303
  Turkey **2:**59
  Uzbekistan **2:**352
  West Bank and Gaza **2:**114–15
  illus. **2:**16
Arafat, Yasir (Palestinian leader) **2:**55, 115
Arafura Sea (Pacific Ocean) **2:**532
Aragats, Mount (Armenia) **2:**76
Aragón (historic region and former kingdom, Spain) **4:**113–14
Arakan Mountains (India–Myanmar) **2:**266, 267
Araks River (Azerbaijan–Iran) **2:**87
Aral Sea (Asia) **2:**347, 350
  table(s)
    largest lakes **6:**347
Aramaeans (Semitic people) **2:**93
Arapaho (Indians of North America) **5:**301, 303, 316, 317, 319, 320
Ararat, Mount (Turkey) **2:**76, 77
Ararat Plain (Armenia) **2:**74
Araucana, La (poem by Ercilla y Zúñiga) **6:**302

Araucanians (Indians of South America) **6:**302, 305, 307, 320, 321
  Argentina **6:**270
Aravalli Range (India) **2:**166
Arawaks (Indians of South and Central America) **5:**428–29, 434
  Antigua and Barbuda **5:**494
  Barbados **5:**479–80
  Jamaica **5:**475
  Puerto Rico **5:**167
  Saint Vincent **5:**492
  Trinidad and Tobago **5:**486
Arbenz Guzmán, Jacobo (president of Guatemala) **6:**33
Arbil (Iraq) **2:**149
Arbore (Romania) **4:**252
Arcadia (region, Greece) **4:**189
Arc de Triomphe (Paris, France) **3:**195–96
  illus. **3:**60
Arce, Manuel José (Salvadoran patriot and president) **6:**16
Archaeology *see also* Prehistoric people
  Arizona **5:**329
  Armenia **2:**74
  Brazil **6:**188
  Chavín de Huántar **6:**221
  Easter Island **6:**323
  England **3:**92, 112
  England: Stonehenge **3:**114
  Hadrian's Wall **3:**92
  Hallstatt (Austria) **3:**320
  Honduras **6:**40
  Inca Empire **6:**223
  Israel **2:**108
  Maya **6:**28
  Mesopotamia **2:**51
  Mexico **5:**375–76
  Moche **6:**223
  Mohenjo-Daro **2:**190–91
  Mound Builders **5:**272, 274
  Nevada **5:**332
  New Mexico, most ancient New World cultures **5:**321
  North America **5:**173
  Oaxaca **5:**417
  Oceania **2:**519
  Peru **6:**219–20, 221–22
  Romania **4:**254
  Roman subway excavations **4:**170
  Sardinia **4:**131
  Teotihuacán **5:**413
  Thailand **2:**279
  Thera **4:**190
  Tlaxcala (Mexico) **5:**415
  Wales **3:**128
  Zimbabwe Ruins **1:**361
  illus.
    Chinese tomb sculptures **2:**394
    Colombian stone statues **6:**127
    Copán (Honduras) **6:**40
    Great Serpent Mound (Ohio) **5:**273
    ruins at Selinunte (Italy) **4:**155
    ruins of Roman Forum **3:**47
    ruins on Delos **3:**46
Arches National Park (Utah) **5:**323
Archipiélago de Colón *see* Galápagos Islands
Architecture *see also* Housing
  Armenia **2:**76
  Barcelona (Spain) **4:**102–3
  Berlin **3:**281
  Brazil **6:**160, 161, 166, 182

Budapest (Hungary) **4:**242
Cairo **1:**115
Chicago (Illinois), home of the world's first skyscraper **5:**283
Chile **6:**310
Colombia **6:**120
Costa Rica **6:**64
Ecuador **6:**199
Egypt **1:**107
Egyptian tombs and temples **1:**110–11
Europe **3:**14
France **3:**177
Germany **3:**255
Greece, ancient **4:**203
Helsinki (Finland) **4:**59
Incas **6:**223
Italy **4:**158
Lisbon (Portugal) **4:**71
Mexico **5:**29, 410l
Moorish Spain **4:**113
Moscow (Russia) **4:**327, 328
New England **5:**180
Palermo (Sicily) **4:**146
Paraguay **6:**248–49
Persia, ancient **2:**160
Peru **6:**213–14
Prague (Czech Republic) **4:**227, 229
Roman Spain **4:**111
St. Petersburg (Russia) **4:**330
South Australia's underground structures **2:**523
Spanish colonial style **5:**381; **5:**399, 403, 405, 417
Sweden **4:**43
Sydney Opera House **2:**511
Thailand **2:**276
Toledo (Spain) **4:**98
Uruguay **6:**257–58
Venezuela **6:**142
Vienna (Austria) **3:**316
Washington, D.C. **5:**170
world's tallest buildings **2:**403
illus.
  ancient Armenian buildings **2:**79
  art deco style in Miami Beach **5:**239
  Chinese construction **2:**412
  contemporary European **3:**63
  European castle **3:**48
  Franciscan mission **5:**403
  Greek church **4:**204
  half-timber style in England **3:**99
  Kenyan village **1:**310
  Mexican luxury resort **5:**355
  Monticello (home of Thomas Jefferson) **5:**225
  Moorish mosaic designs **4:**114
  Moorish style in Peru **6:**214
  mural painted on Egyptian house **1:**104
  New York City landmarks **5:**201
  Papua New Guinea community house **2:**590
  Peruvian homes on stilts **6:**218
  Saudi Arabian airport terminal **2:**53
  Spanish colonial style **5:**401, 405
  Spanish missions in North America **5:**309
  Sudanese thatched porches **1:**127
  Tirana (Albania) **4:**268
  underground construction **2:**521
  Victorian homes in Savannah **5:**236
  Victorian houses in San Francisco **5:**344
  Victorian-style cottages **5:**491
  world's tallest buildings **2:**253

Arciniegas, Germán (Colombian historian) **6:**122
ARCTIC 5:53–64
  Alaska **5:**348
  Greenland **5:**10
  Lapland **4:**35–37
  Norway **4:**24–25
  Nunavut **5:**138
  Russian tundra **4:**307
  illus.
    midnight sun **5:**53
  map(s) **5:**54
Arctic Archipelago (Canadian Arctic Islands) **5:**69–70, 134
  Nunavut **5:**137
Arctic Circle 5:55, 142
Arctic Lowlands (North America) **5:**5
Arctic National Wildlife Refuge 5:59
Arctic Ocean 5:53, 55, 56, 349
  table(s)
    oceans of the world **6:**347
Ardennes (region, Belgium, Luxembourg, France) **3:**28, 207, 208, 212, 213, 215, 217
Ardra (early African kingdom) **1:**214
Arequipa (Peru) **6:**218
Arévalo, Juan José (Guatemalan political leader) **6:**33
ARGENTINA 6:266–301
  Andes **6:**100–101
  "dirty war" **6:**301
  economy **6:**88, 103–4, 289, 296
  education **6:**106
  Euro-American culture **6:**95, 96, 97
  Falkland Islands claims **3:**90; **6:**286, 287
  gauchos **6:**274–75
  Mercosur **6:**262
  middle class **6:**272
  political history **6:**114
  population **6:**7, 8
  poverty **6:**105
  Río de la Plata **6:**284
  Uruguay, cultural kinship **6:**258
  illus.
    Andes **6:**282
    automobile industry **6:**294
    Buenos Aires **6:**267, 268, 278, 279, 288–89, 291
    cattle **6:**294–95
    city life **6:**273
    fishing industry **6:**293
    flag **6:**vi
    gauchos **6:**275
    Iguaçú Falls **6:**281
    Mar del Plata **6:**292
    people **6:**269
    sheep in Patagonia **6:**285
    university students **6:**279
    Ushuaia **6:**290
    vineyard **6:**282
    wheat growing **6:**296
  map(s) **6:**283
Argüedas, Alcides (Bolivian writer) **6:**237
Ariadne (in Greek mythology) **4:**190
Arias Sánchez, Oscar (president of Costa Rica) **6:**71
  illus. **6:**71
Arica (Chile) **6:**311
Aristide, Jean-Bertrand (president of Haiti) **5:**440; **5:**470
Aristotle (Greek philosopher) **3:**47

ARIZONA 5:163, 327–29
  Sonoran Desert **5**:329
  illus.
    Grand Canyon **5**:327
    Mission San Xavier del Bac **5**:309
    Sunset Crater National Monument **5**:9
  map(s) **5**:328
Arizona Memorial
  illus. **5**:353
ARKANSAS 5:266–67
  diamonds **5**:159
  map(s) **5**:267
Arkansas River (U.S.) **5**:256, 266, 305
  table(s)
    longest rivers of the world **6**:346
Arlberg Tunnel (Austria) **3**:304
Arles (France) **3**:160, 180
Arlit (district in Niger) **1**:148
Armada, Spanish (1588) **4**:115
Armadillo
  illus. **5**:251
Armagnac (region, France) **3**:156
Armed forces
  Africa's military spending **1**:2, 3
  Antarctica demilitarized **6**:337
  Arctic's strategic importance **5**:55, 64
  Black Sea Fleet **4**:337
  Northern Ireland's "Troubles" **3**:148, 149
  Sweden **4**:50
  Switzerland **3**:298
  United States in Central America **6**:12–13
  U.S. base at Guantánamo Bay (Cuba) **5**:450
  Venezuela's "Bolivarian schools" **6**:140
  illus.
    Chinese troops enter Hong Kong **2**:410–11
    Colombian surveillance of drug trade **6**:129
    Gulf War **5**:171
    U.S. in Central America **6**:13
    U.S. troops in Germany **3**:282
    U.S. troops in Kuwait **2**:31
    World War I **5**:171
    World War II **5**:171
ARMENIA 2:74–79
  early history **2**:50–51
  Russia, intervention in **2**:55
  Yerevan **2**:47
  illus.
    ancient architecture **2**:79
    caves in mountains **2**:78
    church officials with president **2**:77
    factory **2**:77
    flag **2**:vii
    Yerevan **2**:74
  map(s) **2**:75
Armenian Apostolic Church 2:76
  illus.
    church officials **2**:77
Armenian Church of America 2:75
Armenian language 2:76
Armenians (people) **2**:75
  Azerbaijan **2**:87
  Nagorno-Karabakh **2**:32, 74, 86, 89
  Syria **2**:91
Armería River (Mexico) **5**:408
Armstrong, Neil (American astronaut) **5**:273
Arnesen, Liv (Norwegian explorer) **6**:337
Arnhem Land Plateau (Australia) **2**:483, 484, 532
Arno (Marshall Islands) **2**:575
Arno River (Italy) **4**:129, 148–50
Arosa (Switzerland) **3**:289
Arpád dynasty (kings of Hungary) **4**:245

Arrau, Claudio (Chilean pianist) **6**:310
Arreola, Juan José (Mexican author) **5**:374
Arroyo, Gloria Macapagal (president of Philippines) **2**:338, 340
Art *see also* Architecture; Handicrafts
  Aborigines, Australian **2**:512, 518
  Argentina **6**:278
  Ashanti of Ghana **1**:198
  Bolivia **6**:238
  Brazil **6**:181–82
  Buddhist statues destroyed in Afghanistan **2**:179
  Bulgaria **4**:262
  Cameroon **1**:233
  cave paintings **3**:167; **4**:110
  Chile **6**:309–10
  Colombia **6**:122
  Cuban policies **5**:451
  Easter Island sculptures **6**:323
  Ecuador **6**:199, 200
  Europe **3**:14
  Florence flood damage **4**:149
  France **3**:177–79
  Gabon **1**:254
  Germany **3**:254–55
  Haiti **5**:465
  Indonesia **2**:319
  Japan **2**:459–62
  Khmer Rouge tried to eradicate Cambodian culture **2**:289–90
  London's schools **3**:111
  Maori carving **2**:550
  Mayan sculpture **5**:376
  Mexican folk art **5**:365
  Mexico **5**:371–73, 381–82
  New Zealand **2**:546
  Niger **1**:146
  Norway **4**:28
  Persia, ancient **2**:160
  Peru **6**:214
  pre-Columbian artifacts in Oaxaca **5**:417
  Renaissance **3**:55
  Romania **4**:252
  Russia **4**:314
  Spain **4**:97, 98, 115–16
  Sri Lanka **2**:248
  Sweden **4**:43
  Tunisia **1**:88
  Ukrainian folk arts **4**:335
  UNESCO headquarters **3**:202
  Uruguay **6**:257
  Vatican City **4**:181
  Venezuela **6**:141–42
  illus.
    Aborigines, Australian **2**:518
    African sculpture **1**:52, 53
    ancient Benin sculpture **1**:220
    Chimú sculpture **6**:222
    Chinese scroll art **2**:406
    Chinese tomb sculptures **2**:394
    Colombian stone statues **6**:127
    contemporary North American displays **5**:48–49
    Costa Rican oxcart **6**:67
    depiction of Kublai Khan **2**:24
    Ghanaian artisan painting on cloth **1**:201
    illuminated manuscript **3**:176
    Mayan sculpture **6**:15
    Mexican folk art **5**:365
    mural painted on Egyptian house **1**:104
    painting of Japanese invasion of Korea **2**:21

    sidewalk show in Lima (Peru) **6**:215
    Zapotec jaguar sculpture **5**:375
Arthur, King (legendary king of Britons) **3**:114, 129
Arthur, Owen (prime minister of Barbados) **5**:480
Artibonite River (Hispaniola) **5**:462
Artigas, José Gervasio (Uruguayan patriot) **6**:260, 263
Aruba (island, Caribbean Sea) **3**:235
  map(s) **5**:429
Arusha National Park (Tanzania)
  illus. **1**:338
Arvada (Colorado) **5**:320
Arviat (settlement, Nunavut) **5**:139
Arvon, Mount (Michigan) **5**:275
Arwad (ancient Phoenician city) **2**:101
Aryans (ethnic groups) **2**:13–14
  Indo-Aryans in Asia **2**:21, 171
  Iran **2**:155, 156, 162
  Pakistan **2**:191
Arzú, Alvaro (president of Guatemala) **6**:33
Asahan (Indonesia) **2**:322
Ascalon (Israel) **2**:109
Aschach Dam (Danube River) **3**:326
Asen, John and Peter (Bulgarian rulers) **4**:265
Ashanti (African people) **1**:198, 202, 204; **6**:21
  illus. **1**:203
Ashanti (early African kingdom) **1**:197, 201, 202
Ashanti (region, Ghana) **1**:57, 194, 195
Asheville (North Carolina)
  illus.
    Biltmore **5**:228
Ashkenazi Jews (people) **2**:105, 106
Ashkhabad (capital, Turkmenistan) **2**:357, 358
Ashmore Island (Timor Sea) **2**:488
Ashoka *see* Asoka
Ashur (ancient city, Assyria) **2**:49
ASIA 2:1–40 *see also* names of countries
  Asia, East **2**:367–76
  Asia, Southeast **2**:253–64
  Asia, Southwest **2**:41–55
  Australia, trade with **2**:491, 503
  Central and North **2**:341–45
  Europe's geographic relation to Asia **3**:5
  Ganges River **2**:168
  Himalayas **2**:166–67
  Indus River **2**:170, 183
  Kashmir **2**:172–73
  Mekong River **2**:256–57
  origin of name **2**:5
  South **2**:165–73
  Tigris and Euphrates Rivers **2**:50–51
  Yangtze River **2**:368–69
  Yellow River **2**:370–71
  illus.
    flags of the countries **2**:vii–ix
  map(s) **2**:2–3, 8–9
    population density **2**:5
    precipitation **2**:5
  table(s)
    area and population **6**:344
    continental extremes **6**:345
    countries and territories **2**:4
    great mountain peaks **6**:348
Asia Minor (Anatolia) (peninsula, Asia) **2**:57; **3**:46
Asians (peoples of Asia) *see also* articles on individual countries, regions, and states
  Africa **1**:30, 39
  California **5**:347

Kenya **1:**310–12
Middle Atlantic States **5:**200
Northern Territory (Australia) **2:**533, 534
South Africa **1:**58, 59, 400, 404
Uganda **1:**318, 323
United States population **5:**169, 171
Vancouver (Canada) **5:**130
Asir (region, Saudi Arabia) **2:**123, 127
Askania-Nova (Ukraine) **4:**333
Asmara (capital, Eritrea) **1:**293, 294, 295, 296
Asoka (Mauryan king of India) **2:**20, 171, 192, 214, 243
Asphalt
Pitch Lake (Trinidad) **5:**485
Assab (Eritrea) **1:**287, 294, 296
Assad, Bashar al- (Syrian leader) **2:**96
Assad, Hafiz al- (Syrian leader) **2:**96
Assam (state, India) **2:**199, 200, 228
Assam-Burma ranges (Asia) **2:**167
Assamese language 2:199
Assassinations
Armenia **2:**79
Bangladesh **2:**244
Burundi: Ndadaye, Melchior **1:**331
Ecuador: Alfaro, Eloy **6:**205
Egypt: Sadat, Anwar el- **1:**123
India: Gandhi, Indira **2:**218
India: Gandhi, Rajiv **2:**218
Israel: Rabin, Yitzhak **2:**115
Jordan: Abdullah **2:**121
Kenya: Mboya, Tom **1:**315
Korea, South: Park Chung Hee **2:**438
Lebanon: Gemayel, Bashir **2:**103
Mexico: Villa, Pancho **5:**393
Mozambique: Mondlane, Eduardo **1:**368
Myanmar: Aung San **2:**271–72
Nicaragua **6:**58, 60
Philippines: Aquino, Benigno **2:**340
Sri Lanka: Premadasa, Ranasinghe **2:**250
Sweden: Palme, Olaf **4:**48
World War I, start of **4:**280, 289
Assateague Island (Maryland–Virginia) **5:**217, 223
Assawoman Bay (Maryland) **5:**217
Assiniboia (early settlement in Manitoba) **5:**117
Assiniboin (Indians of North America) **5:**111, 112, 115, 117, 121, 124, 311
Assiniboine River (Canada) **5:**112, 116
Assisi (Italy)
illus. **4:**157
Association of Southeast Asian Nations (ASEAN) 2:292, 300, 302, 308
Assoumani, Azali (president of Comoros) **1:**384
Assumption, Cathedral of the (Mexico City) **5:**381
illus. **5:**381
Assumption Cathedral (Moscow, Russia) **4:**327
Assyria (ancient empire in Asia) **2:**12
Hebrews overcome by **2:**50
Iraq **2:**153
Middle East **2:**49
Tigris and Euphrates Rivers **2:**51
Astana (formerly **Akmola**) (Kazakhstan) **2:**348
Astrodome (Houston, Texas) **5:**253
Astronomy
Antarctic observatory **6:**337
illus.
Australian observatory **2:**474
Caracol, El (Mayan observatory) **5:**26
Asturias (region, Spain) **4:**113
Asturias, Miguel Ángel (Guatemalan novelist) **6:**29

Astypalaia (island, Greece)
illus. **4:**191
Asunción (capital, Paraguay) **6:**242, 244, 249, 290, 297
Río de la Plata **6:**284
illus. **6:**242, 244
Aswan (Egypt) **1:**39, 114, 116
Aswan High Dam (Egypt) **1:**39, 105, 114, 116, 129
Atacama (Chile) **6:**241
Atacama, Puna de (plateau in the Andes) **6:**101
Atacama Desert (Chile) **6:**3, 86, 312, 345
Peruvian extension **6:**207
illus. **6:**84, 312
Atahualpa (Inca ruler) **6:**204, 220, 224
Atakapa (Indians of North America) **5:**222, 249
Atakora Mountains (Benin) **1:**211
Atar (Mauritania) **1:**136, 137
Atatürk, Mustafa Kemal (Turkish statesman) **2:**66–67
Atbara River (east Africa) **1:**294
Aten (ancient Egyptian god) **1:**118
Ath (Belgium) **3:**215
Athabasca Lake (Canada) **5:**4, 12, 118, 122
table(s)
largest lakes **6:**347
Athabascan language group 5:148
Athabascans (Indians of North America) **5:**292
Athabasca River (Canada) **5:**122
Athabasca tar sands 5:71, 127
Athena (Greek goddess) **4:**195, 196
Athens (capital, Greece) **4:**193, 195–97, 200, 202, 203, 205
Europe, ancient history of **3:**46
tourism **3:**15
illus. **4:**196
Old Palace **4:**211
Parthenon **4:**185
Plaka **4:**197
Athens (Georgia) **5:**235
Athens and Thebes, Duchy of 4:205
Athi River (east Africa) **1:**307
Athletics *see* Sports
Athos, Mount (religious state, Greece) **4:**198
illus. **4:**198
Atitlán (lake, Guatemala) **6:**30
Atlanta (capital, Georgia) **5:**49, 222, 235
illus. **5:**235
Atlantic City (New Jersey) **5:**210
illus. **5:**207
Atlantic Ocean
Europe's climate **3:**30
Graveyard of the Atlantic **5:**229
Panama Canal **6:**78
shoreline and coastal plains of North America **5:**9, 12
table(s)
oceans of the world **6:**347
ATLANTIC PROVINCES (Canada) **5:**77–93 *see also* names of provinces, territories, cities
Appalachian Mountains **5:**6
population **5:**78
illus. **5:**77
Atlantic Sahara (Mauritania) **1:**134, 139
Atlantis (legendary continent)
illus.
Thera (Greek island) **4:**200
Atlas Mountains (northern Africa) **1:**18, 66, 89
Algeria **1:**75, 76
illus. **1:**16, 65
Atmosphere 6:3, 317
ozone layer **6:**327

Atolls (coral islands) **2:**251, 559, 560, 610
Atomic energy *see* Nuclear power
Atomic weapons *see* Nuclear weapons
Aton (Egyptian god) *see* Aten
Atrato River (Colombia) **6:**125
Atrek River (Iran–Turkmenistan) **2:**356
Atsina (Gros Ventre) (Indians of North America) **5:**121, 311
Attar of roses 4:264
Attica (region, Greece) **4:**188
Attikamek (Indians of North America) **5:**99
Auburn (Maine) **5:**183
Auckland (New Zealand) **2:**540, 544, 547, 548
illus. **2:**547
Auckland, University of (New Zealand) **2:**545
Audiencias (Spanish colonial government) **6:**224
Audubon Swamp Garden (Charleston, South Carolina) **5:**232
Augusta (capital, Maine) **5:**183
Augusta (Georgia) **5:**235
Augustine, Saint (died 604; 1st archbishop of Canterbury) **3:**50
Augustine, Saint (354–430; church father) **1:**75, 91
Augustus (emperor of Rome) **1:**119; **4:**130, 165
Aung San (Burmese leader) **2:**271, 272
Aung San Suu Kyi (Myanmar political leader) **2:**272
Aunnu (island in American Samoa) **2:**602–3
Aurangabad (India) **2:**216
Aurangzeb (Mogul emperor of India) **2:**188
Aura River (Finland) **4:**55, 64
Aurès Massif (mountains, Algeria) **1:**76, 78
Aurora (Colorado) **5:**320
Aurora (Illinois) **5:**282
Aurora australis 2:539
Aurora borealis 5:57
illus. **5:**57
Ausa (Aussa) (stream, San Marino) **4:**174
Auschwitz (Nazi concentration camp, Poland) **3:**278; **4:**221
Austin (capital, Texas) **5:**254
Austin (Minnesota) **5:**289
Austin, Stephen F. (American pioneer) **5:**255
Austral (island, Polynesia) **2:**601
AUSTRALIA 2:473–79, 480–535 *see also* articles on individual states
Antarctic research **6:**335
East Timor, peacekeepers in **2:**328
flag **2:**474–75
island dependencies **2:**488
Nauru **2:**579
Oceania, continental islands of **2:**519
Papua New Guinea **2:**590
illus. **2:**480
astronomical observatory **2:**474
beaches **2:**485
Bungle Bungle Mountains **2:**524
Christmas in summer **2:**484
coat of arms **2:**514
Darwin's art and culture festival **2:**532
flag **2:**ix
Great Barrier Reef **2:**506
Hobart **2:**530
Melbourne **2:**516
Mount Kosciusko **2:**484
rancher with sheep and dog **2:**520
strip-mining for copper **2:**489
Uluru (Ayers Rock) **2:**481
Wall of Remembrance **2:**514

AUSTRALIA (cont.)
map(s) **2:**482
table(s)
  area and population **6:**344
  continental extremes **6:**345
  great mountain peaks **6:**348
  prime ministers **6:**362
  states and territories **2:**499
Australia Day 2:499
Australian Alps (mountains, Australia) **2:**484,
  516–17
Australian Broadcasting Commission 2:497
AUSTRALIAN CAPITAL TERRITORY (ACT)
  (Australia) **2:513–15**
illus.
  Canberra **2:**513
Australoids (people) **2:**562
AUSTRIA 3:308–25
  Alps **3:**299–304
  Czech nuclear plant opposed by **4:**229
  Danube River **3:**326–27
  Germany, history of **3:**277
  Italy, history of **4:**157, 158
  Polish Partitions **4:**220
  Rhine River **3:**244
  Slovenia, history of **4:**284
illus.
  country church **3:**308
  flag **3:**vi
  Grossglockner **3:**312
  Hallstatt **3:**320
  haying **3:**319
  Salzburg **3:**313
  Seefeld **3:**314
  Vienna **3:**309, 316, 322, 323, 328
map(s) **3:**311
Austria-Hungary (dual monarchy, 1867–1918)
  3:324–25; **4:**246
  Bohemia and Moravia **4:**227
  Bosnia and Herzegovina **4:**290
  Italy **4:**160
  Ukraine **4:**332
Austro-Hungarian empire *see* Austria-Hungary
Automobiles
  Brazilian industry **6:**104
  California has world's greatest concentration
  5:341
  Czech industry **4:**227–28
  Europe **3:**41
  French industry **3:**157, 202
  German industry **3:**261, 264
  Italian driving habits **4:**170
  Le Mans auto race **3:**175–76
  Monaco Grand Prix **3:**205
  U.S. industry **5:**277, 278
illus.
  antique cars in Uruguay **6:**257
  Argentine industry **6:**294
  automated assembly line **5:**51
  Chinese industry **2:**409
  European industry **3:**38
  German industry **3:**260
  Italian industry **4:**151
  Japanese industry **2:**470
  Le Mans auto race **3:**175
  Polish industry **4:**219
  Spanish industry **4:**106
  state-of-the-art manufacturing **5:**94
  vintage cars in Havana **5:**446
Auyán-tepui (mountain, Venezuela) **6:**134
Avalanches
  Switzerland **3:**286–87

Avars (Tatar people) **3:**50, 321
Avarua (capital, Cook Islands) **2:**561
Avellaneda, Nicolás (president of Argentina)
  6:295, 299
Aventine Hill (Rome, Italy) **4:**165
Aviation
  Amsterdam's airport is below sea level
  3:226–27
  Arctic communities linked by small aircraft
  5:64
  Brazil **6:**160
  California's industry **5:**51
  Europe **3:**42
  first airline in Western Hemisphere **6:**120
  French aerospace industry **3:**162
  Northwest Territories' primary transportation
  5:144
  Oklahoma City, major aviation center **5:**306
  Paris' airports **3:**199
  terrorism's effect on airlines **3:**221, 289
illus.
  airborne ambulance service **2:**508
  Australian outback **2:**496
  Canada's Far North **5:**134
  Denver (Colorado) airport **5:**22
  European aircraft industry **3:**39
  float plane **5:**143
  French aerospace industry **3:**161
  Indonesian industry **2:**323
  military aircraft **5:**174
  Saudi Arabian airport terminal **2:**53
  U.S. troops in Germany **3:**282
Aviero (Portugal) **4:**71
Avignon (France) **3:**154, 160, 167, 181–82
Ávila (Spain) **4:**98
Ávila Camacho, Manuel (president of Mexico)
  5:370; **5:**388
Avila Mountain (Venezuela) **6:**136
Avril, Prosper (president of Haiti) **5:**470
Awami League (Bangladesh) **2:**193, 243, 244
Axis Powers (Germany, Italy, Japan) (World
  War II) **1:**122; **3:**277
Axum (early Ethiopian kingdom) *see* Aksum
Ayacucho (town and department, Peru) **6:**214
Ayacucho, Battle of (1824) **6:**226, 240
Ayar (legendary founding family of the Incas)
  6:222
Ayers Rock (Australia) *see* Uluru
Aylwin Azócar, Patricio (president of Chile)
  6:323
Aymará (Indians of South America) **6:**235
Aymará language 6:82, 91, 211, 236, 239
Ayodhya (India) **2:**219
Ayub Khan, Mohammed (Pakistani political
  leader) **2:**193
Ayutthaya Kingdom (Thailand) **2:**279
Azad Kashmir (Pakistani occupied territory)
  2:172, 181
Azande (African people) **1:**128
Azande (early African state) **1:**268
AZERBAIJAN 2:86–89
  Armenia, conflict with **2:**77
  Baku **2:**47
  Nagorno-Karabakh **2:**32, 74, 79
illus.
  Baku **2:**86
  farmer **2:**88
  flag **2:**vii
  oil refinery **2:**88
map(s) **2:**87
Azerbaijan (region, Iran) **2:**87
Azerbaijani (Turkic people) **2:**75, 87, 156

Azeri Turkish (language) **2:**87
Azizia (Libya) **6:**345
Aznar, José María (prime minister of Spain)
  4:95, 118
Azores (islands) **4:**66, 68, 72
Aztecs (Indians of North America) **5:**24, 25, 26,
  377–79, 380
  Mexico City **5:**410, 411
  Morelos **5:**412
  Oaxaca **5:**417
  Querétaro **5:**403
illus. **5:**376
Azuay (province, Ecuador) **6:**196
Azuela, Mariano (Mexican author) **5:**373
Azuero Peninsula (Panama) **6:**72, 75
Azure Coast (Côte d'Azur) (France) *see* Riviera

• • • B • • •

Baalbek (Lebanon) **2:**98
illus. **2:**99
Baath party (Syria–Iraq) **2:**92, 93, 96, 150, 154
Babangida, Ibrahim (Nigerian political leader)
  1:228, 229
Babe (motion picture)
illus. **2:**498
Babelthuap (Babeldoab) (island, Palau) **2:**571
Babenberg family (rulers of duchy of Austria)
  3:321, 325
Baber (Mogul emperor of India) **2:**178
Babi Yar (site of 1941 massacre, Ukraine)
  3:278; **4:**337
Babur (Islamic king) **2:**172
Babylonia (ancient Mesopotamian empire)
  2:12, 48–49, 51
  Hammurabi **2:**20
  Hebrews overcome by **2:**50
  Iraq **2:**153
Bacău (Romania) **4:**255
Baccarat (France) **3:**157
Bach, Johann Sebastian (German composer)
  3:256, 268
Bacharach (Germany)
illus. **3:**244
Bachchan, Amitabh (Indian film star) **2:**204
Backbone Mountain (Maryland) **5:**218
Bacolod (Philippines) **2:**336
Bactra (ancient city) *see* Balkh
Bactrians (Asian people) **2:**156
Baden-Württemberg (state, Germany) **3:**258,
  266
Badlands (North America) **5:**123, 127, 291, 297,
  299, 300, 301
illus. **5:**123, 297
Badlands National Park (South Dakota) **5:**300
Badoglio, Pietro (Italian general) **4:**161
Badshahi Masjid (Imperial Mosque) (Lahore,
  Pakistan) **2:**188
Bafata (Guinea-Bissau) **1:**164
Baffin, William (English navigator) **5:**61
Baffin Island (Canada) **5:**4, 136, 137; **5:**140
table(s)
  largest islands of the world **6:**346
Bafing River (Guinea) **1:**166
Bafour (African people) **1:**138
Bagabandi, Natsagiin (president of Mongolia)
  2:366
Baganda (African people) *see* Ganda

Bagaza, Jean-Baptiste (president of Burundi)
1:331
Baghdad (capital, Iraq) 2:46–47, 50, 148, 150,
154
illus.
Gulf War damage 2:149
Bagpipes
illus. 3:131
Bagratid dynasty (republic of Georgia) 2:84
Bagratuni dynasty (Armenia) 2:78
Baguirmi (early African kingdom) 1:244
Baha'i faith 2:109, 582
BAHAMAS 5:423–25
illus.
flag 5:vi
map(s) 5:425
Baharna (Bahraini people) 2:140
Bahasa Indonesia (language) 2:28, 260, 318
Bahasa Malaysia (Malay) (language) 2:260, 305
Bahia (Baia) (state, Brazil) 6:173, 175, 177–78,
179, 182, 183
Salvador 6:164, 186
Bahía Blanca (Argentina) 6:293
Bahía de Portete (Colombia) 6:125
BAHRAIN 2:140–41; 2:143
illus. 2:140
flag 2:vii
map(s) 2:141
Bahr el Ghazal (river, Africa) 1:242
Bahr el Jebel (section of the Nile river) 1:38
Bahutu (African people) *see* Hutu
Baikal, Lake (Russia) 2:1; 4:308
table(s)
largest lakes 6:347
Baikonur space center (Kazakhstan) 2:346
BAJA CALIFORNIA (state, Mexico) 5:30, **390**
illus. 5:15
BAJA CALIFORNIA SUR (state, Mexico) 5:391
Bajans (Barbadians) (people) 5:479
Baja Peninsula (North America) 5:358, 390, 391
Ba Jin (Pa Chin) (Chinese writer) 2:406
Bajío (region, Mexico) 5:403, 405
Bajrakli Džamija (mosque, Belgrade, Serbia)
4:277
Bajuvars (people) 3:321
Bakau (Gambia) 1:160
Baker, Sir Samuel (English explorer) 1:322
Bakhtiari (Asian people) 2:157
Bakongo (African people) 1:258, 266, 343, 344
Bakota (African people) 1:253
Baku (capital, Azerbaijan) 2:47, 87, 88, 89;
4:309
illus. 2:86
BaKuba (early African kingdom) 1:268
Balaguer, Joaquín (president of Dominican
Republic) 5:460
Bala Lake (Llyn Tegid) (Wales) 3:122
Balante (African people) 1:164
Balaton, Lake (Hungary) 4:237
Balboa (Panama) 6:76, 78
Balboa, Vasco Nuñez de (Spanish explorer)
6:15, 78, 82, 97
illus.
monument in Panama City 6:81
Balbuena, Bernardo de (Mexican poet) 5:381
Balcones Escarpment (Texas) 5:250
Bald eagle (bird, symbol of U.S.)
illus. 5:163
Baldy Mountain (Manitoba) 5:115
Balearic Islands (Spain) 4:80, 84, 88, 90, 113
Europe 3:8, 28

illus.
Majorca 4:84
Balewa, Sir Abubakar Tafawa (Nigerian politi-
cal leader) 1:227
Balfour Declaration (1917) 2:112, 113
Bali (Indonesia) 2:315, 319, 320
terrorist bombing 2:326, 503
Balkan Mountains 3:28; 4:260, 264
Balkans (peninsula, Europe) 3:9
Albania 4:268–73
Bosnia and Herzegovina 4:288–90
Bulgaria 4:258–67
Croatia 4:285–87
Greece 4:185–211
Romania 4:248–57
saying about Belgrade and the Balkans 3:328
Slovenia 4:282–84
Yugoslavia 4:274–81
Balkan Wars (1912–1913) 4:160, 207, 256, 265
Balkh (Afghanistan) 2:176
Balkhash, Lake (Kazakhstan)
table(s)
largest lakes 6:347
Ballarat (Victoria, Australia) 2:518
Ballet
Denmark 4:16
Russia 4:314
illus. 4:17
Ballet Folklórico de Mexico 5:374
Balmat, Jacques (French mountain climber)
3:302
Balmoral Castle (Scotland) 3:138
Balsas River Valley (Mexico) 5:416
Balsas-Tepalcatepec River (Mexico) 5:409
Baltic Sea (Europe)
Denmark 4:9, 10
Finland 4:51
Hanseatic League 3:273
Kiel Canal 3:243
Poland 4:212, 213
Sweden 4:48, 49
illus.
German resort 3:242
table(s)
major seas of the world 6:347
BALTIC STATES 3:19, 20
Estonia 4:293–96
Latvia 4:297–300
Lithuania 4:301–4
Baltimore (Maryland) 5:46, 199, 219
illus. 5:198
Baltimore, Lord (George Calvert) (English
holder of Maryland charter) 5:219
Baltistan (Pakistan) 2:182
Baluba (African people) 1:266
Baluchi (Asian people) 2:157, 183
Baluchi language 2:187
Baluchistan (province, Pakistan) 2:181, 182, 190
Balzac, Honoré de (French writer) 3:178
Balzers (Liechtenstein) 3:305
Bamako (capital, Mali) 1:50, 142
illus. 1:143
Bambara (African people)
illus.
sculpture 1:52
Bambari (Central African Republic) 1:247, 248
Bamiléké (African people) 1:233
Bamoun (African people) 1:233
Bana (waterway, Yemen) 2:132
Banaba (Ocean Island) (island, Kiribati) 2:560,
577, 580–81, 582
Banana Belt (region in southern Ontario) 5:105

Bananas
Central America 6:12, 17
Colombia 6:124
Costa Rica 6:69
Ecuador 6:200
Guinea 1:168
Honduras 6:39
Jamaica 5:473
Nicaragua 6:55
Panama 6:77
Tabasco (Mexico) 5:419
illus. 6:37
Costa Rica 6:69
Ecuador 6:200
shipping 6:13
Banat (province, Romania) 4:248, 249
Banda (African people) 1:247
Banda, Hastings Kamuzu (president of Malawi)
1:279, 280, 281
Bandama River (west Africa) 1:186
Bandaranaike, Sirimavo (prime minister of Sri
Lanka) 2:250
Bandaranaike, Solomon W. R. D. (prime min-
ister of Sri Lanka) 2:250
Bandar Seri Begawan (capital, Brunei) 2:329,
330
illus.
sultan's palace 2:329
Bandeira, Manuel (Brazilian poet) 6:180, 181
Bandeirantes (Brazilian pioneers) 6:189
Bandjabi (African people) 1:253
Bandung (Indonesia) 2:323
Banff National Park (Alberta) 5:126
Bang (Dravidian people) 2:243
Bangalore (India) 2:203, 227
Bangka Island (Indonesia) 2:322
Bangkok (capital, Thailand) 2:261–62, 275,
278–79
railroad link to Vientiane (Laos) 2:282
illus. 2:273, 278
Temple of the Emerald Buddha 2:279
BANGLADESH 2:228, **237–44** *see also* Pakistan
creation of nation 2:27, 30, 193
Ganges River 2:168
people in Myanmar 2:268
illus.
Dhaka 2:244
flag 2:viii
flooding 2:239
pottery making 2:242
rice growing 2:241
rickshaws in Dhaka 2:237
map(s) 2:238
Bangla language *see* Bengali
Bangor (Northern Ireland) 3:147
Bangui (capital, Central African Republic)
1:247, 248, 249, 250
illus. 1:246
Banja Luka (Bosnia and Herzegovina) 4:290
Banjarmasin (Indonesia) 2:323
Banjul (capital, Gambia) 1:160
Banking and finance
Africa's foreign debts 1:3, 63, 64
El Salvador adopts U.S. dollar as second cur-
rency 6:47
Hungarian Westernization 4:244
Luxembourg 3:210
Netherlands 3:232
Switzerland 3:288
Banks, Sir Joseph (English naturalist) 2:552
Banks Island (Arctic Ocean) 5:141
Bann River (Northern Ireland) 3:83, 143

Bantu (language group) **1:**264, 329, 330, 352, 358, 398
Bantu (peoples of Africa) **1:**15, 36
  Angola **1:**343–44, 346
  Basotho people of Lesotho **1:**391
  Botswana **1:**351
  central Africa **1:**44, 47
  Congo, Democratic Republic of **1:**264, 268
  Congo, Republic of **1:**258
  Fang in Equatorial Guinea **1:**235
  Malawi **1:**278, 280
  Mozambique **1:**365
  Somalia **1:**302
  southern Africa **1:**357–59, 360, 361–62, 403, 404
  Swaziland **1:**386, 388
  Uganda **1:**318, 322
  Zambia **1:**273
  Zimbabwe Ruins **1:**361
Bantustans (South Africa) *see* Homelands
Banyankole (African people) **1:**318
Banyoro (African people) **1:**318
Banzer Suárez, Hugo (president of Bolivia) **6:**241
Banziri (African people) **1:**247
Baobab trees 2:486, 525
  illus. **2:**486
Bapounou (African people) **1:**253
Baqqara Arabs (African people) **1:**127
Bara (people) **1:**373, 374
Baracoa (Cuba) **5:**444
Barak, Ehud (prime minister of Israel) **2:**115
Barantu (Eritrea) **1:**295
BARBADOS 5:427, 438, **478–80**
  English language **5:**435
  slavery **5:**483
  illus.
    flag **5:**vi
  map(s) **5:**479
Barbarian invasions (Europe) **3:**48, 49
Barbarossa (Barbary pirates) **1:**83
Barbary States 1:97
Barbeau Peak (Nunavut) **5:**138
Barbecues 6:256, 274
Barbour, John (Scottish author) **3:**137
Barbuda *see* Antigua and Barbuda
Barcelona (province, Spain) **4:**107
Barcelona (Spain) **4:**89, 90, 101–3, 108, 110
  illus. **4:**102, 103
Barcelonnette (France) **3:**173
Barents, William (Dutch navigator) **5:**62
Barents Sea 5:64
Bariba (African people) **1:**213
Bariba (language) **1:**213
Barkley, Lake (Kentucky) **5:**261
Barlach, Ernst (German artist) **3:**255
Barnaul (Russia) **2:**342
Baro River (Ethiopia) **1:**283
Barossa Valley (Australia) **2:**522
Barotseland (region, Zambia) **1:**273
Barquisimeto (Venezuela) **6:**137
Barranquilla (Colombia) **6:**120
Barre (Vermont) **5:**187
Barre, Mohammed Siad (president of Somalia) *see* Siad Barre, Mohammed
Barrett, Peter J. (New Zealand geologist) **6:**329
Barrientos Ortuño, René (president of Bolivia) **6:**241
Barrier islands 5:153, 217, 227
Barrios, Justo Rufino (Guatemalan leader) **6:**32
Barrow (Alaska) **5:**57, 64

Barrow, Errol (prime minister of Barbados) **5:**480
Bartók, Béla (Hungarian composer) **4:**241
Barú (mountain, Panama) **6:**72
Baseball 2:463; **6:**142
  Montreal **5:**100
  illus. **5:**164
    Dominican Republic **5:**454
    Japanese cheerleader **2:**464
Basel (Switzerland) **3:**245, 288, 293, 295
Bashir, Omar Ahmed al- (president of Sudan) **1:**131
Bashō (Japanese poet) **2:**460
Basic Law (Germany, 1949) **3:**284
Basil II (Byzantine emperor) **4:**292
Basin and range (landform) **5:**31, 333, 342
Basketball 5:191
Basotho (African people) **1:**391, 392, 398
Basque language 3:20; **4:**88
Basques (people) **3:**18
  North America, immigrants to **5:**331
  Spain **4:**87, 89, 90, 94, 107–8
Basra (Iraq) **2:**148
Bassari (African people) **1:**206
Basse (Gambia) **1:**160
Basseterre (capital, St. Kitts and Nevis) **5:**495
Bass Strait (Australia) **2:**490, 516, 528, 530
Bastidas, Rodrigo de (Spanish explorer) **6:**15
Bastille, Fall of the (1789) **3:**184
Bastille, Place de la (Paris, France) **3:**198
Bastille Day (July 14) **3:**196
  illus. **3:**197
Basuto (African people) **1:**47
Basutoland *see* Lesotho
Baťa, Tomáš (Czech industrialist) **4:**228
Bata (Equatorial Guinea) **1:**235
Batak (people) **2:**318
Batang (China) **2:**369
Batavi (ancient Germanic people) **3:**235
Batavian Republic (Dutch history) **3:**236
Batéké (African people) **1:**253, 258, 260
Batéké Plateaus (Congo) **1:**257, 259
Bath (England) **3:**113
  illus. **3:**115
Bathurst (New Brunswick) **5:**86
Bathurst Island (Australia) **2:**532
Batidas, Rodrigo de (Spanish explorer) **6:**126
Batik (cloth design) **2:**307, 319
  illus. **2:**320
Batista y Zaldívar, Fulgencio (Cuban dictator) **5:**447
Batlle, Jorge (president of Uruguay) **6:**265
Batlle y Ordóñez, José (Uruguayan statesman) **6:**264
Baton Rouge (capital, Louisiana) **5:**248
Batoro (African people) **1:**318
Batswana (people) **1:**351, 352
Battle Born State (nickname for Nevada) **5:**330
Batumi (republic of Georgia) **2:**84
Batutsi (African people) *see* Tutsi
Batwa (African people) *see* Twa
Bau (island, Fiji) **2:**599
Baudelaire, Charles (French poet) **3:**178
Baudó, Serranía de (mountains, Colombia) **6:**116
Baudouin I (king of Belgium) **3:**224
Bauhaus (German art school) **3:**255
  illus. **3:**255
Baule (African people) **1:**187
  illus.
    sculpture **1:**52

Bauxite
  Appalachian Mountains **5:**7
  France **3:**157
  Guinea **1:**169
  Guyana **6:**151
  Hungary **4:**238
  Jamaica **5:**473–74
  Suriname **6:**159
  illus.
    carried by barge from Guyana mine **6:**151
    processing **6:**159
  map(s)
    world production **6:**355
Bavaria (state, Germany) **3:**247, 249, 250, 270–72, 273
  Ludwig I and his castles **3:**257
  illus.
    Neuschwanstein **3:**257
Bavarian Christian Social Union (German political party) **3:**284
Baya (African people) **1:**247
Bayamo (Cuba) **5:**443
Bay Chimo (settlement, Nunavut) **5:**139
Bayinnaung (Burman king) **2:**271
Bay Islands (Honduras) **6:**37, 41
Bay of Pigs invasion (Cuba, 1961) **5:**448
Bayous 5:245, 247
Bayreuth (Germany) **3:**257, 259
  illus.
    music festival **3:**256
Bazaars *see* Markets
Bazile, Castera (Haitian artist) **5:**465
Beaches
  Africa **1:**19
  Australia **2:**504
  Europe **3:**24
  Hawaii **5:**351, 353
  Jamaica **5:**471
  New Jersey **5:**207
  illus.
    Atlantic City (New Jersey) **5:**207
    Australia **2:**485
    Belize **6:**19
    Brazil **6:**186
    Bulgaria **4:**266
    Cape Verde **1:**150
    Chile **6:**315
    Denmark **4:**13
    Germany **3:**242
    Kiribati **2:**580
    Miami Beach **5:**239
    Netherlands **3:**14
    Portugal **4:**70
    Queensland (Australia) **2:**507
    Saint-Malo (France) **3:**174
    Sicily **4:**129
    Somalia **1:**301
    Spain **4:**84, 85
    Yalta (Ukraine) **4:**339
Beaconsfield, Earl of *see* Disraeli, Benjamin
Beaker people 3:112
Beale Street (Memphis, Tennessee)
  illus. **5:**263
Beardmore Glacier (Antarctica) **6:**325, 329
Bears
  Bern (Switzerland) **3:**292
  dancing bears popular in Turkey **2:**60
  illus.
    polar bear **5:**6
    spectacled bear **6:**89
    in Swiss zoo **3:**291
Beas River (India) **2:**170, 183

Beatles (English musical group)
illus. **3**:108
Beaubourg Center (Georges Pompidou National Center of Art and Culture) (Paris, France) **3**:198–99
Beaufort Sea (Arctic Ocean) **5**:134, 143, 145
Beaver (Indians of North America) **5**:125
Beavers (animals)
illus. **5**:72
Beaver State (nickname for Oregon) **5**:339
Becal (Campeche, Mexico) **5**:420
Beccaria, Cesare (Italian writer) **4**:158
Bechuanaland see Botswana
Becket, Saint Thomas (English churchman) **3**:117
Bédié, Henri Konan (president of Ivory Coast) **1**:188
Bedouins (nomadic Arabs)
Iraq **2**:149
Israel **2**:109
Jordan **2**:117, 118
Morocco **1**:67
Saudi Arabia **2**:126
Yemen **2**:133
illus. **2**:118, 124
Beehive State (nickname for Utah) **5**:323
Beer (beverage)
Belgium **3**:215
Denmark **4**:15–16
Germany **3**:250, 270, 272
millet beer of Chad **1**:241
Munich's Oktoberfest **3**:271
illus.
Danish brewery **4**:15
Milwaukee brewery **5**:285
Beersheba (Israel) **2**:109
Beethoven, Ludwig van (German composer) **3**:256, 267
illus.
home in Bonn **3**:256
Begin, Menachem (prime minister of Israel) **2**:114–15
Béhanzin (king of Dahomey) **1**:214
Beida (Libya) **1**:96, 98
Beijing (Peking) (capital, China) **2**:378, 380, 397, 403, 404
dialect **2**:402
national library **2**:407
student protests **2**:381, 399–400
illus.
Forbidden City **2**:14
Tiananmen Square demonstrations **2**:418
Beijing Opera 2:406
Beira (Mozambique) **1**:46, 364
Beirut (capital, Lebanon) **2**:47, 71, 100, 103
illus. **2**:97, 103
Beja (African people) **1**:127
Beja (language) **1**:109
Bekaa (plateau in Lebanon) **2**:97, 98
Békésy, Georg von (Hungarian-American scientist) **4**:241
Belalcázar, Sebastián de see Benalcázar, Sebastián de
BELARUS 3:2, 35; **4**:341–43, 343
Russia, history of **4**:309
illus.
flag **4**:vi
Minsk **4**:341
map(s) **4**:342
Belau see Palau
Belaúnde Terry, Fernando (Peruvian political leader) **6**:227

Belavezhskaya Pushcha (natural reserve, Belarus–Poland) **4**:341–42
Belawan (Sumatra) **2**:323
Belém (area, Lisbon, Portugal) **4**:71–72
Belém (capital, Pará state, Brazil) **6**:169, 182, 183, 187
Bélep Islands (Pacific Ocean) **2**:585
Belfast (capital, Northern Ireland) **3**:145–46, 149
illus. **3**:148
Grand Opera House **3**:143
restaurant **3**:145
Belfast Agreement (1998) **3**:95, 149
Belfast Lough (Northern Ireland) **3**:143
Belgae (ancient European people) **3**:235
Belgian Congo see Congo, Democratic Republic of
BELGIUM 3:20, **211–24**
Luxembourg, relations with **3**:210
Netherlands, history of **3**:236
illus.
Antwerp **3**:217
Bruges **3**:211
Brussels **3**:216, 222
cattle grazing at Waterloo **3**:218
flag **3**:vi
Ghent **3**:219
Ostend **3**:220
map(s) **3**:213
Belgrade (capital, Yugoslavia) **3**:328; **4**:277
illus. **4**:277
BELIZE 6:**19–24**
Central America **6**:9, 10
English language **6**:7
history **6**:15, 16
population **6**:11
Xunantunich **6**:14
illus.
Belize city **6**:21
flag **6**:vi
Half Moon Cay **6**:19
sugarcane harvest **6**:23
map(s) **6**:20
Belize City (Belize) **6**:20
illus. **6**:21
Bella Coola (British Columbia) **5**:131, 164
Bella Coola (Indians of North America) **5**:130, 132
Belle Isle, Strait of (Canada) **5**:81
Bellevue (Nebraska) **5**:302
Bellingshausen, Fabian von (Russian explorer) **6**:331
Bell Island (Newfoundland) **5**:7
Bello, Andrés (Venezuelan poet) **6**:141
Bellona (Solomon Islands) **2**:592
Bellotto, Bernardo (Italian artist) **3**:268; **4**:215
Belmopan (capital, Belize) **6**:20
Belo, Carlos Ximenes (East Timorese bishop) **2**:328
Belo Horizonte (capital, Minas Gerais state, Brazil) **6**:160, 186–87
Belorussian language (Byelorussian) 4:342
Belorussians (Slavic people) **4**:342
Belver (dam, Portugal) **4**:73
Bemba (African people) **1**:273
Benalcázar, Sebastián de (Spanish conquistador) **6**:204
Ben Ali, Zine el-Abidine (president of Tunisia) **1**:92
Ben Bella, Ahmed (Algerian leader) **1**:84
Bendern (Liechtenstein) **3**:305
Bendery (Moldova) **4**:346

Benelux (economic union) **3**:8, 210, 212, 221, 224, 232
Beneš, Eduard (Czech leader) **4**:235
Bengal (region, India–Bangladesh) **2**:243
Bengal, Bay of (Indian Ocean) **2**:165, 199, 205, 266
Bangladesh **2**:237, 238
Ganges River **2**:168
Madras (Chenai) **2**:207
Bengali (Bangla) (language) **2**:28, 199, 240, 243
Bengalis (people) **2**:30, 239–40, 243
Benghazi (Libya) **1**:95, 96, 98
Benguela (Angola) **1**:46, 343
Benguela highland (plateau, Angola) **1**:342
Beni Amer (language) **1**:295
Beni Hassan (Bedouin Arabs) **1**:139
Benin (ancient kingdom in Africa) **1**:226
illus.
sculpture **1**:220
BENIN (Dahomey) 1:50, 53, **210–14**
illus.
craftsmen illustrating cloths **1**:212
flag **1**:xxiii
houses on stilts **1**:210
sculpture **1**:53
map(s) **1**:211
Benin, Bight of (west Africa) **1**:215
Benin City (Nigeria) **1**:219
Beni River (South America) **6**:231
Benítez, Manuel (Spanish matador) see Cordobes, El
Benito, Rio (Equatorial Guinea) see Mbini River
Benjedid, Chadli (Algerian political leader) **1**:84
Ben Nevis (mountain, Scotland) **3**:83, 132
Benoit, Rigaud (Haitian artist) **5**:465
Benue River (west Africa) **1**:50, 216, 233–34
Beothuk (people of North America) **5**:82, 83
Beowulf (epic poem) **3**:104
Berbera (Somalia) **1**:301, 303, 304
Ethiopian shipping through **1**:287
Berbérati (Central African Republic) **1**:247
Berber language 1:86, 87, 109
Berbers (African peoples)
Algeria **1**:77–78, 83
Libya **1**:97, 99
Mauritania **1**:139
Morocco **1**:65, 67–68, 72, 73
Sahara Desert **1**:25
Tunisia **1**:86, 91, 92
Western Sahara **1**:132; **4**:86
Berbice River (Guyana) **6**:149
Berengar II (king in Italy) **4**:155
Berezina River (Belarus) **4**:341
Bergen (Belgium) see Mons
Bergen (Norway) **4**:33
illus. **4**:31
Bergman, Ingmar (Swedish film director) **4**:44
Beria, Lavrenti (Soviet leader) **2**:84
Bering, Vitus (Danish navigator) **5**:62
Bering Sea (North Pacific Ocean) **5**:348
table(s)
major seas of the world **6**:347
Berisha, Sali (president of Albania) **4**:273
Berkner, Lloyd V. (American scientist) **6**:333
Berkshire Hills (Massachusetts–Connecticut) **5**:156, 189, 195
Berlanga, Tomás de (Spanish bishop and explorer) **6**:202
Berlin (capital, Germany) **3**:275, 279, 280–81, 282, 283
Love Parade music festival **3**:252

Berlin (cont.)
unified Berlin became state **3:**284
illus.
Berlin Wall **3:**62, 280
Brandenburg Gate **3:**253
people **3:**264
Reichstag Building **3:**281
World Time Clock **3:**281
Berlin, Conference of (1884–1885) **1:**268–69, 322, 367
Berlin, Congress of (1878) **2:**72; **4:**265
Berlin airlift (1948–1949) **3:**280, 282
Berliner Ensemble (German theater company) **3:**281
Berlin Wall 3:62, 239–40, 246, 259, 280, 282
illus. **3:**62, 280
Berlusconi, Silvio (prime minister of Italy) **4:**154, 162, 163
Bermejo River (South America) **6:**231, 280
Bermuda 3:90; **5:**32–33
illus. **5:**33
map(s) **5:**32
Bermuda Island (Bermuda) **5:**32
Bermúdez, Juan de (Spanish explorer) **5:**32
Bern (capital, Switzerland) **3:**291–92, 295
illus.
bears in zoo **3:**291
Bernadette, Saint (French religious figure) **3:**165
Bernadotte, Count Folke (Swedish statesman) **4:**50
Bernadotte, Jean-Baptiste *see* Charles XIV John
Bernese Alps (mountains, Switzerland) **3:**286
Berni, Antonio (Argentine painter) **6:**278
Bernina Pass (Alps) **4:**126
Bernini, Giovanni Lorenzo (Italian artist) **4:**181
Bernoulli family (Swiss scientists) **3:**293
Bertinoro (Italy) **4:**138
Bessarabia (region, Europe) **4:**256, 347
Bessemer, Sir Henry (English inventor) **3:**107
Betancourt, Rómulo (Venezuelan president) **6:**147
Béthencourt, Jean de (Norman navigator) **1:**33
Bethlehem (Jordan) **2:**114
Bethlehem (Pennsylvania) **5:**213
Betsiboka River (Madagascar) **1:**371
Betsileo (people) **1:**372, 374, 375, 377
Betsimisaraka (people) **1:**372–73, 377
Bettendorf (Iowa) **5:**294
Beverly Hills (California) **5:**345
Beyeglou (sector of Istanbul, Turkey) **2:**62–63
Beyla (Guinea) **1:**169
Béziers (France)
illus. **3:**31
Bhaktapur (Bhadgaon) (Nepal) **2:**232
Bhotias (Bhotes) (Asian people) **2:**235
Bhumibol Adulyadej (king of Thailand) **2:**276
BHUTAN 2:27, 166, 167, 169, **234–36**
illus.
flag **2:**viii
royal palace and women in costume **2:**234
map(s) **2:**235
Bhutto, Benazir (prime minister of Pakistan) **2:**193, 194
illus. **2:**192
Bhutto, Zulfikar Ali (Pakistani political leader) **2:**194
Biafra (eastern region, Nigeria) **1:**58, 219, 228
Biafra, Bight of (west Africa) **1:**215, 235
Białowieża Forest (Poland) **3:**33; **4:**213
Biarritz (France) **3:**165
Bibi Khanym Mosque (Samarkand, Uzbekistan) **2:**351

Bible 3:119, 130
Bicycling 3:41, 176
illus.
Chile **6:**308
China **2:**401
Germany **3:**251
Italian race **4:**140
Bié (plateau, Angola) **1:**342
Bieler, Manfred (German author) **3:**251
Biermann, Wolf (German author) **3:**251
Big Apple (nickname for New York City) **5:**203
Bigaud, Wilson (Haitian artist) **5:**465
Big Ben (clock tower, London, England)
illus. **3:**111
Big Bend Nation Park (Texas)
illus. **5:**250
Big Cypress Swamp (Florida) **5:**238
Bighorns (Rocky Mountain sheep)
illus. **5:**126
Big Island, The (nickname for the island of Hawaii) **5:**351
Big Muddy (nickname for Missouri River) **5:**160
Big Sky Country (nickname for Montana) **5:**311
Big Stone Lake (South Dakota) **5:**299
Big Sur (California) **5:**157, 342
illus. **5:**333
Bihar State (India) **2:**216
Bikini (atoll, Pacific Ocean) **2:**570, 575
Bilbao (Spain) **4:**108
Bilbies (animals) **2:**505
Billings (Montana) **5:**312
Bill of Rights, English (1689) **3:**120
Billy the Kid (American outlaw) **5:**322
Bilma (Niger) **1:**148
Biloxi (Mississippi) **5:**246
Biltmore (Vanderbilt mansion in North Carolina)
illus. **5:**228
Binch (Belgium) **3:**215
Binger, Louis (French territorial governor) **1:**188
Bingham, Hiram (American archaeologist) **6:**220
Bini *see* Edo
Bin Laden, Osama **2:**174, 179
Bintan Island (Indonesia) **2:**322
Binue River *see* Benue River
Bío-Bío River (Chile) **6:**315
Bioko (Fernando Po) (island, Equatorial Guinea) **1:**55, 235, 236; **4:**85
Biosphere (environmental museum, Montreal)
illus. **5:**98
Biotechnology 3:138, 141
Biqa (plateau in Lebanon) *see* Bekaa
Birch trees
bark used by American Indians **5:**23
Bird, Lester (prime minister of Antigua and Barbuda) **5:**494
Bird, Vere (prime minister of Antigua and Barbuda) **5:**494
Birds
Alaska **5:**349
Andean condors **6:**231
Antarctica **6:**327–28
Arctic **6:**60, 135, 142, 146
Australia **2:**489
Brazilian rain forest **6:**172, 173
California **5:**343
Danube Delta **3:**329
England on migratory routes **3:**102
Europe **3:**33
fossil birds **6:**330

Galápagos Islands **6:**203
Hawaii **5:**351
Hungary **4:**237
Madagascar **1:**369
Nayarit **5:**400
New Zealand **2:**477, 542, 550
North Carolina **5:**227
Romanian waterfowl **4:**250
South America **6:**87
Tobago sanctuary **5:**483
United Kingdom **3:**85
Venezuela **6:**134
illus.
blue-footed booby **6:**203
nesting waterfowl **5:**111
parrots **6:**10
scarlet macaw **6:**89
Birendra (king of Nepal) **2:**233
Birkenau (Nazi concentration camp, Poland) **4:**221
Birmingham (Alabama) **5:**49, 243
illus.
"Praying Ministers" (sculpture) **5:**242
Birmingham (England) **3:**106
Birobidzhan (autonomous region, Russia) **4:**309
Birunga (mountains) *see* Virunga
Biruni, al- (Arab scholar) **2:**351
Biscay, Bay of (Atlantic Ocean) **4:**107–8
Biscayne Bay (Florida) **5:**239
Bishkek (capital, Kyrgyzstan) **2:**353
Bishop, Maurice (prime minister of Grenada) **5:**482
Bislama language 2:595
Bismarck (capital, North Dakota) **5:**298
Bismarck, Otto von (the Iron Chancellor) (German statesman) **3:**186, 275
Bismarck Archipelago (islands, Pacific Ocean) **2:**559, 587, 600
Bison (animal)
American Indians **5:**23, 300
European **3:**33; **4:**342
illus. **5:**162
Bissau (capital, Guinea-Bissau) **1:**164
Bitterroot Mountains (Idaho–Montana) **5:**38, 313
Bitumen 5:123
Biya, Paul (president of Cameroon) **1:**234
Bizerte (Tunisia) **1:**90
Bjørnson, Bjørnstjerne (Norwegian playwright) **4:**28
Black Americans *see also* articles on individual countries, regions, and states
Alabama **5:**243, 244
Atlanta **5:**235
Canada **5:**75
civil rights movement **5:**176
cotton plantations **5:**221
Kentucky **5:**261
Louisiana **5:**247
Michigan **5:**277
Middle Atlantic States **5:**199–200
Mississippi **5:**245, 246
Oberlin College **5:**274
slavery **5:**166–67
Southern States **5:**222
Texas **5:**253
United States population **5:**171
Virginia **5:**224–25
illus.
Kwanzaa festival **5:**44
Black Death (disease) **3:**118; **4:**25

Blackfeet (Indians of North America) *see* Blackfoot

Blackfoot (Indians of North America) **5:**23, 111, 115, 121, 124, 125, 126, 164, 311

Black Forest (Germany) **3:**28, 242, 245, 258, 326

Black Hawk (Sauk chief) **5:**293, 294

Black Hawk War (1832) **5:**283, 286, 294

Black Hills (South Dakota–Montana) **5:**299, 300, 315

Black homelands *see* Homelands

Black magic 5:465

Black Mountain (Kentucky) **5:**260

Black Mountains (North Carolina) **5:**156

Black Power (Trinidadian militants) **5:**486

Black Prince *see* Edward (prince of Wales)

Black Rock Desert (Utah) **5:**323

Blacks
  Africa **1:**12, 13 *see also* Apartheid
  apartheid **1:**58–59
  Argentina **6:**270–71
  Caribbean self-government **5:**437
  Cuba **5:**445
  Haitian independence **5:**461, 468, 469
  Jamaica **5:**474, 475, 476
  South Africa **1:**398–99, 400
  South and Central America **6:**11, 92–95, 111, 112, 165, 177–78, 186
  Toronto **5:**106
  Trinidad and Tobago **5:**484
  United States *see* Black Americans
  illus.
    South America **6:**94

Black Sea (Europe–Asia) **2:**5, 57
  Crimea **4:**336
  Danube River **3:**326, 329
  Rhine-Main-Danube Canal **3:**243
  Romania **4:**250, 254
  illus.
    Bulgarian beach **4:**266
  table(s)
    major seas of the world **6:**347

Black Sea Fleet 4:337

Blackshirts (Italian Fascists) **4:**160

Black States (in South African history) *see* Homelands

Blackstone River and Valley (Massachusetts–Rhode Island) **5:**190, 192

Black Volta River *see* Volta River

Blair, Tony (prime minister of United Kingdom) **3:**95, 96
  illus. **3:**95

Blaize, Herbert A. (prime minister of Grenada) **5:**482

Blanc, Mont (France) **3:**151, 299, 302
  tunnel **3:**41, 304
  illus. **3:**151, 301

Blantyre (Malawi) **1:**278

Blarney Castle (County Cork, Ireland) **3:**73

Blaue Reiter (Blue Rider) group (German artists) **3:**255

Blechen, Karl (German artist)
  illus.
    Mill Valley near Amalfi **3:**254

Bled, Lake (Slovenia) **4:**282

Bligh, William (English naval officer) **2:**605–6

Blitzkrieg (German tactics in World War II) **3:**277; **4:**221

Blixen, Baroness Karen *see* Dinesen, Isak

Block Island (Rhode Island) **5:**192, 193

Bloemfontein (judicial capital, South Africa) **1:**398

Bloody Friday (bombing in Belfast, 1972) **3:**149

Bloody Mary (queen of England) *see* Mary I

Bloomington (Minnesota) **5:**288

Blücher, Gebhard von (Prussian field marshal) **3:**185

Bluebonnet (Texas' state flower)
  illus. **5:**252

Bluefields (Nicaragua) **6:**54, 55, 56
  illus.
    reggae music **6:**55

Bluegrass Country (Kentucky–Tennessee) **5:**260, 262
  illus. **5:**262

Bluegrass State (nickname for Kentucky) **5:**260

Blue Grotto (Capri, Italy) **4:**130

Blue Hen's Chickens (nickname for Delaware's soldiers) **5:**216

Blue Mosque (Cairo, Egypt) **1:**115

Blue Mosque (Istanbul, Turkey) **2:**62

Blue Mountain (St. Croix, U.S. Virgin Islands) **5:**172

Blue Mountains (Jamaica) **5:**442, 471
  illus. **5:**472

Blue Mountains (Oregon–Washington) **5:**336, 339

Blue Nile (river, Africa) **1:**39, 125, 283

Blue Nile Falls (Tisisat Falls) (Ethiopia)
  illus. **1:**284

Blue Range (Arizona) **5:**327

Blue Ridge Mountains (U.S.) **5:**156, 219, 224, 227, 230, 263
  illus. **5:**223

Blue Ridge Parkway (Georgia–North Carolina–Virginia) **5:**156, 229
  illus. **5:**157

Bo (Sierra Leone) **1:**171
  illus. **1:**172

Boadicea (Boudicca) (ancient British queen) **3:**110, 113, 128

Boas (snakes)
  illus. **6:**10

Boat people (Vietnamese refugees) **2:**31

Boats *see also* Ships and shipping
  Asian floating market **2:**257
  Bangladesh's transportation **2:**242
  Danube River **3:**327
  Europe's water transportation **3:**42
  Mayan dories **6:**22
  reed boats on Lake Titicaca **6:**230–31
  yachting Auckland (New Zealand) **2:**547
  illus.
    barge traffic on Seine River **3:**154
    Belgian fishing boats **3:**220
    crew teams on the Thames (England) **3:**106
    ferry crossing Congo River **1:**269
    ferry on Mono River **1:**207
    French marina **3:**164
    German fishing boats **3:**263
    Greek fishing boats **4:**199
    Iceland **4:**6
    Japanese fishing boats **2:**468
    Malaysian river ferry **2:**307
    Maldivian fishing boat **2:**251
    reed boats **6:**231
    sailboat in Papua New Guinea **2:**587
    St.-Tropez (France) **3:**168
    South Asian river **2:**7
    steamboat **5:**147
    Thai riverboat **2:**278
    tourist boat on Rhine River **3:**244
    traditional Portuguese fishing boat **4:**66

Bobo (African people) **1:**191

Bobo-Dioulasso (Burkina Faso) **1:**192
  illus. **1:**191

Boca de Apiza (Colima, Mexico) **5:**408

Bocas del Toro (Panama) **6:**77

Boccaccio, Giovanni (Italian writer) **4:**157

Bocuse, Paul (French chef) **3:**159

Bodensee *see* Constance, Lake of

Bodrum (Turkey)
  illus. **2:**62

Boeotia (region, Greece) **4:**188, 189

Boers (Dutch settlers in South Africa) **1:**354, 392, 404

Boer War (1899–1902) *see* Anglo-Boer War

Boggy Peak (mountain, Antigua and Barbuda) **5:**493

Bogong, Mount (Australia) **2:**516

Bogotá (capital, Colombia) **6:**97, 116, 119, 122
  Andes, life in **6:**100, 101
  history **6:**126, 127
  illus. **6:**117, 119, 122

Bogs 5:208, 349 *see also* Marshes; Swamps

Bohemia (region, Czech Republic) **3:**322; **4:**224, 225, 226, 227, 229, 230

Bohemian Basin (Czech Republic) **3:**28

Bohemian Forest (mountains, Germany–Czech Republic) **3:**315

Bohr, Niels (Danish physicist) **4:**16

Boii (Celtic tribe) **4:**225

Bois de Boulogne (Paris, France) **3:**201–2

Bois de Vincennes (Paris, France) **3:**202

Boise (capital, Idaho) **5:**314

Bokassa, Salah Eddine Ahmed (Jean Bedel Bokassa) (emperor of the former Central African Empire) **1:**250

Bolama (Guinea-Bissau) **1:**164

Bolaños, Enrique (president of Nicaragua) **6:**60

Boleyn, Anne (2d queen of Henry VIII of England) **3:**119

Bolívar, Pico (La Columna) (mountain, Venezuela) **6:**132

Bolívar, Simón (South American liberator) **6:**98, 99
  Bolivia **6:**240
  Colombia **6:**127
  Congress of Angostura **6:**138
  Gran Colombia **6:**204
  holiday honoring him **6:**199
  La Libertad, University of **6:**218
  San Martín and Bolívar **6:**226
  Venezuela **6:**136, 141, 146

BOLIVIA 6:229–41
  Amazon River **6:**168
  Andes **6:**100–101
  criollos **6:**236
  economy **6:**88, 102–3
  education **6:**107
  Guevara, Ernesto (Ché) **6:**240
  Indo-American culture **6:**89, 90, 91
  Mercosur **6:**262
  Río de la Plata **6:**284
  illus.
    fashionable neighborhood **6:**236
    festival **6:**234
    flag **6:**vi
    La Paz **6:**90, 229, 232
    llamas **6:**230
    pre-Columbian sculpture **6:**238
    reed boats **6:**231
    Santa Cruz **6:**234
    Sucre **6:**233
  map(s) **6:**235

Bolkiah, Muda Hassanal (leader of Brunei)
2:329
Böll, Heinrich (German author) 3:251
Boll weevil 5:221
Bologna (Italy) 4:136
    illus. 4:159
Bolsena, Lake (Italy) 4:128
Bolshevik Revolution *see* Russian Revolution
    and Civil War
Bolsheviks (Communist supporters of Lenin)
    4:310, 322
Bolyai, János (Hungarian scientist) 4:241
Bolzano (province, Italy) 4:134
Bombay (Mumbai) (India) 2:203, 204, 206–7,
    228
    motion pictures 2:204
    Parsis 2:209
    illus. 2:207
Bomi Hills (Liberia) 1:182
Bon (traditional religion of Xizang) 2:386
Bonaire (island, West Indies) 3:235
    map(s) 5:429
Bonampak (ancient Mayan city, Mexico) 5:418
Bonaparte, Joseph (king of Naples and Spain,
    brother of Napoleon I) 4:116
Bonaparte, Louis *see* Louis (king of Holland)
Bonaparte, Napoleon *see* Napoleon I
Bondoukou (Ivory Coast) 1:185
Bone (Algeria) *see* Annaba
Bongo, Omar (Gabonese political leader)
    1:253, 255
Boniface, Saint (Benedictine missionary) 3:50
Bonifacio, Andres (Philippine hero) 2:340
Bonn (Germany) 3:245, 267
    illus.
        house of Ludwig von Beethoven 3:256
Bonnie Prince Charlie *see* Stuart, Charles
Bonny, Bight of *see* Biafra, Bight of
Bon Pays (region, Luxembourg) 3:207
Boobies (birds)
    illus. 6:203
Boone, Daniel (American pioneer) 5:224, 257,
    262, 296
Boone, Daniel M. (son of pioneer) 5:296
Bophuthatswana (black state in South African
    history) 1:58–59, 404
Borbón *see* Bourbon
Borchgrevink, Carsten (Norwegian explorer)
    6:332
Bordaberry, Juan M. (president of Uruguay)
    6:265
Bordeaux (France) 3:152, 156, 162
Border disputes *see also* names of specific
    countries
Borges, Jorge Luis (Argentine author) 6:277
Borghese Gardens (Rome, Italy) 4:170
Borgou (plain, Benin) 1:211
Borinage (region, Belgium) 3:212
Borja Cevallos, Rodrigo (president of Ecuador)
    6:205
Borneo (island, Southeast Asia)
    Brunei 2:329, 330
    Indonesia 2:314, 315, 323
    Malaysia 2:303, 304
    table(s)
        largest islands of the world 6:346
Bornholm (island in Denmark) 4:8, 10, 12
Bornu (early African kingdom) 1:244
Borromean Islands (Lake Maggiore, Italy) 4:128
Borucas (Indians of Central America) 6:66
Börzsöny Mountains (Hungary) 4:237

Bosch, Juan (president of Dominican Republic)
    5:460
BOSNIA AND HERZEGOVINA 3:1, 2;
    4:288–90
    Croatia 4:287
    ethnic wars 4:275, 280, 281
    Joint Endeavor operation 4:247
    illus.
        flag 4:vi
        Mostar bridge 4:288
    map(s) 4:289
Bosporus, Strait of (Turkey) 2:5, 57, 61; 3:45
    illus. 2:61
Boston (capital, Massachusetts) 5:46, 181, 189,
    190
    illus. 5:188, 190
Boston Massacre (1770) 5:191
Boston Mountains (Arkansas)
    illus. 5:266
Boston Tea Party (1773) 5:191
Bosumtwi, Lake (Ghana) 1:196
Botany Bay (Australia) 2:485
    illus.
        penal colony 2:500
Botero, Fernando (Colombian artist) 6:122
Bothnia, Gulf of (Baltic Sea) 4:39, 51
Botrange (mountain, Belgium) 3:212
BOTSWANA 1:47, **351–54**
    illus.
        flag 1:xxiv
        Gaborone 1:351
        San hunter 1:12
        village 1:352
    map(s) 1:353
Bouaké (Ivory Coast) 1:185
Bouar (Central African Republic) 1:247, 248
Boudiaf, Muhammad (Algerian political leader)
    1:84
Boudicca *see* Boadicea
Bougainville (island, Pacific Ocean) 2:586, 587,
    588, 590, 591
Boulder Dam *see* Hoover Dam
Boulogne (France) 3:164
Boulogne-Billancourt (France) 3:202
Boumedienne, Houari (Algerian military leader)
    1:84
Bounty, H.M.S. (British ship) 2:488, 562–63, 606
Bourbon (French royal family)
    Bourbon and Orléans kings, list of 6:363, 364
    Italy, history of 4:158
    Spanish Carlists 4:91, 116
Bourguiba, Habib (Tunisian leader) 1:87, 88, 92
Bouteflika, Abdelaziz (president of Algeria)
    1:84
Bouterse, Désiré (military leader of Suriname)
    6:158, 159
Bouvet (island near Antarctica) 4:24
Bovine spongiform encephalopathy *see* Mad
    cow disease
Bowen Island (Australia) 2:515
Bowie (Maryland) 5:218
Bowie, Jim (American soldier) 5:252
Bow River (Alberta) 5:125
Boxer Rebellion (China, 1900) 2:24–25
Boyacá (Colombia) 6:127
Boyars (Russian hereditary nobility) 4:320
Boyer, Jean Pierre (Haitian political leader)
    5:469
Boyne, Battle of the (1690) 3:76, 148
Bracciano, Lake (Italy) 4:128
Bradshaw Mountains (Arizona) 5:327
Braga (Portugal) 4:72

Braganza Dynasty (Portugal; 1640–1910)
    6:189–90
Brahe, Tycho (Danish astronomer) 4:16
Brahma (Hindu god) 2:21
Brahman (Hindu caste) 2:21, 210–11
    illus. 2:210
Brahmaputra River (Asia) 2:168, 198, 238
    Himalayas, source in 2:167
    table(s)
        longest rivers of the world 6:346
Brahms, Johannes (German composer) 3:258
Brahui language 2:187
Braila (Romania) 4:249
Braille, Louis (French teacher) 3:199
Braithwaite, Nicholas (prime minister of
    Grenada) 5:482
Branch Davidians (religious cult) 5:255
Brancusi, Constantin (Romanian artist) 4:252
Brandberg (mountain peak, Namibia) 1:347
Brandeis, Louis (American justice) 5:261
Brandenburg Gate (Berlin)
    illus. 3:253
Brandon (Manitoba) 5:116
Brandt, Willy (West German chancellor) 3:282,
    283
Brandywine Creek (Pennsylvania–Delaware)
    5:215
Bransfield, Edward (British explorer) 6:331
Braque, Georges (French painter) 3:177
Bras d'Or Lake (Nova Scotia) 5:91
Brasília (capital, Brazil) 6:160, 174, 182, 184
    illus. 6:161
Braşov (Romania) 4:254
Brasstown Bald Mountain (Georgia) 5:233
Bratislava (capital, Slovakia) 3:327; 4:234
    illus. 4:232
Brazauskas, Algirdas (Lithuanian political
    leader) 4:304
BRAZIL 6:160–91 *see also* names of cities
    Acre area acquired from Bolivia 6:241
    Afro-American culture 6:91, 93, 94–95, 112
    Amazon River 6:168–69
    Carnival 6:178
    economy 6:88, 103, 104
    education 6:106
    Euro-American culture 6:95, 96, 97
    evangelical movement 6:162
    family names 6:110
    history 6:100
    Japanese immigrants 6:95
    Mercosur 6:262
    political history 6:114
    population 6:8
    Portugal, history of 4:76, 77
    Portuguese language 6:82
    poverty 6:105
    rain forest 6:172
    Río de la Plata 6:284
    social position and race relations 6:112
    Treaty of Tordesillas 6:82
    Yanomamo Indians 6:140
    Zumbi 6:188
    illus.
        Brasília 6:161
        coffee harvesting 6:171
        college students 6:175
        flag 6:vi
        gold mine 6:174
        Iguaçú Falls 6:281
        Itaipú Dam 6:167
        Manaus 6:181

rain forest **6**:172
Recife **6**:163
Rio de Janeiro **6**:178, 183, 186
Salvador **6**:185
São Paulo **6**:7, 83, 165, 182, 184
soccer **6**:179
soccer fans **6**:113
stock market **6**:114
map(s) **6**:170
Brazil, Vital (Brazilian scientist) **6**:177
Brazza, Pierre Savorgnan de (French explorer) **1**:260
Brazzaville (capital, Congo, Republic of) **1**:43, 256, 257, 258, 259, 260
illus. **1**:256
Bread and Butter State (nickname for Minnesota) **5**:287
Breadbasket of America (nickname for Kansas) **5**:303
Brecht, Bertolt (German playwright) **3**:280, 281
Brecon Beacons (mountains, Wales) **3**:122
Breda, Treaty of (1667) **6**:155
Bregenz (Austria) **3**:244, 312
Bremen (Germany) **3**:273
illus. **3**:265
Bremerhaven (Germany) **3**:262
Brenner Pass (Alps) **3**:304; **4**:126
Brescia (Italy) **4**:152
Brest (Belarus) **4**:343
Brest (France) **3**:164
Brest-Litovsk, Treaty of (1918) **4**:322
Breytenbach, Breyten (South African poet) **1**:401
Brezhnev, Leonid (Soviet political leader) **4**:323
Brian Boru (high king of Ireland) **3**:75
Briançon (France) **3**:163
Briand, Aristide (French statesman) **3**:3
Bricks
illus. **1**:376
Bridal Veil Falls (Australia)
illus. **2**:509
Bridgeport (Connecticut) **5**:196
Bridger, James (American frontiersman) **5**:325
Bridges
Avignon (France) **3**:154
Mostar (Bosnia and Herzegovina) **4**:290
Oresund Bridge (Denmark–Sweden) **4**:10
Panama Canal **6**:72
Paris (France) **3**:195
Roman bridges in France **3**:180
Sydney Harbour Bridge **2**:511
Zambezi River railroad bridge **1**:355
illus.
Atlantic Provinces **5**:78
Bridge of Sighs (Venice, Italy) **4**:147
Cameroon bridge building **1**:233
covered bridge **5**:186
Lucerne (Switzerland) **3**:296
Mostar (Bosnia and Herzegovina) **4**:288
Pont Neuf (Paris) **3**:194
rope footbridge **1**:164
Royal Gorge Bridge (Colorado) **5**:318
Bridgetown (capital, Barbados) **5**:480
Brielle (the Netherlands) **3**:236
Brighton (England)
illus. **3**:120
Brikama (Gambia) **1**:160
Brindabella Range (Australia) **2**:514, 515
Brink, André (South African author) **1**:401
Brisbane (capital, Queensland, Australia) **2**:505, 507–8
illus. **2**:504

Bristlecone pine (tree) **5**:343
BRITISH COLUMBIA (province, Canada) **5**:42, 128–33
illus.
Vancouver **5**:36–37, 130
Victoria **5**:133
map(s) **5**:131
British Commonwealth of Nations *see* Commonwealth of Nations
British East India Company *see* East India companies
British Empire (English history) **3**:91–93 *see also* Commonwealth of Nations
India **2**:216–17, 219–20
Jamaica **5**:477
South Asia **2**:172–73
Trinidad and Tobago **5**:483, 486
Yemen **2**:135
British Guiana *see* Guyana
British High Commission Territories (former name of south African nations) **1**:47
British Honduras *see* Belize
British Indian Ocean Territory **1**:47; **3**:90
British Mountains (Canada) **5**:145
British North America **5**:34–39, 80, 165, 174
British Somaliland *see* Somalia
British South Africa Company **1**:49, 276, 362
British Straits Settlements **2**:312
British Togoland (trusteeship territory, west Africa) **1**:194, 209
British Virgin Islands *see* Virgin Islands, British
Britons (people) **3**:18
Brittany (region, France) **3**:18, 162, 164
Brizan, George (prime minister of Grenada) **5**:482
Brno (Czech Republic) **4**:225
Broken Hill (Zambia) *see* Kabwe
Brong-Ahafo (African people) **1**:198
Bronx, The (borough, New York City) **5**:203
Bronze
Ashanti art **1**:198
Thailand, history of **2**:279
Bronze Age **4**:198
Brooke, Rupert (English poet) **4**:190
Brooklyn (borough, New York City) **5**:203, 205
Brooks Range (Alaska) **5**:7, 56, 157, 348
Brownell, Charles DeWolf (American painter)
illus.
Connecticut's Charter Oak **5**:197
Brownsville (Texas) **5**:255
Broz, Josip *see* Tito, Josip Brož
Bruce, The (epic poem, Barbour) **3**:137
Bruges (Belgium) **3**:215, 217, 219
illus. **3**:211
Brulé, Étienne (French explorer) **5**:109
BRUNEI **2**:258, 308, 315, **329–30**
illus. **2**:262, 329
flag **2**:viii
map(s) **2**:330
Brunei Town *see* Bandar Seri Begawan
Brünn (Czechoslovakia) *see* Brno
Brussels (capital, Belgium) **3**:211–12, 214, 215–16, 219, 223, 224
illus. **3**:216, 222
Brussig, Thomas (German author) **3**:251
Bryce Canyon National Park (Utah) **5**:323
Brythons (Brythonic Celts) (people) **3**:124
Bubi (African people) **1**:235
Bubonic plague *see* Black Death
Bucaram, Abdala (president of Ecuador) **6**:205
Bucaramanga (Colombia) **6**:121
Buccaneers *see* Pirates and buccaneers

Bucerias (Nayarit, Mexico) **5**:400
Buchanan (Liberia) **1**:180, 182
Bucharest (capital, Romania) **3**:328; **4**:252, 253, 255
illus.
Palace of the People **4**:253
Bucharest, Treaty of (1812) **4**:347
Buckeye State (nickname for Ohio) **5**:271
Buckingham Fountain (Chicago, Illinois)
illus. **5**:281
Buckingham Palace (royal residence, London)
illus. **3**:79
changing of the guard **3**:103
Buda (now part of Budapest, Hungary) **3**:327; **4**:242, 245
Budapest (capital, Hungary) **3**:327; **4**:242
illus. **3**:329; **4**:236, 238
Buddhism **2**:14, 19 *see also* Lamaism
Afghanistan statues destroyed **2**:179
Asia, East **2**:373
Asia, South **2**:169, 171
Asia, Southeast **2**:18, 254, 260, 261, 295
Asoka **2**:20
Bhutan **2**:235, 236
Cambodia **2**:288–89, 290, 291
China **2**:15, 381, 389, 420
India **2**:214, 216
Indonesia **2**:324
Japan **2**:17, 443, 452
Korea **2**:437
Laos **2**:283
Myanmar **2**:268, 269, 270, 271
Nepal **2**:230, 232
Pakistan **2**:191
Sri Lanka **2**:247, 248, 249
Thailand **2**:275
illus.
Chinese ceremony **2**:388
Great Buddha (Kamakura, Japan) **2**:451
monks **2**:263
Myanmar priest restoring statue **2**:268
Southeast Asian temple **2**:18
Sri Lankan shrine **2**:247
statues of Buddha **2**:373, 389
Buea (Cameroon) **1**:232–33
Buenaventura (Colombia) **6**:121, 124
Buene River (Albania) **4**:269
Bueno, Maria Ester (Brazilian tennis player) **6**:180
Buenos Aires (capital, Argentina) **6**:266, 270, 271, 285, 288–90, 297
history **6**:298, 299
Jockey Club **6**:274
library **6**:277
Montevideo, cultural kinship **6**:258
population **6**:8, 272
poverty **6**:105
Teatro Colón **6**:276
university **6**:278
illus.
Avenida 9 de Julio **6**:288
La Boca **6**:278
Palace of the National Congress **6**:268
Plaza de Mayo and Casa Rosada **6**:291
port **6**:289
Teatro Colón **6**:267
Buenos Aires (province, Argentina) **6**:266, 271, 285, 292
Buffalo (animal) *see* Bison; Water buffalo
Buffalo (New York) **5**:37, 46, 205
Buffalo National River (Arkansas)
illus. **5**:266

Buganda (former kingdom, now a district of Uganda) **1:**38, 318, 322
Buginese (people) **2:**318
Bug River, Southern (Ukraine) **4:**333
Bug River, Western (Ukraine–Poland) **4:**213
Buhari, Mohammed (Nigerian political leader) **1:**228
Building construction see Architecture
Bujumbura (capital, Burundi) **1:**330
Buka (island, Pacific Ocean) **2:**587, 591
Bukhara (emirate) **2:**352, 358
Bukhara (Uzbekistan) **2:**342, 351
Turkmenistan **2:**357
Bukit Barisan (mountains, Indonesia) **2:**314–15
Bükk Mountains (Hungary) **4:**237
Bukovina (province, Romania) **4:**248
Bulawayo (Zimbabwe) **1:**357, 362
BULGARIA 3:2; **4:**258–67
conversion to Christianity **4:**205
Romania, history of **4:**256
illus.
  beach **4:**266
  flag **4:**v
  modern hotel **4:**267
  Monks (mountain formation) **4:**260
  Roman ruins **4:**259
  rose growers **4:**264
  Sofia **4:**258, 263
map(s) **4:**261
Bulgars (nomadic people) **3:**18, 49; **4:**260, 265
"bullet trains" 2:439
Bullfighting
Costa Rica **6:**67
Peru has oldest bullring in Americas **6:**217
Portugal **4:**70
Spain **4:**93
Venezuela **6:**141
illus. **4:**93; **5:**369
  Venezuela **6:**139
Bulls (animals)
illus.
  Pamplona (Spain) **4:**94
Bulu language 1:234
Bunbury (Australia) **2:**527
Bundesrat (of German parliament) **3:**284
Bundestag (of German parliament) **3:**284
Bungee jumping 2:545
Bungle Bungle Mountains (Australia) **2:**525
illus. **2:**524
Bunraku theater (of Japan) **2:**460
Bunyan, Paul (folk hero) **5:**80
Bunyoro (kingdom in Africa) **1:**38, 322
Bureaucracy, German government 3:264
Burgas (Bulgaria) **4:**264
Burgenland (province of Austria) **3:**310, 315
Burgtheater (Vienna, Austria) **3:**318
illus. **3:**322
Burgundians (Germanic tribe) **3:**180, 296
Burgundy (region, France) **3:**156, 235
BURKINA FASO (Upper Volta) 1:52–53, **189–93**
illus.
  Bobo-Dioulasso **1:**191
  farmers **1:**193
  flag **1:**xxii
  man carrying brooms to market **1:**189
map(s) **1:**190
Burley Griffin, Lake (Australia) **2:**514
Burlington (Vermont) **5:**187
Burma see Myanmar
Burmese language see Myanmar language

Burnham, Forbes (prime minister of Guyana) **6:**152
Burns, Robert (Scottish poet) **3:**137
Burns-Paiutes (Indians of North America) **5:**339
Bursa (Turkey) **2:**46, 63
Burton, Richard F. (British explorer) **1:**268
Buru (island, Indonesia) **2:**315
BURUNDI 1:37, **328–31**
Congo, Democratic Republic of **1:**270
illus.
  drummers **1:**328
  flag **1:**xxiv
map(s) **1:**329
Buryats (people) **2:**363
Busansi (African people) **1:**192
Busch, Germán (president of Bolivia) **6:**241
Bush (African landscape) **1:**307
Bush, George (41st president of the U.S.) **4:**184; **5:**253
Bush, George W. (43rd president of the U.S.) **2:**154, 433; **5:**253
illus. **3:**95
Bushire (Iran) **2:**156
Bushmanoid race (of Africa) **1:**12
Bushmen (African people) see San
Bush people (of Suriname) **6:**155, 158
Bushveld (region, South Africa) **1:**395
Busia, Kofi A. (Ghanaian leader) **1:**204
Busoga (district of Uganda) **1:**322
Bussa (Nigeria) **1:**148
Bussa Rapids (Niger River) **1:**50
Bustamante, Anastasio (president of Mexico) **5:**416
Bustamente, Sir William Alexander (prime minister of Jamaica) **5:**477
Bus transportation 6:75
illus. **2:**227
Butare (Rwanda) **1:**325
Buthelezi, Mangosuthu (Zulu chief) **1:**405
Butler, Horacio (Argentine artist) **6:**278
Buyoya, Pierre (president of Burundi) **1:**331
Bwaka (African people) **1:**247
Byarezina River see Berezina River
Byblos (ancient city, Lebanon) **2:**101
illus. **2:**99
Byelorussian see Belorussian language
Bygdøy Peninsula (Norway) **4:**32
Byrd, Richard E. (American explorer) **5:**64; **6:**332
illus. **5:**62
Byron, Cape (New South Wales, Australia) **2:**481
Byron, George Gordon, Lord (English poet) **3:**295; **4:**206
Byzantine Empire (Eastern Roman Empire) (330–1453)
Africa **1:**83, 119
Asia **2:**64, 72
Europe **3:**48–49, 53–54; **4:**185–87, 192, 205, 265
Hagia Sophia (Istanbul) **2:**22
Kiev (Ukraine) **4:**337
Macedonia **4:**292
Russia **4:**320
Turkey **2:**61–62
Byzantium (later **Constantinople,** now **Istanbul) 2:**61 see also Constantinople; Istanbul

· · · **C** · · ·

Caacupé (Paraguay) **6:**248
Cabaret (motion picture) **3:**280
Cabbages
illus. **2:**306
Cabinda (exclave district of Angola) **1:**343, 344, 345
Cable cars
Alps **3:**304
Valparaíso (Chile) **6:**314
Venezuela **6:**132
illus. **5:**399; **6:**131
Cabora Bassa Dam (Zambezi River) **1:**366
Cabo San Lucas (Baja California Sur, Mexico)
illus. **5:**391
Cabot, John (Italian explorer for England) **3:**119; **5:**75, 78, 83, 93, 173, 183
Cabot, Sebastian (Italian explorer) **6:**284, 296
Cabral, Amílcar (political leader, Guinea-Bissau) **1:**165
Cabral, Pedro Álvares (Portuguese navigator) **4:**75–76; **6:**82, 97, 187
Cabramatta (district, Sydney, Australia) **2:**495
Cabrera, Miguel (Mexican artist) **5:**382
Cabrillo, Juan Rodríguez (Portuguese navigator) **5:**335, 341, 346
Caburni Falls (Cuba) **5:**442
Cacahuamilpa Caves (Mexico) **5:**416
Cacao beans 1:188, 200, 224, 234
Cacaxtla (archaeologic site, Mexico) **5:**415
Cacheu (Guinea-Bissau) **1:**164
Cacheu River (west Africa) **1:**164
Caddo (Indians of North America) **5:**249, 250, 253
Cadillac Mountain (Maine) **5:**182
Cádiz (Spain) **4:**104, 109, 110
Caelian Hill (Rome, Italy) **4:**165
Caerphilly Castle (Wales)
illus. **3:**129
Caesar, Gaius Julius (Roman general and statesman) **3:**180
Britain, invasion of **3:**113
Corinth (Greece) **4:**199
Forum, place of his assassination **4:**165
Nile River **1:**38
Switzerland **3:**295
Caetano, Marcello (premier of Portugal) **4:**77, 78
Cafés (restaurants) **3:**23–24, 25, 311; **4:**93
illus. **3:**59
  Argentina **6:**292
  outdoor dining in Uruguay **6:**257
  Venezuela **6:**111
Cagliari (Sardinia, Italy) **4:**131
Caillié, René Auguste (French explorer) **1:**141
Cairns (Queensland, Australia) **2:**508
Cairo (capital, Egypt) **1:**39, 102, 106, 114–15, 116, 119
Islamic architecture **1:**111
population **1:**30
universities **1:**108–9
illus. **1:**31, 107
  Mohammed Ali Mosque **1:**108
Cajamarca (Peru) **6:**220, 224
Cajuns (French Canadian settlers in Louisiana) **5:**80, 247
Cakobau (Fijian chief) **2:**599
Calabar (Nigeria) **1:**219

Calabria (Italy) **4:**138

Calacala (Bolivia) **6:**233

Calais (France)
illus. **3:**164

Calamity Jane (American frontierswoman) **5:**299, 300

Calcutta (India) **2:**203, 204, 205–6
illus. **2:**206

Caldera Rodríguez, Rafael (president of Venezuela) **6:**148

Calderón de la Barca, Pedro (Spanish playwright) **4:**115

Calderón Fournier, Rafael (president of Costa Rica) **6:**71

Calderón Sol, Armando (president of El Salvador) **6:**50

Caledonian Canal (Scotland) **3:**132

Calendar 2:153

Calgary (Alberta) **5:**125, 126, 127
illus. **5:**125

Calgary Stampede (rodeo and exhibition) **5:**125, 127

Cali (Colombia) **6:**119–20, 124, 129

CALIFORNIA 5:162, 163, **341–47**
earthquakes **5:**335
economy **5:**335
resources **5:**50–52
Spanish North America **5:**27
illus.
Big Sur **5:**333
border crossing **5:**362
Carmel **5:**1
Los Angeles **5:**345
Mojave National Preserve **5:**343
San Diego **5:**345
San Francisco **5:**344
wine country **5:**346
Yosemite Valley **5:**149, 341
map(s) **5:**342

California, Gulf of 5:358
illus. **5:**390

Calima (pre-Columbian culture) **6:**126

Caliphates (Muslim rulers) **1:**119

Calistoga (California) **5:**346

Callao (Peru) **6:**211, 218, 227

Calle-Calle River (Chile) **6:**316

Calles, Plutarco (president of Mexico) **5:**387, 388

Calusa (Indians of North America) **5:**238

Calypso (music) **5:**484, 485

Camacho, Manuel Ávila *see* Ávila Camacho, Manuel

Camagüey (Cuba) **5:**443

Camargue (region, France) **3:**168

CAMBODIA 2:286–92
Angkor Wat **2:**21–22
Asia, Southeast **2:**254, 259, 264
border disputes **2:**31
Mekong River **2:**256–57
Vietnam, relations with **2:**298, 302
illus.
Angkor ruins **2:**286
flag **2:**viii
Khmer Rouge violence **2:**291
marketplace **2:**288
schoolchildren **2:**289
map(s) **2:**287

Cambodians (Asian people) *see* Khmer

Cambrian Mountains (Wales) **3:**83, 122

Cambridge Bay (settlement, Nunavut) **5:**139

Cambridge University (England) **3:**105
illus. **3:**105

Cambyses (king of Persia) **1:**119

Camden Yards (Maryland)
illus.
Oriole Park **5:**219

Camels 1:71, 96, 303; **2:**363
illus. **1:**106, 297; **2:**6
being washed **2:**135
caravan in Sahara **1:**24
India **2:**198
Indian camel fair **2:**205
Niger **1:**147
racing in Alice Springs (Australia) **2:**535

CAMEROON 1:54, **230–34**
illus.
bridge building **1:**233
children **1:**13
flag **1:**xxiii
mountains **1:**230
Yaoundé **1:**232
map(s) **1:**231

Cameroon Mountain 1:232

Camões, Luis Vaz de (Portuguese poet) **4:**71

Campbell, Kim (prime minister of Canada) **5:**76

Campbell Hill (Ohio) **5:**272

Camp David (presidential retreat, Maryland) **5:**219

Camp David accords (Israel–Egypt) **1:**123; **2:**115

Campeche (capital, Campeche state, Mexico) **5:**420

CAMPECHE (state, Mexico) **5:420**
Yucatán **5:**421

Campeche, Bay of (Mexico) **5:**420

Campero, Narciso (president of Bolivia) **6:**241

Campine (district, Belgium) **3:**212

Camus, Albert (French writer) **1:**80; **3:**179

CANADA 5:65–148 *see also* names of provinces, territories, cities
Arctic **5:**61, 64
bi-national and multi-cultural system **5:**39
climate **5:**70–71
history *see* Canadian history
Inuit **5:**58
national emblem **5:**105
population concentration **5:**104
resources **5:**39–42, 71–73
Rocky Mountains **5:**38
Ukrainian community **4:**333
illus.
border with U.S. **5:**71
flag **5:**vi
map(s) **5:**66, 68
table(s)
prime ministers **6:**360

Canadian Arctic Islands *see* Arctic Archipelago

Canadian Confederation 5:89, 109
Charlottetown **5:**88
Manitoba **5:**113
illus.
Confederation Room **5:**88

Canadian history 5:75–76 *see also* articles on individual provinces and regions
British North America **5:**37–39
Confederation *see* Canadian Confederation

Canadian National Railway 5:92

Canadian Pacific Railway 5:85, 125, 126, 132

Canadian River (U.S.) **5:**321

Canadian Rockies *see* Rocky Mountains

Canadian (Laurentian) Shield (North America) **5:**4, 67, 94, 268, 284
Alberta **5:**122
Ontario **5:**104
Prairie Provinces **5:**110
Quebec **5:**98–99
United States **5:**45, 287

Canaletto (Venetian painter) *see* Bellotto, Bernardo

Canals *see also* Erie Canal; Panama Canal
Amsterdam's concentric canals **3:**233
Caledonian canal **3:**132
Corinth Canal **4:**188
England **3:**106
Europe, importance to **3:**42, 154, 243
Gota Canal (Sweden) **4:**39
Grand Canal (China) **2:**371
Kara Kum Canal **2:**356, 358
Moselle River **3:**208
Netherlands **3:**226, 229
New York **5:**37
Nicaragua possible canal site **6:**57
North America **5:**13, 44
Panama Canal **6:**78–79
Rhine River **3:**245
Saimaa Canal (Finland–Russia) **4:**52
St. Lawrence Seaway **5:**96, 99
Sudan's Jonglei Diversion **1:**125, 129
Suez Canal **1:**120–21
Thailand **2:**275
United Kingdom **3:**83
United States **5:**5, 177
Venice **4:**148
illus.
Corinth Canal **4:**186
Erie Canal **5:**204
Ethiopian irrigation canal **1:**287
Great Lakes **5:**270
Venice **4:**147

Canal Zone *see* Panama Canal Zone

Canary Islands (off northwest Africa) **1:**32–33, 35; **4:**80, 84–85

Canaveral, Cape (Florida) **5:**241

Canberra (capital, Australia) **2:**512, 513, 514, 515
illus. **2:**513

Cancún (island, Mexico) **5:**358, 422

Candlewood Lake (Connecticut) **5:**195

Cannes (France) **3:**160, 162

Cannibalism 2:551, 552, 599; **5:**430

Canoes 1:375
illus. **1:**281; **5:**287

Canso, Strait of (Canada) **5:**90

Cantabrian Mountains (Spain) **4:**82, 83

Canterbury Plains (New Zealand) **2:**539

Canterbury Tales (stories, Chaucer) **3:**104

Canton (China) *see* Guangzhou

Canton River (China) *see* Pearl River

Cantons (Swiss political districts) **3:**297, 298

Canute II (Canute the Great) (Danish king) **4:**20

Canyonlands National Park (Utah) **5:**323

Cão, Diogo (Portuguese explorer) **1:**43, 260, 346, 350

Cao Dai (Vietnamese sect)
illus. **2:**296

Cape (for the geographic feature) *see* names of capes, as Horn, Cape

Cape Breton (Nova Scotia) **5:**92–93

Cape Breton Highlands National Park 5:91

Cape Breton Island (Nova Scotia) **5:**78, 80, 90, 91, 93
illus. **5:**91
Cape Coast (Ghana) **1:**198, 199
Cape Cod (Massachusetts) **5:**188
Cape Cod National Seashore 5:189
illus. **5:**189
Cape Colony (province, South Africa) *see* Cape of Good Hope
Cape Coloureds (African people) *see* Coloureds
Cape Hatteras National Seashore 5:229
Cape Henry Memorial (Virginia Beach, Virginia) **5:**225
Cape Lookout Lighthouse (North Carolina) **5:**229
illus. **5:**227
Cape Lookout National Seashore 5:229
Cape of Good Hope (historic province, South Africa) **1:**350, 392, 404
Cape Province (South Africa) *see* Cape of Good Hope
Capetian kings (France) **3:**181
list of **6:**363
Cape Town (legislative capital, South Africa) **1:**396, 397, 398, 400, 401, 402
illus. **1:**5, 397
CAPE VERDE 1:54, **150–51**
illus.
beach **1:**150
beaches **1:**55
flag **1:**xxii
map(s) **1:**151
Cape York Peninsula (Queensland, Australia) **2:**481, 484, 495
Cap-Haïtien (Haiti) **5:**468
Capitalism *see also* Socialism
Italian fascism **4:**160
Mexico's combination with socialism **5:**364
origins **2:**23
Capitol Building (Washington, D.C.) **5:**170
illus. **5:**159, 170
Capitoline Hill (Rome, Italy) **4:**165
Capitol Reef National Park (Utah) **5:**323
Cappadocia (Turkey)
illus. **2:**57
Capri (island, Italy) **4:**130
Caprivi Strip (Namibia) **1:**347, 348
Caprock Escarpment (Texas) **5:**251
Carabobo, Battle of (1821) **6:**146
Caracalla (Roman emperor) **2:**97; **4:**167
Caracalla, Baths of (Rome, Italy) **4:**167, 172
Caracas (capital, Venezuela) **6:**132, 136, 138, 144
Andes, life in **6:**100
arts **6:**141, 142
University City **6:**142
illus. **6:**130, 136
Capitol **6:**145
Central University of Venezuela **6:**138
sidewalk café **6:**111
subway **6:**137
Caracas Company (in Latin American history) **6:**145
Caracol, El (ancient observatory, Mexico) **5:**421
illus. **5:**26
Caral (ancient city, Peru) **6:**221
Caratasca Lagoon (Honduras) **6:**35
Carballido, Emilio (Mexican playwright) **5:**374
Carcassonne (France) **3:**16, 160, 163
illus. **3:**162
Cárdenas, Lázaro (president of Mexico) **5:**388

Cardiff (capital, Wales) **3:**124, 126–27
illus. **3:**52
Cardiff Castle (Wales)
illus. **3:**126
Cardigan Bay (Wales) **3:**122
Cardoso, Fernando Henrique (president of Brazil) **6:**191
illus. **6:**191
Cargados Carajos (archipelago dependency of Mauritius) **1:**379
Cargo cults (Pacific islands) **2:**558, 595–96
Carib (Indians of South America) **5:**429–30, 434, 487, 490, 492
Barbados **5:**480
Black Caribs of Belize **6:**22
Grenada **5:**482
Puerto Rico **5:**167
Caribbean Community *see* CARICOM
CARIBBEAN SEA AND ISLANDS 5:426–40 *see also* names of countries and islands
European settlements **6:**97
Florida's climate **5:**238
North America, considered part of **5:**2, 4
Venezuela's island territories **6:**131, 148
illus.
colonial architecture **5:**432
cruise ship **5:**431
cutting sugarcane **5:**434
markets **5:**428
wooden houses **5:**427
map(s) **5:**429
table(s)
major seas of the world **6:**347
Caribbees (islands) *see* Lesser Antilles
Cariboo Mountains (Canada) **5:**131
Caribou *see* Reindeer
CARICOM (Caribbean Community) 5:440
Carinthia (province of Austria) **3:**314, 320
Cariocas (inhabitants of Rio de Janeiro, Brazil) **6:**177, 184
Carl XVI Gustaf (king of Sweden) **4:**47
Carlists (Spanish Borbón royalty) **4:**91
Carlota (empress of Mexico) **5:**384
Carlsbad (Czech Republic) *see* Karlovy Vary
Carlsbad Caverns (New Mexico)
illus. **5:**321
Carlsberg (Danish brewery) **4:**15–16
Carmel (California)
illus. **5:**1
Carmel, Mount (Israel) **2:**109
Carmona, António Oscar de Fragoso (Portuguese statesman) **4:**77
Carnegie, Andrew (American industrialist) **5:**214
Carnival (Mardi Gras; Shrove Tuesday) (religious holiday)
Brazil **6:**178
Colombia **6:**120
Ecuador **6:**199
Germany's Fasching **3:**249, 270
Mazatlán **5:**397
New Orleans **5:**248, 249
Panama **6:**75
Peru **6:**213
Trinidad and Tobago **5:**484–85
Uruguay **6:**255–56
Venezuela **6:**138, 141
illus.
New Orleans Mardi Gras **5:**249
Trinidad and Tobago **5:**483
Carol II (Romanian king) **4:**256
Caroline (princess of Monaco) **3:**206

Caroline Islands (Pacific Ocean) **2:**568, 569, 570, 573, 574
Palau **2:**571–72
Carolingian kings (France) **6:**363
Caroní River (Venezuela) **6:**146
Carpathian Mountains (Europe) **4:**232
Europe's alpine regions **3:**28, 31; **4:**212–13, 275
migration of Magyars to Hungary **4:**238
Romania **4:**248–49
Ukraine **4:**333
Carpentaria, Gulf of (Australia) **2:**483, 505
Carpentaria Basin (Australia) **2:**483
Carpenters Hall (landmark, Philadelphia, Pennsylvania) **5:**213
Carrantuohill (mountain peak in Ireland) **3:**65–66
Carranza, Venustiano (Mexican statesman) **5:**386–87, 394
Carrara (Italy) **4:**133
Carreño, Maria Teresa (Venezuelan pianist-composer) **6:**142
Carrera, José Miguel (Chilean patriot) **6:**321
Carrera, Rafael (Guatemalan political leader) **6:**32
Carrera Andrade, Jorge (Ecuadorian writer) **6:**200
Carriacou (Caribbean island) **5:**481
Carrillo, Braulio (Costa Rican statesman) **6:**68
Carsi (mosque, Priština) **4:**277
Carson, Kit (American frontiersman) **5:**332
Carson City (capital, Nevada) **5:**332
illus. **5:**331
Carstensz, Mount (Indonesia) *see* Puncak Jaya
Cartagena (Colombia) **6:**120–21
Cartagena (Spain) **4:**110
Cartago (Costa Rica) **6:**63, 64, 67, 70
illus. **6:**65
Carter, Jimmy (39th president of U.S.) **5:**234, 452; **6:**18, 79, 80
illus. **5:**451
Carthage (ancient city, North Africa) **1:**33, 72, 83, 91
modern city **1:**90
Rome, its rise and fall **3:**47
Carthaginians (people) **4:**68–69, 110
Cartier, Jacques (French explorer) **5:**75, 85, 89, 96, 101
Cartier Island (Timor Sea) **2:**488
Casablanca (Morocco) **1:**66–67, 68, 71, 72
illus. **1:**69
Casablanca Conference (1943) **1:**74
Casamance (Senegal) **1:**158, 165
Casamance River (Senegal) **1:**152, 153, 154
Casa Rosada (Buenos Aires) **6:**288
illus. **6:**291
Casbah (old section of a north African city) **1:**67, 77
Cascade Range (North America) **5:**8, 156, 333–34, 336, 338, 339, 342
Casemates (tunnels, Luxembourg) **3:**207
Casimir Palace (Warsaw, Poland) **4:**216
Casino gambling 3:205, 206; **5:**196, 300, 332
Macau **2:**416
Mississippi **5:**246
Casiquiare River (Venezuela) **6:**134, 146
Casper (Wyoming) **5:**316
Caspian Depression (Caucasus Mountains) **3:**8
Caspian Sea (Europe–Asia) **2:**42; **4:**308; **6:**345
Asia, lakes of **2:**156, 161
Europe's eastern boundary area **3:**8

oil reserves **2:**53, 88, 89
plant and animal life **3:**33
table(s)
    largest lakes **6:**347
Cassava *see* Manioc
Caste (social class) **2:**14, 21
    Hutu and Tutsi **1:**331
    India **2:**169, 171, 210–11, 212–13, 214
    Sri Lanka **2:**247
Casteau (Belgium) **3:**216
Castel Gandolfo (Italy) **4:**170, 178
    illus. **4:**181
Castelo do Bode (dam, Portugal) **4:**73
Castel San Pietro (Italy) **4:**138
Castel Sant'Angelo (Rome, Italy) **4:**165
Castes, War of the (1847) **6:**24
Castile (historic region and former kingdom in Spain) **4:**80, 107, 113
Castilian Spanish (language) **4:**88
Castilla, Ramón (Peruvian leader) **6:**227
Castillo, Jesús (Guatemalan composer) **6:**28
Castillo Armas, Carlos (Guatemalan leader) **6:**33
Castillo de San Juan de Ulúa (fortress, Mexico) **5:**407
Castle Rock (Edinburgh) **3:**134
Castle Rock (Kansas) **5:**303
Castries (capital, Saint Lucia) **5:**489
Castro, Cipriano (Venezuelan dictator) **6:**147
Castro, Fidel (Cuban dictator) **5:**440, 447–49, 451, 452
    illus. **5:**444, 448
Castro, José María (president of Costa Rica) **6:**67
Castro, Raúl (vice president of Cuba) **5:**447, 452
Catalán language 4:88, 89, 90, 121
Catalonia (historic region, Spain) **4:**88, 89–90, 94, 113
    physical differences among Spaniards **4:**87
Catawba (Indians of North America) **5:**230
Catawba River (South Carolina) **5:**230
Catemaco, Lake (Mexico)
    illus. **5:**407
Cathedrals *see* Churches
Catherine of Aragon (1st queen of Henry VIII of England) **3:**119
Catherine the Great (empress of Russia) **3:**57; **4:**321
Catholic Church *see* Roman Catholic Church
Cato, F. Milton (prime minister of St. Vincent and the Grenadines) **5:**492
Catoche, Cape (Mexico) **5:**422
Catskill Mountains (New York) **5:**156, 199, 202
Cattle
    African society **1:**13, 14
    Argentina **6:**275, 285, 295
    Bantu life **1:**358
    blessing of the cattle **3:**168
    Channel Islands **3:**87
    Colombia **6:**125
    Egyptian farms **1:**103
    El Salvador **6:**47
    France **3:**155
    Honduran economy **6:**39
    India's sacred cows **2:**201, 213
    Madagascar **1:**376
    Masai **1:**310
    Rwanda **1:**326
    South Africa **1:**401
    South America **6:**95

Sudan **1:**127–28
Uganda **1:**318–19
United States **5:**48
Venezuela **6:**134
illus.
    Africa **1:**54, 62
    Argentina **6:**294–95
    Belgium **3:**218
    dairy farm in Wales **3:**123
    Kazakhstan **2:**348
    Pamplona, Spain **4:**94
    Paraguay **6:**247
    sacred cow in India **2:**202
    Tunisia **1:**89
    Uruguay **6:**259
    Venezuela **6:**132
    western U.S. **5:**40–41
Cauca River (Colombia) **6:**86, 116, 119, 120, 124, 125
Caucasian languages 2:44
Caucasoid race 1:12
Caucasus (area and mountains, Europe–Asia) **4:**307 *see also* Transcaucasia
    Europe separated from Middle East **3:**28
    languages **2:**44
    longevity of inhabitants **2:**46
    illus.
        Georgia **2:**83
Caudillos (provincial political leaders) **6:**102, 298
Caura River (Venezuela) **6:**146
Cauto River (Cuba) **5:**442
Cauvery (Kaveri) River (India) **2:**198–99
Cavaço Silva, Aníbal (president of Portugal) **4:**78
Cavally River (west Africa) **1:**179, 186
Cavelier, Robert *see* La Salle, Robert Cavelier, Sieur de
Cavendish (Prince Edward Island)
    illus.
        Anne of Green Gables house **5:**87
Cave paintings
    Altamira caves (Spain) **3:**16; **4:**110
    Lascaux Caves (France) **3:**167, 177
    Libya **1:**93, 99
Caves
    Blue Grotto (Capri) **4:**130
    Hungary **4:**237
    Missouri **5:**295
    New Zealand **2:**538
    Postojna Cave (Slovenia) **4:**282
    illus.
        Armenia **2:**78
        Carlsbad Caverns (New Mexico) **5:**321
        Waitomo Caves (New Zealand) **2:**540
Cavour, Camillo di (Italian statesman) **4:**158
Cayenne (capital, French Guiana) **6:**92
    illus. **6:**93
Cayman Islands (Atlantic Ocean) **3:**90
Cayuga (Indians of North America) **5:**95, 202
Cayuse (Indians of North America) **5:**340
Ceará (state, Brazil) **6:**179, 182
Ceauşescu, Elena (wife of Romanian political leader) **4:**257
Ceauşescu, Nicolae (Romanian political leader) **4:**248, 253, 255, 256–57
Cebu City (Philippines) **2:**336
Cedar Rapids (Iowa) **5:**294
Cedars of Lebanon (trees) **2:**98
Cédras, Raoul (Haitian military leader) **5:**470
Celaya (Guanajuato, Mexico) **5:**405
Celebes *see* Sulawesi

Celestún National Wildlife Refuge (Yucatán, Mexico) **5:**421
Cell phones 4:55
Celsius scale 6:376
Celtiberians (people) **4:**69, 110
Celtic language *see* Gaelic languages
Celts (people) **3:**18, 67, 74–75
    Austria **3:**314, 315, 320
    Belgium **3:**213
    Belgrade (Yugoslavia) **4:**277
    Budapest, remains of settlements in **4:**242
    Celtiberian people of Spain and Portugal **4:**68, 69, 86–87, 110
    Czech Republic, history of **4:**225
    England **3:**102, 112, 113, 114
    Germany **3:**246
    Netherlands, history of **3:**235
    Northern Ireland **3:**147
    Scotland **3:**135, 139, 140
    Switzerland **3:**296
    United Kingdom, the peoples of **3:**86
    Wales **3:**124, 128
Cenac, Winston (prime minister of St. Lucia) **5:**490
Centennial State (nickname for Colorado) **5:**318
Central Africa 1:42–44 *see also* names of countries
CENTRAL AFRICAN REPUBLIC 1:44, **245–50**
    illus.
        Bangui **1:**246
        cotton bales **1:**250
        farmer burning brush **1:**247
        flag **1:**xxiii
        mosque **1:**245
    map(s) **1:**249
CENTRAL AMERICA 6:1–8, **9–18** *see also* Latin America; names of countries
    Declaration of Independence **6:**38
    North America, geographical divisions of **5:**4
    Panama Canal **6:**78–79
    United States, relations with the **6:**12–13
    illus.
        children on donkeys **6:**9
        church interior **6:**14
        ethnic diversity **6:**11
        flags of the countries **6:**vi
        Pan-American Highway **6:**16
    map(s) **6:**4–5, 11
    table(s)
        countries **6:**16–17
Central America, United Provinces of (short-lived federation) **6:**16, 32, 41, 49, 58
Central American Common Market 6:18, 47
CENTRAL AND NORTH ASIA 2:341–45
    Asia, Central **2:**6–7, 27, 341, 343–45; **4:**316
    Asia, North **2:**7, 341–43, 345
Central Basin (region, Australia) **2:**483
Central Intelligence Agency, U.S. 6:13, 33, 320
Central Lowland (North America) **5:**268–69, 276, 290–91, 301, 303
    Minnesota **5:**287
    Ohio **5:**271
Central Lowlands (region, Scotland) **3:**133, 137–38
Central Plateau (region, Mexico) **5:**356–57, 363
Central Powers (Austria-Hungary, Bulgaria, Germany, Turkey) (World War I) **3:**324
Central Till Plain (North America) **5:**279
Central Valley (California) **5:**157, 334, 342, 346
Centre d'Art (Port-au-Prince, Haiti) **5:**465
Century plant *see* Maguey

Cephalonia (Greek island) **4:**190
Ceram (island, Indonesia) **2:**315
Cerezo Arévalo, Marco Vinicio (president of Guatemala) **6:**33
Cerrejón mine (Colombia) **6:**125
Cervantes Saavedra, Miguel de (Spanish author) **4:**92
Cesky Krumlov (Czech Republic)
  illus. **4:**227
Cestos River (west Africa) **1:**179
Ceuta (Spanish city, enclave in Morocco) **1:**74; **4:**86, 118
Ceylon *see* Sri Lanka
Cézanne, Paul (French painter) **3:**177
  illus.
    Mont Sainte-Victoire **3:**177
Chaamba (African people) **1:**25
Chacabuco (Chile) **6:**298, 321
Chaco (region, South America) **6:**241, 243–44, 250, 270, 280, 284
  Mennonites **6:**248
  illus.
    cattle raising **6:**247
Chaco War (1932–1935; Bolivia–Paraguay) **6:**241, 250
  Bolivian literature about **6:**237
CHAD 1:43, 44, **239–44**
  Libya **1:**100
  Sahara **1:**24
  illus.
    Aozou Strip **1:**243
    flag **1:**xxiii
    Fulani villager **1:**244
    N'Djamena **1:**240
    nomads **1:**239
    oasis **1:**242
  map(s) **1:**241
Chad, Lake (Africa) **1:**25, 240, 242, 244
  table(s)
    largest lakes **6:**347
Chaga (African people) **1:**334–35
Chagos Archipelago (Indian Ocean) **3:**90
Chagres River (Panama) **6:**78, 80
Chakmas (people) **2:**240
Chalcidice (peninsula, Greece) **4:**188, 198
Chalk cliffs
  Denmark **4:**10
  England **3:**100
Chambly Canal (Quebec) **5:**13
Chameleons 1:369
Chamonix (France) **3:**173, 304
  illus. **3:**151
Chamorro (people) **2:**569
Chamorro, Pedro Joaquín (Nicaraguan political figure) **6:**60
Chamorro, Violeta Barrios de (president of Nicaragua) **6:**60
  illus. **6:**59
Champa (kingdom in central Vietnam) **2:**302
Champagne (region, France) **3:**156, 163
Champagne Castle (mountain peak, South Africa) **1:**395
Champaign-Urbana (Illinois) **5:**282
Champlain, Lake (New York–Vermont) **5:**186, 202
Champlain, Samuel de (French explorer in America) **5:**109, 187, 206
  New Brunswick **5:**85
  Quebec City **5:**96, 101
Champlain Lowlands (New York–Vermont) **5:**202

Champs-Élysées, Avenue des (Paris, France) **3:**188, 195, 196
  illus. **3:**198
Chams (Asian people) **2:**295, 302
Chan Chan (ancient city, Peru) **6:**222
Chandler (Arizona) **5:**328
Chandni Chauk (street, Delhi, India) **2:**208
Changan (China) *see* Xian
Chang Jiang (river, China) *see* Yangtze River
Channel Islands (English Channel) **3:**8, 81, 87
Chanpasak (kingdom of Laos) **2:**285
Chao Phraya River (Thailand) **2:**274, 278
  illus. **2:**278
Chapala, Lake (Mexico) **5:**402, 409
Chapel Hill (North Carolina) **5:**228, 229
Chapman, Sydney (English geophysicist) **6:**333
Chapultepec (fortress, Mexico City) **5:**383
Chapultepec Park (Mexico City) **5:**411
Charcas (Bolivia) **6:**216
Chardzhou (Turkmenistan) **2:**357
Charing Cross (district, London) **3:**111
Chari River (central Africa) *see* Shari River
Charlemagne (Charles I; Charles the Great) (ruler of the Franks) **3:**181, 272
  Aachen (Germany) **3:**267
  Andorra **4:**121
  Austria, his *Ostmark* ("east mark") boundary **3:**308, 321
  Europe, history of **3:**50–51
  first emperor of Holy Roman Empire **4:**155
Charleroi (Belgium) **3:**219
Charles (archduke, Austria) **4:**284
Charles (Prince of Wales)
  illus. **3:**118; **5:**70
Charles, Mary Eugenia (prime minister of Dominica) **5:**488
Charles I (emperor of Austria, last of Habsburgs) **3:**325
Charles I (king of England) **3:**118, 119
Charles II (king of England)
  British North America **5:**96–97
  Canadian fur trade **5:**111, 117, 121
  Connecticut charter **5:**197
  granted Pennsylvania to William Penn **5:**214
Charles VII (king of France) **3:**183
Charles X (king of France) **3:**185
Charles IV (Charles of Luxembourg) (Holy Roman emperor, king of Germany and Bohemia) **4:**226, 229
Charles V (Holy Roman emperor) **3:**235; **4:**115
  Habsburg marriage plan **3:**321, 322
  Malta given to Knights of St. John of Jerusalem **4:**183
  Panama Canal route surveyed **6:**78
  Protestant Reformation **3:**56
  Venezuela grant to Welser banking house **6:**144
Charles VI (Holy Roman emperor) **3:**306, 323
Charles V (duke of Lorraine) **3:**323
Charles I (king of Spain) *see* Charles V (Holy Roman emperor)
Charles II (king of Spain) **4:**116
Charles IV (king of Spain) **4:**116
Charles V (king of Spain) **1:**97
Charles XII (king of Sweden) **4:**49
Charles XIV John (king of Sweden and Norway) **4:**49
Charles Bridge (Prague) **4:**229
Charles de Gaulle, Place (Place de l'Étoile) (Paris, France) **3:**195, 196
Charles Robert (Charles I) (Hungarian king) **4:**245

Charleston (capital, West Virginia) **5:**259
Charleston (South Carolina) **5:**230, 231, 232
  illus.
    historic waterfront **5:**230
Charlestown (Rhode Island) **5:**193
Charles University (Prague, Czech Republic) **4:**229
Charlotte (North Carolina) **5:**229
Charlotte Amalie (capital, U.S. Virgin Islands) **5:**172
  illus. **5:**172
Charlotte Pass (Australia) **6:**345
Charlottesville (Virginia) **5:**225
Charlottetown (capital, Prince Edward Island) **5:**88, 89
  illus.
    Confederation Room in Province House **5:**88
Charolais cattle 3:155
Charrúa (indigenous people of South America) **6:**252, 262
Charter 77 (Czechoslovakian human rights movement) **4:**230
Charter Oak (landmark, Hartford, Connecticut) **5:**197
  illus. **5:**197
Chartres (France) **3:**165
Château Frontenac (Quebec City)
  illus. **5:**99
Châteauneuf-du-Pape (France)
  illus. **3:**167
Chatham Islands (New Zealand) **2:**537, 543, 544, 550
Chattahoochee River (Alabama–Georgia) **5:**234, 235
Chattanooga (Tennessee) **5:**264
Chaucer, Geoffrey (English poet) **3:**88, 104, 118
  illus. **3:**89
Chaudhry, Mahendra (prime minister of Fiji) **2:**599
Chávez, Carlos (Mexican composer) **5:**373
Chávez, Hugo (president of Venezuela) **6:**115, 131, 148
Chavín (early civilization in the Andes) **6:**221, 222
Chavín de Huántar (Peru) **6:**221
Cheaha Mountain (Alabama) **5:**242
Chechnya (Russian republic) **2:**85; **3:**1, 64; **4:**324, 325
  illus.
    Grozny **4:**326
Checkpoint Charlie (entry point to East Berlin) **3:**281
Cheese
  France **3:**173
  Netherlands **3:**230–31
  Switzerland **3:**288
  Wisconsin, America's Dairyland **5:**286
  illus.
    Dutch market **3:**228
Cheetahs
  illus. **1:**40
Cheikh Anta Diop University (Dakar, Senegal) **1:**156
Cheju Island (South Korea) **2:**368, 435
Chemical industry 5:210
  Delaware **5:**216
  West Virginia **5:**259
Chenab (tributary of the Indus River) **2:**170, 183
Chenai (India) *see* Madras
Cheng Ch'eng-kung (Koxinga) (Chinese general) **2:**427

Chengchow (China) *see* Zhengzhou
Chenonceaux, Château of (France)
  illus. 3:181
Chen Shui-bian (president of Taiwan) 2:428
Cheops (king of Egypt) 1:110, 117
Chepo (Panama) 6:73
Cherbourg (France) 3:154, 164
Chernobyl nuclear reactor (Ukraine) 3:37;
  4:50, 332, 338, 340, 343
  illus.
    official closing 4:340
Cherokee (Indians of North America) 5:23, 165,
  221, 222, 242, 264
  Arkansas 5:257
  Georgia 5:234, 236
  North Carolina 5:227–28, 229
  Oklahoma 5:305, 306
  Texas 5:253
  Trail of Tears 5:174
Cherrapunji (India) 2:199
Chesapeake (Virginia) 5:226
Chesapeake Bay (U.S.) 5:153, 198, 215, 223
  Maryland 5:217, 218, 219
Cheshire Plain (England) 3:82
Chesterfield Inlet (settlement, Nunavut) 5:139
Chesterfield Islands (dependency of New
  Caledonia) 2:585
Chetniks (in Yugoslavian history) 4:280
Chetumal (capital, Quintana Roo, Mexico)
  5:422
Chevron (oil company) 2:349
Chewa (African people) 1:44, 278, 280
Cheyenne (capital, Wyoming) 5:316, 319, 320
Cheyenne (Indians of North America) 5:164,
  292, 301, 303, 311, 317
Chhattisgarh (state, India) 2:221
Chiang Ching-kuo (president of Taiwan) 2:428
Chiang Kai-shek (Jiang Jieshi) (president of
  Taiwan) 2:396–97, 428
Chiang Mai (Thailand) 2:279
CHIAPAS (state, Mexico) 5:30, 418
Chiapas-Guatemala Highlands 5:418, 419
Chibcha (indigenous people of Colombia) 6:90,
  97, 126
Chicago (Illinois) 5:46, 162, 282, 283
  illus. 5:283
    Buckingham Fountain 5:281
Chicago Board of Trade 5:283
Chicago Drainage Canal *see* Sanitary and Ship
  Canal
Chicago-Illinois River Canal *see* Sanitary and
  Ship Canal
Chicago of the North (nickname for Winnipeg)
  5:116
Chicago River (Illinois) 5:283
Chicanos (Southwest U.S. name for people of
  Mexican-American ancestry) 5:252
Chicha (alcoholic beverage) 6:212, 309
Chichén Itzá (ancient Mayan city, Mexico)
  5:377, 421
Chichewa language 1:279
Chichicastenango (Guatemala) 6:28
Chichimec Indians 5:401, 404, 415
Chickahominy (Indians of North America)
  5:224
Chickasaw (Indians of North America) 5:165,
  242, 246, 305
Chicle 5:358; 6:10, 29
Chicoutimi-Jonquière (Quebec) 5:101
Chiem, Lake (Germany) 3:244
Chignecto Bay (Canada) 5:79
Chignecto Isthmus (Canada) 5:90

Chihli, Gulf of (north China) 2:370
Chihuahua (capital, Chihuahua state, Mexico)
  5:393
CHIHUAHUA (state, Mexico) 5:27, 393
Chihuahua-Pacific Railroad 5:393
Children
  Africa 1:28, 29
  Canada's Far North population 5:138, 142
  Chinese education 2:404–5
  Germany's young people 3:248–49
  Jamaican children malnourished 5:472
  Japan 2:454–55, 456–57
  Nigeria 1:220
  United Kingdom, abolition of child labor in
    3:92
CHILE 6:302–23
  Allende Gossens, Salvador 6:320
  Andes 6:100–101
  Atacama acquired from Bolivia 6:241
  Easter Island 6:322–23
  economy 6:88, 102, 103, 104
  Euro-American culture 6:95, 96, 97
  Mercosur 6:262
  ozone hole 6:317
  Peru, relations with 6:226
  political history 6:114
  South American coastline 6:84
  illus.
    Andes 6:316
    Atacama Desert 6:84, 312
    copper mine 6:319
    copper smelting 6:104
    fishing industry 6:318
    flag 6:vi
    huaso (cowboy) 6:307
    Magellan, Strait of 6:317
    poncho market 6:310
    Santiago 6:311, 314
    sheep raising 6:318
    university students on bicycles 6:308
    Valparaíso 6:315
    Viña del Mar 6:315
    vineyard 6:304
    waterfall in the Andes 6:303
  map(s) 6:306
Chillon, Castle of (Switzerland) 3:295
Chilpancingo (capital, Guerrero, Mexico) 5:416
Chilpancingo, Congress of 5:412
Chiltern Hills (England) 3:82, 100
Chiluba, Frederick (president of Zambia) 1:276
Chimanimani (mountains, Zimbabwe) 1:356
Chimborazo (mountain, Ecuador) 6:193–94
Chimú (pre-Columbian civilization) 6:222
  illus.
    sculpture 6:222
Chin (Asian people) 2:259, 269
CHINA 2:377–422
  Albania, relations with 4:271, 273
  Asia, North 2:341
  border disputes 2:31
  Boxer Rebellion 2:24–25
  climate 2:369–70, 380–81
  early civilizations 2:373–74
  economy 2:34–35, 375, 376
  energy needs 2:37
  history, important dates in 2:420–21
  Hong Kong 2:410–11
  impact on Korean and Japanese civilizations
    2:372, 443
  India, relations with 2:228
  Japan, relations with 2:446

  Kashmir 2:173
  Korea 2:431, 433
  Lamaism 2:386–87
  landforms 2:368
  language 2:402
  Macau 2:416
  migration to Southeast Asia 2:254
  Ming dynasty 2:23
  Mongolia 2:362, 366
  nationalism 2:25–26
  people 2:371
  population 2:7
  population control 2:40
  Southeast Asia, relations with 2:255
  Taiwan 2:425–28
  urban growth 2:36
  Vietnam, history of 2:301, 302
  way of life 2:372
  Xinjiang 2:380–81
  Yangtze River 2:368–69
  Yellow River 2:370–71
  Yellow River Valley civilization 2:14–16
  illus.
    army in Hong Kong 2:410–11
    automobile industry 2:409
    Beijing 2:14
    Buddhist ceremony 2:388
    Communist wall poster 2:396
    construction 2:412
    demonstrations (1989) 2:28
    exercise group 2:393
    family-owned business 2:413
    flag 2:ix
    folk-dance troupe 2:407
    Great Wall of China 2:377
    Great Wall souvenir store 2:417
    Guangxi 2:382
    Guangzhou 2:401
    gymnasts 2:408
    horses in Inner Mongolia 2:382
    hospital 2:391
    kindergarten class 2:404
    Lamaist monastery 2:386
    population 2:384
    religious statues 2:389
    retailing 2:392
    rice growing 2:414
    rural housing 2:400
    scroll art 2:406
    Shanghai 2:367, 403
    sheep in Inner Mongolia 2:343
    steel industry 2:415
    terraced fields 2:382
    textile industry 2:415
    Tiananmen Square demonstrations 2:418
    tomb sculptures 2:394
    workers eating lunch 2:398
    Young Pioneers 2:399
  map(s) 2:379
    Yangtze River 2:368
    Yellow River 2:370
  table(s)
    dynasties and states 6:369
    important dates in history 2:420–21
China, People's Republic of (Communist) *see*
  China
China, Republic of *see* Taiwan
Chincha Islands (Peru) 6:213, 227
Chincoteague Bay (Maryland–Virginia) 5:217
Chindwin River (Myanmar) 2:267

Chinese (people) **2:**385–87
Asia, Southeast **2:**255, 258–59, 260, 275, 287
Australia **2:**495
Brunei **2:**329
Christmas Island **2:**488
Indonesia **2:**318
Jamaica **5:**474
Latin America **6:**95
Madagascar **1:**373
Malaysia **2:**305
Mauritius **1:**381
Myanmar **2:**268
New Zealand **2:**544
Philippines **2:**335
Singapore **2:**310
Taiwan **2:**424
United States **5:**169
Vancouver (Canada) **5:**131
Vietnam **2:**295, 296
illus.
dancers at Winnipeg's Folklorama **5:**116
Taiwanese children **2:**17
Chinese-Japanese War (1937–1945) **2:**447
Chinese languages 2:16, 28, 371, 395, 425
language reforms **2:**402
Vietnamese, influence on **2:**296
Chinese New Year 2:425
Ch'ing dynasty (China) *see* Manchu dynasty
Chingola (Zambia) **1:**272
Chin Hills (Myanmar–India) **2:**198, 266
Chinook (Indians of North America) **5:**164, 337, 340
Chinook winds 5:124, 125
Ch'in Shih-huang-ti (Chinese emperor)
illus. **2:**394
Chios (Greek island) **4:**191
Chipewyan (Indians of North America) **5:**121, 124, 125, 142
Chippewa (Indians of North America) *see* Ojibwa
Chirac, Jacques (president of France) **3:**191
Chiriquí (province, Panama) **6:**12, 74, 76
Chiriquí Lagoon (Panama) **6:**73
Chirripó Grande (mountain, Costa Rica) **6:**63
Chişinău (capital, Moldova) **4:**346
Chisos Mountains (Texas) **5:**251
Chissano, Joaquim (president of Mozambique)
1:368
Chita (Russia) **2:**343
Chitimacha (Indians of North America) **5:**222, 249
Chittagong (Bangladesh) **2:**238, 239
Chittagong Hills (Bangladesh) **2:**239, 240
Chitumbuka language 1:279
Chitungwiza (Zimbabwe) **1:**357
Chobe River (Africa) *see* Cuando River
Chocó (Indians of South America) **6:**75, 77
Chocolate 3:295; **5:**368–69
Choctaw (Indians of North America) **5:**165, 242, 245, 246, 305
Choibalsan (Mongolia) **2:**366
Choiseul (Solomon Islands) **2:**591
Cholera (disease) **6:**228
Cholon (Vietnam) **2:**295, 297
Choltitz, Dietrich von (German general)
3:192–93
Cholula (Puebla, Mexico) **5:**414
Cholula Pyramid (Puebla, Mexico) **5:**376, 414
Choluteca (Honduras) **6:**35
Choluteca River (Honduras) **6:**35
Chongjin (North Korea) **2:**431

Chongqing (Chungking) (China) **2:**369, 380, 403
Chopin, Frédéric (Polish composer) **4:**215
Choptank (Indians of North America) **5:**218
Choqueyapu River (South America) **6:**232
Chorotega (Indians of Central America) **6:**66
Choson (Land of Morning Calm) (Korean), or **Chosen** (Japanese) (name for Korea) **2:**433
Choson dynasty (Korea) **2:**437
Chou dynasty *see* Zhou (Chou) dynasty
Chowringhee (avenue, Calcutta, India) **2:**205
Chrétien, Jean (prime minister of Canada) **5:**76
Christchurch (New Zealand) **2:**540, 548, 553
Christian IV (king of Denmark) **4:**19
Christian Democratic Party (Italy) **4:**154, 162
Christian Democratic Union (German political party) **3:**284
Christianity *see also* Churches; Protestantism; Roman Catholic Church
Armenian Apostolic Church **2:**76
Armenia was first to adopt as state religion **2:**51
Asia **2:**19–20
Asia, East **2:**373
Asia, South **2:**169
Asia, Southeast **2:**260, 437
Asia, Southwest **2:**50
Belize **6:**22
Carthage **1:**91
China **2:**389–90
Coptic Church **1:**36, 108
England, history of **3:**112, 115
Ethiopian Christianity **1:**285
Europe, growth and influence in **3:**13, 48, 49, 54
Greece, early **4:**205
Haitian voodoo includes Christian elements **5:**464
icons **4:**262
India **2:**209
Ireland **3:**75
Japan **2:**444, 452
Jerusalem holy places **2:**46, 104
Lebanon **2:**100, 102
missionaries in Oceania **2:**603, 612
Northern Ireland **3:**147
North Korean persecution **2:**431
Philippines **2:**333, 335
Polynesia **2:**602
Rome, center of Christendom **4:**167
St. John the Evangelist on Patmos **4:**191
slavery **5:**434
Spain **4:**111–12, 113–14
Syria **2:**92, 94, 95
illus.
altar boy **1:**223
dignitaries **2:**46
Melanesia **2:**584
Samoan pastor and children **2:**607
Zimbabwean congregation **1:**359
Christiansborg Castle (governmental seat of Ghana) **1:**197
Christiansen, Ole Kirk (Danish toymaker) **4:**12
Christie, Perrie (prime minister of Bahamas) **5:**425
Christina River (Delaware) **5:**216
Christmas
Brazil **6:**179
Costa Rican bullfight **6:**67
Italy **4:**136
Japan **2:**452

Mexico **5:**366–67
Nuremberg's Christmas fair **3:**272
traditional German dinner **3:**250
Venezuela **6:**141
illus.
in Australia **2:**484
decorated tree **5:**44
Christmas Island (Indian Ocean) **2:**488
Christmas Island (Kiribati) **2:**580, 582
Christophe, Henry (king of Haiti) **5:**461, 469
Christ the Redeemer (sculpture) **6:**185
Christ the Redeemer, Cathedral of (Moscow, Russia) **4:**328
Chrysler Building (New York City) **5:**201
Chuang (Asian people) *see* Zhuang
Chuang-tzu (Daoist teacher) *see* Zhuangzi
Chuan Leekpai (prime minister of Thailand) **2:**280
Chubut River (Argentina) **6:**281
Chuche (North Korean policy) **2:**429
Chukchi (Asiatic people) **4:**309; **5:**60
Chukchi Peninsula (Russia) **4:**309
Chulalongkorn (Rama V) (king of Thailand) **2:**280
Chumash (Indians of North America) **5:**346
Chun Doo Hwan (president of South Korea) **2:**438
Chungking (China) *see* Chongqing
Chungyang (mountains, Taiwan) **2:**423
Chunnel *see* English Channel—tunnel
Chuquicamata (copper mine, Chile) **6:**312
illus. **6:**319
Chuquisaca (department, Bolivia) **6:**233
Chur (Switzerland) **3:**289
Churches *see also* Hagia Sophia
Brazilian architecture **6:**182
Bucharest (Romania) **4:**253
Chartres (France) **3:**165
Echmiadzin (Armenia) **2:**76
Ethiopian churches carved from solid rock **1:**288
French architecture **3:**177
Haitian cathedral murals **5:**465
Italy **4:**135, 143
Kremlin (Moscow, Russia) **4:**327, 328
Mexico **5:**399, 415
Nidaros Cathedral (Trondheim, Norway) **4:**33
Os Jeronimos (Lisbon, Portugal) **4:**71
Paraguay **6:**249
Rheims Cathedral **3:**163
St. Peter's Basilica **4:**180–81
St. Stephen's (Vienna) **3:**316
Seville (Spain) **4:**104
Temple of the Holy Family (Barcelona, Spain) **4:**102–3
illus.
Austria **3:**308
Brazzaville (Congo) **1:**256
Cartago (Costa Rica) **6:**65
Central American church interior **6:**14
Church of England in Australia **2:**495
Cologne Cathedral **3:**268
colonial New England architecture **5:**179
Colonia Tovar (Venezuela) **6:**133
Cuzco (Peru) **6:**213
Georgetown (Guyana) **6:**150
Gothic cathedral **3:**21
Granada (Nicaragua) **6:**51
Greece **4:**204
Guatemala City's cathedral **6:**31
Haitian cathedral murals **5:**466

Iceland **4:**1
Kiev (Ukraine) **4:**332
Latin America **6:**1
Lutheran cathedral (Helsinki) **4:**59
Lutheran church in Germany **3:**247
Madagascar **1:**373
Moscow (Russia) **4:**305
Norwegian stave church **4:**29
onion-domed church in Alaska **5:**348
Ronchamp (France) **3:**169
Sacré-Coeur (Paris, France) **3:**201
Sainte-Chapelle (Paris) **3:**194
San Francisco (Tlaxcala, Mexico) **5:**415
Spanish chapel in Coahuila, Mexico **5:**394
Spanish style in South America **6:**96
Tegucigalpa (Honduras) **6:**34
Temple of the Holy Family (Barcelona) **4:**103
Westminster Abbey (London, England) **3:**102
Churchill (Manitoba) **5:**115
illus. **5:**117
Churchill, Sir Winston (English statesman and author)
appeals for a Europe united against Communism **3:**3
Casablanca Conference (1943) **1:**74
quoted on Finland **4:**58
quoted on the English language **3:**113
quoted on Uganda **1:**316
Churchill Downs (Louisville, Kentucky) **5:**261, 262
Churchill River and Falls (Canada) **5:**81, 118
Church of England *see* England, Church of
Church of God **2:**581
Church of Jesus Christ of Latter-day Saints *see* Mormons
Chu River (Kyrgyzstan–Kazakhstan) **2:**353, 355
Churriguera, José (Spanish architect) **4:**98
Churún River (Venezuela) **6:**134
Chuuk (Truk) (state, Federated States of Micronesia) **2:**569, 570, 573, 574, 579
Cibao (region, Dominican Republic) **5:**454, 457
Cibele (fountain, Madrid, Spain) **4:**97
Ciboneys (Indians of South America) **5:**475
Cicero, Marcus Tullius (Roman orator and statesman) **4:**165
Cid, El (Spanish hero) **4:**113
Ciego de Ávila (Cuba) **5:**443
Ciller, Tansu (prime minister of Turkey) **2:**67
Cimarrones **5:**238
Cinchona bark **6:**121
Cincinnati (Ohio) **5:**48, 273
Cinco de Mayo (festival) **5:**345
Cinecittá (Italian moviemaking center) **4:**169
Cintra (Portugal) **4:**72
Circassians (people) **2:**59, 117–18
Circus Circus (hotel, Las Vegas, Nevada) **5:**332
Circuses
illus. **4:**315
Circus Maximus (ancient Rome) **4:**167
Ciskei (black state in South African history) **1:**58–59, 404
Citadel (fortress, Halifax, Nova Scotia) **5:**92
Citadel, The (military college, South Carolina) **5:**232
Citadelle Laferrière (fortress, Haiti) **5:**461
illus. **5:**461

Cities and city life *see also* articles on individual countries; names of major world cities
African cities **1:**30–31, 31, 63
Asia **2:**36, 46–47, 261–62
Australia **2:**473, 496
Canada's population center **5:**95, 97
China **2:**383, 401–3
Columbus, one of first planned cities in U.S. **5:**273
Egyptian urban life **1:**106–7
Europe **3:**21–24, 26, 44
garden-city, Tapiola (Finland) **4:**64
grid plan for Utah's cities **5:**324
Hammerfest (Norway) is northernmost city in world **4:**33
India, city life in **2:**202–5
Japan **2:**440, 442
Latin American migration to cities **6:**8, 104–5
Middle Atlantic States **5:**200
Monaco urban renewal **3:**205–6
North America's megalopolis areas **5:**46
Ohio's urban renewal **5:**274
Peruvian population **6:**211
Syria **2:**93
Teotihuacán **5:**413
U.S. urban clusters **5:**149, 152, 158, 163
Venezuela **6:**139
illus.
Mexico **5:**361, 384
table(s)
countries and capitals **6:**342–44
large cities of the world **6:**345
Citizenship
American Samoans not U.S. citizens **2:**603
Estonia **4:**294
Latvia **4:**298
City of Brotherly Love (Philadelphia, Pennsylvania) **5:**213
City of London (district, London, England) **3:**111
City-states
ancient Greece **3:**46; **4:**185, 198, 202–4
Hausa, in west Africa **1:**225, 226
Italy **4:**156–57
Mesopotamia **2:**51
Phoenicians in Lebanon **2:**99–100, 102
Ciudad Bolívar (Venezuela) **6:**135, 138, 147
Ciudad de Carmen (Campeche, Mexico) **5:**420
Ciudad Guayana (Venezuela) *see* Santo Tomé de Guayana
Ciudad Juárez (Chihuahua, Mexico) **5:**393
Ciudad Pemex (Tabasco, Mexico) **5:**419
Ciudad Trujillo (Dominican Republic) *see* Santo Domingo
Ciudad Victoria (capital, Tamaulipas, Mexico) **5:**396
Civilizations, Ancient *see* Ancient civilizations
Civil rights and liberties *see also* Religious freedom
American Indian Movement **5:**299
Argentina **6:**278, 300, 301
Asia **2:**30
Bill of Rights, English (1689) **3:**120
Black Americans **5:**175, 176
Central America **6:**18
Chile **6:**322
China, People's Republic of **2:**419
Europe **3:**26
Japan **2:**471
Korea, South **2:**438

Magna Carta **3:**117
Menchú, Rigoberta **6:**33
Nigerian abuses **1:**229
Northern Ireland **3:**148
Romania **4:**257
women in the U.S. **5:**175
Civil rights movement (in the United States) **5:**176, 222, 244, 267
Civil War, Chinese **2:**397
Civil War, English (1642–1649) **3:**119–20, 140–41
Civil War, Spanish (1936–1939) **4:**86, 117
Catalonia, Navarre, and Basque provinces **4:**89, 91
Italian intervention **4:**161
monument, Valley of the Fallen **4:**98
University of Madrid damage **4:**98
Civil War, U.S. (1861–1865)
Alabama **5:**244
Arkansas **5:**267
Bermudians as blockade runners **5:**33
Canadian soldiers **5:**75
cotton **5:**221
Georgia **5:**236
North Carolina **5:**229
South Carolina **5:**232
Southern States **5:**222
Tennessee **5:**264–65
Virginia **5:**226
Civil wars
Afghanistan **2:**174, 179
Africa **1:**43, 61
Angola **1:**341, 343, 344, 345, 346
Bangladesh **2:**243
Bosnia and Herzegovina **4:**288, 290
Cambodia **2:**287, 292
Chad **1:**44, 244
Colombia **6:**124, 128, 129
Congo, Democratic Republic of **1:**43, 270
Congo, Republic of **1:**260
Costa Rica **6:**70–71
El Salvador **6:**48–49, 50
Ethiopia **1:**292, 295, 296
European religious wars **3:**56
Georgia (republic) **2:**80, 85
Greece **4:**209
Guatemala **6:**33
Guinea-Bissau **1:**165
Italy **4:**161
Lebanon **2:**97, 100, 102, 103
Liberia **1:**178, 180, 181, 183
Mexico **5:**383, 386
Mozambique **1:**365–66, 368
Nicaragua **6:**51, 56, 58–60
Nigeria **1:**58, 228
Pakistan **2:**193, 228, 243
Portugal **4:**77
Rwanda **1:**324, 327
Sierra Leon **1:**173, 176, 177
Somalia **1:**300, 305
Sri Lanka **2:**250
Sudan **1:**128, 131
Tajikistan **2:**359, 360, 361
Wars of the Roses, England **3:**118–19
Yugoslavia **4:**274–75, 276, 281
illus.
Sierra Leone, victims of rebels in **1:**175
Clans and clan systems
African communities **1:**28, 29, 30–31
Bantu **1:**358
Congo, Democratic Republic of **1:**266

Clans and clan systems (cont.)
  Marshall Islands **2:**576
  Polynesian *ramages* **2:**601, 602
  Somalia **1:**300, 302, 303
  Tuvalu **2:**612
Clare Morison (novel, Spence) **2:**501
Clark, Helen (prime minister of New Zealand)
  illus. **2:**553
Clark, William (American explorer) *see* Lewis
  and Clark Expedition
Clark Air Force Base (Philippines) **2:**340
Clarke County (Georgia) **5:**235
Classes, social *see* Social classes
Claudius I (Roman emperor) **3:**113
Clavijero (Clavigero), Francisco Javier (Mexi-
  can historian) **5:**381
Clay tablets
  illus. **2:**50
Clemenceau, Georges (French statesman)
  3:187
Clement V (pope) **3:**181
Cleopatra VII (queen of Egypt) **1:**38, 119
Cleveland (Ohio) **5:**46, 273
Cleveland, Grover (22nd president of U.S.)
  5:354
Click languages 1:352
Cliff dwellings
  Arizona **5:**329
  illus.
    Georgia (republic) **2:**85
Climate *see also* articles on individual conti-
  nents, countries, and regions
  Antarctic studies **6:**336
  Arctic cold results from Earth's tilt **5:**55
  Colombia's climate affected by altitude **6:**117
  Ethiopia's climate determined by elevation
    1:283
  Galápagos Islands' mixture of climates **6:**202
  Great Lakes modify region's weather **5:**269,
    270
  Japan (Kuroshio) Current **5:**14
  Latin America's vertical climate **6:**3, 84
  map(s)
    world climates **6:**354
Clingmans Dome (mountain, Tennessee) **5:**263
Clinton, Bill (42nd president of the U.S.) **2:**422;
  3:95, 105; **5:**354
  Northern Ireland **3:**149
  illus. **5:**267; **6:**191
Clinton, George (governor of New York) **5:**206
Clitandre, Pierre (Haitian writer) **5:**466
Cloaca Maxima (ancient Roman sewer) **4:**165
Cloncurry (Australia) **6:**345
Clontarf, Battle of (1014) **3:**75
Clothing *see also* Hats
  Afghanistan **2:**177
  Algeria **1:**79–80
  Asia, Southeast **2:**263–64
  Bangladesh **2:**240–41
  Bhutan's compulsory national dress **2:**236
  Bolivia **6:**237
  buccaneers **5:**432
  Chilean huasos **6:**307
  Ecuador **6:**197
  Egypt **1:**103–4, 107
  French fashion industry **3:**158, 196
  Ghana **1:**198
  Greek traditional costume **4:**193
  Guatemalan Indians **6:**26
  Indo-American culture **6:**91
  Inuit **5:**21

Iran **2:**159
Italian fashion industry **4:**169
Jordan **2:**118
Kyrgyzstan **2:**354
Liberia **1:**181
Madagascar **1:**373
Malaysia **2:**306
Muslim women's veils **2:**38
Myanmar **2:**269
Nigeria **1:**220, 221, 222
Pakistan **2:**186
Paraguay **6:**246–47
Peru **6:**212
Philippines **2:**335–36
Saudi Arabia **2:**125
Somalia **1:**302
Sri Lanka **2:**248
Suriname **6:**155–56, 157, 158
Swaziland **1:**386
Turkey **2:**60
Turkmenistan **2:**357
Uygurs of Xinjiang **2:**381
Western Samoa **2:**608
Yemen **2:**134
illus.
  Asia, Southeast **2:**254
  Bhutan **2:**234
  Chilean ponchos **6:**310
  China, modern **2:**392
  German traditional costume **3:**239, 249
  Greek traditional costume **4:**193
  Japanese traditional costume **2:**452
  Muslim women **2:**191
  Myanmar **2:**265
  Panamanian dress **6:**77
  Syria **2:**92
  Welsh traditional costumes **3:**124
Clovis I (king of the Franks) **3:**180, 296
Cluj (Romania) **4:**253–54
Clutha River (New Zealand) **2:**539
Clwydian Range (Wales) **3:**122
Clyde River (Scotland) **3:**83, 133, 138
CN Tower (Toronto) **5:**108
Coahuayana River (Mexico) **5:**408
COAHUILA (state, Mexico) **5:**394
Coal
  Antarctica **6:**329
  Australia **2:**490, 520
  Canada **5:**123
  China **2:**383, 418
  Colombia **6:**125
  England **3:**102
  Europe **3:**36–37
  France **3:**157
  Germany **3:**244–45
  Kentucky **5:**260
  Mexico **5:**30
  Montana **5:**312
  Nigeria **1:**224
  Pennsylvania **5:**211, 213, 214
  South Africa **1:**402
  United Kingdom **3:**85
  United States **5:**160
  Wales **3:**123, 124, 128, 130
  West Virginia **5:**258, 259
  map(s)
    world production **6:**355
Coastal Lowland (region, New England) **5:**179
Coastal plains (North America) **5:**9, 12, 215,
  223, 237, 242, 263
  eastern coastal plain **5:**152–53

Georgia **5:**233
Mexico **5:**358
Middle Atlantic States **5:**198–99
Mississippi **5:**245
New Jersey **5:**207
Pennsylvania **5:**211
South-Central States **5:**256
Southern States **5:**220
Coast Mountains (Alaska–British Columbia) **5:**8,
  69, 129, 130
Coast Ranges (North America) **5:**69, 157, 334,
  336, 339, 342, 348–49
Coatimundi
  illus. **6:**89
Coatzacoalcos (Veracruz, Mexico) **5:**407
Cobble Hill (neighborhood, New York City)
  5:205
Cobequid Mountains (Nova Scotia) **5:**90
Coca-Cola 4:263, 271
Cocaine
  Colombia **6:**128–29
  Peru leads world in coca production **6:**220
  South American Indians chew coca leaves
    6:212, 237
Cochabamba (Bolivia) **6:**233–34
Cockpit Country (Jamaica) **5:**471, 476
Cockscomb Mountains (Belize) **6:**20
Coco, Isla del (island, Pacific Ocean) **6:**62
Coconuts 1:340; **2:**565
  illus. **2:**560
Coco River (Central America) **6:**35
Cocos Islands (formerly **Keeling Islands**)
  (Indian Ocean) **2:**488
Coelho Pereira, Duarte (Portuguese colonist)
  6:164
Coetzee, J. M. (South African author) **1:**401
Coffee
  Austrian cuisine **3:**323
  Brazil **6:**103, 173, 175, 184, 190
  Colombia **6:**102, 120, 123–24
  Costa Rica **6:**68–69
  El Salvador **6:**43, 45–46
  Ethiopia **1:**284, 286
  Haiti **5:**467
  Jamaica **5:**473
  Latin America **6:**12, 88
  Nicaragua **6:**55
  illus. **6:**102
    Brazil **6:**171
    Costa Rica **6:**68
    Guatemala **6:**13
    Kenya **1:**313
    New Caledonia **2:**584
Coffeehouses *see* Cafés
Cognac (France) **3:**156
Cohansey Aquifer (New Jersey) **5:**208
Coimbra (Portugal) **4:**71
Colbert, Edwin H. (American paleontologist)
  6:329
Colchis (ancient region, Caucasus) **2:**84
Cold War (international relations) **3:**62; **4:**323,
  325; **5:**176
  Africa, influence on **1:**1, 61
  Arctic development **5:**64
  Gorbachev's policies led to its end **3:**64
Cole, Thomas (American painter) **5:**204
Cole, USS **2:**135
Colima (capital, Colima state, Mexico) **5:**408
COLIMA (state, Mexico) **5:**408
Colima (volcano, Mexico) **5:**408
Colima Massif (Mexico) **5:**408
Colla (ancient Bolivian empire) **6:**239

Collective farms *see also* Kibbutz
Asia, East **2:**375
Cambodia **2:**290
China **2:**409
Czechoslovakian cooperatives **4:**229
East Germany **3:**260
Hungary **4:**243
Korea, North **2:**432
Laotians resisted **2:**284
Poland **4:**217, 222
Romania **4:**255
Russia, history of **4:**322
Tunisia **1:**90
Ukrainian famine (1930s) **4:**340
Collor de Mello, Fernando (president of Brazil)
6:191
Coloane (island, part of Macau) **2:**416
Cologne (Germany) **3:**241, 245, 266
illus. **3:**268
COLOMBIA 6:116–29
Afro-American culture **6:**91
Amazon River **6:**168
Andes **6:**100–101
cocaine crisis **6:**128–29
economy **6:**88, 102, 103
Indo-European culture **6:**89
land reform **6:**105
Panama, history of **6:**72, 78, 80
illus.
Bogotá **6:**117, 119, 122
flag **6:**vi
flower growing **6:**123
Marwamaque **6:**118
military surveillance of drug trade **6:**129
Sanctuary of the Virgin of Las Lajas **6:**121
Spanish architecture **6:**106
stone figures **6:**127
map(s) **6:**124
Colombo (capital, Sri Lanka) **2:**249
illus. **2:**245, 247
Colón (Panama) **6:**74, 77
Colonia (capital, Yap, Federated States of
Micronesia) **2:**573
Colonia (Uruguay) **6:**258, 261–62, 263
illus. **6:**264
Colonialism
Africa **1:**1, 11, 23, 36, 51, 57–58, 60
Asia **2:**24
Asia, Southeast **2:**264
Germany **3:**275
Colonial Williamsburg (restoration)
illus. **5:**226
Colonia Tovar (Venezuela)
illus. **6:**133
Colons (French-Algerians) **3:**190
COLORADO 5:38, **318–20**
illus.
Royal Gorge Bridge **5:**318
map(s) **5:**319
Colorado, Cerro (mountain, Panama) **6:**76
Colorado, Río (Argentina) **6:**285
Colorado Desert (California) **5:**342
Colorado Party (Paraguay) **6:**250
Colorado Piedmont (region, Colorado) **5:**318
Colorado Plateau (North America) **5:**156,
308–9, 310
canyons **5:**321, 323, 327
Colorado **5:**319
Colorado River (U.S.) **5:**8, 319, 323
California **5:**343
Grand Canyon **5:**309, 327

illus.
Grand Canyon **5:**12–13
table(s)
longest rivers of the world **6:**346
Colorado River Plateau (U.S.) **5:**7
Colorado Springs (Colorado) **5:**320
illus.
U.S. Air Force Academy Cadet Chapel
5:319
Coloreds *see* Coloureds
Colosseum (Roman arena) **4:**165, 167
illus. **4:**172
Colossi of Memnon (ruins, Thebes, Egypt)
1:111
Colossus of Rhodes 4:191
Coloureds (Coloreds) (people) **1:**58, 59, 348,
358, 398, 400, 404
Colt, Samuel (American inventor) **5:**196
Columbia (capital, South Carolina) **5:**231
Columbia (Maryland) **5:**218
Columbia (Missouri) **5:**296
Columbia Ice Field (Canada) **5:**123
Columbia Mountains (Canada) **5:**7
Columbia Plateau (U.S.) **5:**155, 309, 330, 333,
336
Oregon **5:**339
Washington (state) **5:**337
Columbia River (Canada–U.S.) **5:**336, 338, 339,
340
agriculture **5:**50
exploration **5:**39
gaps and passes **5:**8
Columbus (capital, Ohio) **5:**273
illus. **5:**271
Columbus (Georgia) **5:**235
Columbus, Christopher (discoverer of America)
3:55; **5:**173; **6:**6
Antigua and Barbuda **5:**494
Barcelona, scene of return from first voyage
4:102
Caribbean exploration and discovery **5:**428–
29, 430, 496
Central America **6:**15
Cuba **5:**441, 444
Genoa (Italy), birthplace **4:**147
Grenada **5:**482
Guianas **6:**153
Hispaniola **5:**455, 467
Honduras **6:**34, 41
Jamaica **5:**471
misidentification of Native Americans **5:**1
New World discovered for Spain **4:**114
Orinoco River **6:**82, 147
possible burial place, Seville (Spain) **4:**104
Puerto Rico **5:**166, 167
San Salvador (Bahamas) **5:**423
tomb in Santo Domingo (Dominican Repub-
lic) **5:**456
Venezuela **6:**131, 144
illus.
statue in Nassau (Bahamas) **5:**423
Columbus, Diego (son of Christopher Colum-
bus and governor of Hispaniola) **5:**455
Colvin, Marta (Chilean sculptor) **6:**310
Comanche (Indians of North America) **5:**253,
292, 303, 319, 320
Comayagua (Honduras) **6:**35
COMECON *see* Council for Mutual Economic
Assistance
Comédie-Française 3:178
Comino (island, Malta) *see* Kemmuna
Cominotto (island, Malta) *see* Kemmunett

Common Market *see* CARICOM; Central
American Common Market; European Eco-
nomic Community; European Union; Mer-
cosur
Commons, House of (British Parliament) **3:**96
Commons, House of (Canadian Parliament)
illus. **5:**74
Commonwealth, English (1649–1660) **6:**361
Commonwealth of Independent States 2:345;
4:341
troops on Tajik-Afghan border **2:**361
Commonwealth of Nations 3:94 *see also*
United Kingdom; names of individual mem-
bers and dependencies
Australia **2:**474, 479, 501
Canada **5:**70
New Zealand **2:**474, 479
Nigeria's suspension from **1:**229
Zimbabwe's suspension from **1:**362
Commonwealth Trans-Antarctic Expedition
(1957–1958) **6:**334
Communes (in People's Republic of China)
2:391, 409, 413
Communication satellites 5:136, 140
Communism
Albania **4:**271, 273
Asia **2:**29, 35
Asia, East **2:**375
Bulgaria **4:**261, 264
Cambodia **2:**286, 292
China **2:**397–400
Chinese economy **2:**409, 412–15, 417–18
Chinese society **2:**400–408
Cuba **5:**449
Czechoslovakia **4:**230–31
Ethiopia **1:**290, 291
Europe **3:**1, 3, 12, 59, 62, 63–64
Greece **4:**209
Guevara, Ernesto (Ché) **6:**240
Hungary **4:**239, 243, 246–47
Indonesia **2:**325
Laos **2:**285
Lenin **4:**322
manufacturing systems **3:**40
Marx, Karl **3:**254
Mongolia **2:**366
Philippines **2:**331, 338, 340
Poland **4:**217, 218, 222–23
religion discouraged in China **2:**390
Romania **4:**255, 256–57
Russian Revolution **4:**321–22
San Marino **4:**175
Vietnam **2:**301
Yugoslavia **4:**279, 280
Communism, Mount (Tajikistan) **2:**359
Communist Party, Chinese 2:396–97, 419, 422
Communist Party, French 3:189
Communist Party, Italian 4:154
Communist Party, Romanian 4:256
Communist Party, Tajik 2:361
Communist Party of the Soviet Union 4:310
Como, Lake (Italy) **4:**128, 133
illus. **3:**1; **4:**128
Comodoro Rivadavia (Argentina) **6:**283
Comoé River (west Africa) **1:**186
Comoran language 1:384
Como River (Gabon) **1:**252, 254
COMOROS 1:48, **383–84**
illus.
flag **1:**xxiv
Moroni **1:**383
map(s) **1:**384

Compaore, Blaise (government leader of Burkina Faso) **1:**193

Compton, Sir John (prime minister of St. Lucia) **5:**490

Computers 3:210 *see also* Information technology; Internet
illus.
    Costa Rica **6:**68
    India **2:**220
    industry **5:**51
    Inuit among most computer-literate **5:**58
    South America **6:**109
    United States **5:**175

Comstock Lode (Nevada) **5:**332

Conakry (capital, Guinea) **1:**167–68, 169
illus. **1:**166

Conca d'Oro (plain, Palermo, Italy) **4:**146

Concentration camps 2:431; **3:**61, 278; **4:**300, 343
illus.
    Dachau **3:**278
    Latvian memorial **4:**299

Concepción (Chile) **6:**315–16

Concepción (Paraguay) **6:**244

Concepción del Oro (Zacatecas, Mexico) **5:**399

Concord (capital, New Hampshire) **5:**185

Concord (Massachusetts) **5:**190

Concordat of 1801 3:185, 187

Concorde (supersonic airliner) **3:**42, 162

Concorde, Place de la (Paris, France) **3:**195
illus. **3:**196

Condorcanqui, José Gabriel (Indian chief) **6:**225

Condors 6:231

Confederate States of America (during U.S. Civil War, 1861–1865) **5:**242, 244

Confederate White House 5:225

Confederation Bridge (Prince Edward Island–New Brunswick, Canada)
illus. **5:**22

Confederation Centre of the Arts (Prince Edward Island) **5:**88

Confederation of Canada *see* Canadian Confederation

Confederation of the Rhine (1806–1815, association of German states) **3:**306

Confucianism 2:15, 372, 373
    China **2:**19, 388–89, 395, 420
    Japan **2:**452
    Korea **2:**436, 437
illus.
    Taiwan **2:**373, 425

Congaree River (South Carolina) **5:**231

CONGO, DEMOCRATIC REPUBLIC OF (Zaïre) **1:**42–43, 261–70; **3:**223
    Congo Crisis **1:**269
    ferry service to Brazzaville **1:**256
    First World War of Africa **1:**270
    Rwanda backs rebels **1:**327
    Rwandans in refugee camps **1:**325
    Ugandan troops in **1:**323
illus.
    Congo River **1:**264
    ferry crossing Congo River **1:**269
    flag **1:**xxiii
    Kinshasa **1:**265
    Kivu Falls **1:**261
    Mount Nyiragongo eruption **1:**267
    pelicans **1:**263
    rain forest **1:**17
map(s) **1:**262

Congo, People's Republic of *see* Congo, Republic of

CONGO, REPUBLIC OF 1:43–44, **256–60**
illus.
    Brazzaville **1:**256
    flag **1:**xxiii
    Pointe-Noire **1:**259
map(s) **1:**257

Congo Crisis (1960–1963) **1:**269

Congo Free State (former African state) **1:**269; **3:**223

Congonhas (Brazil) **6:**187

Congo River (Africa) **1:**42–43, 257
    Angola **1:**342
    Central African Empire **1:**246
    Congo, Democratic Republic of **1:**262, 268
illus. **1:**264
table(s)
    longest rivers of the world **6:**346

Congress of Vienna *see* Vienna, Congress of

Congress Party (India) **2:**218

CONNECTICUT 5:195–97
illus. **5:**195
map(s) **5:**196

Connecticut River and Valley (U.S.) **5:**179, 184, 195, 196, 197
    Massachusetts **5:**189

Conquistadores (Spanish and Portuguese soldiers) **6:**82, 90
    Aztec civilization's overthrow **5:**25
    Incas, conquest of **6:**224
    Nicaragua **6:**58
    Spanish character traits **4:**92

Conroy, Pat (American writer) **5:**235

Conservative Party (Great Britain) **3:**95, 96

Constance, Lake of (central Europe) **3:**286, 295
    Alps **3:**243, 304, 312
    Rhine River **3:**244

Constanţa (Romania) **4:**254, 255

Constantine (Algeria) **1:**77, 80

Constantine, Basilica of (Rome, Italy) **4:**172

Constantine I (Greek king) **4:**207, 208

Constantine II (Greek king) **4:**210

Constantine I (Roman and Byzantine emperor) *see* Constantine the Great

Constantinescu, Emil (president of Romania) **4:**257

Constantine the Great (Constantine I) (Roman and Byzantine emperor) **3:**48, 321
    Byzantium became Constantinople **4:**205
    Christian era in Egypt **1:**119
    Christianity made a state religion **2:**50
    Jerusalem **2:**46
    Niš (Yugoslavia), birthplace **4:**277
    Saint Peter's Basilica **4:**181

Constantinople (Byzantium) (now Istanbul) **4:**186, 187 *see also* Byzantium; Istanbul
    Catalán seapower against the Turks **4:**113
    Europe, history of **3:**53, 54
    Hagia Sophia, church and museum **2:**22
    Napoleon's comment **2:**56
    Ottoman Empire **2:**57, 61–62, 64; **4:**205–6, 208
    Russia, history of **4:**320

Constantinople Convention (1888) **1:**121

Constellation (U.S. Navy's first ship) **5:**219

Constitution (American warship) **5:**190

Constitution, U.S. *see* United States Constitution

Constitutional Act (Canada, 1791) **5:**109

Constitutions
    Argentina **6:**298–99
    China, People's Republic of **2:**418–19
    Italy **4:**154
    Japan **2:**471
    Korea, South **2:**438
    Mexico (1857) **5:**383
    Mexico (1917) **5:**385–86, 386–87, 403
    Mongolia **2:**366
    Philippines **2:**338
    Portugal **4:**78
    United States *see* United States Constitution
    Uruguay **6:**265
    Venezuela, presidential power in **6:**148

Constitution State (nickname for Connecticut) **5:**195

Construction *see* Architecture

Conté, Lansana (president of Guinea) **1:**170

Continental Congress (U.S. history) **5:**174

Continental Divide 5:155, 310; **6:**78, 79

Continents
    continental islands, Oceania **2:**559
    Europe and Asia, as Eurasia **3:**5
table(s)
    area and population **6:**344
    extremes **6:**345

Contras (Nicaraguan guerrillas) **6:**18, 54, 56, 60

Coober Pedy (South Australia, Australia) **2:**523

Cook, James (English navigator) **2:**478, 485, 499, 586
    Antarctic regions **6:**330
    Australia **2:**506, 508, 512, 519
    British Columbia **5:**131
    Hawaii **5:**354
    New Zealand **2:**552
    Tonga **2:**604, 605

Cook, Mount (New Zealand) **2:**539

Cooking *see* Cuisine

Cook Inlet (Alaska) **5:**350

Cook Islands (Pacific Ocean) **2:**560–61, 567, 601, 603

Cook Strait (New Zealand) **2:**546

Cooperatives 2:109, 110–11, 262; **4:**11 *see also* Collective farms

Coosa River (Alabama) **5:**6

Copacabana Beach (Rio de Janeiro)
illus. **6:**186

Copán (Honduras) **6:**14, 40
illus. **6:**40

Copenhagen (capital, Denmark) **4:**10, 13, 16, 20
illus.
    Amalienborg **4:**19
    canal **4:**18
    Tivoli Gardens **4:**18

Copernicus, Nicolaus (Polish astronomer) **4:**216–17

Copiapó River (Chile) **6:**313

Coppename River (Suriname) **6:**154

Copper 5:30
    Africa **1:**5, 20
    Arizona **5:**160
    Chile **6:**102, 312, 318–19
    Cyprus **2:**71
    Montana **5:**312
    North America **5:**9
    Panama **6:**76–77
    South America **6:**103
    Uganda **1:**321
    Zambia **1:**274, 275
illus.

Chilean mine **6**:319
Chilean smelting **6**:104
ingots **1**:274
strip-mine in Australia **2**:489
map(s)
world production **6**:355
Copper Age (period of human culture) **4**:242
Copper Canyon (Mexico) **5**:393
Coppermine (Canada) **5**:135
Copşa Mică (Romania)
illus. **4**:254
Coptic Church 1:36, 108
Coptic language 1:109
Coquí (frog, symbol of Puerto Rico) **5**:167
Coquimbo (Chile) **6**:313
Coral 2:506, 560, 610; **5**:358
Hawaii **5**:354
illus. **2**:506, 583
Australian reef **2**:485
Coral Sea Islands (Pacific Ocean) **2**:488
Corcovado (mountain peak, Rio de Janeiro, Brazil) **6**:185
Cordero Rivadeneira, León Febes (president of Ecuador) **6**:205
Cordillera (group of mountain systems) **5**:7, 38
see also names of systems, as Andes
Cordillera Central (Andes) **6**:116, 120, 123
Cordillera Central (Panama) **6**:72
Cordillera Occidental (Andes) **6**:116, 230
Cordillera Oriental (Andes) **6**:116, 119, 121, 123, 125, 126, 230
Cordilleras, Central, Oriental, and Setentrional (Dominican Republic) **5**:454
Cordilleras Oriental, Central, and Occidental (Peru) **6**:208
Córdoba (Argentina) **6**:278, 280, 292, 297
Córdoba (province, Argentina) **6**:266, 285
Córdoba (Spain) **4**:109, 113
Córdoba (Veracruz, Mexico) **5**:407
Córdoba, Francisco Hernández de (Spanish explorer) **5**:420
Córdoba, Sierra de (mountains, Argentina) **6**:292
Cordobes, El (Spanish matador) **4**:93
Corfu (Greek island) **4**:190
illus. **4**:210
Corinth (Greece) **4**:199, 205
illus. **4**:203
Corinth, Gulf of (Mediterranean Sea) **4**:188, 198
Corinth Canal (Greece) **4**:188
illus. **4**:186
Corinto (Nicaragua) **6**:55, 56, 57
Corisco (island, Equatorial Guinea) **1**:235
Cork (botany) **4**:67
illus. **4**:108
Cork (Ireland) **3**:69, 73, 75
illus. **3**:74
Corn (Maize) 5:30
American Indians **5**:24
Mexico **5**:355, 361, 368
Midwestern states **5**:47
South Africa **1**:401
South America **6**:91
illus. **5**:43, 302
map(s)
world production **6**:355
Corn belt (region, U.S.) **5**:291
Corneille, Pierre (French playwright) **3**:178
Corner Brook (Newfoundland) **5**:83
Cornish (people) **3**:86
Corno Grande (mountain, Italy) **4**:126

Cornwall (county, England) **3**:114
illus. **3**:99
Tintagel Castle **3**:115
Coromandel Peninsula (New Zealand) **2**:538
Coronado, Francisco (Spanish explorer) **5**:173; **5**:392
Coronado, Juan (Spanish conquistador) **6**:64
Corot, Jean Baptiste Camille (French painter) **3**:167, 177
Corpus Christi Day (June 10) **6**:141
Correa, Julio (Paraguayan author) **6**:249
Corrientes (Argentina) **6**:284
Corrientes (province, Argentina) **6**:271, 280, 284
Corsica (island in Tyrrhenian Sea) **3**:8, 28, 167; **4**:125
Cortés, Hernán (Spanish conqueror of Mexico) **5**:377, 380, 407, 422, 445
Baja Peninsula **5**:391
Mexico City **5**:410
Tlaxcalan Indians **5**:415
illus. **5**:379
Cortés Palace (Cuernavaca, Mexico) **5**:412
illus. **5**:412
Cortez, Sea of *see* California, Gulf of
Corubal River (west Africa) **1**:164
Cossacks (Slavic adventurers) **4**:339; **5**:62
Costa, Cordillera de la (mountains, Chile) **6**:313, 316
Costa, Lúcio (Brazilian architect) **6**:182, 184
Costa Brava (Spain) **3**:41; **4**:107
Costa del Sol (resort area, Spain) **3**:41; **4**:109
illus. **4**:85
Costa do Sol (resort area, Portugal) **4**:72
Costa Norte (region, Honduras) **6**:35, 36, 38
COSTA RICA 6:61–71
Central America **6**:9
democracy **6**:17
economy **6**:14
history **6**:16, 18
land ownership **6**:13
population **6**:7, 11
illus.
banana harvest **6**:69
Cartago **6**:65
coffee plantation **6**:68
cruise ship **6**:64
decorated oxcart **6**:67
flag **6**:vi
Guanacaste Woodland **6**:63
San José **6**:61, 64
schoolchildren **6**:12, 68
train on jungle route **6**:62
map(s) **6**:66
Costineşti (Romania) **4**:254
Costume *see* Clothing
Côte d'Azur (Azure Coast) (France) *see* Riviera
Cotini (Celtic tribe) **4**:225
Cotonou (Benin) **1**:212, 214
Cotopaxi (volcano in the Andes) **6**:193
Cotswold Hills (England) **3**:82, 100
Cotton
Brazil **6**:175
Chad **1**:243
China is world's largest producer **2**:417
early American economy **5**:221
Georgia (state) **5**:236
Mexico **5**:361–62
Nicaragua **6**:55
Turkmenistan **2**:358
Uzbekistan **2**:352

illus.
Alabama **5**:244
Egypt **1**:116
harvesting **6**:57
shipment **1**:250
Couffo River (Benin) **1**:211
Council for Mutual Economic Assistance (COMECON) 3:63
Council of Europe 3:3, 62
Germany **3**:283
Strasbourg headquarters **3**:161
Counter-Reformation (16th century; in Roman Catholic Church) **3**:56, 310
Countries of the world
table(s)
capitals, largest cities, and areas **6**:342–44
Country Music Hall of Fame (Nashville, Tennessee) **5**:265
Courantyne River (Suriname) **6**:154
Courchevel (France) **3**:173
Courtrai (Belgium) **3**:219
Coushatta (Indians of North America) **5**:253
Covadonga (Spain) **4**:113
Coveñas (Colombia) **6**:121
Covered bridges
illus. **5**:186
Cowboys
Chilean huasos **6**:305, 307–8
gauchos **6**:253, 255, 269, 273–75
Venezuelan llaneros **6**:138–39
illus.
Chilean huasos **6**:307
gauchos **6**:259, 275
Kazakhstan **2**:348
Paraguay **6**:247
Saskatchewan rodeo rider **5**:121
Venezuela **6**:132
Cows *see* Cattle
Cozumel (island, Mexico) **5**:358, 422
Crabeater seals 6:328
Cracow (Poland) **4**:213, 216–17
illus. **4**:216
Cradle of Liberty (Philadelphia, Pennsylvania) **5**:213
Crafts *see* Handicrafts
Craiova (Romania) **4**:252
Cranach the Elder, Lucas (German artist) **3**:255
Crans (Switzerland) **3**:289
Cranston (Rhode Island) **5**:194
Crater Lake (Oregon) **5**:339
Crater of Diamonds State Park (Arkansas) **5**:267
Craters of the Moon National Monument (Idaho) **5**:314
Crazy Horse (Sioux chief) **5**:299
Crazy Horse Memorial (South Dakota) **5**:300
Crécy, Battle of (1346, Hundred Years' War) **3**:182
Cree (Indians of North America) **5**:95, 105, 109
Plains Indians of the U.S **5**:164, 298
Prairie Provinces of Canada **5**:111, 117, 121, 124, 125
Quebec **5**:99
Riel rebellions **5**:112
Creek (Indians of North America) **5**:23, 165, 221, 234, 236, 242, 305
Creole (French dialect)
Africa **1**:339, 378
Caribbean islands **5**:435
Haiti **5**:464, 466

Creoles (people) **6:**15
    Belize **6:**20–21, 22
    Cuba, colonial-born Spaniards **5:**445
    French Guiana **6:**92
    Louisiana **5:**247
    Mauritius **1:**381
    Sierra Leone **1:**55, 173, 174, 175–76
    Suriname **6:**155–56
    Venezuela **6:**146
Cresson, Edith (prime minister of France) **3:**190
Crete 3:45; **4:**187, 192, 201
    illus. **4:**192, 201
Crete, Sea of 4:187
Cricket (sport) **3:**104
    illus. **2:**544; **3:**107
Crickets (insects) **5:**325
Crime
    Colombia **6:**120, 129
    Moscow **4:**329
    Palermo (Sicily) **4:**146
    Russia **4:**318
Crimea (peninsula, Ukraine) **4:**336–37
    illus. **4:**336
Crimean Mountains (Ukraine) **4:**333
Crimean War (1854–1856)
    France and Italy **3:**186; **4:**158
    some Finns fought for Britain **4:**56
Criollos (Latin-Americans of Spanish descent)
    6:70, 97–98
    Argentina **6:**270
    Bolivia **6:**236
    Mexico **5:**382
    Peru **6:**224, 225
Cristal, Sierra del (mountains, Cuba) **5:**442
Cristóbal (Panama) **6:**74, 78
CROATIA 3:1, 2; **4:**285–87
    ethnic wars **4:**275, 280, 281
    World War II **4:**280
    illus.
        Dubrovnik **4:**285
        flag **4:**vi
    map(s) **4:**286
Croatian language 4:286
Croats (people) **4:**277, 280, 286, 287
    Bosnia and Herzegovina **4:**288, 289
Crocker Mountains (north Borneo) **2:**304
Crockett, Davy (American frontiersman) **5:**252,
    264
Crocodile River (Africa) *see* Limpopo River
Crocodiles
    illus. **1:**41; **5:**163
Cromwell, Oliver (Lord Protector of England)
    3:76, 120
Crow (Indians of North America) **5:**311, 312,
    317
Crowe, Russell (Australian actor)
    illus. **2:**498
Crown colonies (British) *see* United Kingdom
    Overseas Territories
Crown dependencies (United Kingdom) **3:**84,
    87, 90 *see also* United Kingdom Overseas
    Territories
Crowsnest Pass (British Columbia–Alberta) **5:**8
Cruces River (Chile) **6:**316
Crusades (expeditions to the Holy Land, 1096–
    1291) **3:**53, 54
    Bulgaria, Roman road to Holy Land **4:**258
    Byzantine lands annexed **4:**205
    Crusader castles in Lebanon **2:**98
    Cyprus **2:**72
    Italian cuisine, influences on **4:**136

Lebanon **2:**102
Muslim world **2:**51
Rhodes **4:**191
Saladin, Muslim ruler in Egypt **1:**119
Syria **2:**95
illus. **4:**207
Crystal glassware 3:157
    illus. **3:**71; **4:**43
Crystal Mountains (west coast of Africa) **1:**235
Cserhát (mountains, Hungary) **4:**237
Cuando River (Chobe River) (Africa) **1:**353
Cuauhtémoc (Aztec chief) **5:**380
CUBA 5:426, 427, 428, 433, 438, **441–52**
    Angola **1:**346
    immigration to Puerto Rico **5:**167
    Organization of American States **6:**110
    Spanish language and culture **5:**435
    United States, history of **5:**440
    illus.
        flag **5:**vi
        Havana **5:**441, 445, 446
        seventh-grade class **5:**447
        tobacco farm **5:**442
        tourist resort **5:**449
    map(s) **5:**443
    table(s)
        largest islands of the world **6:**346
Cubagua Island (Caribbean Sea) **6:**144
Cuban-Americans 5:239
Cubango River (Africa) *see* Okavango River
Cubas Grau, Raúl (president of Paraguay)
    6:250
Cubism 3:177
Cuchulain (legendary Irish hero) **3:**70
Cuckoo clocks 3:258
    illus. **3:**258
Cúcuta (Colombia) **6:**121
Cuenca (Ecuador) **6:**196
Cuernavaca (Morelos, Mexico) **5:**412
Cuevas, José Luis (Mexican artist) **5:**372
Cuisine
    Algeria **1:**80
    Argentina **6:**268, 274, 289
    Asia, Southeast **2:**263
    Austria **3:**310–11, 323
    Belgium **3:**215
    Botswana **1:**352
    Brazil **6:**93, 183–84
    Bulgaria **4:**263
    Central African Republic **1:**248
    Chad **1:**241
    Chile **6:**309
    Costa Rica **6:**65–66
    Czech Republic **4:**226
    Denmark **4:**15
    Dominican Republic **5:**457
    Ecuador **6:**199
    El Salvador **6:**45
    Finland **4:**62
    France **3:**162, 173
    Georgia (republic) **2:**82
    Germany **3:**250, 271
    Guatemalan Indians **6:**27
    Honduras **6:**38
    Hungary **4:**240
    India **2:**201, 202
    Iran **2:**158
    Iraqi diet **2:**150
    Israel **2:**107
    Italy **4:**136–38, 170
    Japan **2:**456

Jordan **2:**119
Korea **2:**431
Madagascar **1:**373
Malaysia **2:**306
Mexico **5:**368–69
Morocco **1:**68–69
Nicaragua **6:**55
Pakistan **2:**185–86
Paraguay **6:**247
Peru **6:**215–16
Poland **4:**217
Portugal **4:**69
Romania **4:**252–53
Slovenia **4:**283
Spain **4:**94
Sri Lanka **2:**248
Sudan **1:**128
Sweden **4:**42
Switzerland **3:**290
Thailand **2:**276
Tunisia **1:**88
Turkey **2:**60–61
Ukraine **4:**335–36
Uruguay **6:**256
Venezuela **6:**142
Western Samoa **2:**608
illus.
    Chinese workers' lunch **2:**398
    German marzipan confections **3:**267
    Greek Easter breads **4:**194
    Italian **4:**137
    Japanese meal **2:**453
    Togo bakery **1:**205
    Venezuela **6:**139
Cuitlahuac (Aztec chief) **5:**380
Cuitzeo, Lake (Mexico) **5:**409
Cul-de-Sac plain (Haiti) **5:**462
Culebra Cut *see* Gaillard Cut
Culiacán (capital, Sinaloa, Mexico) **5:**397
Culiacán River (Mexico) **5:**397
Cultural Revolution (1966–1969, China) **2:**390,
    398–99, 403, 405, 407, 412
Cumaná (Venezuela) **6:**144
Cumberland Falls (waterfall, Kentucky) **5:**260
Cumberland Gap (passageway through Appala-
    chian Mountains) **5:**224, 257, 260, 262
    illus. **5:**256
Cumberland Mountains (U.S.) **5:**156
Cumberland National Seashore (Georgia)
    5:234
    illus. **5:**233
Cumberland Plateau (U.S.) **5:**6
Cumberland River (U.S.) **5:**263
Cuna (Indians of South America) **6:**74, 75, 77
Cundinamarca basin (Colombia) **6:**125
Cuneiform (ancient writing system) **2:**11–12, 48,
    153
    illus. **2:**12
Cunene River (Namibia) **1:**348, 350
Curaçao (island, West Indies) **3:**235
    map(s) **5:**429
Curepipe (Mauritius) **1:**379
Curie, Marie (Polish-French scientist) **4:**216
Curling (sport)
    illus. **5:**69
Cuscus (animal) **2:**487
Cush (Kush) (early African kingdom) **1:**33, 127,
    130
Cushites (African peoples) **1:**36, 321, 322
    language **1:**15, 285
Custer's Last Stand *see* Little Bighorn, Battle of
Cutuco (El Salvador) **6:**44

Cuyuna Mountains (North America) **5**:4
Cuyutlán (Colima, Mexico) **5**:408
Cuzco (Peru) **6**:213, 216, 219, 224
arts center **6**:214
Inca capital **6**:222
illus. **6**:213, 219
Cwezi (kings of Kitara, early kingdom in Africa) **1**:322
Cyclades (Greek islands) **4**:187, 190
illus. **3**:46
Cyclones 2:239, 534, 535, 592
Cymraeg language *see* Welsh language
Cynulliad Cenedlaethol i Gymru *see* National Assembly for Wales
Cypress (tree)
illus. **5**:1
Cypress Gardens (South Carolina) **5**:232
Cyprian, Saint (Christian martyr) **1**:91
Cypriots (people) **2**:68, 69–70, 73
CYPRUS 2:67, **68–73**; **3**:2; **4**:209–10
illus.
apartment buildings **2**:71
flag **2**:vii
icon painting **2**:69
Nicosia **2**:68
ruins **2**:72
United Nations troops **2**:73
map(s) **2**:70
Cyrenaica (region, Libya) **1**:94, 95, 97, 99
Cyril, Saint (missionary to the Slavs) **4**:265
Cyrus the Great (king of the Medes and Persians) **2**:49, 162
Czar (title of Russian rulers) **4**:320
Czech language 4:225
Czechoslovakia (1918–1992) **4**:224, 230–31
Germans **3**:279, 282
Prague Spring **3**:63
Ukraine, history of **4**:332
World War II **3**:277
illus.
Prague Spring **4**:230
"Velvet Revolution" **4**:231
CZECH REPUBLIC 3:2, 25; **4**:**224–31**
nuclear power **3**:37
illus.
Cesky Krumlov **4**:227
flag **4**:v
Prague **4**:224, 228
map(s) **4**:226
Czechs (Slavic people) **4**:225, 230, 231, 233, 234
Częstochowa, Miracle of (Polish history) **4**:220

• • • D • • •

Dacca (Bangladesh) *see* Dhaka
Dachau (Germany)
illus.
concencentration-camp site **3**:277
Dachstein Peak (Austria) **3**:315
Dacia (Roman province in southeastern Europe) **4**:250, 256
Dacko, David (president of Central African Republic) **1**:250
Da Costa, Manuel Pinto (president of São Tomé and Príncipe) **1**:238
Daddah, Moktar Ould (president of Mauritania) **1**:139
Dagbani language 1:199
Dagestani (people) **2**:87

Dagomba (African people) **1**:189, 192, 198
Dahna (region, Saudi Arabia) **2**:123
Dahomey (early African kingdom) **1**:214
Dahomey (modern nation) *see* Benin (Dahomey)
Dairyland of America (nickname for Wisconsin) **5**:284
Dairy products
France **3**:155
Midwestern states **5**:47
Netherlands **3**:230–31
Switzerland **3**:288
Wisconsin **5**:286
illus.
Dutch cheese market **3**:228
Fulani villager churning butter **1**:244
Dakar (capital, Senegal) **1**:53, 153, 155, 156, 158
illus. **1**:154
Dakota Sioux (Indians of North America) **5**:164, 269, 288, 289, 291, 298, 299, 300, 301, 317
Northwest Rebellion **5**:112
illus. **5**:292
Dalai Lama (head of Tibetan Lamaism) **2**:387
illus. **2**:19
Dalarna (province, Sweden) **4**:39
Dalits (social class) **2**:169, 211
Asia, social classes in **2**:21
Hindu society **2**:211, 212–13, 221
Dallas (Texas) **5**:49, 254
illus. **5**:254
Dalmatia (region, Croatia) **4**:274, 280, 285
Daloa (Ivory Coast) **1**:185
Dalriada, Kingdom of 3:140
Damara (African people) **1**:349
Damascus (capital, Syria) **2**:47, 90, 91, 93, 94, 95
illus. **2**:90
bazaar **2**:95
Damietta channel (Nile delta) **1**:39, 114
Dammam (Saudi Arabia) **2**:125
Dams
Cabora Bassa Dam **1**:366
Danube River **3**:326, 328; **4**:275
environmental damage **5**:71
Indus River **2**:183
Kariba Dam **1**:275, 276
Nile River **1**:38, 39
Owen Falls Dam **1**:318, 320
Portugal **4**:73
Volta River **1**:195–96, 200, 204
Yangtze River **2**:369
illus.
Eastern Scheldt Sea Barrier **3**:226
Hoover Dam **5**:24
Itaipú Dam **6**:167
Owen Falls Dam **1**:321
Wales **3**:122
Danae, Mount (New Zealand)
illus. **2**:537
Danakil (African people) *see* Afar
Danakil Depression (Eritrea) **1**:294
Danam (India) **2**:220
Da Nang (Vietnam) **2**:282, 297
Dance
Argentina **6**:275
Bolivian devil dance **6**:233, 239
Cambodia **2**:290
Chile **6**:307
Colombia **6**:122, 123
Costa Rica **6**:66
Denmark **4**:16

Ghana **1**:194
Honduras **6**:37–38
Nepal's rice dance **2**:232
Paraguay **6**:248
Russian ballet **4**:314
Sri Lankan art form **2**:248
Tuvalu's *fatele* **2**:611
Venezuela **6**:141
illus.
Bolivian festival **6**:90, 234
Chinese folk dance **2**:407
Danish ballet students **4**:17
Folklorama, Winnipeg (Canada) **5**:116
Greek folk dance **4**:193
Hawaiian hula **5**:353
Highland Games **3**:139
Indonesia **2**:317
Korean circle dance **2**:436
Mexico **5**:372
Panama's *tamborito* **6**:77
Philippine folk dance **2**:333
Spanish flamenco **4**:95
tango **6**:277
whirling dervishes **2**:59
Dancers Practicing at the Bar (painting, Degas)
illus. **3**:177
Dandara (Egypt) **1**:111
Danelaw (English history) **3**:116
Danes (people) **3**:18, 51, 247; **4**:13–17
England, history of **3**:102, 115–16
rulers of England, list of **6**:360
Dan-Guro (African people) **1**:186
D'Annunzio, Gabriele (Italian poet and patriot) **4**:160
Dante Alighieri (Italian poet) **4**:134, 157
Danube Delta Biosphere Reserve (Romania) **3**:329
DANUBE RIVER (Europe) **3**:42, 45, 308, **326–29**; **4**:275
Austria **3**:315–16, 318
Croatia **4**:285
delta **4**:250
Germany **3**:242
Hungary **4**:236, 237, 242
Iron Gate gorge **3**:37
Romania **4**:249
Slovakia **4**:232, 234
Ukraine **4**:333
illus. **3**:327, 328, 329
table(s)
longest rivers of the world **6**:346
Danube Spring (Donauquelle) (Donaueschingen, Germany) **3**:326
Danzig (Poland) *see* Gdánsk
Daoism (religion) **2**:389, 420
Daoud Khan, Mohammed (political leader of Afghanistan) **2**:178, 179
Dardanelles, Strait of the (Turkey) **2**:57, 61
Dare, Virginia (first English child born in the New World) **5**:229
Dar es Salaam (capital, Tanzania) **1**:333, 335
illus. **1**:334
Dargo Plateau (Australia) **2**:517
Darien region (Panama–Colombia) **6**:72, 73–74, 77
Darigangas (people) **2**:363
Dari language 2:175
Darío, Rubén (Nicaraguan writer) **6**:55
Darius the Great (Darius I) (king of Persia) **2**:20
Dark Ages (early Middle Ages) **3**:49; **4**:155–56
"Dark continent" (the myth of Africa) **1**:6

Darling Range (Australia) **2:**524–25, 526
Darling River (Australia) **2:**483, 509
Darrit (Marshall Islands) **2:**575
Dartmoor (plateau, Devonshire, England) **3:**100
Dartmouth (Nova Scotia) **5:**92
Darwin (capital, Northern Territory, Australia) **2:**533–34, 535
  illus.
    art and culture festival **2:**532
Darwin, Charles (British naturalist) **3:**105; **6:**203, 270
Darwin, Cordillera de (Chile) **6:**316
Dasht-i-Kavir (salt desert, Iran) **2:**156
Dasht-i-Lut (salt desert, Iran) **2:**156
Da Silva, Luiz Inacio Lula (president of Brazil) **6:**191
Dates (fruit) **2:**150
Daugava River (Latvian portion of Western Dvina) **4:**297, 299
Daugavpils (Latvia) **4:**299
Dauphin (title of the eldest son of a French king) **3:**183
Dauphin Island (Alabama) **5:**242
Davao (Philippines) **2:**336
Davenport (Iowa) **5:**294
David (king of Israel) **2:**46
David (Panama) **6:**74
David II (king of Scotland) **3:**134
Davidson County (Tennessee) **5:**265
Davis, Edward (British explorer) **6:**322
Davis, Jefferson (American political leader) **5:**261
Davis, John (English explorer) **6:**287
Davis Mountains (Texas) **5:**251
Davis Strait (Greenland–Baffin Island) **5:**134
Davos (Switzerland) **3:**288
Davys, John (English explorer) *see* Davis, John
Dawson City (Yukon Territory) **5:**146, 147, 148
  illus.
    Klondike gold rush **5:**148
Dayaks (Asian people) **2:**318, 329
Dayton (Ohio) **5:**273
Dayton Accords (1995) **3:**1; **4:**281, 287, 288, 290
D Day (June 6, 1944, World War II) **3:**188, 279
Dead Sea (salt lake, Israel–Jordan) **2:**105, 117; **6:**345
Deadwood (South Dakota) **5:**300
Death Valley (California) **5:**341, 342; **6:**345
De Beers (South African diamond organization) **1:**402
Debrecen (Hungary) **4:**242–43
Debt-for-nature swap **6:**172
Debundscha (Cameroon) **1:**231
Deby, Idriss (president of Chad) **1:**244
Decamere (Eritrea) **1:**294
Deccan Plateau **2:**166
Decembrists (Russian revolutionaries) **4:**321
Decision making (in Japan) **2:**449
Declaration of Independence (July 4, 1776) **5:**188, 213
Declaration of the Rights of Man and of the Citizen, French **3:**184; **6:**127
Deep Creek Lake (Maryland) **5:**218
Deep South (U.S.) *see* South-Central States
Deer farming **2:**548
Dee River (Wales) **3:**122
Deeside Valley (Scotland) **3:**138
Degas, Edgar (French painter) **3:**177
  illus.
    Dancers Practicing at the Bar **3:**177

De Gaulle, Charles (French statesman) **3:**188–89, 190
    French colonies **1:**34, 84
Deir el Bahri (site of Egyptian temple) **1:**111
De Klerk, Frederik W. (South African political leader) **1:**405, 406
  illus. **1:**406
Delap (Marshall Islands) **2:**575
de la Rúa, Fernando (president of Argentina) **6:**301
DELAWARE 5:200, **215–16**
  illus.
    Henry Clay Mill **5:**215
  map(s) **5:**216
Delaware (Indians of North America) *see* Lenape
Delaware Bay (U.S.) **5:**198
Delaware River and Valley (U.S.) **5:**208, 210, 211, 212, 213, 216
Delaware Water Gap (valley, New Jersey) **5:**208
De La Warr, Baron (colonial governor, Virginia) **5:**215
De León Carpio, Ramiro (president of Guatemala) **6:**33
Delgado, José Matías (Salvadoran patriot) **6:**48–49
Delhi (India) **2:**203, 208–9, 215, 216
  illus.
    Qutb Minar **2:**214
Delhi, Sultanate of 2:172
Delmarva Peninsula (U.S.) **5:**215
Delos (island, Aegean Sea) **4:**190
  illus. **3:**46
Delphi (Greece) **4:**198
  illus. **4:**202
Delta Works project (the Netherlands) **3:**228
Demarcation, Line of (South American history) **6:**82
Demavand, Mount (Iran) **2:**156
De Menezes, Fradique (president of São Tomé and Príncipe) **1:**238
Demerara River (Guyana) **6:**149
Demirel, Suleyman (prime minister of Turkey) **2:**67
Democracy
    African governments **1:**2, 61, 62
    Asian governments **2:**29
    Australia's early achievements **2:**501
    Brazil, history of **6:**168
    former Communist countries **3:**26
    origins **2:**23; **3:**12
    parliamentary system **3:**93, 96
    Philippines under Marcos **2:**338
    South America **6:**113–14, 115
    Switzerland **3:**298
    Venezuela **6:**131
Democratic Republic of Congo *see* Congo, Democratic Republic of
Democratic Socialism, Party of (Germany) **3:**284
Demonstrations *see* Riots and demonstrations
Demotic Greek (language) **4:**195
Dendi language **1:**213
Déné (Indians of North America) **5:**73–74, 136, 138, 142, 143, 148
Deng Xiaoping (Chinese political leader) **2:**398–99, 404, 421
    economic modernization **2:**398, 412, 418
DENMARK 3:26; **4:8–22**
    Greenland **5:**10, 11

    Iceland **4:**5, 6
    Norway, early relations with **4:**26
  illus.
    ballet students **4:**17
    beach at Holbaek **4:**13
    brewery **4:**15
    children in day-care **4:**14
    Copenhagen **4:**18, 19
    farm **4:**10
    flag **4:**v
    Fredriksborg Castle **4:**8
    Hvide Sande **4:**21
    Ribe **4:**9
  map(s) **4:**11
D'Entrecasteaux Islands (Papua New Guinea) **2:**587
Denver (capital, Colorado) **5:**48, 320
  illus.
    airport **5:**22
    capitol building **5:**320
Denver, John (American singer) **5:**258
Depression of the 1930's
    Europe **3:**61, 188, 276
    United States **5:**176
Derg (Ethiopian military committee) **1:**290, 291
Derg, Lough (lake in Ireland) **3:**66
Derna (Libya) **1:**96
Derry (Northern Ireland) *see* Londonderry
Derwent River (Australia) **2:**530
Desaguadero River (South America) **6:**231
Desai, Morarji (prime minister of India) **2:**218
Desalination (of seawater) **2:**129, 140, 142, 144
Descartes, René (French philosopher) **3:**178, 199
Deseret, State of 5:323, 325 *see also* Utah
Deserts *see also* names of deserts
    Arctic **5:**56, 59, 138
    Asia **2:**10
    Australia **2:**483, 485, 486, 525
    California **5:**342, 343
    Egypt **1:**112–13
    Great Basin (North America) **5:**309, 330
    great deserts of the world, list of **6:**347
    Middle East **2:**123
    Oregon **5:**339
    Utah **5:**323
  illus.
    Afghanistan **2:**176
    Atacama **2:**312
    California **5:**343
    caravan in Sahara **1:**24
    Egypt **1:**112
    White Sands National Monument **5:**15
  map(s)
    world climate **6:**354
    world vegetation **6:**353
Des Moines (capital, Iowa) **5:**294
De Soto, Hernando (Spanish explorer) **5:**246, 248, 267, 445
Dessalines, Jean-Jacques (Haitian leader) **5:**469
Detroit (Michigan) **5:**46, 277, 278
  illus. **5:**277
Detroit River (Michigan–Ontario) **5:**107, 276, 277
De Valera, Eamon (Irish statesman) **3:**77
Devil's Island (French Guiana) **3:**187; **6:**92
Devil's Tower National Monument (Montana) **5:**315–16
Devon Island (Northwest Territories, Canada) **5:**7
Devonport (Tasmania, Australia) **2:**531

Devote, Saint 3:204
Dhahran (Saudi Arabia) **2:**125
  illus.
    University of Petroleum **2:**128
Dhaka (Dacca) (Bangladesh) **2:**239, 243
  illus. **2:**237, 244
Dhlakama, Afonso (Mozambican rebel leader)
  1:368
Dhofar (province of Oman) **2:**137
Diaguita (Indians of South America) **6:**267–68
Diamond Mountains (Korea) **2:**430
Diamonds
  Africa **1:**5
  Arctic **5:**64
  Arkansas **5:**159
  Australia **2:**490
  Botswana **1:**353, 354
  Congo, Democratic Republic of **1:**270
  Crater of Diamonds State Park **5:**267
  Guinea **1:**169
  Namibia **1:**46, 350
  Netherlands **3:**232, 233
  Sierra Leone **1:**173
  South Africa **1:**20, 45, 402
  Tanzania **1:**336
  illus.
    Angolan mine **1:**345
Diana (Princess of Wales) **3:**118
Dias, Bartholomeu (Portuguese navigator)
  1:403; **4:**75, 76
Dias, Diogo (Portuguese sea captain) **1:**377
Diaspora (dispersal of the Jews) **2:**112
Díaz, Porfirio (president of Mexico) **5:**384, 385,
  386, 393, 417
Díaz de Guzmán, Ruy (Argentine author) **6:**276
Díaz de Vivar, Roderigo *see* Cid, El
Dib, Mohamed (Algerian writer) **1:**80
Dibai *see* Dubai
Didi sultanate (dynasty of Maldives) **2:**252
Diégo-Suarez (Madagascar) *see* Antsiranana
Dien Bien Phu (Vietnam) **2:**302
Dieppe (France) **3:**164
Diet (eating habits) *see* Cuisine
Diet (Japanese legislative assembly) **2:**471
Dikhil (Djibouti) **1:**298
Dili (capital, East Timor) **2:**327
  illus.
    independence celebration **2:**327
Dinan (France) **3:**157
Dinaric Alps (Bosnia and Herzegovina) **3:**28;
  4:288
Dinesen, Isak (Danish author) **4:**16
Dingaan (Zulu chief) **1:**404
Dingo (wild Australian dog) **2:**522, 529
Diniz (king of Portugal) **4:**75
Dinka (African people) **1:**127–28
Dinkelsbuhl (Germany)
  illus. **3:**249
Dinosaur National Monument (Utah) **5:**323
Dinosaur Provincial Park (Alberta) **5:**127
Dinosaurs 2:10; **5:**299, 312, 323
  illus. **5:**127
Diocletian (Roman emperor) **1:**119; **3:**48;
  4:171
Diola (African people) **1:**155
Diouf, Abdou (president of Senegal) **1:**158
Dioula (African people) **1:**188
Diourbel (Senegal) **1:**153
Directory (French history) **3:**184
Diredawa (Ethiopia) **1:**285
Diriamba Highlands (Nicaragua) **6:**52
"Dirty war" (in Argentina) **6:**301

Disappeared, The 6:301
Discovery, Age of *see* Exploration and Discov-
  ery, Age of
Disease *see* Medicine and health
Disneyland (Anaheim, California)
  illus. **5:**347
Disneyland (France) *see* Euro Disneyland
Disneyland (near Tokyo, Japan) **2:**464
Disney World (Orlando, Florida) **5:**241
Disraeli, Benjamin (1st Earl of Beaconsfield)
  (English statesman) **3:**93
Dissected Till Plains (North America) **5:**293
Divehi (language of the Maldives) **2:**251
Divine right (absolute power of monarch)
  1:202; **3:**57
Divorce
  Hungary's high rate **4:**239
  Iran **2:**158, 159
  Islam **2:**45
  Italy **4:**163
  Portugal, barred in **4:**72
  Spain **4:**89
  Uruguay **6:**252
Djajawidjaja Mountains (Indonesia) *see* Jayaw-
  iyaya Mountains
Djakarta (capital, Indonesia) *see* Jakarta
Djebel (Arab word for mountain) *see* the main
  element of the name
Djemila (Algeria) **1:**75
  illus. **1:**83
Djenné (Mali)
  illus. **1:**140
Djerba (Tunisia) **1:**90
Djerid, Chott (salt lake, Tunisia) **1:**89
Djerlap Hydroelectric Dam (Yugoslavia–
  Romania) **4:**275
Djerma-Songhai (African people) **1:**51, 146
DJIBOUTI 1:37, 297–99, 304
  illus. **1:**297
    flag **1:**xxiii
  map(s) **1:**299
Djibouti (capital, Djibouti) **1:**287, 298
Djourab (lowlands, Chad) **1:**240
Dlamini clan (Swaziland) **1:**388
Dmowski, Roman (Polish leader) **4:**220
Dnieper River (Europe) **4:**308, 333, 341
  table(s)
    longest rivers of the world **6:**346
Dniester River (Moldova–Ukraine) **4:**333, 345
Dobruja (province, Romania) **4:**248, 249, 256
Doctor Zhivago (motion picture) **4:**331
Dodecanese (Greek islands) **4:**187, 190–91
Dodo (extinct bird) **1:**382
Dodoma (Tanzania) **1:**334
Doe, Samuel K. (Liberian political leader)
  1:178, 183
Dog Fence (barrier in South Australia) **2:**522
Dogra (Hindu people) **2:**173
Dogrib (Indians of North America) **5:**142
Dog River (Lebanon) **2:**97
Dogsleds
  illus. **4:**308; **5:**140; **6:**333
Doha (capital, Qatar) **2:**142
Doi moi (Vietnamese economic reform)
  2:298–99
Dolder Hills (Zurich, Switzerland) **3:**292
Doldrums (windless areas) **2:**561
Dolisie (Congo) **1:**257
Dolly (sheep) **3:**141
Dolores (Guanajuato, Mexico) **5:**382, 383, 405
Dolphins
  illus. **2:**525

Dome of the Rock (mosque, Jerusalem) **2:**47
Domesday Book (England's 1st census) **3:**117
Dominguez, Francisco Atanasio (Spanish
  explorer) **5:**325
DOMINICA 5:427, 438, **487–88**
  Carib Indians **5:**430
  Creole patois **5:**435
  illus. **5:**487
    flag **5:**vi
  map(s) **5:**488
DOMINICAN REPUBLIC 5:426, 427, 438, 440,
  453–60
  Haiti, history of **5:**469
  immigration to Puerto Rico **5:**167
  Spanish language **5:**435
  Venezuela, history of **6:**145
  illus.
    baseball **5:**454
    flag **5:**vi
    housing **5:**456
    Santo Domingo **5:**453
    sugarcane harvesting **5:**457
    University of Santo Domingo **5:**458
  map(s) **5:**455
Donaueschingen (Germany) **3:**326
Donets Basin (industrial area, Ukraine) **3:**40;
  4:338
Donets River (Ukraine) **4:**333
Donkeys
  illus. **6:**9
Don River (Russia) **4:**308
Door Peninsula (Wisconsin) **5:**285
Dorians (Greek people) **3:**46
Dornach (France) **3:**297
Dorpat (Estonia) *see* Tartu
Dorsale (region, Tunisia) **1:**89
Dortmund (Germany) **3:**244
Dos Santos, José Eduardo (president of
  Angola) **1:**346
Dosso (Niger) **1:**144
Dostoyevsky, Fyodor (Russian writer) **4:**313,
  330
Douala (Cameroon) **1:**232, 234
Double Ten (Taiwanese holiday) **2:**425
Doubtful Sound (New Zealand)
  illus. **2:**537
Douglas (capital, Isle of Man) **3:**84
Douglas, Denzil (prime minister of St. Kitts and
  Nevis) **5:**496
Douglas, Rosie (prime minister of Dominica)
  5:488
Douglas, Thomas (Scottish colonizer) **5:**117
Douglas Island (Alaska) **5:**350
Douro River (Spain–Portugal) **4:**66, 67, 73, 74,
  82
Dover (capital, Delaware) **5:**216
Dover (England)
  illus. **3:**81
Dover, Strait of (England–France) **3:**80
Down East (coastal Maine) **5:**182
Downs (hills, England) **3:**82, 100
Dracula (Transylvanian prince) **4:**249
Drake, Sir Francis (English sea captain) **3:**119;
  5:335; **6:**121
  Caribbean Sea and islands **5:**431
Drakensberg Mountains (South Africa) **1:**18,
  390, 395, 396
Drama *see* Theater
Dra River (Morocco) **1:**66
Dravidian languages 2:28
Dravidians (Asian people) **2:**13, 171, 187, 191,
  243

Dreamtime (Australian aboriginal legend) **2:**499
Dreifuss, Ruth (president of Switzerland) **3:**298
Dresden (Germany) **3:**241, 243, 268
Dreyfus, Alfred (French army officer) **3:**187
Driftless Area (region, North America) **5:**281, 293
Drift Prairie (region, North Dakota) **5:**297
Drina River (Bosnia and Herzegovina) **4:**288
Drnovšek, Janez (Slovenian political leader) **4:**284
Droughts
  Africa **1:**23, 284
  Angola **1:**345
  Botswana **1:**354
  Dust Bowl **5:**307
  Eritrea **1:**294
  Mexico **5:**394
  Mongolia **2:**363
  South Africa **1:**401
  Tunisia **1:**90
Drug addiction 6:129
Drug trade, International 2:359; **6:**124, 128–29
Druids (ancient Celtic priests) **3:**113, 128, 129
  Northern Ireland **3:**147
  Stonehenge **3:**114
Drumlins 5:202, 284
Druze (Muslim sect) **2:**91, 100, 102, 105
Drygalski, Erich von (German explorer) **6:**332
Duars plain (Bhutan–India) **2:**234, 235
Dubai (United Arab Emirates) **2:**138, 139
Dubček, Alexander (Czechoslovakian leader) **4:**230, 235
Dublin (capital, Ireland) **3:**69, 72–73, 75
  illus. **3:**72, 78
    horse show **3:**73
    Trinity College **3:**69
Dubrovnik (Croatia) **4:**285, 286
  illus. **4:**285
Duck-billed platypus *see* Platypus
Dueling 3:270
Dufourspitze (mountain, Switzerland) **3:**286, 299
Duhalde, Eduardo (president of Argentina) **6:**301
Duisburg (Germany) **3:**244
Dukhan (oil field region, Qatar) **2:**142
Dulce River (South America) **6:**280
Duluth (Minnesota) **5:**46, 288
Duma (Russian national assembly) **4:**321
Dumas, Alexandre (French author) **3:**178
Dumont d'Urville, Jules (French sea captain) **6:**332
Dunant, Jean Louis (Swiss businessman) **3:**293
Duncan I (king of Scotland) **3:**140
Dundee (Scotland) **3:**138
Dunedin (New Zealand) **2:**548, 553
Dunkers (German religious sect) **5:**212
Dunkirk (France) **3:**152, 154, 164
Du Pont, E. I. (French-American industrialist) **5:**216
  illus.
    site of gunpowder works **5:**215
Durán Ballén, Sixto (president of Ecuador) **6:**205
Durango (capital, Durango state, Mexico) **5:**398
DURANGO (state, Mexico) **5:**31, **398**
Durazzo (Albania) **4:**271
Durban (South Africa) **1:**397, 398, 400, 402
Durbets (people) **2:**363
Dürer, Albrecht (German artist) **3:**254, 272
  illus.
    Self-Portrait **3:**254

Durham (North Carolina) **5:**228, 229
Durmitor Range (Yugoslavia) **4:**275
Dürnstein Castle (Austria) **3:**315, 326
Durrës (Albania) *see* Durazzo
Dušan (Dushan), Stephen *see* Stephen Dušan
Dushanbe (capital, Tajikistan) **2:**359
Düsseldorf (Germany) **3:**261, 266
Dust Bowl (U.S.) **5:**307
  illus. **5:**307
Dutch (people) **3:**225, 229–30
  North America **5:**37, 174, 206, 210
  South Africa **1:**45
Dutch Borneo *see* Kalimantan
Dutch East India Company 1:399, 403; **2:**324
Dutch East Indies *see* Netherlands East Indies
Dutch Guiana *see* Suriname
Dutch language 3:214, 229; **6:**7
Dutch Reformed Church (South Africa) **1:**399
Dutch West India Company 6:154
Duvalier, François (president of Haiti) **5:**470
Duvalier, Jean-Claude (president of Haiti) **5:**470
Dvina (name for either of two rivers, Northern Dvina and Western Dvina rivers, Russia) **4:**308
  Daugava River (Latvia) **4:**297
Dvořák, Antonín (Czech composer) **4:**225
Dyaks *see* Dayaks
Dyerma-Songhai *see* Djerma-Songhai
Dzaoudzi (Comoros) **1:**383
Dzongkha (language of Bhutan) **2:**235

• • • E • • •

Eagle, Mount (St. Croix, U.S. Virgin Islands) **5:**172
Eagle Mountain (California) **5:**8
Eagle Mountain (Minnesota) **5:**287
Eagles 2:201
  illus. **5:**163
Earthquake Park (Anchorage, Alaska) **5:**350
Earthquakes
  Anchorage (Alaska) **5:**350
  Ankara **2:**63
  Armenia **2:**75
  and Chile's architecture **6:**310
  Colombia **6:**120
  Concepción (Chile) **6:**315–16
  Costa Rica **6:**63
  Ecuador **6:**196, 200
  El Salvador **6:**43, 45, 49, 50
  Europe **3:**28
  Greece **4:**199
  Guatemala **6:**31
  Iceland **4:**2
  India **2:**229
  Iran **2:**1
  Italy **4:**128
  Latin America **6:**2
  Lisbon (Portugal) **4:**77
  Macedonia **4:**291–92
  Mexico City **5:**410
  New Zealand **2:**537, 538
  Nicaragua **6:**51
  Oceania **2:**558–59
  Pakistan **2:**188–89
  Peru **6:**210, 212–13
  Philippines **2:**332, 336
  San Andreas fault **5:**342

Turkmenistan 2:357
U.S. Pacific States 5:157, 333, 335
Uzbekistan 2:351
Venezuela 6:142
Washington (state) **5:**338
Earth Summit (1992) **6:**174, 336
Eas a Chual (waterfall, Scotland) **3:**132
East Africa 1:11, 36–41
East African Community 1:3, 321
East Africa Protectorate (now Kenya and Uganda) **1:**315, 322
EAST ASIA 2:6, 25–26, **367–76**, 395
East Bengal *see* Bangladesh
East Berlin *see* Berlin
East China Sea (Pacific Ocean) **2:**368, 369
Easter
  Italy **4:**136
  Mexico **5:**366
  illus.
    Greek Easter breads **4:**194
Easter Island 2:600, 601; **6:**322–23
  illus. **6:**323
  map(s) **6:**322
Easter Monday Rebellion (1916) **3:**77
Eastern Cape Province (South Africa) **1:**396
Eastern Catholic Church 4:256
Eastern Desert *see* Arabian Desert
Eastern Ghats *see* Ghats, Eastern and Western
Eastern Highlands (Australia) *see* Great Dividing Range
Eastern Highlands (mountainous region, Zimbabwe) **1:**356
Eastern Orthodox churches
  Europe, history of **3:**49
  Georgia (republic) **2:**82
  Greece **4:**193, 194–95, 205, 206
  Lebanon **2:**100
  Russia **4:**310, 320
  Serbia **4:**277
  Ukraine **4:**334
  U.S. population **5:**171
  illus.
    Georgian worshipers **2:**81
    Russian service **4:**310
Eastern Province (Saudi Arabia) **2:**123, 128
Eastern Roman Empire *see* Byzantine Empire
Eastern Samoa *see* American Samoa
Eastern Townships (Quebec) **5:**102, 103
East Falkland Island 6:286
East Germany (1949–1990) *see* German Democratic Republic
East India companies 2:24, 207, 215, 216, 309, 324
East Indians (immigrants from India and Pakistan in the Caribbean) **5:**427, 484
  Belize **6:**22
  Jamaica **5:**474
  Latin America **6:**95
East Indies *see* Indonesia; Southeast Asia
East Lansing (capital, Michigan) **5:**278
East London (South Africa) **1:**398, 401, 402
Eastman, George (American inventor) **5:**205
Easton (Pennsylvania) **5:**213
East Pakistan *see* Bangladesh
East Prussia (former German province) **3:**279
East Slavs (European people) **4:**333
EAST TIMOR 2:27, 30, 264, 326, **327–28**
  Indonesia **2:**313
  Portugal **4:**68
  map(s) **2:**328
Eau Claire (Wisconsin) **5:**286
Ebano (San Luis Potosí, Mexico) **5:**401

Ebro River (Spain) **4:**82
Ecevit, Bulent (prime minister of Turkey) **2:**67
Echandi Jiménez, Mario (president of Costa Rica) **6:**71
Echevarría, Aquileo (Costa Rican poet) **6:**67
Echidnas 2:477, 489, 505
Echmiadzin (Armenia) **2:**76
Economic Commission for Africa 1:36
Economic Cooperation and Development, Organization for (OECD) 3:63
Economic Monetary Union (Europe) *see* European Monetary Union (EMU)
ECUADOR 6:192–205
  Amazon River **6:**168
  Andes **6:**100–101
  education **6:**107
  Galápagos Islands **6:**202–3
  Indo-American culture **6:**89, 91, 112
  Peru, relations with **6:**227, 228
  population **6:**7
  illus.
    banana growing **6:**200
    flag **6:**vi
    Galápagos Islands **6:**202
    Guayaquil **6:**195
    livestock **6:**200
    oil pipeline **6:**201
    Otavalo market **6:**198
    Quilotoa Crater **6:**192
    Quito **6:**195, 196, 204
    sierra region **6:**193
  map(s) **6:**194
    Galápagos Islands **6:**202
Eden, Garden of 2:50
Eden, Mount (New Zealand) **2:**547
Edfu (Egypt) **1:**111
Edinburgh (capital, Scotland) **3:**134, 136, 137, 138
  illus.
    Military Tattoo **3:**134
Edinburgh, University of (Scotland) **3:**134
Edinburgh Castle (Scotland) **3:**134
  illus. **3:**134
Edjeleh (oil field, Algeria) **1:**76
Edmond (Oklahoma) **5:**306
Edmonton (capital, Alberta) **5:**124, 125, 126, 127
Edo (Bini) (African people) **1:**219
Edo (Japan) **2:**445
Edom (ancient kingdom in the Middle East) **2:**120
Education
  Africa: school attendance **1:**3
  Arctic schools access Internet **5:**64, 140
  Australia: students in isolated areas **2:**497, 508
  Belgium's church schools **3:**224
  Cambodia **2:**289
  Central and South America **6:**8
  Chinese Communism **2:**403–5
  Denmark **4:**12, 16
  English system **3:**103–4
  Europe **3:**26
  European universities **3:**13
  India **2:**221, 222, 223
  Japan **2:**456–57, 457–58, 458–59
  Kiribati's Marine Training Centre **2:**582
  Latin America **6:**106–8
  Massachusetts scholars and scientists **5:**191
  Peru's University of San Marcos **6:**216
  Philippine universities **2:**264, 335

  Roman Catholic Church in Canada **5:**95
  Scotland's local schools **3:**137
  Swiss universities **3:**294
  Turkey: reforms of Kemal Atatürk **2:**66
  Tuvalu's Maritime Training School **2:**612
  Venezuela's "Bolivarian schools" **6:**140
  illus.
    adult classes in Tanzania **1:**335
    African open-air classroom **1:**29
    Argentine university students **6:**279
    Asian women at universities **2:**39
    Australia: lessons via satellite **2:**497
    Brazilian college students **6:**175
    Cambodian schoolchildren **2:**289
    Catholic University of Ecuador **6:**196
    Central University of Venezuela **6:**138
    Chinese kindergarten **2:**404
    Christian school in India **2:**221
    classes for immigrants to Israel **2:**113
    Costa Rican schoolchildren **6:**12, 68
    Cuban students **5:**447
    German vocational school **3:**248
    Honduran schoolchildren **6:**38
    Iranian schoolchildren **2:**158
    Japanese students **2:**458
    Lebanese teacher in war-damaged classroom **2:**102
    outdoor classroom in India **2:**222
    Peruvian students **6:**216
    Saudi students training for oil industry **2:**128
    South American coeducation **6:**111
    South American schoolroom **6:**108
    Sudanese schoolchildren **1:**126
    Trinity College (Dublin) **3:**69
    uniforms on students in Trinidad and Tobago **5:**485
    Uruguay's national university **6:**255
Eduskunta (Finnish legislature) **4:**58
Edward, Lake (Africa) **1:**19, 262, 316
  illus.
    pelicans **1:**263
Edward I (king of England) **3:**117, 129, 140
Edward III (king of England) **3:**117, 182
Edward VI (king of England) **3:**119
Edwards Bello, Joaquín (Chilean author) **6:**309
EEC *see* European Economic Community
Efate (island, Vanuatu) **2:**594, 596
Efik (African people) **1:**51, 219
Eforie (Romania) **4:**254
Egadi Islands (Italy) **4:**130
Egbert (king of England) **3:**118
Egede, Hans (Norwegian missionary) **5:**11
Eggenberg Castle (Graz, Austria) **3:**315
Egmont, Mount (New Zealand) **2:**538
  illus. **2:**536
EGYPT (Arab Republic of Egypt) **1:101–23**
  Arab-Israeli wars **2:**113–15
  Islam **2:**342
  Muslim Brotherhood **1:**123
  Nile River **1:**38–39
  North African countries **1:**35
  peace treaty with Israel **2:**54
  Suez Canal **1:**120–21
  United Arab Republic **2:**55
  illus.
    Alexandria **1:**115
    Cairo **1:**31, 107, 108
    cotton picking **1:**116
    desert **1:**112
    family returning from field work **1:**105

    fishing **1:**114
    flag **1:**xxii
    irrigation **1:**106
    men playing dominoes **1:**102
    mural painted on house **1:**104
    Muslims at prayer **1:**109
    Nile River **1:**113
    petroleum production **1:**116
    pyramids **1:**118
    ruins **1:**110–11
  map(s) **1:**103
Egypt, Ancient 1:110–11, 117–19
  Asia, Southwest **2:**49
  Nile River **1:**38
  North Africa, Egyptian influences **1:**32–33
  illus.
    art **1:**101
Ehécatl (Tlaxcalan god) **5:**415
Ehrenburg, Ilya (Soviet author) **4:**314
Eidsvoll (Norway) **4:**26
Eiffel Tower (Paris, France) **3:**203
  illus. **3:**203
Eiger (mountain, Switzerland) **3:**286
Eilat (Israel) **2:**109, 114
Eindhoven (the Netherlands) **3:**232
Einstein, Albert (German-American scientist) **3:**290
Eisenhower, Dwight D. (34th president of U.S.) **5:**267
Eisteddfod (Welsh national festival) **3:**125
  illus. **3:**125
Ejidos (Mexican communal farms) **5:**361
El (in names) *see* the main element in name for entries not listed below
El Alamein (Egypt) **1:**122
Elath (Israel) *see* Eilat
Elba (island, Italy) **3:**185; **4:**125, 131
Elbe River (eastern Europe) **3:**243; **4:**224
  Germanic peoples, eastern boundary of **3:**18
  Hamburg (Germany) **3:**265
El Borma (Tunisia) **1:**90
Elbow River (Alberta) **5:**125
Elbrus, Mount (Russia) **4:**307; **6:**345
Elburz (mountains, Iran) **2:**42, 156
  illus. **2:**155
El Callao (gold mine, Venezuela) **6:**135
El Cangrejo (Panama) **6:**74
Elchibey, Abulfaz (president of Azerbaijan) **2:**89
El-Djem (Tunisia) **1:**90
El Dorado ("the Gilded One") (legendary South American ruler and kingdom) **6:**135, 147
Elections *see also* individual country articles
  Bhutan has one vote per family **2:**236
  Israel's differ from those in U.S. **2:**111
  illus.
    Mongolia **2:**365
Electric power *see also* Geothermal-power plants; Hydroelectricity
  Asia **2:**37
  Chinese shortages **2:**418
  France **3:**157
  Italy **4:**132
  Laos' sale to Thailand **2:**285
  Ukraine **4:**338
  illus.
    geothermal (steam)-power plant **4:**131
Elena (Spanish princess)
  illus. **4:**91
Elephants 2:201, 277
  Myanmar **2:**269

Elephants (cont.)
  Sri Lanka **2:**246
  illus. **1:**4, 314; **2:**200, 267
Elephant seals 6:328
Eleuthera (island, Bahamas) **5:**424
Eleutherian Adventurers (Caribbean colonists)
  5:424
El Garrafón National Underwater Park (Quin-
  tana Roo, Mexico) **5:**422
El Gassi (oil field, Algeria) **1:**76
Elgin Marbles (sculpture from Parthenon) **4:**196
Elgon, Mount (Kenya–Uganda) **1:**18, 308, 317
El Greco (Spanish painter) *see* Greco, El
El Imposible National Park (El Salvador) **6:**44
Elisabeth (princess of Belgium) **3:**224
Elisabethville (Congo, Democratic Republic of)
  see Lubumbashi
Elizabeth (New Jersey) **5:**210
  illus. **5:**210
Elizabeth (South Australia. Australia) **2:**523
Elizabeth I (queen of England) **3:**91, 110, 118,
  140
  Drake's plunder in the Caribbean **5:**431
  England of her time **3:**119
  Irish lands given to Sir Walter Raleigh **3:**76
  Welsh language **3:**130
  illus. **3:**119
Elizabeth II (queen of Great Britain and North-
  ern Ireland) **3:**118
  illus. **2:**479, 502; **3:**118; **4:**180
Ellesmere Island (northwest of Greenland) **5:**4,
  7, 70, 137, 138
  illus. **5:**67
  table(s)
    largest islands of the world **6:**346
Ellice Islands (Pacific Ocean) *see* Tuvalu
Ellis Island (New York) **5:**169
Ellora (India) **2:**216
  illus. **2:**215
Elmina Castle (Ghana)
  illus. **1:**194
Elobey Chico (island, Equatorial Guinea) **1:**235
Elobey Grande (island, Equatorial Guinea)
  1:235
El Paso (Texas) **5:**254
Elqui River (Chile) **6:**313
EL SALVADOR 6:9, 11, 14, **42–50**
  civil war **6:**48–49
  history **6:**16, 18
  Honduras, relations with **6:**41
  land distribution **6:**17
  illus.
    Bahía de Jiquilisco **6:**42
    farming **6:**46
    flag **6:**vi
    San Salvador **6:**44, 49
    shopping mall **6:**46
    street vendors **6:**45
    war destruction **6:**48
  map(s) **6:**47
Elsner, Gisela (German author) **3:**251
El Turbio (Argentina) **6:**283
Elysée Palace (Paris, France) **3:**196
Elytis, Odysseus (Greek author) **4:**194
El Zerqa (Jordan) **2:**118, 119
Emancipation Day (Texas state holiday) **5:**253
Emerald Buddha, Temple of (Bangkok, Thai-
  land) *see* Wat Phra Keo
Emerald Isle (name for Ireland) **3:**65
Emeralds 6:125
Emigration *see* Immigration and emigration
Emi Koussi (mountain, Chad) **1:**25

Emmerich (Germany) **3:**245
Emperor penguins 6:327–28
  illus. **6:**325
Empire State (nickname for New York) **5:**201
Empire State Building (New York City)
  illus. **5:**201
Empire State of the South (nickname for Geor-
  gia) **5:**233
Employment
  Albanian economy **4:**271
  Algerian economy **1:**81, 82
  Asian recession **2:**34
  Central America **6:**14
  China **2:**414, 415
  Dominican Republic **5:**458–59
  East Asian workweek **2:**40
  Europe **3:**22, 44
  European Union **3:**25
  foreign workers in Qatar **2:**142
  Germany **3:**246, 263, 264, 276
  Japanese system **2:**449, 467–70
  Ohio, labor regulations **5:**274
  Philippine underemployment **2:**335
  Saudi unemployment **2:**129
  South American economy **6:**104
  Spain **4:**106, 108
  Sweden **4:**40
  United Kingdom **3:**90, 91
  Yemen **2:**133
Empty Quarter (desert, Arabia) *see* Rub' al-
  Khali
Emu (bird) **2:**489
  illus. **2:**487
Encarnación (Paraguay) **6:**244
Encomienda system (Spanish colonial govern-
  ment) **6:**225
Endara, Guillermo (president of Panama) **6:**81
Endeavour (ship) **2:**552
Enderby Land (Antarctica) **6:**332
Energy *see* Electric power
Enesco, Georges (Romanian-French composer)
  4:252
Engel, C. L. (German architect) **4:**59
ENGLAND 3:80–81, 87, **97–120** *see also*
  Commonwealth of Nations; England, history
  of; United Kingdom
  Europe, history of **3:**54
  London **3:**110–11
  illus.
    Cambridge University **3:**105
    Cornwall beach **3:**99
    country village **3:**85
    farms **3:**98
    fields **3:**17
    Hadrian's Wall **3:**92
    Liverpool **3:**91
    sporting events **3:**107
    Stonehenge **3:**114
    waterfalls **3:**98
    Westminster Abbey **3:**102
    Windsor Castle **3:**43
  map(s) **3:**101
England, Church of (Anglican Church) **3:**119
  British North America **5:**34
England, history of 3:112–20
  Asia, colonialism in **2:**24
  British North America **5:**34–39
  Caribbean Islands, colonialism in **5:**434, 436,
    437, 438
  contributions to world governments **3:**12
  Hadrian's Wall **3:**92

South America, history of 6:97, 98
  United Kingdom and how it was created
    3:91
  table(s)
    British rulers and prime ministers **6:**360–62
English Channel (England–France) **3:**80, 151,
  152, 164
  tunnel **3:**42
  illus.
    White Cliffs of Dover **3:**81
English East India Company *see* East India
  companies
English Harbour (Antigua and Barbuda)
  illus. **5:**493
English history *see* England, history of; United
  Kingdom
English language 3:104, 117–18
  Africa **1:**15
  Anglo-Irish writers **3:**70
  archaic forms Newfoundland **5:**79
  Asia, second language in **2:**28, 200
  Australian English **2:**494
  Barbadians' way of speaking **5:**479
  British Empire **3:**93
  Caribbean islands **5:**435
  English and U.S. usage, examples **3:**113
  "Jamaica talk" **5:**474
  Latin America **6:**7
  Malawi **1:**279
  New Zealand expressions **2:**551
  Nicaragua **6:**55
  Nigeria **1:**223
  Philippines **2:**334
  Scots English **3:**136
English people 3:86
Eniwetok (Pacific coral atoll) **2:**575
Enkhbayar, Nambariin (prime minister of Mon-
  golia) **2:**366
Enlightenment, The (18th century) **3:**57, 58;
  4:158
Enmerkar (priest-king of Sumeria) **2:**41
Ennedi Plateau (Chad) **1:**240, 243
Enns River (Austria) **3:**318
Enosis (union of Cyprus with Greece) **2:**73
Enron Corporation 5:255
Ensenada (Argentina) **6:**292
Ensenada (Baja California, Mexico) **5:**390
Entebbe (Uganda) **1:**318
Enterprise (Alabama)
  illus.
    Boll Weevil Monument **5:**221
Entre Ríos (province, Argentina) **6:**271, 272, 280
Enugu (Nigeria) **1:**219
Environment *see also* Pollution; Rain forests
  Amazon River **6:**201
  Antarctic regulations **6:**337
  Bhutanese policies **2:**235
  Brazilian rain forest **6:**172
  Canadian conservation **5:**109
  Denmark had first forest protection law **4:**12
  Dust Bowl **5:**307
  Everglades **5:**240
  French planning **3:**168–69
  Galápagos Islands **6:**203
  Hawaii's coral reefs **5:**354
  hydroelectric dams **5:**71
  Japanese standards **2:**440
  Mercosur's planned waterway **6:**262, 284
  New Zealand **2:**542–43
  Norway's healthy environment **4:**34
  ozone layer **6:**317, 327

Suriname's protected area **6:**159
Swedish problems **4:**50
U.N. conference (1992) **6:**174, 336
EOKA (Greek Cypriot underground movement) **2:**73
Eora (aboriginal tribe, Australia) **2:**512
Epcot Center (Walt Disney World, Florida)
illus. **5:**241
Ephesus (Turkey)
illus. **2:**66
Epiphany (religious holiday) **4:**136
Epirus (region, Greece) **4:**187, 188
Equality State (nickname for Wyoming) **5:**315
Equator 1:262; **6:**192
EQUATORIAL GUINEA 1:55, 235–36; **4:**85
illus.
flag **1:**xxiii
map(s) **1:**236
Equatorial Islands *see* Line Islands
Erasmus, Desiderius (Dutch scholar) **3:**293
Erbakan, Necmettin (Turkish political leader) **2:**67
Ercilla y Zúñiga, Alonso de (Spanish poet) **6:**302
Ergs (desert sands) **1:**24
Eric IX (king of Sweden) **4:**55
Ericson, Leif (Norse mariner) **4:**25; **5:**75
Eric the Red (Norse chieftain) **5:**10, 61
Erie (Indians of North America) **5:**274
Erie (Pennsylvania) **5:**213
Erie, Lake (Canada–U.S.) **5:**37, 270, 271, 272
Cleveland (Ohio) **5:**273
megalopolis area **5:**46
table(s)
largest lakes **6:**347
Erie Canal (New York) **5:**177, 206, 283 *see also*
New York State Barge Canal
Michigan, settlement of **5:**278
New York City trade **5:**37
North American inland navigation routes **5:**5, 13
illus. **5:**204
Eriksson, Leif *see* Ericson, Leif
ERITREA 1:36–37, 282, 287, 291, 292, **293–96;**
4:159
independence **1:**11
illus. **1:**293, 295
flag **1:**xxiii
map(s) **1:**294
Erivan *see* Yerevan
Erne, Lough (Northern Ireland) **3:**143
Erosion
Ethiopia **1:**283
Italy **4:**128
Lesotho **1:**391, 392
Panama **6:**74
Venice (Italy) **4:**148
illus. **6:**88
Ershad, Hossein Mohammed (political leader of Bangladesh) **2:**244
Erzberg (Ore Mountain) (Styria province, Austria) **3:**314, 318
Erzgebirge Mountains (Czech Republic–Germany) **3:**242; **4:**224, 227
Escalante, Silvestre Vélez de (Spanish explorer) **5:**325
Escalante Desert (Utah) **5:**323
Esch-sur-Sûre (Luxembourg)
illus. **3:**207
Escobar, Marisol (Venezuelan sculptor) **6:**142
Escondido (river, Nicaragua) **6:**57
Escorial (palace, near Madrid, Spain) **4:**98

Esdraelon (plain, Israel) **2:**105
Eskimo *see* Inuit
Esmeralda (Ecuador) **6:**146
Esperanza (Palmer Peninsula, Antarctica) **6:**345
Espiritu Santo (island, Vanuatu) **2:**594–95, 596
Espoo (Finland) **4:**64
Esquemeling (Dutch buccaneer) **5:**432
Esquiline Hill (Rome, Italy) **4:**165
Essen (Germany) **3:**244, 265
Essequibo River (Guyana) **6:**149
Estates-General (French history) **3:**184
Estelí (Nicaragua) **6:**55
Estenssoro, Victor Paz *see* Paz Estenssoro, Victor
Estevánico (Moorish explorer) **5:**322
ESTONIA 3:2, 25; **4:293–96**
illus. **4:**293, 295
flag **4:**vi
map(s) **4:**294
Estonians (Baltic people) **4:**293
Estoril (Portugal) **4:**72
Estrada, Joseph (president of Philippines) **2:**338, 340
Estrada Cabrera, Manuel (Guatemalan leader) **6:**33
Estrêla, Serra da (mountains, Portugal) **4:**66
Estremadura (historic region, Spain) **4:**94, 108
ETA (Basque separatist organization) **4:**90
ETHIOPIA 1:36, 282–92
African plateau regions **1:**18
Blue Nile's headwaters at Lake Tana **1:**39
early human fossils **1:**6
Egypt, Ethiopian rulers of **1:**118
Eritrea, war with **1:**295, 296
Franco-Ethiopian Railroad **1:**298
Italy, history of **4:**160
Mengistu and the Derg **1:**290
Ogaden **1:**288
illus.
Blue Nile Falls **1:**284
castle of King Fasiladas **1:**290
flag **1:**xxiii
market at Gondar **1:**286
rain/fertilization ceremony **1:**291
refugees **1:**292
ruins at Aksum **1:**289
village **1:**282
water supply from irrigation canal **1:**287
map(s) **1:**283
Ethiopian Orthodox Christianity 1:285, 288, 295
Ethnic groups *see also* articles on individual countries, regions, and states
Africa's First World War **1:**118
Asia, areas of conflict in **2:**30, 40, 55
Bosnia and Herzegovina **4:**288, 290
Croatia **4:**287
Los Angeles's neighborhoods **5:**345
New Jersey **5:**207, 209
New York City **5:**204, 205
Ontario's changing mix **5:**105–6
Solomon Islands **2:**557
Sri Lanka, violence in **2:**249
U.S. minority populations **5:**171, 173
Winnipeg's many groups **5:**116
Yugoslav wars **4:**274, 276–77, 280, 281
Étienne, Jean-Louis (French explorer) **6:**337
Etna, Mount (Sicily) **4:**128, 129
Etruscans (people) **3:**47; **4:**134, 154–55
Euboea (Greek island) **4:**187, 189–90
Eucalyptus (tree) **1:**282, 284; **2:**486, 492, 510
ghost gums **2:**533

Eugene (Oregon) **5:**340
Eugene Onegin (novel, Pushkin) **4:**312
Eugénie (French empress) **3:**196
Eulalia, Saint (patron saint of Barcelona) **4:**102
Euphrates River (Asia) **2:**11–12, 50–51, 91, 147–48
table(s)
longest rivers of the world **6:**346
Eurasia (name for Europe and Asia when considered as one continent) **2:**5; **3:**5
Ireland, the western boundary **3:**65
Russia **4:**305–6
Euro (European currency) **3:**1, 2, 4, 44
illus.
symbol on sign at Eiffel Tower **3:**172
Euro Disneyland (Marne-la-Vallée, France) **3:**172, 202
Euromast (tower, Rotterdam, the Netherlands) **3:**233
EUROPE 3:1–64
Alps **3:**299–304
Danube River **3:**326–29
Rhine River **3:**244–45
illus.
flags of the countries **3:**vi; **4:**v–vi
map(s) **3:**6–7, 10–11
population density **3:**29
precipitation **3:**29
table(s)
area and population **6:**344
continental extremes **6:**345
great mountain peaks **6:**348–49
nations **3:**13
Europe, Council of *see* Council of Europe
European Coal and Steel Community (ECSC) 3:3, 190; **4:**162
European Commission for Nuclear Research 3:293
European Community *see* European Union
European Court of Human Rights 3:161
European Economic Area 3:298; **4:**34
European Economic Community (EEC, Common Market) 4:152, 162 *see also* European Union
France **3:**190
Germany **3:**260, 283
Netherlands **3:**231, 232–33
European Free Trade Association (EFTA) 3:2
European Monetary Union (EMU) 3:2, 4, 64; **4:**58
Belgium **3:**221
Germany **3:**262
Spain **4:**118
European Parliament 3:161, 210
European Recovery Program (1948–1952) *see* Marshall Plan
European Union (formerly **European Community**) (collective name for various cooperative organizations) **3:**1, 2, 4, 64, 78
Andorra, agreement with **4:**121
Austria temporarily isolated by **3:**325
Belgium **3:**212, 221, 224
defense **3:**64
Denmark **4:**13, 22
European Investment Bank **3:**210
Finland **4:**55, 58
formation of EEC **3:**62
Greece **4:**200, 211
Ireland's economic growth **3:**71
Netherlands **3:**238
Norway's trade with **4:**34

European Union (cont.)
Portugal **4:**78
social welfare legislation **3:**40
Spain **4:**118
Sweden **4:**50
Swiss agreements with **3:**298
Turkey **2:**64
United Kingdom **3:**95
workers move between countries **3:**25
illus.
offices in Brussels **3:**222
Europoort (harbor, Rotterdam, Netherlands)
3:42, 233
Evangelical movement (in Brazil) **6:**162
Evangeline (poem, Longfellow)
illus.
statue of Evangeline **5:**93
Evans, Gwynfor (Welsh member of British Parliament) **3:**130
Evansville (Indiana) **5:**280
Everest, Mount (Tibet–Nepal) **2:**166, 167, 231;
6:345
Asia, landforms of **2:**10
illus. **2:**1
Everglades (swamp in Florida) **5:**238, 240
illus. **5:**240
Evergreen State (nickname for Washington)
5:336
Évora (Portugal) **4:**72
Evzones (Greek soldiers) **4:**193
Ewe (African people) **1:**198, 199, 206
Ewe language 1:207
Ewondo language 1:234
Exploits River (Newfoundland) **5:**81–82
Exploration and discovery *see also* names of
individual explorers, and history section of
country and regional articles
Africa's interior difficult to access **1:**19
Antarctic **6:**330–32, 337
Arctic **5:**61–62
Asia, Marco Polo's travels in **2:**16
Atlantic Provinces of Canada **5:**78–79
Canada **5:**75
Central America **6:**15
Mississippi River **5:**161
Monument of Discoveries (Lisbon, Portugal)
4:72
North America **5:**1–2, 173
Oceania **2:**563–66
Polynesia **2:**602–3
Portuguese explorers **4:**75–76
South America **6:**82, 97–98
U.S. Pacific States **5:**335
illus.
Spanish founding of St. Augustine **5:**169
Exploration and Discovery, Age of (15th–17th
centuries) **3:**55–56
Extraterritoriality
Vatican's colonies **4:**178
Eyadéma, Gnassingbe (president of Togo)
1:209
Eyre, Lake (South Australia, Australia) **2:**482,
483, 521; **6:**345
table(s)
largest lakes **6:**347
Eyre Basin (Australia) **2:**483
Ezana (emperor of Aksum) **1:**288

· · · **F** · · ·

Fabini, Eduardo (Uruguayan composer) **6:**257
Factories *see* Manufacturing
Fada (Chad) **1:**242
Fados (Portuguese songs) **4:**69
Faeroe Islands (Denmark) **3:**8; **4:**8, 20
Fahd (Saudi Arabian king) **2:**127
Fahrenheit scale 6:376
Fairbanks (Alaska) **5:**349, 350
Fairfax (Virginia) **5:**225
Fair Isle (Scotland) **3:**135
Fairweather, Mount (British Columbia) **5:**129
illus. **5:**129
Faisal (Saudi Arabian king) **2:**127, 129
Faisalabad (Lyallpur) (Pakistan) **2:**188
Faisal Ibn Hussein (Syrian king) **2:**95, 96
Faisal Masjid (Faisal Mosque) (Islamabad, Pakistan) **2:**187
Faith, Age of *see* Middle Ages
Faiyum (oasis, Egypt) **1:**112
Falasha (African people) **1:**36, 285
Falkland Islands (Islas Malvinas) (Atlantic
Ocean) **3:**90; **6:**84, 280, 286–87
illus. **6:**286, 287
map(s) **6:**287
Falkland Islands War (Britain–Argentina, 1982)
3:90; **6:**287, 300
Fall line (geological area) **5:**199, 224
Fall Line Hills (Georgia) **5:**233
Falster (island, Denmark) **4:**8
Falun Gong (Chinese meditation sect) **2:**422
Famagusta (Cyprus) **2:**70, 71
Famagusta Bay (Cyprus) **2:**69, 70
Family *see also* Clans and clan systems
Africa **1:**28–29
Algeria **1:**78–79
Arab Muslims **2:**45
Brazil **6:**163
Burkina Faso **1:**191
China **2:**390–91
Congo, Democratic Republic of **1:**266
Costa Rica **6:**65
Gambia **1:**160
Hindu Codes (India) **2:**221
Iran **2:**158
Ireland **3:**68
Japan **2:**448, 452–55, 456–57
Latin America **6:**8, 109–10
Liberia **1:**181
Myanmar **2:**269
Nigeria **1:**220
Oceania **2:**563
Senegal **1:**156
Sierra Leone **1:**174
Suriname **6:**156, 157
Syria **2:**91
illus. **2:**38
Famine
Africa **1:**23
Biafra **1:**228
Cambodia (1970s) **2:**290
China (1950s–1960s) **2:**412
Eritrea **1:**294
Ethiopia **1:**286, 287
Europe **3:**35
Iceland (1783) **4:**3
Ireland (1840s) **3:**76
Korea, North **2:**431, 433

Somalia (1990s) **1:**305
Sudan **1:**128
Ukraine (1930s) **4:**340
Faneuil Hall (Boston, Massachusetts) **5:**190
Fang (African people) **1:**235, 253
Fa Ngoun (historic ruler of Laos) **2:**285
Fanon, Frantz (Algerian writer) **1:**80
Fanti (African people) **1:**198, 199
Farabundo Martí National Liberation Front (El
Salvador) **6:**48
Farafra (oasis, Egypt) **1:**112
Far East *see* East Asia
Fargo (North Dakota) **5:**298
Farim (Guinea-Bissau) **1:**164
Farms *see also* Collective farms; Subsistence
farming
African society **1:**10, 13–14, 22–23, 26, 27
Atlantic Provinces of Canada **5:**80
Australia **2:**483, 491, 518–19, 520, 535
Central Valley of California **5:**342
Dust Bowl **5:**307
Egypt **1:**102–3, 116
Europe **3:**15, 25, 33–36
fertility of Central Lowland **5:**269
Florida's citrus orchards **5:**241
Honduran poverty **6:**37
Iowa **5:**293
Jamaica, ownership in **5:**472, 473
Malawi **1:**280
Mexico **5:**356, 361–62
Midwestern states **5:**47
New Zealand, agricultural science in
2:548–49
North Dakota **5:**298
Pacific coastal valleys **5:**42, 157
Pennsylvania **5:**211–12, 214
Russian production **4:**317, 318, 319
Saskatchewan **5:**119, 120
strip farms in French North America **5:**34
U.S. growing seasons **5:**158, 159
Wisconsin, America's Dairyland **5:**286
illus.
Africa **1:**63
agricultural technology **5:**174–75
Amish traditional methods **5:**211
Australian sheep ranch **2:**520
Austria **3:**319
Azerbaijan farmer **2:**88
Burkinabe farmers drying vegetables **1:**193
Central African Republic **1:**247
Chile **6:**318
Chinese terraced fields **2:**382
corn harvest **5:**43
Crete **4:**192
Cuban tobacco **5:**442
dairy farm in Wales **3:**123
dairy farm in Wisconsin **5:**284
Denmark **4:**10
El Salvador **6:**46
England **3:**17, 98
Finland **4:**56
fish cultivation **2:**476
Florida's citrus orchards **5:**237
Germany **3:**262
grain harvest in the Prairie Provinces **5:**110
Great Lakes dairy farm **5:**269
Guatemala **6:**30
Haitian rice harvesting **5:**462
hay crop in South Dakota **5:**299
Iowa family farms **5:**293
Iranian women working in field **2:**161

Israel's kibbutzim **2:**110
Japanese rice growing **2:**466
Kenya **1:**308
Mexico **5:**27
Moldova **4:**345
Nigeria **1:**219
North American heartland **5:**7
Ohio's Till Plains **5:**274
Pakistan **2:**184
Peru **6:**208
Russia **4:**316
Russian greenhouse **4:**318
Saskatchewan **5:**120
South America **6:**102
Southeast Asian farm women **2:**255
Spain **3:**32
Swaziland **1:**387
Sweden **4:**42
Ukrainian farm woman **4:**334
Zambian farmer at well **1:**271
map(s)
  world map **6:**352
Faro (Yukon Territory) **5:**147
Faro, El (lighthouse, Mazatlán, Mexico) **5:**397
Faroe Islands *see* Faeroe Islands
Farouk I (king of Egypt) **1:**35, 122
Farsi *see* Persian
Far West (U.S.) *see* Pacific States
Fasching (German pre-Lenten carnival) **3:**270
Fascism
  Croatia **4:**280, 287
  Italy **4:**153, 154, 160–61
Fashion *see* Clothing
Fashoda (Sudan) *see* Kodok
Fasiladas (king in ancient Ethiopia)
  illus.
    castle **1:**290
Fasting 2:126
Fataka (Solomon Islands) **2:**591
Fátima (Portugal) **4:**72
Fatimid (Muslim dynasty) **1:**114, 119
Faya (Chad) *see* Largeau
F'Dérik (Mauritania) **1:**137, 138
Fear, Cape (North Carolina) **5:**229
Fearn, John (English whaling captain) **2:**579
Federal District (Mexico) **5:**410
Federal Republic of Germany *see* Germany, Federal Republic of
Federation of— *see* the main element of the name
Feldberg (mountain, Germany) **3:**258
Fellahin (peasant farmers of Egypt) **1:**102–6
Fenchenko Glacier (Tajikistan) **2:**359
Fenian Cycle (in Irish literature) **3:**70
Fennoscandian Peninsula (Europe) **4:**51
Fen River (China) **2:**371
Fens (swamps, England) **3:**82, 99
Ferdinand II (Ferdinand V of Castile) (king of Aragon) **4:**114–15; **5:**445
Ferdinand III (king of Castile) **4:**103–4
Ferdinand VII (king of Spain) **4:**116
Fergana Valley (central Asia) **2:**350, 352, 353, 355, 359
Fernandes de Queirós, Pedro (Portuguese explorer) **2:**596
Fernández, Mauro (Costa Rican educator) **6:**68
Fernández Reyna, Leonel (president of Dominican Republic) **5:**460
Fernando de la Mora (Paraguay) **6:**244
Fernando Po (island province of Equatorial Guinea) *see* Bioko

Ferris wheel
  illus. **3:**94
Fertile Crescent (region between the Tigris and Euphrates Rivers) **2:**42, 90, 147
Festivals *see also* Parades and processions; articles on individual countries
  Belgium **3:**215
  Berlin's music festival **3:**252
  Bolivia **6:**239
  Brazil **6:**177–79
  Costa Rica **6:**67
  Ghana **1:**194
  Guatemala's Conquista **6:**27
  Honduras **6:**38
  Italy **4:**136, 138–40
  Latin America **6:**306–7
  Mauritius **1:**381–82
  Mexico **5:**366–68
  Munich's Oktoberfest **3:**271
  Pakistani holidays **2:**186–87
  Panama **6:**75
  Sri Lanka **2:**248
  Swaziland **1:**389
  Thailand **2:**277
  Venezuela **6:**140–41
  Wales' National Eisteddfod **3:**125
  Zurich (Switzerland) **3:**293
  illus.
    Bayreuth Festival **3:**256
    Bolivia **6:**90
    celebrations in U.S. **5:**44–45
    Gambia **1:**159
    Nigeria **1:**215
    Oktoberfest **3:**271
    running the bulls in Pamplona (Spain) **4:**94
    Senegal **1:**152
    Seville (Spain) **4:**105
    Wales' National Eisteddfod **3:**125
Feudalism
  Brazil **6:**164
  Burundi **1:**329–30
  England **3:**114–15
  Europe **3:**51–52, 53
  Japan **2:**444, 446
  Tonga **2:**605
Fez (Morocco) **1:**67, 70, 71, 73
  illus. **1:**72
Fez, Treaty of (1912) **1:**74
Fezzan (region, Libya) **1:**94, 95
Fianna Fáil (Irish political party) **3:**77
Fiat (Italian automobile company) **4:**145
Fig trees
  illus. **1:**395
Figueres Ferrer, José (president of Costa Rica) **6:**71
Figueres Olsen, José María (president of Costa Rica) **6:**71
FIJI 2:565, 583, 585, 586, **597–99**
  high islands of Oceania **2:**560
  Polynesian migrations **2:**600
  violence **2:**567
  illus. **2:**597
    flag **2:**x
  map(s) **2:**598
Filfla (island, Malta) **4:**182
Filipinos (people) **2:**333–35
Fillmore, Millard (13th president of U.S.) **2:**445
Films *see* Motion pictures
"Final Solution" (code name for Nazi plan to annihilate European Jews) **3:**278
Finance *see* Banking and finance
Finches (birds) **6:**203

Finger Lakes (New York) **5:**23, 202
FINLAND 4:51–64
  Estonia, relations with **4:**295
  Europe, history of **3:**19
  Lapland **4:**35, 37
  Sweden, history of **4:**48, 49
  illus.
    farm **4:**56
    flag **4:**v
    Helsinki **4:**59, 60, 61, 62
    lake **4:**52
    Marimekko textiles **4:**61
    Olavinlinna **4:**53
    pottery making **4:**60
    reindeer pulling sleds **4:**51
    Tapiola **4:**63
    timber floating downstream **4:**54
  map(s) **4:**57
Finnbogadóttir, Vigdís (president of Iceland) **4:**7
Finnish language 4:55
Finn Mac Cool (legendary Irish hero) **3:**70
Finns (people) **4:**40, 55
Finsteraarhorn (mountain, Switzerland) **3:**286
Fiordland (region, New Zealand) **2:**539
Fiordland National Park (New Zealand)
  illus. **2:**537
Fiords *see* Fjords
Firdausi (Persian poet) **2:**159
Fire Island (New York)
  illus. **5:**199
Fires 5:314; **6:**172
  Great Fire of London **3:**110
Firestone Tire and Rubber Company 1:183
First International Polar Year (1882–1883) **6:**333
First Nations (indigenous people of Canada) **5:**136, 139, 146, 148
First Reich (German history) **3:**272
First State (nickname for Delaware) **5:**215
First World War of Africa 1:270
Fish 6:3, 52, 134
  illus.
    technological cultivation **2:**476
Fishing
  African lakes **1:**19
  Arctic waters **5:**57–58
  Atlantic Provinces of Canada **5:**77
  Chesapeake Bay **5:**219
  Denmark **4:**12
  Europe **3:**33, 36
  French industry **3:**164
  Germany **3:**262
  Grand Banks **5:**78–79, 80, 82, 83
  Greenland **5:**11
  Iceland **4:**2
  Luo of Kenya **1:**309–10
  Mauritania **1:**138
  Morocco **1:**72
  Netherlands **3:**231
  New Brunswick **5:**84, 86
  Norway **4:**28
  Peru **6:**221
  Portugal **4:**72
  Rhode Island **5:**193
  St. Pierre and Miquelon **5:**28–29
  salmon canneries in British Columbia **5:**133
  Sierra Leone **1:**175
  Western Samoa **2:**607
  illus.
    Argentine industry **6:**293

Fishing
   illus. (cont.)
      Atlantic Provinces **5:**80
      Belgian fishing boats **3:**220
      Chile **6:**318
      cooking fish in Iraq **2:**151
      Egypt **1:**114
      French fish market **3:**160
      German fisherman **3:**263
      Ghana **1:**197
      Greece **3:**8; **4:**199
      Haiti **5:**468
      Japanese industry **2:**465
      Kodiak Island (Alaska) **5:**41
      lobster processing **5:**89
      Malawi **1:**281
      Maldives **2:**251
      Morocco **1:**34
      oyster diver in Acapulco **5:**368
      Pakistan **2:**190
      Portuguese fish market **4:**69
      Senegalese fishermen **1:**157
      South American Indians **6:**103
      traditional Portuguese fishing boat **4:**66
      Tuvalu **2:**610
      Uganda **1:**320
      using nets on Lake Pátzcuaro **5:**409
      Vietnam **2:**298
   map(s)
      world map **6:**352
Fish meal 6:207, 221
Fish River (Africa) **1:**348, 403, 404
Fito, Mount (Western Samoa) **2:**608
Fitrat, Abdalrauf (Uzbek author) **2:**351
Fiume (Yugoslavia) *see* Rijeka
Fiumicino (Italy) **4:**171
Five Civilized Tribes (Nation Indians) (group of North American Indian tribes) **5:**305, 306
   see also Cherokee; Chickasaw; Choctaw; Creek; Seminole
Five Dynasties (Wu Tai) (China) **2:**420
Five Pillars of Islam 2:126
Five-year plans (China's economy) **2:**409
Fjords (long narrow bays) **5:**12
      Chile **6:**84
      Norway **4:**24
   illus. **4:**23; **5:**81, 334
Flagler, Henry (American industrialist) **5:**239
Flags of the world
   illus.
      Africa **1:**xxii–xxiv
      Asia **2:**vii–ix
      Central America **6:**vi
      Europe **3:**vi; **4:**v
      North America **5:**vi
      Oceania **2:**ix–x
      Russian tricolor adopted **4:**305
      South America **6:**vi
Flaming Gorge Reservoir (Wyoming) **5:**315
Flanders (region, Belgium) **3:**211, 213–15, 219, 220, 221, 224
Flathead (Indians of North America) **5:**311
Flemings (people) **3:**211, 212, 213–15, 221
Flemish language *see* Dutch language
Flinders Island (Tasmania, Australia) **2:**528
Flinders Ranges (Australia) **2:**483, 521
Flint (Michigan) **5:**278
Flint Hills (Kansas) **5:**303
Floods and flood control
      Algiers **1:**84
      Bangladesh **2:**242

Chinese myth **2:**1
Elbe River **3:**243
Florence (Italy) **4:**149–50
Mekong River **2:**257
Mississippi River **5:**161
Mozambique **1:**366
Netherlands **3:**228
Nile River **1:**39
Peru's *huaycos* **6:**208
Venezuela **6:**148
Venice **4:**148
Yellow River (China) **2:**370–71
illus.
   Bangladesh **2:**239
Florence (Italy) **4:**129, 134, 136, 139, 142, 148–50, 156
   illus. **4:**149
Flores (island in Lesser Sunda group) **2:**315
Flores, Francisco (president of El Salvador) **6:**50
Flores, José Asunción (Paraguayan composer) **6:**248
Flores, Juan José (Ecuadorian soldier and statesman) **6:**50
Flores Facusse, Carlos Roberto (president of Honduras) **6:**41
Florewood River Plantation (Mississippi) **5:**246
FLORIDA 5:12, 163, **237–41**
   population **5:**222
   illus.
      Everglades **5:**240
      Miami Beach **5:**239
      orange grove **5:**237
   map(s) **5:**238
Florida, Straits of (Florida–Cuba) **5:**424
Florida Keys 5:238
Florida Plateau 5:237
Flowers
      Arctic **5:**59
      Colombian economy **6:**125
      Guatemala's national flower **6:**29
      Japanese flower arranging **2:**461
      Netherlands is largest producer **3:**231
      United Kingdom **3:**84–85, 101
      Western Australia's wildflower species **2:**524, 525
   illus.
      Colombian economy **6:**123
      Dutch tulips **3:**231
      Japanese flower arranging **2:**454
      wildflower garden in Perth **2:**526
Fly River (Papua New Guinea) **2:**588
Foggaras (underground water channels) **1:**25
Fogo, Pico do (volcano, Cape Verde) **1:**150
Folklorama (festival, Winnipeg) **5:**116
Folklore *see* Legends and folklore
Folk schools (Scandinavia) **4:**12, 16, 40
Fon (African people) **1:**212
Fon language 1:213
Fonseca, Gonzalo (Uruguayan sculptor) **6:**257
Fonseca, Gulf of (Central America) **6:**35, 42
Fontainebleau (France) **3:**165, 167
   illus. **3:**166
Font-Romeu (France) **3:**173
Fontvielle (Monaco) **3:**206
Food *see also* Cuisine; Famine
      Africa's food supply **1:**2, 63–64
      Bolivian Indians' inadequate diet **6:**237
      Europe's food supply **3:**33–36
      India's Green Revolution **2:**225–26
      Jamaica, malnutrition in **5:**472
      malnutrition in Brazil **6:**169

North Korean shortages **2:**429
Russian shortages **4:**317
staple foods introduced to Africa **1:**14–15
   illus.
      French pastry shop **3:**15
   map(s)
      world grain production **6:**355
Forbidden City (Beijing, China)
   illus. **2:**14
Ford, Henry (American manufacturer) **5:**278
Forests and forestry *see also* Lumber and lumbering; Rain forests
      Antarctica's tropical past **6:**329
      Congo, Republic of **1:**258, 259
      Denmark had first protection law **4:**12
      England, forests cleared from **3:**101
      Europe's vegetation **3:**32–33
      Fontainebleau **3:**165, 167
      Germany's Black Forest **3:**258
      Great Lakes States **5:**268
      Haiti's treeless hillsides **5:**463
      Honduran deforestation **6:**39
      Iceland's reforestation experiments **4:**4
      Idaho fire (1910) **5:**314
      Italy's reforestation program **4:**128
      New Zealand **2:**541–42
      North America **5:**16, 17–18
      Norwegian students plant saplings **4:**28
      Ontario **5:**107, 109
      Pakistan's juniper forest **2:**182
      Portuguese forests planted by King Diniz **4:**75
      South-Central States **5:**256
      Tennessee **5:**263
      United Kingdom **3:**84
      Vermont **5:**186
   illus.
      Sherwood Forest **3:**86
   map(s)
      world map **6:**352, 353
Formosa *see* Taiwan
Fortaleza, La (fortress and governor's residence in Puerto Rico) **5:**168
Fort-Archambault (Chad) *see* Sarh
Fort Chipewyan (Alberta) **5:**113
Fort Christina (Delaware) **5:**216
Fort Collins (Colorado) **5:**320
Fort Gouraud (Mauritania) *see* F'Dérik
Forth River (Scotland) **3:**133
Fort Jackson (South Carolina) **5:**231
Fort Jesus (Kenya) **1:**314
Fort-Lamy (Chad) *see* N'Djamena
Fort McHenry (Baltimore, Maryland) **5:**219
Fort Raleigh National Historic Site (North Carolina) **5:**229
Fort Rouge (early trading post in Winnipeg area, Manitoba) **5:**112, 113
Fort St. George (now **Chenai**) (India) **2:**207
Fort Salisbury (Zimbabwe) **1:**357, 362
Fort Smith (Arkansas) **5:**267
Fort Snelling (Minnesota) **5:**289
Fortune telling 1:230–31
Fortuyn, Pim (Dutch politician) **3:**234
Fort Victoria (Zimbabwe) **1:**362
Fort Wayne (Indiana) **5:**280
Fort Western (Augusta, Maine) **5:**183
Fort Worth (Texas) **5:**49, 254
Forum (Rome, Italy) **4:**165, 167
   illus. **3:**47
Forum des Halles (market complex, Paris, France) **3:**198–99
Forza Italia (Italian political party) **4:**154, 162

Fos (France) **3:**168
Fossey, Dian (American naturalist) **1:**325
Fossils
  Antarctica's tropical fossils **6:**329–30
  dinosaur fossils in Australia **2:**482
  Dinosaur National Monument **5:**323
  human ancestors in Africa **1:**6, 244, 336
  Montana's dinosaurs **5:**312
  Sahara Desert **1:**24
  South Dakota: treasure trove of fossils **5:**299
Foumban (Cameroon) **1:**233
Fountains **3:**293; **4:**173
  illus.
    Buckingham Fountain (Chicago) **5:**281
    Paris' Place de la Concorde **3:**196
    Petrodvorets (Russia) **4:**319
Fourah Bay College (Freetown, Sierra Leone)
  1:176
Four Modernizations (Chinese history) **2:**412
Fouta Djallon Plateau (west Africa) **1:**50, 167,
  168, 216
Fox (Indians of North America) *see* Sauk and
  Fox
Foxe Basin (Northwest Territories, Canada) **5:**4
Fox Glacier (New Zealand) **2:**539
Fox hunting **3:**105
Fox Quesada, Vicente (president of Mexico)
  5:386, 388
  illus. **5:**386
Fox River (Wisconsin) **5:**286
Foyle, Lough (Northern Ireland) **3:**143
Foyle River (Northern Ireland) **3:**83, 143, 146
FRANCE 3:150–203
  Algeria **1:**81, 83–84
  Alps **3:**299–304
  Antarctic research **6:**335
  Asia, colonialism in **2:**24
  Caribbean Islands, colonialism in **5:**435, 436,
    437–38
  Chad **1:**244
  Europe, history of **3:**54, 57–58
  exploration and colonization of North Amer-
    ica **5:**31–34, 174
  French Guiana **6:**92–93
  Germany, military personnel in **3:**247
  Haiti, history of **5:**468–69
  Italy, history of **4:**158
  nuclear testing **2:**559
  overseas departments and territories **3:**191
  Paris **3:**192–203
  president serves as prince of Andorra **4:**121
  railroads **3:**41
  Réunion **1:**46–47
  Rhine River **3:**245
  Saint Pierre and Miquelon **5:**28–29
  South America, history of **6:**97, 98
  tourism **3:**40–41
  Vietnam **2:**302
  women get right to vote **3:**26
  illus.
    aerospace industry **3:**161
    antiques market **3:**158
    barge traffic on Seine River **3:**154
    Béziers **3:**31
    Calais **3:**164
    Carcassonne **3:**162
    Chamonix and Mont Blanc **3:**151
    Châteauneuf-du-Pape **3:**167
    Château of Chenonceaux **3:**181
    cognac production **3:**156
    flag **3:**vi

Fontainebleau palace **3:**166
Honfleur **3:**189
Le Mans auto race **3:**175
Lyons **3:**63
Marseilles **3:**159
Mont-Saint-Michel **3:**163
Nice fish market **3:**160
Orléans **3:**182
Paris **3:**58, 60, 150, 194, 196, 197, 198, 201,
  203
pilgrims at Lourdes **3:**165
Pont du Gard aqueduct **3:**180
Ronchamp chapel **3:**169
Saint-Malo beach **3:**174
Saint-Tropez harbor **3:**168
sheep grazing **3:**155
skiers at Montgenèvre **3:**174
Versailles **3:**57, 166
vineyard **3:**34
map(s) **3:**153
  political divisions **3:**152
  regions **3:**152
table(s)
  rulers and presidents **6:**363–64
Franceville (Gabon) **1:**252, 253, 254
Francia (kingdom of the Franks, now France)
  3:181
Francia, José Gaspar (Paraguayan dictator)
  6:249
Francis I (king of France) **3:**165
Francis Ferdinand (Franz Ferdinand) (archduke
  of Austria) **3:**275, 317, 324; **4:**280, 289
Francis Joseph I *see* Franz Joseph I
Francis Stephen *see* Franz Stefan
Francistown (Botswana) **1:**353
Francis Xavier, Saint *see* Xavier, Saint Francis
Franco, Francisco (Spanish chief of state) **4:**86,
  89, 91, 117
  Canary Islands **1:**33
Franco, Itamar (president of Brazil) **6:**191
Franco-Ethiopian Railroad **1:**298
Franconia (region, Germany) **3:**273
Franconian (dynasty of German rulers)
  Holy Roman emperors, list of **6:**366
Franco-Prussian War (1870–1871) **3:**157, 186,
  275
Frankfort (capital, Kentucky) **5:**261
Frankfurt (Germany) **3:**269–70
  illus. **3:**269, 283
Franklin (Idaho) **5:**314
Franklin, Benjamin (American statesman) **5:**213
Franklin, Sir John (English explorer) **5:**62, 148
Franks (Germanic people) **3:**18, 49, 50, 180–81,
  272, 273
  Frankish Holy Roman emperors, list of **6:**366
  Germany and Switzerland **3:**296
  Holy Roman Empire **4:**155
Františkovy Lázně (Czech Republic) **4:**225
Franz Ferdinand *see* Francis Ferdinand
Franz Josef Glacier (New Zealand) **2:**539
Franz Joseph I (emperor of Austria) **3:**316, 324;
  4:246
Franz Joseph II (prince of Liechtenstein) **3:**306
Franz Stefan (Holy Roman emperor) **3:**323
Fraser, Dawn (Australian athlete) **2:**492
Fraser, Simon (fur trader in Canada) **5:**132
Fraser River and Valley (Canada) **5:**8, 129
Fray Bentos (Uruguay) **6:**261
Frederick (Maryland) **5:**218
Frederick III (Holy Roman emperor) **3:**321

Frederick II (Frederick the Great) (king of
  Prussia) **3:**57, 265–66, 274
  illus. **3:**274
Frederick the Great (king of Prussia) *see* Freder-
  ick II
Frederick William (duke of Prussia) **3:**274
Fredericton (capital, New Brunswick) **5:**85, 86
  illus. **5:**86
Frederik (Danish prince) **4:**22
Frederik V (king of Denmark) **4:**19
Frederik IX (king of Denmark) **4:**22
Frederiksborg Castle (Denmark)
  illus. **4:**8
Free Democratic Party (Germany) **3:**284
Freedom Alliance (Italy) **4:**163
Freedom Trail (Boston, Massachusetts) **5:**190
Free French Movement (World War II) **3:**188
Free market *see* Market economy
Free ports **1:**298; **2:**410
  Indonesia **2:**336
Free State (nickname for Maryland) **5:**217
Free State Province (formerly **Orange Free
  State**) (province, South Africa) **1:**401, 402,
  404
  Bloemfontein **1:**398
Freetown (capital, Sierra Leone) **1:**55, 171, 173,
  176, 177
  illus. **1:**171
Free trade
  Argentina **6:**301
  Caribbean Islands **5:**440
  Central America **6:**47
  Latin America **6:**104, 126
  Mercosur **6:**262
  North American Free Trade Agreement **5:**362
  Panama **6:**77
  Pan-Americanism **6:**115, 323
  St. Lucia **5:**490
Free University (Berlin, Germany) **3:**281
Frei Montalva, Eduardo (president of Chile)
  6:318
Frei Ruíz-Tagle, Eduardo (president of Chile)
  6:323
Frelimo (Mozambican nationalist movement)
  1:368
Fremont culture (Native American people)
  5:309
French Afar Territory *see* Djibouti
French Alps **3:**151
French and Indian Wars (1689–1763) **5:**38, 97,
  109, 206, 214, 274 *see also* Seven Years'
  War
  Minnesota **5:**289
  Quebec **5:**101
French Canadians **5:**74, 97, 100, 101, 102, 103
  Atlantic Provinces of Canada **5:**78, 85
  Manitoba **5:**115
French Community (association of overseas
  states, territories, departments, and Metro-
  politan France) **3:**190, 191
  Africa **1:**143, 158, 188, 214, 255, 260, 377
French Congo *see* French Equatorial Africa
French Equatorial Africa (former French colo-
  nies) **1:**43, 244, 250, 255, 256, 260
French Guiana **3:**191; **6:**7, 92–93
  illus. **6:**92, 93
  map(s) **6:**93
French Indochina (Southeast Asia) **2:**24, 264,
  285, 291, 294
French language **3:**150, 178
  Africa **1:**15

French language (cont.)
Belgium **3:**214
Benin **1:**213
Caribbean islands **5:**435
Congo, Democratic Republic of **1:**265
Congo, Republic of **1:**258
French Guiana **6:**7
Guinea **1:**167
Quebec **5:**95, 100
Switzerland **3:**290
Vietnam **2:**296
French North America 5:31–34, 79–80, 96, 174
French Polynesia 2:601, 602, 603; **3:**191
Tahiti **2:**558–59
French Revolution (1789–1799) **3:**57, 178, 184, 198
Haiti, effect on **5:**468
Italy, influence on **4:**158
slavery **5:**435–36
French Somaliland see Djibouti
French Sudan see Mali
French Territory of the Afars and the Issas see Djibouti
French Togoland see Togo
French West Africa (former French possessions, Africa) **1:**52–53, 139, 143, 149, 193
Fresnillo (Zacatecas, Mexico) **5:**399
Fresno (California) **5:**346
Fretilin (Timorese independence movement) **2:**328
Freyre, Gilberto (Brazilian historian) **6:**180
Fria (Guinea) **1:**169
Friedrich der Grosse (king of Prussia) see Frederick II
Friendly Island see Molokai
Friendly Islands see Tonga
Friesland (province of the Netherlands) **3:**228, 229
Frisian language 3:229
Frisians (people) **3:**235
Frissell, Mount (Connecticut) **5:**195
Friuli-Venezia Giulia (region, Italy) **4:**152, 154
Frobisher, Martin (English sea captain) **3:**119; **5:**61, 136
Frontera (formerly **Álvaro Obregón**) (Tabasco, Mexico) **5:**419
Frontier Days (rodeo, Cheyenne, Wyoming) **5:**316
Frontlands (raised river banks) **5:**247
Front Range (Colorado) **5:**318
Froude, James A. (British historian) **5:**437
Frunze (Kyrgyzstan) see Bishkek
Fuad I (king of Egypt) **1:**122
Fuchs, Vivian (British explorer) **6:**335
Fuego (volcano, Guatemala) **6:**30, 31
Fuentes, Carlos (Mexican writer) **5:**374
Fuerteventura (Canary Islands) **1:**32; **4:**85
Fujaira (United Arab Emirates) **2:**138
Fuji, Mount (Fujiyama) (Japan) **2:**440, 442
illus. **2:**439
Fujian (province of China) **2:**427
Fujimori, Alberto (president of Peru) **6:**228
illus. **6:**227
Fulani (Fula; Fulbe) (African people) **1:**51
Benin **1:**213
Burkina Faso **1:**191
Cameroon **1:**233
Gambia **1:**160, 161
Guinea **1:**167, 168
Guinea-Bissau **1:**164
Mauritania **1:**135, 136

Niger 1:148
Nigeria 1:57–58, 215, 219, 221–22, 223, 226
Senegal **1:**154–55, 158
Sierra Leone **1:**173, 174–75
illus. **1:**244
Fulfulde language 1:136
Fuller, R. Buckminster
illus.
Montreal's Biosphere **5:**98
Funafuti (capital, Tuvalu) **2:**610, 611
Funafuti (island, Tuvalu) **2:**612
Funan (Khmer kingdom) **2:**290
Funchal (Madeira Islands) **4:**68
FUNCINPEC (Cambodian political party) **2:**292
Fundamental Orders of Connecticut (1639) **5:**197
Fundy, Bay of (Canada) **5:**79, 84, 85
illus. **5:**79
Fundy Isles (New Brunswick) **5:**84
Fundy National Park (New Brunswick) **5:**85
Funeral customs
Ganges River **2:**168
Honduras' cave of the glowing skulls **6:**40
Madagascar **1:**374
Moche **6:**223
Funj (African people) **1:**130
Furious Fifties (wind) **6:**325
Fur seals 6:328
illus. **5:**348
Fur trade
Arctic exploration **5:**62
beaver trapping **5:**310
British Columbia **5:**132
Canada's Far North **5:**136
French North America **5:**96, 101
Great Lakes region **5:**269
mountain men **5:**39
Oregon **5:**340
Prairie Provinces **5:**111–13, 117, 121
Washington (state) **5:**338
Wyoming **5:**317
Furtwanger (Germany) **3:**258
Futuna Islands see Wallis and Futuna Islands
Fyn (Fünen) (island, Denmark) **4:**8

· · · G · · ·

Ga (African people) **1:**198, 199
Gabès (Tunisia) **1:**90
Gabès, Gulf of (Tunisia) **1:**90
GABON 1:43, **251–55**
illus.
flag **1:**xxiii
Libreville **1:**251
oil pump **1:**255
Port-Gentil **1:**253
map(s) **1:**252
Gaborone (capital, Botswana) **1:**352, 353
illus. **1:**351
Gaelic languages 3:20, 87
Ireland **3:**69
Irish language and early literature **3:**70
Isle of Man **3:**84
Northern Ireland **3:**144, 145
Nova Scotia **5:**78, 80
Scotland **3:**136
Gagarin, Yuri (Soviet cosmonaut) **4:**312
Gagauz (people) **4:**345, 346
Gagik Bagratuni I (king of Armenia) **2:**78

Gagnoa (Ivory Coast) **1:**185
Gaillard Cut (Panama Canal) **6:**78, 79
Gairy, Eric (prime minister of Grenada) **5:**482
Gaithersburg (Maryland) **5:**218
Galápagos Islands (Ecuador) **6:**84, 192, 202–3
illus. **6:**202, 203
map(s) **6:**202
Galaţi (Romania) **3:**329; **4:**249
Galicia (region, Spain) **4:**87, 89, 91, 108, 113
illus. **4:**90
Galilee (hilly region, Israel) **2:**105, 113
Galilee, Sea of (Lake Tiberias; Yam Kinneret) (Israel) **2:**105
Galileo (Italian astronomer) **4:**158
Galindo, Sergio (Mexican writer) **5:**374
Galla (African people) see Oromo
Gallega Island (Mexico) **5:**407
Gallegos, Rómulo (Venezuelan writer and statesman) **6:**141, 147
Gallen-Kallela, Akseli (Finnish artist) **4:**64
Galleria Vittorio Emanuele II (Milan) **4:**143
illus. **4:**142
Gallipoli campaign (1916–1916) **2:**502
Galway (Ireland) **3:**69, 74
Gama, Vasco da (Portuguese navigator) **3:**55; **4:**71, 75
Asia opened to European trade **2:**23, 215
Cape of Good Hope **1:**403
East Africa **1:**314, 336, 337, 366–67
GAMBIA 1:56, 152, **159–63**
illus. **1:**159, 163
flag **1:**xxii
map(s) **1:**161
Gambia River (west Africa) **1:**160
illus. **1:**163
Gambier (island, Polynesia) **2:**601
Gambling 2:416; **3:**206; **5:**332
Native American reservations **5:**196, 300
Gamelan (Indonesian orchestra) **2:**319
Game reserves and parks
Alaska **5:**349
Australia **2:**488
Belavezhskaya Pushcha **4:**341–42
Camargue region of France **3:**168
Central African Republic **1:**246
Great Dismal Swamp **5:**223
Hawaii **5:**351
Kenya **1:**307
Mexico **5:**421, 422
Nevada's wild burros and horses **5:**331
New Zealand **2:**542–43
Padre Island (Texas) **5:**250
Pine Barrens (New Jersey) **5:**208
Rwanda **1:**324–25
Tanzania **1:**338
Trinidad and Tobago **5:**483
Uganda **1:**321
Zambia **1:**276
illus.
Cumberland National Seashore **5:**233
Mozambique **1:**367
South Africa **1:**395
Tanzania **1:**338
Games see Sports; Toys
Gamsakhurdia, Zviad (president of Georgia) **2:**85
Ganda (African people) **1:**318, 322
Gandhi, Indira (Indian political leader) **2:**218
illus. **2:**217

Gandhi, Mohandas Karamchand ("Mahatma") (Indian political and spiritual leader) **2:**27, 216, 217
Raj Ghat, shrine **2:**208
Gandhi, Rajiv (Indian political leader) **2:**218, 222
Ganges River (India–Bangladesh) **2:**168, 198, 238
Himalayas, source in **2:**167
holy site at joining of Jumna River **2:**208
illus. **2:**199, 208–9
map(s) **2:**168
table(s)
longest rivers of the world **6:**346
Gangetic Plains (India) **2:**198, 199, 226
Gang of Four (in Chinese history) **2:**398–99
Gante, Pedro de (Franciscan missionary, educator) **5:**381–82
Gao (early African kingdom) **1:**169
Gao (Mali) **1:**50, 142, 148
Garay, Juan de (Spanish soldier) **6:**270, 290, 297
Garcia Granados, Miguel (Guatemalan political leader) **6:**32
García Márquez, Gabriel (Colombian author) **6:**122
García Moreno, Gabriel (Ecuadorian leader) **6:**205
García Pérez, Alan (president of Peru) **6:**228
Garcilaso de la Vega (Peruvian historian) **6:**214
Garda, Lake (Italy) **3:**301; **4:**128, 133
Gardel, Carlos (Argentine singer) **6:**275–76
Garden Isle *see* Kauai
Garden of the Gods (rock formation, Colorado) **5:**318
Gardens *see* Parks and gardens
Garden State (nickname for New Jersey) **5:**207
Garfield, James (20th president of U.S.) **5:**273
Garibaldi, Giuseppe (Italian patriot) **4:**158, 175; **6:**264
Garonne River (France) **3:**152
Garoua (Cameroon) **1:**233–34
Gary (Indiana) **5:**46, 280
Gash River (east Africa) *see* Mareb
Gaspé Peninsula (Quebec) **5:**99, 101
illus. **5:**102
Gastineau Channel (Alaska) **5:**350
Gateway Arch (St. Louis, Missouri)
illus. **5:**295
Gateway to India (stone arch, Bombay, India) **2:**206
Gathering Place *see* Oahu
Gatineau River (Quebec) **5:**107
Gatún Lake (Panama) **6:**78
Gauchos (South American horsemen) **6:**95, 253, 255, 269, 273–75, 294, 295
Argentine literature **6:**276
illus. **6:**259, 275
Gaudí y Cornet, Antonio (Spanish architect) **4:**102–3
Gauguin, Paul (French artist) **2:**559
Gauguin, Paul (French painter) **3:**177
Gaul (Gallia) (Roman name for France and parts of bordering countries) **3:**180
Italy, history of **4:**155
Gayoom, Maumoon Abdul (president of Maldives) **2:**252
Gaza Strip (Egypt) **1:**123; **2:**32, 105, 113, 114–15
Gbango, Laurent (president of Ivory Coast) **1:**188
Gbarnga (Liberia) **1:**180

Gdańsk (Danzig) (Poland) **4:**221
illus. **4:**218
Gdynia (Poland) **4:**221
Geba River (west Africa) **1:**164
Gebel (Arab word for mountain) *see* the main element of the name
Gediminas (early ruler, Lithuania) **4:**303, 304
Geelong (Victoria, Australia) **2:**518
Geez language **1:**288
Gefara (sandy plain in Libya) **1:**95
Gelati (republic of Georgia) **2:**83
Gemayel, Bashir (president of Lebanon) **2:**103
Gemsbok (antelope)
illus. **1:**19
General Motors (GM) **5:**278
General Sherman Tree **5:**342
Geneva (Switzerland) **3:**285, 293–94, 295, 297
illus. **3:**61, 294
Geneva, Lake (France–Switzerland) **3:**286, 304
Genevieve, Saint (patron saint of Paris, France) **3:**199
Genghis Khan (Mongol warrior and empire builder) **2:**57, 362, 366
Afghanistan **2:**174, 178
Asia **2:**16, 162, 345
Gennaro (Italian saint) *see* Januarius, Saint
Genoa (Italy) **4:**142, 146–47, 152, 156
illus. **4:**146
Genocide (attempt to kill an entire people)
Armenians **2:**78
Cambodia's Pol Pot regime **2:**292
Holocaust **3:**61, 278
Geographic terms, list of 6:350–52
George, Lake (Africa) **1:**316
George, Lake (New York) **5:**202
George V (king of Great Britain and Northern Ireland) **3:**77
George VI (king of Great Britain and Northern Ireland) **4:**184
George I (king of Greece) **4:**207
George II (king of Greece) **4:**208, 209
George Cross (English award) **4:**184
George of Poděbrad (Bohemian king) **4:**229
Georgetown (capital, Guyana) **6:**150
illus. **6:**149, 150
Georgetown (Gambia) **1:**160
Georgetown (neighborhood, Washington, D.C.) **5:**170
George Tupou I (king of Tonga) **2:**606
GEORGIA (republic) **2:**51, 55, **80–85**
Tbilisi **2:**47
illus. **2:**80
Caucasus Mountains **2:**83
flag **2:**vii
Orthodox worshipers **2:**81
Vardzia cliff dwellings **2:**85
map(s) **2:**82
GEORGIA (state) **5:**233–36
illus.
Atlanta **5:**235
Cumberland National Seashore **5:**233
Savannah's historic homes **5:**236
map(s) **5:**234
Georgia, Strait of (Canada)
illus. **5:**130
Georgian language **2:**44, 81
Georgian Military Highway (Georgia–Russia) **2:**81
Georgians (Asian people) **2:**81
Georgia O'Keeffe Museum (Santa Fe, New Mexico)
illus. **5:**48

Geothermal-power plants **2:**541; **4:**132
illus. **4:**131
Gerlache, Adrien de (Belgian explorer) **6:**332
German-Americans **5:**285
German Democratic Republic (East Germany) (1949–1990) **3:**239, 259–60, 261, 282, 283
government **3:**284
population **3:**246
Soviet domination **3:**63
sports **3:**250
German East Africa (former German colonies) **1:**326, 331
Germanic languages **3:**20
Germanic peoples
Europe **3:**18–19, 49
Germans in Canada **5:**39
Germans in South Australia **2:**522, 523
Kazakhstan **2:**347
Sudeten-Germans **4:**228
German language **3:**248, 252–53
Austrian German **3:**310
Mennonites in the Chaco **6:**248
Switzerland **3:**290
German South West Africa (now Namibia) **1:**350
GERMANY 3:239–84
Alps **3:**299–304
cities **3:**265–72 *see also* names of cities
Danube River **3:**326
reunification (1990) **3:**64, 239, 252, 263–64, 283–84
Rhine River **3:**244–45
states **3:**284
Thirty Years' War **3:**56
World War I **3:**60
illus.
automobile industry **3:**260
Baltic Sea beach **3:**242
Berlin **3:**62, 264, 280, 281
Bremen **3:**265
coastal fishing **3:**263
Cologne **3:**268
Dinkelsbuhl (Germany) **3:**249
farms **3:**262
flag **3:**vi
Frankfurt **3:**269, 283
Hamburg **3:**266
Heidelberg **3:**270
Iron Curtain **3:**282
Lübeck **3:**267
Lutheran Church **3:**247
religious procession **3:**22
Roman ruins at Trier **3:**273
sports **3:**251
tourist boat on Rhine River **3:**244
Ulm **3:**327
vocational school **3:**248
Zugspitze **3:**243
map(s) **3:**241
Germany, East (1949–1990) *see* German Democratic Republic
Germany, Federal Republic of (West Germany) (1949–1990) **3:**239, 260, 282–83, 284
Germany, West (1949–1990) *see* Germany, Federal Republic of
Geronimo (Apache chief) **5:**329
Gessler (legendary Swiss governor) **3:**297
Gettysburg, Battle of (1863) **5:**214
Geysers 4:4; **5:**317
illus. **4:**3; **6:**84
Lady Knox Geyser (New Zealand) **2:**540
Gezira (area, Sudan) **1:**39, 125, 129

GHANA 1:11, 56–57, **194–204**
Ashanti nation **1:**202
illus.
　Accra **1:**196
　artisan painting on cloth **1:**201
　Ashanti **1:**203
　cocoa to be exported **1:**200
　Elmina Castle **1:**194
　fishing **1:**197
　flag **1:**xxiii
　University of Ghana **1:**199
map(s) **1:**195
Ghana (early African kingdom) **1:**140, 142, 169
Islam **1:**139
Ghardaïa (Algeria)
illus. **1:**78
Ghats, Eastern and Western (mountains, India)
2:166, 198, 199
Ghawar (oil field, Saudi Arabia) **2:**128
Ghegs (people) **4:**270
Ghent (Belgium) **3:**214, 217, 219
illus. **3:**219
Gheorghiu-Dej, Gheorghe (Romanian political
leader) **4:**256
Ghéris River (Morocco) **1:**66
Ghibellines (Italian political party) **4:**157
Giant's Causeway (Northern Ireland) **3:**146
illus. **3:**146
Gibbon, Edward (English historian) **4:**268
GIBRALTAR 3:90; **4:**86, **123**
illus. **3:**90
map(s) **4:**123
Gibraltar, Strait of 4:80, 123
Gibson Desert (Australia) **2:**483, 525
Gilaki (Asian people) **2:**157
Gila National Forest (New Mexico) **5:**310
Gila River (New Mexico–Arizona) **5:**327, 329
Gilbert (Arizona) **5:**328
Gilbert (hurricane, 1988) **5:**388; **5:**477
Gilbert and Ellice Islands Colony 2:582, 612
Gilbertese language 2:581
Gilbert Islands (Pacific Ocean) *see* Kiribati
Gilded Age (in U.S. history) **5:**206
Gilead (ancient kingdom in the Middle East)
2:120
Gilgit (region, Kashmir) **2:**173
Ginastera, Alberto (Argentine composer) **6:**276
Ginza (district, Tokyo, Japan)
illus. **2:**34, 445
Giolitti, Giovanni (Italian statesman) **4:**159
Giralda (bell tower, Seville, Spain) **4:**104, 113
Girl with Green Eyes (painting, Matisse)
illus. **3:**176
Gironde (estuary, France) **3:**152
Giscard d'Estaing (president of France) **3:**190
Gist, Christopher (American explorer) **5:**262
Giurgiu (Romania) **4:**249, 255
Giza (Egypt) **1:**39, 114
　Great Pyramids **1:**110
　North African ancient civilizations **1:**33
Gizo (Solomon Islands) **2:**592
Gjirokastër (Albania)
illus. **4:**269
Glacier National Park (Montana) **5:**310, 311
Glaciers
Alaska **5:**348, 349
Alps **3:**302
Beardmore Glacier (Antarctica) **6:**325
Canada **5:**123
Fenchenko Glacier (Tajikistan) **2:**359
Greenland **5:**10–11

Jostedalsbre **4:**25
Kyrgyzstan **2:**353
New Zealand **2:**538, 539
North America **5:**12–13, 310, 311
Pacific States **5:**333
illus. **3:**28
　Alaska **5:**334
　Ellesmere Island **5:**67
　ice tunnel **3:**303
　pilgrims at Colqueounka Glacier **6:**211
Glasgow (Scotland) **3:**136, 138
illus. **3:**137
Glasnost (Soviet policy) **4:**310, 323, 324
Glendale (Arizona) **5:**328
Glendower, Owen (Welsh chief) **3:**130
Glen More (Scotland) **3:**132
Glenn, John (American astronaut and senator)
5:273
Glens of Antrim (Northern Ireland) **3:**143
Glinka, Mikhail (Russian composer) **4:**314
Global warming 5:63; **6:**172, 336
ocean levels **2:**610–11
Globe Theatre (London, England) **3:**116
Glyndwr, Owain *see* Glendower, Owen
Goa (India) **4:**68
Goats
illus. **4:**133
Gobi Desert (central Asia) **2:**10, 362, 378
Godafoss (waterfall, Iceland) **4:**3
Godavari River (India) **2:**198–99
Gododdin (Welsh epic, Aneirin) **3:**125
Godoy, Manuel de (Spanish minister) **4:**116
Godthaab (Greenland) *see* Nuuk
Godwin Austen, Mount (K2) (Karakoram
Mountains, central Asia) **2:**173, 182
Goethals, George W. (American engineer) **6:**79
Goethe, Johann Wolfgang von (German writer)
3:253, 269, 270
Gogebic Range (North America) **5:**4
Gogol, Nikolai (Ukrainian-Russian writer)
4:312–13, 335
Gogra River (India) **2:**168
Goh Chok Tong (Singapore political leader)
2:312
Goiás (state, Brazil) **6:**183, 184
Golan Heights (area annexed by Israel) **2:**96,
105
Gold *see also* Gold rushes
Africa **1:**5, 20
Ashanti art **1:**198
Brazil **6:**188, 189
Canada **5:**4
Nicaragua **6:**53
North America **5:**8–9
Oceania **2:**566
Papua New Guinea **2:**588
South Africa **1:**45, 395, 402
Venezuela **6:**135
Western Australia **2:**527
illus.
　Brazilian mine **6:**174
　South Africa **1:**45, 403
　tourists in Australian mine **2:**533
Gold Beach (Oregon) **5:**339
Gold Coast (former name of Ghana) **1:**11,
201–2, 203
Golden Age (of Spanish arts) **4:**115–16
Golden Gate Bridge (San Francisco, California)
5:345
Golden Hind (ship of Francis Drake) **5:**431
Golden Horde (Mongol invaders of Russia)
3:53; **4:**339

Golden Horn (inlet of the Bosporus, Turkey)
2:62, 63
Golden State (nickname for California) **5:**341
Golden Stool (Ashanti tradition) **1:**202
Golden Temple (Amritsar, India)
illus. **2:**218
Gold rushes
Alaska **5:**51, 350
Australia **2:**479, 500, 520
British Columbia **5:**42, 132
California **5:**51, 347
Colorado **5:**320
Montana **5:**312
Mountain States **5:**310
Nevada **5:**332
New Zealand **2:**479, 553
Panama Railroad **6:**78, 80
South Dakota **5:**299, 300
Yukon Territory **5:**136, 147, 148
Goma (Congo, Democratic Republic of) **1:**270,
325
Gomel (Belarus) **4:**343
Gomera (island, Canary Islands) **1:**32; **4:**84
Gomes, Antônio Carlos (Brazilian composer)
6:180
Gómez, Juan Vicente (Venezuelan dictator)
6:147
Gomułka, Władysław (Polish leader) **4:**222
Gonâve (island, Haiti) **5:**462
Gonâve, Gulf of (Haiti) **5:**462
Gonçalves, André (Portuguese explorer) **6:**184
Göncz, Árpád (president of Hungary) **4:**247
Gondar (Ethiopia)
illus. **1:**286
　castle of King Fasiladas **1:**290
Gondwanaland (hypothetical supercontinent)
2:475, 541; **6:**330
Gonsalves, Ralph (prime minister of St. Vincent
and the Grenadines) **5:**492
González, Elián (Cuban refugee) **5:**452
González, Felipe (prime minister of Spain)
4:118
González Prada, Manuel (Peruvian author)
6:214–15
González Víquez, Cleto (Costa Rican states-
man) **6:**68
Goober State (nickname for Georgia) **5:**233
Good Friday accord (1998) *see* Belfast Agree-
ment
Good Hope, Cape of (South Africa) **1:**45, 396,
403, 404
Good Neighbor Policy (1933; U.S.–Latin Amer-
ica) **6:**113
Goodyear, Charles (American inventor) **5:**196
Goose Lake Prairie State Park (Illinois) **5:**281
Goražde (Bosnia and Herzegovina) **4:**290
Gorbachev, Mikhail Sergeyevich (Soviet politi-
cal leader) **3:**64; **4:**6, 184, 323–24
perestroika **4:**317–18
illus. **4:**325
Gorée (Senegal) **1:**158
illus. **1:**155
Gorgas, William C. (American Army doctor)
6:79
Gorgi, Abdelaziz (Tunisian artist) **1:**88
Gorillas 1:324–25
illus. **1:**327
Gorky (Russia) *see* Nizhny Novgorod
Gorky, Maksim (Russian author) **4:**330
Gorm the Old (Danish king) **4:**20
Gorno-Badakshan Autonomous Region (Tajiki-
stan) **2:**360

Gorongoza National Reserve (Mozambique) *illus.* **1:**367
Gorostiza, José (Mexican poet) **5:**374
Gosiute (Indians of North America) **5:**325
Gota Canal (Sweden) **4:**39
Gotaland (region, Sweden) **4:**38
Gota River (Sweden) **4:**45
Göteborg (Sweden) **4:**39, 44, 45 *illus.* **4:**46
Gothic architecture 3:177 *illus.* **3:**268
Goths (Germanic people) **3:**18
  Gotaland (Sweden) **4:**38, 39, 48
  Ostrogoths **3:**49
  Visigoths in France **3:**180
  Visigoths in Spain **4:**87, 98, 112, 113
Gotland (island, Sweden) **4:**39
Götzen, G. A. Von (German explorer) **1:**326
Goulart, João (president of Brazil) **6:**190–91
Goulburn Island (Australia) **2:**532
Gould, Lawrence (American geologist) **6:**329
Gouled Aptidon, Hassan (president of Djibouti) **1:**299
Government, forms of *see also* articles on individual countries
  absolute monarchy of Louis XIV **3:**183–84
  African community decision making **1:**11, 27
  ancient Greek political philosophy **3:**46
  Asia **2:**29–30
  caste system **2:**210–11
  centralization, as in China **2:**395
  commonwealth status of Puerto Rico **5:**166, 168
  constitutional monarchies **2:**606; **3:**96; **5:**70
  divine right of kings **3:**57
  enlightened despotism **3:**57
  Europe's legacies of how to govern **3:**12
  federal system in Australia **2:**502–3
  federal system of India **2:**220
  Iceland's Althing **4:**5
  Mexico's one-party democracy **5:**386, 387
  "Oregon System" **5:**340
  parliamentary **3:**93, 96
  regional governments, Italy **4:**154
  single-party system **1:**1, 60
  Swiss commune **3:**298
  town meeting **5:**181, 185
  Uganda: a nonparty system **1:**323
Gowda, H. D. Deve (prime minister of India) **2:**218
Gower Peninsula (Wales) **3:**122
Gowon, Yakubu (Nigerian political leader) **1:**228
Goya, Francisco (Spanish artist) *illus.*
  Majas on a Balcony **4:**99
Gozo (island, Malta) **4:**182
Grace (princess of Monaco) *see* Kelly, Grace
Graceland (Elvis Presley's home, Memphis, Tennessee) **5:**264
Graham Land (part of Antarctic Peninsula) **6:**331
Grampian Hills (Scotland) **3:**83, 133
Granada (Nicaragua) **6:**54, 58 *illus.* **6:**51
Granada (Spain) **4:**109, 113, 114 *illus.*
  Alhambra **4:**79, 112
Gran Chaco (region, South America) *see* Chaco
Gran (Great) Colombia, Republic of (South American history) **6:**127, 146, 204

Grand Banks (off Newfoundland) **5:**77, 78, 82, 83
  Portuguese fishing fleets **4:**72
  Saint Pierre and Miquelon **5:**28
Grand Canal (China) **2:**371
Grand Canary (island, Canary Islands) **1:**32, 33; **4:**85
Grand Canyon (Arizona) **5:**156, 309, 327; **6:**345 *illus.* **5:**12–13, 327
Grand Canyon of the Yellowstone River (Wyoming) **5:**317
Grand Canyon State (nickname for Arizona) **5:**327
Grande Comore (Comoros) **1:**383
Grand Etang (lake, Grenada) **5:**481
Grand Forks (North Dakota) **5:**298
Grand Hassan II Mosque (Casablanca, Morocco) **1:**66–67
Grand Ole Opry (Nashville, Tennessee) *illus.* **5:**265
Grand' Place (Brussels) **3:**215, 216 *illus.* **3:**216
Grand-Pré National Historic Site (Nova Scotia, Canada) **5:**78 *illus.* **5:**93
Grand Rapids (Michigan) **5:**278
Grand Teton National Park (Wyoming) **5:**316 *illus.* **5:**315
Granite 5:185, 187
Granite State (nickname for New Hampshire) **5:**184
Granma (province, Cuba) **5:**443
Gran Paradiso (mountain, Italy) **4:**125
Gran Paradiso National Park (Italy) **4:**33
Gran Sabana (region, Venezuela) **6:**135–36
Gran Sasso d'Italia (mountains, Italy) **4:**126
Grant, James (English explorer) **1:**316, 322
Grant, Ulysses S. (18th president of U.S.) **5:**273
Grapes *see also* Wine
  Georgia (republic) **2:**84
Graphite 3:318
Grass, Günter (German author) **3:**251 *illus.* **3:**252
Grasse (France) **3:**168
Grasslands
  Dust Bowl **5:**307
  Illinois tallgrass prairie **5:**281
  Indiana's protected area **5:**279
  Minnesota's tallgrass prairie **5:**287
  Missouri **5:**295
  Nebraska **5:**301
  North America **5:**5, 18
  Saskatchewan **5:**118
  Texas **5:**251 *illus.* **5:**313
Grau San Martín, Ramón (president of Cuba) **5:**447
Graveyard of the Atlantic 5:229
Gray, Robert (American explorer) **5:**338, 340
Graz (capital, Styria, province of Austria) **3:**310, 314
Great Artesian Basin (Australia) **2:**483, 505, 508
Great Australian Bight 2:485, 521, 524
Great Barrier Reef (Australia) **2:**481, 506, 508 *illus.* **2:**506
Great Basin (geologic region, U.S.) **5:**7, 155, 156, 309, 323, 330, 339
Great Bay (New Hampshire) **5:**184
Great Bear Lake (Northwest Territories, Canada) **5:**4, 12, 141, 144 *table(s)*
  largest lakes **6:**347

Great Bitter Lake (Egypt) **1:**120
Great Britain (island, Atlantic Ocean) **3:**80, 91, 112 *table(s)*
  largest islands of the world **6:**346
Great Britain and Northern Ireland, United Kingdom of *see* United Kingdom
Great Cypress Swamp (Delaware) **5:**199, 215
Great Dismal Swamp (Virginia–North Carolina) **5:**223, 227
Great Dividing Range (Eastern Highlands) (Australia) **2:**483–84, 504–5, 509, 510, 516
Greater Antilles (Caribbean Island group) **5:**426 *map(s)* **5:**429
Greater Moravia (former Slavic state) **4:**234
Greater Serbia (nationalist movement) **4:**276, 280
Greater Sunda Islands (Indonesia) **2:**314–15
Great Escarpment (region, South Africa) **1:**395
Great Falls (New Jersey) **5:**208
Great Lakes (North America) **5:**4, 268, 270
  Canada **5:**94; **5:**105
  climate **5:**105; **5:**269
  Ice Ages **5:**12, 13
  Michigan shoreline **5:**275
  port cities **5:**270
  St. Lawrence Seaway **5:**96
GREAT LAKES STATES (region, U.S.) **5:**47, 48, **268–89**
Great Leap Forward (Chinese history) **2:**398, 403, 409, 412
Great Plague (1665, London) **5:**291
Great Plains (North America) **5:**5, 155, 290, 299, 301, 303, 318
  buffalo hunting by Plains Indians **5:**23
  elevation **5:**308
  glaciation **5:**12
  Montana **5:**315
  New Mexico **5:**321
  Oklahoma **5:**305, 307
  Texas **5:**251
Great Plateau (Australia) *see* Western Shield
Great Rift Valley (Africa) **1:**285, 307–8
  eastern Africa **1:**262, 277–78, 283, 316, 317, 328
  Manyara, Lake, wildlife park **1:**338 *illus.* **1:**27
Great Saint Bernard Pass (Alps) **3:**289; **4:**126
Great Salt Lake (Utah) **5:**309, 325, 326 *illus.* **5:**326
Great Sandy Desert (Australia) **2:**525
Great Scarcies River (Guinea–Sierra Leone) **1:**172
Great Serpent Mound (Ohio) **5:**274 *illus.* **5:**273
Great Slave Lake (Northwest Territories, Canada) **5:**4, 12, 141, 143, 144 *illus.* **5:**143 *table(s)*
  largest lakes **6:**347
Great Smoky Mountains (North Carolina–Tennessee) **5:**156
Great Smoky Mountains National Park (North Carolina–Tennessee) **5:**263, 264
Great Swamp Fight (American history) **5:**194
Great Trek (South Africa, 1836–1838) **1:**404
Great Uprising (Sepoy Mutiny) (1857, India) **2:**216
Great Valley of California 5:51, 52
Great Valley of Virginia 5:224
Great Victoria Desert (Australia) **2:**521, 525

Great Wall of China
illus. **2:**377, 417
Great Zab River (Asia) **2:**50
Greco, El (Spanish painter) **4:**98, 115–16, 192
illus.
   View of Toledo **4:**100
Gredos, Sierra de (mountains, Spain) **4:**82
GREECE 4:185–211
Cyprus **2:**68, 73
farms **3:**36
Macedonian republic's name opposed by **4:**291
illus.
   Astypalaia **4:**191
   Athens **4:**185, 196, 197, 211
   baking Easter breads **4:**194
   church at Mistras **4:**204
   Corfu **4:**210
   Corinth **4:**203
   Corinth Canal **4:**186
   Crete **4:**192
   Crusaders' castle **4:**207
   Delphi **4:**202
   fishing industry **3:**8; **4:**199
   flag **4:**v
   monastery on island **4:**208
   Mount Athos **4:**197
   Mykonos **4:**189
   Rhodes **4:**190
   ruins on Delos **3:**46
   theater ruins **4:**209
   Thera **4:**200
   traditional costume and dance **4:**193
   village square **4:**187
map(s) **4:**188
Greece, ancient 4:201–5
concept of democracy **3:**12
contributions to science **3:**15
culture brought to Spain by Muslims **4:**113
Europe's classical civilizations **3:**45–47
Georgia (republic) **2:**84
Middle East **2:**49
Sicily **4:**129, 154
Spanish outposts **4:**110
Greek language 4:195
Greek Orthodox Church 4:193, 194–95, 205, 206
illus.
   icon painting **2:**69
Green Bay (bay, Michigan–Wisconsin) **5:**285, 286
Green Bay (Wisconsin) **5:**286
Greenhouse effect *see* Global warming
Greenland 5:10–11
Arctic exploration **5:**61
continental extremes **6:**345
glaciers **5:**56
Iceland, relations with **4:**5
Inuit **5:**58
Kalmar Union **4:**20
Norway, history of **4:**25, 26
shrimp grounds are largest in world **4:**12
Viking settlements **5:**14
winter temperatures **5:**57
illus. **5:**10
map(s) **5:**10
table(s)
   largest islands of the world **6:**346
Green Mountain (Libya) *see* Akhdar, Gebel el
Green Mountains (Vermont) **5:**156, 180, 186, 187
Green Party (Germany) **3:**284

Green Revolution (India) **2:**225–26
Green River (Wyoming) **5:**315
Greensboro (North Carolina) **5:**229
Greenville (Liberia) **1:**180
Greenville (Mississippi) **5:**246
Greenville (South Carolina) **5:**232
Greenwich Village (neighborhood, New York City) **5:**205
Gregory, Lady Augusta (Irish playwright) **3:**70
Gregory, Saint (Gregory I; Gregory the Great) (pope) **3:**50, 256
GRENADA (island, West Indies) **5:**427, 438, **481–82,** 488
Caribs **5:**430
Creole patois **5:**435
U.S. invasion of **5:**440
illus.
   flag **5:**vi
   St. George's **5:**481
map(s) **5:**482
Grenadines (islands in the Caribbean Sea) **5:**481, 491
Grey, Sir George (New Zealand statesman) **2:**553
Greylock, Mount (Massachusetts) **5:**189
Grieg, Edvard (Norwegian composer) **4:**28
Griffin, Walter Burley (American architect) **2:**514
Grijalva, Juan de (Spanish explorer) **5:**407, 419
Grijalva River (Mexico) **5:**419
Grimaldi family (rulers of Monaco) **3:**206
Grimm, Jacob and Wilhelm (German collectors of fairy tales) **3:**253
Grimsson, Olafur Ragnur (Icelandic president) **4:**7
Grindelwald (Switzerland)
illus. **3:**285
Gripsholm Castle (Sweden)
illus. **4:**49
Grise Fiord (settlement, Nunavut) **5:**139
Groningen (province, Netherlands) **3:**229
Groote Eylandt (island, Australia) **2:**532
Gropius, Walter (German-American architect)
illus.
   Bauhaus **3:**255
Gros Piton (mountain, St. Lucia)
illus. **5:**489
Grossglockner (mountain, Austria) **3:**312
illus. **3:**312
Gros Ventre (Indians of North America) *see* Atsina
Group Areas Act (South Africa, 1966) **1:**58
Group of Three (trade organization) **6:**115
Grozny (capital, Chechnya)
illus. **4:**326
Grundtvig, Nikolai Frederik Severin (Danish theologian) **4:**12
Grünewald, Matthias (German artist) **3:**254
illus.
   Temptation of Saint Anthony **3:**254
Grunitzky, Nicolas (president of Togo) **1:**209
Grünwald, Battle of (1410) **4:**304
Gstaad (Switzerland) **3:**288
illus. **3:**303
Guadalajara (capital, Jalisco, Mexico) **5:**31, 356, 389, 402
illus. **5:**402
Guadalcanal (island, Solomon Islands) **2:**557; **2:**591, 592
Guadalquivir River (Spain) **4:**82, 103, 110
Guadalupe, Basilica of the Virgin of (Mexico City) **5:**411

Guadalupe Mountains (Texas) **5:**251
Guadalupe Peak (Texas) **5:**251
Guadarrama, Sierra de (mountains, Spain) **4:**82
Guadeloupe (Caribbean island) **3:**191; **5:**430, 436, 438
French language **5:**435
map(s) **5:**429
Guadiana River (Spain–Portugal) **4:**66, 82
Guadiana Valley (Mexico) **5:**398
Guajira Peninsula (Colombia) **6:**117, 125
Guam (island, Pacific Ocean) **2:**568–69, 570
illus. **2:**568
Guanabara Bay (Brazil) **6:**160, 184, 185
Guanacache (lake district, Argentina) **6:**269
Guanacaste (province in Costa Rica) **6:**66
illus. **6:**63
Guanacaste, Cordillera de (mountains, Costa Rica) **6:**63
Guanaco (animal) **6:**87
Guanaja (island, Honduras) **6:**41
Guanajuato (capital, Guanajuato state, Mexico) **5:**405
GUANAJUATO (state, Mexico) **5:**403, **405**
Guanajuato River (Mexico) **5:**405
Guanches (people) **1:**33
Guangxi Autonomous Region (China) **2:**385
illus. **2:**382
Guangzhou (Canton) (China) **2:**374
illus. **2:**401
Guano (seabird droppings used as fertilizer) *see* Phosphate
Guantánamo Bay (Cuba) **5:**446, 450
illus.
   U.S. Navy base **5:**450
Guaporé River (South America) **6:**231
Guaraní (Indians of South America) **6:**245, 248, 269
Guaraní language 6:245–46, 269, 271
Guardia, Tomás (Costa Rican political leader) **6:**69
GUATEMALA 6:25–33
Belize, history of **6:**24
Central America **6:**9, 10, 15
Central America, culture of **5:**24, 25
civil war **6:**33
economy **6:**14
history **6:**16, 18
land distribution **6:**17
Maya, mystery of the **6:**27
population **6:**7, 11
Tikal **6:**14
United States, relations with the **6:**13
illus.
   Antigua **6:**32
   coffee picking **6:**13
   farms **6:**30
   flag **6:**vi
   Guatemala City **6:**31
   marimba **6:**27
   market **6:**25
   step pyramid at Tikal **6:**29
map(s) **6:**26
Guatemala City (capital, Guatemala) **6:**11, 31
illus. **6:**31
Guaviare River (South America) **6:**146
Guayana (region, Venezuela) **6:**132, 134–36
Guayaquil (Ecuador) **6:**194–95, 199
meeting of Bolívar and San Martín **6:**226
illus. **6:**195
Guayaquil, Gulf of 6:224
Guayas River (Ecuador) **6:**194

Guaymallen (legendary chief of Huarpe Indians) 6:269
Guaymí (Indians of South America) 6:75, 77
Gudmundsson, Einar Már (Icelandic author) 4:7
Guei, Robert (president of Ivory Coast) 1:188
Guelfs (Italian political party) 4:157
Guelleh, Ismael Omar (president of Djibouti) 1:299
Guernsey (island, Channel Islands) 3:87
GUERRERO (state, Mexico) 5:416
Guerrero, Vicente (Mexican patriot) 5:383, 416
Guerrillas (engaging in irregular warfare)
  antiapartheid movement 1:59
  Colombia 6:128
  Maquis in World War II 3:188
  Shining Path 6:226, 228
  Zimbabwe, history of 1:49–50
Guerzi (African people) 1:167
Guevara, Ernesto (Ché) (Latin American revolutionary) 5:447; 6:240
  illus. 6:240
Guhayna (African people) 1:126
Guiana Highlands (South America) 6:86
  Venezuela's Guayana 6:132, 134–36
Guianas, The 6:153 *see also* French Guiana;
  Guyana; Suriname
  Afro-American culture 6:91
  European colonization 6:97, 98
  immigration 6:95
Guilds (medieval unions) 3:39, 117
GUINEA 1:50, 52, 53, **166–70**
  illus.
  choral group 1:168
  Conakry 1:166
  flag 1:xxii
  Independence Day parade 1:167
  map(s) 1:169
Guinea (coin) 5:434
Guinea, Gulf of (Africa) 1:50, 166, 215
GUINEA-BISSAU (Portuguese Guinea) 1:54, **164–65**; 4:77
  illus. 1:164
  flag 1:xxii
  map(s) 1:165
Guinea Coast (region of Africa) 5:434–35
Guipúzcoa (Basque province of Spain) 4:88, 107–8
Guipuzcoana Company (in Latin American history) *see* Caracas Company
Güiraldes, Ricardo (Argentine author) 6:276
Gujarat (state, India) 2:229
Gujarati language 2:199
Gujral, Inder Kumar (prime minister of India) 2:218
Gulab Singh (ruler, Kashmir) 2:173
Gulfport (Mississippi) 5:246
Gulf Stream (Atlantic Ocean current)
  British Isles 3:66–67
  Europe warmed by 3:29, 152, 213; 4:10
  Norway 4:25
  Nova Scotia 5:92
  Sweden 4:39
  United Kingdom 3:83
Gulf War (1991) 2:32, 55; 5:176
  Egypt a leader of multinational coalition 1:123
  Iran remained neutral 2:164
  Iraq 2:151, 152, 154
  Jordan, effects on 2:119
  Kurds 2:148

  Kuwait 2:144, 146
  Oman 2:137
  Qatar 2:143
  refugees 2:31
  Saudi Arabia 2:129
  Shi'ites fled Iraq 2:149
  Syria 2:96
  Yemen 2:135
  illus. 5:171
  war damage 2:149
Gullfoss (waterfall, Iceland) 4:3
Gum arabic 1:129
Gumti River (India) 2:168
Gum tree *see* Eucalyptus
Gunpowder 2:421
  illus.
  site of du Pont works in Delaware 5:215
Guomindang (Kuomintang) (nationalist party in China) 2:25–26, 396, 397, 428
Gupta Empire (India) 2:172, 214, 243
Gurk (Austria) 3:314
Gurkhas (Gurungs) (Asian people) 2:231–32, 233
Gurunsi (African people) 1:191
Gusmão, Alexandre (East Timorese leader) 2:328
Gustav VI Adolf (king of Sweden) 4:47
Gustavus I (Gustavus Vasa) (king of Sweden) 4:48–49
Gustavus II (Gustavus Adolphus) (king of Sweden) 4:49
Gutenberg, Johann (German inventor) 3:253
Guterres, Antonio (prime minister of Portugal) 4:78
Gutiérrez Nájera, José Gorostiza (Mexican poet) 5:374
GUYANA 6:7, 131, **149–52**
  illus.
  barge carrying bauxite 6:151
  flag 6:vi
  Georgetown 6:149, 150
  Muslims 6:152
  Rupununi savanna and Kanuku Mountains 6:150
  map(s) 6:151
Guyandotte River (West Virginia) 5:259
Guzmán, Augusto (Bolivian writer) 6:237
Guzmán Reynoso, Abimael (Peruvian terrorist) 6:226, 228
  illus. 6:226
Gwembe Valley (Zambia) 1:271
Gweru (Gwelo) (Zimbabwe) 1:357
Gwich'in (Indians of North America) 5:142
Gyandzha (Azerbaijan) 2:88
Gyanendra (king of Nepal) 2:233
Gymnasium (German secondary school) 3:248
Gypsies
  Czech Republic 4:225
  Danube River, "the dustless road" 3:329
  Hungary 4:239, 241
  Romania 4:251
  Slovakia 4:232

· · · H · · ·

Haakon VII (king of Norway) 4:26
Ha'apai (island group, Tonga) 2:605, 606
Haarlem (the Netherlands) 3:231
Habibie, B. J. (president of Indonesia) 2:326

Habré, Hissène (president of Chad) 1:244
Habsburg family (German-Austrian rulers, 1278–1918)
  Austria-Hungary 3:309, 313, 321–25; 4:245–46
  Holy Roman emperors, list of 6:366
  Netherlands 3:235
  Reformation in Bohemia 4:229
  Spanish Habsburgs 4:115, 116
  Switzerland 3:296, 297
  Thirty Years' War 3:56, 183
Habyarimana, Juvénal (president of Rwanda) 1:327
Haciendas (Latin American estates) 5:26; 6:126
Hackett, A. J. (New Zealand sportsman) 2:545
Hadhramaut (waterway, Yemen) 2:132
Hadith (Islamic traditions) 2:128
Hadrian (Roman emperor) 3:92, 113; 4:111, 165
Hadrian's Wall (England) 3:92, 139
  illus. 3:92
Hafiz (Persian poet) 2:159
Hafsids (Berber dynasty) 1:92
Hagia Sophia (building, Istanbul, Turkey) 2:22, 61–62
Hague, The (seat of government of the Netherlands) 3:3, 233–34, 235
  illus. 3:238
Haida (Indians of North America) 5:130, 132, 164, 349, 350
Haifa (Israel) 2:109
  illus. 2:109
Haiku (Japanese poetry) 2:460
Haile Selassie I (title of **Ras Tafari Makonnen**) (emperor of Ethiopia) 1:289, 291
Hainan (China) 2:368
Hainchu industrial science park (Taiwan) 2:426
Haiphong (Vietnam) 2:297
HAITI 5:426, 427, 436, 440, **461–70**
  Dominican Republic compared with 5:453, 457–58
  French language 5:435
  immigration to Florida 5:240
  Santo Domingo, history of 5:459
  illus.
  Citadelle Laferrière 5:461
  flag 5:vi
  harvesting rice 5:462
  Port-au-Prince 5:464, 469
  map(s) 5:463
Hajar Mountains (United Arab Emirates) 2:138
Hajj (Muslim pilgrimage to Mecca) 2:126
Hakka (Asian people) 2:425
Haleakala (dormant volcano, Hawaii) 5:352
Haleakala National Park (Hawaii) 5:352
Half Moon Cay (Belize)
  illus. 6:19
Halifax (capital, Nova Scotia) 5:40, 92, 93
  illus. 5:92
Halla, Mount (South Korea) 2:435
Halle (Germany) 3:241
Hallett Station (Antarctica) 6:334
Hallormsstadur (Iceland) 4:4
Hallstatt (Austria) 3:320
  illus. 3:320
Halmahera (island, Indonesia) 2:315
Halonen, Tarja (president of Finland) 4:58
Halphoolaren (people) *see* Tukulor
Hama (Syria) 2:91
Hamas (militant branch of Muslim Brotherhood) 1:123

Hamburg (Germany) **3:**243, 250, 265
illus. **3:**266
Hämeenlinna (Finland) **4:**64
Hamersley Range (Australia) **2:**483, 524–25
Hamhung (North Korea) **2:**431
Hamilcar Barca (Carthaginian general) **4:**110
Hamilton (capital, Bermuda) **5:**32
Hamilton (Ontario) **5:**41, 107
Hamito-Semitic languages *see* Semitic languages
Hammadas (desert uplands) **1:**24
Hammarskjöld, Dag (Swedish diplomat) **1:**269; **4:**50
Hammerfest (Norway) **4:**33
Hammersmith Farm (estate in Newport, Rhode Island) **5:**194
Hammocks (for sleeping) **6:**142, 166
Hammond, James (American senator) **5:**221
Hammurabi (king of Babylon) **2:**20, 48
illus. **2:**12
Hamsun, Knut (Norwegian writer) **4:**28
Han (Indians of North America) **5:**146
Han-Chinese (people) **2:**371, 380, 385, 386
Hancock, John (American patriot) **5:**188
Handel, George Frideric (German-English composer) **3:**256
Handicrafts
  Asia, ancient **2:**20
  Asian women **2:**39
  Austrian master craftsmen **3:**319
  Bhutan **2:**236
  Black Forest cuckoo clocks **3:**258
  Brazil **6:**182–83
  Indo-American culture **6:**91
  Indonesia **2:**319
  Malaysian batik **2:**307
  Maldives **2:**252
  Mexico **5:**365
  North Carolina **5:**228
  Peru **6:**214
  Sri Lanka **2:**248
  Venezuela **6:**142
  illus.
    Beninese cloth illustration **1:**212
    Mexico **5:**365
    painting vases in Taiwan **2:**426
    Polynesian crafts fair **2:**600
    traditional Micronesian crafts **2:**568
Han dynasty (China) **2:**15–16, 385, 394, 420
Hanga Roa (Easter Island) **6:**322
Hanging Gardens (Babylon) **2:**153
Hangzhou (Hangchow) Bay (China) **2:**380
Hannibal (Carthaginian general) **4:**110, 126, 128
Hanoi (capital, Vietnam) **2:**262, 295, 297, 299
illus. **2:**297
    flower vendors **2:**293
    Ho Chi Minh's tomb **2:**301
Hanover, House of (British dynasty)
  British rulers, list of **6:**361
Han River (China) **2:**368
Han River (South Korea) **2:**435
Hans Adam (prince of Liechtenstein) **3:**306
Hanseatic League (trade organization of north European cities, Middle Ages) **3:**273
  Lübeck (Germany) **3:**265
  Norway **4:**25–26
  Riga (Latvia) **4:**298
Han Wudi (Chinese emperor) **2:**420
Hapsburg family *see* Habsburg family
Harappa (ancient city, Pakistan) **2:**13, 171, 180, 191
  India, history of **2:**203, 213

Harare (capital, Zimbabwe) **1:**357, 360
illus. **1:**355, 357
Harbour Grace (Newfoundland) **5:**83
Harding, Warren (29th president of U.S.) **5:**273
Hargeisa (Somalia) **1:**301, 303, 304, 305
Hargreaves, James (English inventor) **3:**108
Harmattan (desert wind) **1:**172, 190, 196, 217
Harold Bluetooth (Danish king) **4:**20
Harold the Fairhaired (king of Norway) **4:**25
Harper (Liberia) **1:**180, 181
Harpers Ferry (West Virginia) **5:**258
Harrisburg (capital, Pennsylvania) **5:**213
Harrison, Benjamin (23rd president of U.S.) **5:**273
Harry (English prince)
illus. **3:**118
Hartford (capital, Connecticut) **5:**196
Hartford Courant (newspaper) **5:**196
Harvard University (Cambridge, Massachusetts) **5:**188, 190
illus. **5:**31
Haryana (state, India) **2:**220
Harz Mountains (Germany) **3:**241–42
Hašek, Jaroslav (Czech writer) **4:**226–27
Hashemite family (rulers of Jordan) **2:**121
Hashemite Kingdom of Jordan *see* Jordan
Hashimoto Ryutaro (prime minister of Japan) **2:**472
Hasina Wazed, Sheikh (prime minister of Bangladesh) **2:**244
Hassan, Abdiqasim Salad (president of Somalia) **1:**305
Hassan, Mohammad Abdullah (Somali leader) *see* Abdullah Hassan, Mohammad
Hassan II (king of Morocco) **1:**74
Hassaniyya Arabic (language) **1:**136
Hassawis (Bahraini people) **2:**140–41
Hassi Messaoud (oil field, Algeria) **1:**76
Hassi R'Mel (Algeria) **1:**76
Hata Tsutomu (prime minister of Japan) **2:**472
Hato Rey (district, San Juan, Puerto Rico) **5:**168
Hats
  Botswana **1:**352
  Campeche: woven palm **5:**420
  Panama hats **6:**196
  Tajik skullcap **2:**360
  Turkey: reforms of Kemal Atatürk **2:**66
  illus.
    Lesotho **1:**393
    Niger headgear **1:**144
    Panama hats **6:**197
    Turkmenistan **2:**356
Hatshepsut (queen of ancient Egypt) **1:**111, 117–18
Hatta, Mohammed (Indonesian leader) **2:**325
Hatteras, Cape (North Carolina) **5:**229
illus. **5:**227
Hattiesburg (Mississippi) **5:**246
Hauraki Gulf (New Zealand) **2:**547
Hausa (African people) **1:**51, 57–58, 145–46, 148, 215, 221–22, 223, 228
  ancient city-states **1:**225, 226
Hausa language **1:**15, 199, 223
Haussmann, Baron Georges (French administrator) **3:**186, 197, 201
Havana (capital, Cuba) **5:**431, 443–44, 448, 451
illus. **5:**441, 445, 446
Havana (province, Cuba) **5:**443
Havana City (province, Cuba) **5:**443
Havel, Václav (president of the Czech Republic) **4:**230, 231
Havel River (eastern Europe) **3:**243

HAWAII 5:157, 351–54
  climate **5:**159
  Oceania **2:**600, 602
  volcanoes **5:**335
  illus.
    hula dancer **5:**353
    Waipo Valley **5:**351
  map(s) **5:**352
Hawaii (largest of the islands of Hawaii) **5:**351–52
Hawkes, "Trigger" (American airman) **6:**335
Hawkeye State (nickname for Iowa) **5:**293
Hawkins, John (English sea captain) **5:**434
Hay
illus. **5:**299
Haya de la Torre, Victor Raúl (Peruvian political leader) **6:**227
Hay–Bunau-Varilla Treaty (1903) **6:**78–79, 80
Hayes, Rutherford (19th president of U.S.) **5:**273
Hay-Herrán Treaty (1903) **6:**78, 80
Hay River (Northwest Territories) **5:**143
Hayward fault (earthquake belt, California) **5:**157
Hazara (Asian people) **2:**175
Health *see* Medicine and health
Heaney, Seamus (Northern Irish poet) **3:**145
Heard Island (Indian Ocean) **2:**488
Heart of Dixie (nickname for Alabama) **5:**242
Heather (plant)
illus. **3:**81
Heathrow Airport 3:42
Heaven Mountain (Denmark) **4:**9
Hebrew language 2:28, 44
illus.
    classes for immigrants to Israel **2:**113
Hebrews (Semitic people) **2:**18–19, 49–50 *see also* Jews
    Moses found at the Nile **1:**38
Hebrides (islands west of Scotland) **3:**8, 81, 134, 135
Hebron (Jordan) **2:**114
Heidelberg (Germany) **3:**270
illus. **3:**270
Heimaey (island, Iceland) **4:**2
Heine, Heinrich (German poet) **3:**253
Hejaz (region, Saudi Arabia) *see* Hijaz
Hekla, Mount (Iceland) **4:**3
Helen (legendary Spartan queen) **4:**202
Helena (capital, Montana) **5:**312
Helgafell (volcano, Iceland) **4:**2
Helios (Greek god) **4:**191
Hellenes (Greeks' name for themselves) **4:**193
Hellenistic civilization (Greek history) **4:**204
Hells Canyon (Snake River) **5:**313, 339; **6:**345
Helsinki (capital, Finland) **4:**55, 59, 62–64
illus.
    harbor in winter **4:**62
    Lutheran cathedral **4:**59
    Sibelius Memorial **4:**61
    statue of Paavo Nurmi **4:**60
Helvetii (people) **3:**295
Hemingway, Ernest (American writer) **5:**448
Henday, Anthony (fur trader in Canada) **5:**112, 125
Hendaye (France) **3:**152
Henderson (Nevada) **5:**332
Heng Samrin (Cambodian political leader) **2:**292
Henri (crown prince of Luxembourg) **3:**210
Henry, Patrick (American patriot) **5:**225
Henry II (king of England) **3:**75, 147–48

Henry V (king of England) **3:**202
Henry VII (king of England) **3:**91, 119, 130
Henry VIII (king of England)
Act of Union (1536, Wales and England) **3:**130
Reformation imposed on Ireland **3:**76
illus. **3:**119
Henry IV (Henry of Navarre) (king of France) **3:**56, 183, 192, 195
Henry Clay Mill (museum, Delaware)
illus. **5:**215
Henry of Burgundy (count of Portugal) **4:**74
Henry of Navarre see Henry IV (king of France)
Henry the Navigator (prince of Portugal) **4:**72, 75
Henson, Matthew (American explorer) **5:**64
Herculaneum (Italy) **4:**144
Herero (African people) **1:**349
Hermitage, The (Andrew Jackson's estate, Tennessee) **5:**265
Hermitage Museum (St. Petersburg, Russia) **4:**330
illus. **4:**331
Hermosillo (capital, Sonora, Mexico) **5:**392
Hernández, José (Argentine poet) **6:**276
Herodotus (Greek historian) **1:**30, 33, 113
Heroes Like Us (book, Brussig) **3:**251
Herrenchiemsee, Castle (Germany) **3:**257
Herrera Campíns, Luis (president of Venezuela) **6:**148
Herrerra y Reissig, Julio (Uruguayan poet) **6:**256
Herzegovina see Bosnia and Herzegovina
Hesling, Edouard (French colonial governor) **1:**193
Hesse, Hermann (German-Swiss author) **3:**290
Heyerdahl, Thor (Norwegian ethnologist and writer) **4:**32
Hickok, Wild Bill (American frontiersman) **5:**299, 300
HIDALGO (state, Mexico) **5:406**
Hidalgo del Parral (Chihuahua, Mexico) **5:**393
Hidalgo y Costilla, Miguel (Mexican priest and patriot) **5:**382–83, 403, 405, 406
illus. **5:**382
Hidatsa (Indians of North America) **5:**291
Hidrovia (proposed waterway, South America) **6:**262
Hierro (island, Canary Islands) **1:**32; **4:**84
Highland Games 3:139
illus. **3:**139
Highlands (Scotland) **3:**132–33, 135
High Tatra (mountains, Europe) see Tatra
Highveld (region, South Africa) **1:**395, 403
Zimbabwe **1:**356
Highways see Roads and highways
Hiiumaa (island, Estonia) **4:**293
Hijaz (region, Saudi Arabia) **2:**123, 127
Hiking 3:24; **5:**187, 233
illus. **5:**183
Hildesheimer, Wolfgang (German dramatist) **3:**251
Hillaby, Mount (Barbados) **5:**478
Hillary, Sir Edmund P. (New Zealand mountain climber) **6:**334–35
Hillbillies (name for people of Appalachia) **5:**257
Hill people (of southeast Asia) **2:**275, 283, 295
Hillsborough Bay (Prince Edward Island) **5:**88
Hilton Head Island (South Carolina) **5:**232

Himalayas (mountains, central Asia) **2:**166–67, 197–98, 231, 232, 234
animal life **2:**200
Asia, landforms of **2:**7, 10
Indus River **2:**170
Nepal **2:**230
illus. **2:**1, 166, 197, 230
Himmelbjaerget (Denmark) see Heaven Mountain
Himyarite (ancient kingdom) **2:**134
Hinayana Buddhism 2:295
Hindemith, Paul (German composer) **3:**259
Hindenburg, Paul von (German general and statesman) **3:**276
Hindi language 2:28, 199, 200
motion pictures **2:**204
Hindu Codes of 1954–56 2:221
Hinduism 2:210–12
Angkor Wat, temple to Brahma **2:**21–22
Asia **2:**14, 18, 19, 169, 171
Bangladesh **2:**243
Bhutan **2:**235
Cambodia **2:**290
caste system **2:**211–12
cave temples (Ellora, India) **2:**216
cows, sacred **2:**201, 213
Ganges River **2:**168, 198, 208
India **2:**209, 219
Indonesia **2:**319, 324
Mauritius **1:**381
Nepal **2:**230, 232
origins of **2:**213–14
Pakistan **2:**191
Sri Lanka **2:**247
illus.
Indian monks **2:**213
pilgrims bathing in Ganges **2:**208–9
priest **2:**210
Sri Lankan temple **2:**247
wedding ceremony **2:**211
Hindu Kush (mountains, central Asia) **2:**10, 42, 170, 174–75, 183
Hindustani (Asian Indian people in Suriname) **6:**155, 156–57
Hindustani language 2:199–200
Hippolyte, Hector (Haitian artist) **5:**465
Hippopotamus
illus. **1:**40
Hirohito (emperor of Japan)
illus.
funeral **2:**472
Hiroshima (Japan) **2:**447
illus.
war memorial **2:**448
Hispania (Roman province, now Spain) **4:**110–11
Hispanic Americans see also Cuban-Americans; Mexican-Americans; articles on individual countries, regions, and states
California **5:**344
Florida **5:**239
Middle Atlantic States **5:**200
New Mexico **5:**321
Puerto Rico **5:**167
United States population **5:**171
Hispaniola (island, West Indies) **5:**426, 428, 431, 432, 433, 462
Dominican Republic **5:**453, 456
Haiti **5:**467
table(s)
largest islands of the world **6:**346

History see also articles on individual continents and countries
important dates in world history, list of **6:**370–74
History, Ancient see Ancient civilizations
Hitler, Adolf (German dictator) **3:**61, 276
autobahns **3:**41
Blitzkrieg on Poland **4:**221
Nietzsche's superman idea incorrectly applied **3:**253–54
suicide **3:**279
World War II **3:**188
illus. **3:**277
Hittites (people) **2:**49, 56
HIV see Human Immunodeficiency Virus
Hmong (Asian people) see Meo
Hobart (capital, Tasmania, Australia) **2:**530
illus. **2:**530
Hobson, William (English government official) **2:**552
Hochhuth, Rolf (German playwright) **3:**251
Ho Chi Minh (Vietnamese political leader) **2:**302
illus.
tomb **2:**301
Ho Chi Minh City (Saigon) (Vietnam) **2:**257, 262, 295, 297
illus. **2:**259
Hockey (sport) **4:**226; **5:**100, 104
illus. **5:**46, 69
Hodeida (Yemen) **2:**131, 133
Hofburg (Imperial Palace) (Vienna, Austria) **3:**316, 317
illus. **3:**309
Hogan, Paul (Australian actor)
illus. **2:**498
Hoggar Mountains (Algeria) see Ahaggar Mountains
Hohenstaufen (German princely family)
Holy Roman emperors, list of **6:**366
Hohenzollern dynasty (rulers of Prussia and Germany) **3:**274, 280
Hohokam (Indians of North America) **5:**329
Hokkaido (island, Japan) **2:**440, 444
table(s)
largest islands of the world **6:**346
Holbaek (Denmark)
illus. **4:**13
Holbein, Hans, the Younger (German artist) **3:**255
Holguín (Cuba) **5:**443
Holland see Netherlands
Holland (Michigan) **5:**276
illus.
Tulip Festival **5:**278
Holland, Kingdom of (Dutch history) **3:**236
Hollé (Congo) **1:**259
Hollywood (California) **5:**51, 345, 347
Holmes, Oliver Wendell (American author)
quoted on Paris **3:**159
Holocaust (mass murder of Jews in World War II) **3:**61, 278, 279
factors shaping modern Israel **2:**104
Swiss banks held victims' assets **3:**298
Wiesel, Elie **4:**252
Holography
illus. **5:**49
Holstein (former duchy, south Jutland) **4:**20–21
see also Schleswig-Holstein
Holy Land see Palestine

Holy Roman Empire (A.D. 800 with interregnums to 1806) **3:**272, 273, 274
　Charlemagne, first emperor **3:**181
　emperors, list of **6:**366
　Europe **3:**50–51, 54
　Italy **4:**155–56
　Netherlands **3:**235
　Reformation and Counter Reformation **3:**56
　Switzerland **3:**296, 297
Holyrood Castle (Edinburgh, Scotland) **3:**134
Holy Sepulcher, Church of the (Jerusalem) **2:**46
Holy Trinity (Saint-Trinité), Episcopal Cathedral of the (Port-au-Prince, Haiti) **5:**465
　illus. **5:**466
Home Insurance Building (Chicago, Illinois) **5:**283
Homelands (in South African history) **1:**58, 59, 404, 406
Homelessness
　India **2:**203–4
Homer (Greek poet) **4:**201–2
　birthplace **2:**63
　Iliad, first record of war in Europe **3:**45–46
Home rule
　Basques in Spain **4:**90
　Ireland **3:**77, 148
Homes *see* Architecture; Housing
Homesteaders (U.S. history) *see* Land rushes
Homs (Syria) **2:**91
HONDURAS 6:34–41
　cave of the glowing skulls **6:**40
　Central America **6:**9
　claims to parts of the Mosquito Coast **6:**56
　Copán **6:**14
　El Salvador, relations with **6:**50
　history **6:**16, 18
　land ownership **6:**17
　population **6:**11
　United States, relations with the **6:**12, 13
　illus. **6:**37, 38
　　banana industry **6:**13, 37
　　Copán **6:**40
　　flag **6:**vi
　　Tegucigalpa **6:**34, 36
　map(s) **6:**39
Honecker, Erich (East German political leader) **3:**282, 283
Honfleur (France)
　illus. **3:**189
Hong Kong 2:410–11
　British acquisition of **2:**24, 374
　economy **2:**375, 376
　way of life **2:**372
　illus.
　　Chinese troops move into city **2:**410–11
　map(s) **2:**411
Honiara (capital, Solomon Islands) **2:**592, 593
Honolulu (capital, Hawaii) **5:**353
Honshu (island, Japan) **2:**440, 442
　table(s)
　　largest islands of the world **6:**346
Hood, Mount (Oregon) **5:**339
　illus. **5:**339
Hooghly River (India) **2:**205
Hoosier State (nickname for Indiana) **5:**279
Hoover Dam (Boulder Dam) (Arizona–Nevada) **5:**24
　illus. **5:**24
Hopatcong, Lake (New Jersey) **5:**208
Hopetown (South Africa) **1:**402
Hopewell culture (Native American people) **5:**269, 272, 274

Hopi (Indians of North America) **5:**328
Horlich Mountains (Antarctica) **6:**329
Hormuz, Strait of 2:136, 138
Horn, Cape (Chile) **6:**78, 316, 317
　Antarctic trade and exploration **6:**330
Horn of Africa (northeastern Africa) **1:**298, 300
Horses
　Argentina **6:**274
　Assateague Island **5:**223
　English sports **3:**105
　Iceland **4:**2
　Indians of North America **5:**292
　Irish horse racing **3:**68
　Italian festivals **4:**139–40
　Kentucky's horse farms **5:**262
　Lippizaner horses **4:**284
　Mongolia **2:**363, 364
　Nevada refuges **5:**331
　Turkmenistan **2:**357
　illus.
　　Bluegrass Country breeding farm **5:**262
　　buggies in Colonial Williamsburg **5:**226
　　Chilean *huaso* and his horse **6:**307
　　Cumberland National Seashore **5:**233
　　horse-drawn sleigh in Russia **4:**308
　　Irish horse show **3:**73
　　Italian horse race **4:**139
　　Mongolia **2:**382
　　polo **2:**20
Horsham (Victoria, Australia) **2:**518–19
Horthy, Miklós (Hungarian ruler) **4:**246
Hosokawa, Morihiro (prime minister of Japan) **2:**472
Hostages
　Fijian parliament building **2:**599
　U.S. embassy seizure in Iran **2:**163
Hotham, Mount (Australia) **2:**516–17
Hot springs *see* Thermal springs
Hot Springs National Park (Arkansas) **5:**267
Hottentots (African people) *see* Khoikhoi
Houphouët-Boigny, Félix (president of Ivory Coast) **1:**188
Housatonic River (Connecticut–Massachusetts) **5:**195
Housing
　Afghanistan **2:**176–77
　Algeria **1:**79
　Asia, Southeast **2:**263
　Bantu houses **1:**359
　Botswana **1:**352
　Brazil **6:**161–62
　Brunei **2:**329
　Burundi **1:**329
　China **2:**400, 401, 402
　Egyptian fellahin's houses **1:**104
　Fiji **2:**598
　Iraq **2:**149–50
　Japan **2:**440, 442, 455
　Jordan **2:**118
　Laos **2:**283
　Madagascar **1:**375
　Malaysia **2:**306
　mansions of Newport, Rhode Island **5:**194
　Morocco **1:**68
　Moscow **4:**329
　Pakistan **2:**184–85
　shortage in Shanghai **2:**401, 402
　shortages in Venezuela **6:**139
　Sierra Leone **1:**174
　Sri Lanka **2:**247
　Sweden **4:**40–41

　Thailand **2:**276
　Tunisia **1:**88
　Turkey **2:**59–60
　Tuvalu **2:**611
　Western Samoa **2:**608
　illus.
　　Asian houses on stilts **2:**270, 321, 336
　　Austrian public housing **3:**316
　　Barbados **5:**478
　　Beninese houses on stilts **1:**210
　　Botswana village **1:**352
　　Cappadocia (Turkey) **2:**57
　　Caribbean Islands **5:**427
　　Colombia **6:**106
　　construction in India **2:**228
　　Cyprus apartment buildings **2:**71
　　Dominican Republic **5:**456
　　Ivory Coast houses on stilts **1:**184
　　Kenya **1:**27
　　Mexico **5:**385
　　Pakistan **2:**185
　　pre-Civil War Mississippi **5:**245
　　Rome apartment buildings **4:**169
　　rural Chinese houses **2:**400
　　Solomon Islands **2:**591
　　South American apartment complex **6:**107
　　Southern plantation house **5:**220
Houston (Texas) **5:**49, 253
　illus. **5:**253
Houston, Samuel (American statesman) **5:**255, 264
Howel the Good *see* Hywel Dda
Hoxha, Enver (Albanian political leader) **4:**272
Hoyte, Desmond (president of Guyana) **6:**152
Hron River (Slovakia) **4:**232
Huallaga River (Peru) **6:**209
Huambo (Nova Lisboa) (Angola) **1:**343
Huanacache (lake district, Argentina) *see* Guanacache
Huancayo (Peru) **6:**213, 214, 220
Huang He (river, China) *see* Yellow River
Huarpe (Indians of South America) **6:**268–69
Huáscar (Inca prince) **6:**224
Huascarán, Mount (Peru) **6:**208
Huaso (Chilean horseman) **6:**305, 307–8
　illus. **6:**307
Huastec Indians 5:401, 407
Hudson, Henry (English sea captain) **5:**201, 206
　Arctic exploration **5:**61
Hudson Bay (Canada) **5:**4, 61, 94, 97, 104–5
　Manitoba's rivers **5:**114
　illus. **5:**97
　table(s)
　　major seas of the world **6:**347
Hudson-Champlain gap (Appalachian Mountain pass) **5:**6, 38
Hudson Highlands (New York) **5:**202
Hudson-Mohawk gap (geographical gateway to the west of North America) **5:**37
Hudson River (New York) **5:**6, 43, 44, 45, 202, 204, 208
Hudson's Bay Company (fur traders) **5:**136
　Alberta **5:**125
　British Columbia **5:**132
　Northwest Territories **5:**143
　Prairie Provinces **5:**111, 113, 117, 121
　Yukon Territory **5:**148
Hue (Vietnam) **2:**297
　illus. **2:**300
Huerta, Victoriano (Mexican general) **5:**386; **5:**393
Hugh Capet (king of France) **3:**181

Hugo (hurricane, 1989) 5:232
Hugo, Victor (French author) 3:178, 199
Huguenots (French Protestants) 3:183, 184; 5:165
  Henry IV 3:192
  South Africa 1:403
Hui (Asian people) 2:385
Huichol Indians 5:402
Huitzilopochtli (Aztec god) 5:377, 378, 379
Hukbalahaps (Huks) (Philippine Communist movement) 2:338
Hula (dance)
  illus. 5:353
Hulagu (Mongol Khan) 2:154
Hull (Quebec) 5:95, 101
Human Immunodeficiency Virus (HIV) 1:319
  see also AIDS
Human rights see Civil rights and liberties
Human sacrifice
  Aztecs 5:378–79
  Egypt, ancient 1:101
  Inca Empire 6:223
  Mexico, ancient 5:376, 377
  Tahiti 2:559
  illus.
    Aztec ritual 5:376
Humayun (Mogul emperor of India) 2:216
Humber River (England) 3:83, 99
Humber River (Newfoundland) 5:81–82, 83
Humboldt Current see Peru (Humboldt) Current
Hume, David (Scottish philosopher) 3:137
Hume, John (political leader in Northern Ireland) 3:149
Humor (Romania) 4:252
Hundertwasser, Friedrich (Austrian architect) 3:318
Hundred Days (of Napoleon I) 3:185
Hundred Years' War (1337–1453) 3:54, 182–83
  British Empire, early extent 3:117
Hungarian language 4:236, 240
Hungarians (people) see Magyars
HUNGARY 3:2; 4:236–47
  Croatia, history of 4:287
  Danube River 3:327
  economy 3:25
  Germans 3:279, 282, 283
  Romania, relations with 4:250–51, 257
  Slovakia 4:233, 234, 235
  Soviet domination 3:63
  illus.
    Budapest 3:329; 4:236, 238
    bus factory 4:246
    flag 4:v
    religious procession 4:241
    shepherds 4:243
    town 4:237
    vineyards 4:244
  map(s) 4:239
Hungnam (North Korea) 2:431
Huns (people) 3:18
  Austria 3:308, 321
  Pakistan 2:192
Hun Sen (Cambodian political leader) 2:292
Hunting
  illus. 1:12
Huntington (West Virginia) 5:259
Huntsville (Alabama) 5:243
  illus.
    U.S. Space and Rocket Center 5:243
Hunyadi, János (Hungarian general) 4:245
Hurling (sport) 3:68

Huron, Lake (Canada–U.S.) 5:270
  table(s)
    largest lakes 6:347
Hurons (Indians of North America) 5:32, 96, 99; 5:105, 108
Hurricanes 5:159
  Australia 2:485
  Belize 6:20
  Central America 6:10
  Cuba 5:443
  Florida 5:241
  Gilbert (1988) 5:477
  Honduras 6:40
  Hugo (1989) 5:232
Husavik (Iceland)
  illus. 4:6
Huss, John (Czech religious reformer) 4:229
Hussein, Saddam (president of Iraq) 2:21, 55, 154
Hussein, Taha (Egyptian minister of education) 1:108
Hussein I (king of Jordan) 2:115, 116, 117, 121
Husseinite dynasty (Tunisia) 1:92
Hussites (religious sect) 4:229, 235
Hutchinson, Anne (American founder of Portsmouth colony) 5:194
Hutterites (religious sect) 5:300
Hutu (African people) 1:37
  Burundi 1:329–30, 331
  militias in refugee camps 1:270
  Rwanda 1:324, 325, 326, 327
Hveragerdi (Iceland) 4:4
Hwang Chini (Korean poet) 2:432
Hwang Ho (river, China) see Yellow River
Hyderabad (India) 2:203, 204, 227
  illus. 2:205
Hydroelectricity
  Alps 3:301
  Argentina 6:280
  Asia 2:37–38
  Austria 3:318
  British Columbia 5:133
  Canada 5:71
  Chile 6:319
  Congo River 1:42
  Danube River 3:326
  Egypt 1:105
  Europe 3:37
  Finland 4:64
  France 3:157
  Ghana 1:196, 200
  Iceland 4:3
  Italy 4:132
  Labrador 5:81
  Liechtenstein 3:307
  Mekong River 2:257
  Mozambique 1:366
  New Zealand 2:550
  Nicaragua 6:57
  Norway 4:28
  Ontario 5:109
  Pakistan 2:183
  Portugal 4:73
  Quebec 5:102–3
  Scotland 3:135
  Siberia 5:64
  Spain 4:84
  Switzerland 3:288
  Tasmania 2:531
  Uganda 1:320
  Ukraine 4:333

  Volga River 4:317
  Wales 3:124
  Yugoslavia 4:275
  Zambia 1:44
Hydrogen bombs 4:110
Hyksos (Asian people) 1:117
Hywel Dda (Howel the Good) (Welsh king) 3:129

• • • **|** • • •

Ibadan (Nigeria) 1:217–18
  illus. 1:222
Ibadhi (branch of Islam) 2:137
Iberia (region of republic of Georgia) 2:84
Iberian Peninsula (Europe) 3:9
  Arabs, conquest by 3:18
  Gibraltar 4:123
  Portugal 4:66–67
  Spain 4:80
Iberians (people) 3:112, 124, 128; 4:68, 87, 110
Ibibio (African people) 1:51, 219
Ibn (Arabic word meaning son) see the main part of the name for entries not listed below
Ibn Batuta (Arab scholar) 1:30
Ibn-Khaldun (Arab historian) 1:92
Ibn-Saud (Abdul Aziz Al-Saud) (king of Saudi Arabia) 2:122, 127
Ibo (African people) 1:58, 215, 219–20, 223, 228
Iboundji, Mount (Gabon) 1:252
Ibsen, Henrik (Norwegian playwright) 4:28
Ice
  Antarctica 6:324, 325, 327, 336, 338
  Greenland 5:10, 11
Ice Ages
  Europe's northwestern uplands 3:27; 4:51–52
  North America 5:12, 13
Icebergs 5:82; 6:325
  illus. 5:56
Icebreakers (ships)
  illus. 6:335
Ice islands 5:56
ICELAND 3:8, 36, 37; 4:1–7
  emigration to Canada 5:39, 115–16
  Kalmar Union 4:20
  Norway, history of 4:25, 26
  illus.
    flag 4:v
    geyser 4:3
    Husavik harbor 4:6
    Reykjavik 4:7
    Thingvellir 4:1
  map(s) 4:4
  table(s)
    largest islands of the world 6:346
Ice lenses 5:56
Icons (religious art) 4:262
  illus. 2:69; 4:262
IDAHO 5:313–14
  map(s) 5:314
Idaho Falls (Idaho) 5:314
Id al Adha (Muslim festival) 2:187
Id al Fitr (Muslim festival) 2:186–87
Idanha (dam, Portugal) 4:73
Idris I (king of Libya) 1:98, 100
Idris I (Moroccan ruler) 1:73
Idris II (Moroccan ruler) 1:73
Ife (Nigeria) 1:219, 221, 226

Ifni (Morocco) **1:**34, 74; **4:**85
Ifrane (Morocco) **6:**345
Iglesia ni Kristo (Philippine church) **2:**335
Iglesias, Rafael (Costa Rican statesman) **6:**69
Igloos (snow houses)
  illus. **5:**61
Ignatius Loyola, Saint *see* Loyola, Saint Ignatius
Iguaçu (Iguazú; Iguassú) Falls (South America)
  6:160, 266, 280
IGY *see* International Geophysical Year
Ijaw (Ijo) (African people) **1:**219
IJsselmeer (lake, Netherlands) **3:**228
Ikalto (republic of Georgia) **2:**83
Ikhshidids (Turkish rulers in Egypt) **1:**119
I-Kiribati (language) **2:**611
Île de la Cité (Paris, France) **3:**193, 195
Île Saint-Louis (Paris, France) **3:**195
Iliad (epic poem by Homer) **3:**45–46; **4:**201–2
Iliescu, Ion (Romanian president) **4:**257
Illampú (mountain, Bolivia) **6:**231
Illimani (mountain, Bolivia) **6:**231, 232
Illiniwek (Indians of North America) **5:**281, 282
ILLINOIS 5:281–83
  illus.
    Chicago **5:**281
  map(s) **5:**282
Illinois (Indians of North America) **5:**269
Illinois and Michigan Canal *see* Sanitary and
  Ship Canal
Illiteracy
  Africa **1:**2, 5
  Bangladesh **2:**240
  Benin **1:**213
  Brazil **6:**106, 169, 177
  Cambodia **2:**289
  China **2:**402
  Ghana **1:**199
  Guinea **1:**167
  Haiti **5:**466
  India **2:**221
  Mexico **5:**370
  Nepal **2:**232
  Nicaraguan literacy campaign **6:**59
  Pakistan **2:**193
  Peru's remote areas **6:**216
  Sierra Leone **1:**176
  South Africa **1:**400
  Syria **2:**93
  Tunisia **1:**87
  Venezuela **6:**140
  Yemen **2:**134
Illuminated manuscripts 2:76
  illus. **3:**176
Illyria (ancient country, Balkan peninsula of
  Europe) **4:**272
Illyria (province created by Napoleon) **4:**284
Iloilo (Philippines) **2:**336
Ilopango, Lake (El Salvador) **6:**43, 44
Imam (Muslim ruler) **2:**135
Imatong Mountains (Sudan–Uganda) **1:**125
Imbabura (province, Ecuador) **6:**197
Imhotep (Egyptian vizier) **1:**110
Immigration and emigration
  Albania to Italy and Greece **4:**268
  Argentina **6:**271–72, 279, 299
  Armenians **2:**75
  Asians of Kenya **1:**311–12
  Asians to Vancouver (Canada) **5:**130, 131
  Australia **2:**495, 496, 502, 518, 519
  Barbadian emigration **5:**480
  Belorussians to other countries **4:**343

Brazil **6:**161
Bulgarian Turks to Turkey **4:**260
Canada **5:**97, 106, 108, 109, 111, 115, 117,
  125, 142
Central America to U.S. **6:**12
Cubans to U.S. **5:**449, 451
El Salvador **6:**44
England **3:**102, 111
Ethiopians from Africa **1:**286
European restrictions **3:**64
Europeans to South America **6:**95, 97
Europe's food supply, population, and emi-
  gration **3:**35
Florida's Hispanic population **5:**239
former USSR to Israel **2:**106
France **3:**170
Germany **3:**246, 248–49, 259, 263, 279, 282,
  283
Greece **4:**189
Haitians seeking employment **5:**463–64
Ireland **3:**65, 76, 78
Italy **4:**159, 162
Jamaicans to U.S. and U.K. **5:**472
Lithuanians in U.S. **4:**302
London residents **3:**111
Michigan, waves of settlement **5:**276–77
Netherlands **3:**229
New England **5:**181
New York **5:**204, 206
Northern Ireland, emigration from **3:**144, 147
Norway to U.S. **4:**23
Pennsylvania **5:**212–13
Prairie Provinces **5:**113
Puerto Rico **5:**167, 168
Quebec **5:**102
Scotland, emigration from **3:**136, 141
Slovaks to U.S. **4:**234
Somalia **1:**302
South America **6:**95
Sweden **4:**40, 46
Ukrainians to other countries **4:**333–34
United Kingdom **3:**86
United States **5:**125, 165–67, 169, 171
Uruguay **6:**253–54, 264
Venezuela **6:**138
Wales, migration from **3:**130
  illus.
    Canada **5:**76
    classes for immigrants to Israel **2:**113
Imperialism *see* Colonialism
Imperial Mosque (Lahore, Pakistan) *see* Bad-
  shahi Masjid
Impressionism (in art) **3:**177
Inca (Indians of South America) **6:**90, 97, 206,
  207, 222–24
  Andes, mines in **6:**101
  Atahualpa **6:**204, 220
  customs maintained in Bolivia **6:**236, 239
  Cuzco (Peru), ancient Inca capital **6:**219
  legend, the "chopped-off" mountain **6:**231
  Machu Picchu, fortress city **6:**219–20
  reed boats on Lake Titicaca **6:**230–31
  Royal Commentaries of Peru **6:**214
  illus. **6:**94
    Machu Picchu **6:**220
Inchon (South Korea) **2:**436
Incwala (Swazi festival) **1:**389
Indentured labor 5:35–36
Independence (Missouri) **5:**296
Independence National Historical Park (Phila-
  delphia, Pennsylvania) **5:**213

INDIA 2:27, 170, **195–229**
  animal life **2:**200–201
  Asoka **2:**20
  Bangladesh **2:**243
  border disputes **2:**31
  British colonialism **2:**24
  education **2:**222
  energy needs **2:**37
  Ganges River **2:**168
  government **2:**29
  Himalayas **2:**166–67
  Hindu caste system **2:**21, 210–11
  Indonesia, influence on **2:**324
  Indus River **2:**183
  Indus River civilization **2:**13, 14
  Kashmir **2:**172–73
  monuments to the past **2:**216
  motion pictures **2:**204
  Pakistan, relations with **2:**32, 193, 194
  people in Caribbean *see* East Indians
  people in Fiji **2:**598, 599
  people in Guyana **6:**150
  people in Myanmar **2:**268
  people in New Zealand **2:**544
  people in Singapore **2:**310
  people in South Africa **1:**398, 400
  people in Southeast Asia **2:**255
  people in Suriname **6:**155
  population **2:**6, 7
  population control **2:**39, 171
  Portuguese arrival **2:**23
  religion **2:**169
  Sikh nationalism **2:**169
  Southeast Asia, relations with **2:**255
  Sri Lanka **2:**250
  television **2:**40
  urban growth **2:**36
  illus.
    Bombay (Mumbai) **2:**207
    bus transportation **2:**227
    Calcutta **2:**206
    cave temples **2:**216
    computer scientists **2:**220
    Delhi **2:**214
    drying fabrics in sun **2:**224
    Ellora temples **2:**215
    flag **2:**viii
    Gandhi, Indira **2:**217
    Ganges River **2:**199
    Golden Temple at Amritsar **2:**218
    Himalayas **2:**197
    Hindu monks **2:**213
    Hindu priest **2:**210
    Hindu wedding **2:**211
    housing construction **2:**228
    irrigation **2:**225
    markets **2:**205
    New Delhi mosque **2:**212
    nuclear-power plant **2:**229
    outdoor classroom **2:**222
    pilgrims bathing in Ganges **2:**208–9
    population control advertisement **2:**223
    Republic Day celebration **2:**219
    river transportation **2:**201
    rural poverty **2:**200
    sacred cow **2:**202
    school **2:**221
    Sikh demonstration **2:**27
    street cleaning **2:**226
    Taj Mahal **2:**195
    Thar Desert **2:**198
    Udaipur **2:**203

water storage **2:**201
map(s) **2:**196
INDIANA 5:279–80
illus.
Indianapolis **5:**279
map(s) **5:**280
Indianapolis (capital, Indiana) **5:**48, 280
illus.
War Memorial Plaza **5:**279
Indian Desert see Thar Desert
Indian National Congress 2:216–17
Indian Ocean
Africa's historic trading community **1:**6, 36
Asia, South **2:**165
Comoros **1:**383–84
Madagascar **1:**369–77
Maldives **2:**251
Mauritius **1:**378
Réunion **1:**46–47
Seychelles **1:**339
table(s)
oceans of the world **6:**347
Indian River Bay (Delaware) **5:**215
Indians of Central and South America 6:6, 7,
11, 14–15, 82, 89–91, 92, 95, 111, 112 see
also articles on individual countries and
regions; names of tribes
Amazon River **6:**169
Andes, life in **6:**100
Araucanians of Chile **6:**302, 305
Argentina **6:**267–70, 299
Bolivia **6:**235, 236–37, 239, 240
Brazil **6:**163, 165, 166, 167
Caribbean islands **5:**428–30
Chiapas (Mexico) **5:**418
Colombia **6:**126
Ecuador **6:**196–97, 201
Guatemala **6:**26–27
Guyana **6:**150
music and musical instruments **6:**213
Panama **6:**75
Peru **6:**206, 211–12, 215–16, 224–25, 228
slave-hunting bandeirantes **6:**189
Suriname Amerindians **6:**153, 155, 158
Venezuela **6:**135, 138, 144, 146
Yanomamo **6:**140
illus.
fishing **6:**103
Incas **6:**94
Venezuela's Yanomamo **6:**140
Indians of North America 5:1, 375 see also
articles on individual countries, regions, and
states; names of tribes
American Indian Movement **5:**299
Arizona **5:**328
British Columbia **5:**132
Canada **5:**39, 73–74, 78, 95, 111
culture areas **5:**164–65
displacement **5:**174
environmental impact of early civilizations
5:21–25
French North America **5:**32–33
Illinois **5:**283
Mexico **5:**355, 368–69, 417, 418
Middle Atlantic States **5:**199
migration from Asia **5:**163
Montana **5:**311, 312
Mountain States **5:**309
New Brunswick **5:**85
New Mexico **5:**321

Oklahoma **5:**306, 307
Pacific coast region **5:**22, 334
Plains States **5:**291–92
Prairie Provinces **5:**113, 119, 120–21
Quebec **5:**99
sign language **5:**164
Tabasco (Mexico) **5:**419
Teotihuacán **5:**413
United States population **5:**171
illus. **5:**173
Plains Indians **5:**292
powwow **5:**106
Indian Territory (U.S. history) **5:**174, 294, 302,
304
Louisianna Purchase **5:**292
Indo-America (regional culture of South and
Central America) **6:**89–91, 112
Indo-Aryans (Asian people) **2:**21, 213–14
Indochina (area, Southeast Asia) **2:**294 see also
Cambodia; French Indochina; Laos; Malay-
sia; Myanmar; Thailand; Vietnam
France, history of **3:**187, 190
Mekong River **2:**256–57
Indo-European languages 3:20
Asia **2:**28, 44, 187, 191
Southwest Asian culture enters Europe **3:**45
Indo-Gangetic Plain 2:167–68
INDONESIA 2:313–26
Asia, Southeast **2:**254, 255, 258, 260, 264
Dutch exploration **3:**237–38
East Timor, history of **2:**327, 328
political instability **2:**29
Polynesians, origin of **2:**600
illus.
agriculture **2:**321
aviation industry **2:**323
batik **2:**320
ethnic dance **2:**317
flag **2:**viii
houses on stilts **2:**321
industry **2:**37
Jakarta **2:**260, 313, 318
people **2:**17
petroleum industry **2:**322
volcano **2:**314
map(s) **2:**316
Indonesian language see Bahasa Indonesia
Indonesians (people) see Malays
Indus River (Asia) **2:**170, 183
Asia, history of **2:**12–14
Himalayas, source in **2:**167
India, rivers of **2:**198
Kashmir **2:**173
Pakistan **2:**182
map(s) **2:**170
table(s)
longest rivers of the world **6:**346
Industrial Revolution (18th century) **3:**92
England **3:**99, 106, 108
Europe, contributions to the world **3:**15, 37,
39, 58–59
New England **5:**181
Scotland **3:**141
United States **5:**194
Industry see Manufacturing
Indus Valley civilization 2:12–14, 171, 213
Pakistan **2:**180, 190–91
Infanticide 2:436
Infant mortality
Africa **1:**2, 3, 5
Asia **2:**37

Bolivia **6:**237
Malawi **1:**279
South Africa **1:**400
Inflation (economics)
China **2:**414
Estonia **4:**295
Germany (1920s) **3:**276
Israel **2:**111
Peru (1980s) **6:**228
petroleum prices (1970s) **5:**177
Ukraine (1990s) **4:**338
Information technology (IT) see also Comput-
ers; Internet
Arctic **5:**64, 140
Czech Republic **4:**229
Germany **3:**264
Luxembourg **3:**210
Sweden **4:**47
Inga Falls (Congo River) **1:**42
Ingraham, Hubert A. (prime minister of Baha-
mas) **5:**425
Inhambane (Mozambique) **1:**364
Initiation rites see Passage rites
Initiative, Legislative 3:298; **4:**154
Inkatha (Zulu movement) **1:**405
"Inland Empire" (region, U.S.–Canada) **5:**337
Inland Ice (Greenland) **5:**10
Inner Alster (lake, Hamburg, Germany) **3:**265
Inner Asia see Central and North Asia—Asia,
Central
Inner Mongolian Autonomous Region (China)
see Nei Monggol Autonomous Region
Inn River (central Europe) **3:**286, 318
Innsbruck (capital, Tyrol province of Austria)
3:310, 313
Innu (people of North America) **5:**78, 82
Innuinan Mountains (North America) **5:**7
Innuitian Region (North America) **5:**138
Inquisition (organization set up to defend
Christianity) **4:**114, 158
In Salah (Algeria) **1:**76
Institute for Industrial Reconstruction (Italy)
4:152, 160
Institutional Revolutionary Party (PRI)
(Mexico) **5:**386, 387, 388
Insular Mountains (British Columbia) **5:**129
Integration see Segregation
Inter-American Development Bank 6:110
Inter-American Highway 5:406; **6:**69, 72, 73
Interglacials 5:13
Intergovernmental Conference 3:4
Interior Lowlands (North America) **5:**5
Interior Low Plateaus (North America) **5:**272
Interlaken (Switzerland) **3:**288
illus. **3:**5
International Council of Scientific Unions
6:333
International Court of Justice (World Court)
(The Hague) **3:**233–34; **6:**358
International Geophysical Year (IGY) (1957–
1958) **6:**330, 334–35
International Labor Organization (ILO) 3:293
International Museum of the Horse (Lexing-
ton, Kentucky) **5:**262
International Peace Garden (Canada–U.S.)
illus. **5:**34
International polar years 6:333
International Red Cross 3:293
International trade see also Free trade
Africa **1:**2, 3
Asia **2:**36

International trade (cont.)
  Asia, East **2:**376
  China **2:**418
  Dutch transshipment industry **3:**231–32
  Hong Kong **2:**410, 411
  Indonesia, history of **2:**323–24
  Japan **2:**440, 445, 470–71
  New Zealand's changing market **2:**550, 554
  North American Free Trade Agreement **5:**362
  Singapore **2:**311
  Somalia, history of **1:**301
  South Africa **1:**46
  Syria, history of **2:**90
  United States, history of **5:**43, 45, 177
  U.S. embargo against Cuba **5:**452
  U.S. embargo against Vietnam lifted **2:**300
Internet 4:47; **5:**64, 140 see also Computers;
    Information technology
  Tuvalu's economy **2:**612
  illus.
    Inuit users **5:**58
Interstadials 5:13
Inthanon Peak (Thailand) **2:**274
Intifada (Arab uprising) **2:**54, 55, 114, 115
  illus. **2:**54
Intracoastal Waterway 5:229
Inuit (Eskimo) 5:60–61, 78, 101, 135, 136, 137,
    334
  Alaska **5:**349, 350
  Alberta **5:**124
  computer use **5:**140
  Greenland **5:**10, 11
  industries **5:**64
  Labrador **5:**82
  North America **5:**20, 21
  Northwest Territories **5:**142, 143
  Nunavut **5:**138, 139
  population **5:**115, 117
  Prairie Provinces **5:**111
  Quebec **5:**95, 99
  Yukon **5:**148
  illus. **5:**136
    building snow houses **5:**61
    children **5:**139
    computer use **5:**58
    with dogsled **5:**140
    Inukshuk (rock cairn) **5:**137
    mending fishing nets **5:**6
    snowmobiles **5:**20
Inukshuk (Inuit rock cairn)
  illus. **5:**137
Inuktitut language 5:138, 139, 140
Inuvik (Northwest Territories, Canada) **5:**143
Invalides, Hôtel des (Paris, France) **3:**199–200
Inyanga Mountains (Zimbabwe) **1:**356, 357
Inyangani, Mount (Zimbabwe) **1:**357
Inylchek Glacier (Kyrgyzstan) **2:**353
Iolani Palace (Hawaii) **5:**354
Ionesco, Eugène (Romanian-French playwright)
    4:252
Ionian Islands (Greece) **4:**187, 190, 206
Ionian Sea (Mediterranean Sea) **4:**187
IOWA 5:293–94
  illus.
    family farm **5:**293
  map(s) **5:**294
Iowa (Indians of North America) **5:**291, 294
Iowa City (Iowa) **5:**294
Ioway (Indians of North America) see Iowa
Ipiales (Colombia)
  illus. **6:**121
Ipin (China) see Yibin

Iqaluit (capital, Nunavut) **5:**138, 139, 140
Iquique (Chile) **6:**312–13
Iquitos (Peru) **6:**168, 169, 210, 218–19
  illus. **6:**218
IRAN 2:155–64 see also Persia
  cities **2:**46
  Iraq **2:**148
  Iraq, war with see Iran-Iraq War
  Islam **2:**45
  illus.
    Abadan refinery **2:**160
    flag **2:**viii
    Khomeini's funeral **2:**164
    Persepolis **2:**15, 162
    schoolchildren **2:**158
    Teheran **2:**155
    women working in field **2:**161
  map(s) **2:**157
Iran-Iraq War (1980–1988) **2:**32, 154, 164
  Kurds **2:**148
  Saudi Arabia **2:**129
  Shi'ites expelled from Iraq **2:**149
  Syria **2:**96
  illus.
    captured Iraqis **2:**19
Irapuato (Guanajuato, Mexico) **5:**405
IRAQ 2:55, 147–54
  Baghdad **2:**46–47
  international trade **2:**33
  Iran, war with see Iran-Iraq War
  Kuwait **2:**144, 145, 146
  Saudi Arabia, relations with **2:**129
  Syria, relations with **2:**93
  Tigris and Euphrates rivers **2:**50
  illus.
    Baghdad **2:**149
    cooking fish **2:**151
    flag **2:**viii
    Monument of Saddam's Qadissiya **2:**147
    ruins **2:**153
    ruins of Great Mosque at Samarra **2:**152
  map(s) **2:**150
Irazú (volcano, Costa Rica) **6:**63
Irbid (Jordan) **2:**118, 119
IRELAND 3:65–78 see also Northern Ireland
  Celts **3:**114
  early Arctic exploration **5:**61
  England, history of **3:**117
  Europe's grasslands **3:**32
  language **3:**87
  Northern Ireland, negotiations with **3:**149
  United Kingdom, relations with **3:**91, 93
  Viking occupation **3:**51
  illus.
    Cork **3:**74
    Dublin **3:**69, 72, 78
    flag **3:**vi
    green peninsula **3:**65
    horse show **3:**73
    peat cutting **3:**66
    Powerscourt gardens **3:**75
    pub **3:**68
    Waterford crystal **3:**71
  map(s) **3:**67
  table(s)
    largest islands of the world **6:**346
Ireland, Northern see Northern Ireland
Irianese (Asian people) **2:**317–18
Irian Jaya (Indonesia) **2:**313, 314, 315, 317, 322,
    326, 587
Irigoyen, Hipólito (president of Argentina)
    6:299–300

Irish-Americans 5:180–81, 189
Irish Free State 3:148
Irish language 3:69
Irish people 3:86
Irish Republican Army (IRA) 3:77, 78, 149
Irkutsk (Russia) **2:**343; **4:**315–16
Iron
  Australia **2:**483
  Brazil **6:**103
  Europe **3:**37
  France **3:**157
  Guinea **1:**169
  Hittites **2:**56
  Labrador **5:**82
  Lapland **4:**37
  Mauritania **1:**138
  Mexico **5:**398
  Minnesota **5:**160, 287, 289
  North America **5:**4, 7, 8
  Sweden **4:**40
  Venezuela **6:**131, 135
  map(s)
    world production **6:**355
Iron Age (archaeology) **1:**361; **3:**320
  Northern Ireland **3:**147
  Zimbabwe Ruins **1:**361
Iron Curtain (political division between Eastern
    and Western Europe) **3:**62, 282; **4:**323
  illus. **3:**282
Iron Gate (gorge, Danube River) **3:**37, 328;
    4:249, 275
Iron Guard (Romanian terrorists) **4:**256
Iron sands 2:549
Ironsi, Johnson Aguiyi (Nigerian leader)
    1:227–28
Iron Springs (Utah) **5:**8
Iroquois (Indians of North America) **5:**23, 33,
    96, 101, 164, 199, 202, 205, 206, 212, 227,
    272, 274
  Canada **5:**95, 108
Irrawaddy River (Southeast Asia) **2:**267, 270
  table(s)
    longest rivers of the world **6:**346
Irrigation
  Aral Sea **2:**347, 350
  Armenia **2:**74
  Asia **2:**11
  Cambodia, ancient **2:**291
  Egypt **1:**114, 116
  Gezira Scheme **1:**129
  Huarpe people of Argentina **6:**269
  Inca Empire **6:**90, 223
  Indus River **2:**183
  Italy **4:**128
  Kara Kum Canal **2:**356
  Kazakhstan **2:**346
  Mountain States **5:**49–50
  Nile River **1:**39
  Pueblo Indians **5:**24–25
  Saudi Arabia **2:**129
  Spain **4:**110
  Sri Lanka **2:**246, 249
  Sumerians **2:**48
  Tagus River **4:**73
  Turkmenistan **2:**358
  illus.
    Africa **1:**63
    Bahrain **2:**140
    Egypt **1:**106
    India **2:**225
    Mexico **5:**357

Nebraskan corn field **5:**302
Nigerian rice farm **1:**219
Irtysh River (Russia) **4:**308
Isabela Island (Galápagos Islands) **6:**202
Isabella I (queen of Castile) **4:**114–15; **5:**444
Isabella Indian Reservation (Michigan) **5:**276
Ischia (island, Italy) **4:**130
  illus. **4:**130
Ischl (resort center, Austria) **3:**315
Iseo (lake, Italy) **4:**128
Isère River (France) **3:**154
Isfahan (Iran) **2:**46, 159, 163
Isidore, Saint (Spanish patron saint of Madrid)
  4:97
Islam *see also* Mosques
  Afghanistan **2:**175, 176
  Africa **1:**6, 32, 33–34, 225–26
  Albania **4:**270
  Algeria **1:**78, 84
  Asia **2:**18, 20, 38, 40
  Asia, East **2:**373
  Asia, South **2:**169, 172
  Asia, Southeast **2:**254, 260
  Asia, Southwest **2:**55
  Azerbaijan **2:**87
  Bangladesh **2:**240, 243
  Bosnia and Herzegovina **4:**289, 290
  Chad **1:**244
  China **2:**380, 381, 385, 389, 390
  Crusades against **3:**54
  Egypt **1:**107–8, 116, 119
  Ethiopia **1:**285, 288
  Europe **3:**19
  festivals **2:**186–87
  Five Pillars **2:**126
  former Soviet Union **2:**342
  India **2:**212–13
  Indonesia **2:**318, 319, 324
  Iran **2:**155, 157, 159, 162–63, 164
  Iraq **2:**148–49, 153–54
  Italy **4:**162
  Jerusalem holy places **2:**47, 104
  Kashmir **2:**172
  Koran **1:**109
  Kyrgyzstan, militants' invasion of **2:**355
  Lebanon **2:**100, 102
  Libya, modern reform movements in **1:**98
  Malaysia **2:**305
  Mauritania **1:**139
  Mauritius **1:**381
  Middle East **2:**45
  Mongolia **2:**365
  Moors in Spain **4:**112–13
  Morocco **1:**68
  Muslim Brotherhood **1:**123
  Muslim world **2:**51
  Nigeria **1:**223
  North Africa **1:**61
  Oman **2:**137
  Pakistan **2:**180, 183–84, 192–93, 219
  Philippines **2:**333–34, 338, 339, 340
  Saudi Arabia **2:**123, 125, 126–27, 128, 129
  Shi'a branch of Islam *see* Shi'a
  Sierra Leone **1:**173
  Somalia **1:**302
  Spain **4:**89, 114
  Sudan **1:**128, 131
  Sunni branch of Islam *see* Sunni
  Syria **2:**91–92, 94
  Tajikistan **2:**360
  Tunisia **1:**88

  Turks in Bulgaria **4:**260
  U.S. population **5:**171
  Uzbekistan **2:**352
  Yemen **2:**133
  Yugoslavia **4:**277, 280
  illus.
    Guyana Muslims **6:**152
    Muslims praying **1:**80, 109; **2:**42
    women in Tunisia **1:**12
    worshipers at mosque **2:**342
Islamabad (capital, Pakistan) **2:**187
  illus. **2:**185
Islamic Salvation Front (FIS) (Algeria) **1:**84
Islands and island groups *see also* names of
    islands and island groups
  Arctic **5:**56
  Arctic Archipelago **5:**134
  Asia, East **2:**368–69
  Asia, Southeast **2:**256
  Europe's islands **3:**8
  Greenland, world's largest **5:**10–11
  Newfoundland, North America's largest **5:**81
  North America **5:**2, 4
  Oceania **2:**555–67
  table(s)
    largest of the world **6:**346
Islas Canarias (Spain) *see* Canary Islands
Islas Malvinas *see* Falkland Islands
Islay (island, Scotland) **3:**134
Isle of Man *see* Man, Isle of
Isle of Pines (dependency of New Caledonia)
  2:585
Isle Royale National Park (Michigan) **5:**269,
  275
Ismail I (ruler of Egypt) **1:**121
Ismailia (Egypt) **1:**114
Ismailis (Muslim sect) **1:**311
Isola Bella (Lake Maggiore, Italy) **4:**128
Isonzo River (Italy) **4:**129
ISRAEL 2:104–15 *see also* Arab-Israeli wars
  Arab-Israeli wars **2:**116
  creation of modern state **2:**52
  disputed lands **2:**114–15
  Egypt, history of **1:**122, 123
  Jerusalem, Israeli capital **2:**46–47
  Jordan **2:**121
  Lebanon **2:**103
  Palestinians **2:**54–55
  Suez Canal **1:**121
  illus.
    flag **2:**vii
    Haifa **2:**109
    immigrants **2:**108, 113
    Jerusalem **2:**26, 107
    kibbutz **2:**110
    Masada **2:**112
    Tel Aviv-Jaffa **2:**104
  map(s) **2:**106
Israeli-Arab wars *see* Arab-Israeli wars
Israelites *see* Hebrews
Issas (African people) **1:**37, 298, 299
Issyk Kul Lake (Kyrgyzstan) **2:**353
Istanbul (formerly **Constantinople**) (Turkey)
  2:46, 60, 61–63 *see also* Constantinople
  Napoleon's comment **2:**56
  illus. **2:**61
    Suleymaniye Mosque **2:**56
Istiqlal Party (Morocco) **1:**74
Istria (Istrian Peninsula) (Adriatic Sea) **4:**160,
  285
Itaipú Dam (Brazil–Paraguay)
  illus. **6:**167

Italian-Americans 5:181, 189, 209, 216
Italian East Africa 1:296
Italian language 3:290; **4:**134, 170
Italian Somaliland *see* Somaliland
ITALY 4:124–73
  Alps **3:**299–304
  history *see* Italy, history of
  power resources **3:**37
  San Marino **4:**174–76
  Vatican City **4:**177–81
  illus.
    Alps **4:**126
    Amalfi coast **4:**124
    Apuane marble quarries **4:**132
    Assisi **4:**157
    automobile industry **4:**151
    bicycle race **4:**140
    Bologna **4:**159
    Como, Lake **4:**128
    flag **4:**v
    Florence **4:**149
    Genoa **4:**146
    goats grazing near sulfur plant **4:**133
    hotel near *autostrade* **4:**163
    Ischia **4:**130
    Lake Como **3:**1
    Leaning Tower of Pisa **4:**135
    Milan **4:**141, 142
    Naples **4:**143, 144
    Pompeii **4:**156
    Rome **4:**161, 166, 168, 169, 171, 172, 173
    ruins at Selinunte **4:**155
    ruins of Roman Forum **3:**47
    Sicilian beach **4:**129
    steam-power plant **4:**131
    textile industry **4:**152
    Turin **4:**145
    Venice **3:**43; **4:**147, 148
    vineyards and olive groves **4:**150
  map(s) **4:**127
Italy, history of 4:154–63
  Albania, relations with **4:**272
  Ethiopia, invasion of (1935–1936) **1:**289
  Greece, invasion of **4:**209
  Libya, history of **1:**100
  Papal States (754–1870) **4:**178
Itasca, Lake (Minnesota) **5:**160
Itauguá (Paraguay) **6:**248
Ithaca (Greek island) **4:**190
Iturbide, Agustín de (Mexican emperor) **5:**383
Ituri Forest (Congo, Democratic Republic of)
  1:264
Ivan III (the Great) (Russian ruler) **3:**53; **4:**320
Ivan the Great Bell Tower (Moscow, Russia)
  4:327
Ivan the Terrible (Ivan IV Vasilievich) (czar of
  Russia) **4:**320, 327, 328
Ivindo River (Gabon) **1:**252
Iviza (island, Balearic Islands) **4:**84
Ivory 1:20
  illus. **1:**53
Ivory-billed woodpecker 5:227
IVORY COAST 1:53, **184–88**
  illus. **1:**184, 187
    Abidjan **1:**186
    flag **1:**xxii
    sculpture **1:**52
  map(s) **1:**185
Ivvavik National Park (Yukon Territory)
  illus. **5:**146
Ixchel (Mayan goddess) **5:**422
Ixmiquilpan (Hidalgo, Mexico) **5:**406

Ixtacihuatl (extinct volcano, Mexico) **5**:357
Ixtlilxochitl, Fernando de Alva (Mexican historian) **5**:381
Izabal, Lake (Guatemala) **6**:30
Izmir (Smyrna) (Turkey) **2**:46, 60, 63, 66; **4**:208

• • • J • • • •

Jabal (Arab word for mountain) see the main element of the name
Jáchymov (Czech Republic) **4**:224, 227
Jackson (capital, Mississippi) **5**:246
Jackson, Andrew (7th president of U.S.) **5**:264, 265
Jackson, Maynard (mayor of Atlanta, Georgia) **5**:235
Jackson Purchase (area, Kentucky) **5**:261
Jacksonville (Florida) **5**:240–41
Jacob (Congo) **1**:257
Jacobite uprising (Scottish history) **3**:141
Jadwiga (queen of Poland) **4**:304
Jaffa (Israel) see Tel Aviv-Jaffa
Jagan, Cheddi (president of Guyana) **6**:152
Jagan, Janet Rosenberg (president of Guyana) **6**:152
Jagas (African people) **1**:346
Jagdeo, Bharrat (president of Guyana) **6**:152
Jagiellonian dynasty (Poland) **4**:219, 304
Jagiellonian University (Cracow, Poland) **4**:216
Jaguars
   illus. **6**:10
Jainism (religion) **2**:169, 209, 212, 214
Jakarta (capital, Indonesia) **2**:261, 314, 323, 324
   illus. **2**:260, 313, 318
Jakin (Porto-Novo) (early African kingdom) **1**:214
Jalapa (capital, Veracruz, Mexico) **5**:407
Jalapa Anthropology Museum (Tabasco, Mexico)
   illus. **5**:419
JALISCO (state, Mexico) **5**:402
Jaluit (Marshall Islands) **2**:575
JAMAICA 5:426, 432, 438, **471–77**
   British colonialism **5**:427, 433, 435
   illus. **5**:471
      Blue Mountains **5**:472
      flag **5**:vi
      Kingston **5**:474
      processing sugarcane **5**:473
      school children **5**:477
   map(s) **5**:475
Jama Masjid (mosque, Delhi, India) **2**:208
James, Edison (prime minister of Dominica) **5**:488
James, Henry (American writer) **4**:168
James, Saint (the Elder or Greater) (one of the Twelve Apostles) **4**:112
James I (James VI of Scotland) (king of Great Britain) **3**:91, 119, 140
James II (king of Great Britain) **3**:76, 120, 141, 148
James River (South Dakota) **5**:300
James River (Virginia) **5**:43, 223, 225
Jamestown (New York) **5**:226
Jamestown (Virginia) **5**:173–74, 225
Jammeh, Yahya (president of Gambia) **1**:163
Jammu (Kashmir) **2**:173
Jammu and Kashmir (state, India) **2**:172, 181, 228

Janáček, Leoš (Czech composer) **4**:225
Janissaries (Turkish soldiers) **2**:64, 65
Jan Mayen Island (island, Arctic Ocean) **4**:24
Januarius, Saint (patron saint of Naples, Italy) **4**:136
JAPAN 2:439–72
   Ainu **2**:444
   China **2**:372, 374, 396, 397, 421
   climate **2**:370
   economy **2**:6, 32–33, 34, 375, 376
   "education mamas" **2**:456–57
   energy needs **2**:37
   ethnic Koreans **2**:30
   Fuji, Mount **2**:442
   government **2**:29
   history since the 1400s **2**:25
   Korea **2**:433
   Kuril Islands dispute **2**:31
   landforms **2**:368
   mandated territories **2**:566
   Palau, history of **2**:572
   people **2**:371
   population control **2**:40
   spread of civilization **2**:16–17
   Taiwan, history of **2**:427
   Wales, investment in **3**:128
   way of life **2**:372
   illus.
      Ainu **2**:444
      automobile industry **2**:470
      cheerleader **2**:464
      company picnic **2**:449
      fishing boats **2**:468
      flag **2**:ix
      flower arranging **2**:454
      Great Buddha in Kamakura **2**:451
      Hirohito's funeral **2**:472
      Hiroshima **2**:448
      kabuki theater **2**:459
      Kyoto market **2**:455
      mealtime **2**:453
      mother and children **2**:456
      Mount Fuji **2**:439
      old painting of invasion of Korea **2**:21
      opening trade with West **2**:25
      rice growing **2**:466
      Shinto ceremony **2**:451
      steel industry **2**:469
      students **2**:458
      sumo wrestling **2**:463
      tea ceremony **2**:461
      Tokyo **2**:34, 445, 447
      traditional costume **2**:452
      writing on scrolls **2**:460
   map(s) **2**:441
   table(s)
      emperors, shoguns, and other leaders **6**:369
Japan, Sea of 2:442
   table(s)
      major seas of the world **6**:347
Japan (Kuroshio) Current (Pacific Ocean) **5**:14, 129
Japanese (people) **2**:443; **6**:95, 236
Japanese-Americans 5:347
Japanese language 2:28, 372, 450, 460–61
Jaruzelski, Wojciech (Polish government official) **4**:222
Jasna Góra (monastery, Poland) **4**:220
Jassy (Romania) **4**:254

Java (Indonesian island) **2**:314, 318, 320, 322, 323, 324
   table(s)
      largest islands of the world **6**:346
Java Man (prehistoric human being) **2**:323
Javanese (people) **2**:318; **6**:155
   Suriname **6**:157–58
Javanese dialect 2:318
Jawara, Sir Dawda (president of Gambia) **1**:163
Jayawiyaya Mountains (Snow Mountains) (Indonesia) **2**:315
Jazirat al Azl (Bahrain) **2**:140
Jazirat Jabal Zuqar (island, Red Sea) **2**:130
Jebba (Nigeria) **1**:50
Jebel (Arab word for mountain) see the main element of the name
Jefferson, Thomas (3rd president of U.S.) **5**:225, 226, 258
Jefferson City (capital, Missouri) **5**:296
Jehovah's Witnesses 4:225
Jekyll (island, Georgia) **5**:234
Jemez Mountains (New Mexico) **5**:321
Jericho (Jordan) **2**:114, 115
Jersey (island, Channel Islands) **3**:87
Jersey City (New Jersey) **5**:210
Jerusalem (capital, Israel) **2**:46–47, 104, 105, 108, 109, 115
   Arab-Israeli wars **2**:116
   Crusades **3**:54
   international city in divided Palestine **2**:113
   illus. **2**:26, 107
JERVIS BAY TERRITORY (Australia) **2**:513–15
   illus.
      Point Perpendicular Lighthouse **2**:515
Jesuits (Society of Jesus) (religious order)
   China **2**:389–90
   South America **6**:176, 189, 245
   illus.
      Bolivian mission **6**:234
Jesus Christ 2:50
Jews see also Hebrews; Holocaust
   Austria **3**:310
   Babi Yar massacre (1941) **4**:337
   Brazil **6**:165, 168
   Bulgaria **4**:266
   Colombia **6**:120
   Czech Republic **4**:225
   Denmark's rescue of (World War II) **4**:22
   Dreyfus case **3**:187
   Egypt, history of **1**:118
   Europe, history of **3**:18
   Falasha of Ethiopia **1**:36, 285
   Germany, history of **3**:61, 272, 276
   Holocaust **3**:278, 279
   Hungary **4**:240
   Inquisition in Spain **4**:114
   Israel **2**:104, 105–6, 108, 111–15
   Jerusalem **2**:46
   Lithuania **4**:301–2
   Miami **5**:239
   Montreal **5**:100
   Morocco **1**:68
   Netherlands **3**:237
   New Jersey **5**:209
   Poland **4**:219, 221
   Prague has one of Europe's oldest synagogues **4**:227
   Romania **4**:251
   Russia **4**:309, 310
   Spain **4**:89
   Ukraine **4**:335

U.S. population **5:**171
Yiddish spoken in Europe **3:**20
illus.
Ethiopia **1:**285
Jharkhand (state, India) **2:**221
Jhelum River (Kashmir–Pakistan–India) **2:**170, 183
Jialing River (China) **2:**368
Jiang Jieshi (president of Taiwan) *see* Chiang Kai-shek
Jiang Qing (Chiang Ching) (Chinese political leader) **2:**398–99, 407
Jiangsu (province, China) **2:**383
Jiang Zemin (president of China) **2:**421, 422
Jicaque (Indians of Central America) **6:**41
Jichang (China) **2:**369
Jiddah (Saudi Arabia) **2:**47, 125
Jim Crow laws 5:222
Jiménez, Jesús (Costa Rican statesman) **6:**68
Jiménez, Marcos Pérez *see* Pérez Jiménez, Marcos
Jiménez de Quesada, Gonzalo (Spanish explorer) **6:**97, 126
Jiménez Oreamuno, Ricardo (Costa Rican statesman) **6:**68
Jimmu (emperor of Japan) **2:**443
Jinan (Tsinan) (China) **2:**370
Jinja (Uganda) **1:**317, 318, 320
Jinnah, Mohammed Ali (Muslim statesman) **2:**193, 217
Jiquilisco, Bahía de (waterway, El Salvador)
illus. **6:**42
Jiu River (Romania) **4:**255
Jívaros (Indians of South America) **6:**194
Joanna (Spanish queen) *see* Juana
Joan of Arc, Saint (French national heroine) **3:**182–83, 198, 200
Jochenstein Dam (Danube River) **3:**326
Jogaila (king of Poland) *see* Władysław
Jogjakarta (Indonesia) *see* Yogyakarta
Johannesburg (South Africa) **1:**18, 30, 397, 398, 401, 402
illus. **1:**12, 399
John (king of England) **3:**54, 117
John, Elton (English musician)
illus. **3:**89
John, Saint (Saint John the Evangelist) **4:**191
John III Sobieski (Polish king) **3:**323; **4:**220
John III (king of Portugal) **6:**164, 187
John IV (king of Portugal) **4:**76; **6:**189
John VI (king of Portugal) **6:**100, 189
John F. Kennedy Memorial Plaza (Dallas, Texas) **5:**254
John of Luxemburg (king of Bohemia) **4:**229
John of the Cross, Saint (Spanish mystic) **4:**98
John Paul II (pope) **4:**177, 194, 214, 222, 334; **5:**388
illus. **4:**180; **5:**448
Johnson, Lyndon (36th president of U.S.) **5:**253
Johnson, Prince (Liberian leader) **1:**183
Johnson, Uwe (German author) **3:**251
Johnson Space Center *see* Lyndon B. Johnson Space Center
Johnston Island (atoll in the Pacific) **2:**568–69
Johore Strait (Singapore–Malaysia) **2:**309
Joinville-le-Pont (France) **3:**202
Jókai, Mór (Hungarian novelist) **4:**240
Jola (African people) **1:**160, 162
Joliba River (name for section of Niger River) **1:**50
Jolliet, Louis (Canadian-born French explorer) **5:**101, 274

Jonassaint, Émile (Haitian leader) **5:**470
Jonathan, Leabua (prime minister of Lesotho) **1:**392
Jones Sound (between Ellesmere and Devon islands) **5:**61
Jonglei Canal (Sudan) **1:**125, 129
Jooss, Kurt (Chilean dancer) **6:**310
JORDAN 2:47, 113, 114, 115, **116–21**
Israel, relations with **2:**55
illus.
Amman **2:**116
Bedouins **2:**118
flag **2:**vii
Palestinian Arab refugees **2:**119
Petra **2:**120
map(s) **2:**117
Jordan River (Israel–Jordan) **2:**105, 116, 117
Jos (Nigeria) **1:**219
Joseph II (Holy Roman emperor) **3:**57
Joseph I (king of Spain) *see* Bonaparte, Joseph
Jospin, Lionel (president of France) **3:**191
Jos Plateau (Nigeria) **1:**216, 225
Josquin des Prez (Flemish composer) **3:**179
Jostedalsbre Glacier (Norway) **4:**25
Joubert, Elsa (South African author) **1:**401
Joyce, James (Irish writer) **3:**69, 70
József, Attila (Hungarian poet) **4:**240
Juana (Joanna) (Spanish queen) **3:**321; **4:**115
Juana Inés de la Cruz (Mexican nun, writer) **5:**381
Juan Carlos I (Spanish king) **4:**117, 118
illus. **4:**91
Juan de Fuca Strait (Pacific Northwest coast) **5:**336
Juan Fernández Islands (Pacific Ocean) **6:**84, 311
Juan-les-Pins (France) **3:**160
Juárez, Benito (Mexican statesman) **5:**383, 384, 417
Juàzeiro (Brazil) **6:**173
Juba (Sudan) **1:**129
Jubail (Saudi Arabia) **2:**125
Juba River (East Africa) **1:**283, 301
Judaism 2:18–19, 104, 108
Asia, Southwest **2:**49–50
illus. **5:**165
Judea (area, Israel–Jordan) **2:**109, 114
Jugnauth, Aneerood (prime minister of Mauritius) **1:**382
Jujuy (province, Argentina) **6:**266
Juliana (queen of the Netherlands) **3:**237
Julian Alps (Italy–Slovenia) **4:**160, 282
Julianehaab (Greenland) **5:**11
Jumna (Jamuna) River (India) **2:**168, 208
Juneau (capital, Alaska) **5:**350
Juneau, Mount (Alaska) **5:**350
Jungfrau (mountain, Switzerland) **3:**286, 299
illus. **3:**302
Junín (department, Peru) **6:**220
Jupiter (Romania) **4:**254
Jura Mountains (Switzerland–France) **3:**151, 173, 286, 295
Jūrmala (Latvia) **4:**299
Juruá River (Peru–Brazil) **6:**168
Justus Lipsius Council Building (Brussels, Belgium)
illus. **3:**222
Jute (fiber) **2:**241
Jutes (Germanic people) **3:**18, 49, 113
Jutland (peninsula, Denmark) **4:**8, 9–10, 20, 21
Amber Road **3:**320
Jwaneng (Botswana) **1:**353

• • • K • • •

K2 (mountain, central Asia) *see* Godwin Austen, Mount
Kaaba (sacred shrine of Islam, in Mecca) **2:**125
illus. **2:**127
Kabaka (title of kings of Buganda) **1:**318
Kabala (Sierra Leone) **1:**174
Kaba River (Guinea–Sierra Leone) *see* Little Scarcies River
Kabbah, Ahmed Tejan (president of Sierra Leone) **1:**177
Kabila, Laurent (president, Congo, Democratic Republic of) **1:**270
Kabrai (African people) **1:**206
Kabuki theater **2:**460
illus. **2:**459
Kabul (capital, Afghanistan) **2:**179
Kabwe (Broken Hill) (Zambia) **1:**271, 272
Kabylia (region, Algeria) **1:**78, 79
Kachin (Asian people) **2:**259, 269
Kachlet Dam (Danube River) **3:**326
Kádár, János (Hungarian premier) **4:**247
Kaduna (Nigeria) **1:**218
Kaduna River (Africa) **1:**50, 216
Kaédi (Mauritania) **1:**137
Kaesong (North Korea) **2:**433
Kafirs (Asian people) **2:**176
Kafka, Franz (Austrian writer) **4:**227
Kafue National Park (Zambia) **1:**276
Kagera National Park (Rwanda) **1:**324
Kagera River (Africa) **1:**38, 324
Kahoolawe (island, Hawaii) **5:**352
Kaieteur Falls (Guyana) **6:**149
Kaifeng (China) **2:**370
Kainji (Nigeria) **1:**148
Kairouan (Tunisia) **1:**90
illus.
Great Mosque **1:**92
Kaiulani (Hawaiian princess) **5:**354
Kaka (African people) **1:**230–31
Kalaallit 5:58
Kalahari Desert (Africa) **1:**47, 348
Bushmen of Botswana **1:**351
Kalambo Falls (Zambia) **1:**271
Kalemegdan (fortress, Belgrade, Yugoslavia) **3:**328; **4:**277
Kalevala (Finnish national epic) **4:**55
Kalgoorlie-Boulder (Australia) **2:**527
Kalimantan (Indonesia) **2:**314, 315, 318, 320
Kaliningrad (Russia) **4:**301, 315
Kalistan (proposed Sikh nation) **2:**169
Kalmar Union (1397, of Denmark, Norway, and Sweden) **4:**20, 26, 48
Kalomo (Zambia) **1:**271
Kaloum Peninsula (Guinea) **1:**169
Kamadja (African people) **1:**243
Kamakura (Japan)
illus. **2:**451
Kamaran (island, Red Sea) **2:**130
Kamba (African people) **1:**306
Kambu Svayambhuva (king of Cambodia) **2:**290
Kamchatka (Russia) **2:**343
Kamehameha I (Hawaiian king) **5:**353–54
Kamloops (British Columbia) **5:**131
Kampala (capital, Uganda) **1:**317, 318
illus. **1:**316
Kampuchea *see* Cambodia

Kampucheans (Asian people) see Khmer
Kanakas (people) **2:**567
Kanara (Kanarese) (language) see Kannada
Kanawha River (U.S.) **5:**259
Kandi (plain, Benin) **1:**211
Kandy (Sri Lanka) **2:**248
Kanem (early African kingdom) **1:**244
Kanem-Bornu (early state in west Africa) **1:**225
Kangaroo 2:317, 487
  illus. **2:**487
Kangaroo Island (Australia) **2:**521
Kankan (Guinea) **1:**168, 169
Kannada (Kanarese) language 2:199
Kano (Nigeria) **1:**218
  illus.
    festival **1:**215
    mosque **1:**56–57
    palace **1:**227
Kanpur (India) **2:**203
Kansa (Indians of North America) **5:**291, 303
KANSAS 5:303–4
  map(s) **5:**304
Kansas City (Kansas) **5:**304
Kansas City (Missouri) **5:**296
Kanuku Mountains (Guyana)
  illus. **6:**150
Kanuri (African people) **1:**219
Kanye (Botswana) **1:**353
Kao (island in Tonga group, Pacific) **2:**559
Kaohsiung (Taiwan) **2:**424
Kaokoveld Hills (Namibia) **1:**347
Kaolack (Senegal) **1:**153
Kappel am Albis (Switzerland) **3:**297
Kapsukas (Lithuania) **4:**302
Karachi (Pakistan) **2:**187–88
Karakalpak (Asian people) **2:**347, 351
Karakoram (mountains, central Asia) **2:**10, 167, 173
Karakul sheep 1:349; **2:**178, 352, 358
Kara Kum (desert, Turkmenistan) **2:**10, 343, 356
Kara Kum Canal (Turkmenistan) **2:**356, 358
Karamanlis, Constantine (prime minister of Greece) **4:**209–10, 211
Karamoja (area, Uganda) **1:**321
Karamojong (African people) **1:**318
Kara Mustafa (Turkish grand vizier) **3:**323
Karanga (African people) **1:**361
Karankawa (Indians of North America) **5:**253
Karaouine University (Fez, Morocco) **1:**70
Karavanke Mountains (Slovenia–Austria) **4:**282
Karbala (Iraq) **2:**149
Karen (Asian people) **2:**259, 275
Kariba Dam (Zimbabwe–Zambia) **1:**44, 275, 276
  illus. **1:**275
Karikal (India) **2:**220
Karimov, Islam A. (president of Uzbekistan) **2:**352
Karisimbi, Mount (Rwanda) **1:**324
Karl Johans Gate (Oslo, Norway) **4:**31
Karlovy Vary (Karlsbad) (resort and spa, Czech Republic) **4:**225
Karmal, Babrak (Afghan political leader) **2:**179
Karnak (Egypt) **1:**111
Karnaphuli River (India–Bangladesh) **2:**238
Karnataka (state, India) **2:**201
Karroos, Great and Little (plateaus, South Africa) **1:**395, 401
Karsts
  Laos **2:**281
  illus. **2:**382
Karthala, Mount (Comoros) **1:**383

Kartvelians see Georgians
Karun River (Iran) **2:**156
Karzai, Hamid (president of Afghanistan) **2:**179
Kasavubu, Joseph (Congolese leader) **1:**269
Kashmir (region, Asia) **2:**170, 172–73, 194 see also Jammu and Kashmir
  map(s) **2:**172
Kaska (Indians of North America) **5:**146
Kassala (Sudan)
  illus. **1:**129
Katahdin, Mount (Maine) **5:**233
Katanga (Shaba) (province, Congo, Democratic Republic) **1:**43, 269
  Congo River **1:**42
  Lubumbashi **1:**263
Katherina, Gebel (Egypt) **1:**113
Katmandu (Kathmandu) (capital, Nepal) **2:**231, 232
  illus. **2:**233
Kattegat (strait, North Sea) **4:**9, 45
Kauai (Garden Isle) (island, Hawaii) **5:**352
Kaunas (Lithuania) **4:**303
Kaunda, Kenneth David (Zambian leader) **1:**276
Kauri tree 2:477
  illus. **2:**542
Kautokeino (Norway) **4:**34
Kaveri River (India) see Cauvery River
Kawasaki (Japan) **2:**440
Kayes (Mali) **1:**142
Kayibanda, Grégoire (president of Rwanda) **1:**327
Kazakhs (Asian people) **2:**344, 347, 348, 349, 363, 365, 380
KAZAKHSTAN 2:341, **346–49,** 362
  land **2:**343
  population **2:**344
  record high temperature **2:**344
  illus. **2:**346
    bazaar **2:**348
    cattle roundup **2:**348
    flag **2:**ix
  map(s) **2:**347
Kazán Defile (Danube River) **3:**328
Kazantzakis, Nikos (Greek author) **4:**194
Kazimiyah (Iraq) **2:**149
Keats, John (English poet) **4:**172
Kebnekaise (mountain, Sweden) **4:**39
Keeling Islands see Cocos Islands
Keelung (Taiwan) **2:**424
Keetmanshoop (Namibia) **1:**348
Keflavik (Iceland) **4:**6
Keita, Modibo (president of Mali) **1:**143
Kejimkujik National Park (Nova Scotia) **5:**91
Kékes, Mount (Hungary) **4:**237
Kells, Book of 3:72
Kelly, Grace (American actress and princess of Monaco) **3:**206
Kelly Ingram Park (Birmingham, Alabama)
  illus. **5:**242
Kelowna (British Columbia) **5:**131
Kelsey, Henry (English fur trader) **5:**121
Kemal Atatürk (Turkish statesman) see Atatürk, Mustafa Kemal
Kemerovo (Russia) **2:**342
Kemmuna (Comino) (island, Malta) **4:**182
Kemmunett (Cominotto) (island, Malta) **4:**182
Kenema (Sierra Leone) **1:**171
Kennebec River (Maine) **5:**183
Kennedy, John F. (35th president of U.S.)
  Alliance for Progress **6:**86

  Cuba **5:**448
  Memorial Plaza in Dallas, Texas **5:**254
  wedding reception in Rhode Island **5:**194
Kennedy Space Center (Florida) **5:**241
Kenosha (Wisconsin) **5:**286
KENTUCKY 5:260–62
  map(s) **5:**261
Kentucky Derby 5:261, 262
Kentucky Lake (Kentucky) **5:**261
KENYA 1:36, 39–40, **306–15**
  anthropology **1:**6
  early human ancestors **1:**312
  regional cooperation **1:**3
  topography **1:**18
  illus.
    coffee processing and shipping **1:**313
    elephants **1:**314
    farm **1:**308
    flag **1:**xxiii
    Great Rift Valley **1:**27
    Kikuyu village **1:**310
    Nairobi **1:**309, 311
    rites of passage **1:**306
  map(s) **1:**307
Kenya, Mount (Kenya) **1:**18, 306, 307, 309
Kenyatta, Jomo (president of Kenya) **1:**39–40, 315
Kenyatta, Uhuru (son of Jomo Kenyatta) **1:**315
Kérékou, Mathieu (president of Benin) **1:**214
Keren (Eritrea) **1:**294
Kerki (Turkmenistan) **2:**357
Kérouané (Guinea) **1:**169
Ketterer, Franz Anton (German clock maker) **3:**258
Kettles (land form) **5:**284
Key, Francis Scott (American lawyer, poet) **5:**219
Keystone Province (nickname for Manitoba) **5:**114
Keystone State (nickname for Pennsylvania) **5:**211
Key West (Florida) **5:**239
  Havana (Cuba), proximity of **5:**442
Kgalagadi (African people) **1:**351
Kha (Asian people) **2:**283
Khabarovsk (Russia) **2:**343
Khabur River (Asia) **2:**51
Khachaturian, Aram (Armenian composer) **2:**76
Khalid (king of Saudi Arabia) **2:**127
Khalifa family (Bahraini rulers) **2:**141
Khalkhas (Asian people) **2:**363, 365
Khama, Sir Seretse (Botswana political leader) **1:**354
Khamenei, Ali (Iranian Muslim leader) **2:**164
Khami Ruins (Zimbabwe) **1:**357
Khamsin (wind) **1:**114
Khan (ruler of the Mongols) **2:**366
Khan, Ghulam Ishaq (president of Pakistan) **2:**194
Kharga (oasis, Egypt) **1:**112
Kharkov (Ukraine) **4:**338
Khartoum (capital, Sudan) **1:**124, 125, 126, 128–29, 130
  Nile River **1:**38, 39
  illus. **1:**124
Khartoum North (Sudan) **1:**126
Khat (shrub) **2:**131
  illus. **2:**133
Khatemi, Mohammed (president of Iran) **2:**164
Khayyám, Omar (Persian poet) see Omar Khayyám
Khmelnitsky, Bogdan (Cossack leader) **4:**339

Khmer (Cambodians; Kampucheans) (Asian people) **2:**254, 259, 275, 279, 286, 287–88, 290, 295, 302
Khmer Rouge (Cambodian Communists) **2:**288, 289, 292
Khoikhoi (Hottentots) (African people)
Namibia **1:**343, 349, 350
South Africa **1:**45, 403, 404
Khoisan (African people) **1:**349
Khoisan ("click") language 1:15, 352
Khomeini, Ayatollah (Iranian Muslim leader) **2:**163
illus.
funeral **2:**164
picture displayed by captured Iraqis **2:**19
Khone Falls (Mekong River, Laos) **2:**257
Khorasan (province, Iran) **2:**159
Khorat Plateau (Thailand) **2:**274
Khorenatsi, Moses (Armenian historian) **2:**76
Khotons (Turkic people) **2:**363, 365
Khrushchev, Nikita (Soviet political leader) **4:**323
Crimea "given" to Ukraine **4:**337
Cuba **5:**448
Khufu *see* Cheops
Khurramshahr (Iran) **2:**156
Khybur Pass (Afghanistan–Pakistan)
illus. **2:**176
Kiangsu (province, China) *see* Jiangsu
Kibbutz (collective settlement in Israel) **2:**109, 110–11
illus. **2:**110
Kickapoo (Indians of North America) **5:**282, 286
Kicking Horse Pass (British Columbia–Alberta) **5:**8
Kiel, Treaty of (1814) **4:**49
Kiel Canal (Germany) **3:**42, 243
Kierkegaard, Søren (Danish philosopher) **4:**16
Kiev (capital, Ukraine) **4:**309, 333, 336–37
Russia, history of **4:**319
Swedish Viking trading settlement **3:**51
illus.
St. Sophia Cathedral **4:**332
Kievan Rus (Kievan Russia) (medieval state) **4:**319, 332, 339
literature **4:**335
Kiev Mohyla Academy (Ukraine) **4:**334
Kigali (capital, Rwanda) **1:**325
Kija (founder of Chinese culture in Korea) **2:**431
Kikuyu (African people) **1:**40, 306, 309, 315
illus. **1:**310
Kikuyu language 1:312
Kilauea (volcano, Hawaii) **5:**335, 351
Kildare (Ireland) *see* Maynooth
Kilembe (Uganda) **1:**321
Kilimanjaro, Mount (Tanzania) **1:**18, 307, 332, 337, 338; **6:**345
illus. **1:**4, 338
Kilindini (Kenya) **1:**309
Kiliya Channel (Danube River) **3:**329
Kilkenny, Statutes of (1366) **3:**75–76
Killarney (Ireland) **3:**73
Killer whale
illus. **5:**59
Kilwa (ancient city, Africa) **1:**30
Kimberley (South Africa) **1:**398, 402
Kimberley Plateau (Australia) **2:**483, 484, 525, 527
Kimbundu (African people) **1:**343, 344, 346
Kim Dae Jung (president of South Korea) **2:**433, 438

Kim Il Sung (North Korean leader) **2:**429, 431
Kim Jong Il (North Korean leader) **2:**429, 433
Kimpech (ancient Mayan site) *see* Campeche
Kim Young Sam (president of South Korea) **2:**438
Kindia (Guinea) **1:**168
King, B. B. (American musician) **5:**263
King, Martin Luther, Jr. (American civil-rights leader) **5:**176, 222, 234, 235, 236, 244, 265
illus. **5:**173
King Island (Tasmania, Australia) **2:**528
Kings Canyon National Park (California) **5:**342
Kingston (capital, Jamaica) **5:**472, 476
illus. **5:**474
Kingston Harbor (Norfolk Island) **2:**488
Kingstown (capital, Saint Vincent and the Grenadines) **5:**491
Kinneret, Yam (Israel) *see* Galilee, Sea of
Kinsale, Battle of (1601) **3:**76
Kinshasa (Leopoldville) (capital, Congo, Democratic Republic of) **1:**43, 263, 270
ferry service to Congo **1:**256
illus. **1:**265
Kinyarwanda language 1:325
Kinyeti, Mount (Sudan) **1:**125
Kiowa (Indians of North America) **5:**292, 303
Kipchak khanate 2:352
Kiranti (Asian people) **2:**231
Kirchner, Ernst Ludwig (German artist)
illus.
People on the Street **3:**254
Kirdi (African people) **1:**233
Kirghizia *see* Kyrgyzstan
KIRIBATI 2:569, 570, 580–82, 611, 612
economy **2:**567
Gilbert Islands **2:**568
illus. **2:**580
flag **2:**x
map(s) **2:**581
Kirkenes (Norway) **4:**37
Kirkuk (Iraq) **2:**148, 149
Kirovabad (Azerbaijan) *see* Gyandzha
Kirthar Range (Asia) **2:**167
Kiruna (Sweden) **4:**37
Kirundi language 1:330
Kis Alföld (region, Hungary) **4:**237
Kisangani (Congo, Democratic Republic of) **1:**43, 263–64
Kishinev (Moldova) *see* Chişinău
Kishon River (Israel) **2:**105
Kismayu (Somalia) **1:**301
Kissi (African people) **1:**167
Kissinger, Henry (American government official) **2:**114
Kistna (Krishna) River (India) **2:**198–99
Kisumu (Kenya) **1:**308
Kitara (early kingdom in Africa) **1:**322
Kitchener (Ontario) **5:**107
Kitchener, Horatio Herbert (British general) **1:**130
Kittatinny Mountains (New Jersey) **5:**199
Kittredge, Benjamin (American landowner) **5:**232
Kitty Hawk (North Carolina) **5:**229
Kitwe (Zambia) **1:**272, 274
Kivu (province, Congo, Democratic Republic of) **1:**266
Kivu, Lake (Africa) **1:**19, 262, 324, 326
Kivu Falls (Congo, Democratic Republic of)
illus. **1:**261
Kiwi (bird)
illus. **2:**542

Kladno (Czech Republic) **4:**224
Klaipėda (Lithuania) **4:**303
Klamath (Indians of North America) **5:**339
Klamath Mountains (California–Oregon) **5:**8, 51, 339, 341–42, 343
Klaus, Václav (Czech finance minister) **4:**228–29, 231
Klestil, Thomas (president of Austria) **3:**325
Klondike, S.S. (steamship)
illus. **5:**147
Klondike Days (celebration, Edmonton) **5:**127
Klondike gold rush 5:136, 147, 148
illus. **5:**148
Kluane National Park (Yukon Territory) **5:**145
Knesset (Israeli parliament) **2:**107, 111
Knife River Indian Village National Historic Site (Iowa) **5:**298
Knights Hospitalers of St. John of Jerusalem (Knights of Malta) 4:183
Knobs (region, Kentucky) **5:**260–61
Knokke-sur-Mer (Belgium) **3:**217
Knossos (Crete) **4:**192
illus. **4:**201
Knox, John (Scottish preacher) **3:**140
Knoxville (Tennessee) **5:**264
Koala
illus. **2:**487
Kobe (Japan) **2:**440
Koblenz (Germany) **3:**245
Koch, Ed (mayor of New York City) **5:**204
Kocharian, Robert (president of Armenia) **2:**79
illus. **2:**77
Kochis (people) **2:**178
Kodály, Zoltán (Hungarian composer) **4:**241
Kodiak Island (Alaska)
illus. **5:**41
Kodok (Sudan) **1:**128
Koestler, Arthur (Hungarian-born writer) **4:**240–41
Kohl, Helmut (German statesman) **3:**263, 284
Koizumi Junichiro (prime minister of Japan) **2:**472
Kok, Willem (premier of Netherlands) **3:**238
Kokand khanate 2:355
Kola Gulf (Barents Sea) **5:**64
Kolahun (Liberia) **1:**180
Kola Peninsula (White Sea–Arctic Ocean)
Lapland **4:**35
Kold, Kristen (Danish educator) **4:**12
Kolingba, André (president of Central African Republic) **1:**250
Kolkhida Plain (republic of Georgia) **2:**80
Kollwitz, Käthe (German artist) **3:**255
Kolwezi (Congo, Democratic Republic of) **1:**263
Komati River (southeast Africa) **1:**385–86
Komondo Island (Indonesia)
illus. **2:**321
Komsomolsk-na-Amure (Russia) **2:**343
Konaré, Alpha Oumar (president of Mali) **1:**143
Konbaung (Burman dynasty, 16th century) **2:**271
Kong (early capital of Senufo people, Ivory Coast) **1:**188
Kongo (early African kingdom) **1:**43, 260, 268, 344, 346
Königsberg (Russia) *see* Kaliningrad
Konkomba (African people) **1:**206
Konkouré River (west Africa) **1:**166
Kono (African people) **1:**173
Konrad, György (Hungarian writer) **4:**241
Kon-Tiki Museum (Oslo, Norway) **4:**32

Konvicki, Tadeusz (Polish author) **4:**215
Kookaburra (bird) **2:**489, 510
Koolau Mountains (Hawaii) **5:**353
Koori (aboriginal tribe, Australia) **2:**493
Kopet Dagh (mountains, Iran–Turkmenistan)
  2:343, 356
Korab, Mount (Albania) **4:**269
Koran (Arabic: **Qu'ran**) (holy book of Islam)
  1:109; **2:**51, 128
Koranko (African people) **1:**173, 174
Kordofan plateau (region, Sudan) **1:**130
Korea 2:429–38
  civilization influenced by China **2:**372
  division of **2:**26
  Japanese control **2:**374, 446, 447
  people **2:**371
  Russo-Japanese War **2:**25
  illus.
    old painting of invasion by Japanese **2:**21
    reunification march **2:**374
Korea, Democratic People's Republic of *see*
  North Korea
Korea, Republic of *see* South Korea
Korean language 2:372, 431, 437
Korean Peninsula 2:368, 370, 434–35
Koreans (people)
  Japan **2:**30, 443
Korean War (1950–1953) **2:**430, 436, 438
Korhogo (Ivory Coast) **1:**185
Koroma, Johnny Paul (president of Sierra
  Leone) **1:**177
Koror (capital of Palau) **2:**571
Koro Sea (South Pacific) **2:**597
Koryo dynasty (Korea) **2:**433
  pottery **2:**432
Kosciuszko, Mount (New South Wales, Austra-
  lia) **2:**481, 484, 509; **6:**345
  illus. **2:**484
Kosciusko, Thaddeus (Polish general) **4:**220
Košice (Slovakia) **4:**234
Kosinski, Jerzy (Polish-American author) **4:**215
Kosi River (India) **2:**168
Kosovo (province, Serbia) **4:**275, 278, 281
  Albanian population **4:**270, 276
  ethnic conflict **3:**1, 2
  Italy **4:**163
  refugees from **4:**273, 292
Kosovo Field, Battle of (1389) **4:**278, 279
Kosrae (Kusaie) (state, Federated States of
  Micronesia) **2:**569, 570, 573, 574
Kossuth, Lajos (Hungarian leader) **4:**245–46
Kostunica, Vojislav (president of Yugoslavia)
  4:275
Kota Kinabalu (capital, Sabah, Malaysia) **2:**307
Kotokoli (African people) **1:**206
Kotor, Gulf of (Yugoslavia) **4:**276
  illus. **4:**274
Kouchibouguac National Park (New Bruns-
  wick) **5:**85
Kouilou River (Congo) **1:**257
Kouranke (African people) **1:**167
Kourou (French Guiana) **6:**92
Kowloon Peninsula (Hong Kong) **2:**410, 411
Koxinga *see* Cheng Ch'eng-kung
Kpémé (Togo)
  illus. **1:**208
Kraftwerk (German music group) **3:**252
Krajina (region, Croatia) **4:**287
Krakatau (Krakatoa) (volcano, Indonesia) **2:**313
Krasnoyarsk (Russia) **2:**343
Kreda (African people) **1:**242

Kremlin (Moscow, Russia) **4:**327
  illus. **4:**327
Kreshchatik (main street, Kiev, Ukraine) **4:**336
Krestovy Pass (Georgian Military Highway) **2:**81
Krill 6:338
Krimml Falls (Austria) **3:**314
Krishna (Hindu god) **2:**201
Krivoi Rog (Ukraine) **3:**38
Kru (African people) **1:**186
Kruger, Paul (South African statesman) **1:**388
Krugersdorp (South Africa) **1:**402
Krujë (Albania) **4:**272
Kshatriyas (caste, India) **2:**21, 210
Kuala Lumpur (capital, Malaysia) **2:**262, 305,
  307
  illus. **2:**303
    Petronas Towers **2:**253
Kuan Yin (Chinese goddess)
  illus. **2:**389
Kublai Khan (Mongol ruler of China) **2:**324,
  366, 394, 421
  Lamaism adopted as state religion **2:**387
  Myanmar **2:**271
  illus. **2:**24
Kučan, Milan (president of Slovenia) **4:**284
Kuching (capital, Sarawak, Malaysia) **2:**307
Kuchma, Leonid (president of Ukraine) **4:**332,
  338
  illus. **4:**340
Kufour, John (president of Ghana) **1:**204
Kufra (Libya) **1:**95
Kumaratunga, Chandrika (president of Sri
  Lanka) **2:**250
Kumasi (Ghana) **1:**197, 199, 201, 202
Kum River (South Korea) **2:**435
Kunama (African people) **1:**295
Kundera, Milan (Czech writer) **4:**230
Kunene River (Africa) *see* Cunene River
Kuntaur (Gambia) **1:**160
Kunze, Reiner (German author) **3:**251
Kuomintang (nationalist party in China) *see*
  Guomindang
Kupe (Maori chief) **2:**550
Kura Valley (Azerbaijan) **2:**88
Kurdistan (region, Middle East) **2:**148
Kurds (Asian people) **2:**30, 59, 91, 117, 118, 157
  Iraq **2:**148, 154
Kurfürstendamm (street, Berlin, Germany)
  3:281
Kuril Islands (Pacific Ocean) **2:**31, 343
Kuropaty Forest (Belarus) **4:**342
Kurosawa, Akira (Japanese movie director)
  2:463
Kuroshio Current *see* Japan (Kuroshio) Current
Kurs (early European tribe) **4:**298
Kusaie (island, Pacific Ocean) *see* Kosrae
Kush (early African kingdom) *see* Cush
Kushan (Asian people) **2:**192
Küssnacht (Switzerland) **3:**297
Kutchin (Indians of North America) **5:**146
Kutenai (Indians of North America) **5:**130, 311
KUWAIT 2:144–46
  Iraq, invasion by **2:**55, 154
  refugees from **2:**31
  illus.
    flag **2:**vii
    refugees **2:**30
  map(s) **2:**145
Kuwait City (capital, Kuwait) **2:**144
Kuznetsk Basin (Kuzbas) (industrial area, Rus-
  sia) **4:**308, 309
Kuznetsov, A. Anatoli (Soviet author) **4:**337

Kwajalein (atoll, Pacific Ocean) **2:**575
Kwakiutl (Indians of North America) **5:**132
Kwakwani (Guyana) **6:**151
Kwa language 1:180
Kwaluseni (Swaziland) **1:**388
Kwangju (South Korea) **2:**435, 436, 438
Kwangsi-Chuang Autonomous Region (China)
  see Guangxi Autonomous Region
Kwanzaa
  illus. **5:**44
Kwa River (Africa) **1:**42
Kwaśniewski, Aleksander (president of Poland)
  4:223
KwaZulu/Natal (province, South Africa) **1:**396,
  400, 401, 405, 406
Kyoga, Lake (Africa) **1:**317
Kyoto (Japan) **2:**440, 443, 457
  illus. **2:**455
Kyrenia Mountains (Cyprus) **2:**68, 70
Kyrgyz (Turkic people) **2:**344, 354, 355, 380
  Kazakhstan **2:**347
Kyrgyz language 2:354
KYRGYZSTAN 2:341, **353–55**
  land **2:**343
  illus. **2:**353
    flag **2:**ix
  map(s) **2:**354
Kyushu (island, Japan) **2:**440, 444, 445, 457
Kyzyl Kum (desert, Uzbekistan) **2:**10, 343, 350

• • • L • • •

L1 (mountain, Canada) **5:**81
Labé (Guinea) **1:**168
Labe River *see* Elbe River
La Boca (port area, Buenos Aires, Argentina)
  6:290
  illus. **6:**278
Labor unions
  Chicago, labor movement centered in **5:**283
  Italy **4:**153, 162
  Japan **2:**468–69
  Manitoba **5:**117
  Pennsylvania **5:**214
Labour Party (Great Britain) **3:**95, 96
Labrador (Canada) **5:**12, 78, 80 *see also* New-
  foundland and Labrador
Labrador City (Labrador) **5:**83
Labrador Current (Atlantic Ocean) **5:**78, 82
Lacalle, Luis Alberto (president of Uruguay)
  6:265
La Ceiba (Honduras) **6:**38
Lacemaking 3:295; **6:**248
  illus. **6:**245
Lachlan River (Australia) **2:**483
La Condamine (Monaco) **3:**206
La Coruña (Spain) **4:**111
Ladakh (region, Kashmir) **2:**173
La Digue (island in the Seychelles group) **1:**339
Ladinos (Guatemalans who live according to
  Spanish tradition) **6:**27–28
Ladoga, Lake (Russia) **4:**308
  table(s)
    largest lakes **6:**347
Lady Knox Geyser (New Zealand)
  illus.
    Lady Knox Geyser (New Zealand) **2:**540
Lae (Papua New Guinea) **2:**589
Laetolil (Tanzania) **1:**6

LAFTA *see* Latin American Free Trade Association
Lagan River (Northern Ireland) **3:**83, 143, 145
Lagerkvist, Pär (Swedish playwright) **4:**43
Lagerlöf, Selma (Swedish writer) **4:**43
Lagoa dos Patos *see* Patos, Lagoa dos
Lagos (Nigeria) **1:**217, 227
   illus.
     medical clinic **1:**229
     shopkeepers **1:**218
Lagos Escobar (president of Chile) **6:**323
La Grande River (Quebec) **5:**102
La Guaira (Venezuela) **6:**133, 137
Laguna de Cuyutlán (Colima, Mexico) **5:**408
Laguna de Perlas (Nicaragua) **6:**56
Laguna Mountains (California) **5:**342
Lahore (Pakistan) **2:**188
Lake District (England) **3:**83, 98, 101
Lake Ontario-Mohawk gap (Appalachian Mountain pass) **5:**6, 38
Lake Placid (resort town, New York) **5:**204
Lake Plains (Ohio) **5:**271
Lakes
   African rift valleys **1:**19
   Finland's **4:**52
   glaciation in North America **5:**12–13, 297
   Great Basin **5:**309
   Sahara Desert **1:**25
   table(s)
     largest of the world **6:**347
Lake Shore Drive (street, Chicago, Illinois) **5:**283
Lakewood (Colorado) **5:**320
Laki, Mount (Iceland) **4:**3, 5
Lalibela (emperor of Ethiopia) **1:**288
Lallans (Lowland Scots) (language) **3:**136
Lamaism (Tibetan form of Buddhism) **2:**169, 235, 365, 385, 386–87
   Mongolia **2:**344
   illus.
     Dalai Lama **2:**19
La Mancha (Spain) *see* Mancha, La
Lambaréné (Gabon) **1:**43, 253
Lanai (Pineapple Island) (island, Hawaii) **5:**352
Lancang Jiang (Chinese name for Mekong River) **2:**256
Lancaster, House of (English dynasty)
   rulers of England, list of **6:**360
Lancaster County (Pennsylvania)
   illus. **5:**211
Lancaster Sound (Northwest Territories, Canada) **5:**5, 61
Lan Chang (Lan Xang) (former kingdom of Laos) **2:**285
Lanchow (China) *see* Lanzhou
Land *see also* Land reclamation; Land reform
   African land rights **1:**26–28
   Brazilian distribution **6:**164
   Central American distribution **6:**13–14, 17
   Ecuadorian ownership **6:**198
   French North America **5:**33–34
   Honduran plantations **6:**39–40
   Lesotho land use **1:**392
   Mexican distribution **5:**28
   Micronesia, Federated States of **2:**574
   Oceania social system **2:**563–64
   Philippine distribution **2:**337–38
   Samoan communal system **2:**603
   Scottish land rights **3:**141
   Solomon Islands ownership **2:**593
   South American distribution **6:**105

Spanish North America **5:**27, 28
   Tonga's feudal system **2:**605
   Zimbabwe's land division **1:**360–61
Land Acts (South Africa, 1913 and 1936) **1:**58
Land Between the Lakes (recreation area, Kentucky) **5:**261
Lander, Richard and John (English explorers) **1:**51
Land of Enchantment (nickname for New Mexico) **5:**321
Land of Lincoln (nickname for Illinois) **5:**281
Land of 1,000 Lakes (nickname for Manitoba) **5:**114
Land of Opportunity (nickname for Arkansas) **5:**266
Land of 10,000 Lakes (nickname for Minnesota) **5:**287, 289
Land reclamation
   Belgium **3:**212
   Hong Kong **2:**410
   Mexico City **5:**410
   Monaco **3:**206
   Netherlands **3:**227, 228
   Spain **4:**110
Land reform
   Chile **6:**319
   China **2:**397, 409
   Colombia **6:**125
   Egypt **1:**102
   El Salvador **6:**46, 47, 48, 50
   Iran **2:**163
   Ireland **3:**71
   Mexico **5:**361
   Nicaragua **6:**59, 60
   Panama **6:**77
   South America **6:**105
   Taiwan **2:**426
Land rushes (U.S. history) **5:**302, 306–7
Landsbergis, Vytautas (president of Lithuania) **4:**304
Land's End (England) **3:**100
Landuman (African people) **1:**167
Langeberg (mountains, South Africa) **1:**395
Langi (African people) **1:**319
Lango (African people) **1:**323
Language and languages *see also* articles on individual continents and countries; names of principal languages and language groups
   Africa **1:**6, 15
   Asia **2:**27–28
   Asia: East **2:**371–72
   Asia: India **2:**199–200
   Asia: South **2:**170
   Asia: Southeast **2:**259–60
   Asia: Southwest **2:**44
   Belgium, language boundary line in **3:**211, 214, 224
   Canada's official languages **5:**74
   Caribbean islands **5:**435
   Chinese language reforms **2:**402
   "click" languages **1:**352
   Easter Island's lost language **6:**323
   Europe **3:**20
   European Union, official languages of **3:**4
   Iceland **4:**5
   modern Italian **4:**134
   Oceania **2:**563
   Paraguay's bilingualism **6:**245–46
   sign language of North American Indians **5:**164
   Switzerland's four languages **3:**290
Languedoc (region, France) **3:**160, 180

Langurs **2:**234
L'Anse aux Meadows (Newfoundland) **5:**78
L'Anse-aux-Meadows (Newfoundland) **5:**83
L'Anse Indian Reservation (Michigan) **5:**276
Lansing (capital, Michigan) **5:**278
Lan Xang *see* Lan Chang
Lanzarote (island, Canary Islands) **1:**32; **4:**85
Lanzhou (Lanchow) (China) **2:**370
Lao (Asian people) **2:**259, 275, 283, 285
Lao language **2:**260
LAOS **2:**254, 259, 264, **281–85**
   Mekong River **2:**256–57
   illus. **2:**281, 284
     flag **2:**viii
   map(s) **2:**282
La Palma (island, Canary Islands) **1:**32; **4:**84
La Pampa (province, Argentina) **6:**266, 272, 285
La Paz (capital, Baja California Sur, Mexico) **5:**391
La Paz (official capital, Bolivia) **6:**232, 239
   illus. **6:**90, 229, 232
LAPLAND **4:**34, **35–37**, 39
   Europe's tundra area **3:**32
   illus. **4:**36
   map(s) **4:**35
La Plata (Argentina) **6:**292, 299
La Plata (Spanish viceroyalty at Buenos Aires) **6:**90, 99
Lappeenranta (Finland) **4:**52
Lappland *see* Lapland
Lapp language **4:**37
Lapps (Sami) (people) **4:**34, 35, 37, 40, 58; **5:**60
   illus. **4:**36; **5:**61
Lara, Agustín (Mexican composer) **5:**373
Laramie Mountains (Wyoming) **5:**315
Larderello (Italy) **4:**132
Largeau (Faya) (Chad) **1:**242
Larnaca (Cyprus) **2:**70, 72
La Salle, Robert Cavelier, Sieur de (French explorer) **5:**101
La Scala (opera house, Milan) **4:**143
Lascaux Caves (France) **3:**167, 177
Las Cruces (New Mexico) **5:**322
La Serena (Chile) **6:**313
Las Hadas (Colima, Mexico)
   illus. **5:**408
Las Palmas (Canary Islands) **1:**32; **4:**84–85
Lassen Volcanic National Park (California) **5:**342
Last Frontier (nickname for Alaska) **5:**348
Las Vegas (Nevada) **5:**50, 331, 332
   illus. **5:**330
Latakia (Syria) **2:**91
Lateran Treaty (1929) **4:**163, 167, 178
Laterite (rock) **1:**22, 266
Latgallians (early European tribe) **4:**298
Latham Island (Northwest Territories) **5:**144
Latifundia (landholding system) **4:**67, 151; **6:**105, 164, 198
Latin America **6:**1–8 *see also* Central America; South America
Latin American Free Trade Association (LAFTA) **6:**115
Latin American Integration Association (LAIA) **6:**115
Latin American tower (Mexico City) **5:**411
Latin language **3:**49; **4:**111, 134
Latin Quarter (Paris, France) **3:**199
La Tirana (Chile) **6:**306
Latrobe Valley (Australia) **2:**520
Lattgalians (early European tribe) *see* Latgallians

LATVIA 3:2; **4:**297–300
  illus. **4:**297, 299
  flag **4:**vi
  map(s) **4:**298
Latvians (people) **4:**297–98
Lau Group (Fiji) **2:**597
Launceston (Tasmania, Australia) **2:**530
La Unión (El Salvador) **6:**44
Laurentian Shield *see* Canadian (Laurentian) Shield
Lausanne (Switzerland) **3:**294, 295
Lausanne, Treaty of (1923) **2:**66
Lava
  Giant's Causeway **3:**146
  illus. **5:**352
Laval, Pierre (French politician) **3:**188
La Valette, Jean Parisot de (French-born defender of Malta) **4:**183
Lavalleja, Juan Antonio (Uruguayan patriot) **6:**261, 263
La Vega (Dominican Republic) **5:**454
La Vega Real (region, Dominican Republic) **5:**454
Lavena River (Europe) **3:**307
La Venta (Tabasco, Mexico) **5:**419
La Venta Island (Mexico) **5:**419
Lavín, Joaquín (Chilean politician) **6:**323
Law
  Code of Hammurabi **2:**48
  Islamic law in Iran **2:**164
  Islamic law in Pakistan **2:**183
  Islamic law in Qatar **2:**142–43
  Islamic law in Saudi Arabia **2:**128
  Islamic law in Sudan **1:**128, 131
  legal codes introduced to Oceania **2:**566
  Napoleonic Code **3:**185
  Netherlands **3:**235
  Pakistani women **2:**193
  Scotland **3:**141
  Stephen Dušan, Code of **4:**277
  Turkey: reforms of Kemal Atatürk **2:**66–67
  illus.
    Code of Hammurabi **2:**12
Lawn bowling
  illus. **2:**544
Lawrence, T. E. (Lawrence of Arabia) (British soldier and writer) **2:**95
Laxness, Halldór (Icelandic author) **4:**7
Lazo, Francisco (Peruvian artist) **6:**214
Lead (mineral) **5:**160
League of Nations
  African mandates **1:**46, 326, 331, 337, 350
  Europe **3:**60, 293
  Middle East **2:**102, 113, 121, 154
  Nauru **2:**579
  Oceania **2:**566
  Palau **2:**572
  Southwest Asia **2:**52
Leakey, Louis S. B. (British-Kenyan anthropologist) **1:**312
Leakey, Richard (Kenyan anthropologist)
  illus. **1:**312
Leaning Tower of Pisa (Italy)
  illus. **4:**135
Leather 1:222
  illus.
    Moroccan workers dye leather **1:**72
LEBANON 2:96, **97–103**, 115
  illus.
    Baalbek **2:**99
    Beirut **2:**97, 103

Byblos 2:99
    flag **2:**vii
    Pigeon Rock **2:**99
    shepherd with sheep **2:**99
    teacher in war-damaged classroom **2:**102
  map(s) **2:**98
Lebanon Mountains 2:97
Lebowans (African people) **1:**398
Lebu (African people) **1:**154
Leclerc, Charles (French general) **5:**469
Le Corbusier (French architect)
  illus.
    Ronchamp chapel **3:**169
Leduc (Alberta) **5:**127
Leeds (England) **3:**106–7
Lee Kuan Yew (Singapore political leader) **2:**312
Lee River (Ireland) **3:**73
Lee Teng-hui (president of Taiwan) **2:**428
Leeward Islands (Caribbean Sea) **5:**426, 433
  Antigua and Barbuda **5:**493
  Montserrat **5:**439
  St. Kitts and Nevis **5:**495
Left Bank (Paris, France) **3:**193, 199–200
Legal codes *see* Law
Legends and folklore
  Ashanti's Golden Stool **1:**202
  Belize **6:**21
  Bolivian mountain legend **6:**231
  Brazil **6:**166
  Bulgarian superstitions **4:**259
  Chilean *huaso* **6:**307
  Chinese flood myth **2:**1
  Finland **4:**55
  Garden of Eden located **2:**50
  German literature **3:**253
  Huarpe people of Argentina **6:**269
  Inca Empire, founding of **6:**222
  Indonesia **2:**316
  Jamaica **5:**475
  Japan, founding of **2:**16–17, 443
  Lapland **4:**37
  Liechtenstein **3:**306
  Lorelei of Rhine River **3:**245
  Madagascar, island of the great roc **1:**377
  Manas (Kyrgyz epic) **2:**355
  Netherlands: boy at dike **3:**225
  Northern Ireland's heroes **3:**145, 146
  Romania **4:**252
  Rome, founding of **4:**164–65
  Rome's Trevi Fountain **4:**173
  Saint Vincent and grapevines **3:**156
  Spain, first settlers in **4:**110
  Suriname **6:**156
  Swiss religious history **3:**297
  Tell, William **3:**295, 297
  Theseus and the Minotaur **4:**190
  Venezuela's Guayana **6:**135
  illus.
    lovers' leap at Pigeon Rock (Lebanon) **2:**101
    Thera thought to be site of Atlantis **4:**200
Leghari, Farooq (president of Pakistan) **2:**194
Lego Company 4:12–13
Legon (Ghana) **1:**199
  illus. **1:**199
Lehár, Franz (Hungarian composer) **4:**241
Le Havre (France) **3:**152, 154, 164
Leipzig (Germany) **3:**241, 268
Lekhanya, Justin (political leader of Lesotho) **1:**392–93
Le Loi (Vietnamese national hero) **2:**301
Lelu (island, Micronesia) **2:**573

Lem, Stanisław (Polish author) **4:**215
Le Mans auto race (France) **3:**175–76
  illus. **3:**175
Lemberg (Ukraine) *see* Lviv
Lemmings 5:60
Lempa River (Central America) **6:**43
Lempira (Indian chief) **6:**36, 41
Lemurs (animals) **1:**369
Lenape (Indians of North America) **5:**199, 209, 210, 212, 216, 274
Lena River (Russia) **4:**308; **5:**56
  table(s)
    longest rivers of the world **6:**346
Lendl, Ivan (Czech tennis player) **4:**226
L'Enfant, Pierre Charles (French engineer) **5:**170; **6:**186
Leni-Lenape (Indians of North America) *see* Lenape
Lenin, Vladimir Ilich (Russian leader) **4:**322, 328
Leningrad (Russia) *see* St. Petersburg
Leo III (pope) **4:**155
Leo Africanus (Spanish Moorish geographer) **1:**30
León (Guanajuato, Mexico) **5:**405
León (Nicaragua) **6:**54, 58
León (region and former kingdom, Spain) **4:**113
Leonardo da Vinci (Italian artist) **4:**143
Leoni, Raúl (president of Venezuela) **6:**148
Leopard seals 6:327, 328
Leopold I (margrave of duchy of Austria) **3:**321
Leopold I (king of Belgium) **3:**223
Leopold II (king of Belgium) **1:**42–43, 261, 268, 269; **3:**223
Leopold III (king of Belgium) **3:**224
Leopoldville (Congo, Democratic Republic of) *see* Kinshasa
Lepanto, Battle of (1571) **2:**65; **4:**115
Le Pen, Jean-Marie (French politician) **3:**191
Leptis Magna (Libya)
  illus. **1:**10, 93
Lerma River (Mexico) **5:**405, 409
Lermontov, Mikhail (Russian poet) **2:**81
Les Baux (France) **3:**38, 157
Lesbos (Greek island) **4:**191
Les Escaldes (Andorra) **4:**121
LESOTHO 1:47, **390–93**
  illus.
    flag **1:**xxiv
    traditional hat **1:**393
  map(s) **1:**391
Lesseps, Ferdinand, Vicomte de (French businessman) **1:**120, 121; **3:**186; **6:**78
  Panama Canal **6:**80
Lesser Antilles (Caribbean island group) **5:**426, 487, 489, 493, 495
  map(s) **5:**429
Lesser Sunda Islands (Indonesia) **2:**315
Lessing, Gotthold (German playwright) **3:**253
Lethbridge (Alberta) **5:**124
L'Etoile *see* Arc de Triomphe
Letsie III (king of Lesotho) **1:**393
Letts (people) *see* Latvians
Letzeburgisch language *see* Luxembourgian
Levant (old name for the Middle East) **2:**43
Levy, Uriah (American purchaser of Monticello) **5:**225
Lewis, Sir Arthur (St. Lucian economist) **5:**489
Lewis, Jerry Lee (American musician) **5:**263
Lewis, Meriwether (American explorer) *see* Lewis and Clark Expedition

Lewis, Vaughan (prime minister of St. Lucia) **5:**490

Lewis and Clark Expedition (1804–1806) **5:**39, 298, 310, 340

Lewiston (Maine) **5:**183

Lexington (Kentucky) **5:**261, 262

Lexington (Massachusetts) **5:**190

Lhasa (capital, Xizang) **2:**387

Liamuiga, Mount (St. Kitts and Nevis) **5:**495
  illus. **5:**495

Liaodong Peninsula (China) **2:**380

Liaquat Ali Khan (prime minister of Pakistan) **2:**193

Liberec (Czech Republic) **4:**224

LIBERIA 1:55, 177, **178–83**
  illus.
    flag **1:**xxii
    market **1:**181
    Monrovia **1:**178
    rice harvest **1:**180
  map(s) **1:**179

Libertad (department, Peru) **6:**218

Liberty, Statue of *see* Statue of Liberty

Liberty Bell
  illus. **5:**213

Libraries
  Alexandria **1:**115, 119
  Armenian manuscripts **2:**76
  China **2:**407
  Vatican Library **4:**181
  illus.
    Africa **1:**28

Libreville (capital, Gabon) **1:**253, 254
  illus. **1:**251

LIBYA 1:34–35, **93–100**
  Barbary pirates **1:**97
  Chad, history of **1:**244
  Egypt, Libyan rulers of **1:**118
  Sahara **1:**24
  terrorism **1:**98
  illus.
    flag **1:**xxii
    Leptis Magna ruins **1:**10, 93
    Libyans with picture of Qaddafi **1:**100
    oasis **1:**96
    oil refinery **1:**99
    Tripoli **1:**95
  map(s) **1:**94

Libyan Desert (north Africa) **1:**94, 112

Lidingo (Sweden) **4:**43

LIECHTENSTEIN 3:305–7
  illus. **3:**305
    flag **3:**vi
  map(s) **3:**307

Liechtenstein, Johann Adam von (Austrian prince, founder of Liechtenstein) **3:**306

Lied Discovery Children's Museum (Las Vegas, Nevada) **5:**332

Liège (Belgium) **3:**217, 219

Liepāja (Latvia) **4:**297, 299

Life expectancy
  Africa **1:**3, 5
  Burkina Faso **1:**52
  United Arab Emirates **2:**139
  Yemen **2:**134
  table(s)
    Central America **6:**17
    South America **6:**99

Lighthouses
  Mazatlán **5:**397
  North Carolina **5:**229

Pharos of Alexandria 1:115
  illus. **2:**515; **5:**227

Ligurian Alps 4:126

Likasi (Congo, Democratic Republic of) **1:**263

Likiep Atoll (Marshall Islands) **2:**575

Liliuokalani (Hawaiian queen) **5:**354
  illus. **5:**354

Lille (France) **3:**162

Lilongwe (capital, Malawi) **1:**278

Lima (capital, Peru) **6:**207, 211, 215, 217
  education **6:**106, 216
  festivals **6:**212–13
  history **6:**224
  terrorist attacks **6:**228
  illus. **6:**105, 215, 218
    flea market **6:**6
    guard at Government Palace **6:**224
    Palace of the Archbishop **6:**214
    San Martín, statue of **6:**217

Limassol (Cyprus) **2:**70, 71

Limay River (Argentina) **6:**281

Limba (African people) **1:**173, 174

Limba trees 1:259

Limbe (Malawi) **1:**278

Limburg (province, Netherlands) **3:**229

Limerick (Ireland) **3:**69, 74, 75

Limestone
  illus. **6:**88

Limmat River (Switzerland) **3:**292
  illus. **3:**292

Limoges (France) **3:**157

Limón (Costa Rica) **6:**64

Limón (San Luis Potosí, Mexico) **5:**401

Limousin (region, France) **3:**155

Limpopo River (Africa) **1:**355, 356, 364, 396

Lincoln (capital, Nebraska) **5:**301, 302

Lincoln, Abraham (16th president of U.S.) **5:**174–75, 214, 261, 283

Lincoln Memorial (Washington, D.C.)
  illus. **5:**170

Linderhof Castle (Germany) **3:**257

Line Islands (Kiribati) **2:**569, 580

Linz (capital, Upper Austria province) **3:**315

Lions
  illus. **1:**41

Lipari Islands (Italy) **4:**130

Li Peng (premier of China) **2:**422

Lipica (Lippiza) (Slovenia) **4:**284

Lippizaner horses 4:284

Liquefied natural gas 2:321, 330

Lisbon (capital, Portugal) **4:**71–72, 73, 77
  illus. **4:**73
    Monument of Discoveries **4:**76

Lisburn (Northern Ireland) **3:**147

Lissouba, Pascal (president of Congo) **1:**260

Liszt, Franz (Hungarian composer) **4:**241

Literature *see also* Poetry
  Afrikaners **1:**401
  Argentina **6:**276–77
  Armenia **2:**76
  Bangladesh **2:**240
  Bolivia **6:**237–38
  Brazil **6:**180
  Bulgaria **4:**261
  Chile **6:**309
  China **2:**406–7
  Colombia **6:**122
  Costa Rica **6:**67
  Czech Republic **4:**226–27
  Denmark **4:**16
  Ecuador **6:**199–200

England **3:**104
  England: Elizabethan Age **3:**119
  England: Shakespeare **3:**116
  Europe **3:**14
  France **3:**178–79
  Germany **3:**253–54
  Greek, ancient **4:**201–2
  Greek, modern **4:**193–94
  Guatemala **6:**29
  Haiti **5:**465–66
  Honduras **6:**38
  Hungary **4:**240–41
  Iceland **4:**7
  Iran **2:**159–60
  Ireland **3:**70, 75
  Japan **2:**460, 462
  Korea **2:**431–32
  Kyrgyzstan **2:**355
  Latin's Silver Age **4:**111
  Liberia's oral literature **1:**181
  Mexico **5:**373–74, 381
  New Zealand **2:**546
  Nicaragua **6:**55
  Northern Ireland **3:**145
  Norway **4:**28
  Paraguay **6:**249
  Peru **6:**214–15
  Poland **4:**215
  Portugal's *Os Lusíadas* **4:**71
  Renaissance **3:**55
  Russia **4:**312–13, 314–15, 331
  Scotland **3:**137
  Senghor and Negritude **1:**158
  Sweden **4:**42–43
  Ukraine **4:**335
  United Kingdom **3:**88
  Uruguay **6:**256–57
  Uzbekistan **2:**351
  Venezuela **6:**135, 141
  Wales **3:**125–26
  illus.
    illuminated manuscript **3:**176

LITHUANIA 3:2; **4:301–4**
  Belarus, history of **4:**343
  illus. **4:**301
    flag **4:**vi
  map(s) **4:**302

Little Bighorn, Battle of 5:312

Little Bitter Lake (Egypt) **1:**120

Little Ice Age 5:14

Little Rock (capital, Arkansas) **5:**267

Little Saint Bernard Pass (Alps) **4:**126

Little Scarcies River (Guinea–Sierra Leone) **1:**172

Little Zab River (Asia) **2:**50

Liu Shaoqi (Liu Shao-chi) (Chinese Communist leader) **2:**398

Liverpool (England) **3:**107–8, 109
  illus.
    Royal Liver Building **3:**91

Livestock *see also* Cattle; Horses; Sheep
  England, epidemic-disease crisis **3:**109
  Mongolia **2:**363, 365
  illus.
    Ecuador **6:**200

Living Buddha (spiritual and secular ruler of the Mongols) **2:**365

Livingstone (Zambia) **1:**272

Livingstone, David (Scottish missionary and explorer) **1:**268, 276, 280, 331

Livingstone Falls (Congo River) **1:**42

Livs (early European tribe) **4:**298

Ljubljana (capital, Slovenia) **4:**283, 284
Llamas 6:87, 231
illus. **6:**89, 206, 230
Llanos (grasslands of South America) **6:**132, 133–34
Lleyn Peninsula (Wales) **3:**122
Llyn Tegid *see* Bala Lake
Llywelyn ap Gruffudd (Welsh prince) **3:**129
Lobamba (traditional capital, Swaziland) **1:**389
Lobatse (Botswana) **1:**353
Lobengula (leader of the Matabele) **1:**362
Lobi (African people) **1:**186, 191
Lobito (Angola) **1:**343
Lobsters
illus. **5:**468
Lobster traps
illus. **5:**182
Locks (of a canal) **6:**78
illus. **6:**73
Locmariaquer (France) **3:**164
Łódź (Poland) **4:**218
Loess (soil) **5:**290, 293
Loess Hills (Nebraska) **5:**301
Logan (Utah) **5:**324
Logan, Mount (Yukon Territory) **5:**69, 145
Logging *see* Lumber and lumbering
Logone River (central Africa) **1:**240, 241
Loire River (France) **3:**152
Loja (province, Ecuador) **6:**197
Loko (African people) **1:**173
Lokoja (Nigeria) **1:**216
Lolang (early Chinese colony in Korea) **2:**433
Lolland (island in Denmark) **4:**8
Lomami River (Congo, Democratic Republic of) **1:**266
Lomati River (southeast Africa) **1:**385–86
Lombards (Germanic tribe) **3:**18, 50; **4:**155
Lombardy (region, Italy) **4:**142, 152, 158
Lombok (island, Indonesia) **2:**315
Lomé (capital, Togo) **1:**206, 208, 209
illus. **1:**209
Lomond, Loch (Scotland) **3:**83, 132
Lomwe (African people) **1:**278
Londinium (Roman town, now London, England) **3:**110, 113
LONDON (capital, United Kingdom) **3:**16, 104, 106, 109, 110–11
freedom of speech in Hyde Park **3:**26
Heathrow airport **3:**42
illus. **3:**100
Buckingham Palace **3:**79
changing of the guard at Buckingham Palace **3:**103
Houses of Parliament and Big Ben **3:**111
London Eye (Ferris wheel) **3:**94
Piccadilly Circus **3:**109
Royal Opera House **3:**104
Trafalgar Square **3:**97
traffic **3:**110
underground (subway) **3:**112
London (Ontario) **5:**41, 107
London Bridge 3:110
Londonderry (Derry) (Northern Ireland) **3:**146, 148
London Eye (Ferris wheel, London, England)
illus. **3:**94
Lone Star State (nickname for Texas) **5:**250
Long Beach (California) **5:**346
Longfellow, Henry Wadsworth (American poet) **5:**183
Long House (Narragansett tribal headquarters) **5:**193

Long Island (New York) **5:**201
Long Island Sound (New York–Connecticut) **5:**193, 195, 196
Long March (in Chinese history) **2:**397
Long Range Mountains (Canada) **5:**81
Long Trail (Green Mountains, Vermont) **5:**187
Lon Nol (Cambodian political leader) **2:**291–92
Lönnrot, Elias (Finnish folklorist) **4:**55
Lookout, Cape (North Carolina) **5:**229
Lope de Vega (Spanish playwright) *see* Vega Carpio, Lope Félix de
Lopez, Cape (Gabon) **1:**252
López, Carlos Antonio (Paraguayan dictator) **6:**250
López, Francisco Solano (Paraguayan dictator) **6:**190, 250
López y Planes, Vicente (Argentine poet) **6:**276
Lords, House of (British Parliament) **3:**96
Loreto (department, Peru) **6:**218
Lorikeets
illus. **2:**533
Lorraine (historical region, France) **3:**37, 154, 155, 157, 273 *see also* Alsace and Lorraine
Los Angeles (California) **5:**51, 52, 344–45
earthquake (1994) **5:**335
illus. **5:**345
Los Angeles Ranges (California) **5:**342
Los Mochis (Chihuahua, Mexico) **5:**393
Lost Colony (Roanoke Island, North Carolina) **5:**227, 229
Lothian region (Scotland) **3:**133
Lotus-Eaters (legendary people) **1:**90
Louang-Phrabang (Laos) *see* Luang Prabang
Louis I (le Debonnaire; le Pieux) (king of France and Holy Roman emperor) **4:**121
Louis IX (Saint Louis) (king of France) **3:**54, 193, 200
Louis XIII (king of France) **3:**179, 183
Louis XIV ("the Sun King") (king of France) **3:**57, 167, 183–84
court was artistic center of the world **3:**177
Louis XV (king of France) **3:**184
Louis XVI (king of France) **3:**184, 195, 324
Louis XVIII (king of France) **3:**185
Louis (king of Holland) **3:**235, 236
Louise, Lake (Alberta) **5:**126
Louisiade Islands (Papua New Guinea) **2:**587
LOUISIANA 5:162, 247–49
illus. **5:**247, 248
map(s) **5:**248
Louisiana Purchase (1803) **5:**174, 292, 294, 296
Louisiana Purchase Exposition (1904) **5:**296
Louis Napoleon *see* Napoleon III
Louis Philippe (king of France) **3:**185–86
Louis the Great (Louis I) (Hungarian king) **4:**245
Louisville (Kentucky) **5:**261
illus. **5:**260
Louisy, Allan (prime minister of St. Lucia) **5:**490
Lourdes (France) **3:**165
illus. **3:**165
Lourenço Marques (Mozambique) *see* Maputo
Louvain (Belgium) **3:**214, 217
L'Ouverture, Toussaint *see* Toussaint L'Ouverture
Louvre (art museum, Paris, France) **3:**195, 200
Love Parade (music festival in Berlin, Germany) **3:**252, 281
illus. **3:**253
Low Countries (Belgium and the Netherlands) **3:**211–24, 225–38; **4:**115
Lower Austria (province of Austria) **3:**315

Lower California *see* Baja California
Lower Canada 5:97, 102, 109
Lowland Scots language *see* Lallans
Loyalists (Unionists) (Northern Ireland) **3:**144, 148, 149
Loyalists, British (American Revolution) *see also* United Empire Loyalists
Bahamas **5:**424
Loyalty Islands (dependency of New Caledonia) **2:**585
Loyola, Saint Ignatius (Spanish founder of Jesuits) **4:**97
Lozi (Rozi) (African people) **1:**273, 357, 362
Lualaba (another name for Congo River) **1:**42
Luanda (capital, Angola) **1:**342–43, 344
illus.
refugees **1:**341
Luang Prabang (Laos) **2:**257, 282, 285
illus. **2:**281
Luanshya (Zambia) **1:**272
Luapula (another name for Congo River) **1:**42
Luba (early African kingdom) **1:**268, 346
Lubbers, Ruud (premier of Netherlands) **3:**238
Lübeck (Germany) **3:**265, 273
illus. **3:**267
Lubumbashi (Elisabethville) (Congo, Democratic Republic of) **1:**263
Lucerne (Switzerland) **3:**295
illus. **3:**296
Lucerne, Lake of (Switzerland) **3:**286, 295, 296
illus. **3:**304
Lucy (early human fossil) **1:**6
Lüderitz (Namibia) **1:**348, 350
Ludwig I (king of Bavaria) **3:**271; **4:**206
Ludwig II (king of Bavaria) **3:**257
Luftwaffe (German air force) **3:**277
Lugano, Lake (Italy–Switzerland) **3:**286; **4:**128
Lugbara (African people) **1:**319
Luhya (African people) **1:**309
Luhya language 1:312
Lukacs, György (Hungarian writer) **4:**241
Lukashenko, Aleksandr (president of Belarus) **3:**2; **4:**341, 343
Lula da Silva, Luiz Inacio (president of Brazil) *see* Da Silva, Luiz Inacio Lula
Lulua (African people) **1:**266
Lumber and lumbering *see also* Forests and forestry
Appalachia **5:**257
Atlantic Provinces of Canada **5:**80
British Columbia **5:**42, 133
Canada **5:**71
Finland **4:**52–53
Guyana **6:**151
Malaysia **2:**304
Nicaragua **6:**56–57
North America **5:**17–18
Ottawa **5:**107
Pacific States **5:**50
Pennsylvania hardwood **5:**214
Quebec **5:**99
illus.
logs awaiting export in Gabon **1:**253
Myanmar's use of elephants **2:**267
Swaziland **1:**389
timber floating downstream in Finland **4:**54
Lumumba, Patrice E. (Congolese leader) **1:**269
Lumut (Brunei) **2:**330
Lund (Sweden) **4:**40
Lunda (African people) **1:**269
Lunda (early African kingdom) **1:**266, 268, 346
Lundström, J. E. (Swedish inventor) **4:**46

Lüneburger Heide (Germany) **3:**241, 245
Lunenburg (Nova Scotia) **5:**93
Lungi (Sierra Leone) **1:**171
Lunging Island (New Hampshire) **5:**184
Luo (African people) **1:**309–10, 315, 322
Luo language 1:312
Luostarinmäki (section of Turku, Finland) **4:**64
Luque (Paraguay) **6:**244
Luque, Hernando de (Spanish priest and explorer) **6:**224, 240
Lur (Asian people) **2:**157
Lusaka (capital, Zambia) **1:**272, 274, 275
illus. **1:**272
Lushai Hills (Assam, India) **2:**198, 266
Lusinchi, Jaime (president of Venezuela) **6:**148
Lusitanians (people) **4:**69; **6:**165
Lutetia Parisiorum (ancient town, now Paris, France) **3:**193
Luther, Martin (German leader of Protestant Reformation) **3:**56, 253, 273, 322
Lutheranism (religion) **4:**40, 49
illus.
German church **3:**247
LUXEMBOURG 3:207–10
illus.
Esch-sur-Sûre **3:**207
flag **3:**vi
Luxembourg city **3:**208
Vianden **3:**208
map(s) **3:**209
Luxembourg (capital, Luxembourg) **3:**207
illus. **3:**208
Luxembourg Garden (Paris, France) **3:**199
Luxembourgian language 3:209
Luxor (Egypt) **1:**111
massacre of tourists **1:**116
Lu Xun (Lu Hsun) (Chinese writer) **2:**406
Luzon (island in the Philippines) **2:**332, 336
table(s)
largest islands of the world **6:**346
Lviv (Lvov; Lwów) (Ukraine) **4:**337–38
Lyallpur (Pakistan) *see* Faisalabad
Lyndon B. Johnson Space Center (Houston, Texas) **5:**253
Lynn, Loretta (American singer) **5:**261
Lyons (France) **3:**157, 160–61, 180
illus. **3:**63
Lyttelton (New Zealand) **2:**548

• • • M • • •

Maas River (the Netherlands) *see* Meuse River
Maastricht Treaty (1991) **3:**1, 4, 64, 238
MacAlpin, Kenneth (Gaelic chieftain) **3:**140
MacArthur, Douglas (American general) **2:**340, 447
Macassar (Indonesia) *see* Ujung Pandang
Macau (Macao) (Portuguese territory) **2:**416; **4:**66, 68
economy **2:**375
map(s) **2:**416
Macaw (bird)
illus. **6:**89
MacBeth (king of Scotland) **3:**140
MacCool, Finn (Irish legendary character) **3:**146
MacDonald, Flora (Scottish hero) **3:**141
Macdonnell Ranges (Australia) **2:**483, 532, 534
Macedonia (ancient kingdom) **4:**203–4, 291
Armenia **2:**78

Macedonia (region, south Europe) **4:**187, 188
MACEDONIA (republic) **3:**2; **4:**280, **291–92**
Albanian population **4:**270
Greece, relations with **4:**211
illus. **4:**291
flag **4:**vi
map(s) **4:**292
Macedonians (people) **4:**277
Macgillycuddy's Reeks (mountains, Ireland) **3:**65–66
Machado de Assís, Joaquim Maria (Brazilian author) **6:**112, 180
Machado y Morales, Gerardo (Cuban politician) **5:**447
Machel, Samora (Mozambican leader) **1:**368
Machiavelli, Niccolò (Italian political commentator) **4:**157
Machismo (cult of exaggerated masculinity) **5:**370
Machu Picchu (ancient Inca city, Peru) **6:**90, 219–20
illus. **6:**220
Macías Nguema, Francisco (president of Equatorial Guinea) **1:**236
Mackenzie (district, Northwest Territories, Canada) **5:**43
Mackenzie (Guyana) **6:**151
Mackenzie, Sir Alexander (Scottish explorer in North America) **5:**62, 113, 132, 143
Rocky Mountains **5:**39
Mackenzie Highway (Canada) **5:**144
Mackenzie Lowlands (North America) **5:**5
Mackenzie Mountains (Canada) **5:**7, 69, 141, 142, 145
Mackenzie River (Canada) **5:**56, 134–35, 141
table(s)
longest rivers of the world **6:**346
Mackinac, Straits of (Michigan) **5:**275
Mackinac Bridge (Michigan) **5:**275
MacMahon, Patrice de (French field marshal) **3:**187
Mada (people) *see* Medes
Madách, Imre (Hungarian writer) **4:**240
MADAGASCAR 1:50, **369–77**
illus.
Ambodirafia **1:**371
Antananarivo **1:**369, 373
bricks drying in sun **1:**376
flag **1:**xxiv
people in streets **1:**374
Toamasina **1:**372
winnowing rice **1:**375
map(s) **1:**370
table(s)
largest islands of the world **6:**346
Mad cow disease 3:35
Madden Lake (Panama) **6:**78
Madeira Islands (Portugal) **4:**66, 68
Madero, Francisco I. (president of Mexico) **5:**385, 386, 394
Madison (capital, Wisconsin) **5:**286
Madison, James (4th president of U.S.) **5:**226
Madjapahit (ancient kingdom in Southeast Asia) **2:**308, 319
Madl, Ferenc (president of Hungary) **4:**247
Mad Mullah (Somali leader) *see* Abdullah Hassan, Mohammad
Madras (Chenai) (India) **2:**203, 204, 207–8, 227
Madras cloth 2:207
Madrassas (Islamic schools) **2:**87, 342, 351
Madras State (India) *see* Tamil Nadu
Madre, Sierra (mountains, Guatemala) **6:**29

Madre, Sierra (mountains, Wyoming) **5:**315
Madre de Dios River (South America) **6:**231
Madre del Sur, Sierra (mountains, Mexico) **5:**30, 357, 416
Madre Occidental, Sierra (mountains, Mexico) **5:**8, 30, 357
continental divide **5:**310
minerals **5:**27
mining **5:**363
volcanic peaks **5:**409
Madre Oriental, Sierra (mountains, Mexico) **5:**7, 357
minerals **5:**27, 30, 398
Orizaba, Pico de **5:**407
volcanic peaks **5:**402
Madrid (capital, Spain) **4:**87, 94, 96–98, 108, 115
illus.
National Palace **4:**117
Prado **4:**97
Puerta del Sol **4:**96
Madrid (province, Spain) **4:**106–7
Madrid, Treaty of (1670) **5:**476
Madriz, José (president of Nicaragua) **6:**12
Madura (Indonesian island) **2:**320
Madura, Ricardo (president of Honduras) **6:**41
Maestra, Sierra (mountains, Cuba) **5:**442, 447
Maestral (wind) **4:**285
Magallanes (province, Chile) **6:**317
Magaña, Sergio (Mexican playwright) **5:**374
Magar (Asian people) **2:**231
Magdalena River (Colombia) **6:**86, 116, 120, 125, 126, 127, 128
Magellan, Ferdinand (Portuguese explorer) **3:**55; **6:**97
Philippines **2:**339
Río de la Plata Basin **6:**296
Tehuelche Indians **6:**270
Magellan, Strait of (South America) **6:**316
illus. **6:**317
Magenta (Italy) **4:**158
Maggiore, Lake (Italy–Switzerland) **3:**286; **4:**128
Maghreb (region, north Africa) **1:**89
Maginot Line (French fortifications) **3:**188
Magna Carta (great charter of English liberty) **3:**54, 117
Magnolia Plantation and Garden 5:232
Maguey (plant) **5:**359, 378
Magyars (Hungarians) (people) **3:**18, 49; **4:**236, 238–39, 244
Austria **3:**308, 321
language **3:**20
Romania **4:**250, 257
Serbia **4:**276, 277
Slovakia **4:**232, 235
Mahafaly (people) **1:**373, 374
Maharashtra (state, India) **2:**206–7
Mahathir Mohammed (prime minister of Malaysia) **2:**308
Mahavansa (epic of Sri Lanka) **2:**249
Mahayana Buddhism 2:235, 295, 389
Lamaism based on **2:**387
Mahdi, The *see* Mohammed Ahmed
Mahé (India) **2:**220
Mahé (island in the Seychelles group) **1:**339
Mahébourg (Mauritius) **1:**379
Mahendra Bir Bikram Shah Deva (king of Nepal) **2:**233
Mahican (Indians of North America) **5:**202
Mahmud II (Ottoman sultan) **2:**65
Mahuad, Jamil (president of Ecuador) **6:**205
Maidan (park, Calcutta, India) **2:**206

MAINE 5:182–83
illus. **5:**182, 183
map(s) **5:**183
Maine (ship) **5:**446
Maipú (Chile) **6:**298, 321
Maisí, Cape (Cuba) **5:**442
Maize *see* Corn
Majapahit (kingdom in Indonesia) **2:**324
Majas on a Balcony (painting, Goya)
illus. **4:**99
Majlis (Iranian legislature) **2:**164
Major, John (prime minister of United Kingdom) **3:**95
Majorca (island, Spain) **4:**84, 90
illus. **4:**84
Majuro Atoll (Marshall Islands) **2:**575
Makarikari Salt Pans (Botswana) **1:**353
Makarios, Archbishop (Cypriot Orthodox prelate) **2:**73; **4:**210
Makassar (Indonesia) *see* Ujung Pandang
Makassarese (people) **2:**318
Makatea (French Polynesia) **2:**577
Makeni (Sierra Leone) **1:**171
Makerere (Uganda) **1:**320
Makhkamov, Kakhar M. (president of Tajikistan) **2:**361
Malabar Hill (Bombay (Mumbai), India) **2:**206
Malabo (capital, Equatorial Guinea) **1:**235, 236
Malacca (Malaysia) **2:**23, 264, 308, 312, 324
Málaga (Spain) **4:**109
Malagarasi River (Africa) **1:**328
Malagasy language 1:373–74
Malagasy Republic *see* Madagascar
Malaita (island, Solomon Islands) **2:**591, 593
Malan, Daniel François (South African political leader) **1:**404
Malange (Angola) **1:**343
Malapoa College (Port-Villa, Vanuatu) **2:**595
Malar, Lake (Sweden) **4:**39, 44
Malaria 2:240; **6:**78, 79, 137, 140
Malaspina Glacier (Alaska) **5:**348
MALAWI 1:44, **277–81,** 365
illus.
driving on the left **1:**277
fishermen **1:**281
flag **1:**xxiii
Mozambican refugees **1:**279
map(s) **1:**278
Malawi, Lake 1:18, 277, 278, 280, 363
illus. **1:**281
table(s)
largest lakes **6:**347
Malaya *see* Malaysia
Malaya, Federation of 2:308
Malayalam language 2:199
Malay-Indonesian language *see* Bahasa Indonesia
Malay language *see* Bahasa Indonesia; Bahasa Malaysia
Malayo-Polynesian language 2:28, 296
Malay Peninsula (Southeast Asia) **2:**303
Singapore **2:**309
Thailand **2:**273, 274, 277
Malays (Asian people) **2:**254, 258, 259, 301, 305, 308, 310
Brunei **2:**329
Indonesia **2:**317, 323
Philippines **2:**334–35, 339
South African Coloureds **1:**400, 403, 404
Thailand **2:**275

MALAYSIA 2:303–8, 315
Asia, Southeast **2:**254, 258, 259, 260, 264
Singapore, history of **2:**309, 312
illus.
agriculture **2:**306
flag **2:**viii
Kuala Lumpur **2:**303
river ferry **2:**307
tin mining **2:**305
map(s) **2:**304
Malcolm III (king of Scotland) **3:**140
MALDIVES 2:27, 165, **251–52**
illus.
fishing **2:**251
flag **2:**viii
map(s) **2:**252
Maldonado (Uruguay) **6:**258
Male (capital, Maldives) **2:**251
Malecite (Indians of North America) **5:**78, 85
Malekula (island, Vanuatu) **2:**594–95
MALI 1:52–53, **140–43**
Niger River **1:**50, 51
Sahara **1:**24
Sahel **1:**142
illus.
Bamako **1:**143
Djenné **1:**140
flag **1:**xxii
sculpture **1:**52
map(s) **1:**141
Mali (early African kingdom) **1:**142, 162, 169
Mali Federation 1:143, 158
Malinche (Aztec wife of Cortés) **5:**380
Malindi (Kenya) **1:**314
Malinke (African people) **1:**167, 186
Malmo (Sweden) **4:**10, 38, 44, 45
Maloja Pass (Alps) **4:**126
MALTA 3:2, 8; **4:182–84**
illus. **4:**182
flag **4:**v
map(s) **4:**183
Maltese language 4:183
Maluku (islands, Indonesia) *see* Moluccas
Mamaia (Romania) **4:**254
Mambilla Plateau (Cameroon) **1:**233
Mamluks (Mamelukes) (Egyptian military class occupying the sultanate) **1:**119, 120
Mammoth Cave National Park (Kentucky) **5:**261
Mamoré River (South America) **6:**231
Mamprusi (African people) **1:**198
Man (town, Ivory Coast) **1:**185
Man, Isle of (Irish Sea) **3:**8, 81, 84
Managua (capital, Nicaragua) **6:**51, 52, 53–54, 57, 58
Managua, Lake (Nicaragua) **6:**52
Manama (capital, Bahrain) **2:**140
Manas (Kyrgyz epic poem) **2:**355
Manassas (Virginia) **5:**225
Manassas Park (Virginia) **5:**225
Manaus (capital, Amazonas state, Brazil) **6:**169, 173, 187
illus.
Opera House **6:**181
Manawatu River (New Zealand) **2:**538
Mancha, La (historic region, Spain) **4:**108
Mancham, James (president of Seychelles) **1:**340
Manchester (England) **3:**42, 108, 109
Manchester (New Hampshire) **5:**185

Manchu (Ch'ing; Qing) dynasty (China) **2:**381, 394, 395–96, 421
Asia, history of **2:**366, 427, 433
Manchuria (northeast area, China) **2:**368, 378, 381, 382, 383
Japanese control **2:**396, 446, 447
Manco Capac (legendary founder of Inca Empire) **6:**222
Mandalay (Myanmar) **2:**270
Mandan (Indians of North America) **5:**23
Mandate system (international relations)
Africa **1:**46, 209, 326, 331, 337
Iraq **2:**154
Jordan **2:**121
Lebanon **2:**102
Namibia **1:**46, 350
Nauru **2:**579
Oceania **2:**566
Palau **2:**572
Palestine **2:**112–13, 121
Papua New Guinea **2:**590
Southwest Asia **2::**52
Syria **2:**95–96
Mande (African people) **1:**191
Mandela, Nelson (president of South Africa) **1:**394, 405, 406
illus. **1:**59, 406
Mande language 1:180
Mandingo (African people) **1:**140, 142, 160–61, 162, 164
Mandingo language 1:136
Mandinka-Bambara (African people) **1:**155
Mandjia (African people) **1:**247
Manet, Edouard (French painter) **3:**177
Manganese 2:84
Mangbetu (early African state) **1:**268
Mangla Dam (Indus River) **2:**183
Mangoky River (Madagascar) **1:**371
Manhattan (borough, New York City) **5:**202, 203, 205
Manica (mountains, Zimbabwe) **1:**356
Manicouagan River (Quebec) **5:**102
Manifest Destiny (American history) **5:**169
Manigat, Leslie F. (president of Haiti) **5:**470
Manila (capital, Philippines) **2:**262, 336
illus. **2:**261, 331
Manioc (Cassava) 1:248, 254; **6:**55–56, 91, 166
MANITOBA (province, Canada) **5:**113, **114–17**
history **5:**112; **5:**143
population **5:**115–16
illus. **5:**114
map(s) **5:**115
Manitoba, Lake 5:114
Manizales (Colombia) **6:**120
Manley, Michael (Jamaican leader) **5:**477
Mann, Thomas (German author) **3:**254
Mannerheim, Carl Gustav Emil von (Finnish field marshal) **4:**58
Manning, Patrick (prime minister of Trinidad and Tobago) **5:**486
Manoa Valley (Hawaii) **5:**353
Manolete (Spanish matador) **4:**93
Mano River (west Africa) **1:**179
Mansart, François (French architect) **3:**177
Mansfield, Katherine (New Zealand born writer) **2:**546
Mansôa River (Guinea-Bissau) **1:**164
Mantaro River (Peru) **6:**220
Manuel I (king of Portugal) **4:**71
Manufacturing
African industrialization **1:**64

American manufacturing belt **5:**45–46
Asia, East **2:**375–76
Asian industrialization **2:**35–36
Canadian industry **5:**97
China **2:**415, 417–18
Communist management **3:**40
Czech Republic **4:**227–28
England **3:**109
Europe **3:**26, 39–40
France **3:**157–58
Germany **3:**261, 264
high-tech industry centers **5:**162
India **2:**226–27
Industrial Revolution **3:**58–59
"Japanese model" **2:**34
Korea, South **2:**437
Mexico **5:**363–64, 392
Middle Atlantic States **5:**200
Pakistan **2:**189–90
Russia **4:**316–17
South America **6:**103–4
Southern States **5:**222
Sweden **4:**46
Taiwan **2:**426
United States, history of **5:**177
illus.
   aircraft industry **3:**39
   American industry **5:**50–51
   Armenian factory **2:**77
   automobile industry **2:**409; **3:**38
   Canadian industry **5:**94
   German industry **3:**246, 260, 261
   Indonesian aviation industry **2:**323
   Japanese steel industry **2:**469
   robots assemble cars **5:**51
   Russian VCR factory **4:**313
   U.S. industry **5:**174, 175
map(s)
   world map **6:**352
Manus Island (Pacific Ocean) **2:**587
Manx cat 3:84
  illus. **3:**84
Manx language 3:84
Manyara, Lake (Tanzania) **1:**338
Manych Depression *see* Caspian Depression
Manzanillo (Colima, Mexico) **5:**408
Manzanillo Bay (Mexico) **5:**408
Manzini (Swaziland) **1:**385
Maori (people) **2:**478, 479, 543, 550, 553, 600
  art and artifacts **2:**546
  Europeans, early encounters with **2:**551–52
  land claims **2:**554
  illus. **2:**543
Maori language 2:543, 545
Mao Zedong (Mao Tse-tung) (leader of Communist China) **2:**390, 397, 405, 407, 409
  Cultural Revolution **2:**398–99
Maps *see also* individual countries and continents
  world **1:**xviii–xix
  world climate **6:**354
  world economic activities **6:**352
  world grain production **6:**355
  world mineral production **6:**355
  world population **6:**353
  world precipitation **6:**354
  world time zones **6:**356–57
  world vegetation **6:**353
Mapuche language 6:305
Maputo (capital, Mozambique) **1:**364, 366
  illus. **1:**363
Maquiladoras (assembly plants) **5:**390, 392

Maquis (French underground) **3:**188
Maqurra (early African kingdom) **1:**130
Maracaibo (Venezuela) **6:**133, 137
Maracaibo, Lake (Venezuela) **6:**86, 136, 137, 144
  illus.
   oil derricks **6:**2, 144
  table(s)
   largest lakes **6:**347
Maracay (Venezuela) **6:**132, 137
Maradi (Niger) **1:**145
Marais (section of Paris, France) **3:**198
Maralinga Tjarutja (aboriginal tribe, Australia) **2:**522
Marano (stream, San Marino) **4:**174
Marañón River (Peru) **6:**168, 209
Marathi language 2:199
Maravi (African people) **1:**280
Marbella (resort town, Spain) **4:**109
Marble 4:132–33
  illus. **4:**132
March to the Sea (campaign in U.S. Civil War) **5:**236
Marconi, Guglielmo (Italian inventor) **4:**180
Marco Polo *see* Polo, Marco
Marcos (Zapatista leader) **5:**418
Marcos, Ferdinand (president of Philippines) **2:**331, 337, 338, 340
Marcus Aurelius (Roman emperor) **4:**111
  place of death, Vindobona (Vienna) **3:**315
  triumphal arch in Tripoli **1:**95–96
Marcy, Mount (New York) **5:**204
Mar del Plata (Argentina) **6:**292–93
  illus. **6:**292
Mardi Gras *see* Carnival
Mareb (Gash) River (east Africa) **1:**294
Margai, Albert (prime minister of Sierra Leone) **1:**176
Margai, Milton (prime minister of Sierra Leone) **1:**176
Margaret (Romanian princess) **4:**257
Margaret Island (Danube River, at Budapest) **4:**242
Margarita Island (Venezuela) **6:**131
  map(s) **5:**429
Margherita, Mount (Congo, Democratic Republic of) **1:**262
Margrethe I (queen of Denmark) **4:**20, 26, 48
Margrethe II (queen of Denmark) **4:**22
Mariachi bands 5:366
Mariana (Brazil) **6:**187
Marianas (islands, Pacific Ocean) **2:**568, 569, 570
Marianas Trench (North Pacific Ocean) **6:**345
Marianna Lowlands (Florida) **5:**237
Mariánské Lázně (Czech Republic) **4:**225
Maria of Burgundy (wife of Maximilian of Austria) **3:**321
Mariátegui, José Carlos (Peruvian journalist) **6:**215
Maria Theresa (Austrian empress) **3:**323–24
Marib (ancient city, Yemen) **2:**132
Marie Antoinette (queen of France) **3:**184, 195, 324
Marie de Médicis (queen of France) **3:**183
Marie Louise (empress of the French) **3:**324
Marienbad (Czech Republic) *see* Mariánské Lázně
Marien Ngouabi University (Brazzaville, Congo, Republic of) **1:**258
Marietta (Ohio) **5:**274
Marignano (Italy) *see* Melegnano

Marimba (musical instrument) **6:**37, 123
  illus. **6:**27
Marina (road, Madras (Chenai), India) **2:**207–8
Marinus, Saint (founder of San Marino) **4:**174
Marisol (Venezuelan sculptor) *see* Escobar, Marisol
Maritime Provinces (Canada) *see* Atlantic Provinces
Maritsa River (eastern Europe) **4:**260
Market economy
  Angola **1:**345
  Asia, East **2:**376
  Chinese reforms **2:**413–15
  Cuba **5:**452
  Czech Republic **4:**228–29
  Ghana **1:**200
  Hungary **1:**243
  Russian reforms **4:**318–19
  Tunisia **1:**90
  Vietnam **2:**293, 298–99, 300
Markets
  Aztec society **5:**378
  Ecuador **6:**198–99
  Egypt **1:**105
  German shopping hours **3:**264
  Guatemala **6:**27
  Kumasi (Ghana) **1:**197
  Leipzig Fair **3:**268
  Nuremberg's Christmas fair **3:**272
  Peru **6:**220
  South America **6:**109
  Southeast Asian floating market **2:**257
  illus.
   Abu Dhabi **2:**138
   Afghanistan **2:**177
   Asia, South **2:**165
   Asian shop **2:**36
   Brazilian shopping mall **6:**165
   Cambodia **2:**288
   Cameroon **1:**232
   Caribbean Islands **5:**428
   Chile **6:**310
   China **2:**392
   Chinese family-owned business **2:**413
   Damascus bazaar **2:**95
   Dutch cheese market **3:**228
   Ecuador **6:**198
   El Salvador shopping mall **6:**46
   Ethiopia **1:**286
   French Guiana **6:**93
   Great Wall souvenir store **2:**417
   Guatemala **6:**25
   India **2:**205
   Japan **2:**455
   Kazakh bazaar **2:**348
   Laos **2:**284
   Latin America **6:**7
   Liberia **1:**181
   mall in Northern Ireland **3:**147
   Mexico: shopping mall **5:**27
   Morocco **1:**67, 70
   Nigeria **1:**218, 220, 221
   north African bazaar **1:**35
   Oaxaca **2:**417
   Pakistan **2:**186
   Peruvian flea market **6:**6
   Portuguese fish market **4:**69
   San Salvador (El Salvador) **6:**45
   shopping mall in U.S. **5:**164
   Somalia **1:**304
   South American village **6:**105

Markets
illus. (cont.)
  Sudan **1**:129
  Turkmen street vendor **2**:356
  vendors at Angolan train stop **1**:343
  Vietnamese flower vendors **2**:293
  Yemen **2**:134
Markham River (Papua New Guinea) **2**:588
Marley, Bob (Jamaican musician) **5**:476
Marmara, Sea of (Turkey) **2**:57, 61
Marmas (people) **2**:240
Marne-la-Vallée (France) **3**:202
Marne River (France) **3**:163
Maroni River (South America) *see* Marowijne
  River
Maronites (Christian religious sect) **2**:100, 102
Maroons (Jamaican people) **5**:476
Marostica (Italy) **4**:139
Maroua (Cameroon) **1**:233
Marowijne River (South America) **6**:154
Marquesas Islands (Pacific Ocean) **2**:600, 601
Marquette, Jacques (French missionary-explorer) **5**:101
Marra, Jabal (Sudan) **1**:125
Marrakesh (Morocco) **1**:65, 67, 73
  illus. **1**:67
Marriage
  Africa **1**:28
  Bantu **1**:359
  Brazil **6**:163
  China **2**:391–92
  divorce barred in Portugal **4**:72
  Hindu caste system **2**:210
  India **2**:221
  Iran **2**:158
  Japan **2**:452–53
  Nigeria **1**:220
  polygyny in Swaziland **1**:387
  Saudi arranged marriages **2**:125
  Suriname **6**:156–57
  illus.
    Hindu ceremony **2**:211
Marseilles (France) **3**:46, 154, 159–60
  illus. **3**:159
MARSHALL ISLANDS (Pacific Ocean) **2**:567,
  568, 570, **575–76**, 611
  Kiribati's first settlers came from **2**:582
  illus. **2**:575
    flag **2**:ix
  map(s) **2**:576
Marshall Plan (1948–1952) **3**:39–40, 63, 190,
  237, 260; **4**:22, 162
Marshall Space Flight Center (Huntsville, Alabama) **5**:243
Marshes **5**:91, 93, 208 *see also* Bogs; Swamps
  Belarus **4**:341
  Ukraine **4**:333
Marsupial animals **2**:487
Martha's Vineyard (Massachusetts) **5**:188
Martí, Farabundo (Salvadoran peasant leader)
  6:48
Martí, José (Cuban statesman) **5**:446
Martial law
  Korea, South **2**:438
  Kuwait **2**:146
  Myanmar **2**:272
  Pakistan **2**:194
  Philippines **2**:338, 340
  Poland **4**:222
  Taiwan **2**:428

Martinique (island, West Indies) **3**:191; **5**:435,
  436, 438
  map(s) **5**:429
Marx, Karl (German philosopher) **3**:59, 254
Marx, Roberto Burle (Brazilian architect) **6**:182
Marxism in Latin America **6**:60, 114, 320, 322
Mary I (Bloody Mary) (queen of England) **3**:76,
  119
Mary II (queen of England) **3**:120, 141
MARYLAND **5**:170, 200, **217–19**
  illus.
    Baltimore **5**:198
  map(s) **5**:218
Mary Queen of Scots (Mary Stuart) **3**:140
  illus. **3**:139
Marzipan (almond paste) **3**:265
  illus. **3**:267
Masada (ancient fortress in Israel)
  illus. **2**:112
Masai (African people) **1**:14, 309, 310, 332, 334
Masai language **1**:312
Masaryk, Tomás Garrigue (Czech leader) **4**:235
Mascarene Islands (Indian Ocean) **1**:46
Mascarenhas, Pedro (Portuguese explorer) **1**:47
Maseru (capital, Lesotho) **1**:391, 393
Mashantucket Pequot (Indians of North America) **5**:196
Mashhad (Iran) **2**:46
Mashona (African people) **1**:49, 357, 358
Mashonaland (region absorbed by Rhodesia)
  1:357, 362
Masira (island, Oman) **2**:136
Masire, Quett (president of Botswana) **1**:354
Mason, John (English colonist) **5**:184
Mason-Dixon Line **5**:217
Massa (African people) **1**:239
MASSACHUSETTS **5**:181, **188–91**
  illus.
    Boston **5**:188, 190
  map(s) **5**:189
Massachusetts Bay **5**:188
Massachusetts Bay Colony **5**:174, 191
Massamba-Débat, Alphonse (president of
  Congo) **1**:260
Massawa (Eritrea) **1**:287, 293, 294, 296
Massif Central (region, France) **3**:28
Mastoc, Mesrop (Armenian monk) **2**:76
Masur, Kurt (German conductor) **3**:259
Masuria region (Poland) **4**:213
Matabele (Ndebele) (African people) **1**:49, 357,
  358, 359, 362, 398
Matabeleland (region absorbed by Rhodesia)
  1:362
Matadi (Congo, Democratic Republic of) **1**:263
Matamoros (Tamaulipas, Mexico) **5**:396
Matanzas (Cuba) **5**:443
Maté (beverage) *see* Yerba maté
Matisse, Henri (French painter)
  illus.
    Girl with Green Eyes **3**:176
Mato Grosso (state, Brazil) **6**:284
Matopo Hills (area, Zimbabwe) **1**:356
Matos Rodríguez, Gerardo H. (Uruguayan
  composer) **6**:257
Matozinhos (Portugal) **4**:73
Matrah (Oman) **2**:136
Mátra Mountains (Hungary) **4**:237
Matsu (island off China's mainland) **2**:423
Matta Echaurren, Roberto (Chilean painter)
  6:309–10
Mattaponi (Indians of North America) **5**:224

Matterhorn (mountain, Switzerland) **3**:286, 299,
  304
  illus. **3**:289, 300
Matthias Corvinus (king of Hungary) **4**:245
Maui (Valley Isle) (island, Hawaii) **5**:352
Maule River (Chile) **6**:222
Mau Mau (secret organization in Kenya) **1**:40,
  315
Mauna Loa (volcano, Hawaii) **5**:335, 351
Maurice (Byzantine emperor) **2**:75
Maurice (prince of Nassau) **1**:382
MAURITANIA **1**:53, **134–39**
  Sahara **1**:24
  Senegal border conflicts **1**:158
  Western Sahara **1**:132, 133
  illus.
    Akjoujt **1**:134
    flag **1**:xxii
    Moorish woman serving tea **1**:135
    Muslims at mosque **1**:138
  map(s) **1**:137
MAURITIUS **1**:47, 60, 340, **378–82**
  illus. **1**:379, 380
    flag **1**:xxiv
    Port Louis **1**:378
  map(s) **1**:381
Maurya Empire (Asia) **2**:171, 192, 214, 243
Maximilian (Austrian archduke, and emperor of
  Mexico) **3**:186; **5**:384, 403, 412
Maximilian I (Holy Roman emperor) **3**:321
Maya (Indians of North America) **5**:30, 376,
  377, 419
  Belize **6**:20, 22, 24
  Cacaxtla murals of **5**:415
  Campeche **5**:420
  Central America **6**:11, 14
  Chiapas **5**:418
  farming and cities **5**:24, 25
  Guatemala **6**:28
  Honduras **6**:40
  mystery of the Maya **6**:28
  Quintana Roo **5**:422
  Tazumal ruins **6**:43
  Yucatán **5**:421
  illus.
    Caracol, El **5**:26
    Copán **6**:40
    pyramids **5**:418; **6**:29
    sculptures **5**:374; **6**:15
    temple **5**:374
Mayagüez (Puerto Rico) **5**:168
Maya Mountains (Belize) **6**:19
Mayan language **5**:355
Mayapán (ancient Mayan capital) **5**:421
Mayflower (Pilgrims' ship) **5**:191
  illus. **5**:191
Maynooth (Kildare) (Ireland) **3**:69
Mayombé Escarpment (Congo) **1**:256–57
Mayon, Mount (Philippines)
  illus. **2**:337
Mayotte (island, Comoros) **1**:48, 383, 384;
  3:191
Mazanderani (Asian people) **2**:157
Mazapil (Zacatecas, Mexico) **5**:399
Mazarin, Cardinal (French statesman) **3**:183
Mazatlán (Sinaloa, Mexico) **5**:397
Mazowiecki, Tadeusz (prime minister of
  Poland) **4**:222
Mazzini, Giuseppe (Italian patriot) **4**:158
Mba, Léon (president of Gabon) **1**:253, 255
Mbabane (capital, Swaziland) **1**:385, 389

Mbandaka (Congo, Democratic Republic of) **1:**43

Mbeki, Thabo (South African political leader) **1:**406

Mbem (area, Cameroon) **1:**230

Mbini River (Equatorial Guinea) **1:**235

M'Bochi (African people) **1:**258

Mboya, Tom (Kenyan leader) **1:**315

Mbuji-Mayi (Congo, Democratic Republic of) **1:**263

McAleese, Mary (president of Ireland) **3:**77

McAuliffe, Christa (American teacher, *Challenger* crew member) **5:**185

McClure, Sir Robert (English explorer) **5:**62

McCourt, Frank (Irish-American writer) **3:**70

McDonald Islands (Indian Ocean) **2:**488

McDonald's (restaurant chain) **4:**329
illus.
Japan **2:**34

McKinley, Mount (Alaska) **5:**8, 157, 348, 349; **6:**345
illus. **5:**8–9, 349

McKinley, William (25th president of U.S.) **5:**273, 354

McMurdo Sound (Antarctica) **6:**332, 334

Meath (county, Ireland) **3:**74

Mecca (holy city of Islam, Saudi Arabia) **2:**47, 123, 125, 126, 127
illus. **2:**127

Mechlin (Belgium) **3:**218, 219

Mečiar, Vladimír (Slovak political leader) **4:**235

Medan (Indonesia) **2:**323

Medellín (Colombia) **6:**120, 125, 129

Medes (Asian people) **2:**21, 49, 156, 162

Medici family (Florence, Italy) **4:**137, 150, 156

Medicine and health
Africa **1:**2–3, 5, 26
AIDS in Africa **1:**319
AIDS in Haiti **5:**467
Australia's Royal Flying Doctors **2:**508
Bangladesh **2:**240
Bohemian spas **4:**225
cancer resulting from Chernobyl disaster **4:**332, 340
diseases among Panama Canal workers **6:**78, 79
France rated best by World Health Organization **3:**170
Korea, North **2:**431
Native Americans died from European diseases **6:**6
Nicaragua's health care **6:**59
Norwegian health program **4:**30
ozone hole and health problems **6:**317
Pakistani women **2:**193
Peruvian cholera epidemic **6:**228
Rwandan refugees **1:**325
Saskatchewan socialized medicine **5:**121
South Africa, facilities overwhelmed **1:**400
Vienna, history of **3:**317–18
Yanomamo Indians, threats to **6:**140
illus.
African clinic **1:**26
AIDS **1:**319
airborne ambulance service **2:**508
Asian hospital **2:**37
Brazilian research **6:**176
Chinese exercise group **2:**393
Chinese hospital **2:**391
Nigerian clinic **1:**229
pilgrims at Lourdes **3:**165

Medicine Hat (Alberta) **5:**124–25

Médicis, Marie de *see* Marie de Médicis

Medina (Saudi Arabia) **2:**47, 51, 125, 126

Medinet Habu (Egyptian temple) **1:**111

Mediterranean Sea and islands 2:5
Azure Coast (Côte d'Azur) **3:**163–64, 204
development of civilization **3:**29
fishing's lack of importance **3:**36
Gibraltar **4:**123
Greek islands **4:**187
Italian peninsula **4:**125
northern Africa **1:**32–33
part of Europe **3:**8, 167; **4:**129–31, 182–84
table(s)
major seas of the world **6:**347

Megaliths
illus. **3:**114, 133

Megalopolis (very large urbanized area) **3:**44

Megawati Sukarnoputri 2:326

Mégève (France) **3:**173

Meghna River (Bangladesh) **2:**238

Mehemet Ali (viceroy of Egypt) **1:**120, 130

Meija, Hipolito (president of Dominican Republic) **5:**460

Meiji (emperor of Japan) **2:**445

Meiji Restoration (Japan) **2:**446, 448

Meissen (Germany) **3:**245, 268

Meistersingers (German musicians) **3:**256

Meknès (Morocco) **1:**67, 71

Mekong River (Southeast Asia) **2:**256–57, 294
Cambodia **2:**287
hydroelectric power **2:**38
Laos **2:**281, 282, 283
Thailand **2:**273
Vietnam **2:**295
map(s) **2:**256
table(s)
longest rivers of the world **6:**346

Melaka (Malaysia) *see* Malacca

MELANESIA (islands, Pacific Ocean) **2:**562, 565, 567, **583–86**
illus. **2:**583, 584
table(s) **2:**520

Melanesian pidgin (language) *see* Pidgin, Melanesian

Melanesians (people) **2:**561–62, 584–85, 589, 592, 594

Melbourne (capital, Victoria, Australia) **2:**497, 517, 519, 520
illus. **2:**516

Melbourne Cup 2:492

Melegnano (Marignano) (Italy) **3:**297

Meles Zenawi (Ethiopian political leader) **1:**292

Melik-Agopias, Hagop (Armenian author) **2:**76

Melilla (Spanish city, enclave in Morocco) **1:**74; **4:**86, 118

Melrhir, Shott (lake, Algeria) **1:**25

Melville Island (Australia) **2:**532

Memel (Lithuania) *see* Klaipėda

Memphis (Tennessee) **5:**264
illus.
Beale Street **5:**263

Menai Strait (Wales) **3:**122

Menam River (Thailand) *see* Chao Phraya River

Menchú, Rigoberta (Guatemalan human-rights advocate) **6:**33

Mendana y Neyra, Alvaro de (Spanish explorer) **2:**593

Mende (African people) **1:**55, 173, 174

Mendeleyev, Dmitry (Russian chemist) **4:**311

Mendelssohn, Felix (German composer) **3:**256, 258

Mendès-France, Pierre (French statesman) **3:**190

Méndez Manfredini, Aparicio (president of Uruguay) **6:**265

Mendota, Lake (Wisconsin) **5:**286

Mendoza (Argentina) **6:**280, 293

Mendoza (province, Argentina) **6:**281, 298
Aconcagua, mountain peak **6:**266
Huarpe Indians **6:**268–69
wine-growing district **6:**293
illus. **6:**282

Mendoza, Alonso de (founder of La Paz, Bolivia) **6:**232

Mendoza, Jaime (Bolivian writer) **6:**237

Mendoza, Pedro de (Spanish explorer) **6:**290, 296

Menelik II (emperor of Ethiopia) **1:**284, 288

Menem, Carlos Saúl (president of Argentina) **6:**301

Menes (king of Upper Egypt) **1:**117

Mengele, Josef (German Nazi) **4:**221

Mengistu Haile Mariam (Ethiopian political leader) **1:**290, 291

Menin (Belgium) **3:**214

Mennonites (German religious sect) **5:**300
Belize **6:**22
Paraguay's Chaco region **6:**245, 248
Pennsylvania Dutch **5:**212
Russian Mennonites in Manitoba **5:**115–16
illus. **5:**248

Menominee (Indians of North America) **5:**269, 285, 286

Meo (Hmong; Miao) (Asian people) **2:**259
Laos **2:**283
Thailand **2:**275
Vietnam **2:**295

Merca (Somalia) **1:**301

Mercado, Cerro del (Durango, Mexico) **5:**398

Mercedes (Uruguay) **6:**261

Mercosur (Southern Common Market) 6:115, 191, 250, 262, 301, 323

Mer de Glace (glacier, Mont Blanc) **3:**302

Mergui (Myanmar) **2:**269

Meri, Lennart (president of Estonia) **4:**296

Mérida (capital, Yucatán, Mexico) **5:**421

Mérida (Spain) **4:**111

Mérida (Venezuela) **6:**132, 138
illus.
cable cars **6:**131

Mérida, Sierra Nevada de (branch of the Andes) **6:**132

Merina (people) **1:**372, 373, 374, 375, 377

Merkel, Angela (German political leader) **3:**249, 284

Meroë (ancient city, Sudan) **1:**30, 33, 38, 130

Merrick, Mount (Scotland) **3:**133

Merrimack River (New Hampshire) **5:**184, 185

Mersey River (England) **3:**83, 108
illus. **3:**91

Mertert (Luxembourg) **3:**208

Meru, Mount (Tanzania) **1:**18

Mesa (Arizona) **5:**328

Mesabi Range (North America) **5:**4

Mesa del Norte (plateau, Mexico) **5:**393

Mesa Verde National Park (Colorado) **5:**320

Meseta (upland country, Spain) **3:**28, 31; **4:**80, 82, 88, 96

Meshed (Iran) **2:**159

Mesič, Stjepan (president of Croatia) **4:**285

Mesilla Valley (New Mexico–Arizona) **5:**383

Mesopotamia (region, Argentina) **6:**280

Mesopotamia (region, southwestern Asia) **2:**12, 48–49, 147
Mesquakie (Indians of North America) *see* Sauk and Fox
Messaoria plain (Cyprus) **2:**68–69, 70
Messina, Strait of 4:125, 126, 153
Messina Conference (1955) **3:**3–4
Mestizos (Latin Americans of Indian and European ancestry) **5:**27; **6:**7, 15 *see also* the people section of Latin-American countries
   Chiapas **5:**418
   Morelos, José Maria **5:**383
Meta, Ilir (prime minister of Albania) **4:**273
Meta River (South America) **6:**146
Metaxas, John (Greek dictator) **4:**209
Methodist Church 2:605
Methodius, Saint (bishop to the Slavs) **4:**265
Métis (Canadians of mixed Indian and European heritage) **5:**73, 95, 111
   Manitoba **5:**115, 116
   Northwest Territories **5:**142
   Ontario **5:**105
   Riel rebellions **5:**112, 117, 121
Metric system 6:375–76
Metro Manila (Philippines) **2:**336
Metternich, Klemens Wenzel Lothar von (Austrian statesman) **4:**158
Meuse River (Europe) **3:**212–13, 217, 219
   Netherlands **3:**226, 228, 229
Mexicali (capital, Baja California, Mexico) **5:**30, 390
Mexicali Valley (Mexico) **5:**390, 391
Mexican-Americans 5:252–53, 328
Mexican highlands 5:415
Mexican War (1846–1848) **5:**264, 310, 390, 391, 395, 396
   Mexico **5:**383
   Texas **5:**255
MEXICO 5:355–422 *see also* names of cities, states
   civilizations, early **5:**14, 24, 25
   climate **5:**359, 361
   maquiladoras **5:**392
   Maximilian **3:**186
   North American Free Trade Agreement **5:**362
   people **5:**355, 365
   PRI's rule **5:**386
   resources **5:**27–28, 30–31
   states of Mexico **5:**389
   transportation **5:**365
   Villa, Pancho **5:**393
   wars of independence **5:**383, 405, 412, 416
   illus.
      Baja California **5:**15
      border crossing **5:**362
      Caracol, El (Aztec observatory) **5:**26
      farms **5:**27, 357
      flag **5:**vi
      garment workers **5:**363
      housing **5:**385
      luxury resort **5:**355
      Mexico City **5:**356, 373
      people **5:**365, 366
      Popocatepetl **5:**357
      Sonoran Desert **5:**358
      tropical coastline **5:**359
      University of Mexico **5:**371
      urban housing **5:**361
   map(s) **5:**360
      states of Mexico **5:**389
   table(s)
      presidents since 1917 **6:**360

MÉXICO (state, Mexico) **5:**413
   history **5:**406
Mexico, Gulf of 5:12, 250
   climate **5:**158, 238
   petroleum **5:**358, 362, 363
   illus. **5:**421
   table(s)
      major seas of the world **6:**347
Mexico, National Autonomous University of
   see National Autonomous University of Mexico
Mexico, Valley of 5:31, 356–57, 410, 413
   archaeological sites **5:**375, 376
MEXICO CITY (capital, Mexico) **5:**28, 29, 31, 356, 389, **410–11**
   climate **5:**359
   mayoral elections **5:**388
   México State **5:**413
   Tenochtitlán **5:**378
   tower designed by Gonzalo Fonseca **6:**257
   illus.
      Cathedral of the Assumption **5:**381
      Plaza de la Reforma **5:**356
      Plaza of the Three Cultures **5:**373
      suburbs **5:**413
Miami (Florida) **5:**49, 239
Miami (Indians of North America) **5:**269, 272, 274, 280, 282
Miami Beach (Florida)
   illus. **5:**239
Miami River (Ohio) **5:**44, 272
Miao (Asian people) *see* Meo
Michael (czar of Russia) **4:**320
Michael I (Romanian king) **4:**256, 257
Michael the Bold (Romanian prince) **4:**256
Michelangelo (Italian artist) **4:**180, 181
MICHIGAN 5:275–78
   illus.
      Detroit **5:**277
      Holland (Michigan) Tulip Festival **5:**278
      Pictured Rocks National Lakeshore **5:**275
   map(s) **5:**276
Michigan, Lake (U.S.) **5:**269, 270, 279
   Chicago, citylife shaped by lake **5:**283
   megalopolis area **5:**46
   table(s)
      largest lakes **6:**347
Michigan Basin (geological region) **5:**276
MICHOACÁN (state, Mexico) **5:**409
Mickiewicz, Adam (Polish author) **4:**215
Micmac (Indians of North America) **5:**78, 95
   New Brunswick **5:**85
   Newfoundland **5:**82
   Nova Scotia **5:**91, 92, 93
   Prince Edward Island **5:**88, 89
   Quebec **5:**99
Micomber, Michel (president of Burundi) **1:**331
MICRONESIA (islands, Pacific Ocean) **2:**562, 567, **568–70**
   illus. **2:**568
   table(s) **2:**520
MICRONESIA, Federated States of (Pacific Ocean) **2:**567, 570, **573–74**
   illus. **2:**574
      flag **2:**ix
   map(s) **2:**573
Micronesians (people) **2:**561–62, 575, 592
Mid-Atlantic States (U.S.) *see* Middle Atlantic States
Middle Ages (8th–14th centuries) **3:**39, 49–54, 181–82

Middle America *see* Central America
MIDDLE ATLANTIC STATES (region, U.S.) **5:**37, 198–219
Middle East 2:41–55 *see also* Southwest Asia; names of countries
   use of term **2:**43
   map(s) **2:**43
Middle Guinea *see* Fouta Djallon Plateau
Middle passage (Atlantic crossing of slave ships) **5:**435
Middleton, Arthur (American landowner) **5:**232
Middleton Place (gardens, South Carolina) **5:**232
Midlands (area, England) **3:**99, 109
Midlands (area, England) **3:**82
Midnight sun 5:55
   Canada's Far North **5:**135
   Finland **4:**53
   Russia **4:**330
   Scandinavia **4:**35, 37, 39
   illus. **5:**53
Midway, U.S.A. (nickname for Kansas) **5:**303
Midway Islands (atolls in the Pacific) **2:**569
Midwest (U.S.) *see* Great Lakes States; Plains States
Midwest City (Oklahoma) **5:**306
Mies van der Rohe, Ludwig (German-American architect) **3:**281
   illus.
      German architecture **3:**255
Mieszko (Polish prince) **4:**219
Migration of people *see also* Immigration and emigration
   California's population growth **5:**347
   China's restrictions on urban migration **2:**383
   Europeans, origin of **3:**17–19
   Italy **4:**162
   Magyars to Hungary **4:**238–39
   North America, Ice Ages **5:**13, 20
   North American mountain passes **5:**6
   Southeast Asia **2:**253, 268, 285, 301
Mikhalkov, Nikita (Russian film director) **4:**315
Milan (Italy) **4:**133, 135, 141, 142–43, 152, 156, 168
   illus. **4:**141, 142
Mile High City (nickname for Denver, Colorado) **5:**320
Miles City (Montana) **5:**311
Military forces *see* Armed forces
Millay, Edna St. Vincent (American poet) **5:**183
Milles, Carl (Swedish sculptor) **4:**43, 45
Millet, Jean François (French painter) **3:**167
Mill Valley near Amalfi (painting, Blechen)
   illus. **3:**254
Milošević, Slobodan (president of Yugoslavia) **4:**275, 279, 280, 281, 290
   International Tribunal **3:**2
   illus. **4:**281
Miłosz, Czesław (Polish poet) **4:**215
Milwaukee (Wisconsin) **5:**285–86
   illus. **5:**268
      brewery **5:**285
Mina (African people) **1:**212
Minangkabau (people) **2:**318
Minas (Uruguay) **6:**261
Minas Channel (Nova Scotia, Canada) **5:**79
Minas Gerais (state, Brazil) **6:**173, 182, 184, 186–87, 188
Mindanao (island in the Philippines) **2:**332, 333, 339
   table(s)
      largest islands of the world **6:**346

Mindaugas (Lithuanian nobleman) **4:**303–4
Mindêlo (Cape Verde) **1:**150
Minerals see also Mines and mining; names of
    minerals
    Africa **1:**5
    Alaska **5:**349
    Arctic **5:**55, 58
    Australia **2:**483, 490
    Brazilian rain forest **6:**172
    British Columbia **5:**133
    Canada **5:**71
    coastal plains of North America **5:**12
    Congo, Democratic Republic of **1:**267
    Czech Republic **4:**227
    England **3:**102
    Europe **3:**37–39
    Madre Occidental, Sierra **5:**27
    Madre Oriental, Sierra **5:**27, 398
    Mexico **5:**30–31
    Mountain States **5:**310, 316, 317
    Nevada's vast wealth **5:**331
    Newfoundland and Labrador **5:**82
    Northern Territory (Australia) **2:**532–33, 535
    Nunavut **5:**138
    Ontario **5:**105, 109
    Philippines **2:**303
    Rocky Mountains **5:**39
    Russia's mineral resources **4:**308–9
    Spain's impressive variety **4:**83–84
    Sri Lanka's gemstones **2:**246
    U.S. Pacific States **5:**335
    U.S. resources **5:**159–60
    map(s)
        world production **6:**355
Mines and mining
    Antarctic mining moratorium **6:**337, 338
    Appalachia **5:**257
    Arctic **5:**64
    Chuquicamata copper mine **6:**312
    Georgia (republic) has world's largest manga-
        nese mines **2:**84
    Incan mines in Andes **6:**101
    Indonesia **2:**320–22
    Mexico **5:**363, 393, 401
    New Brunswick **5:**86
    Northwest Territories **5:**142, 144
    Nunavut **5:**140
    Papua New Guinea copper mine **2:**589
    Saskatchewan **5:**121
    South Africa **1:**402
    South America **6:**88
    South Dakota **5:**300
    Western Australia **2:**527
    West Virginia history **5:**259
    Yukon Territory **5:**148
    Zambia **1:**274–75
    illus.
        Angolan diamond mine **1:**345
        Brazilian gold mine **6:**174
        Chilean copper mine **6:**319
        Malaysian tin mine **2:**305
        open-pit mine in Utah **5:**9
        strip-mining for copper **2:**489
        Togo phosphate mine **1:**208
        tourists in Australian gold mine **2:**533
        Venezuelan iron mine **6:**143
Ming dynasty (China) **2:**23, 394, 421
Minho (Portugal) **4:**71
Minho River (Spain–Portugal) **4:**66, 74
Mining see Mines and mining
Minneapolis (Minnesota) **5:**48, 160, 289
Minnesingers (German musicians) **3:**256

MINNESOTA 5:287–89
    illus. **5:**287
        St. Paul's Winter Carnival **5:**289
    map(s) **5:**288
Minnesota River (Minnesota) **5:**287
Minoan civilization (ancient Crete) **3:**45; **4:**192,
    201
Minorca (island, Spain) **4:**84
Minorities see Ethnic groups
Minos (legendary king of Crete) **3:**45; **4:**192
    illus.
        Palace of Minos **4:**201
Minot (North Dakota) **5:**298
Minotaur (in Greek legend) **4:**190
Min River (China) **2:**368
Minsk (capital, Belarus) **4:**342, 343
    illus. **4:**341
Minute Maid Park (Houston, Texas) **5:**253
Miquelon (island) see Saint Pierre and Mique-
    lon
Mirador Nacional Mountain (Uruguay) **6:**259
Miraflores (Panama) **6:**78
    illus. **6:**73
Miramichi (New Brunswick, Canada) **5:**84
Miranda, Francisco de (Venezuelan patriot)
    6:146
Mirim, Lake (Uruguay) **6:**259
Mirror Peak (near Mérida, Venezuela) **6:**132
Misiones (province, Argentina) **6:**266, 270, 280,
    284
Miskito (Indians of Central America) **6:**35, 56
Miskolc (Hungary) **4:**242
Missing persons of Argentina 6:301
Missions, Spanish 5:403
    illus. **5:**309, 403; **6:**163, 234
Mississauga (Indians of North America) **5:**108
MISSISSIPPI 5:222, 245–46
    map(s) **5:**246
Mississippi River (U.S.) **5:**160–61, 220–21, 245,
    247, 249, 260, 284, 295
    Arkansas **5:**266
    delta **5:**12, 153, 160
    drainage basin **5:**154–55
    South-Central States **5:**256
    illus. **5:**161
    map(s) **5:**160
    table(s)
        longest rivers of the world **6:**346
MISSOURI 5:295–96
    map(s) **5:**296
Missouri (Indians of North America) **5:**294, 301
Missouri Plateau (region, North Dakota) **5:**297
Missouri River (U.S.) **5:**290, 293, 295, 299, 300
    Mississippi River **5:**160
    table(s)
        longest rivers of the world **6:**346
Misti, El (volcano, Peru) **6:**218
Mistral (wind) **3:**151
Mistral, Gabriela (Chilean poet) **6:**309
Mitch (hurricane, 1998) **6:**40, 50
Mitchell, George (American senator, peace
    negotiator) **3:**149
Mitchell, Sir James (prime minister of St. Vin-
    cent and the Grenadines) **5:**492
Mitchell, Keith (prime minister of Grenada)
    5:482
Mitchell, Mount (North Carolina) **5:**156
Mitla (archaeologic site, Mexico) **5:**417
Mitre, Bartolomé (Argentine statesman) **6:**276,
    299
Mittelland Canal (Germany) **3:**243

Mitterrand, François (president of France)
    3:190
Mixtec (Mexican Indian dialect) **5:**355
Mixtecs (Mexican people) **5:**376, 414, 417
Mkapa, Benjamin William (president of Tanza-
    nia) **1:**338
Mkhulumngcandi (traditional Swazi god) **1:**387
Mlanje, Mount (highest point in Malawi) **1:**278
Moa (bird) **2:**541, 550
Moab (ancient kingdom, Middle East) **2:**120
Moa River (Sierra Leone) **1:**172
Mobile (Alabama) **5:**243
Mobile Bay (Alabama) **5:**243, 244
Mobile River (Alabama) **5:**242
Mobutu Sese Seko (president of Congo, Demo-
    cratic Republic of) **1:**269, 270
Moçâmedes (Angola) see Namibe
Mocha (Yemen) **2:**131
Moche (Mochica) (people) **6:**222, 223
Moctezuma River (Mexico) **5:**406
Modekngei (Modignai) (Palauan religion) **2:**571
Modoc (Indians of North America) **5:**340
Moen (capital, Chuuk, Federated States of
    Micronesia) **2:**573
Moffat, Robert (Scottish missionary) **1:**354
Mogadishu (capital, Somalia) **1:**301, 304, 305
    illus. **1:**300
Mogae, Festus (president of Botswana) **1:**354
Mogilev (Belarus) **4:**343
Mogollon Rim (Arizona) **5:**327
Mogul Empire (India) **2:**172, 192, 208, 215
Mohács, Battle of (1526) **3:**327; **4:**245
Mohammad, Ali Mahdi (Somalian warlord)
    1:305
Mohammad Abdullah Hassan (Somali leader)
    see Abdullah Hassan, Mohammad
Mohammad Reza Pahlavi (Shah of Iran) **2:**155,
    163
Mohammed (founder of Islam) see Muhammad
Mohammed V (king of Morocco) **1:**74
Mohammed VI (king of Morocco) **1:**74
Mohammed II (Ottoman sultan) **4:**206, 245
Mohammed V (Ottoman sultan) **2:**65
Mohammed VI (Ottoman sultan) **2:**66
Mohammed Ahmed (the Mahdi) 1:121, 130
Mohammed Ali Mosque (Cairo, Egypt)
    illus. **1:**108
Mohammed ibn Abd al-Wahhab (Arab reli-
    gious reformer) **2:**127
Mohammed Zahir Shah (king of Afghanistan)
    2:178, 179
Mohawk (Indians of North America) **5:**95, 99,
    202
Mohawk River and Valley (New York) **5:**6, 46
Mohegan (Indians of North America) **5:**196
Mohéli (island, Comoros) **1:**383, 384
Mohenjo-Daro (ancient city of Indus Valley
    civilization) **2:**13, 171, 190–91
    India, history of **2:**203, 213
    Pakistan **2:**180
    illus. **2:**13
Moher, Cliffs of (Ireland) **3:**74
Moi, Daniel arap (president of Kenya) **1:**315
Mojave (Indians of North America) **5:**164, 332,
    344
Mojave Desert (California) **5:**342
    illus. **5:**158–59
Mojave National Preserve (California)
    illus. **5:**343
Moldau River see Vltava River
Moldavia (former Soviet republic) see Moldova
Moldavia (medieval principality) **4:**345

Moldavia (province, Romania) **4:**248, 249, 256
Moldavian Carpathians (mountains, Romania) **4:**249
MOLDOVA 3:1, 2; **4:345–47**
illus.
    farm **4:**345
    flag **4:**vi
    map(s) **4:**346
Moldovan language 4:345
Moldovița (Romania) **4:**252
Molière (French playwright) **3:**178
Moline (Illinois) **5:**294
Molnár, Ferenc (Hungarian playwright) **4:**240
Molokai (Friendly Island) (island, Hawaii) **5:**352
Molonglo River (Australia) **2:**514
Moluccas (Maluku; Spice Islands) (Indonesia) **2:**315, 318, 323, 324, 326
Molybdenum (mineral) **5:**160
Momase (region, Papua New Guinea) **2:**587
Mombasa (Kenya) **1:**39, 309, 312, 314
illus.
    coffee loaded at port **1:**313
Momoh, Joseph (president of Sierra Leone) **1:**176–77
Momotombito (volcano, Nicaragua)
illus. **6:**52
Momotombo (volcano, Nicaragua) **6:**51
illus. **6:**52
Møn (island in Denmark) **4:**10
Mona, Mother of Wales (island) *see* Anglesey
Monacan (Indians of North America) **5:**224
MONACO (principality) **3:204–6**
illus. **3:**204, 205
    flag **3:**vi
    map(s) **3:**205
Monaco-Ville (capital, Monaco) **3:**204
Monarchy (form of government) **3:**96; **4:**47; **5:**70
    England **3:**118
Monasteries *see* Monks and monasteries
Monastery of the Caves (Kiev, Ukraine) **4:**337
Monclova (Coahuila, Mexico) **5:**394
Moncton (New Brunswick) **5:**85, 86
Mondlane, Eduardo (Mozambican leader) **1:**368
Monet, Claude (French painter) **3:**177
Monfalcone (Italy) **4:**152
Mongkut (Rama IV) (king of Thailand) **2:**280
Mongol dynasty (China) *see* Yüan dynasty
MONGOLIA 2:341, 345, **362–66**
    government **2:**29
    land **2:**343
    people **2:**344
    illus.
        election **2:**365
        flag **2:**ix
        rock music group **2:**363
        Ulaanbaatar **2:**362
    map(s) **2:**364
Mongolian Plateau 2:362
Mongoloids (racial group of Asia) **2:**363, 371 *see also* Inuit
    Asia, Southeast **2:**258–59, 268
    Japan **2:**443
Mongols (people) **2:**345, 362, 366 *see also* Tatars
    China (Nei Monggol Autonomous Region) **2:**385–86
    Chinese civilization **2:**16, 394
    Georgia (republic) **2:**84

Iran **2:**162
Iraq **2:**154
Java **2:**324
Kazakhstan, history of **2:**349
Korea **2:**433
Russia invaded by **3:**53
Tatar (Tartar) invaders of Hungary **4:**245
Ukraine **4:**339
Monica, Saint (mother of Saint Augustine) **1:**91
Monkey Mia (Australia) **2:**525–26
Mon-Khmer (Asian people) **2:**268–69
Mon-Khmer language 2:282, 283, 296
Monks and monasteries
    Austria **3:**315, 321
    Buddhism **2:**269, 275, 295
    Convent of Guadalupe (Zacatecas, Mexico) **5:**399
    Europe, history of **3:**50, 51–52
    Ireland **3:**75
    Lamaism **2:**386–87
    Monastery of the Caves (Kiev, Ukraine) **4:**337
    Mount Athos (Greece) **4:**198
    Romania **4:**252
    illus.
        Buddhist monks **2:**263
        Greek island **4:**208
        Hindu monks **2:**213
        Sucevița monastery (Romania) **4:**250
Monnet, Jean (French economist) **3:**190
Monoliths (prehistoric stone monuments) *see* Megaliths
Monoma Lake (Wisconsin) **5:**286
Monomotapa (early African kingdom) **1:**361–62
illus. **1:**10
Monongahela (Indians of North America) **5:**212
Monongahela River (Pennsylvania) **5:**212, 213
Mono River (Togo–Benin) **1:**205, 211
illus. **1:**207
Monotremes 2:489
Monroe, James (5th president of U.S.) **5:**226
illus. **1:**182
Monroe Doctrine (American foreign policy)
    South America, history of **6:**100
Monrovia (capital, Liberia) **1:**180, 181, 183
illus. **1:**178
Mons (Asian people) **2:**271
Mons (Bergen) (Belgium) **3:**215
Monsoons 2:11
    Asia, Southeast **2:**256
    Bangladesh **2:**238–39
    India **2:**199
    Liberia **1:**179
    Pakistan **2:**183
    Sri Lanka **2:**245–46
    Thailand **2:**274
Montagnais (Indians of North America) **5:**95, 99
Montagnards (people) **2:**259, 295
Montaigne, Michel de (French essayist)
    quoted on Paris **3:**203
Montaigne, Michel de (French writer) **3:**178
MONTANA 5:311–12
illus. **5:**311
map(s) **5:**312
Montaña (plains, Peru) **6:**208–9
Mont-aux-Sources (mountain peak, South Africa) **1:**395
Mont Blanc Pass (Alps) **4:**126
Mont Blanc Tunnel 3:41, 304
Mont Cenis Pass (Alps) **3:**301, 304; **4:**126
Mont Cenis tunnel 3:304

Monte Albán (ancient Indian ruins, Mexico) **5:**375–76, 417
Monte Carlo (Monaco) **3:**206
illus. **3:**205
Montecristo Cloud Forest (El Salvador) **6:**44
Montego Bay (Jamaica) **5:**471
Montejo, Francisco de (Spanish soldier) **5:**419
Montenegrins (people) **4:**276
Montenegro (Yugoslav state) **4:**276, 279, 280, 281 *see also* Yugoslavia
illus.
    Gulf of Kotor **4:**274
Monterey (California) **5:**342
Montero, José Luis (Peruvian artist) **6:**214
Monte Rosa group (Pennine Alps) **3:**286, 299
Monterrey (capital, Nuevo León, Mexico) **5:**27–28, 389, 395
Montevideo (capital, Uruguay) **6:**254–55, 258, 260–61, 263
illus. **6:**251, 254, 255, 260
Montezuma II (Aztec ruler of Mexico) **5:**379–80, 410, 412
illus. **5:**379
Montgenèvre (France)
illus. **3:**174
Montgomery (capital, Alabama) **5:**243, 244
Monticello (home of Thomas Jefferson) **5:**225
illus. **5:**225
Montmartre (section of Paris, France) **3:**200–201
Montpelier (capital, Vermont) **5:**187
Montreal (Quebec) **5:**6, 95, 96, 99, 100, 101, 102
    French North America, center of **5:**34, 41
    illus. **5:**35, 100
        Biosphere **5:**98
        Notre Dame Basilica **5:**75
Montreal Island (Montreal) **5:**99, 100
Montreux (Switzerland) **3:**295
Mont Sainte-Victoire (painting, Cézanne)
illus. **3:**177
Mont-Saint-Michel (abbey, France) **3:**164
illus. **3:**163
Montserrat (island, West Indies) **3:**90; **5:**439
illus. **5:**439
map(s) **5:**429
Monument of Discoveries (Lisbon, Portugal) **4:**72
illus. **4:**76
Monument Rocks (Kansas) **5:**303
Monument Valley (Arizona) **5:**327
Moon, Mountains of the *see* Ruwenzori Mountains
Moore, Michael (American director) **5:**278
Moors (landform) **3:**84, 101
illus. **3:**86
Moors (people) **4:**87, 96, 98, 103, 109, 112–13
    Gibraltar **4:**123
    Mali **1:**142
    Mauritania **1:**135, 136, 139
    Peruvian architecture, influence on **6:**213–14
    Portugal and Brazil **4:**69, 74–75, 76; **6:**164–65
    trans-Saharan caravan route **1:**157
    illus.
        mosaic designs **4:**114
        woman serving tea **1:**135
Mopti (Mali) **1:**142
Mora, Juan Rafael (president of Costa Rica) **6:**70
Morães Barros, Prudente José de (president of Brazil) **6:**190

Moraines 3:27; **5:**12, 276, 279, 284
Morales, Evo (Bolivian political candidate) **6:**241
Morant Bay uprising (Jamaica) **5:**476
Morar, Loch (Scotland) **3:**132
Morava River (Czech Republic) **3:**45; **4:**224–25, 275
Moravia (region, Czech Republic) **3:**322; **4:**224–25, 227, 228, 229
Moravian Church 6:55, 56
Morazán, Francisco (Honduran statesman) **6:**32, 41
Morea (peninsula, Greece) *see* Peloponnesus
Morelia (capital, Michoacán, Mexico) **5:**409
MORELOS (state, Mexico) **5:**412
Morelos y Pavon, José María (Mexican priest and patriot) **5:**383
Morelos y Pavón, José María (Mexican patriot) **5:**409, 412
Morena, Sierra (mountains, Spain) **4:**82, 83
Moreno, Gabriel García *see* García Moreno, Gabriel
Moreno, Gabriel René (Bolivian historian) **6:**237
Moreton Bay (Australia) **2:**507
Morgan, Henry (English buccaneer) **6:**74
Morgarten (Switzerland) **3:**297
Moriori (people) **2:**543, 550
Moriscos (converted Muslims) **4:**115
Mori Yoshiro (prime minister of Japan) **2:**472
Mormons (religious sect) **5:**43, 314, 323, 324, 325, 326
illus.
Mormon Temple **5:**325
Morne La Selle (mountain, Haiti) **5:**462
Moro, Aldo (Italian politician) **4:**162
MOROCCO 1:34, 65–74
France, history of **3:**187, 190
Sahara **1:**24
Spanish Morocco, history of **4:**85
Spanish territories **4:**86
Western Sahara **1:**132, 133
illus.
Atlas Mountains **1:**16
carpet making **1:**71
Casablanca **1:**69
fishing industry **1:**34
flag **1:**xxii
leatherworkers **1:**72
Marrakesh **1:**67
Rabat **1:**71
Saharan oasis **1:**22–23
Telouet **1:**65
Volubilis **1:**73
wall enclosing Western Sahara **1:**133
map(s) **1:**66
Moroni (capital, Comoros) **1:**383
illus. **1:**383
Morphou Bay (Cyprus) **2:**70
Morro Castle (El Morro) (fortress, Havana, Cuba) **5:**444
Moscoso, Mireya (president of Panama) **6:**81
MOSCOW (capital, Russia) **4:**320, 324, **327–29**
manufacturing center **3:**40; **4:**316
Napoleonic wars **3:**185
tourism **3:**15–16
winter climate **3:**30
illus.
boutiques **3:**16
Kremlin **4:**327
St. Basil's Cathedral **4:**305
university **4:**311

Moselle River (Europe) **3:**208, 245
Moses (Hebrew law giver and prophet) **1:**38
Moshoeshoe (Basotho chief) **1:**392
Moshoeshoe II (king of Lesotho) **1:**393
Mosisile, Pakalitha (prime minister of Lesotho) **1:**393
Moslem League 2:193, 243
Mosotho *see* Basotho
Mosques 2:212
Algiers (Algeria) **1:**76–77
Badshahi Masjid (Lahore, Pakistan) **2:**188
Bosnia and Herzegovina **4:**289
Cairo **1:**115
Casablanca (Morocco) **1:**66–67
Dome of the Rock (Jerusalem) **2:**47
Faisal Mosque (Pakistan): world's largest **2:**187
Istanbul (Turkey) **2:**62
Kairouan (Tunisia) **1:**90
Kano (Nigeria) **1:**218
Mustapha Pasha (Skopje, Macedonia) **4:**292
Tunis (Tunisia) **1:**86
Yugoslavia **4:**277
illus.
Bobo-Dioulasso (Burkina Faso) **1:**191
Cairo **1:**108
Central African Republic **1:**245
Djenné (Mali) **1:**140
Hussein mosque (Amman, Jordan) **2:**116
Kairouan (Tunisia) **1:**92
Kano (Nigeria) **1:**56–57
Mauritania **1:**138
Moroni (Comoros) **1:**383
Nairobi (Kenya) **1:**311
New Delhi (India) **2:**212
Pakistan **2:**180
Paramaribo (Suriname) **6:**153
Riyadh (Saudi Arabia) **2:**122
ruins at Samarra (Iraq) **2:**152
Suleymaniye Mosque (Istanbul) **2:**56
Mosquito Coast (Honduras–Nicaragua) **6:**35, 53, 54, 56
Mossadegh, Mohammed (prime minister of Iran) **2:**163
Mossi (African people) **1:**189, 190–91, 192, 193
Mostar (Bosnia and Herzegovina) **4:**290
illus.
war damage to bridge **4:**288
Mosul (Iraq) **2:**50, 148
Motagua River (Guatemala) **6:**29
Mother of Presidents (nickname for Virginia) **5:**223
Mother of States (nickname for Virginia) **5:**223
Motion pictures
Australia **2:**498
Brazil **6:**112
China **2:**407–8
Europe **3:**24
France **3:**179, 202
Hollywood **5:**51, 347
India **2:**204
Italy **4:**141, 169
Japan **2:**463
Poland **4:**215
Repentance **2:**83
Russia **4:**315
St. Petersburg **4:**331
Sweden **4:**44
Motor City (nickname for Detroit, Michigan) **5:**277
Motown Records 5:277
Motu language 2:589

Moudang (African people) **1:**239
Moulouya River (Morocco) **1:**66
Mound Builders (American archaeology) **5:**234, 267, 269, 272, 274
illus. **5:**273, 282
Mound cactus
illus. **5:**343
Moundou (Chad) **1:**240
Mountain climbing
Alps **3:**302, 304
Fujiyama **2:**442
illus. **2:**166; **3:**299; **5:**349
Mountain men (in U.S. history) **5:**39, 310, 317
Mountains *see also* articles on individual continents and countries; names of mountains and mountain ranges
Africa not generally mountainous **1:**18
Asia, East **2:**368
mountain building **3:**28
North America **5:**5–9
in Sahara Desert **1:**25
table(s)
great mountain peaks of the world **6:**348–49
Mountains of the Moon *see* Ruwenzori Mountains
Mountain State (nickname for West Virginia) **5:**258
MOUNTAIN STATES (region, U.S.) **5:**308–32
resources **5:**49–50
Mount Desert Isle (Maine) **5:**182
illus. **5:**182
Mounties *see* Royal Canadian Mounted Police
Mount Pearl (Newfoundland) **5:**83
Mount Pleasant (South Carolina) **5:**232
Mount Royal Park (Montreal, Quebec) **5:**100
Mount Rushmore National Memorial (South Dakota) **5:**300
Mourne Mountains (Northern Ireland) **3:**143
Mouse deer 2:316
Movies *see* Motion pictures
MOZAMBIQUE 1:48, 363–68
Cold War end accelerated peace process **1:**1
Portugal's former overseas provinces **4:**77
refugees to Malawi **1:**280
Zimbabwe, relations with **1:**355
illus.
flag **1:**xxiv
Gorongoza National Reserve **1:**367
Maputo **1:**363
Mozambican refugees in Malawi **1:**279
women walking to market **1:**364
map(s) **1:**365
Mozambique (Mozambique) **1:**364
Mozambique Channel 1:370, 383
Mozambique National Resistance Movement (Renamo) 1:368
Mozart, Wolfgang Amadeus (Austrian composer) **4:**226
MPLA *see* Popular Movement for the Liberation of Angola
Mros (people) **2:**240
Mswati (king of Swaziland) **1:**388
Mswati III (king of Swaziland) **1:**389
Muara (Brunei) **2:**330
Mubarak, Hosni (Egyptian leader) **1:**123
Muchinga Mountains (Zambia) **1:**272
Mugabe, Robert (Zimbabwean political leader) **1:**362
Muhajirs (Indian refugees in Pakistan) **2:**183

Muhammad (founder of Islam)
  Dome of the Rock **2:**47
  Islam's prophets **1:**108
  Mecca and Medina **2:**51, 125, 126
Muhammad ibn Ali al-Sanusi see Sanusi, Sayyid Muhammad ibn Ali as-
Muharraq (island, Bahrain) **2:**140
Muisca (indigenous people of Colombia) see Chibcha
Mujahidin (Afghan freedom fighters) **2:**174, 179, 360
Mujeres (island, Mexico) **5:**358, 422
Mujibur Rahman (Mujib) (prime minister of Bangladesh) **2:**243–44
Mukammal, al-, Mount (Lebanon) **2:**98
Mulatas see San Blas (Mulatas) Islands
Mulattoes (Haitian people) **5:**468, 469–70
Mule (animal) **6:**87
Mulhacén (mountain peak, Spain) **4:**82
Mulroney, Brian (prime minister of Canada) **5:**76
Multan (Pakistan) **2:**188
Muluzi, Bakili (president of Malawi) **1:**281
Mumbai (India) see Bombay
Mumtaz Mahal (wife of Shah Jahan) **2:**216
Munch, Edvard (Norwegian painter) **4:**28
Munich (capital, Bavaria, Germany) **3:**16, 265, 270–72
  illus.
    Oktoberfest **3:**271
Munich Pact (1938) **3:**271, 277; **4:**230
Munsee (Indians of North America) **5:**202
Muong (Asian people) **2:**295
Murayama Tomiichi (prime minister of Japan) **2:**472
Murchison Falls (White Nile River) **1:**38, 317
Murcia (historical region and modern province, Spain) **4:**94
Murgab River (Afghanistan–Turkmenistan) **2:**356
Murillo, Bartolomé (Spanish artist) **4:**115
Murillo, Pedro Domingo (Bolivian patriot) **6:**240
Müritz, Lake (Germany) **3:**244
Murmansk (Russia) **4:**306–7; **5:**64
Murray Basin (Australia) **2:**483
Murray River (Australia) **2:**483, 509, 517, 519, 520
  South Australia **2:**521
  Victoria **2:**516
  table(s)
    longest rivers of the world **6:**346
Mur River (Croatia–Hungary) **4:**285
Mururata (mountain, Bolivia) **6:**231
Mururoa (atoll in Pacific Ocean) **2:**559
Musandam Peninsula (Oman–United Arab Emirates) **2:**136, 138
Muscat (capital, Oman) **2:**136
  illus. **2:**136
Muscat and Oman see Oman (Muscat and Oman)
Muscogee County (Georgia) **5:**235
Musée D'Orsay (Paris, France) **3:**195
Museums
  Amsterdam (the Netherlands) **3:**233
  Australia **2:**498
  Boston (Massachusetts) **5:**190
  Europe **3:**16
  Hermitage (St. Petersburg, Russia) **4:**330
  Hôtel des Invalides (Paris) **3:**199–200
  London (England) **3:**111

Louvre (Paris, France) **3:**195, 200
Oslo (Norway) **4:**32, 34
Picasso museum (Barcelona, Spain) **4:**102
Prado (Madrid) **4:**97
Vatican **4:**181
Zwinger (Dresden, Germany) **3:**268
illus.
  Hermitage (St. Petersburg, Russia) **4:**331
  National Museum of Natural History (Paris) **3:**58
Museveni, Yoweri Kaguta (president of Uganda) **1:**323
Musgrave Ranges (Australia) **2:**483, 521
Musharraf, Pervez (president of Pakistan) **2:**194
Music
  Albanian folk songs **4:**270
  Argentina **6:**275–76
  Australia **2:**497–98
  Austria **3:**317
  Belgium **3:**215
  Bolivia **6:**238–39
  Brazil **6:**93, 180–81
  Bulgaria **4:**262, 263
  Cambodia **2:**289–90
  Chile **6:**307, 310
  Chinese opera **2:**421
  Colombia **6:**122–23
  Costa Rica **6:**66
  Czech Republic **4:**225, 226
  Dominican Republic **5:**457
  Ecuador **6:**199
  Europe **3:**14
  France **3:**172, 179
  Germany **3:**252, 255–56, 258–59
  Guatemala **6:**28
  Honduras **6:**37
  Hungary **4:**241
  Indonesia **2:**319
  Italy **4:**141
  Jamaica **5:**476
  Korea **2:**432
  Lithuanian singing festivals **4:**302
  Lucerne (Switzerland) music festival **3:**295
  Mexican mariachi bands **5:**366
  Mexico **5:**373
  Moldova **4:**346
  New Zealand **2:**546
  Nicaragua **6:**55
  Paraguay **6:**248
  Peru **6:**213
  Poland **4:**215
  Portuguese fados **4:**69
  Russia **4:**313–14
  Senegalese minstrels **1:**155
  Sweden's pop-music industry **4:**50
  Tennessee, center for American music **5:**263, 264, 265
  Trinidad and Tobago **5:**485
  United Kingdom **3:**89
  Uruguay **6:**256
  Venezuela **6:**141, 142
  Wales **3:**125
  illus.
    Beale Street (Memphis, Tennessee) **5:**263
    Burundi drummers **1:**328
    Estonian choral group **4:**295
    Guinean choral group **1:**168
    marimba **6:**27
    Mongolian rock group **2:**363
    reggae music in Nicaragua **6:**55
    Senegalese instruments **1:**152
    Teatro Colón (Buenos Aires) **6:**267

Muskogeans (Indians of North America) **5:**249
Muslim Brotherhood **1:**123
Muslim League see Moslem League
Muslims (followers of Islam) see Islam
Mussolini, Benito (Italian political leader) **3:**61, 277; **4:**153, 160–61
Mustafa Kemal see Atatürk, Mustafa Kemal
Mustapha Pasha Mosque (Skopje, Macedonia) **4:**292
Mutalibov, Ayaz (president of Azerbaijan) **2:**89
Mutarara (Mozambique) **1:**364
Mutare (Umtali) (Zimbabwe) **1:**357
Mutesa I (king of Buganda) **1:**322
Mutesa II (Sir Edward Mutesa) (president of Uganda) **1:**322
Muzorewa, Abel (Zimbabwean political leader) **1:**362
Mwadui (Tanzania) **1:**336
Mwanawasa, Levy (president of Zambia) **1:**276
Mwanga (king of Buganda) **1:**322
Mwinyi, Ali Hassan (president of Tanzania) **1:**338
MYANMAR (Burma) **2:**24, **265–72**
  Asia, Southeast **2:**258, 259, 264
  Buddhism **2:**254
  illus.
    Buddhist priest restoring statue **2:**268
    elephant moving lumber **2:**267
    flag **2:**viii
    houses on stilts **2:**270
    people **2:**17
    Yangon **2:**265, 271
  map(s) **2:**266
Myanmar (people) **2:**254, 269
Myanmar language **2:**268, 269
Mycenae (ancient Greek city) **4:**198–99
Mycenaean civilization (ancient Greece, 1600–1200 b.c.) **3:**45–46; **4:**201
Mykonos (island, Greece) **4:**190
  illus. **3:**8; **4:**189
Myrtle Beach (South Carolina) **5:**232
Mystery Island see Niihau
Mystic (Connecticut)
  illus. **5:**195
Mythology see Legends and folklore
Mytilene (island, Greece) see Lesbos
Myvatn, Lake (Iceland) **4:**3–4
Mzab (region of oases, Algeria) **1:**78
Mzilikaze (leader of the Matabele) **1:**362

• • • N • • • •

Naafkopf (mountain peak, Liechtenstein) **3:**306
Nabiyev, Rakhman (president of Tajikistan) **2:**361
Nablus (Jordan) **2:**114
Nacala (Mozambique) **1:**278, 364
Nader, Ralph (American consumer advocate) **5:**196
Nadir Shah (king of Persia) **2:**163, 178
Näfels (Switzerland) **3:**297
NAFTA see North American Free Trade Agreement
Nafud Desert **2:**10, 123
Naga Hills (India–Myanmar) **2:**198, 266
Nagasaki (Japan) **2:**445, 447
Nagorno-Karabakh (Armenian enclave in Azerbaijan) **2:**32, 55, 74, 75, 79, 86, 89

Naguib, Mohammad (Egyptian political leader) **1**:122

Nagy, Imre (Hungarian premier) **4**:246, 247

Nahua (Indians of North America) **5**:377

Nahuatl language 5:355, 376, 415, 419

Nahuel Huapí, Lake (Argentina) **6**:266

Nahuel Huapí National Park (Argentina) **6**:283

Naipaul, V.S. (Trinidad-born writer) **5**:440

Nairobi (capital, Kenya) **1**:308–9, 313, 314
  illus. **1**:309
    mosque **1**:311

Nairobi National Park (Kenya) **1**:314

Naismith, James (American inventor of basketball) **5**:191

Naismith Memorial Basketball Hall of Fame 5:191

Naivasha, Lake (Kenya) **1**:308

Najd (Nejd) (region, Saudi Arabia) **2**:123

Najibullah, Mohammad (Afghan political leader) **2**:179

Nakhichevan (autonomous region, Azerbaijan) **2**:87

Naktong River (South Korea) **2**:435

Nakuru, Lake (Kenya) **1**:308

Nama (African people) *see* Khoikhoi

Nambung National Park (Australia)
  illus. **2**:527

Names, personal
  Bulgarian Turks forced to take Christian names **4**:260
  Latin America **6**:109–10
  Turks adopted family names **2**:67

Namgyal, Ngawang (king of Bhutan) **2**:236

Namib Desert (Africa) **1**:348, 350, 396
  illus. **1**:347

Namibe (Moçâmedes) (Angola) **1**:343

NAMIBIA (South-West Africa) 1:46–47, **347–50**
  apartheid **1**:31
  Congo, Democratic Republic of **1**:270
  Walvis Bay **1**:350
  illus.
    flag **1**:xxiv
    gemsbok in desert **1**:19
    Namib Desert **1**:347
    San (Bushmen) **1**:349
    Windhoek **1**:349
  map(s) **1**:348

Nampa (Idaho) **5**:314

Namphy, Henry (Haitian political leader) **5**:470

Nanaimo (British Columbia) **5**:131

Nanchao (Thai kingdom in China) **2**:269

Nan River (Thailand) **2**:274

Nansemond (Indians of North America) **5**:224

Nansen, Fridtjof (Norwegian explorer) **4**:32; **5**:11, 62

Nantes, Edict of (1598, French religious decree) **3**:183, 184

Nanticoke (Indians of North America) **5**:216, 218

Nantucket (Massachusetts) **5**:188

Nanumanga (island, Tuvalu) **2**:610

Nanumea (island, Tuvalu) **2**:610, 612

Napata (ancient city, Egypt) **1**:130

Napa Valley (California) **5**:342, 346

Naperville (Illinois) **5**:282

Naples (Italy) **4**:114, 141, 143–44, 158
  San Gennaro (Januarius), patron saint **4**:136
  illus. **4**:143, 144

Naples, Bay of 4:130
  illus. **4**:130, 144

Napoleon I (emperor of France) **3**:184–85
  Andorra must be preserved **4**:119
  Arc de Triomphe (Paris) **3**:195–96
  Berezina River, battle at **4**:341
  Caribbean Islands **5**:436
  Corsica **3**:167
  Egyptian campaign **1**:120
  Elba, island (Italy) **4**:131
  Europe, history of **3**:41, 57–58, 324
  Haiti, history of **5**:468–69
  Holy Roman Empire crushed **3**:274
  Italy **4**:158, 167
  Malta **4**:184
  Paris memorials **3**:195–96, 197
  quoted on Constantinople **2**:56
  quoted on Spain **4**:80
  Russian invasion **4**:321
  San Marino **4**:174
  Slovenia, history of **4**:284
  Switzerland **3**:297
  tomb in the Invalides (Paris) **3**:200

Napoleon III (Louis Napoleon) (emperor of France) **3**:186, 197, 201; **4**:158; **5**:384

Napoleonic Code (French legal code) **3**:185

Napoleonic Wars (1803–1815) **3**:184–85
  Denmark **4**:20, 21
  Norway **4**:26
  Spain **4**:116

Narekatsi, St. Grigor (Armenian poet) **2**:76

Narragansett (Indians of North America) **5**:193, 194

Narragansett Bay (Rhode Island) **5**:193, 194
  illus. **5**:192

Narva (Estonia) **4**:296

Naryn River (Kyrgyzstan–Uzbekistan) **2**:353

NASA *see* National Aeronautics and Space Administration

Nashua (New Hampshire) **5**:185

Nashville (capital, Tennessee) **5**:265

Näsi, Lake (Finland) **4**:64

Nasir, Ibraham (president of Maldives) **2**:252

Naskapi (Indians of North America) **5**:99

Nassau (capital, Bahamas) **5**:424–25
  illus. **5**:423

Nassau-Siegen, Count John Maurice (Dutch general) **6**:168

Nassau-Weilburg, House of (Luxembourg) **3**:210

Nasser, Gamal Abdel (president of Egypt) **1**:122, 123
  Suez Canal **1**:121

Nasser, Lake (Egypt)
  Abu Simbel temple **1**:111
  Sudan, irrigation in **1**:129

Natal (historic province, South Africa) **1**:404, 405

Natchez (Indians of North America) **5**:222, 246

Natchez Trace Parkway (Mississippi–Tennessee) **5**:246, 265

Nathan, S.R. (president of Singapore) **2**:312

National Aeronautics and Space Administration (NASA) 5:243, 253

National anthems 5:219

National Assembly for Wales 3:130

National Autonomous University of Mexico 5:371, 373, 381, 411
  illus. **5**:30, 371, 411

National Civil Rights Museum (Memphis, Tennessee) **5**:265

Nationalism
  African independence, problems of **1**:60–61

Asia, Southeast **2**:264
Bosnia and Herzegovina **4**:290
China **2**:24–25, 25–26, 386
Europe **3**:17
Georgia (republic), history of **2**:84, 85
Ghana **1**:203
"Greater Serbia" movement **4**:276, 280
Habsburg empire destroyed **3**:324
India's national movement **2**:216–17
Kazakhstan **2**:349
Latin America **6**:112–13
Lithuania **4**:301
Morocco **1**:74
Nazi appeal to **3**:276
Nigeria **1**:227
Quebec **5**:97, 102, 103, 112
Sikhs in India **2**:169
Slovakia **4**:233, 235
Somalia **1**:304
Spain **4**:89–91
Ukraine **4**:332, 334, 340

Nationalist China *see* Taiwan

Nationalist Party (China) *see* Guomindang

Nationalists (Republicans) (Northern Ireland) **3**:144, 148, 149

Nationalization
  Algeria **1**:81–82
  Chilean copper mining **6**:318–19
  Cuba **5**:451
  Ethiopia **1**:286
  Germany, East **3**:259
  Iran **2**:160–61, 163
  South African mineral resources **1**:402
  Uganda **1**:323
  Venezuelan heavy industry **6**:143, 148

National Liberation Front (FLN) (Algeria) **1**:84

National parks
  Alaska **5**:349
  Argentina: Nahuel Huapí **6**:283
  Australia: Jervis Bay Territory **2**:514
  Bhutan **2**:235
  Canada **5**:85, 91
  Canada: Banff **5**:126
  Ecuador: Galápagos Islands **6**:203
  El Salvador: El Imposible **6**:44
  England **3**:98–99
  Haiti **5**:462
  Honduras: United Nations National Park **6**:36
  Kenya **1**:314
  New Zealand **2**:542–43
  Panama **6**:74
  Poland **4**:213
  Rwanda **1**:324–25
  Tanzania **1**:338
  United States *see* individual park names
  Utah **5**:323, 326
  Wales **5**:122
  Zambia: Kafue **1**:276
  illus.
    Australia **2**:484
    Tanzania **1**:338

National Salvation Front (political organization, Romania) **4**:257

National seashores 5:189, 229
  Cumberland National Seashore **5**:233, 234

National Union for the Total Independence of Angola (UNITA) 1:343, 346

Nation Indians *see* Five Civilized Tribes

Native Americans *see* Indians of Central and South America; Indians of North America

Native Title Act (Australia, 1993) **2**:502

NATO *see* North Atlantic Treaty Organization
Nat Turner's Rebellion (1831) **5:**226
Natural gas *see also* Liquefied natural gas
  Algeria **1:**76
  Australia **2:**490
  California **5:**51
  Canada **5:**123, 127
  China **2:**383
  England **3:**102, 109
  Iran **2:**156, 161
  Louisiana **5:**247
  Netherlands **3:**36
  New Zealand **2:**541, 550
  Norway **4:**26, 28
  Pakistan **2:**189
  Qatar **2:**143
  Romania has largest reserves in Europe **4:**255
  Russia **4:**309
  Scotland **3:**135
  Turkmenistan **2:**358
  Western Australia **2:**527
  illus.
    Venezuela **6:**104
  map(s)
    world production **6:**355
Nature
  Japanese appreciation of **2:**460–61
  Lapps' deep feeling for **4:**37
Naugatuck River (Connecticut) **5:**195
Nauplia (Greece) **4:**195
NAURU 2:560, 569, 570, **577–79,** 612
  economy **2:**567
  illus. **2:**577
    flag **2:**x
  map(s) **2:**578
Nautilus (nuclear submarine) **5:**64
Navajo (Indians of North America) **5:**309, 321,
    322, 324, 325, 328, 329
  illus.
    weaving **5:**328
Navarre (historic region, Spain) **4:**89, 91, 108,
    113
Navratilova, Martina (Czech tennis player)
    4:226
Naxos (Greek island) **4:**190
NAYARIT (state, Mexico) **5:400, 402**
Nazarbayev, Nursultan (president of Kazakh-
    stan) **2:**346, 349
Nazaré (Portugal) **4:**72
Nazas River (Mexico) **5:**398
Nazism 3:276
  Austria **3:**325
  Czechoslovakia **4:**230
  German intellectual life stifled **3:**254, 280
  Holocaust **3:**278
  Munich **3:**271
  neo-Nazis **3:**249
  Nuremberg (Germany) **3:**272
  Poland **4:**220–21
  Stalin's dealings with Germany **4:**323
  World War II **3:**61
  illus.
    party rally **3:**277
Ndadaye, Melchior (president of Burundi)
    1:331
Ndebele (African people) *see* Matabele
Ndebele language *see* Sindebele
N'Djamena (capital, Chad) **1:**240, 241, 243
  illus. **1:**240
N'Djolé (Gabon) **1:**252
Ndola (Zambia) **1:**272
Neagh, Lough (Northern Ireland) **3:**82, 143, 146

Near East *see* Middle East
NEBRASKA 5:301–2
  illus.
    Omaha **5:**301
  map(s) **5:**302
Nebuchadnezzar II (king of Babylon) **2:**153
  name carved on cliff in Lebanon **2:**97
Nefta (Tunisia) **1:**90
Nefusa (plateau in Libya) **1:**95
Negev Desert (Israel) **2:**105, 109
Negoi (mountain peak, Romania) **4:**249
Negritos (Asian people) **2:**334
Négritude (African culture) **1:**158
Negro, Cerro (volcano, Nicaragua) **6:**51
Negroes *see* Blacks
Negropont (Greek island) *see* Euboea
Negro River (Brazil–Colombia) **6:**134
  Amazon River **6:**168
  link with Orinoco River **6:**146
Negro River (Uruguay) **6:**259, 261
Nehru, Jawaharlal (prime minister of India)
    2:217–18
**Nei Monggol Autonomous Region (Inner
    Mongolia)** (China) **2:**378, 385–86
  climate **2:**370
  Mu Us loop, Yellow River **2:**371
  population **2:**383
  way of life **2:**372
  illus. **2:**343, 382
Neisse River (Europe) **3:**243; **4:**213
Nejd (region, Saudi Arabia) *see* Najd
Nelson, Horatio, Lord (English admiral)
  Antigua and Barbuda **5:**493
  Trafalgar, Battle of (1805) **4:**116
  wounded in attack on the Canary Islands
    1:33
Nelson River (Manitoba) **5:**111–12
Nelson's Dockyard (Antigua and Barbuda)
    5:493
Neman (Nemunas) River (Belarus–Lithuania)
    4:301
Nendo (Solomon Islands) **2:**591, 593
Nentsi (people) *see* Samoyeds
NEPAL 2:27, **230–33**
  Buddhism **2:**169
  Himalayas **2:**166–67
  illus. **2:**230
    flag **2:**viii
    Katmandu **2:**233
    people **2:**16
  map(s) **2:**231
Nepalese (Asian people) **2:**235
Nepali language **2:**231, 235
Neptun (Romania) **4:**254
Neretva River (Bosnia and Herzegovina) **4:**288,
    289, 290
Neri, Saint Philip (Italian priest) **4:**97
Neruda, Pablo (Chilean poet) **6:**309
Nervo, Amado (Mexican poet) **5:**374
Ness, Loch (Scotland) **3:**132
Netanyahu, Benjamin (prime minister of Israel)
    2:115
NETHERLANDS 3:225–38
  Belgium, history of **3:**223
  Brazil, history of **6:**167–69, 188, 189
  climate **3:**30
  farms **3:**35
  Indonesia, history of **2:**324, 325
  natural gas **3:**36
  Polynesia, history of **2:**602
  Rhine River **3:**245

  South America, history of **6:**97, 98
  illus.
    Amsterdam **3:**225
    beach **3:**14
    canal **3:**55
    cheese market **3:**228
    Eastern Scheldt Sea Barrier **3:**226
    flag **3:**vi
    The Hague **3:**238
    Rotterdam **3:**232
    tulips **3:**231
  map(s) **3:**227
Netherlands Antilles (Dutch outlying depen-
    dency) **3:**235
Netherlands East Indies (former possessions of
    Netherlands in Malay archipelago) **2:**23, 313
Netherlands Guiana *see* Suriname
Neto, António Agostinho (president of Angola)
    1:346
Neuchâtel (Switzerland) **3:**295, 297
Neuchâtel, Lake (Switzerland) **3:**286
Neuquén (province, Argentina) **6:**266
Neuquén River (Argentina) **6:**281
Neuschwanstein (castle, Germany) **3:**257
  illus. **3:**257
Neusiedler, Lake (Austria–Hungary) **3:**315
Neutral (Indians of North America) **5:**105
Neutrality
  Austria **3:**325
  Belgium **3:**224–25
  Sweden **4:**50
  Switzerland **3:**298
NEVADA 5:330–32
  illus.
    Carson City **5:**331
    Lake Tahoe **5:**332
  map(s) **5:**331
Nevada, Sierra (mountains, California) **5:**8, 51,
    156, 330, 332, 333, 342
  tree line **5:**16
  illus. **5:**158
Nevada, Sierra (mountains, Spain) **3:**28; **4:**80,
    82
  illus. **4:**83
Nevada de Santa Marta, Sierra (mountains,
    Colombia) **6:**117
  illus. **6:**118
Neva River (Russia) **4:**308, 330
Neves, Tancredo de Almeida (Brazilian politi-
    cal leader) **6:**191
Nevis (island in the Caribbean) *see* Saint Kitts
    and Nevis
Nevis Peak (St. Kitts and Nevis) **5:**495
Nevsky Prospect (street, St. Petersburg, Russia)
    4:330
New Amsterdam (Dutch settlement in America,
    now New York City) **5:**206
New Amsterdam (Guyana) **6:**150
Newar (Asian people) **2:**231
Newark (New Jersey) **5:**210
Newark Bay (New Jersey) **5:**210
New Bedford (Massachusetts) **5:**181
New Britain (island, Pacific Ocean) **2:**587
New Britain Trench (Solomon Islands) **2:**592
NEW BRUNSWICK (province, Canada) **5:**77,
    80, **84–86**
  illus.
    Fundy, Bay of **5:**79
  map(s) **5:**86

New Caledonia (island, Pacific Ocean) **2:**559, 567, 583, 584–85, 586; **3:**191
illus.
drying coffee **2:**584
New Castile (historical region, Spain) **4:**80
Newcastle (England) **3:**108
Newcastle (New Brunswick) **5:**86
Newcastle (New South Wales, Australia) **2:**509, 512
New Delhi (capital, India) **2:**208–9
illus.
mosque **2:**212
New Echota (Georgia) **5:**236
New Economic Policy (USSR, 1921) **4:**322
NEW ENGLAND (region, U.S.) **5:178–97**
Appalachian Mountains **5:**6
British North America **5:**36–37
illus.
autumn foliage **5:**178–79, 184
colonial-era church **5:**179
covered bridge **5:**186
stone walls **5:**180
New England Uplands 5:179
New Jersey **5:**208
New York **5:**201–2
Rhode Island **5:**192
Newfoundland (island, Canada) **4:**25; **5:**78, 79
table(s)
largest islands of the world **6:**346
NEWFOUNDLAND AND LABRADOR (province, Canada) **5:**77, 80, **81–83**
map(s) **5:**82
New France (early Canada) **5:**96, 101
New Georgia (island, Solomon Islands) **2:**591
New Granada (Spanish viceroyalty at Bogotá) **6:**90, 99, 127, 225
Venezuela **6:**145
New Guinea (island in Malay archipelago) **2:**315, 559, 583
Papua New Guinea **2:**587–90
table(s)
largest islands of the world **6:**346
New Guinea, Territory of (Pacific Ocean) **2:**590
NEW HAMPSHIRE 5:184–85
illus. **5:**184
map(s) **5:**185
New Haven (Connecticut) **5:**196, 197
New Hebrides *see* Vanuatu
Ne Win (Burmese head of government) **2:**265, 268, 272
New Ireland (island, Pacific Ocean) **2:**587
NEW JERSEY 5:200, 207–10
illus.
Atlantic City **5:**207
Elizabeth **5:**210
Pine Barrens **5:**208
Trenton **5:**209
map(s) **5:**209
New London (Connecticut) **5:**195
Newly industrialized economies (NIEs) 2:34, 278
NEW MEXICO 5:321–22
illus.
Carlsbad Caverns **5:**321
White Sands National Monument **5:**15
map(s) **5:**322
New Orleans (Louisiana) **5:**49, 247, 248
Mardi Gras **5:**249
illus.
French Quarter **5:**248
Mardi Gras **5:**249

Newport (Rhode Island) **5:**194
illus.
Rosecliff **5:**194
Newport (Wales) **3:**127
New Providence Island (Bahamas) **5:**424, 425
New River Gorge (West Virginia)
illus. **5:**258
New Siberian Islands (Russia) **5:**62
New South (U.S.) **5:**220, 235
economic growth followed air conditioning **5:**222
Piedmont region **5:**153
NEW SOUTH WALES (state, Australia) **2:**485, 491, **509–12**
Australian Capital Territory **2:**514
illus.
Bridal Veil Falls **2:**509
Sydney **2:**511, 512
map(s) **2:**510
New Spain (Spanish viceroyalty at Mexico City) **6:**90
Newspapers
Canada **5:**71
China **2:**407
Japan **2:**462
United Kingdom **3:**89
Vatican daily paper **4:**180
New Stone Age 4:110
New Territories (area, Hong Kong) **2:**410, 411
New Toledo (colonial name for Chile) **6:**320
Newton, Sir Isaac (English scientist) **3:**105
Newtonabbey (Northern Ireland) **3:**147
New Valley Canal (Egypt) **1:**116
New Waterway (canal, Netherlands) **3:**42, 245
New World
Caribbean islands, settlement of **5:**430–33
Central and South America, discovery and settlement of **6:**15, 82, 97
New Year celebrations
Chinese New Year **2:**425
Iran **2:**159
NEW YORK (state) **5:**200, **201–6** *see also* New York City
history **5:**37
illus.
Adirondack Mountains **5:**204
Erie Canal **5:**204
Fire Island **5:**199
map(s) **5:**202
New York City 5:6, 203
early trade center **5:**37
megalopolis area **5:**46
metropolitan-area population **5:**200
multicultural population **5:**204
population **5:**205
wildlife **5:**202
illus.
architecture **5:**201
Rockefeller Center **5:**203
Times Square **5:**36
New York State Barge Canal 5:45
NEW ZEALAND 2:473–79, **536–54**
Antarctic research **6:**334–35
flag **2:**474
Oceania **2:**519
Polynesia **2:**600
Western Samoa **2:**609
illus.
Auckland **2:**547
coastline **2:**474
Fiordland National Park **2:**537

flag **2:**ix
Mount Egmont **2:**536
sheep **2:**536, 549
sports **2:**544
Stewart Island **2:**538
Sutherland Falls **2:**537
vineyard **2:**549
map(s) **2:**539
table(s)
prime ministers **6:**363
Nez Percé (Indians of North America) **5:**314, 337, 340
Ngaanyatjarra (aboriginal tribe, Australia) **2:**522
N'Gaoundéré (Cameroon) **1:**233
Ngauruhoe, Mount (volcano, New Zealand) **2:**538
Ngio (Asian people) **2:**275
Ngoc Linh (mountain peak, Vietnam) **2:**294
Ngonde Yao (African people) **1:**278
Ngoni (African people) **1:**273, 278
Ngoni language 1:47
Ngorongoro Crater (Tanzania) **1:**338
illus. **1:**332
N'Gounié River (Gabon) **1:**252
Nguema Mbasogo, Teodoro Obiang (president of Equatorial Guinea) **1:**236
Nguni (African people) **1:**354, 398
Ngwavuma River (southeast Africa) **1:**385–86
Niagara Escarpment (Canada) **5:**105
Niagara Falls (Canada–U.S.) **5:**105, 270
New York **5:**202, 205
Ontario's hydroelectric power **5:**109
illus. **5:**205
Niagara River (Ontario–New York) **5:**205
megalopolis area **5:**46
Niamey (capital, Niger) **1:**145, 146, 147, 148
illus. **1:**149
Niari River (Congo) **1:**257, 258
Nibelungenlied (German epic) **3:**253
Nibelungs (legendary family in Norse mythology) **3:**245
NICARAGUA 6:51–60
Central America **6:**9, 10
history **6:**16, 18
Honduras, relations with **6:**41
land distribution **6:**17
population **6:**11
United States, relations with the **6:**12, 13
illus.
cotton harvesting **6:**57
farmers fording a stream **6:**52
flag **6:**vi
Granada **6:**51
Momotombo and Momotombito **6:**52
Puerto Cabezas **6:**56
reggae music in Bluefields **6:**55
map(s) **6:**54
Nicaragua, Lake 6:3, 52, 58
table(s)
largest lakes **6:**347
Nicaraguan Depression (Nicaragua) **6:**51, 52, 53
Nice (France) **3:**160, 162, 186; **4:**158
illus.
fish market **3:**160
Nicholas II (czar of Russia) **4:**321, 322
Nickel
Manitoba **5:**116, 117
Sudbury (Ontario) **5:**4
illus. **5:**71
Nicolet, Jean (French explorer) **5:**286

Nicosia (capital, Cyprus) **2:**70, 71
   illus. **2:**68
Nieman River *see* Neman River
Niemeyer, Oscar (Brazilian architect) **6:**182, 184
   illus.
      Latin American Memorial **6:**7
Nietzsche, Friedrich (German philosopher) **3:**253–54
Nieuw Amsterdam (Suriname) **6:**154
Nieuw Nickerie (Suriname) **6:**154
NIGER 1:144–49
   Niger River **1:**50–51
   Sahara **1:**24
   western Africa **1:**52–53
   illus.
      camel transportation **1:**147
      flag **1:**xxii
      headgear **1:**144
      Niamey **1:**149
      Niger River **1:**146
   map(s) **1:**145
NIGERIA 1:56–58, **215–29**
   Biafra **1:**228
   Niger River **1:**50–51
   illus.
      altar boy **1:**223
      extracting palm oil **1:**226
      festival **1:**215
      flag **1:**xxiii
      Kano **1:**56–57, 227
      Lagos **1:**218, 229
      markets **1:**220
      Niger River delta **1:**217
      oil industry **1:**224
      rice farming **1:**219
      University of Ibadan **1:**222
      women on way to market **1:**221
      workers packing grain **1:**225
   map(s) **1:**216
Niger River (Africa) **1:**50–51, 216
   Guinea **1:**166, 167
   Mali **1:**141, 142
   Niger **1:**144, 148
   Sahara **1:**25
   illus. **1:**146, 217
   table(s)
      longest rivers of the world **6:**346
Nihilists (radical youth of nineteenth-century Russia) **4:**313
Niihau (Mystery Island) (island, Hawaii) **5:**352
Nile River (Africa) **1:**4, 38–39 *see also* Aswan High Dam
   channel for cultural exchange in North Africa **1:**33
   Egypt **1:**113–14, 116, 117
   Egyptian worship of the river **1:**101–2
   Ethiopia **1:**283
   Sahara **1:**25
   Sudan **1:**125, 129
   Uganda **1:**316, 317, 318
   illus. **1:**113
      Cairo **1:**31
   table(s)
      longest rivers of the world **6:**346
Nilgiri Hills (Tamil Nadu, India) **2:**198
Nilo-Hamites (African people) **1:**318–19
Nilotes (African people) **1:**35, 36, 127–28, 264, 318, 319, 322
Nimba Mountains (Africa) **1:**169, 179, 182
Nimeiry, Gaafar Muhammad al- (president of Sudan) **1:**130–31

Nîmes (France) **3:**160, 180
Ningaloo Reef (Australia) **2:**526
Ningsia-Hui (Ningxia Hui) Autonomous Region (China) **2:**385
Niños, Los (cadet defenders of Mexico City at Chapultepec) **5:**383
Niš (Yugoslavia) **4:**277
Nitrate (mineral) **6:**312, 318, 321
Niue (former New Zealand territory) **2:**567, 601, 603
Niulakita (island, Tuvalu) **2:**610
Niutao (island, Tuvalu) **2:**610
Niyazov, Saparmurad (president of Turkmenistan) **2:**358
Niza, Marcos de (Spanish priest and explorer) **5:**322
Nizhny Novgorod (Russia) **4:**320
   Swedish Viking trading settlement **3:**51
Nkrumah, Kwame (Ghanaian statesman) **1:**203, 204
Nobel, Alfred B. (Swedish inventor) **4:**46
Nobel Peace Prize
   1964: King **5:**234
   1971: Brandt **3:**283
   1980: Pérez Esquivel **6:**278
   1983: Wałęsa **4:**222
   1986: Wiesel **4:**252
   1987: Arias Sánchez **6:**71
   1989: Dalai Lama **2:**387
   1992: Menchú **6:**33
   1993: de Klerk and Mandela **1:**406
   1994: Arafat, Peres, and Rabin **2:**55, 115
   1996: Belo and Ramos-Horta **2:**328
   1998: Hume and Trimble **3:**149
Nobel Prize: economics
   1970: Lewis **5:**489
Nobel Prize: literature
   1905: Sienkiewicz **4:**215
   1924: Reymont **4:**215
   1955: Laxness **4:**7
   1963: Seferis **4:**194
   1972: Böll **3:**251
   1978: Singer **4:**215
   1979: Elytis **4:**194
   1980: Miłosz **4:**215
   1990: Paz **5:**373
   1992: Walcott **5:**440, 489
   1995: Heaney **3:**145
   1996: Szymborska **4:**215
   1998: Saramago **4:**78
   2001: Naipaul **5:**440
Nobility (social class)
   England **3:**103, 114–15
   Scotland, land ownership in **3:**141
Noboa, Gustavo (president of Ecuador) **6:**205
Nok (Nigeria) **1:**225
Nokia Corporation 4:55
Nokoué, Lake (Benin) **1:**211
Nomads *see also* Bedouins
   Africa **1:**37, 142, 154, 222, 242–43, 298, 310
   Argentina, early gauchos of **6:**274
   Aryans **2:**13
   Asia, ancient **2:**21
   Asia, North **2:**345
   Bedouins of Jordan **2:**118
   Benin **1:**213
   China **2:**385–86
   Chukchi of Siberia **4:**309
   Eritrea **1:**295
   Inuit **5:**21
   Iran **2:**157–58

Iraq 2:150
   Kazakhstan **2:**348
   Kochis of Afghanistan **2:**178
   Kyrgyz traditions **2:**354
   Lapland migrations ceasing **4:**37
   Libya **1:**97, 98
   Mauritania **1:**136, 137
   Mongol way of life **2:**363–64
   Niger **1:**146
   North Africa and the Sahara **1:**25, 132
   Oman **2:**137
   Paleolithic Europeans **3:**45
   Somalia **1:**302
   Sudan **1:**127
   illus.
      Africa **1:**62
      Chad **1:**239
Nombre de Dios (Panama) **6:**80
Nonaggression Pact (USSR–Germany, 1939) **3:**277; **4:**304, 323
Nonaggression Pact (USSR–West Germany, 1970) **3:**283
Non Nok Tha (Thailand) **2:**279
Nootka (Indians of North America) **5:**132
Nordenskjöld, Nils Adolf Erik (Swedish explorer) **5:**62
Nordenskjöld, Nils Otto Gustaf (Swedish explorer) **6:**332
Nordic Council (Sweden, Norway, Denmark, Finland, and Iceland) **4:**50
Norfolk (Virginia) **5:**225–26
Norfolk Island (Pacific Ocean) **2:**488, 563
   illus. **2:**488
Noricum (ancient Celtic kingdom) **3:**320
Noriega, Manuel (Panamanian political leader) **6:**13, 81
Norilsk (Russia) **5:**64
Norman (Oklahoma) **5:**306
Norman Conquest (England, 1066) **3:**116–17
Normandy (historical region, France) **3:**51
   agriculture **3:**155
   battle and invasion of (1944) **3:**188, 279
Normans (Norman French) (European people) **3:**102
   Ireland **3:**75
   Norman rulers of England, list of **6:**360
Norrland (region, Sweden) **4:**38, 39
Norsemen (early Scandinavians) **4:**23, 25 *see also* Vikings
   Canada **5:**136
   Europe, history of **3:**51
   Greenland settled by Eric the Red **5:**10
North Africa 1:32–35 *see also* names of countries
   Mediterranean influence **1:**11
NORTH AMERICA 5:1–52 *see also* names of countries
   Amerinds *see* Indians of North America
   Cuba is geologically a part of **5:**442
   illus.
      flags of the countries **5:**vi
   map(s)
      physical map **5:**3
      political map **5:**19
      population **5:**5
      precipitation **5:**4
   table(s)
      area and population **6:**344
      continental extremes **6:**345
      countries **5:**21
      great mountain peaks **6:**349
North American Cordillera 5:56

North American Free Trade Agreement 5:45, 362, 364
  Mexico **5:**31, 388
North Asia see Central and North Asia—Asia, North
North Atlantic Drift (section of Gulf Stream) **3:**29
North Atlantic Treaty Organization (NATO) 3:62, 63
  armed forces **3:**2
  Belgium **3:**212, 216
  Bosnia and Herzegovina **4:**288, 290
  Cold War in international relations **4:**323
  France, history of **3:**190
  Germany **3:**260, 283
  Greenland **5:**11
  Hungary **4:**236
  Italy **4:**162, 163
  Keflavik (Iceland) base **4:**6
  Luxembourg **3:**210
  Malta **4:**184
  Netherlands **3:**237
  Norfolk naval base **5:**226
  Norway **4:**34
  Poland **4:**223
  Russia on new council **4:**325
  Spain **4:**118
  Turkey **2:**67
  United Kingdom **3:**94
  Yugoslavia, bombing of **4:**273, 279, 281, 292
North Barren Mountain (Nova Scotia) **5:**91
North Borneo see Sabah
North Cape (Norway) **4:**24
NORTH CAROLINA 5:162, **227–29**
  illus.
    Cape Lookout Lighthouse **5:**227
  map(s) **5:**228
North Channel (Northern Ireland–Scotland) **3:**83
North Charleston (South Carolina) **5:**232
North Chihuahuan Desert (New Mexico)
  illus. **5:**15
North China Plain 2:383
NORTH DAKOTA 5:297–98
  illus.
    Badlands **5:**297
  map(s) **5:**298
North Downs (hills, England) **3:**82, 100
Northeast Passage (to the Orient) **5:**62, 64
Northern Cape (province, South Africa) **1:**406
Northern Hemisphere
  Arctic **5:**53–64
Northern Highlands (Scotland) **3:**83
Northern Highlands (Vietnam) **2:**294
NORTHERN IRELAND 3:81, 87, 142–49 see
  also Ireland; Ulster
  economy **3:**89
  Great Britain, relations with **3:**93, 94, 95, 96
  Ireland, history of **3:**77, 78
  illus.
    Belfast **3:**143, 145, 148
    castle **3:**142
    Giant's Causeway **3:**146
    shopping mall **3:**147
  map(s) **3:**144
Northern Ireland Assembly see Stormont
Northern lights see Aurora borealis
Northern Marianas (islands, Pacific Ocean) **2:**567
Northern Rhodesia (now Zambia) **1:**276, 362
Northern Sporades see Sporades

NORTHERN TERRITORY (Australia) **2:**490, 492, 493, **532–35**
  illus.
    Darwin's art and culture festival **2:**532
    petroleum industry **2:**534
  map(s) **2:**535
North German Confederation (1867) **3:**275
North Island (New Zealand) **2:**544
  precipitation **2:**476
  table(s)
    largest islands of the world **6:**346
NORTH KOREA (Korea, Democratic People's Republic of) 2:26, **429–33,** 438
  border disputes **2:**31
  economy **2:**375, 376
  government **2:**29
  illus.
    flag **2:**ix
    holiday celebration **2:**432
    Pyongyang **2:**429
  map(s) **2:**430
Northland (region, New Zealand) **2:**538
North Las Vegas (Nevada) **5:**332
Northmen see Vikings
North Platte River (U.S.) **5:**8
North Pole 5:62, 64
North Rhine-Westphalia (state, Germany) **3:**261, 266
North Sea (arm of the Atlantic Ocean) **3:**212, 213; **4:**9
  canals connect to other bodies of water **3:**243
  England's coastline **3:**98
  Hanseatic League **3:**273
  Netherlands, flooding and land reclamation **3:**228
  petroleum **3:**36, 135; **4:**26
  Rhine River **3:**245
  table(s)
    major seas of the world **6:**347
North Sea Canal (Amsterdam, Netherlands) **3:**232, 233
North Side (area of Chicago, Illinois) **5:**283
North Slope (arctic region of Alaska) **5:**158, 348, 349
North Thompson River (British Columbia) **5:**131
Northumbria (Anglo-Saxon kingdom) **3:**140
North West Company (fur traders) **5:**113, 125, 132
Northwest culture area (Indians of North America) **5:**22
North-West Frontier Province (Pakistan) **2:**181
Northwest Mounted Police (Canada) see Royal Canadian Mounted Police
Northwest Passage 5:62
North West Rebellion (1885) see Riel Rebellions
NORTHWEST TERRITORIES (Canada) **5:**42, **141–44**
  mines and mining **5:**64
  original territory **5:**136
  map(s) **5:**143
Northwest Territory (U.S. history) **5:**269, 274
North Yemen 2:135
NORWAY 4:23–34
  Denmark, history of **4:**20
  dual monarchy with Sweden **4:**49
  hydroelectricity **3:**37
  Iceland **4:**5
  Lapland **4:**35, 37

  referendum against EU membership **3:**4
  illus.
    Bergen **4:**31
    fjord **4:**23
    flag **4:**v
    Oseberg ship **4:**32
    Oslo **4:**30
    skiers **4:**33
    stave church **4:**29
  map(s) **4:**27
Norway (Norwegian) Current (Atlantic Ocean) **4:**25, 37
Norwegians (people) **4:**28
  Norwegian Vikings **3:**51
No theater (of Japan) **2:**460
Notre Dame, Cathedral of (Paris, France) **3:**193
  illus. **3:**150
Notre Dame Basilica (Montreal)
  illus. **5:**75
Nottaway Plantation (Louisiana) **5:**248
Nouadhibou (Mauritania) **1:**136, 137
Nouakchott (capital, Mauritania) **1:**136, 137, 139
Nouazibou (Mauritania) see Nouadhibou
Nouméa (New Caledonia, Pacific Ocean) **2:**585
Nova Lisboa (Angola) see Huambo
NOVA SCOTIA (province, Canada) **5:**40, 77, 80, **90–93**
  illus.
    Fundy, Bay of **5:**79
  map(s) **5:**91
Novaya Zemlya (two islands in Arctic Ocean) **3:**8; **5:**61
Novgorod (Russia) **4:**315, 319
Novi Sad (Yugoslavia) **4:**277
Novokuznetsk (Russia) **2:**342
Novosibirsk (Russia) **2:**342; **4:**316
Nowa Huta (Poland) **4:**218
Ntare V (king of Burundi) **1:**331
Ntibantuganya, Sylvestre (president of Burundi) **1:**331
Nuba Mountains (Sudan) **1:**125
Nubia (region, Africa) **1:**117, 130
  Nile River **1:**38
  Nubians in Sudan **1:**35
  races and cultures **1:**13
  slave trade **1:**248
Nubian language 1:109
Nubians (African people) **1:**127
Nuclear power see also Radioactive wastes
  Austria's opposition to **3:**319
  Chernobyl accident **3:**37; **4:**50, 332, 343
  Czech Republic **4:**229
  Europe **3:**37
  France **3:**157
  Hungary **4:**238
  India **2:**227
  Japan **2:**37
  Russia **4:**316
  Sweden **4:**40
  Taiwan **2:**424
  Ukraine **4:**338
  illus. **2:**229
Nuclear weapons see also Radioactive wastes
  Belarus **4:**343
  China **2:**228
  French testing **2:**559
  India **2:**32, 173, 227, 228
  Kazakhstan **2:**346
  Korea, North **2:**433
  Marshall Islands testing **2:**570, 575

Nuclear weapons (cont.)
  Nevada testing site **5:**332
  New Mexico, first atomic-test site **5:**322
  New Zealand's antinuclear policy **2:**554
  Pakistan **2:**32, 173, 194, 228
  Soviet Union **4:**312
  submarines in Arctic **5:**55
  U.S.-Soviet agreement (1987) **4:**6
  World War II **2:**447
Nuer (African people) **1:**127, 128
Nueva Cádiz (Spanish settlement, Venezuela) **6:**144–45
Nueva Galicia (Spanish colonial province, Mexico) **5:**402
Nueva Vizcaya (Spanish colonial province, Mexico) **5:**393, 398
Nuevo Laredo (Tamaulipas, Mexico) **5:**396
NUEVO LEÓN (state, Mexico) **5:395**
Nuevo Vallarta (Nayarit, Mexico) **5:**400
Nui (island, Tuvalu) **2:**610, 611
Nujoma, Sam (Namibian political leader) **1:**350
Nuku'alofa (capital, Tonga) **2:**605
Nukufetau (island, Tuvalu) **2:**610, 612
Nukulaelae (island, Tuvalu) **2:**610
Nullarbor Plain (Australia) **2:**482, 521, 525
NUNAVUT (Inuit territory, Canada) **5:**58, 134, 135, 136, **137–40**
  mines and mining **5:**64
  illus. **5:**138, 139
  map(s) **5:**139
Nunavut Land Claims Agreement Act (1993) **5:**139–40
Núñez, Rafael (president of Colombia) **6:**128
Nupe (African people) **1:**219
Nuremberg (Germany) **3:**272
Nuremberg Laws (Germany, 1935) **3:**272, 276, 278
Nurmi, Paavo (Finnish runner)
  illus. **4:**60
Nutmeg (spice) **5:**481
Nuuk (capital, Greenland) **5:**11
Nyabarongo River (Rwanda) **1:**324
Ny-Ålesund (Spitsbergen, Norway) **6:**345
Nyanza (region in Kenya) **1:**308, 309
Nyasa, Lake *see* Malawi, Lake
Nyasaland *see* Malawi
Nyasaland Protectorate (1891–1953) **1:**280
Nyerere, Julius K. (Tanzanian political leader) **1:**337, 338
Nyiragongo, Mount (Congo, Democratic Republic of)
  illus.
    people fleeing eruption **1:**267
Nyoongah (aboriginal tribe, Australia) **2:**493

• • • O • • •

Oahu (Gathering Place) (island, Hawaii) **5:**352, 353
Oakland (California) **5:**52, 344
  earthquake (1989) **5:**335
Oases 1:242–43
  Algeria **1:**78
  Libya **1:**94–95, 97–98
  Libyan Desert **1:**112
  Sahara Desert **1:**24, 25
  Tunisia **1:**89, 90
  illus. **1:**22–23, 77, 96, 242

Oaxaca (capital, Oaxaca state, Mexico) **5:**412, 417
OAXACA (state, Mexico) **5:**375, **417**
Oaxaca, Valley of (Mexico) **5:**417
Obasanjo, Olusegun (president of Nigeria) **1:**229
Obeah men *see* Witch doctors
Oberammergau (Germany) **3:**273–74
Oberlin College (Ohio) **5:**274
Obiang Nguema Mbasogo, Teodoro (president of Equatorial Guinea) *see* Nguema Mbasogo, Teodoro Obiang
Obin, Philomé (Haitian artist) **5:**465
Obock (Djibouti) **1:**298
Obote, Milton (president of Uganda) **1:**322–23
Obregon, Álvaro (Mexican leader) **5:**387, 388
Ob River (Russia) **4:**308; **5:**56
  table(s)
    longest rivers of the world **6:**346
Obuchi Keizo (prime minister of Japan) **2:**472
Óbuda (now part of Budapest, Hungary) **4:**242
OCEANIA (islands, Pacific Ocean) **2:**473, **555–2:567** *see also* names of countries, islands, and island groups
  Australia, trade with **2:**503
  people in New Zealand **2:**544
  illus. **2:**555
    flags of the countries **2:**ix–x
  map(s) **2:**557
  table(s)
    countries and territories **2:**556
Ocean Island *see* Banaba
Oceans (of the world)
  levels predicted to rise **2:**574–75
  table(s) **6:**347
Ocho Rios (Jamaica) **5:**471
Ochrida (Ohrid), Lake (Albania–Macedonia) **4:**269, 291
O'Connell, Daniel (Irish leader) **3:**77
Ocotillo (desert shrub)
  illus. **5:**250
Odeillo (France) **3:**157
Oder-Neisse boundary line (Germany–Poland) **3:**283; **4:**222
Oder River (Europe) **3:**19, 243; **4:**213
Odessa (Ukraine) **4:**309, 333, 338
O'Donnell clan (Northern Ireland) **3:**148
Odyssey (epic poem by Homer) **4:**201, 202
OECD *see* Economic Cooperation and Development, Organization for
Offa (king of Mercia) **3:**128, 129
Offa's Dyke (earthwork, Wales) **3:**128
Official Languages Act (Canada, 1969) **5:**74
Ofu (island in American Samoa) **2:**603
Ogaden (region, Ethiopia) **1:**288, 291
  Somalia **1:**304
Ogallala Aquifer (North America) **5:**291, 303
Ogbomosho (Nigeria) **1:**218
Ogilvie Mountains (Canada) **5:**145
Oglethorpe, James (English colonist) **3:**105; **5:**236
Ogooué River (Gabon) **1:**252, 254
O'Gorman, Juan (Mexican artist)
  illus.
    Panel of Independence **5:**382
Ogou River (Togo) **1:**205
O'Higgins, Bernardo (Chilean soldier and statesman) **6:**97, 298, 321
OHIO 5:271–74
  illus.
    Columbus **5:**271

    Great Serpent Mound **5:**273
    Till Plains **5:**274
  map(s) **5:**272
Ohio and Erie Canal 5:273, 274
Ohio-Great Lakes-Mississippi Lowlands (North America) **5:**5
Ohio River (U.S.) **5:**258, 259, 260, 272, 273, 274, 279
  megalopolis area **5:**46
  Mississippi **5:**160
  Pittsburgh (Pennsylvania) **5:**212, 213
  South-Central States **5:**256
  illus. **5:**260
Ohio State University
  Institute of Polar Studies **6:**329
Ohrid (Macedonia) **4:**292
Ohrid, Lake *see* Ochrida (Ohrid), Lake
Oil (Petroleum) *see* Petroleum and petroleum industry
Oil sands 5:123, 127
Oirats (Asian people) **2:**363
Ojców National Park (Poland) **4:**213
Ojeda, Alonso de (Spanish explorer) **6:**97, 144
Ojibwa (Chippewa) (Indians of North America) **5:**105, 109, 164, 269, 275, 276, 278, 284, 286, 288, 292, 298
  Prairie Provinces **5:**111, 115
Ojocaliente (Zacatecas, Mexico) **5:**399
Ojukwu, C. Odemegwu (Biafran leader) **1:**228
Okanagan Lake (British Columbia) **5:**131
Okanagan River and Valley (Canada) **5:**69, 129
Okanogan (Indians of North America) **5:**130, 337
Okanogan Highlands (region, Washington) **5:**336
Okavango River (Cubango River) (Africa) **1:**342, 348, 351, 353
Okeechobee, Lake (Florida) **5:**238, 240
Okefenokee Swamp (Florida–Georgia) **5:**233–34, 237
Okhotsk, Sea of (Pacific Ocean)
  table(s)
    major seas of the world **6:**347
Okies (Dust Bowl refugees) **5:**307
OKLAHOMA 5:305–7
  illus.
    dust storm **5:**307
    Tulsa **5:**305
  map(s) **5:**306
Oklahoma City (capital, Oklahoma) **5:**306
  bombing of federal building **5:**307
Okoume trees 1:251, 259
Oktoberfest (German festival) **3:**249, 271
  illus. **3:**271
Oland (island, Sweden) **4:**39
Olavinlinna (fortress, Finland) **4:**52
  illus. **4:**53
Old Believers (*Raskolniki*) (Russian religious sect) **4:**310
Old Castile (historical region, Spain) **4:**80
Old Faithful (geyser, Yellowstone National Park) **5:**317
"Old Ironsides" (American warship) *see* Constitution (American warship)
Old Man of the Mountain (rock formation, New Hampshire) **5:**184
Old Man River (nickname for Mississippi River) **5:**160
Old South Meeting House (Boston, Massachusetts) **5:**190
Old Stone Age *see* Paleolithic
Olduvai Gorge (Tanzania) **1:**6, 336, 338

Olentangy River (Ohio) **5:**273
Olinda (Brazil) **6:**188
Olives
 illus. **4:**150
Olmecs (Indians of North America) **5:**375, 407, 419
 illus.
  carving **5:**419
Olosega (island in American Samoa) **2:**603
Olvera Street (Los Angeles, California) **5:**345
Olympia (capital, Washington) **5:**337–38
Olympia (Greece) **4:**198
Olympic Games
 Alps **3:**304
 Athens **4:**197, 211
 Australia **2:**492
 China **2:**385
 East German medal-winning **3:**250
 Japan **2:**463
 illus.
  Sydney (Australia) **2:**503
Olympic Mountains (Washington) **5:**8, 336, 338
Olympic National Park (Washington) **5:**336
 illus. **5:**336
Olympic Peninsula (Washington) **5:**336
Olympic Saddledome (Alberta)
 illus. **5:**125
Olympio, Sylvanus (president of Togo) **1:**209
Olympus, Mount (Washington) **5:**336
Omagh (Northern Ireland) **3:**149
Omaha (Indians of North America) **5:**291, 294, 301, 302
Omaha (Nebraska) **5:**301, 302
 illus. **5:**301
OMAN (Muscat and Oman) (Arabian Peninsula) **2:**136–37
 illus. **2:**136
  flag **2:**vii
 map(s) **2:**137
Oman, Gulf of 2:138
Omar I (second orthodox caliph, Mecca) **1:**119
Omar Khayyám (Persian poet) **2:**159
Omayyad dynasty (Arab dynasty) **2:**94
Omdurman (Sudan) **1:**126, 129
Omiéné (African people) **1:**253
Omsk (Russia) **2:**342
Ona (Indians of South America) **6:**270, 305
Onassis, Jacqueline Kennedy (widow of John F. Kennedy) **5:**194
Onega, Lake (Russia) **4:**308
 table(s)
  largest lakes **6:**347
Oneida (Indians of North America) **5:**95, 202
O'Neill, Susie (Australian athlete)
 illus. **2:**492
O'Neill clan (Northern Ireland) **3:**148
Onetti, Juan Carlos (Uruguayan author) **6:**257
Ong Teng Cheong (president of Singapore) **2:**312
Onilahy River (Madagascar) **1:**371
Onondaga (Indians of North America) **5:**95, 202
ONTARIO (province, Canada) **5:**94, 95, 96, 97, **104–9**
 history **5:**143
 resources **5:**40–41
 illus.
  Native American powwow **5:**106
  Ottawa **5:**104, 107
  Toronto **5:**108
 map(s) **5:**106

Ontario, Lake (Canada–U.S.) **5:**23, 97, 270
 table(s)
  largest lakes **6:**347
Ontario Highlands (Canada) **5:**105
Ontario Science Center (museum, Toronto)
 illus. **5:**105
Ontong Java (atoll, Solomon Islands) **2:**591, 592
OPEC *see* Organization of Petroleum Exporting Countries
Open University (United Kingdom) **3:**88
Opera
 Bulgaria **4:**262
 Europe **3:**24
 France **3:**179
 Germany **3:**258
 Italy **4:**141, 143, 158, 172
 Monaco **3:**205
 Myanmar **2:**264
 Vienna (Austria) **3:**317, 318
 illus.
  Bayreuth Festival **3:**256
Operation Bootstrap (Puerto Rico) **5:**168
Operation Restore Hope (aid to Somalia) **1:**305
Opium War (1839–1842) **2:**374, 395
Oporto (Portugal) **4:**67, 71, 72
 illus. **4:**74
Opryland USA (Nashville, Tennessee) **5:**265
Oran (Algeria) **1:**77, 80
Orange (France) **3:**160
Orange, House of (Netherlands royal family) **3:**234, 236
  William III and Mary II, rulers of England **6:**361
Orange City (Iowa) **5:**294
Orange Day Parade (Northern Ireland) **3:**145, 148
Orange Free State (province, South Africa) *see* Free State Province
Orange River (Africa) **1:**348, 396, 402
Oranges
 Valencia (Spain) **4:**107
 illus.
  Algeria **1:**81
  California groves **5:**42
  Florida **5:**237
  Israel **2:**110
  Valencia **4:**107
Orapa (Botswana) **1:**353
Orbán, Viktor (prime minister of Hungary) **4:**247
Orca *see* Killer whale
Ordaz, Diego de (Spanish explorer) **6:**147
Ordoñez, Antonio (Spanish matador) **4:**93
Ordzhonikidze, Sergo (Soviet leader) **2:**84
OREGON 5:50, **339–40**
 illus.
  Mount Hood **5:**339
  Pacific coast **5:**340
 map(s) **5:**340
Oregon Trail (U.S.) **5:**296, 316
Orellana, Francisco de (Spanish explorer) **6:**169
Ore Mountains *see* Erzgebirge Mountains
Oresund (the Sound) (strait, Sweden–Denmark) **4:**9, 45
Oresund Bridge (Sweden–Denmark) **4:**10
Organization of African Unity (OAU) 1:3, 6, 282
 Tanzania's invasion of Uganda **1:**323

Organization of American States (OAS) 6:110
 Alliance for Progress **6:**261
 Dominican Republic **5:**460
Organization of Eastern Caribbean States 5:440
Organization of Petroleum Exporting Countries (OPEC) 2:55, 129
 Ecuador **6:**200–201
Oribe, Manuel (president of Uruguay) **6:**264
Orient *see* East Asia
Oriente (province, Cuba) **5:**447
Oriente (tropical region of Ecuador) **6:**194
Orinoco River (South America) **6:**86, 146–47
 Columbus, Christopher **6:**82
 Venezuela **6:**132, 136, 144
 map(s) **6:**147
 table(s)
  longest rivers of the world **6:**346
Oriole Park (Camden Yards, Maryland)
 illus. **5:**219
Oriya language 2:199
Orizaba, Pico de (mountain, Mexico) **5:**357, 407
Orkney Islands (off Scotland) **3:**8, 81, 135, 140
 illus.
  monoliths **3:**133
Orlando (Florida) **5:**49, 241
Orléans (France) **3:**152
 illus. **3:**182
Orlich Bolmarich, Francisco J. (president of Costa Rica) **6:**71
Oromo (Galla) (African people) **1:**36, 285, 291
 illus. **1:**282
Oromo language 1:36, 285
Oromo Liberation Front (OLF) (Ethiopia) **1:**292
Orozco, José Clemente (Mexican artist) **5:**372, 402
Ortega Saavedra, Daniel (president of Nicaragua) **6:**59, 60
 illus. **6:**59
Orthodox Churches *see* Eastern Orthodox Churches
Oruro (Bolivia) **6:**233
Osage (Indians of North Americans) **5:**266, 291, 296, 303
Osage Plains (North America) **5:**295, 303
Osaka (Japan) **2:**440
Oseberg ship
 illus. **4:**32
Osei Tutu (Ashanti king) **1:**202
Oshawa (Ontario) **5:**106
Oshkosh (Wisconsin) **5:**286
Oslo (capital, Norway) **4:**30–32
 world's only ski museum **4:**34
 illus. **4:**30
  Oseberg ship **4:**32
Osman (legendary founder of Ottoman empire) *see* Othman
Osmanlis (Ottomans) (ancestors of modern Turks) **2:**57
Ossetia (region, republic of Georgia) **2:**85
Ossetians (Asian people) **2:**80, 82
Ossies (derogatory German name for former East Germans) **3:**252
Ostend (Belgium) **3:**217
 illus. **3:**220
Ostia (Italy) **4:**170
Ostland (historic German province) **4:**300
Ostrava (Czech Republic) **4:**225
Ostrogoths (East Goths) *see* Goths
Oświęcim (Nazi concentration camp, Poland) *see* Auschwitz

Otago (region, New Zealand) **2:**539, 541
Dunedin **2:**548
Otago, University of (New Zealand) **2:**548
Otavalo (Ecuador) **6:**198–99
illus. **6:**198
Otero, Alejandro (Venezuelan painter) **6:**142
Othman (Osman) (legendary founder of Ottoman Empire) **2:**64
Oti River (Togo) **1:**205
Oto (Indians of North America) **5:**291, 294, 301, 302
Otomi (Mexican Indian dialect) **5:**355
Otomí Indians 5:403
Otranto, Strait of (Albania–Italy) **4:**268
Ottawa (capital, Canada) **5:**41, 107
climate **5:**95
illus. **5:**104
House of Commons interior **5:**74
Parliament Building **5:**107
Ottawa (Indians of North America) **5:**108, 276, 278
Ottawa River (Canada) **5:**107
Ottawa Valley (Canada) **5:**102
Otto I (king of Germany) **3:**273; **4:**155
Otto I (king of Greece) **4:**196–97, 206
Otto II (Holy Roman emperor) **3:**321
Ottokar II (king of Bohemia) **3:**321
Ottoman Empire (Turkey) **2:**23, 56–57, 61, 64–67
Africa **1:**83, 92, 121
Armenia **2:**78
Bosnia and Herzegovina **4:**290
Bulgaria **4:**258–59
Eastern Europe **4:**272
Egypt **1:**119
Greece, history of **4:**187, 191, 192, 196, 205–8
Hungary controlled by Turks **3:**327; **4:**245
Israel, history of **2:**112
Libya **1:**100
Macedonia **4:**292
Malta **4:**183
Middle East, history of **2:**51–52, 102, 120–21, 154
Qatar **2:**143
Saudi Arabia **2:**127
Syria **2:**95
Ukraine **4:**339
Vienna, siege of (1683) **3:**322–23
Ouachita Highlands (Mountains) (U.S.) **5:**7, 256, 266, 305
Ouachita National Forest (Tennessee) **5:**267
Ouagadougou (capital, Burkina Faso) **1:**191, 192
Ouagadougou (early African kingdom) **1:**192
Oubri (traditional founder of Ouagadougou, Burkina Faso) **1:**192
Oueddei, Goukouni (president of Chad) **1:**244
Oueds (dry riverbeds) *see* Wadis
Ouegbadja (king of Dahomey) **1:**214
Ouémé River (Benin) **1:**211
Ouerhga River (Morocco) **1:**71
Ouidah (Benin) **1:**212
Oujda (Morocco) **1:**67
Oum er Rbia River (Morocco) **1:**66
Ounianga Kebir (Chad) **1:**242
Ouro Prêto (Brazil) **6:**187
Our River (Luxembourg) **3:**208
Ouse River (England) **3:**99
Outardes River (Quebec) **5:**102
Outback (interior of Australia) **2:**509–10
Outer Alster (lake, Hamburg, Germany) **3:**265

Outer Banks (North Carolina) **5:**227, 229
Ovambo (African people) **1:**348–49
Ovando Candia, Alfredo (Bolivian general) **6:**241
Overland Park (Kansas) **5:**304
Ovid (Roman poet) **4:**254
Oviedo (province, Spain) **4:**108
Ovimbundu (African people) **1:**343, 344, 346
Owen Falls Dam (Uganda) **1:**318, 320
illus. **1:**321
Oxen
illus. **2:**184; **4:**66; **6:**67, 208
Oxford University (England) **3:**105
Oxus River *see* Amu Darya
Oymyakon (Russia) **6:**345
Oyo (ancient city, Nigeria) **1:**214, 221, 226
Özal, Turgut (president of Turkey) **2:**67
Ozark Plateau (U.S.) **5:**7
Great Lakes States **5:**269, 281
Plains States **5:**295, 305
South-Central States **5:**256, 257, 266
Ozarks, Lake of the (Missouri) **5:**295
Özbeg (Kipchak monarch) **2:**352
Ozone layer 6:317, 327

• • • **P** • • •

Paccard, Michel (French mountain climber) **3:**302
Pacheco, Abel (president of Costa Rica) **6:**71
Pachuca (capital, Hidalgo, Mexico) **5:**406
Pacific, War of the (1879–1884) **6:**227, 240–41, 304, 321
Pacific coast Indians *see* Northwest culture area
Pacific Council *see* ANZUS Treaty
Pacific Islands, Trust Territory of the *see* Trust Territory of the Pacific Islands
Pacific islands and island groups 2:555–67 *see also* names of islands
Pacific Ocean
Micronesia **2:**568–70
Panama Canal **6:**78
Polynesia **2:**600–603
table(s)
oceans of the world **6:**347
Pacific Ranges (North America) **5:**8
PACIFIC STATES (region, U.S.) **5:**333–54
geologically active region **5:**157
precipitation **5:**159
resources **5:**50–52
illus.
coastline **5:**1, 333, 340
Paderewski, Ignace (Polish pianist and patriot) **4:**220
Padmasambhava (Buddhist monk) **2:**386
Padre Island (Texas) **5:**250
Paektu, Mount (North Korea) **2:**430
Pagalu (Annobón) (island, Equatorial Guinea) **1:**235
Pagan (Myanmar) **2:**270–71
Pago Pago (seat of government of American Samoa) **2:**602
Paguna copper mine (Papua New Guinea) **2:**589
Pahang River (Malaysia) **2:**303
Pahlavi dynasty (Iran) **2:**163
Paine, Cordillera del (Chile) **6:**316
Painted Desert (Arizona) **5:**327

Paiute (Indians of North America) **5:**21, 324, 325, 331, 332, 339
PAKISTAN 2:27, **180–94** *see also* Bangladesh
Afghanistan, relations with **2:**178
Bangladesh **2:**243
immigration to Northwest Territories **5:**142
India, relations with **2:**32, 219, 228
irrigation **2:**183
Kashmir **2:**170, 172–73
Mohenjo-Daro **2:**190
Muslim nationalism in India **2:**217
refugees to India **2:**203
women in society **2:**192–93
illus.
agriculture **2:**184
carpet weaving **2:**189
fishing **2:**190
flag **2:**viii
housing **2:**185
Islamabad **2:**185
mosque **2:**180
polo **2:**20
Rawalpindi **2:**186
sugarcane processing **2:**188
village **2:**180
women in Muslim dress **2:**191
map(s) **2:**182
Palace of Nations (Geneva, Switzerland) **3:**293
Palacios y Sojo, Pedro (Venezuelan composer) **6:**142
Pala dynasty (Bengal) **2:**243
Palais de Chaillot (Paris, France) **3:**202
Palais des Nations (Geneva, Switzerland) *illus.* **3:**61
Palakir (capital, Pohnpei, Federated States of Micronesia) **2:**573
Palatine Hill (Rome, Italy) **4:**165
PALAU 2:567, 569, 570, **571–72**
illus. **2:**571
flag **2:**ix
map(s) **2:**572
Palazzo Carignano (Turin, Italy) **4:**145
Palazzo Reale (Turin, Italy) **4:**145
Palembang (Indonesia) **2:**323
Palenque (ancient Mayan city, Mexico) **5:**418
Paleolithic (Old Stone Age) 3:45; **4:**110
Palermo (capital, Sicily) **4:**142, 146
Palestine (historic region in the Middle East) **2:**52, 112–15, 116, 121
Crusades **3:**53, 54
Jerusalem **2:**47
Palestine Liberation Organization (PLO) 2:52, 54, 103, 105, 115, 121, 129
Palestinian Arab refugees 2:99, 102, 119, 121
Jordan **2:**117
Lebanese camps attacked **2:**103
Persian Gulf **2:**31
illus. **2:**119
Palestinians 2:32, 52, 54, 55
Kuwait, expulsion from **2:**145
self-rule issue **1:**123; **2:**114–15
workers in Israel **2:**105
illus.
community on West Bank **2:**44
intifada **2:**54
Palimé (Togo) **1:**206
Palisades (cliffs, New York–New Jersey) **5:**202, 208
Palk Strait (Sri Lanka–India) **2:**245
Palma (capital, Balearic Islands, Spain) **4:**84
Palma, Ricardo (Peruvian writer) **6:**214
Palmares (historic republic in Brazil) **6:**188

Palmas, Cape (Liberia) **1:**179
Palme, Olaf (prime minister of Sweden) **4:**48
Palmer, Nathaniel B. (American sea captain)
 6:330–31
Palmer's Land (part of Antarctic Peninsula)
 6:331, 345
Palm trees
 Malaysia is world's largest producer of palm
  oil **2:**304
 Nigeria **1:**224
 illus. **6:**19
  extracting oil from kernels **1:**226
  weaving leaves **2:**574
Palmyra (Syria)
 illus. **2:**96
Palomares (Spain) **4:**110
Palouse Hills (Washington) **5:**336
Pamir (Pamirs) (mountains of central Asia) **2:**7,
 174, 343
 Tajikistan **2:**359
 Xinjiang **2:**380
Pamlico Sound (North Carolina) **5:**229
Pampas (grassy plains of South America) **6:**95,
 285, 295
 Argentina **6:**266, 283
 gauchos **6:**274–75
Pampas (Indians of South America) **6:**269
Pamplona (Spain)
 illus.
  running the bulls **4:**94
Pamunkey (Indians of North America) **5:**224
PANAMA 6:72–81
 Central America **6:**9, 10
 history **6:**15, 16
 Panama Canal **6:**14, 78–79
 population **6:**11
 United States, relations with the **6:**12, 13
 illus.
  flag **6:**vi
  national dance **6:**77
  Panama Canal **6:**73, 79
  Panama City **6:**75, 81
 map(s) **6:**76
  Panama Canal **6:**78
Panama, Gulf of 6:73
Panama, Isthmus of 6:72, 78, 80
Panama Canal 6:3, 14, 72, 78–79, 80
 Panama's income **6:**76
 turned over to Panamanian control **6:**13, 18
 illus. **6:**73, 79
 map(s) **6:**78
Panama Canal Zone (Panama) **6:**79, 80
Panama City (capital, Panama) **6:**72, 74, 76, 80,
 81
 illus. **6:**73, 75
  Balboa monument **6:**81
Panamanian Free Trade Zone 6:77
Panama Railroad 6:78, 80
Pan-American Health Organization 6:110
Pan-American Highway 6:73, 137
 Mexico **5:**365, 406
 illus. **6:**16
Pan-Americanism 6:110
Pan-American Union 6:110
Pan Am flight 103 bombing (1988) **1:**98
Panchimalco Indian Village (El Salvador) **6:**44
Panday, Basdeo (prime minister of Trinidad and
 Tobago) **5:**486
Pankisi Gorge (Georgia, republic of) **2:**85
Pannonia (ancient region, part of Roman
 Empire) **3:**320, 321; **4:**242
Pan-Slavic movement 4:279–80

Pantanal (wetlands, South America) **6:**262
Pantelleria (island, Italy) **4:**130
Panthéon (Paris, France) **3:**199
Pánuco (Veracruz, Mexico) **5:**407
Pánuco River (Mexico) **5:**396
Papaloapam River (Mexico) **5:**30
Papal States (Italian history) **3:**50; **4:**158, 159,
 167, 178
Papandreou, Andreas (prime minister of
 Greece) **4:**211
Papeete (Tahiti) **2:**559
 illus. **2:**558
Papua, Territory of (Pacific Ocean) **2:**590
PAPUA NEW GUINEA 2:315, 583, 585, 586,
 587–90, 593
 northern Solomons **2:**591
 illus. **2:**587, 590
  flag **2:**x
 map(s) **2:**588
Papuans (people) **2:**589
Pará (state, Brazil) **6:**187
Paracas (ancient civilization in Peru) **6:**222
Parades and processions
 Bastille Day in Paris **3:**196
 Finnish Independence Day **4:**63
 Mauritius **1:**381–82
 Mexican saint day celebrations **5:**366
 Northern Ireland's political parades **3:**145,
  148
 Red Square (Moscow, Russia) **4:**327
 Republic Day in Niger **1:**144
 Spanish Holy Week procession **4:**88
 Zurich (Switzerland) **3:**293
 illus.
  Aguascalientes' San Marcos Day **5:**404
  Cinco de Mayo celebration in Puebla
   5:414
  Darwin (Northern Territory, Australia) **2:**532
  German religious procession **3:**22
  Guinea's Independence Day **1:**167
  Hungarian religious procession **4:**241
  India's Republic Day **2:**219
  Korea, North **2:**432
  Polish religious procession **4:**213
  Solidarity parade in Poland **4:**223
  Spanish Holy Week procession **4:**88
  United Kingdom **3:**88
Paradies Glacier (Switzerland) **3:**244
PARAGUAY 6:242–50
 Euro-American culture **6:**95
 Mennonites in the Chaco **6:**248
 Mercosur **6:**262
 political history **6:**114
 Río de la Plata Basin **6:**284
 illus.
  Asunción **6:**242, 244
  cattle raising **6:**247
  children **6:**244
  flag **6:**vi
  lace-making **6:**245
  luxury hotel **6:**247
 map(s) **6:**246
Paraguayan War *see* Triple Alliance, War of the
Paraguay River (South America) **6:**86, 173, 231,
 242, 243, 244, 262
 Río de la Plata Basin **6:**284
Parakou (Benin) **1:**212, 214
Paramaribo (capital, Suriname) **6:**154
 illus. **6:**153, 156
Paraná (Argentina) **6:**299
Paraná (state, Brazil) **6:**171
Paraná-Paraguay river system 6:242

Paraná River (South America) **6:**86, 173, 242,
 262, 280
 Río de la Plata Basin **6:**284
 Rosario (Argentina) **6:**290
Paria, Gulf of (Trinidad and Tobago) **5:**485
Parima Mountains (Sierra Parima) (South
 America) **6:**146
PARIS (capital, France) **3:**159, **192–203**
 climate **3:**30
 fashion industry **3:**157–58
 Haussmann's redesign of **3:**186
 tourism **3:**15
 World War II **3:**188
 illus.
  Arc de Triomphe **3:**60
  Bastille Day **3:**197
  Champs-Élysées **3:**198
  Eiffel Tower **3:**203
  National Museum of Natural History **3:**58
  Notre Dame Cathedral **3:**150
  Place de la Concorde **3:**196
  Pont Neuf **3:**194
  Sacré-Coeur **3:**201
  Sainte-Chapelle **3:**194
 map(s) **3:**192
Paris, Treaty of (1763) **5:**85, 101
Paris, Treaty of (1783) **5:**219
Paris, Treaty of (1814) **1:**139, 382
Paris Commune (1871) **3:**187
Parisii (Gallic tribe) **3:**193
Park, Mungo (Scottish explorer) **1:**51, 149
Park Chung Hee (president of South Korea)
 2:438
Park Range (Colorado) **5:**318
Parks, Rosa (American civil-rights leader) **5:**244
Parks and gardens
 Charleston (South Carolina) **5:**232
 El Salvador **6:**44
 illus.
  Perth (Australia) **2:**526
Park Slope (neighborhood, New York City)
 5:205
Parliament, British 3:96
 England, history of **3:**117, 118, 119, 120
 illus.
  opening ceremony **3:**93
Parliament, Houses of (London)
 illus. **3:**111
Parliament, Scottish 3:141
 illus. **3:**140
Parliaments
 Iceland's Althing **4:**5
 Isle of Man **3:**84
 Italy **4:**153–54, 160
Parma (Ohio) **5:**274
Parnassus, Mount (Greece) **4:**198
Parnell, Charles Stewart (Irish leader) **3:**77
Parnu (Estonia) **4:**295
Parramatta River (Australia) **2:**511
Parrant, Pierre "Pig's Eye" (French settler of
 Minnesota) **5:**289
Parrots
 illus. **6:**10
Parry Islands (Northwest Territories, Canada)
 5:7, 141
Parsis (people) **2:**209
Parthenon (temple, Athens, Greece) **4:**195–96,
 203
 illus. **4:**185
Parthians (ancient Middle Eastern people)
 2:156, 162

Parti Québecois (Canadian political party) **5:**103

Partisans (in Yugoslavian history) **4:**280

Parton, Dolly (American musician) **5:**264

Parvanov, Georgy (president of Bulgaria) **4:**267

Pascua, Isla de see Easter Island

Pashto language 2:175, 187

Pashtoon (Asian people) see Pashtun

Pashtun (Pathan) (Asian people) **2:**175, 178, 181, 183

Passage rites
Togo **1:**207
illus. **1:**306

Passaic River (New Jersey) **5:**208, 210

Passau (Germany) **3:**326

Passover, Feast of 1:118

Passports 5:488

Pasternak, Boris (Soviet author) **4:**314, 331

Pastrana, Andrés (president of Colombia) **6:**129

Patagonia (plateau region, South America) **6:**86, 281–83
sheep ranching **6:**295
Tehuelche Indians **6:**270
Welsh settlers **6:**271, 279, 282
illus. **6:**285

Patan (Nepal) **2:**232

Patassé, Ange-Félix (president of Central African Republic) **1:**250

Patchouli oil 1:340

Paterson (New Jersey) **5:**208, 210

Pathan (Asian people) see Pashtun

Pathet Lao (Communist forces in Laos) **2:**283, 285

Patmos (Greek island) **4:**191

Pato (sport) **6:**274–75

Patos, Lagoa dos (lagoon or lake, Brazil) **6:**187

Patras (Greece) **4:**197

Patrick, Saint (patron saint of Ireland) **3:**75, 147

Patrocinio, José de (Brazilian statesman) **6:**112

Patroons (Dutch land owners in colonial North America) **5:**37

Patterson, Percival J. (prime minister of Jamaica) **5:**477

Patterson Inlet (New Zealand)
illus. **2:**538

Patuca River (Honduras) **6:**35

Patuxent (Indians of North America) **5:**218

Pátzcuaro (Michoacán, Mexico) **5:**409

Pátzcuaro, Lake (Mexico) **5:**409
illus. **5:**409

Paul (prince of Yugoslavia) **4:**280

Paul, Saint 2:94; **4:**112, 183, 205

Paul I (king of Greece) **4:**209, 210

Paulistas (people from São Paulo, Brazil) **6:**189

Paulo Afonso Falls (Brazil) **6:**160, 173

Pavarotti, Luciano (Italian singer) **4:**141

Pavia (Italy) **4:**136

Pavlov, Ivan (Russian physiologist) **4:**311

Pawnee (Indians of North America) **5:**292, 301, 302, 303

Pawtucket (Rhode Island) **5:**194

Paysandú (Uruguay) **6:**261

Paz, Octavio (Mexican author) **5:**373

Paz Estenssoro, Victor (president of Bolivia) **6:**241

Paz Zamora, Jaime (president of Bolivia) **6:**241

Peace River and Valley (Canada) **5:**8, 122
table(s)
longest rivers of the world **6:**346

Peace Tower (Ottawa) **5:**107

Peach State (nickname for Georgia) **5:**233

Peacock Throne 2:163

Pearl Harbor (U.S. naval base, Hawaii)
Japanese attack (December 7, 1941) **2:**447; **3:**277; **5:**353
illus.
U.S.S. *Arizona* Memorial **5:**353

Pearl River (Mississippi) **5:**246

Pearl (Zhu) River (China) **2:**410, 416

Peary, Robert E. (American explorer) **5:**64

Peary Land (region, Greenland) **5:**56

Peasants
China **2:**400–401
Cuba **5:**449
Egypt's fellahin **1:**102–6
Latin America **6:**6
Russia **4:**320, 321, 322
Syria **2:**92
Ukraine **4:**340

Peat 3:66; **4:**341
illus. **3:**66

Peçanha, Nilo (Brazilian statesman) **6:**112

Pecherskaya Lavra see Monastery of the Caves

Pechora River (Russia) **4:**308

Pecos River (New Mexico–Texas) **5:**321

Pécs (Hungary) **4:**242

Pedah (African people) **1:**212

Pedernales (Venezuela) **6:**147

Pedi (African people) **1:**398

Pedias River (Cyprus) **2:**69

Pedicabs
illus. **2:**271

Pedro I, Dom (emperor of Brazil) **6:**100, 189

Pedro II, Dom (emperor of Brazil) **6:**100, 189–90

Pedro Miguel (Panama) **6:**78

Peiping (China) see Beijing

Peipus, Lake (Estonia–Russia) **4:**293

Peking (China) see Beijing

Peking Man (prehistoric human being) **2:**371

Pelé (Brazilian soccer player) **6:**179

Pelevin, Victor (Russian writer) **4:**315

Pelicans
illus. **1:**263

Pella (Iowa) **5:**294

Pelly Mountains (Canada) **5:**145

Peloponnesian War (431–404 B.C.) **3:**47; **4:**203

Peloponnesus (peninsula, Greece) **4:**187, 188, 189, 198–99

Penal colonies 2:479, 488, 499–500; **6:**93
New South Wales **2:**511, 512
Queensland **2:**508
Tasmania **2:**531
illus.
Botany Bay (Australia) **2:**500
Port Arthur (Tasmania) **2:**531

Penal Laws (Great Britain, 1695) **3:**76, 77

Penang (Malaysia) see Pinang

Penghu (islands in the Taiwan Strait) see Pescadores

Penguins 2:517; **6:**327–28
illus. **2:**517; **6:**325, 328

Penn, William (English Quaker and founder of Pennsylvania) **3:**105; **5:**37, 213, 214

Pennacook (Indians of North America) **5:**185

Pennines (mountain chain, England) **3:**83, 98

PENNSYLVANIA 5:211–14
coal **5:**6–7
history **5:**37, 200
illus.
Amish farmer in Lancaster County **5:**211
Philadelphia **5:**214
map(s) **5:**212

Pennsylvania Dutch (people) **5:**212

Pennyroyal (region, Kentucky) **5:**261

People on the Street (painting, Kirchner)
illus. **3:**254

People's Liberation Army (Communist China) **2:**397

Peoria (Arizona) **5:**328

Pepel (Sierra Leone) **1:**171

Pepin III (the Short) (Frankish king) **3:**50; **4:**155

Pequonnock River (Connecticut) **5:**196

Perak River (Malaysia) **2:**303

Percé Rock (Quebec)
illus. **5:**102

Pereljil (Spanish territory, North Africa) **4:**86

Perekop Isthmus (Crimea) **4:**336

Peres, Shimon (Israeli leader) **2:**55, 115

Perestroika (Soviet policy) **4:**317–18, 323

Pérez, Carlos Andrés (president of Venezuela) **6:**148

Pérez, Juan (Spanish explorer) **5:**131

Pérez Balladares, Ernesto (president of Panama) **6:**81

Pérez Esquivel, Adolfo (Argentine sculptor) **6:**278

Pérez Jiménez, Marcos (Venezuelan dictator) **6:**147

Perfume 3:168

Périgueux (France) **3:**167

Perijá, Sierra de (branch of the Andes) **6:**132

Perim (island, Red Sea) **2:**130

Permafrost 5:55, 56, 63, 138, 142

Permanent Court of Arbitration see International Court of Justice

Pernambuco (state, Brazil) **6:**164, 173, 179, 186, 187, 188, 189

Perón, Eva (wife of Juan Perón) **6:**300
illus. **6:**300

Perón, Isabel (president of Argentina) **6:**300

Perón, Juan (Argentinian political leader) **6:**114, 274, 300

Perry, Matthew C. (American naval officer) **2:**445

Persepolis (ancient capital, Persia) **2:**21, 160
illus. **2:**15, 162

Pershing, John J. (American general) **5:**393

Persia (now **Iran**) **2:**153, 155, 162–63 see also Iran
Armenia **2:**78
art and literature **2:**159–60
Asia, history of **2:**21
Darius I **2:**20
Egypt, ancient **1:**119
Greece, history of **3:**46; **4:**203
Middle East, history of **2:**49
Pakistan **2:**192

Persian Gulf (arm of the Arabian Sea)
Bahrain **2:**140
Iran **2:**156
Kuwait **2:**144, 146
Oman **2:**136
Qatar **2:**142
Saudi Arabia **2:**122
Tigris and Euphrates Rivers **2:**50
United Arab Emirates **2:**138

Persian Gulf War (1991) see Gulf War

Persian (Farsi) language 2:44, 157, 159
Tajiks' language is similar **2:**359

Persson, Göran (prime minister of Sweden) **4:**48

Perth (capital, Western Australia, Australia) **2:**526
illus. **2:**526
expressways **2:**491

PERU 6:206–28
Amazon River **6:**168
Andes **6:**100–101
Chavín de Huántar **6:**221
colonial viceroyalty at Lima **6:**90, 100,
224–25
democracy **6:**115
economy **6:**88, 102–3
Ecuador, relations with **6:**192, 201
education **6:**106
immigration **6:**95
Indo-American culture **6:**89, 90, 91, 112
Moche **6:**223
population **6:**7
urban poverty **6:**105
illus.
alpacas **6:**206
Cuzco **6:**213, 219
farms **6:**208
flag **6:**vi
flea market **6:**6
houses on stilts **6:**218
legislative body **6:**225
Lima **6:**105, 214, 215, 217, 218, 224
Machu Picchu **6:**220
religious pilgrims **6:**211
students in uniforms **6:**216
Titicaca, Lake **6:**210
map(s) **6:**209
Peru (Humboldt) Current (Pacific Ocean)
6:207, 221, 315
Galápagos Islands **6:**202
Pescadores (islands in the Taiwan Strait) **2:**423
Peshawar (Pakistan) **2:**188
Pest (section of Budapest, Hungary) **3:**327;
4:242
Pétain, Henri (French field marshal) **3:**188
Petén (province, Guatemala) **6:**27, 29
Peter, Saint 4:180–81
Peter I (czar of Russia) *see* Peter the Great
Peter II (king of Yugoslavia) **4:**280
Peter I (island near Antarctica) **4:**24
Peter and Paul Fortress (St. Petersburg, Russia)
4:330
Peters, DeWitt (American artist) **5:**465
Peter the Great (Peter I) (czar of Russia)
4:320–21, 328
Finland **4:**55
Northeast Passage through the Arctic **5:**62
St. Petersburg **4:**330
Pétion, Alexandre (Haitian political leader)
5:469
Petitcodiac River (Canada) **5:**79, 85
Petite Suisse (region, Luxembourg) **3:**207
Petit Martinique (Caribbean island) **5:**481
Petit Piton (mountain, St. Lucia)
illus. **5:**489
Petőfi, Sándor (Hungarian poet) **4:**240
Petra (Jordan)
illus. **2:**120
Petrarch, Francesco (Italian poet) **4:**157
Petrified Forest National Park (Arizona) **5:**327
Petrodvorets (Russia)
illus. **4:**319
Petrograd (Russia) *see* St. Petersburg
Petroleum and petroleum industry
Aegean Sea **4:**199
African resources **1:**20
Alaska **5:**350
Alberta **5:**123
Algeria **1:**76

Angola **1:**344, 345
Antarctic moratorium **6:**334, 337, 338
Arctic region **5:**58–59, 64, 143
Argentina **6:**281
Asia **2:**33, 37
Asia, Southwest **2:**5, 52–53, 55
Australia **2:**490
Azerbaijan **2:**88, 89
Bahrain **2:**140, 141
Brunei **2:**330
California **5:**51
Cameroon **1:**234
Canada **5:**71, 127
Chad **1:**243
Colombia **6:**125
Congo **1:**259
Cuba **5:**451
Dallas-Fort Worth metropolitan area **5:**254
Ecuador **6:**200–201
Egypt **1:**116
energy crisis of the 1970s **5:**177
England **3:**102, 109
Equatorial Guinea **1:**235
Europe's limited supply and imports **3:**36
France **3:**157
Gabon **1:**254
Houston (Texas) **5:**253
Indonesia **2:**321, 322
Iran **2:**155, 156, 160, 161, 163
Iraq **2:**147, 151, 152, 154
Kazakhstan **2:**349
Kuwait **2:**144, 145–46
Libya **1:**99
Louisiana **5:**247, 248
Malaysia **2:**304
Mexico **5:**27, 28, 362–63, 396, 419
Middle Atlantic States **5:**200
New Brunswick **5:**86
Newfoundland **5:**82, 83
Nigeria **1:**218, 224
North Sea **3:**36, 89, 135
Norway **4:**26, 28, 34
Oklahoma **5:**306
Oman **2:**136, 137
Panama **6:**76, 77
Panama pipeline **6:**78
Pennsylvania **5:**211
Peru **6:**207, 221
Qatar **2:**142, 143
Romania **4:**254, 255
Russia **4:**309
Saskatchewan **5:**121
Saudi Arabia **2:**122, 128–29
Scotland **3:**135, 138, 141
Sicily **4:**130
Southern states **5:**49
Sudan **1:**130
Suez Canal **1:**121
Syria **2:**93
Texas **5:**255
Transcaucasian pipeline **2:**53, 88
Trinidad and Tobago **5:**485
Tunisia **1:**90
Turkmenistan **2:**358
United Arab Emirates **2:**138, 139
United States **5:**160
Venezuela **6:**88, 102, 131, 133, 136, 142–43,
144
Veracruz **5:**407
Yemen **2:**132, 133
illus.
Alaskan pipeline **5:**24, 350

Algeria **1:**82
Arctic **5:**55
Asia, Southwest **2:**6, 41
Ecuadorian pipeline **6:**201
Egypt **1:**116
Indonesia **2:**322
Nigeria **1:**224
Northern Territory (Australia) **2:**534
offshore rig **5:**361
oil derricks **6:**2, 144
oil pump **1:**255
oil refineries **1:**99; **2:**88, 123, 142, 160, 260
Trinidad and Tobago **5:**486
University of Petroleum in Saudi Arabia
2:128
map(s)
world distribution **6:**355
Petronas Towers (Kuala Lumpur, Malaysia)
illus. **2:**253
Peul (Peuhl) *see* Fulani
Pharaohs (rulers of ancient Egypt) **1:**110,
117–18
Pharos (lighthouse at Alexandria, Egypt) **1:**115
Philadelphia (Pennsylvania) **5:**199, 213, 214
history **5:**37
megalopolis area **5:**46
metropolitan-area population **5:**200
illus.
city hall **5:**214
Philhellenes (pro-Greek foreigners in Greek
revolution) **4:**206
Philip (prince of the United Kingdom, duke of
Edinburgh)
illus. **2:**479; **3:**118
Philip IV (king of France) **3:**181
Philip II (king of Macedon) **4:**203
Philip I (king of Spain) **4:**115
archduke of Austria **3:**321
Philip II (king of Spain) **3:**235–36; **4:**96, 98,
115; **6:**188
Philippines named in his honor **2:**339
Philip III (king of Spain) **4:**115
Philip IV (king of Spain) **4:**115
Philip V (king of Spain) **4:**116
Philippe (crown prince of Belgium) **3:**224
Philippeville (Algeria) *see* Skikda
Philippi (Greece) **4:**205
PHILIPPINES 2:331–40
Asia, Southeast **2:**254, 258, 264
government instability **2:**30
Polynesians, origin of **2:**600
religion **2:**255
women's rights **2:**39
illus.
Aquino, Corazon **2:**339
flag **2:**ix
folk dance **2:**333
Manila **2:**261, 331
rice fields near Mount Mayon **2:**337
rural village **2:**336
University of Santo Tomas **2:**334
map(s) **2:**332
Phillip, Captain Arthur (English sea captain)
2:499, 500
Phillip Island (Australia) **2:**517
Philosophes (French writers) **3:**178
Phnom Penh (capital, Cambodia) **2:**257, 262,
287, 291, 302
Phoenicians (people) **2:**49, 98, 101–2
Algeria **1:**83

Phoenicians (cont.)
alphabetical system of writing **2:**94
Cyprus **2:**72
Lebanon **2:**97
Libya **1:**99
Morocco **1:**72
Spanish settlements **4:**110
Tunisia **1:**91
Phoenix (capital, Arizona) **5:**50, 328–29
Phoenix Islands (Kiribati) **2:**569, 580
Phosphate 2:560
Banaba **2:**580–81, 582
Christmas Island **2:**488
Florida **5:**12, 160
Morocco **1:**71
Nauru **2:**577–78, 579
Peru's guano production **6:**103, 221, 226
Togo **1:**54
illus. **2:**577
Togolese mine **1:**208
Phutai (Asian people) **2:**275
Piankashaw (Indians of North America) **5:**280
Piast dynasty (Poland) **4:**219
Piave River (Italy) **4:**129
Piazza del Duomo (Milan, Italy) **4:**135, 143
Picacho Mountain (Tegucigalpa, Honduras)
6:36
Picasso, Pablo (Spanish-born painter) **3:**177;
4:102
bust of Apollinaire **3:**199
Piccadilly Circus (London, England)
illus. **3:**109
Pichincha, Battle of (1822, Ecuador) **6:**194, 199,
204
Pichincha, Cerro (mountain, Ecuador) **6:**194,
195
Pico (in names of mountains) *see* the main part
of the name
Picts (ancient people) **3:**135, 140
Pictured Rocks National Lakeshore (Michigan)
5:269, 275
illus. **5:**275
Pidgin, Melanesian (language) **2:**589, 593
Piedmont (region, Italy) **4:**152, 155, 158
Piedmont (region, U.S.) **5:**153, 215, 230, 242
Georgia **5:**233, 234
Middle Atlantic States **5:**199
New Jersey **5:**207–8
North Carolina **5:**227
Pennsylvania **5:**211
South, The **5:**49
Southern States **5:**220
Pieniny (mountains, Poland) **4:**213
Pierre (capital, South Dakota) **5:**300
Pigs
Vanuatu culture **2:**595
illus. **6:**30
Pike, Zebulon M. (American explorer) **5:**291,
320
Pikes Peak (Colorado) **5:**320
Pilapila (African people) **1:**213
Pilatus, Mount (Switzerland) **3:**295
illus. **3:**304
Pilcomayo River (South America) **6:**231, 280,
284
Pilgrimage Church of the Wies (Bavaria, Ger-
many) **3:**255
Pilgrims (settlers in U.S.) **5:**165, 174, 181, 188,
191
Pilica River (Poland) **4:**213
Pilipino language 2:334
Pillars of Hercules (Gibraltar) **4:**123

Piłsudski, Józef (Polish statesman) **4:**220
Pinang (Penang) (Malaysia) **2:**307, 308, 312
Pinar del Río (city and province, Cuba) **5:**443
Piñata (Mexican custom) **5:**367
Pinatubo, Mount (volcano, Philippines) **2:**336
Pindling, Lynden O. (prime minister of Baha-
mas) **5:**425
Pindus Mountains (Greece) **4:**189
Pineapple Island *see* Lanai
Pine Barrens (New Jersey) **5:**199, 208
illus. **5:**208
Pine Hills (region, Mississippi) **5:**245
Pine Mountains (Kentucky) **5:**260
Pine Ridge (Nebraska) **5:**301
Pine Ridge Indian Reservation (South Dakota)
5:300
Pines, Lake o' the (Texas) **5:**250
Pine trees 5:17–18, 343
Piney Woods (area in Louisiana, Texas, and
Arkansas) **5:**250
Ping River (Thailand) **2:**274
Pinnacle Desert (Western Australia)
illus. **2:**527
Pinochet Ugarte, Augusto (Chilean political
leader) **6:**322, 323
Pinto, Edgar Roquette (Brazilian anthropologist)
6:177
Pinyin System (for writing Chinese in Roman
characters) **2:**402
Pinzón, Vicente (Spanish explorer) **6:**97, 169
Pipestone National Monument (Minnesota)
5:289
Pipil (Indians of Central America) **6:**42, 43
Piraeus (Greece) **4:**195
Pirapóra (Brazil) **6:**173
Pirates and buccaneers
Bahamas **5:**424
Barbary pirates **1:**97
Belize **6:**15, 19
Caribbean Sea and islands **5:**430–32
Costa Rica **6:**62
Haiti **5:**467
Jamaica **5:**476
Outer Banks of North Carolina **5:**229
United Arab Emirates **2:**139
Venezuela **6:**145
Pisa (Italy) **4:**156
illus.
Leaning Tower **4:**135
Piscataway (Indians of North America) **5:**218
Pisco (brandy) **6:**212, 309
Pisco (Peru) **6:**212
Pissarro, Camille (French painter) **3:**177
Pitcairn Islands (Pacific Ocean) **2:**562–63, 601;
3:90
illus. **2:**562
Pitchblende (ore) **4:**227
Pitch Lake (Trinidad) **5:**485
Pitjantjatjara (aboriginal tribe, Australia) **2:**522
Piton de la Fournaise (volcano, Réunion) **1:**46
Piton des Neiges (Réunion) **1:**46
Pitons (mountains, St. Lucia)
illus. **5:**489
Pitt Islands (New Zealand) **2:**537, 544
Pittsburgh (Pennsylvania) **5:**46, 200, 213
Pittsburgh Agreement (1918) **4:**235
Pius IX (pope) **4:**178
Pizarro, Francisco (Spanish conqueror of the
Incas) **6:**90, 97, 204, 217, 218, 224, 240
Pizarro, Gonzalo (Spanish conquistador) **6:**169,
224
Pla (African people) **1:**212

Plague (disease) *see* Black Death
Plaid Cymru (Welsh political party) **3:**130
Plains Indians (North America) **5:**23, 164
Plains of Abraham *see* Abraham, Plains of
Plains regions (North America) **5:**111, 118, 123,
128 *see also* Plains States
Canada **5:**69
Montana **5:**311
Wyoming **5:**315, 316
Plains regions (South America) **6:**251, 253, 259
see also Pampas (grassy plains of South
America)
PLAINS STATES (region, U.S.) **5:**290–307
resources **5:**47, 48
illus.
farm **5:**290
Plaka (section, Athens, Greece) **4:**197
illus. **4:**197
Plankton 6:328–29
Plantagenet family (rulers of England)
list of **6:**360
Plantation system (agriculture)
Brazil **6:**93–95, 164, 167, 190
British North America **5:**35, 36
Ecuador **6:**196, 198
Florida **5:**238, 241
Georgia **5:**236
Latin America **6:**6
Puerto Rico **5:**168
South-Central States **5:**257
Southern States **5:**220, 221, 222
Spanish North America **5:**26
illus.
Southern plantation house **5:**220
Plant life *see also* Flowers; Forests and forestry
Arctic **5:**59, 63, 73
Brazil **6:**172, 173–74
California **5:**343
Cameroon **1:**232
Colombia **6:**117–18
England **3:**101
Ethiopia **1:**284
Europe **3:**32–33
Everglades **5:**240
Galápagos Islands **6:**203
General Sherman Tree **5:**342
Himalayas **2:**167
Indonesia's Wallace Line **2:**315–17
Latin America **6:**3
Liechtenstein **3:**306
Madagascar **1:**50, 369
Nevada **5:**331
New Zealand **2:**477, 541
North Carolina **5:**227
Paraguay **6:**243
Puerto Rico **5:**167
Sonoran Desert **5:**329
Sri Lanka **2:**246
United States **5:**161
illus.
California's deserts **5:**343
map(s)
world vegetation **6:**353
Plata, Río de la (estuary, South America) **6:**86,
173, 284, 296
Argentina **6:**285, 292
Paraguay **6:**242
Uruguay **6:**259, 260, 263
Plate tectonics 2:476, 537
Plato (Greek philosopher) **3:**47
Platt Amendment (U.S., 1901) **5:**446, 450
Plattdeutsch (German dialect) **6:**248

Platte River and Valley (Nebraska) **5:**301
Platypus 2:477, 489
state animal of New South Wales **2:**510
illus. **2:**510
Plaza de la Constitución (Mexico City) *see* Zócalo
Plaza Lasso, Galo (Ecuadorian statesman) **6:**200, 205
Pliny the Elder (Roman historian) **1:**89
PLO *see* Palestine Liberation Organization
Ploeşti (Romania) **3:**36; **4:**254, 255
Plymouth (capital, Montserrat) **5:**439
Plymouth (Massachusetts) **5:**174, 181, 191
Plymouth Rock 5:191
Plzeň (Czech Republic) **4:**224
Po, Fernão do (Portuguese explorer) **1:**236
Poás (volcano, Costa Rica) **6:**63
Pocahontas (Native American) **5:**226
Pocatello (Idaho) **5:**314
Pocomoke (Indians of North America) **5:**218
Podgorica (Yugoslavia) **4:**277
Podor (Senegal) **1:**153
Poetry
Albania **4:**270
Chile **6:**308, 309
France **3:**178
Hungary **4:**240
Japan **2:**460
Korea **2:**431–32
Manas (Kyrgyz epic) **2:**355
Paraguay **6:**249
Russia **4:**314, 315
Sumerians **2:**48
Uruguay **6:**256–57
Pohnpei (Ponape) (state, Federated States of Micronesia) **2:**569, 570, 573
Pointe-Noire (Congo) **1:**257, 258, 259
illus. **1:**259
Point Four (Latin American economic assistance program) **6:**113
Poitiers, Battle of (1356) **3:**182
POLAND 3:2; **4:212–23**
Belarus, history of **4:**341, 343
Belavezhskaya Pushcha **4:**341–42
economy **3:**25
farms **3:**36
Germans **3:**279
Lithuania, history of **4:**304
Nazi invasion (1939) **3:**277
Oder-Neisse boundary line **3:**283
population **3:**19
Ukraine, history of **4:**332, 339
illus.
automobile industry **4:**219
Cracow **4:**216
flag **4:**v
Gdańsk **4:**218
plains **4:**212
religious procession **4:**213
Solidarity parade **4:**223
Warsaw **4:**217
map(s) **4:**214
Polar bears 5:59, 115
illus. **5:**6, 59, 72, 117
Polar continental air mass 5:14
Polar Pacific air mass 5:14–15, 17
Polar regions *see* Antarctica; Arctic
Polder (land reclaimed from the sea) **3:**212, 227, 228
Police
Canadian "Mounties" **5:**73

Haitian Tontons Macoute **5:**470
London's bobbies **3:**110
Romanian secret police **4:**257
Police Motu (language) **2:**589
Polisario Front (Saharan guerrillas) **1:**55, 133
Polish Americans 5:216
Polish Partitions (1772, 1793, 1795) **3:**274; **4:**220
Politburo (in Communist government)
China, People's Republic of **2:**422
Pollution
Black Forest **3:**258
Canadian-U.S. tensions **5:**71
Colombia **6:**119
Czech Republic **4:**225
England's Midlands **3:**99
European cities **3:**23
European rivers **3:**33
Germany **3:**245
Great Lakes cleanup **5:**270
Japan **2:**440
Latvia **4:**299
Netherlands **3:**230
Ohio, restoration of waterways **5:**272, 274
Poland **4:**217
Romania **4:**255
Taiwan **2:**427
illus.
Romania **4:**254
Polo (sport) **3:**104; **6:**274
illus. **2:**20; **3:**107
Polo, Marco (Venetian traveler) **2:**16, 250, 324, 421
Italian cuisine **4:**137
illus. **2:**23
Polotsk (Belarus) **4:**343
Pol Pot (Cambodian political leader) **2:**292
Poltava, Battle of (1709) **4:**49
Polygamy 5:326
Polygons (Arctic soil patterns) **5:**56
illus. **5:**142
POLYNESIA (islands, Pacific Ocean) **2:**562, 567, **600–603**
table(s) **2:**520
Polynesians (Pacific islanders) **2:**561–62, 563, 574, 601–2 *see also* Maori
Auckland (New Zealand) **2:**547
Easter Island **6:**322
Hawaii **5:**352, 353
Solomon Islands **2:**592
Tonga **2:**605
Torres Strait Islands (Australia) **2:**495, 508
Tuvalu **2:**611, 612
Western Samoa **2:**607
Pombal, Marquês de (Portuguese statesman) **4:**71
Pomo (Indians of North America) **5:**346
Pompéia, Raúl (Brazilian writer) **6:**180
Pompeii (Italy) **4:**128, 144
illus. **4:**156
Pompidou, Georges (president of France) **3:**190
Ponape (state, Federated States of Micronesia) *see* Pohnpei
Ponca (Indians of North America) **5:**291, 301, 302
Ponce (Puerto Rico) **5:**168
Ponce de León, Juan (Spanish explorer) **5:**173, 237, 241
Pondicherry (India) **2:**221
Ponies *see* Horses
Pontchartrain, Lake (Louisiana) **5:**247

Pont du Gard (aqueduct, near Nîmes, France) **3:**180
illus. **3:**180
Pont Neuf (bridge, Paris) **3:**195
illus. **3:**194
Pontresina (Switzerland) **3:**288
Poopó, Lake (Bolivia) **6:**86
Popayán (Colombia) **6:**120
Popes (Roman Catholic Church) **4:**177–81 *see also* Papal States
Avignon (France) **3:**181–82
list of **6:**366–68
Popocatepetl (volcano, Mexico) **5:**31, 357, 414
illus. **5:**357
Popular Front (Spanish political party) **4:**117
Popular Movement for the Liberation of Angola (MPLA) 1:346
Population *see also* the fact boxes of continent, country, and state articles
Africa's problems **1:**2, 63
Asia **2:**6
Asia, South **2:**171
Asia has 61 percent of world's population **2:**7
Europe **3:**35
Latin America, problems of a youthful population **6:**107–8
Ohio, America in miniature **5:**271, 272
U.S. Census Bureau projections **5:**173
youthful regions of Canada **5:**124, 138, 142
map(s)
Africa **1:**17
Asia **2:**5
Europe **3:**29
South America **6:**99
world density **6:**353
table(s)
by continent **6:**344
Population control
Asia **2:**39–40
China **2:**384–85
India's program **2:**223–24
Tunisia **1:**87
Vietnam **2:**295
illus.
Indian advertisement **2:**223
Population Registration Act (South Africa, 1950) **1:**58
Porcelain *see* Pottery
Po River (Italy) **4:**128, 132, 133, 151, 152, 160
valley **3:**29
Poro (secret society in Liberia) **1:**181, 182
Portales, Diego (Chilean statesman) **6:**321
Port Anson (Malaysia) *see* Telok Anson
Port Arthur (Tasmania, Australia)
illus. **2:**531
Port-au-Prince (capital, Haiti) **5:**462, 463
illus. **5:**469
Episcopal cathedral murals **5:**466
women cleaning sidewalks **5:**464
Port Elizabeth (South Africa) **1:**398, 401, 402
Porteños (inhabitants of Buenos Aires, Argentina) **6:**266, 290, 297, 298
Port-Gentil (Gabon) **1:**251, 253, 254
illus. **1:**253
Porthan, Henrik Gabriel (Finnish historian) **4:**55
Port Harcourt (Nigeria) **1:**51, 218, 220, 224
illus. **1:**224
Portillo, Alfonso (president of Guatemala) **6:**33
Portinari, Cândido (Brazilian artist) **6:**182
Port Jackson (Sydney, Australia) **2:**511

Portland (Maine) **5:**183
Portland (Oregon) **5:**340
Port Louis (capital, Mauritius) **1:**378, 379, 381
  illus. **1:**378
Port Moresby (capital, Papua New Guinea)
  2:589
  illus.
    sailboat in harbor **2:**587
Pôrto Alegre (Brazil) **6:**187
Portobello Market (antique-shop district, Lon-
  don (England))
  illus. **3:**100
Port of Spain (capital, Trinidad and Tobago)
  5:485
  illus.
    Carnival **5:**483
Pôrto Grande (Cape Verde) **1:**150
Porto-Novo (capital, Benin) **1:**211, 214
Porto-Novo (Jakin) (early African kingdom) *see*
  Jakin
Port Phillip Bay (Australia) **2:**519
Port Royal (Jamaica) **5:**432, 476
Port Royal (Nova Scotia) *see* Annapolis Royal
Port Said (Egypt) **1:**113, 114, 120, 121
Portsmouth (North Carolina) **5:**229
Portsmouth (Rhode Island) **5:**194
Port Stanley (Falkland Islands) *see* Stanley
Port Sudan (Sudan) **1:**126
Port Swettenham (Malaysia) **2:**307
PORTUGAL 4:65–78
  Angola, history of **1:**48, 341, 346
  farms **3:**35
  Guinea-Bissau **1:**165
  Macau **2:**416
  Mozambique **1:**48, 367–68
  overseas provinces and territories **4:**65–66,
    68, 77–78
  São Tomé and Príncipe **1:**237–38
  South America, exploration and colonization
    6:3, 82, 97, 100
  illus.
    beach **4:**70
    flag **4:**v
    Lisbon **4:**73
    Monument of Discoveries **4:**76
    Oporto **4:**74
    traditional fishing boat **4:**66
    vineyards **4:**65
    women at fish market **4:**69
  map(s) **4:**67
Portuguese-Americans 5:181
Portuguese Guinea *see* Guinea-Bissau
Portuguese language
  Africa **1:**15
  Latin America **6:**1, 6, 82, 162, 165–66
  widely used in Age of Exploration **4:**75
Portuguese Timor *see* East Timor
Port-Vila (capital, Vanuatu) **2:**594, 595, 596
  illus. **2:**594
Port Weld (Malaysia) **2:**307
Post, Pieter (Dutch architect) **6:**168
Postojna Cave (Slovenia) **4:**282
Potash 1:259; **3:**38, 245; **5:**121, 160
Potatau (Maori king) **2:**553
Potatoes
  Irish famine (1840s) **3:**35, 76
  South America **6:**91, 215–16
Potawatomi (Indians of North America) **5:**276,
  282
Poteca River (Central America) **6:**35
Potgieter, Andries (Boer leader) **1:**404

Potlatch (American Indian gift-giving feast)
  5:132
Potomac River (U.S.) **5:**43, 218, 223, 258
Potosí (Bolivia) **6:**234
Potsdam (Germany) **3:**265–66
Potsdam Conference (1945) **3:**266, 279
Potsdamer Platz (city square, Berlin, Germany)
  3:281
Pottery
  ancient Asian civilizations **2:**11
  Diaguita Indians **6:**268
  French luxury industries **3:**157
  Korea **2:**432
  Meissen porcelain **3:**268
  New Zealand **2:**545–46
  Peru **6:**214, 222
  illus. **3:**23
    Bangladesh **2:**242
    Finland **4:**60
    Meissen porcelain **3:**269
Poverty
  Africa **1:**2, 5, 62–64
  Asia **2:**33, 36–37
  Bangladesh **2:**240, 241
  Brazil **6:**161–62, 169
  Ecuador **6:**196
  El Salvador **6:**44–45
  Haiti **5:**463, 467
  Honduran farmers **6:**37
  India **2:**197, 224–25
  Jamaica **5:**472; **5:**475
  Nicaragua **6:**55
  Romania **4:**255
  Tunisia **1:**87
  Venezuela **6:**139, 148
  Vietnam **2:**298
Power, Electric *see* Electric power
Powerscourt gardens (Ireland)
  illus. **3:**75
Powhatan (Native American chieftain) **5:**226
Prado (museum, Madrid, Spain) **4:**97
  illus. **4:**97
Prado, Pedro (Chilean author) **6:**309
Prado y Ugarteche, Manuel (Peruvian political
  leader) **6:**227
Prague (capital, Czech Republic) **4:**224, 226–27,
  229
  airport **3:**42
  automobiles **3:**41
  early oil street lamps **3:**36
  tourism **3:**16
  illus. **4:**224, 228
Prague Spring (Czechoslovakian history) **3:**63;
  4:230, 235
  illus. **4:**230
Prahova Valley (Romania) **4:**254
Praia (capital, Cape Verde) **1:**150
Prairie Plain (South Dakota) **5:**299
PRAIRIE PROVINCES (Canada) **5:**39, 41–42,
  110–27
  illus. **5:**110
Prairies *see* Grasslands
Prajadhipok (king of Thailand) **2:**280
Pra River (Ghana) **1:**195
Praslin (island in the Seychelles group) **1:**339
"Praying Ministers" (sculpture, Birmingham,
  Alabama)
  illus. **5:**242
Precipitation
  Arctic **5:**57
  Australia **2:**476, 517, 521–22

  Bangladesh **2:**238–39
  Cherrapunji (India) **2:**199
  Congo, Democratic Republic of **1:**262–63
  Debundscha (Cameroon) is one of the
    world's wettest places **1:**231
  Florida's thunderstorms **5:**238
  Ireland's rainfall **3:**67
  New Zealand **2:**476, 540–41
  Peru's garúa **6:**207
  rain-forest destruction leads to decreased
    rainfall **6:**74
  Sahara Desert **1:**25
  Spain's is lowest in Western Europe **4:**83
  U.S. Pacific Northwest **5:**159
  "wettest place in Europe" **4:**276
  map(s)
    Africa **1:**17
    Asia **2:**5
    Europe **3:**29
    South America **6:**98
    world **6:**354
  table(s)
    extremes **6:**345
Pre-Columbian period (Americas) **6:**90
  Chavín de Huántar **6:**221
  Guatemala **6:**27–28
  Mexico **5:**374–79
  Moche **6:**223
  Peru **6:**221–22
  illus.
    Chimú sculpture **6:**222
    sculpture **6:**238
Prehistoric people
  Africa was first home of **1:**5–6
  Arizona **5:**329
  Asia **2:**11
  Denmark **4:**19–20
  Easter Islanders **6:**323
  humanoid fossils **1:**244, 271, 336, 403
  Java Man **2:**323
  Kenya **1:**312
  Lascaux cave paintings **3:**167, 177
  Libya's cave paintings **1:**93, 99
  migration from Asia to North America **5:**163
  monuments in North America **5:**173
  New Mexico **5:**322
  Oceania **2:**562–63
  Peking Man **2:**371
  Stonehenge **3:**114
  U.S. Pacific States **5:**334–35
Premadasa, Ranasinghe (president of Sri
  Lanka) **2:**250
Premier *see* Prime minister
Prempeh I (Ashanti king) **1:**202
Presbyterian Church
  Scotland **3:**141
Présence Africaine (literary journal) **1:**158
Presidents of France
  list of **6:**364
Presidents of the U.S.
  Ohio, seven U.S. presidents from **5:**273
  table(s) **6:**359
Presley, Elvis (American singer, actor) **5:**263,
  264
  illus.
    birthplace **5:**246
Prespa, Lake (Albania–Macedonia) **4:**269, 291
Pressburg (Slovakia) *see* Bratislava
Pretoria (administrative capital, South Africa)
  1:398, 400, 402
Préval, René (Haitian president) **5:**470

PRI (Mexican political party) *see* Institutional Revolutionary Party
Pribilof Islands (Alaska) **5:**348
Price, George (Belizean political leader) **6:**24
Prigov, D. A. (Russian poet) **4:**315
Prime minister (premier) (government)
  table(s)
    Australian prime ministers **6:**362
    British prime ministers **6:**361–62
    Canada **6:**360
    New Zealand prime ministers **6:**363
PRINCE EDWARD ISLAND (province, Canada) **5:**40, 77, 80, **87–89**
  map(s) **5:**89
Prince George (British Columbia) **5:**131
Prince of Wales (British title) **3:**129–30
Prince William Sound (Alaska) **5:**350
Princip, Gavrilo (Serbian assassin) **3:**324; **4:**280, 289
Principality (country ruled by a prince)
  Andorra **4:**121
  Liechtenstein **3:**305–7
  Monaco **3:**204–6
Príncipe (island, São Tomé and Príncipe) **1:**238
Pripet Marshes (Belarus–Ukraine) **4:**333, 341
Pripyat (Pripet) River (Europe) **4:**333, 341
Priština (Yugoslavia)* **4:**277
Prithwi Narayan Shah (king of Nepal) **2:**233
Privatization *see also* Market economy
  Africa **1:**64
  Bulgaria **4:**264, 265
  Estonia **4:**295
  France **3:**158
  Kazakhstan **2:**349
  Latvia **4:**299
  Mexico **5:**363–64, 388
  Mongolia **2:**364
  Nicaragua **6:**60
  Romania **4:**255
  Russia **4:**318, 319
Processions *see* Parades and processions
Prochorus, Saint **4:**191
Prodi, Romano (prime minister of Italy) **4:**163
Progreso (Yucatán, Mexico) **5:**421
Prohibition era (1920–1933, in U.S. history)
  Bermuda's tourist industry **5:**33
  Tijuana **5:**390
Project Moses (Venice, Italy) **4:**148
Prokofiev, Sergei (Russian composer) **4:**314
Promontory (Utah) **5:**310
Protection of Antarctic Environment (protocol, 1998) **6:**337
Protestantism
  Brazil **6:**162, 168
  Germany **3:**247, 273
  Mennonites in the Chaco **6:**248
  Northern Ireland **3:**87, 144, 145
  Reformation in European history **3:**56, 119, 294
  Spain **4:**89
  Tuvalu **2:**611
  U.S. population **5:**171
  illus. **5:**165
Protestant Reformation *see* Reformation
Protests *see* Riots and demonstrations; Strikes
Proust, Marcel (French author) **3:**178
Provence (region, France) **3:**156, 160, 163
Providence (capital, Rhode Island) **5:**181, 193–94
  illus. **5:**192
Provincetown (Massachusetts) **5:**191
Provo (Utah) **5:**324–25

Prussia (former German state) **3:**186, 273, 274, 275
  Polish Partitions **4:**220
Prut River (Moldova–Romania) **4:**249, 345
Pskov (Russia) **4:**315
Psychology
  Chilean personality **6:**309
  Dutch way of life **3:**229–30
  Japanese group harmony **2:**448–50, 471
  mistral winds said to affect people **3:**151
  Spanish national character **4:**92–93
Ptolemies (kings of Egypt, 323–30 B.C.) **1:**111, 115, 119
Ptolemy I (king of Egypt) **1:**119
Pubs (Public houses) **3:**25
  illus. **3:**68
Pucará (Peru) **6:**214
Puebla (capital, Puebla state, Mexico) **5:**376, 380, 414
PUEBLA (state, Mexico) **5:**414
Pueblo (Colorado) **5:**320
Pueblos (Indians of North America) **5:**24–25, 164, 309, 321, 322
Puerta del Sol (Madrid) **4:**97
  illus. **4:**96
Puerto Ayacucho (Venezuela) **6:**147
Puerto Baquerizo (chief town of Galápagos Islands) **6:**203
Puerto Barrios (Guatemala) **6:**32
Puerto Cabello (Venezuela) **6:**133
Puerto Cabezas (Nicaragua) **6:**56
  illus. **6:**56
Puerto Montt (Chile) **6:**316
  illus. **6:**310
Puerto Páez (Venezuela) **6:**146
Puerto Ricans
  Wilmington (Delaware) **5:**216
Puerto Rico **5:**166–68
  Caribbean islands **5:**426, 431, 433, 438, 440
  commonwealth status **5:**166, 168
  Spanish language **5:**435
  illus.
    Old San Juan **5:**168
  map(s) **5:**166
Puerto Sandino (Nicaragua) **6:**57
Puerto Vallarta (Jalisco, Mexico) **5:**402
Pueyrredón, Juan Martin de (Argentine statesman) **6:**298
Puget Sound (Washington) **5:**12, 50–51, 52, 336, 337, 338
  coastal valley **5:**157
Puig, Manuel (Argentine author) **6:**277
Pulque (alcoholic drink) **5:**359, 378
Puna de Atacama *see* Atacama, Puna de
Puncak Jaya (Mount Carstensz) (Indonesia) **2:**315
Punchbowl (crater, Honolulu, Hawaii) **5:**353
Punic Wars (264–146 B.C.)
  Carthage **1:**90
  Iberian Peninsula **4:**110
  Rome, its rise and fall **3:**47
Punjab (province, Pakistan) **2:**180, 181, 183
Punjab (region, India–Pakistan) **2:**213, 226
Punjab (state, India) **2:**219, 220
Punjabi (people) **2:**183
Punjabi language **2:**187, 199
Punkaharju (area in Finland) **4:**52
Puno (city and department, Peru) **6:**214, 216
Punta, Cerro de (mountain, Puerto Rico) **5:**166
Punta Arenas (Chile) **6:**316–17
Punta del Este (Uruguay) **6:**260–61
  illus. **6:**261

Punta Lara (seaside resort, Argentina) **6:**292
Puntarenas (Costa Rica) **6:**64
Puntjak Djaja (Indonesia) *see* Puncak Jaya
Puppets
  Indonesian shadow plays **2:**264, 319
  Japan's *bunraku* theater **2:**460
Puritans (Protestants who demanded reforms within the Church of England) **5:**165, 174, 180, 181
  British North America settlement **5:**34
  Connecticut **5:**197
  Massachusetts **5:**188, 191
Pusan (South Korea) **2:**436
Pushkin, Aleksandr (Russian poet) **4:**312
Pushtu language *see* Pashto
Pushtun (Asian people) *see* Pashtun
Putin, Vladimir (president of Russia) **3:**2, 25; **4:**310; **4:**319, 324; **4:**325, 326, 331
  illus. **4:**326
Putumayo River (South America) **6:**168
Pygmies (people)
  Africa **1:**258
  Burundi **1:**329–30
  Congo **1:**44
  Congo, Democratic Republic of **1:**264, 265, 268
  Papua New Guinea **2:**589
  Rwanda **1:**325
  Uganda **1:**321
  Zambia **1:**272–73
Pyhä, Lake (Finland) **4:**64
Pyongyang (capital, North Korea) **2:**430, 431
  illus. **2:**429
Pyramids
  Egypt **1:**33, 110, 117
  Guatemala **6:**28
  Mexico **5:**376, 413, 414, 415, 421
  Moche **6:**223
  illus.
    Egypt **1:**118
    Mayan **5:**418
    Mexico **5:**374
Pyrenees Mountains (France–Spain) **3:**28, 151, 152
  Andorra **4:**119
  solar-power station **3:**157
  Spain **4:**79, 80
  illus.
    Andorra **4:**120
    sheep grazing **3:**155
    village **4:**82
Pyu (Asian people) **2:**269

· · · Q · · ·

Qaboos bin Sa'id (sultan of Oman) **2:**137
Qaddafi, Muammar el- (Libyan political leader) **1:**98, 100
  illus. **1:**100
Qadiri, Abdullah (Uzbek author) **2:**351
Qaeda, al- **2:**85; **5:**450
Qajar dynasty (Persia) **2:**163
QATAR **2:**141, **142–43**
  illus.
    flag **2:**vii
    oil refinery **2:**142
  map(s) **2:**143
Qattara Depression (Egypt) **1:**112; **6:**345
Qin dynasty (China) **2:**420

Qing dynasty (China) *see* Manchu dynasty
Qinghai (Tsinghai) (province, China)
  source of Mekong River **2:**256
  Yangtze and Yellow rivers **2:**368, 370
Quad Cities (region, Iowa–Illinois) **5:**294
Quakers (members of the Society of Friends)
  5:165, 212, 214
Quapaw (Indians of North America) **5:**266
Quatre Bornes (Mauritius) **1:**379
QUEBEC (province, Canada) **5:**33, 34, 39, 41,
  76, 94, 95, 96, 97, **98–103**
  history **5:**38, 143
  population **5:**99–101
  resources **5:**40–41
  illus.
    demonstration for Canadian unity **5:**103
  map(s) **5:**101
Quebec Act (1774) **5:**101
Quebec City (capital, Quebec) **5:**41, 96, 97, 99,
  101
  climate **5:**95
  illus.
    Chateau Frontenac **5:**99
Québecois (French speaking residents of Quebec) **5:**98, 103
Quebracho (tree) **6:**246
Quechua (Indians of South America) **6:**235
Quechua language 6:82, 91, 236, 239, 271
  Inca Indians of Peru **6:**211, 222
  Indians of South America **6:**82, 196, 268
Queen Charlotte Island (British Columbia)
  5:69, 129
  illus. **5:**129
Queen Elizabeth Islands (North America) **5:**70,
  138
Queens (borough, New York City) **5:**203
QUEENSLAND (state, Australia) **2:**485, **504–8**
  economy **2:**490, 491
  illus.
    airborne ambulance service **2:**508
    beaches **2:**507
    Brisbane **2:**504
    Great Barrier Reef **2:**506
  map(s) **2:**505
Quelimane (Mozambique) **1:**364
Quemoy (island off China's mainland) **2:**423
Querétaro (capital, Querétaro state, Mexico)
  5:382, 403
QUERÉTARO (state, Mexico) **5:403**
  illus.
    Franciscan mission **5:**403
Queru-Queru (Bolivia) **6:**233
Quetta (capital, Baluchistan, Pakistan) **2:**188–89
Quetzalcoatl (Plumed Serpent) (Olmec and
  Toltec-Aztec god) **5:**376, 377, 380, 421
Quetzalcoatl (Toltec chief) **5:**377, 406
Quezon City (Philippines) **2:**336
Quiché (Indians of North America) **6:**28
Quiet Revolution (Quebec) **5:**102, 103
Quilotoa Crater (Ecuador)
  illus. **6:**192
Quimbaya (indigenous people of Colombia)
  6:126
Quinnipiac River (Connecticut) **5:**196
QUINTANA ROO (state, Mexico) **5:422**
  Yucatán **5:**421
Quipu (Inca system of knotted strings instead of
  writing) **6:**223
Quirinal Hill (Rome, Italy) **4:**165
Quiroga, Jorge (president of Bolivia) **6:**241
Quiroga, Vasco (Spanish missionary) **5:**409
Quisling, Vidkun (Norwegian Nazi) **4:**26

Quito (capital, Ecuador) **6:**101, 195–96, 199,
  200, 204
  illus. **6:**195, 196, 204
Qutb Minar (minaret, Delhi, India) **2:**216
  illus. **2:**214

· · · R · · ·

Rabat (Morocco) **1:**67, 70
  illus. **1:**71
Rabbits 2:489–90
Rabelais, François (French writer) **3:**178
Rabi (Rambi) (island, Fiji group) **2:**581
Rabin, Yitzhak (Israeli leader) **2:**55, 115
Rabuka, Sitiveni (prime minister of Fiji) **2:**599
Race
  Africa **1:**4, 12, 13, 30
  Asia **2:**258–59, 363, 371
  Caribbean islands **5:**427, 434
  Central and South America **6:**7, 95, 111–12,
    161, 164, 165
  Dominican Republic, history of **5:**456–57,
    458
  Puerto Rican homogeneity **5:**167
  Uruguay free of racial tensions **6:**255
Racine (Wisconsin) **5:**286
Racine, Jean (French playwright) **3:**178
Racism
  discrimination against Asian-Americans **5:**347
  at English universities **3:**105
  Jim Crow laws **5:**222
  violence in Germany **3:**248–49
Radama I (Merina king on Madagascar) **1:**377
Radio
  China **2:**408
  Radio Andorra **4:**122
  Radio Luxembourg **3:**210
  Vatican's radio station **4:**180
Radioactive wastes 5:332
Raffi *see* Melik-Agopias, Hagop
Raffles, Sir Stamford (English colonial adminis-
  trator) **2:**309, 312
Rafsanjani, Hojatolislam Hashemi (president
  of Iran) **2:**164
Ragusa (Yugoslavia) *see* Dubrovnik
Railroads
  Bangkok (Thailand) linked to Vientiane (Laos)
    2:282
  bridge across Zambezi River **1:**355
  Canada, history of **5:**113
  Canadian National Railway **5:**92
  Canadian Pacific Railway **5:**85, 132
  Chihuahua-Pacific Railroad **5:**393
  Congo **1:**259
  Europe **3:**41–42
  first U.S. transcontinental railroad **5:**310, 347
  Florida **5:**239, 241
  Franco-Ethiopian Railroad **1:**298
  immigration of workers **5:**169
  Italy **4:**153
  Mount Pilatus (Switzerland) has steepest cog
    railway in world **3:**295
  Nebraska **5:**302
  Panama Railroad **6:**78, 80
  settlement of North and South Dakota **5:**298
  Trans-Gabon Railroad **1:**254
  Trans-Siberian Railway **2:**345
  illus.
    Costa Rican jungle **6:**62

  Sinaloa **5:**397
  vendors at Angolan train stop **1:**343
Rain *see* Precipitation
Rain forests
  Africa **1:**185, 195, 216, 235
  Amazon River **6:**201
  Australia **2:**486, 504
  Bolivia **6:**239
  Brazil **6:**171, 172, 173–74, 175
  British Columbia **5:**71, 129
  Central America **6:**9
  Chile **6:**305, 316
  Gabon **1:**251
  Hawaii **5:**351
  Madagascar **1:**370
  Nicaragua **6:**53, 56–57
  Panama **6:**73–74, 79
  Peru **6:**209
  Puerto Rico **5:**166–67
  Suriname **6:**159
  U.S. Pacific coast **5:**157
  illus. **1:**17; **6:**2
    British Columbia **5:**129
    Cameroon bridge building **1:**233
    destruction **6:**172
    Dominica **5:**487
    South America **6:**87
    Suriname village **6:**157
  map(s)
    world climate **6:**354
Rainier, Mount (Washington) **5:**336, 337
Rainier III (prince of Monaco) **3:**206
Rajasthan (state, India) **2:**201, 216
  illus. **2:**205
Raj Ghat (shrine, Delhi, India) **2:**208
Rakhmonov, Emomali (Tajik political leader)
  2:361
Rákosi, Mátyás (Hungarian dictator) **4:**246
Raleigh (capital, North Carolina) **5:**228, 229
Raleigh, Sir Walter (English soldier, courtier,
  and poet) **3:**76; **5:**227; **6:**135
  Orinoco River **6:**147
Ralik (island chain, Marshall Islands) **2:**575
Rama (Nicaragua) **6:**57
Rama I (king of Thailand) **2:**279
Rama IV (king of Thailand) *see* Mongkut
Rama V (king of Thailand) *see* Chulalongkorn
Ramadan (holy month of Islam) **1:**108; **2:**126,
  159, 186
Ramallah (West Bank city) **2:**114
Rama Thibodi (king of Thailand) **2:**279
Ramganga River (India) **2:**168
Ramgoolam, Navinchandra (prime minister of
  Mauritius) **1:**382
Ramgoolam, Sir Seewoosagur (prime minister
  of Mauritius) **1:**382
Ramiers (fortified site, Haiti) **5:**462
Ramkhamhaeng (king of Thailand) **2:**275
Ramos, Fidel (president of Philippines) **2:**338,
  340
Ramos, Samuel (Mexican author) **5:**373
Ramos-Horta, José (East Timorese leader)
  2:328
Ramses II (king of ancient Egypt) **1:**102, 118;
  2:97
  statues at Abu Simbel **1:**111
Ramses III (king of Egypt) **1:**111, 118
Ramu River (Papua New Guinea) **2:**588
Rana family (Nepal) **2:**233
Ranariddh, Prince Norodom (premier of Cam-
  bodia) **2:**289
Ranavalona III (queen of Madagascar) **1:**377

Rance River (France) **3:**157
Rand (region, South Africa) *see* Witwatersrand
Rangitikei River (New Zealand) **2:**538
Rangitoto Volcano (New Zealand) **2:**547
Rangoon (Myanmar) *see* Yangon
Rankin, Jeannette (American congresswoman) **5:**312
Rao, P. V. Narasimha (prime minister of India) **2:**218
Rapa Nui *see* Easter Island
Raphael (Italian artist) **3:**268
Rapid City (South Dakota) **5:**300
Rappahannock (Indians of North America) **5:**224
Rappahannock River (Virginia) **5:**223
Raritan River (New Jersey) **5:**208
Rarotonga (island, Cook Islands, Pacific Ocean) **2:**561
Ras al Khaima (United Arab Emirates) **2:**138, 139
Raskolniki see Old Believers
Rasmussen, Anders Fogh (prime minister of Denmark) **4:**22
Rasmussen, Poul Nyrup (prime minister of Denmark) **4:**22
Rastafarianism 5:476
Rastrelli, Bartolomeo (Italian architect) **4:**330
Ratak (island chain, Marshall Islands) **2:**575
Rathlin Island (Northern Ireland) **3:**142
Rationing system (in China) **2:**383
Ratsiraka, Didier (president of Madagascar) **1:**377
Ravalomana, Marc (president of Madagascar) **1:**377
Ravenna (Italy) **4:**132
Ravi (tributary of the Indus River) **2:**170, 183
Rawalpindi (Pakistan) **2:**187
    illus. **2:**186
Rawlings, Jerry (Ghanian leader) **1:**204
Ray, Satyajit (Indian movie director) **2:**204
Rayburn, Sam (American legislator) **5:**253
Razdan River (Armenia) **2:**74
Reagan, Ronald (40th president of U.S.) **4:**6
    illus. **4:**325
Rebmann, Johannes (German missionary) **1:**337
Reccaredo (Visigoth king of Spain) **4:**112
Recession (economics)
    Asia (1990s) **2:**34, 307, 437
    Asia (1990s): Indonesia **2:**319, 326
    Asia (1990s): Japan **2:**440, 464, 472
    Latin America **6:**265, 289, 296, 301
    United States (1980s) **5:**177
Recife (Brazil) **6:**160, 167–68, 169, 186, 188
    illus. **6:**163
Red Brigade (Italian terrorist organization) **4:**162, 163
Red Centre (region, Northern Territory, Australia) **2:**532, 533
Red Cross *see* International Red Cross
Red Deer (Alberta) **5:**124
Red Deer River and Valley (Alberta) **5:**127
Redford, Robert (American actor) **5:**324
Red Fort (Delhi, India) **2:**208
Red Guards (Chinese youth organization) **2:**398
Red Lodge (Montana) **5:**311, 312
Redonda (island, Antigua and Barbuda) **5:**493
Red River (southeast Asia) **2:**294, 301
Red River (U.S.) **5:**250, 305
Red River of the North (Canada–U.S.) **5:**4, 112
    glaciation **5:**12

Red River Valley (North Dakota) **5:**297
    Winnipeg **5:**116
Red River Rebellion (1870) *see* Riel Rebellions
Red River Valley (North Dakota) **5:**297
Red Rocks Park (Colorado) **5:**318
Reds (motion picture) **4:**331
Red Sea (Asia–Africa) **2:**122
    Sudan **1:**124
    Yemen **2:**130
    table(s)
        major seas of the world **6:**347
Red Sea Mountains (Sudan–Egypt) **1:**112, 127
Red Square (Moscow, Russia) **4:**327–28
Red Volta River *see* Volta River
Redwood (tree) **5:**157, 161, 343
Ree, Lough (lake in Ireland) **3:**66
Reed, John (American journalist) **4:**331
Referendum, Legislative 3:298; **4:**154
Reform, War of the (1857–1861; Mexico) **5:**383
Reformation (Protestant movement to reform the Christian Church) **3:**56, 273; **4:**229
    church music **3:**256
    French Huguenots **3:**183, 184
    Scotland **3:**140
    Switzerland **3:**294, 297
Refugees
    Afghanistan **2:**177, 188
    Africa **1:**3
    Albanians from Kosovo **4:**290
    Asia **2:**31
    Asia, Southeast **2:**259
    Austria sheltered émigrés from Communist countries **3:**325
    Congo, Democratic Republic of **1:**270
    Croatia **4:**286
    Cuba to U.S. **5:**449, 451
    Cyprus **2:**70
    Djibouti **1:**299
    East to West Germany **3:**259, 279, 282, 283
    Ethiopia **1:**286, 288
    Florida's population growth **5:**239, 240, 241
    Georgia (republic) **2:**80
    Germany **3:**246–47
    India and Pakistan **2:**203, 219, 228
    Indochina **2:**275
    Kenya **1:**314
    Kosovo to Albania **4:**273
    Liberia **1:**178
    Middle East **2:**99, 102, 117, 119, 121
    Mozambicans in Malawi **1:**280
    Mozambique **1:**365
    Nagorno-Karabakh **2:**86
    Nigeria **1:**228
    Rwanda **1:**325
    San Marino **4:**175
    Somalia **1:**300
    Sudan **1:**131
    Yugoslav wars **4:**276
    illus.
        Angola **1:**341
        Ethiopia **1:**292
        Kuwait **2:**30
        Mozambican refugees in Malawi **1:**279
        Palestinian Arabs **2:**119
        Rwanda **1:**61, 324
Regensburg (Germany) **3:**326
Reggae (music) **5:**476
Regina (capital, Saskatchewan) **5:**119–20
    illus.
        Royal Canadian Mounted Police Academy **5:**118

Regionalism
    Asia **2:**170
    India **2:**200–201
Regs (desert plains) **1:**24
Rehoboth Bay (Delaware) **5:**215
Rei-Bouba (Cameroon) **1:**231
Reichenau (Austria) **3:**244
Reichstag building (Berlin, Germany) **3:**281
    illus. **3:**281
Reign of Terror (in French history) **3:**184
Reina, Carlos Roberto (president of Honduras) **6:**41
Reincarnation (religious belief) **2:**212, 261, 387
Reindeer 4:37; **5:**82, 126
    illus. **2:**341; **4:**36, 51; **5:**61, 72
Religions of the world *see also* names of religions
    African forms in the New World **5:**435; **6:**93
    Asia **2:**18–20, 45, 49–50, 169, 260–61, 372–73
    Brazilian evangelical movement **6:**162
    cargo cults of Oceania **2:**558, 595–96
    Chinese values and religion **2:**387–90, 420
    Europe **3:**19
    India **2:**209–13
    Jamaica **5:**475, 476
    Japan's Ainu **2:**444
    Lamaism **2:**386–87
    Mexico, ancient **5:**376–77
    Polynesia **2:**602
    Russia's religious revival **4:**310
    Tonga's Sabbath observation **2:**605
    U.S. denominations **5:**169, 171
    voodoo **5:**464–65
    illus.
        Ethiopian rain/fertilization ceremony **1:**291
        Southeast Asia traditional beliefs **2:**258
        U.S. congregations **5:**165
Religious freedom
    Hungarian history **4:**245
    Rhode Island, history of **5:**193, 194
    United States **5:**165, 219
Religious Toleration, Act of (Maryland, 1649) **5:**219
Remus (Roman legend) *see* Romulus and Remus
Renaissance (European culture) **3:**54–55; **4:**157, 167
    France **3:**177, 178
Renaissance Center (Detroit) **5:**277
Renamo *see* Mozambique National Resistance Movement
René, France-Albert (president of Seychelles) **1:**340
Reng Tlang (mountain, Bangladesh) **2:**238
Rennell Island (Solomon Islands) **2:**591, 592
Reno (Nevada) **5:**331, 332
Renoir, Auguste (French painter) **3:**177
Repentance (motion picture) **2:**83; **4:**315
Republicans (Northern Ireland) *see* Nationalists
Republic of Texas (antigovernment organization) **5:**255
Research Triangle Park (North Carolina) **5:**228, 229
Restigouche River (New Brunswick, Canada) **5:**84
Retailing *see* Markets
Retief, Piet (Boer leader) **1:**404
Retirement
    British Columbia **5:**131, 133
    California **5:**52
    Florida **5:**163, 239, 240

Réunion (island, Indian Ocean) **1:**45, 46–47; **3:**191
Reuss River (Switzerland) **3:**295
   illus. **3:**296
Reventazón River (Costa Rica) **6:**63
Revere, Paul (American patriot) **5:**191
   illus. **5:**169
Reversing falls (Saint John River, Canada) **5:**79, 85
Revilla Gigedo Islands (Mexico) **5:**408
Revolutionary War (1775–1781) **5:**38, 174
   Boston (Massachusetts) **5:**191
   Delaware's soldiers **5:**216
   Loyalists *see* Loyalists, British; United Empire Loyalists
   New Jersey **5:**208, 210
   New York **5:**206
   North Carolina **5:**229
   Philadelphia (Pennsylvania) **5:**213
   Rhode Island **5:**194
   Virginia **5:**226
   illus.
      Paul Revere's ride **5:**169
      Valley Forge **5:**200
Revolution of 1830 (France) **3:**185, 198
Revolution of 1848 (France) **3:**186, 198
Revolution of 1910 (Mexico) **5:**370, 371–72, 385
Reyes, Alfonso (Mexican author) **5:**373
Reyes, José Trinidad (Honduran priest) **6:**38
Reykjavík (capital, Iceland) **4:**4, 6
   illus. **4:**7
Reymont, Władysław S. (Polish author) **4:**215
Reza Khan Pahlavi (ruler of Iran) **2:**163
Rhaeti (early European people) **3:**295, 296, 306
Rhaetia (Roman province) **3:**306, 313
Rhaeto-Romanic language *see* Romansh language
Rheims Cathedral (France) **3:**163, 183
Rheingau (region, Germany) **3:**245
Rhine, Confederation of the *see* Confederation of the Rhine
Rhineland (region, Germany) **3:**274, 276
Rhine-Main-Danube Canal (Europe) **3:**243
RHINE RIVER (Europe) **3:**244–45
   Europe, importance to **3:**42
   France **3:**150, 161
   Germany **3:**242, 243, 258, 266
   Netherlands **3:**226, 233
   Switzerland **3:**286, 293, 296
   illus. **3:**244
   map(s) **3:**245
RHODE ISLAND 5:192–94
   illus. **5:**181, 192
   map(s) **5:**193
Rhodes (Greek island) **4:**191
   illus. **4:**190
Rhodes, Cecil (English financier in Africa) **1:**276, 355, 362, 398, 402
Rhodesia *see* Zambia; Zimbabwe
Rhodesia and Nyasaland, Federation of (1953–1963) **1:**276, 281, 362
Rhodri Mawr (Roderick the Great) (died 877) (Welsh ruler) **3:**129
Rhone Glacier (Switzerland)
   illus. **3:**303
Rhone River (Europe) **3:**152, 154, 157, 160, 168, 286
Ribe (Denmark)
   illus. **4:**9
Ribera, José (Spanish artist) **4:**115

Rice
   Cambodia **2:**287
   China **2:**401, 417
   Thailand **2:**256, 279
   illus.
      Asia, Southeast **2:**10
      Bangladesh **2:**241
      Chinese agriculture **2:**414
      Haitians harvesting **5:**462
      Japanese agriculture **2:**466
      Liberian harvest **1:**180
      Nigerian farmer **1:**219
      Philippines **2:**337
      Sri Lanka **2:**249
      Taiwan's terraced paddies **2:**427
      Thailand **2:**276
      Vietnam **2:**299
      winnowing **1:**375
   map(s)
      world production **6:**355
Richard I ("the Lion-Hearted") (king of England) **3:**117
   Cyprus taken during the Crusades **2:**72
   Dürnstein Castle on the Danube **3:**315, 326
Richard III (king of England) **3:**119
Richards Bay (South Africa) **1:**398, 402
Richardson Mountains (Canada) **5:**7, 56, 141, 142, 145
Richelieu, Cardinal (French statesman) **3:**183
Richelieu River (Quebec) **5:**13
Richmond (capital, Virginia) **5:**49, 225
Richmond County (Georgia) **5:**235
Rickshaws
   illus. **2:**237
Rideau Canal (Ontario) **5:**107
Rideau River (Ontario) **5:**107
Riebeeck, Jan van (Dutch colonist in South Africa) **1:**398, 403
Riel, Louis (Canadian rebel leader) **5:**75–76, 112, 117, 121
Riel Rebellions (1870, 1885) **5:**112, 117, 121
Rif Mountains (Morocco) **1:**66
Rift valleys (landforms, Africa) **1:**18–19 *see also* Great Rift Valley
Riga (capital, Latvia) **4:**298–99, 300
Riga, Gulf of (Baltic Sea) **4:**295, 297
Riga, Treaty of (1921) **4:**343
Right Bank (Paris, France) **3:**193
Rijeka (Croatia) **4:**160, 162, 287
Riksdag (Swedish parliament) **4:**48
Rilsky, Ivan (Bulgarian monk)
   illus.
      icon **4:**262
Rimac River (Peru) **6:**217
Ring of Fire (geologic zone) **5:**335; **6:**51
Ring of Kerry (Ireland) **3:**73
Rio (Spanish or Portuguese word for river) *see* the main element of the name for those not listed below
Rio de Janeiro (Brazil) **6:**105, 161, 179, 180, 182, 184–85
   Brazil, history of **6:**189
   Carnival **6:**178
   Portugal, history of **4:**77
   illus. **6:**183
      Carnival **6:**178
      Copacabana Beach **6:**186
      soccer fans **6:**113
Rio de Janeiro (state, Brazil) **6:**184
Río de la Plata, United Provinces of 6:298
Río de la Plata, Viceroyalty of 6:249, 290, 297

Río de la Plata Basin (South America) **6:**284
   see also Plata, Río de la
   map(s) **6:**284
Rio Grande (river, Mexico–U.S.) **5:**250, 321
   illus. **5:**255
   table(s)
      longest rivers of the world **6:**346
Río Grande (river, Panama) **6:**78
Rio Grande do Sul (Brazil) **6:**180, 184
Rio Grande do Sul (state, Brazil) **6:**171, 183, 187
Río Muni (province of Equatorial Guinea) **1:**55, 235, 236
Rioni River (republic of Georgia) **2:**80, 84
Ríotinto (Spain) **4:**83
Riots and demonstrations
   Albania **4:**273
   Argentina **6:**301
   Bangladesh, history of **2:**243
   Beijing (China) **2:**399–400
   French student protests **3:**190
   German anti-immigrant violence **3:**248–49
   Indonesia **2:**326
   Los Angeles **5:**345
   Myanmar, history of **2:**272
   Poland **4:**222
   Romania **4:**257
   Trinidad and Tobago **5:**486
   Xinjiang **2:**381
   illus.
      Beijing (China) **2:**418
      China (1989) **2:**28
      Sikhs in India **2:**27
Risdon Cove (Tasmania, Australia) **2:**531
Risorgimento (Italian history) **4:**158
Rites of passage *see* Passage rites
Rivadavia (Argentina) **6:**345
Rivadavia, Bernardino (Argentine statesman) **6:**298
Rivas (Nicaragua) **6:**67
Rivas, Battle of (1856) **6:**70
Rivera, Diego (Mexican artist) **5:**372; **5:**412
Rivera y Orbaneja, Miguel Primo de (Spanish dictator) **4:**116
Rivers *see also* articles on individual continents and countries; names of individual rivers
   Africa **1:**19
   Amazon may be world's longest river **6:**168
   Continental Divide determines flow direction **5:**310
   European transportation **3:**42
   in Sahara **1:**24, 25
   U.S. eastern coastal plain **5:**153
   table(s)
      longest of the world **6:**346
Riviera (Mediterranean coastal region, France–Italy) **3:**160, 163–64
   Monaco **3:**204
   illus. **3:**168
Riyadh (capital, Saudi Arabia) **2:**47, 122, 123, 125, 127
   illus. **2:**122
Rizaiyeh, Lake *see* Urmia, Lake
Rizal, José (Philippine hero) **2:**340
Roads and highways
   Arctic's frozen waterways **5:**64
   Bolivian interior **6:**239
   Brazil **6:**160
   Buenos Aires' Avenida 9 de Julio **6:**290
   Europe **3:**41
   Georgian Military Highway **2:**81

German city streets **3:**265
Incan road system **6:**222
Inter-American Highway **6:**69, 72, 73
Italian *autostrade* network **4:**153
Laos to Da Nang **2:**282
Madras (Chenai) (India) **2:**207–8
Panama's *Camino Real* **6:**80
Pan-American Highway **6:**137
Persian empire **2:**49
Roman roads began at Forum **4:**165, 171
Roman roads in Britain **3:**113
Roman roads in France **3:**180
Roman roads in Spain **4:**111
Roman road through Bulgaria **4:**258–59
illus.
  cloverleaf interchange **5:**23
  Germany's autobahn system **3:**240
  hurricane evacuation jams highways **5:**16
  India's street cleaning **2:**226
  Italy's *autostrade* **4:**163
  Pan-American Highway **6:**16
Roanoke Island (North Carolina) **5:**227, 229
Roaring Forties (wind) **2:**529, 540; **6:**325
Robert I (king of Scotland) **3:**140
Robert the Bruce *see* Robert I
Robespierre, Maximilien (French revolutionary leader) **3:**184; **5:**436
Robinson, Arthur N. R. (prime minister of Trinidad and Tobago) **5:**486
Robinson, Jackie (American baseball player) **5:**234
Robinson, Mary (president of Ireland) **3:**77
Robson, Mount (British Columbia) **5:**38
Roca, Julio (president of Argentina) **6:**299
Rocafuerte, Vicente (Ecuadorian educator and president) **6:**204–5
Rochester (Minnesota) **5:**288
Rochester (New York) **5:**46, 205
Rock, The (Gibraltar) **4:**123
Rock and Roll Hall of Fame (Cleveland, Ohio) **5:**273
Rockefeller, John D. (American industrialist) **5:**214
Rockefeller Center (New York City)
  illus. **5:**203
Rocketry industry
  Southern states **5:**49
Rockford (Illinois) **5:**282
Rock Hill (South Carolina) **5:**230, 232
Rockies *see* Rocky Mountains
Rock Island (Illinois) **5:**294
Rockville (Maryland) **5:**218
Rocky Mountains (North America) **5:**7, 9, 38–39, 44, 145, 155, 251, 308, 310, 313, 323, 333, 336, 348
  Alaska **5:**157
  Canada **5:**69, 111, 123, 128
  Colorado **5:**318–19
  Montana **5:**311
  New Mexico **5:**321
  tree line **5:**16
  Wyoming **5:**315
  illus. **5:**38, 318
Rocky Mountain Trench (British Columbia) **5:**128
Rodeo (sport)
  Cheyenne (Wyoming) **5:**316
  Chile **6:**308
  illus. **5:**121, 122
Roderick the Great (Welsh ruler) *see* Rhodri Mawr
Rodó, José Enrique (Uruguayan writer) **6:**256

Rodrigues (island dependency of Mauritius) **1:**379
Rodríguez, Andrés (president of Paraguay) **6:**250
Rodríguez, Miguel Angel (president of Costa Rica) **6:**71
Rodríguez, Simón (Venezuelan author) **6:**141
Rodríguez Lara, Guillermo (president of Ecuador) **6:**205
Rogers, Mount (Virginia) **5:**224
Roggeveen, Jakob (Dutch explorer) **2:**609; **6:**322
Rogue River (Oregon) **5:**339
Roh Tae Woo (president of South Korea) **2:**438
Rojas Pinilla, Gustavo (Colombian general) **6:**128
Rolfe, John (English colonist) **5:**226
Roller coasters
  illus. **5:**47
Roma (Lesotho) **1:**391
Romagna (Italy) **4:**138
Romaji (Japanese writing system) **2:**461
Roman Britain (55 B.C.–5th century A.D.) **3:**92, 113, 139
  London **3:**110
  Wales **3:**128–29
  illus.
    Hadrian's Wall **3:**92
Roman Catholic Church *see also* Vatican City
  Argentina **6:**279, 298
  Asia, Southeast **2:**260
  Austria **3:**310
  Brazil **6:**162–63
  Cameroon **1:**234
  Canadian public education **5:**95
  Ecuador **6:**199
  Europe, history of **3:**49–50, 53, 56
  Fátima (Portugal) shrine **4:**72
  French North America **5:**32
  Germany **3:**247, 273
  Guatemala **6:**26–27
  Hungary **4:**240
  Ireland **3:**67, 76
  Italy **4:**135–36, 155, 156, 160, 163, 168
  Japan **2:**444
  Jesuits **2:**389–90; **6:**176, 189, 245
  Latin America **6:**6, 82, 88, 90, 140
  Maryland colony **5:**165, 219
  Mauritius **1:**382
  Mexico **5:**366–67, 387–88
  Monaco **3:**204
  Netherlands **3:**237
  Northern Ireland **3:**87, 144, 145, 148
  Orthodox Churches, relations with **4:**194
  Peru **6:**212, 216
  Philippines **2:**333
  Poland **4:**214, 220, 222
  popes, list of **6:**366–68
  Portuguese church in Brazil **6:**165
  Spain **4:**88–89, 112, 114
  Ukraine **4:**334
  U.S. population **5:**171
  Vietnam **2:**295
  Yugoslavia **4:**277
  illus.
    African priest **1:**37
    Central American church interior **6:**14
    Franciscan mission in Brazil **6:**163
    German religious procession **3:**22
    Hungarian religious procession **4:**241

    Mexican nuns in Holy Week procession **5:**367
    pilgrims at Lourdes **3:**165
    pilgrims in Peru **6:**211
    Polish religious procession **4:**213
    Sanctuary of the Virgin of Las Lajas **6:**121
    South American church **6:**96
    United States **5:**165
Romance languages **3:**20
Romanée-Conti vineyards (France) **3:**156
Roman Empire (27 B.C.–A.D. 476) **3:**295–96; **4:**134, 155, 165 *see also* Rome, ancient
  Africa **1:**75, 83, 91, 99
  Asia **2:**49, 102
  Austria **3:**320
  Belgrade **4:**277
  British Isles *see* Roman Britain
  Dacia (now part of Romania) **4:**250
  Danube River **3:**326
  eastern Europe **4:**272
  Egypt, ancient **1:**119
  emperors, list of **6:**365
  Gaul **3:**180, 193
  Germanic tribes and Germany **3:**18, 272
  Greece **4:**204–5
  Greek influence on **4:**185
  Hispania, province (now Spain) **4:**110–12
  Hungary **4:**242
  Macedonia **4:**292
  Moroccan ruins **1:**72–73
  Palestine **2:**112
  Romania **4:**254, 256
  Slovenia **4:**284
  Turkey **2:**56
  illus.
    Bulgarian ruins **4:**259
    Djemila (Algeria) ruins **1:**83
    German ruins **3:**273
    Hadrian's Wall **3:**92
    Lebanese ruins **2:**99
    Leptis Magna ruins **1:**10, 93
    Moroccan ruins **1:**73
    Tunisian ruins **1:**91
ROMANIA **3:**2; **4:**248–57
  Communism, fall of **3:**64
  conversion to Christianity **4:**205
  Danube River **3:**328–29
  Europe, history of **3:**19
  Hungarian minority **4:**239
  Moldova, history of **4:**345, 347
  Ploesti oil fields **3:**36
  shipping canal **3:**42
  illus.
    Black Sea coast **4:**249
    Bucharest **4:**253
    flag **4:**v
    pollution **4:**254
    Sucevița monastery **4:**250
    village **4:**248
  map(s) **4:**251
Romanian language **4:**250
  Moldovan language similar to **4:**345
Romanian Orthodox Church **4:**251
Romanies *see* Gypsies
Romanovs (Russian rulers) **4:**320–21
  list of **6:**364
Romansh (Rhaeto-Romanic) language **3:**20, 290
Romanticism (in art, literature, and music)
  France **3:**178
Romany language **4:**239

ROME (capital, Italy) **4:**129, 141, 142, 159, 164–73
  tourism **3:**15
  Vatican City **4:**177–81
  illus.
    apartment buildings **4:**169
    Colosseum **4:**172
    Piazza del Popolo **4:**168
    ruins of Roman Forum **3:**47
    St. Peter's Basilica **4:**166
    Spanish Steps **4:**171
    Trevi Fountain **4:**173
    Vittorio Emanuele II Monument **4:**161
  map(s) **4:**164
Rome, ancient 4:164–65, 167 *see also* Roman Empire
  agriculture **3:**33–34
  Europe's classical civilizations **3:**47–49
  Georgia (republic) **2:**84
  idea of law and obedience to law **3:**12
  Italian cuisine **4:**136
  roads **3:**41
  Syria **2:**94
Rome, Treaty of (1957) **3:**4
Rome-Berlin-Tokyo Axis *see* Axis Powers
Romulus and Remus (Roman legend) **4:**164–65
Ronchamp (France)
  illus. **3:**169
Rongelap Atoll (Marshall Islands) **2:**575
Roosevelt, Franklin Delano (32nd president of U.S.) **5:**176, 219, 353
  Casablanca Conference (1943) **1:**74
Roosevelt Campobello International Park (New Brunswick) **5:**85
Rosario (Argentina) **6:**290, 292
Rosas, Juan Manuel de Ortiz (Argentine dictator) **6:**190, 263–64, 270, 298
Roseau (capital, Dominica) **5:**487
Rosebud Indian Reservation (South Dakota) **5:**300
Roseires (Sudan) **1:**125
Rose Island (American Samoa) **2:**603
Roses
  illus. **4:**264
Roses, Valley of (Bulgaria) **4:**264
Roses, Wars of the (1455–1485, in English history) **3:**118–19
Rosetta channel (Nile delta) **1:**39, 114
Rosetta Stone (key to understanding Egyptian hieroglyphics) **1:**120
Rosh Hashanah (Jewish religious holiday) **2:**108
Ross, Sir James (Scottish explorer) **6:**332
Ross Barnett Reservoir (Mississippi) **5:**246
Ross Ice Shelf (Antarctica) **6:**325
Rosso (Mauritania) **1:**137
Ross seals 6:328
Rothschild vineyards (France) **3:**156
Rotterdam (the Netherlands) **3:**36, 42, 231–32, 233, 245
  illus. **3:**232
Rotuma (island, Fiji islands) **2:**597
Rouen (France) **3:**157
Rougemont, Denis de (Swiss writer) **3:**3
Rousseau, Jean Jacques (Swiss born French philosopher) **3:**294
Royal Australian Naval College (Jervis Bay Territory, Australia) **2:**513–14
Royal Canadian Mounted Police (Northwest Mounted Police) 5:73, 113, 119, 125, 126
  illus. **5:**73
    academy at Regina **5:**118
Royal Dutch Airlines (KLM) 3:42

Royal family, British
  illus. **3:**118
Royal Gorge Bridge (Colorado)
  illus. **5:**318
Royal Manas National Park (Bhutan) **2:**235
Royal Opera House (London, England)
  illus. **3:**104
Royal Pavilion (Brighton, England) **3:**120
Royal Tyrrell Museum (Alberta) **5:**127
  illus. **5:**127
Rozi (African people) *see* Lozi
Ruanda *see* Rwanda
Ruanda-Urundi *see* Burundi; Rwanda
Ruapehu, Mount (volcano, New Zealand) **2:**538
Rub' al-Khali (Empty Quarter) (desert, Saudi Arabia) **2:**10, 44, 123, 132
Rubber
  African resources **1:**20, 43
  Akron (Ohio) **5:**273
  Brazil **6:**173, 190
  Liberia **1:**183
  Malaysia is world's largest producer **2:**304
  illus. **2:**306
Rubinshteyn, Lev (Russian poet) **4:**315
Rudolf, Lake (Kenya) *see* Turkana, Lake
Rudolf I (Habsburg ruler) **3:**321
Rudolf II (Holy Roman Emperor) **4:**226
Rufisque (Senegal) **1:**153, 158
Rugby (sport)
  illus. **2:**544
Rugova, Ibrahim (president of Kosovo) **4:**278
Rugs and carpets
  Afghan **2:**178
  Bukhara **2:**351
  Persian **2:**160
  Turkmenistan **2:**358
  illus.
    Morocco **1:**71
    Pakistan industry **2:**189
Ruhr (district, Germany) **3:**244, 261, 274
  Düsseldorf **3:**266
  Rhine River **3:**245
Ruisdael, Jacob van (Dutch artist)
  illus.
    painting of windmill **3:**237
Ruiz de Alarcón, Juan (Mexican dramatist) **5:**381
Rukh (Ukrainian independence movement) **4:**332
Rulfo, Juan (Mexican author) **5:**374
Rumailia (oil field, Iraq) **2:**146
Rumania *see* Romania
Rumi (Persian poet) **2:**159
Rupununi savanna (Guyana) **6:**149
  illus. **6:**150
Rurik (Russian ruler) **4:**339
Rurik, House of (Russian rulers)
  list of **6:**364
Rurikid dynasty (Kievan Rus) **4:**339
Rushmore, Mount (South Dakota) **5:**300
RUSSIA 2:362; **3:**2; **4:**305–26 *see also* Union of Soviet Socialist Republics
  administrative units **4:**326
  Alaska, history of **5:**174, 350
  Antarctic research **6:**334
  Arctic **5:**60
  Arctic exploration **5:**62
  Asia, North **2:**341–43, 345
  Belarus, cooperation treaty with (1997) **4:**341
  Belarus, history of **4:**343

  border disputes **2:**31
  Bulgaria, relations with **4:**261
  divided into European and Asian Russia **3:**8
  economy **3:**25; **4:**316–19
  Estonia, relations with **4:**296
  Finland, history of **4:**55, 56–57
  food supply **3:**35
  Georgia (republic), history of **2:**84, 85
  hydroelectricity **3:**37
  Korea, North **2:**433
  Lapland **4:**35, 37
  Latvia, relations with **4:**299, 300
  leaders, list of **6:**364
  Lithuania, relations with **4:**301
  manufacturing **3:**40
  mineral resources **3:**38
  Moldova, history of **4:**347
  Mongolia **2:**362
  Mongols' Golden Horde **3:**53
  Moscow **4:**327–29
  Odessa, history of **4:**338
  petroleum reserves **3:**36
  Polish Partitions **4:**220
  rivers **3:**42, 44
  St. Petersburg **4:**330–31
  Siberia **2:**24
  size **3:**8
  Sweden, history of **4:**48
  Transcaucasia, history in **2:**52, 55
  Turkey, history of **2:**65
  Ukraine, history of **4:**332, 337, 339, 340
  Viking invasions **3:**51
  Volga River **4:**317
  illus.
    church service **4:**310
    dogsled **4:**308
    farm **4:**316
    flag **4:**vi
    greenhouse **4:**318
    horse-drawn sleigh **4:**308
    Moscow **3:**16; **4:**305, 311
    Moscow Circus **4:**315
    "Motherland" monument **4:**320
    Petrodvorets **4:**319
    St. Petersburg **4:**331
    toppled statues **4:**324
    Ural Mountains **4:**307
    VCR factory **4:**313
  map(s) **4:**306
    Volga River **4:**317
Russian Orthodox Church 4:310, 320
  Moscow cathedrals **4:**327, 328
  Uniate Church, merger with **4:**334
  illus. **4:**310
Russian Revolution and Civil War (1917–1921) **4:**321–22
  Reds (motion picture) **4:**331
Russians (Slavic people) **4:**309
  Asia, Central **2:**344, 345
  conversion to Christianity **4:**205
  Estonia **4:**293, 294
  Europe, movements of population **3:**19
  Kazakhstan **2:**347, 348, 349
  Kyrgyzstan **2:**355
  Manitoba **5:**115–16
  Moldova: Trans-Dniester population **4:**345
  illus. **4:**309
Russian State University for the Humanities (RSUH) 4:311
Russo-Japanese War (1904–1905) **2:**25, 374, 446
Russo-Turkish War (1877–1878) **4:**256, 265

Rustaveli, Shota (Georgian writer) **2:**83
Ruth, Babe (American athlete) **5:**219
Ruthenia (Transcarpathia) (region, Ukraine) **4:**338
Ruutel, Arnolt (president of Estonia) **4:**296
Ruwenzori Mountains (Mountains of the Moon) (Africa) **1:**18, 262, 316–17, 321
Ruzizi River (Africa) **1:**324, 328
RWANDA 1:37, **324–27** *see also* Burundi
Congo, Democratic Republic of **1:**270
refugees **1:**325
illus.
flag **1:**xxiv
gorillas **1:**327
refugees **1:**61, 324
map(s) **1:**326
Rybakov, Anatoli (Soviet author) **4:**314–15
Rye (New Hampshire) **5:**185

• • • S • • •

Saadi (Persian poet) **2:**159
Saale River (Eastern Europe) **3:**243
Saar Basin (Germany) **3:**37
Saaremaa (island, Estonia) **4:**293
Saarinen, Eliel and Eero (Finnish-American architects) **4:**59
Saarland (state, Germany) **3:**244
Saba (ancient kingdom, Arabia) **2:**130
Saba (island, Caribbean Sea) **3:**235
Sabah (state of Malaysia) **2:**303, 304, 305, 307, 308, 315
Sabah family (rulers of Kuwait) **2:**146
Sabena (airline) **3:**221
Sabine River (Texas–Louisiana) **5:**250
Sac (Indians of North America) *see* Sauk and Fox
Sacagawea (Shoshone guide) **5:**298
Sacramento (capital, California) **5:**346, 347
Sacramento River and Valley (California) **5:**342, 343, 346
Sacré-Coeur (Basilica of the Sacred Heart) (Paris, France) **3:**200
illus. **3:**201
Sacrifice, Human *see* Human sacrifice
Sadakhlo (republic of Georgia) **2:**77
Sadat, Anwar el- (Egyptian leader) **1:**123; **2:**114–15
Saddam's Qadissiyah, Monument of (Iraq)
illus. **2:**147
Saeima (Latvian parliament) **4:**300
Saek (Asian people) **2:**275
Safaniyah (oil field, Saudi Arabia) **2:**128
Safavid dynasty (Persia) **2:**141, 162–63
Safi (Morocco) **1:**72
Sagas (oral literature) **3:**70; **4:**6, 28
Sagebrush State (nickname for Nevada) **5:**330
Sagres (Portugal) **4:**75
Saguaro cactus 5:161, 329
illus. **5:**162, 329, 392
Sahagún, Bernardino de (Spanish historian in Mexico) **5:**381
Sahara (desert, north Africa) **1:**19, 24–25
Africa's early trading communities **1:**6, 13
Algeria **1:**75, 78
Chad, Sahara zone of **1:**242–43
Egypt, early history of **1:**117
Libya **1:**94, 97
Mauritania **1:**134–35

Morocco **1:**66
Niger **1:**144
Sahel, bordering area **1:**142
Tunisia **1:**89
illus.
caravan **1:**24
oases **1:**22–23, 242
Saharan Atlas Mountains (Algeria) **1:**75, 76
Sahel (eastern coast of Tunisia) **1:**89
Sahel (semi-arid region south of the Sahara) **1:**134, 135, 142
Saibou, Ali (president of Niger) **1:**149
Saida (Sidon) (Lebanon) **2:**101
Sa'id dynasty (Oman) **2:**137
Said Pasha (viceroy of Egypt) **1:**120, 121
Saigon (Vietnam) *see* Ho Chi Minh City
Saimaa, Lake (Finland) **4:**52
Saint *see* names of saints, as Paul, Saint. Place names beginning with Saint are under Saint, as Saint Louis, Missouri
St. Augustine (Florida) **5:**173
illus. **5:**169
St. Basil's Cathedral (Moscow, Russia) **4:**328
illus. **4:**305
Saint Bernard passes (Alps) **3:**289; **4:**126
Saint Brandon (island dependency of Mauritius) **1:**379
St. Catherine, Mount (Grenada) **5:**481
Saint Clair, Lake (Michigan–Ontario) **5:**46
Saint Clair River (Michigan–Ontario) **5:**276
St. Croix (island, U.S. Virgin Islands) **5:**172
St. Croix Island (Maine) **5:**85
St. Croix River (New Brunswick-Maine) **5:**85
Saint-Denis (capital, Réunion) **1:**46
Saint-Domingue (colonial name for Haiti) *see* Haiti
Sainte-Chapelle (church, Paris, France) **3:**193, 195
illus. **3:**194
St. Elias Mountains (North America) **5:**69, 135, 145, 349
illus. **5:**135
Saintes-Maries-de-la-Mer (France) **3:**168
St. Eustatius (island, Caribbean Sea) **3:**235
St. Francois Mountains (Missouri) **5:**295
Saint Gall (Switzerland) **3:**295
St. George (Bermuda) **5:**32
Saint George channel (Danube River) **3:**329
St. George's (capital, Grenada) **5:**481
illus. **5:**481
Saint George's Cay, Battle of (1798) **6:**24
Saint-Germain-des-Prés (church, Paris, France) **3:**199
Saint Gotthard Massif (Lepontine Alps) **3:**286
Saint Gotthard Pass (Alps) **3:**289; **4:**126
Saint Helena (island in the South Atlantic) **3:**90, 185; **4:**131
St. Helens, Mount (volcano, Washington state) **5:**156, 335, 336
illus. **5:**335
St. John, Lake (Quebec) **5:**103
St. John (island, U.S. Virgin Islands) **5:**172
Saint John (New Brunswick) **5:**40, 85, 86
Saint John, Cathedral of (Warsaw, Poland) **4:**216
St. John Baptiste Day (Quebec holiday) **5:**100
St. John River (Africa) **1:**179
Saint John River (Canada) **5:**79, 84, 85
St. John's (capital, Antigua and Barbuda) **5:**493
St. John's (capital, Newfoundland) **5:**83
illus. **5:**83
St. Johns River (Florida) **5:**241

St. Kilda (island group, Scotland) **3:**134
ST. KITTS AND NEVIS 5:427, 438, **495–96**
illus. **5:**495
flag **5:**vi
map(s) **5:**496
St. Lawrence, Gulf of 5:99
Atlantic Provinces of Canada **5:**77, 84
North American paths of immigration **5:**6
St. Lawrence Lowlands (North America) **5:**69, 94, 95–96, 97, 99, 103, 105, 202
St. Lawrence River (North America) **5:**77, 99, 202
illus. **5:**95
table(s)
longest rivers of the world **6:**346
St. Lawrence Seaway 5:45, 96, 97, 99, 205, 270, 273
Michigan **5:**278
Ontario **5:**109
illus. **5:**96
St. Louis (France) **3:**157
St. Louis (Missouri) **5:**48, 296
illus. **5:**295
Saint-Louis (Réunion) **1:**46
Saint-Louis (Senegal) **1:**153, 158
St. Louis Expo *see* Louisiana Purchase Exposition
ST. LUCIA 5:427, 435, 438, **489–90**
illus. **5:**489
flag **5:**vi
map(s) **5:**490
St. Lucia Channel 5:489
Saint-Malo (France)
illus. **3:**174
Saint Martin (island, in the Caribbean) **3:**235
map(s) **5:**429
St. Mary's City (Maryland) **5:**219
St. Mary's River (Michigan–Ontario) **5:**276
Saint Mary the Minor, Cathedral of (Santo Domingo, Dominican Republic) **5:**455
Saint Moritz (Switzerland) **3:**288
Saint-Nazaire (France) **3:**152, 154, 164
St. Ours Canal (Quebec) **5:**13
St. Paul (capital, Minnesota) **5:**48, 160, 289
illus.
Winter Carnival **5:**289
St. Paul River (Africa) **1:**179
Saint Paul's Cathedral (London) **3:**110
St. Peter Port (capital, Guernsey, Channel Islands) **3:**87
Saint Peter's Basilica (Rome, Italy) **4:**177, 180, 181
illus. **4:**166, 177, 178
St. Petersburg (Florida) **5:**241
ST. PETERSBURG (Russia) **4:**307, 320, 328, 329, **330–31**
Finland, history of **4:**55
industry **4:**316
Russian revolutions **4:**322
illus.
Hermitage Museum **4:**331
Nevsky Prospect **4:**330
Saint Peter's Square (Vatican City) **4:**177, 181
illus. **4:**177
Saint Pierre (capital, Saint Pierre and Miquelon) **5:**28
Saint-Pierre (Réunion) **1:**46
St. Pierre and Miquelon (French overseas department) **3:**191; **5:**28–29
illus. **5:**29
map(s) **5:**28
Saint Simons (island, Georgia) **5:**234

St. Sophia Cathedral (Kiev, Ukraine) **4:**337
illus. **4:**332
Sts. Peter and Paul, Cathedral of (St. Petersburg, Russia) **4:**330
Saint Stephen's Cathedral (Vienna, Austria) **3:**316, 318
illus. **3:**322
St. Thomas (island, U.S. Virgin Islands) **5:**172
Saint Thomé Cathedral (Madras (Chenai), India) **2:**207
St.-Tropez (France)
illus. **3:**168
Saint Vincent, Cape (Portugal) **4:**65, 75
St. Vincent, Gulf (Australia) **2:**521
ST. VINCENT AND THE GRENADINES 5:427, 435, 438, **491–92**
illus.
flag **5:**vi
Victorian-style cottages **5:**491
map(s) **5:**492
St. Vincent Passage 5:489
Sáinz, Gustavo (Mexican writer) **5:**374
Saite (Egyptian dynasty, 663?–?525 B.C.) **1:**118
Sajudis (Lithuanian nationalist movement) **4:**301, 304
Sakalava (people) **1:**373, 374, 377
Sakhalin Island (off Siberia) **2:**343; **4:**309
Sakkara (Egypt) **1:**110
Saladin, Yusuf ibn-Ayyub (Muslim sultan of Egypt and Syria) **1:**115, 119; **2:**20–21, 95
Salado River (South America) **6:**280, 281, 293
Salamanca (Guanajuato, Mexico) **5:**405
Salary man (Japanese white-collar worker) **2:**467–68
Salaspils (Latvia) **4:**300
illus.
memorial **4:**299
Salazar, António de Oliveira (Portuguese premier) **4:**77
Saleh, Ali Abdullah (Yemeni political leader) **2:**135
Salem (capital, Oregon) **5:**340
Salem (Massachusetts) **5:**191
Salerno (Italy) **4:**136
Salinas de Gortari, Carlos (president of Mexico) **5:**388
Salinas Valley (California) **5:**342
Salisbury (Zimbabwe) *see* Harare
Salisbury Plain (England) **3:**114
Salish (Indians of North America) **5:**130, 132, 164, 337
Salonika (Greece) **4:**197, 205, 207
Salonika, Gulf of 4:291
Saloum River (Senegal) **1:**153
Salt
Andes Mountains **6:**101
Argentina's *salinas* **6:**281
Austria **3:**313, 314, 320
Botswana **1:**353
Eritrea **1:**294
Europe **3:**38
Mali **1:**140
Salta (Argentina) **6:**293
Salta (province, Argentina) **6:**281
Saltillo (capital, Coahuila, Mexico) **5:**394
Salt Lake (Utah) *see* Great Salt Lake
Salt Lake City (capital, Utah) **5:**50, 324, 325
Salto (Uruguay) **6:**261
Salton Sea (lake, California) **5:**342
Salt River (Arizona) **5:**328, 329
Saluda River (South Carolina) **5:**230

Salvador (Brazil) **6:**186
illus. **6:**185
Salween River (Southeast Asia) **2:**267, 273
Salzach River and Valley (Europe) **3:**318
Salzburg (Austria) **3:**310, 313–14, 320
illus. **3:**313
Samaná Bay (Dominican Republic) **5:**454
Samaria (region, Israel) **2:**114
Samarkand (Uzbekistan) **2:**342, 350, 351, 352
Samarra (Iraq)
illus.
ruins of mosque **2:**152
Sambre River (Belgium–France) **3:**219
Sami (people) *see* Lapps
Samina River (Europe) **3:**307
Samizdat (underground publishing in USSR) **4:**314
SAMOA 2:560, 567, 600, 601, 603, **607–9**
division and annexation **2:**566
Polynesian migrations **2:**612
Tongans thought to have come from **2:**604
illus. **2:**607
flag **2:**x
map(s) **2:**608
Samoans (people) **2:**608
Samos (Greek island) **4:**191
Samoyeds (people) **5:**60
Sampaio, Jorge (president of Portugal) **4:**78
Samper, Ernesto (president of Colombia) **6:**129
Samsun (Turkey) **2:**63
Samuilo (Slavic czar) **4:**292
Samurai (military aristocracy of old Japan) **2:**444, 445
Sana (capital, Yemen) **2:**131
illus. **2:**130
San Andreas fault (earthquake belt, California) **5:**157, 342
San Antonio (Texas) **5:**252, 253–54
San Antonio, Cape (Cuba) **5:**442
San Antonio de Tipichincha (Ecuador) **6:**192
San Bernardino Mountains (California) **5:**342
San Blas (Nayarit, Mexico)
illus. **5:**400
San Blas (Mulatas) Islands (Panama) **6:**74, 77
San Blas River (Mexico) **5:**400
San Carlos de Bariloche (Argentina) **6:**283
Sánchez, Florencio (Uruguayan playwright) **6:**257, 271
Sánchez de Lozada, Gonzalo (president of Bolivia) **6:**239, 241
San Cristóbal (island, Solomon Islands) **2:**591
San Cristóbal (Venezuela) **6:**137
San Cristóbal de las Casas (Chiapas, Mexico) **5:**418
Sancti-Spíritus (Cuba) **5:**444
San Daniele del Friuli (Italy) **4:**138
Sand Creek Massacre (1864) **5:**320
Sande (secret society in Liberia) **1:**181, 182
Sandhill country (region, North Carolina) **5:**227
Sandhill cranes (birds) **5:**301
Sand Hills (Nebraska) **5:**301
Sand Hills (region, South Carolina) **5:**230
San Diego (California) **5:**342, 344
illus. **5:**345
San Diego Bay (California) **5:**342, 344
San Diego Ranges (California) **5:**342

Sandiford, Erskine (prime minister of Barbados) **5:**480
Sandinista government (Nicaragua) **6:**13, 18, 49, 54, 56, 58–60
Sandino, Augusto César (Nicaraguan political figure) **6:**58
illus. **6:**51
Sandstorms 1:124
Sandwich Islands *see* Hawaii
San Francisco (California) **5:**51, 52, 342, 345
illus. **5:**344
San Francisco, Church of (Tlaxcala, Mexico) **5:**415
San Gabriel Mountains (California) **5:**342
Sangangüey (extinct volcano, Mexico) **5:**400
Sanga River (Congo) **1:**42, 257
Sango (African people) **1:**247
Sango language 1:249
Sangre de Cristo Mountains (Colorado–New Mexico) **5:**319, 321
Sanguinetti, Julio María (president of Uruguay) **6:**265
Sanhadja Berbers (group of tribes) **1:**139
San Isidro de Coronado (Costa Rica) **6:**67
Sanitary and Ship Canal (Illinois and Michigan Canal) (part of the Illinois Waterway) **5:**5, 13, 44
San Joaquin River and Valley (California) **5:**342, 343, 346
San Jose (California) **5:**346
San José (capital, Costa Rica) **6:**63–64
illus. **6:**61, 64
San José del Cabo (Baja California Sur, Mexico) **5:**391
San Juan (Argentina) **6:**293
San Juan (capital, Puerto Rico) **5:**168
illus. **5:**168
San Juan (province, Argentina) **6:**266, 268
San Juan del Sur (Nicaragua) **6:**56
San Juan Mountains (Colorado) **5:**319
San Juan Pueblo (New Mexico) **5:**322
San Juan River (Nicaragua–Costa Rica) **6:**52
San Julián de Loria (Andorra) **4:**122
Sankara, Thomas (government leader of Burkina Faso) **1:**193
Sankoh, Foday (rebel leader in Sierra Leone) **1:**177
San Lorenzo (Paraguay) **6:**244
San Lorenzo, Church of (Florence, Italy) **4:**150
San Luis (province, Argentina) **6:**266, 268, 285
San Luis Potosí (capital, San Luis Potosí state, Mexico) **5:**389, 401
illus. **5:**401
SAN LUIS POTOSÍ (state, Mexico) **5:**401
San Marcos, University of (Lima, Peru) **6:**106, 216
SAN MARINO 4:125, **174–76**
illus. **3:**9; **4:**174, 176
flag **4:**v
map(s) **4:**175
San Martín, José de (Argentine general) **6:**98, 226, 298, 321
illus.
statue in Lima (Peru) **6:**217
San Miguel (El Salvador) **6:**43
Sanoquelli (Liberia) **1:**180
San Pedro (San Luis Potosí, Mexico) **5:**401
San Pedro Sula (Honduras) **6:**36, 38, 40
San Remo (Italy) **4:**141
San Salvador (capital, El Salvador) **6:**11, 42, 43, 44
illus. **6:**44, 49

San Salvador (Watling Island) (island, Bahamas) **5:**423
San Sebastián (Spain) **4:**108
Sanskrit language 2:191
San Souci (palace, Haiti) **5:**462
Sans Souci (palace, Potsdam, Germany) **3:**266
San Stefano, Treaty of (1878) **4:**265
Santa Ana (El Salvador) **6:**43
Santa Ana Volcano (El Salvador) **6:**42
Santa Anna, Antonio Lopez de (Mexican general) **5:**255, 383
Santa Catarina (Brazil) **6:**183
Santa Clara (Cuba) **5:**443
Santa Clara Valley (California) **5:**342
Santa Croce (church, Florence, Italy) **4:**150
Santa Cruz (Bolivia) **6:**235
    illus. **6:**234
Santa Cruz, Domingo (Chilean composer) **6:**310
Santa Cruz de Tenerife (Canary Islands) **1:**32; **4:**84
Santa Cruz group (Solomon Islands) **2:**591
Santa Cruz River (Arizona–Mexico) **5:**329
Santa Cruz y Espejo, Eugenio de (Ecuadorian physician and writer) **6:**199
Santa Fe (Argentina) **6:**270, 293
Santa Fe (capital, New Mexico) **5:**174, 322
    illus.
        Georgia O'Keeffe Museum **5:**48
Santa Fe (province, Argentina) **6:**266, 271, 285, 295
        Rosario **6:**290
Santa Fe Trail 5:296, 322
Santa Isabel (Equatorial Guinea) *see* Malabo
Santa Isabel (Solomon Islands) **2:**591
Santa María (volcano, Guatemala) **6:**30
Santa Maria del Fiore (Cathedral of Florence) (Italy) **4:**150
Santa Marta (Colombia) **6:**121, 126
Santander (province, Spain) **4:**108
Santander, Francisco de Paula (president of New Granada) **6:**127
Santarém (Brazil) **6:**169
Santa Rosalía (Baja California Sur, Mexico) **5:**391
Santiago (capital, Chile) **6:**310, 313–14, 321
    illus. **6:**311, 314
Santiago (Santiago de los Caballeros) (Dominican Republic) **5:**454, 456
Santiago de Compostela (Spain) **4:**112
Santiago de Cuba (Cuba) **5:**443, 444, 447
Santiago de Guatemala (early seat of Spanish territories in Central America) **6:**32
Santiago del Estero (Argentina) **6:**271, 297
Santiago del Estero (province, Argentina) **6:**266, 271, 285
        Indian population **6:**268, 270
Santo António (São Tomé and Príncipe) **1:**238
Santo Domingo (capital, Dominican Republic) **5:**455, 456, 460
    illus.
        Alcázar de Colón **5:**453
        University of Santo Domingo **5:**458
Santo Domingo, Audiencia of 6:145
Santo Domingo, Church of (Oaxaca, Mexico) **5:**417
Santo Domingo, University of
    illus. **5:**458
Santorin (Greek island) *see* Thera
Santos (Brazil) **6:**187
Santo Tomás (Costa Rica) **6:**68

Santo Tomas, University of (Philipines)
    illus. **2:**334
Santo Tomé de Guayana (Venezuela) **6:**104, 135, 138, 147
Sanusi, Mohammed Idris el- *see* Idris I (king of Libya)
Sanusi, Sayyid Muhammad ibn Ali as- (Muslim religious leader) **1:**98
San Xavier del Bac (mission, Tucson, Arizona)
    illus. **5:**309
San Ysidro (California)
    illus.
        border crossing to Mexico **5:**362
Sao (African people) **1:**244
São Francisco River (Brazil) **6:**86, 173
    table(s)
        longest rivers of the world **6:**346
Saône River (France) **3:**154, 160
São Paulo (Brazil) **6:**160, 173, 185–86
        arts **6:**180
        Christmas **6:**179
        cuisine **6:**183
        economy **6:**104, 176, 190
        education **6:**106, 107
        history **6:**189
        poverty **6:**105
    illus. **6:**7, 83, 165, 182, 184
São Paulo (state, Brazil) **6:**187
        festivals **6:**178
São Salvador (now Salvador, Brazil) **6:**188
São Tiago (island, Cape Verde islands) **1:**150
São Tomé (capital, São Tomé and Príncipe) **1:**237
    illus. **1:**237
SÃO TOMÉ AND PRÍNCIPE 1:54, 237–38
    illus.
        flag **1:**xxiii
        São Tomé **1:**237
    map(s) **1:**238
São Vicente (Brazil) **6:**187
São Vicente (island, Cape Verde islands) **1:**150
Sappho (Greek poet) **4:**191
Saquisilí (Ecuador) **6:**199
Sara (African people) **1:**239, 247
Sarajevo (capital, Bosnia and Herzegovina) **3:**317, 324; **4:**289–90
Sarakole (African people) **1:**135, 136, 139
Saramago, José (Portuguese writer) **4:**78
Sarawak (state of Malaysia) **2:**303, 304, 305, 307, 308, 315, 329
Sarcee (Indians of North America) **5:**125
Sardinia (island, Italy) **4:**125, 131, 154, 158
        Europe's alpine regions **3:**8, 28
Sardinia, Kingdom of 4:158
Sargon I (Akkadian ruler) **2:**48
Sarh (Chad) **1:**240
Sark (island, Channel Islands) **3:**87
Sarmatians (ancient people) **2:**82
Sarmiento (Argentina) **6:**345
Sarmiento, Domingo F. (Argentine statesman) **6:**276, 295, 299
Sarney, José (president of Brazil) **6:**191
Saronic Gulf (inlet of Aegean Sea) **4:**188
Saroyan, William (American writer) **2:**76
Sartre, Jean-Paul (French writer) **3:**179
SASKATCHEWAN (province, Canada) **5:**112, 113, **118–21**, 143
    illus. **5:**67, 120
    map(s) **5:**119
Saskatchewan River (Canada) **5:**4
Saskatoon (Saskatchewan) **5:**120
Sasolburg (South Africa) **1:**402

Sassandra River (Africa) **1:**186
Sassanians (Asian people) **2:**162
Sassanid dynasty 2:153, 192
Sassou-Nguesso, Denis (president of Congo) **1:**260
Satpura range (India) **2:**166
Saud (king of Saudi Arabia) **2:**127
SAUDI ARABIA 2:44, **122–29**
        cities **2:**47
        Islam **2:**342
        oil production **2:**52
        Yemen-border dispute **2:**135
    illus.
        airport terminal **2:**53
        Bedouins **2:**124
        flag **2:**vii
        Mecca **2:**127
        oil refinery **2:**123
        Riyadh **2:**122
        University of Petroleum **2:**128
    map(s) **2:**124
Sauk and Fox (Indians of North America) **5:**282, 293, 294
Sault Ste. Marie (Ontario) **5:**108
Sauna (Finnish bath) **4:**63
Sausages (food) **3:**250
Saussure, Horace Bénédict de (Swiss scientist) **3:**302
Sauteurs (Grenada) **5:**430
Savai'i (island, Western Samoa) **2:**607, 608
SAVAK (Iranian secret police) **2:**163
Savannah (Georgia) **5:**235, 236
    illus. **5:**236
Savannah River (South Carolina–Georgia) **5:**230, 234
Savannakhet (Laos) **2:**282
Savannas (tropical grasslands) **1:**142, 185, 190, 216, 217, 241, 246, 266, 353
        Burundi **1:**329
        Gabon **1:**251–52
    illus. **1:**18
    map(s)
        world climate **6:**354
        world vegetation **6:**353
Sava River (Bosnia and Herzegovina–Croatia) **4:**275, 285, 288
Save River (Mozambique) **1:**364
Savimbi, Jonas (Angolan political leader) **1:**346
Savonlinna (Finland) **4:**52
Savorgnan de Brazza, Pierre *see* Brazza, Pierre Savorgnan de
Savoy (historical region, France–Italy) **3:**186; **4:**158
Savoy, House of (Italian noble family) **4:**158
Sawatch Range (Colorado) **5:**318
Saw Maung (Myanmar political leader) **2:**272
Saxe-Coburg-Gotha, House of 6:361
Saxon (dynasty of German rulers)
        Holy Roman emperors, list of **6:**366
Saxons (Germanic peoples) **3:**49, 86, 97, 113, 140, 272
        rulers of England, list of **6:**360
Saxony (former duchy, Germany) **3:**273
Say (Niger) **1:**50, 147
Scafell Pike (highest point, England) **3:**98
Scandinavia (region, northern Europe) **3:**8
        Denmark **4:**8–22
        languages **3:**20
        Norway **4:**23–34
        Sweden **4:**38–50
        Viking invaders in Scotland **3:**138
        Vikings in world history *see* Vikings

Scapa Flow (bay, Scotland) **3:**135
Scarcies River (Guinea–Sierra Leone) **1:**172
Scarlet macaw
illus. **6:**89
Schaan (Liechtenstein) **3:**305
Schaffhausen (Switzerland) **3:**244
Scheldt River (Europe)
Belgium **3:**212–13, 216
Netherlands **3:**226, 228
illus. **3:**226
Schellenberg (Liechtenstein) **3:**305, 306
Schenectady (New York) **5:**46
Scheveningen (the Netherlands) **3:**234
Schiller, Friedrich (German playwright) **3:**253
Schiphol International Airport 3:226–27, 233
Schleswig (former Danish duchy, south Jutland)
4:20–21
Schleswig-Holstein (state, Germany) **3:**245
Schmidt, Helmut (West German chancellor)
3:283
Schönbrunn Palace (Vienna, Austria) **3:**324
illus. **3:**323
Schools *see* Education; the education sections
of country and continent articles
Schroeder, Gerhard (chancellor of Germany)
3:284
Schuman, Robert (French statesman) **3:**190
Schumann, Robert (German composer) **3:**256
Schuylkill River (Pennsylvania) **5:**213
Schweitzer, Albert (French medical missionary)
1:43, 253
Schwyz (canton, Switzerland) **3:**296, 297
Science
Antarctic research **6:**333–35, 337
Europe, history of **3:**15, 56
Hungarian scientists **4:**241
International Geophysical Year **6:**333–35
Korea, history of **2:**432
Massachusetts scholars and scientists **5:**191
Russian tradition **4:**311–12
illus.
Antarctic research **6:**337
Brazilian research **6:**176
Scilly, Isles of (England) **3:**81, 100
Scioto River (Ohio) **5:**273
illus. **5:**271
Sciròcco (wind) **4:**134
Scituate Reservoir (Rhode Island) **5:**192
SCOTLAND 3:81, 87, **131–41** *see also* United
Kingdom
government **3:**96
Hadrian's Wall **3:**92
"Silicon Glen" **3:**89
United Kingdom and how it was created
3:91, 119–20
illus.
country road **3:**132
Glasgow **3:**137
heather on mountains **3:**81
Highland Games **3:**139
map(s) **3:**133
Scots (people) **3:**140
Canada **5:**78, 80, 113, 117
United Kingdom **3:**86
illus.
bagpipers parade in Nova Scotia **5:**90
Scott, Robert Falcon (English explorer) **6:**332
Scott, Thomas Alexander (American business-
man) **5:**214
Scott, Sir Walter (Scottish writer)
illus.
home of **3:**136

Scott, Winfield (American general) **5:**383
Scott Base (Antarctica) **6:**334–35
Scottsdale (Arizona) **5:**328
Screaming Sixties (wind) **6:**325
Scutari (Albania) **4:**271
Scutari, Lake (Albania–Yugoslavia) **4:**269, 275
Scythians (people) **2:**156
Seaga, Edward P. G. (Jamaican leader) **5:**477
Seagull (bird) **5:**325
Sea Islands (South Carolina) **5:**230
Seals (animals) **4:**50; **5:**115; **6:**328
illus. **5:**348
Seasons of the year
Southern Hemisphere **2:**476
Venezuela **6:**132, 133
Seattle (Washington) **5:**51, 52, 338
illus.
Space Needle **5:**338
Sebastian (king of Portugal) **4:**76
Sebou River (Morocco) **1:**66
Séchelles, Moreau de (French finance minister)
1:340
Second International Polar Year (1932–1933)
6:333
Second Reich (German history) **3:**275
Secret Army Organization (OAS) (Algeria) **1:**84
Secret societies
Gabon **1:**254
Liberia **1:**181, 182
Seefeld (Austria)
illus. **3:**314
Seferis, George (Greek author) **4:**194
Segesta (Sicily) **4:**129
Ségou (Mali) **1:**50, 142
Segovia (Spain) **4:**99, 101, 111
illus. **4:**111
Alcázar **4:**101
Segregation *see also* Apartheid
European settlements in Africa **1:**30
South African townships **1:**397
United States **5:**176, 222, 267
Zimbabwe, history of **1:**360
Seine River (France) **3:**152, 157
Paris **3:**193, 195
Pont Neuf ("New Bridge") **3:**195
illus. **3:**154
Sejong (Korean king) **2:**437
Sekondi-Takoradi (Ghana) **1:**197
Selebi-Phikwe (Botswana) **1:**353
Self-Portrait (painting, Dürer)
illus. **3:**254
Seljuks (Turkish dynasty) **2:**57
Middle East **2:**51, 95, 162
Selkirk, 5th earl of *see* Douglas, Thomas
Selkirk, Alexander (British sailor) **6:**311
Selma (Alabama) **5:**244
Selonians (early European tribe) **4:**298
Selva (South American rain forest) **6:**173–74,
209, 305, 316
Brazil **6:**171
Sembe (Congo) **1:**259
Semigallians (early European tribe) **4:**298
Seminole (Indians of North America) **5:**222,
238, 241, 305
Seminole Wars (1835–1842) **5:**241
Semitic languages 2:28, 44
Semmelweis, Ignaz (Hungarian scientist) **4:**241
Sempach (Switzerland) **3:**297
Seneca (Indians of North America) **5:**95, 202
SENEGAL 1:53, **152–58**
Sahara **1:**24

Senghor and Négritude **1:**158
illus.
Dakar **1:**154
festival **1:**152
fishermen selling their catch **1:**157
flag **1:**xxii
Gorée **1:**155
people at party **1:**156
map(s) **1:**153
Senegal River (northwest Africa) **1:**137–38, 153,
157, 166
Senegambia (confederation of Senegal and
Gambia) **1:**56, 158, 163
Senghor, Léopold Sédar (president of Senegal)
1:158
Sennar (Sudan) **1:**125, 130
Senoussi (African people) **1:**248
Senufo (African people) **1:**186, 188
Seoul (capital, South Korea) **2:**433, 435, 436
illus. **2:**434
Sephardi Jews (people) **2:**105–6
Sepoy Mutiny (1857, India) *see* Great Uprising
September 11, 2001 terrorist attacks 2:40;
5:176
aviation industry, effect on **3:**221, 289
New York City **5:**203
Saudi participants **2:**129
Somalia's alleged financial links to **1:**303
Sequoia (tree) **5:**161, 343
illus. **5:**158
Sequoia National Park (California) **5:**342
Sequoya (Cherokee scholar) **5:**236, 264
Serahuli (African people) **1:**160, 161
Serbia (Yugoslav state) **4:**279 *see also* Yugoslavia
conversion to Christianity **4:**205
World War I **3:**275
Serbia and Montenegro (Balkan country) *see*
Yugoslavia
Serbian language 4:286
Serbian Orthodox Church 4:277
Serbo-Croatian language *see* Croatian language
Serbs (people) **4:**276, 277, 280
Bosnia and Herzegovina **4:**288, 289, 290
Croatia **4:**285, 286, 287
Kosovo **4:**278
Serbs, Croats, and Slovenes, Kingdom of
4:274, 280, 284, 287, 290
Serengeti National Park (Tanzania) **1:**338
Serengeti Plains (Tanzania) **1:**332
Serer (African people) **1:**154
Serfs (workers bound to a feudal lord) **3:**52
Russia **4:**317, 320, 321
Turgenev's novels **4:**313
Seria (Brunei) **2:**330
Seri Indians 5:392
Serra (Serranía) (words for mountains) *see* the
main element of the name
Serra, Junípero (Spanish missionary) **5:**346–47
Serrá, Pico da (mountain, Portugal) **4:**66
Serrano Elias, Jorge (president of Guatemala)
6:33
Servius Tullius (Roman king) **4:**171
Sesotho language 1:391
Setit River (east Africa) *see* Takkaze
Setswana language 1:352
Seurat, Georges (French painter)
illus.
A Sunday Afternoon at the Grande Jatte
3:176
Sevan, Lake (Armenia) **2:**74
Sevastopol (Ukraine) **4:**337
Seven Hills of Rome 4:165

Seventh-Day Adventist Church 2:563, 581
Seven wonders of the ancient world
  Colossus of Rhodes **4:**191
  Great Pyramid at Giza **1:**110
  Hanging Gardens of Babylon **2:**153
  Pharos of Alexandria (lighthouse) **1:**115
Seven Years' War (1756–1763) **3:**184; **5:**433–34
Severn River (England–Wales) **3:**83, 122
  bridge **3:**127
Seville (Spain) **4:**103–5, 109, 111, 113; **6:**345
  tourism **3:**16
  illus. **4:**104, 105
    Holy Week procession **4:**88
Sèvres (France) **3:**157
Sèvres, Treaty of (1920) **2:**66
Seward, William H. (American statesman)
  5:350
Seward's Folly (purchase of Alaska) **5:**350
Sewa River (Sierra Leone) **1:**172
Sewers
  Rome, ancient **4:**165
SEYCHELLES 1:47, **339–40**
  illus.
    flag **1:**xxiv
  map(s) **1:**340
Seymour Island (Antarctica) **6:**329
Sezer, Necdet (president of Turkey) **2:**67
Sfax (Tunisia) **1:**90
Shaba (province, Congo, Democratic Republic
  of) *see* Katanga
Shackleton, Sir Ernest (English explorer) **6:**329
Shadow plays (of Indonesia) **2:**319
Shafi'i (sect of Islam) **2:**133
Shagari, Alhaji Shehu (president of Nigeria)
  1:228
Shahaptian (Indians of North America) **5:**337
Shah family (rulers of Nepal) **2:**233
Shah Jahan (Mogul emperor of India) **2:**216
Shahjahanbad (former name of Old Delhi,
  India) **2:**208
Shakespeare, William (English playwright)
  3:116
  illus. **3:**116
    home **3:**116
Shamanism (animistic religion) **6:**22, 27
  Korea **2:**437
  Mongolia **2:**365
Shan (Asian people) **2:**259, 269, 275
Shandong Peninsula (China) **2:**380
Shangaan-Tsonga (African people) **1:**398
Shang dynasty (China) **2:**15, 420
Shanghai (China) **2:**380, 381, 383, 403, 404
  housing shortage **2:**401, 402
  illus. **2:**367, 403
Shannon River (Ireland) **3:**66
Shan Plateau (Shan highlands) (Myanmar)
  2:267
**SHAPE (Supreme Headquarters Allied Powers
  Europe)** (Casteau, Belgium) **3:**216
Sharecroppers (tenant farmers) **5:**221, 222
Sharia (Islamic law) **2:**128
Sharif, Nawaz (prime minister of Pakistan)
  2:194
Shari (Chari) River (central Africa) **1:**240, 241,
  247
Sharja (United Arab Emirates) **2:**138
Shark Bay (Australia) **2:**527
  illus. **2:**525
Sharks, freshwater 6:3, 52
Sharon, Ariel (prime minister of Israel) **2:**55,
  115
Sharp, Granville (British abolitionist) **1:**176

Shasta (Indians of North America) **5:**344
Shasta, Mount (California) **5:**342
Shastri, Lal Bahadur (prime minister of India)
  2:218
Shatt al-Arab (river formed by confluence of
  Tigris and Euphrates) **2:**50, 148, 154, 164
Shaw, George Bernard (Irish playwright) **3:**70
Shawnee (Indians of North America) **5:**212, 226,
  253, 272, 274, 280, 282
Shawnee Hills (Illinois) **5:**281
Shaybani, Muhammad (Uzbek leader) **2:**352
Sheba (Biblical kingdom) *see* Saba
Sheep
  Afghanistan's Karakul export **2:**178
  Argentina **6:**295
  Australia **2:**473, 500, 520
  Barbadian sheep have no wool **5:**479
  Karakul sheep **2:**352, 358
  Namibia **1:**349
  New Zealand **2:**473, 548
  South Africa **1:**401
  illus. **2:**475
    Argentina **6:**285
    Australia **2:**520
    Australian ranch **2:**490
    Bighorns **5:**126
    Chile **6:**318
    France **3:**155
    Germany **3:**262
    Hungarian shepherds **4:**243
    Inner Mongolia **2:**343
    Lebanon **2:**99
    New Zealand **2:**536, 549
    Turkish shepherd **2:**63
Sheffield (England) **3:**107
Sheikhdoms (regions ruled by Arab chiefs)
  2:139, 143
Shelburne Museum (Burlington, Vermont)
  5:187
Shelta language 3:144
Shenandoah National Park (U.S.) **5:**224
  illus. **5:**223
Shenandoah River and Valley (U.S.) **5:**6
Shenzen (China)
  illus. **2:**412
Shepard, Alan, Jr. 5:185
Sherbro (African people) **1:**173, 174, 175
Sherbrooke (Quebec) **5:**101
Sherman, William Tecumseh (American gen-
  eral) **5:**236
Sherpas (Asian people) **2:**231, 232
  illus. **2:**166
Sherry (fortified wine)
  illus. **4:**109
Sherwood Forest (England)
  illus. **3:**86
Shetland Islands (northeast of Scotland) **3:**8,
  81, 135, 140
Shevardnadze, Eduard (president, republic of
  Georgia) **2:**83, 85
Shevchenko, Taras (Ukrainian poet) **4:**335
Shi'a (branch of Islam) **2:**342
  Asia, Southwest **2:**45
  Iran **2:**157, 163
  Iraq **2:**148–49, 154
  Lebanon **2:**100, 102
  Pakistan **2:**184
  Saudi Arabia **2:**123
  Syria **2:**91–92
  Yemen **2:**133
Shickshock Mountains (Canada) **5:**69
Shifting cultivation (agriculture) **1:**22–23

Shi Huangdi (Chinese emperor) **2:**420
Shikoku (island, Japan) **2:**440
Shilluk (African people) **1:**127, 128
Shining Path (Peruvian terrorist group) **6:**226,
  228
Shinto (Shintoism) (religion of Japan) **2:**17, 372,
  451, 452
  wedding ceremony **2:**453
  illus. **2:**451
Ships and shipping
  Australia **2:**479
  Belfast (Northern Ireland) **3:**146
  Belgium's transshipment industry **3:**220–21
  Cape Verde refueling stop **1:**150, 151
  Danish merchant marine **4:**13
  Dutch transshipment industry **3:**231–32
  Europe's harbors **4:**44
  Europe's important ports **3:**44
  Finnish shipbuilding industry **4:**57
  Graveyard of the Atlantic **5:**229
  Greek economy **4:**200
  Kiribati's Marine Training Centre **2:**582
  Liberian "flag of convenience" **1:**182
  Mercosur's planned waterway **6:**262
  Mississippi River **5:**161
  New Zealand **2:**479, 554
  Norway **4:**28
  Panama Canal **6:**76, 78–79
  St. Lawrence Seaway **5:**96
  steamboat age **5:**177
  Suez Canal **1:**120–21
  Tuvaluans work on merchant vessels **2:**612
  Veracruz **5:**407
  Viking Ship Museum (Oslo, Norway) **4:**32
  illus.
    Antarctic icebreakers **6:**335
    Calcutta harbor **2:**206
    cruise ships **5:**172, 431; **6:**64
    Gdańsk (Poland) **4:**218
    Havana **5:**441
    Oseberg ship **4:**32
    Panama Canal **6:**73, 79
    Swedish shipyard **4:**46
Shire River (Africa) **1:**278
Shkodër (Albania) *see* Scutari
Shkumbî River (Albania) **4:**270
Shoguns (early Japanese war lords) **2:**443–45
Shona language 1:358, 361
Shortland Islands (Solomon Islands) **2:**591
Shoshone (Indians of North America) **5:**314,
  316, 317, 324, 325, 331, 332
Shostakovich, Dmitri (Russian composer) **4:**314
Show Me State (nickname for Missouri) **5:**295
Shreveport (Louisiana) **5:**248
Shrimp
  Greenland has largest shrimp grounds **4:**12
  Nicaragua **6:**56
  Panama **6:**74
Shrove Tuesday (religious holiday) *see* Carnival
Shuswap (Indians of North America) **5:**130
Shwe Dagon Pagoda (Yangon, Myanmar)
  illus. **2:**268
Siad Barre, Mohammed (president of Somalia)
  1:304, 305
Siam *see* Thailand
Sian Ka'an Biosphere Reserve (Quintana Roo,
  Mexico) **5:**422
Sibelius, Jean (Finnish composer) **4:**64
Siberia (Russia) **2:**341, 342–43
  Arctic development **5:**64
  Birobidzhan (autonomous region) **4:**309

Siberia (cont.)
European advances in Asia **2:**24
manufacturing **4:**316
people **5:**58, 60
population concentrated along railroad **2:**345
illus.
reindeer herding **2:**341
village **2:**344
Sichuan (Szechwan) (province, China) **2:**369
Sicily (island, Italy) **4:**125, 129–30, 132, 134, 138, 158, 161
capture by Aragón **4:**113
Europe's alpine regions **3:**8, 28
government **4:**154
mountains **4:**126
Palermo **4:**146
illus. **4:**129, 133
Sico River (Honduras) **6:**35
Sidon (Lebanon) *see* Saida
Siegfried (founder of Luxembourg) **3:**210
Siena (Italy) **4:**139–40
Sienkiewicz, Henryk (Polish author) **4:**215
Sierra (in names of mountains) *see* the main element of the name
Sierra (region, Peru) **6:**207–8, 209, 211, 212, 216
SIERRA LEONE 1:55–56, **171–77,** 183
illus.
Bo **1:**172
flag **1:**xxii
Freetown **1:**171
tie-dying cloth **1:**177
victims of civil war **1:**175
map(s) **1:**173
Sierra Leone Peninsula 1:172
Sign language, North American Indian 5:164
Siguiri (Guinea) **1:**168
Sigurdsson, Jón (Icelandic statesman and scholar) **4:**6
Sihanouk, Prince Norodom (ruler of Cambodia) **2:**291, 292
Sikaiana (Solomon Islands) **2:**592
Sikasso (Mali) **1:**142
Sikhs (religious sect of India) **2:**169, 209, 219, 220
Kenya **1:**311
illus.
demonstration **2:**27
Golden Temple at Amritsar **2:**218
Si Kiang (West River) (China) *see* Xijiang
Sikkim (state, India) **2:**221
Silesia (former Prussian province) **3:**274; **4:**224, 225
Siles Zuazo, Hernán (president of Bolivia) **6:**241
Silicon Valley (region, California) **5:**346
Silisili, Mount (Western Samoa) **2:**608
Silja, Lake (Sweden) **4:**39
Silk 2:352, 358
Silk Road (trade route) **2:**345, 350, 353, 420
Xinjiang (China) **2:**381
Silla dynasty (Korea) **2:**433
Sillanpää, Frans Eemil (Finnish author) **4:**62
Silva Xavier, Joaquim José da (Brazilian patriot) **6:**189
Silver
Bolivia **6:**234
Mexico **5:**363, 399, 401, 405
Montana **5:**312
Mountain States **5:**310
Nevada **5:**332
North America **5:**9
Silver Spring (Maryland) **5:**218

Silver State (nickname for Nevada) **5:**330
Silvretta Range (Alps) **3:**312
Sima Qian (Chinese historian) **2:**420
Simeon II (prime minister and former king of Bulgaria) **4:**259, 265, 266, 267
Simferopol (Ukraine) **4:**337
Simitis, Costas (prime minister of Greece) **4:**211
Simmonds, Kennedy A. (prime minister of St. Kitts and Nevis) **5:**496
Simplon Pass (Alps) **3:**289, 304
Simpson Desert (Australia) **2:**532
Sinai Peninsula (Egypt) **1:**113, 121, 122, 123
Arab-Israeli wars **2:**105, 114, 115
SINALOA (state, Mexico) **5:**397
Sind (province, Pakistan) **2:**180, 181, 190, 192
history **2:**172
Mohenjo-Daro **2:**213
Sindebele language 1:358
Sindhi (people) **2:**183
Sindhi language 2:187, 199
Sinepuxent Bay (Maryland) **5:**217
Sines (Portugal) **4:**73
SINGAPORE 2:309–12
Asia, Southeast **2:**255, 262, 264
Malaysia, history of **2:**308
people **2:**258, 259
illus. **2:**309, 311
flag **2:**viii
map(s) **2:**310
Singapore Strait (Southeast Asia) **2:**309
Singer, Isaac Bashevis (Polish-American author) **4:**215
Singh, Vishwanath Pratap (prime minister of India) **2:**218
Sinhalese (people) **2:**246–47, 249, 250, 251
Sinhalese language 2:248, 250
Sinkiang (autonomous region, China) *see* Xinjiang-Uygur
Sinn Féin Party (Ireland) **3:**77
Sino-Japanese War (1894–1895) **2:**427
Sino-Tibetan languages 2:28, 282
Sinú (indigenous people of Colombia) **6:**126
Sioux (Indians of North America) *see* Dakota Sioux
Sioux Falls (South Dakota) **5:**300
Sipán (Peru) **6:**223
Siqilli, Jawhar al- (Fatimid general) **1:**108, 115
Siqueiros, David Alfaro (Mexican artist) **5:**372
illus.
mural **5:**371, 411
Sisal (fiber) **1:**336
Sistine Chapel (Vatican, Rome) **4:**181
SiSwati language 1:387
Sittang River (Burma) **2:**267
Sitting Bull (Sioux chief) **5:**299
Siwa (oasis, Egypt) **1:**109, 112
Siwalik Range (Asia) **2:**167
Six Day War (1967) **2:**47, 105, 114, 116
Six Madun (Badus) (peak, Lepontine Alps, Switzerland) **3:**244
Sixtus IV (pope) **4:**181
Sjaelland (island, Denmark) *see* Zealand
Skagerrak (channel, Denmark–Norway) **4:**9
Skane (province, Sweden) **4:**38
Skansen (park, Stockholm, Sweden) **4:**45
Skënderbeg (Albanian national hero) **4:**271, 272
Skiing
France **3:**173, 175
Norway **4:**34
Swiss transportation **3:**290

Vermont **5:**187
illus. **3:**174, 251, 301; **4:**33
Skikda (Philippeville) (Algeria) **1:**77
Skinheads 3:249
Skopje (capital, Macedonia) **4:**291–92
illus. **4:**291
Skuas (birds) **6:**327, 328
Skydome (Toronto) **5:**108
Skye (island, Scotland) **3:**134
Skyros (Greek island) **4:**190
Slash-and-burn agriculture 1:245, 273; **2:**283
Slater, Sam (American industrialist) **5:**194
Slave River (Canada) **5:**122
Slavery
ancient Athens **4:**202
ancient Egypt **1:**118
Antigua and Barbuda **5:**494
Argentina **6:**270
Barbados **5:**480
Brazil **6:**95, 167, 188, 189, 190
captives of Barbary pirates **1:**97
Caribbean islands **5:**427, 434–36, 483, 485
Central and South America **6:**6, 92–95
colonial America **5:**36, 174
cotton plantations **5:**221, 222
Cuba **5:**445
Dominican Republic **5:**457, 458
Five Civilized Tribes **5:**306
Florida **5:**238
freed American blacks resettled in Liberia **1:**178, 182–83
French Guiana **6:**92
Georgia **5:**236
Haiti **5:**461, 467, 468
Jamaica **5:**476
Kansas **5:**304
Mauritius **1:**382
North Carolina **5:**231
Puerto Rico **5:**167, 168
Suriname **6:**155
Tuvaluans kidnapped in 1800s **2:**612
United Kingdom **3:**92
United States **5:**166–67, 174, 257, 274, 286, 435
Vermont, the first free state **5:**187
Virginia **5:**226
Yemen **2:**133
Slave trade
abolished in British colonies (1807) **5:**436
African coastal trade **1:**11, 20, 48, 51, 201–2
Angola and Mozambique to Brazil **1:**367
Central African Republic **1:**248
Congo area **1:**268
Denmark first European state to abolish **4:**14
depot at São Tomé and Príncipe **1:**238
foods introduced into Africa **1:**15
Gambia **1:**161, 163
Malawi, history of **1:**280
Nigeria, history of **1:**226
Slavey (Indians of North America) **5:**142
Slavic languages 3:20
Slavs (European people) **3:**18–19, 321 *see also* South Slavs
Belarus **4:**342, 343
Bosnia and Herzegovina **4:**288, 289, 290
Bulgaria **4:**260, 265
Czechs and Slovaks **4:**225, 230, 232, 233
Germany **3:**246
Macedonia **4:**290
Poland **4:**219
Russia **4:**319

Slovakia **4:**234
Ukraine **4:**333
Yugoslavia **4:**279
Sleeping Bear Dunes National Lakeshore (Michigan) **5:**269
Sleeping sickness 1:26, 216, 248, 332
Slieve Donard (mountain peak, Northern Ireland) **3:**143
Slovak Association 4:233
SLOVAKIA 3:2; **4:232–35**
Czechoslovakia, history of **4:**230, 231
Danube River **3:**327
illus. **4:**232, 233
flag **4:**v
map(s) **4:**234
Slovak language 4:232
Slovaks (Slavic peoples) **4:**225, 230, 231, 232, 233, 234, 235
Slovenes (people) **4:**134, 277, 282
SLOVENIA 3:2, 25; **4:**274, 280, **282–84**
illus. **4:**282
flag **4:**vi
map(s) **4:**283
Slovenian Alps *see* Julian Alps
Slovenian language 4:282
Smarth, Rosny (prime minister of Haiti) **5:**470
Smetana, Bedřich (Czech composer) **4:**225
Smith, Bessie (American singer) **5:**264
Smith, Ian Douglas (prime minister of Rhodesia) **1:**49–50, 362
Smith, John (English soldier and explorer)
Jamestown (Virginia) **5:**173
Maryland **5:**219
New England named by **5:**181
Smith, Joseph (American Mormon) **5:**325
Smith Sound (Greenland–Ellesmere Island) **5:**61
Smokies (mountains, U.S.) *see* Great Smoky Mountains
Smyrna (Turkey) *see* Izmir
Snag (Yukon Territory) **5:**135, 146
Snake River and Plain (U.S.) **5:**7, 313
Snakes 5:252
illus. **6:**10
Snegur, Mircea (president of Moldova) **4:**347
Snow *see* Precipitation
Snowdon (mountain peak, Wales) **3:**122
Snowdonia Mountains (Wales) **3:**122
Snowmobiles
illus. **5:**20, 141
Snow Mountains (Indonesia) *see* Jayawiyaya Mountains
Snow petrels 6:328
Snowy Mountains (Australia) **2:**484, 509, 515
Soares, Mário (premier of Portugal) **4:**78
Soba (Sudan) **1:**130
Sobaek Range (Korea) **2:**435
Sobhuza II (king of Swaziland) **1:**388–89
Sobieski *see* John III Sobieski
Soccer
Argentina **6:**289
Brazil **6:**179–80
Colombia **6:**123
England **3:**104
Europe **3:**24
France **3:**173
Italy **4:**140
Portugal **4:**70
Uruguay **6:**258
World Cup 2002 **2:**463
illus. **6:**45
Brazil **6:**179

Brazilian fans **6:**113
Germany **3:**251
Zimbabwe **1:**360
Soccer War (1969; Honduras–El Salvador) **6:**41, 50
Social classes
Argentina **6:**272
Asia **2:**21
Aztec society **5:**378
Brazil **6:**163, 164, 165
caste system in India **2:**210–11
China **2:**395, 397, 398
Ecuador **6:**196–97, 198
European barriers broken down **3:**26
Japanese concept of status **2:**450
Latin America **6:**6, 8, 108–9, 110–12
medieval society, divisions in **3:**52
Mexico **5:**382
Polynesia **2:**602
Rwanda **1:**325
Senegal **1:**155
Spanish colonial society **6:**224–25
Uruguay's integrated population **6:**254
Yemen **2:**133–34
Social Democratic Party (Germany) **3:**284
Socialism *see also* Capitalism
African agricultural policies **1:**63
Chile **6:**320, 322
Ethiopia **1:**286–87
European origin **3:**12, 59
France **3:**190–91
Libya **1:**96, 100
Mexico's combination with capitalism **5:**364
Spain **4:**117–18
Socialist Realism (Soviet artistic policy) **4:**314
Social welfare
Canada **5:**76
Denmark **4:**13–14
Egypt's rural social centers **1:**106
Europe **3:**44
European Union legislation **3:**40
France **3:**158
Germany **3:**262–63
Hungary, reform of system **4:**244
Kuwait **2:**145
Netherlands **3:**238
northern Europe **3:**25
Norway **4:**29–30
Sweden **4:**48
United Kingdom **3:**94
Uruguay **6:**252, 264
Society Islands (Pacific Ocean) **2:**560, 600, 601
Socotra (island, Gulf of Aden) **2:**130
Socrates (Greek philosopher) **3:**47
Soda ash 1:353
Soda Springs (Idaho) **5:**313
Sofala (Mozambique) **1:**278, 366
Sofia (capital, Bulgaria) **4:**263–64
illus. **4:**258
national theater **4:**263
Sogdians (Asian people) **2:**345
SoHo (neighborhood, New York City) **5:**205
Soignes Forest (Belgium) **3:**215
Soils
Africa **1:**19, 22–23
Arctic **5:**56, 63
Congo, Democratic Republic of **1:**266
Ethiopian erosion **1:**283
New England's rocky landscape **5:**179, 180
North America **5:**18, 20
Ukraine's *chernozem* **4:**333, 334

Sojo, Vicente Emilio (Venezuelan composer) **6:**142
Sokodé (Togo) **1:**206
illus. **1:**205
Solano López, Francisco (Paraguayan dictator) *see* López, Francisco Solano
Solar power 3:157
Solentiname, Archipelago of (Nicaragua) **6:**55
Solferino (Italy) **4:**158
Solidarity (Polish trade union confederation) **4:**222
illus. **4:**223
Solidarity Action (Polish political group) **4:**223
Solifluction 5:56
Solís, Juan Díaz de (Spanish explorer) **6:**262, 296
Solomon (king of Israel) **2:**46, 49
SOLOMON ISLANDS 2:559, 583, 585, 586, 587, **591–93**
illus. **2:**591
flag **2:**x
map(s) **2:**592
Solzhenitsyn, Aleksandr (Soviet author) **4:**314
Somali (African people) **1:**288, 291, 298, 315
colonialism cut across ethnic groups **1:**36, 37
SOMALIA (Somali Democratic Republic) 1:37, **300–305**
clans and subclans **1:**303
Ethiopia, relations with **1:**291
Kenya, relations with **1:**315
refugees in Ethiopia **1:**286
Somaliland Republic **1:**305
illus.
coastline **1:**301
flag **1:**xxiii
marketplace **1:**304
Mogadishu **1:**300
map(s) **1:**302
Somaliland (now **Somalia**) **4:**159
Somaliland Republic 1:305
Somali language 1:37, 285, 301
Somba (African people) **1:**213
Sombrerete (Zacatecas, Mexico) **5:**399
Sombrero (island, West Indies) **5:**495
Somoza (Nicaraguan family) **6:**17
Somoza Debayle, Anastasio (president of Nicaragua) **6:**58
Somoza Garcia, Anastasio (president of Nicaragua) **6:**58
Songhai (early African kingdom) **1:**50, 140, 142, 143, 148, 162
Soninke (African people) *see* Sarakole
Sonoma (California) **5:**347
Sonoma Valley (California) **5:**346
SONORA (state, Mexico) **5:**392
Sonoran Desert (Mexico–U.S.) **5:**30, 327, 329, 358
illus. **5:**329, 358
Son River (India) **2:**168
Son Sann (premier of Cambodia) **2:**292
Sooner State (nickname for Oklahoma) **5:**305
Sorghum 5:304
Soriano, Juan (Mexican artist) **5:**372
Soroche (altitude sickness) **6:**212
Sorokin, Vladimir (Russian writer) **4:**315
Soros, George (Hungarian-American financier) **4:**312
Sotho (African people) **1:**398
Soto, Jesús (Venezuelan painter) **6:**142
Soto, Marco Aurelio (president of Honduras) **6:**41
Soubirous, Bernadette *see* Bernadette, Saint

Soufrière (St. Lucia) **5:**489
Soufrière, Mount (volcano, Saint Vincent) **5:**491
Soufrière Hills (volcano, Montserrat) **5:**439
illus. **5:**439
Sousse (Tunisia) **1:**88, 90
South, The (U.S.) **5:**162 *see also* South-Central States; Southern States
SOUTH AFRICA 1:45, **394–406**
Afrikaners **1:**401
Angola, history of **1:**346
apartheid **1:**31, 58–59
Botswana, relations with **1:**354
democratic elections **1:**1
Inkatha **1:**405
international trade **1:**3, 46
Lesotho **1:**390, 392, 393
Namibia, history of **1:**350
Walvis Bay **1:**350
illus.
Cape Town **1:**5, 397
flag **1:**xxiv
game reserve **1:**395
gold **1:**403
gold refining **1:**45
Johannesburg **1:**12, 399
map(s) **1:**396
South African War (1899–1902) *see* Anglo-Boer War
South Africa Republic *see* Transvaal
SOUTH AMERICA 6:1–8, **82–115** *see also* Latin America; names of countries
Afro-American culture **6:**91–95
Alliance for Progress **6:**86
Amazon River **6:**168–69
Andes (mountains) **6:**100–101
Euro-American culture **6:**95–97
Indo-American culture **6:**89–91
Mercosur **6:**262
Orinoco River **6:**146–47
Río de la Plata Basin **6:**242, 284
illus.
eroded limestone rocks **6:**88
flags of the countries **6:**vi
racial and ethnic groups **6:**94
map(s) **6:**4–5, 85
Andes **6:**101
population **6:**99
precipitation **6:**98
Río de la Plata Basin **6:**284
table(s)
area and population **6:**344
continental extremes **6:**345
countries **6:**98–99
great mountain peaks **6:**349
Southampton (England) **3:**109
South Arabia, Federation of 2:135
SOUTH ASIA 2:6, 27, **165–73**
illus.
boats on river **2:**7
SOUTH AUSTRALIA (state, Australia) **2:**490, **521–23**
illus.
Adelaide Festival of Arts **2:**522
underground construction **2:**521
vineyard **2:**522
map(s) **2:**523
South Bend (Indiana) **5:**280
SOUTH CAROLINA 5:230–32
map(s) **5:**231
South Central L.A. (district, Los Angeles, California) **5:**345

SOUTH-CENTRAL STATES (region, U.S.) **5:256–67**
South China Sea
Malaysia **2:**303
Mekong River Delta **2:**257
table(s)
major seas of the world **6:**347
SOUTH DAKOTA 5:158, **299–300**
map(s) **5:**300
South Downs (hills, England) **3:**82, 100
SOUTHEAST ASIA 2:6, 17–18, 27, **253–64** *see also* names of countries
France's colonial empire in **2:**24
Mekong River **2:**256–57
Oceania, continental islands of **2:**559
illus.
Buddhist temple **2:**18
farming **2:**255
floating market **2:**257
Petronas Towers **2:**253
rice growing **2:**10
traditional clothing **2:**254
traditional religion **2:**258
map(s) **2:**254
Mekong River **2:**256
Southeast Cape (Tasmania, Australia) **2:**481
Southern Africa (region) **1:**11, 44–50
Southern African Development Community 1:46, 354, 388
Southern Alps (New Zealand) **2:**538, 539
Southern Highlanders (name for people of Appalachia) **5:**257
Southern Italy Development Fund 4:151
Southern Rhodesia *see* Zimbabwe
SOUTHERN STATES (region, U.S.) **5:220–55**
Atlanta exemplifies the New South **5:**235
British North America **5:**35, 36
resources **5:**48–49
Southern Uplands (region, Scotland) **3:**83, 133
South Georgia Island (British dependency) **3:**90; **6:**286, 333
South Island (New Zealand) **2:**537, 538–39, 540–41, 544
precipitation **2:**476
table(s)
largest islands of the world **6:**346
SOUTH KOREA (Korea, Republic of) 2:26, 429, **434–38**
Christians fled from North Korea **2:**431
economy **2:**375, 376
energy needs **2:**37
illus.
circle dance **2:**436
flag **2:**ix
Seoul **2:**434
map(s) **2:**435
South Ossetia (region, republic of Georgia) **2:**80
South Platte River (Colorado) **5:**320
South Pole 6:332, 334
South Sandwich Islands (British dependency) **3:**90; **6:**286
South Seas *see* Pacific islands and island groups; Pacific Ocean
South Shetland Islands (Antarctic Ocean) **6:**331
South Side (area of Chicago, Illinois) **5:**283
South Slavs (peoples of Europe) **4:**282, 286, 291 *see also* Slavs
South Thompson River (British Columbia) **5:**131
South Tyrol (Italy) **4:**160

South-West Africa *see* Namibia
SOUTHWEST ASIA 2:5–6, 23, 26–27, **41–55**
illus.
ruins **2:**48
South Yemen 2:135
Soutpansberg (area, South Africa) **1:**395
Souvanna Phouma, Prince (prime minister of Laos) **2:**285
Souza, Thomé de (Brazilian captain-general) **6:**187
Soviets (Russian revolutionary councils) **4:**322
Soviet Union *see* Union of Soviet Socialist Republics
Soweto (South Africa) **1:**398
Space exploration and travel
Baikonur space center **2:**346
Florida **5:**241
French Guiana space center **6:**92, 93
Soviet space program **4:**312
illus.
Sputnik monument **4:**312
U.S. launch **5:**176
U.S. Space and Rocket Center **5:**243
Space Needle (Seattle, Washington)
illus. **5:**338
Space shuttle (U.S. spacecraft)
illus. **5:**176
SPAIN 4:79–118
Canary Islands **1:**32–33
Caribbean Islands **5:**430–33, 434, 438
Central and South America **6:**3, 82
Cuba **5:**444–46
Gibraltar **4:**123
Italy, history of **4:**157
Mexico, conquest of **5:**379–80
overseas territories **4:**85–86
Peru, war with **6:**227
Polynesia, history of **2:**602
Portugal, history of **4:**76
Puerto Rico, history of **5:**168
Santo Domingo, history of **5:**459
Spanish Guinea **1:**236
Spanish North America **5:**25–31, 165, 173, 174
tourism **3:**41
Western Sahara **1:**132–33
illus.
Alhambra **4:**79, 112
Andalusian street **4:**87
automotive industry **4:**106
Barcelona **4:**102, 103
bullfight **4:**93
cork harvesting **4:**108
Costa del Sol **4:**85
field **3:**32
flag **4:**v
flamenco dancers **4:**95
hotel in Galicia **4:**90
Madrid **4:**96, 97, 117
Majorca **4:**84
Moorish architecture **4:**114
orange cultivation **4:**107
royal wedding **4:**91
running the bulls in Pamplona **4:**94
Segovia **4:**101, 111
Seville **4:**104, 105
Seville's Holy Week procession **4:**88
sherry **4:**109
Sierra Nevada **4:**83
Toledo **4:**100
village in Pyrenees **4:**82
map(s) **4:**81

Spanish-American War (1898–1899) **5:**438, 446
  Philippines **2:**339–40
  Spain **4:**116
Spanish Armada *see* Armada, Spanish
Spanish Fork (Utah) **5:**324
Spanish Guinea *see* Equatorial Guinea
Spanish Hispaniola *see* Dominican Republic
Spanish language 4:88
  Argentina **6:**279
  Caribbean islands **5:**435
  Dominican Republic **5:**457
  Latin America **6:**1, 6, 11, 82, 83
  Uruguayan similarities to Argentinian **6:**258
Spanish Main (mainland of South America)
  6:19, 97
Spanish Morocco (former Spanish possessions)
  4:85
Spanish North America 5:25–31
Spanish Sahara *see* Western Sahara
Spanish Steps (Rome, Italy)
  illus. **4:**171
Spanish Succession, War of the (1701–1713)
  4:91, 116
  Spain ceded Gibraltar to England **4:**86, 123
Sparks (Nevada) **5:**332
Sparta (ancient Greek city) **4:**199, 202, 203
Spas (resorts) **3:**24; **4:**225
Speed Art Museum (Louisville, Kentucky) **5:**261
Speke, John H. (English explorer) **1:**268
  Rwanda and Uganda **1:**316, 322, 326
Spence, Catherine Helen (Australian reformer
  and writer) **2:**501
Spencer Gulf (Australia) **2:**521
Sperrin Mountains (Northern Ireland) **3:**83, 143
Sphinx (mythological monster) **1:**39, 110
Spice Islands *see* Moluccas
Spice trade, Portuguese 4:75, 76
Spider divination 1:230–31
Spiny anteaters *see* Echidnas
Spirit worship *see* Animism
Spitsbergen (islands, Arctic Ocean) **3:**8; **4:**24;
  5:61
Spitteler, Carl (Swiss author) **3:**290
Split (Croatia) **4:**285, 287
Spock, Benjamin (American pediatrician) **5:**196
Spokan (Indians of North America) **5:**337
Spokane (Washington) **5:**337
Spokane Falls (Spokane, Washington) **5:**337
Spokane River (Washington) **5:**337
Sporades (Greek islands) **4:**190–91
Sports
  Argentina **6:**274–75, 289
  Australia **2:**492
  "Australian Rules" football **2:**516, 519
  Belgium **3:**215
  Brazil **6:**179–80
  Chile **6:**307
  China **2:**408
  Colombia **6:**123
  Czech Republic **4:**226
  England **3:**104–5
  Europe **3:**24
  Finland's *pesäpallo* **4:**64
  France **3:**173, 175
  Germany **3:**250
  Hungary **4:**240
  Iran **2:**159
  Ireland **3:**68
  Italy **4:**140
  Japan **2:**463
  Kyrgyz horseback games **2:**354

  Mongolia **2:**364
  New Zealand **2:**545
  Portugal **4:**70
  Seattle **5:**338
  Switzerland **3:**288–89
  Thailand **2:**277
  Toronto **5:**104, 108
  Uruguay **6:**258
  Venezuela **6:**142
  illus.
    "Australian Rules" football **2:**519
    Chinese exercise group **2:**393
    Chinese gymnasts **2:**408
    cricket **2:**544; **3:**107
    hockey **5:**46
    lawn bowling **2:**544
    polo **3:**107
    rugby **2:**544
    soccer **6:**45
    tennis **3:**107
    zorbing **2:**545
SPQR (Senate and the People of Rome) **4:**165
Spree River (Germany) **3:**243, 280
Springer Mountain (Georgia) **5:**233
Springfield (capital, Illinois) **5:**282
Springfield (Massachusetts) **5:**189, 190–91
Springfield (Missouri) **5:**296
Springs (South Africa) **1:**402
Sputnik I (Soviet space satellite) **4:**312
  illus.
    monument **4:**312
Spyri, Johanna (Swiss author) **3:**285
Square du Vert Galant (Paris, France) **3:**195
Sranang Tongo (Taki-Taki) language 6:158
Srebrenica (Bosnia and Herzegovina) **4:**290
SRI LANKA 2:27, 245–50
  population control **2:**171
  religious strife **2:**170
  trade routes and colonialism **2:**23, 24
  illus.
    Buddhist shrine **2:**247
    Colombo **2:**245
    flag **2:**viii
    Hindu temple **2:**247
    rice growing **2:**249
    tea plantation **2:**248
  map(s) **2:**246
  table(s)
    largest islands of the world **6:**346
Srinagar (Kashmir) **2:**173
Sriwijaya (ancient Asian kingdom) **2:**308, 324
SS (Nazi security troops) **3:**279
St. (Ste.) (abbreviation for Saint and Sainte) *see*
  names of saints, as Paul, Saint; for names of
  places see under Saint and Sainte, as Saint
  Louis (Missouri)
Stalin, Joseph (Soviet premier) **4:**322–23, 331
  censorship and purges **4:**314, 322
  deportation of Crimean Tatars **4:**336
  de-Stalinization of Soviet life **4:**323
  five-year plans for industrial growth **4:**316
  Georgia (republic) **2:**83, 84
  mass graves of "Great Terror" victims found
    4:342
  Poland never built a monument to him **4:**222
  Rybakov's *Children of the Arbat* **4:**315
Stalingrad (Russia) *see* Volgograd
Stalingrad, Battle of (1942–1943) **3:**278
Stamboul (sector of Istanbul, Turkey) **2:**62, 63
Stamford (Connecticut) **5:**197

Stamps, postage
  Andorra **4:**122
  Liechtenstein **3:**307
  Monaco **3:**206
  Pitcairn Island **2:**563
  San Marino **4:**176
Stanley (capital, Falkland Islands) **6:**286, 287
  illus. **6:**286
Stanley, Henry Morton (English explorer)
  Burundi and Uganda **1:**322, 331
  Congo River area **1:**43, 261, 268
Stanley Falls (Congo River) **1:**42
Stanley Park (Vancouver, British Columbia)
  5:130
Stanleyville (Congo, Democratic Republic of)
  see Kisangani
Star Island (New Hampshire) **5:**184
Star-Spangled Banner (national anthem of the
  U.S.) **5:**219
STASI (secret police of former East Germany)
  3:250
Staten Island (New York) **5:**201, 203
States General (Dutch parliament) **3:**234, 235,
  236
Statue of Liberty 5:169, 203
Stavanger (Norway) **4:**33
Steel
  France **3:**157
  German industry **3:**261
  Luxembourg **3:**207
  Pennsylvania **5:**213, 214
  Pittsburgh **5:**200
  Sheffield (England) **3:**107
  Sweden **4:**46
  Youngstown (Ohio) **5:**273–74
  illus.
    Chinese industry **2:**415
    German industry **3:**246
    Japanese industry **2:**469
    Swedish industry **4:**47
Steel band (music) **5:**485
  illus. **5:**485
Steep Point (Western Australia) **2:**481
Štefánik, M. R. (Slovak general) **4:**235
Steger, Will (American explorer) **6:**337
Stellenbosch (South Africa) **1:**400, 403
Stendhal (French writer) **3:**178
  quoted on Naples **4:**144
Stephanie (princess of Monaco) **3:**206
Stephen, Saint (Stephen I) (king of Hungary)
  4:244–45
Stephen Dušan (king of Serbia) **4:**277, 279
Steppes (plains regions) **3:**33
  Africa **1:**89, 135
  Kazakhstan **2:**343
  Russia **2:**342, 343; **4:**308
  Ukraine **4:**333
  map(s)
    world climate **6:**354
    world vegetation **6:**353
Sterkfontein (South Africa) **1:**403
Sterling Heights (Michigan) **5:**278
Stevens, Siaka (president of Sierra Leone) **1:**176
Stewart Island (New Zealand) **2:**537, 539, 544
  illus. **2:**538
Stirling Range (Australia) **2:**524–25
Stockholm (capital, Sweden) **4:**39, 44–45
  illus. **4:**38, 44
Stockton and Darlington Railroad (England)
  3:41

Stone Age (archaeology)
Malta **4:**182
Maori culture **2:**550
Northern Ireland **3:**147
Zambia, archaeological excavations in **1:**271
Stonehenge (England) **3:**16, 114
illus. **3:**114
Stone walls 5:180
Stoney (Indians of North America) **5:**125
Stóri Geysir (geyser, Iceland) **4:**4
Stormont (parliament, Northern Ireland) **3:**146, 149
Storytelling
illus. **1:**15
Stowe (Vermont) **5:**187
Stowe, Harriet Beecher (American author) **5:**196
Stoyanov, Petar (president of Bulgaria) **4:**267
Strangford Lough (Northern Ireland) **3:**143
Strasbourg (France) **3:**62, 161, 245
Strasser, Valentine (president of Sierra Leone) **1:**177
Stratford-on-Avon (England) **3:**116
illus. **3:**116
Strathclyde, Kingdom of 3:140
Strathmore Valley (Scotland) **3:**133
Strauss, Richard (German composer) **3:**259
Streets *see* Roads and highways
Strikes (labor)
Albania **4:**273
Bulgaria **4:**264–65
France **3:**170
Italy, history of **4:**160
Ohio **5:**274
Poland **4:**222
United Kingdom **3:**95
Strindberg, August (Swedish playwright) **4:**43
Stroessner, Alfredo (president of Paraguay) **6:**114, 250
illus. **6:**249
Stromboli (island, Italy) **4:**130
Stuart, Charles (Bonnie Prince Charlie; the Young Pretender) 3:141
Stuart, House of 6:361
Students' Grove (Oslo, Norway) **4:**31
Stuttgart (Germany) **3:**266–67
Styria (province of Austria) **3:**314–15, 318, 320
Suakoko (Liberia) **1:**181
Subic Naval Base (Philippines) **2:**336, 340
Submarines
polar exploration **5:**64
Subsistence farming 1:26; **6:**14
Congo **1:**44, 258
El Salvador **6:**45
Haiti **5:**467
Moldova **4:**344
Nicaragua **6:**55
Nigeria **1:**58
Tanzania **1:**41
Venezuela **6:**135
Subways
Paris (France) **3:**200
Rome (Italy) **4:**170
illus.
Caracas (Venezuela) **6:**137
London (England) **3:**112
Suceviţa (Romania) **4:**252
illus.
monastery **4:**250
Sucksdorff, Arne (Swedish film director) **4:**44
Sucre (constitutional capital, Bolivia) **6:**232, 233
illus. **6:**233

Sucre, Antonio José de (South American liberator) **6:**204, 226, 240
SUDAN 1:124–31
Egypt **1:**121
Nile River **1:**38–39
North African countries **1:**32, 35
refugees **1:**286
Sahara **1:**24
United States bombing of **1:**308
illus.
carved stones **1:**131
flag **1:**xxii
Khartoum **1:**124
market **1:**129
schoolchildren **1:**126
thatched porches **1:**127
map(s) **1:**125
Sudanese Republic *see* Mali
Sudbury (Ontario) **5:**4, 108
Sudd (swamp region, Nile) **1:**38, 125
SUDENE (Superintendency for the Development of the Northeast Region) (Brazil) **6:**169
Sudetenland (Czechoslovakia) **3:**277; **4:**228, 230
Sudetes Mountains (Europe) **4:**212, 213, 224
Sudras (caste, India) **2:**21, 210
Suez (Egypt) **1:**113, 114
Suez, Gulf of (Red Sea) **1:**120
Suez Canal (Egypt) **1:**112, 113, 120–21
Arab-Israeli wars **1:**123; **2:**114
England's purchase **3:**93
French interests in the canal **3:**186
nationalization **1:**122
North Africa and Asia **1:**35, 298; **2:**52
Suffrage
Australia **2:**501, 502
Belgium **3:**214
Belgium women **3:**224
Black Americans **5:**222
Canadian women **5:**117
Costa Rican women **6:**71
French women **3:**26
Iranian women **2:**158, 159
Liechtenstein women **3:**307
Mexican women **5:**388
New Zealand women **2:**554
Panama's mandatory voting **6:**81
Portuguese women **4:**77
Swiss women **3:**26, 298
United Kingdom, women in **3:**93
Uruguay **6:**252, 265
U.S. women **5:**176, 312
Wyoming women first to vote **5:**317
Sugar
Barbados **5:**479, 480
Brazilian plantations **6:**94–95, 164, 167, 173
Caribbean economy **5:**433–34, 436
Colombia **6:**124
Congo, Republic of **1:**258
Cuba **5:**451, 452
Dominican Republic **5:**454, 459
Jamaica **5:**473, 476
Trinidad and Tobago **5:**485
illus.
harvesting sugarcane **5:**434, 457; **6:**23
processing in Pakistan **2:**188
processing sugarcane **5:**473
stands of sugarcane **1:**380
Sugar Islands (early name for Caribbean islands) **5:**427

Sugarloaf Mountain (Rio de Janeiro, Brazil) **6:**185
illus. **6:**183
Suharto (president of Indonesia) **2:**325–26
Suicide rate in Hungary 4:239
Sui dynasty (China) **2:**420
Suipacha, Battle of (1810) **6:**397
Sukarno (Indonesian political leader) **2:**324, 325
Sukhe Bator (Mongolia) **2:**366
Sukhumi (republic of Georgia) **2:**84
Sukumuland (region, Tanzania) **1:**332
Sulaiman Range (Asia) **2:**167
Sulawesi (island, Indonesia) **2:**314, 315, 318, 322, 323
table(s)
largest islands of the world **6:**346
Suleiman I (the Magnificent) (sultan of Turkey) **2:**65
Sulfur
illus.
Italian industrial plant **4:**133
Sulina channel (Danube River) **3:**329
Sumatra (Indonesian island) **2:**314–15, 318, 320, 322, 323, 324
table(s)
largest islands of the world **6:**346
Sumba (island, Indonesia) **2:**315
Sumerians (people) **2:**11–12, 41, 48, 152–53
Sumgait (Azerbaijan) **2:**88, 89
Summerside (Prince Edward Island) **5:**88
Sumo wrestling 2:463
illus. **2:**463
Sunda Islands (Indonesia) **2:**314–15
Sundance (Film) Institute 5:324
Sundanese (people) **2:**318
Sundarbans (region, Bangladesh) **2:**238, 239
Sunda Strait 2:313
Sunday Afternoon at the Grande Jatte (painting, Seurat)
illus. **3:**176
Sunflower State (nickname for Kansas) **5:**303
Sun King *see* Louis XIV
Sunni (branch of Islam)
Asia, Central **2:**344
Asia, Southwest **2:**45
China **2:**380
former Soviet republics **2:**342
Iran **2:**157
Iraq **2:**148–49
Jordan **2:**118
Lebanon **2:**100, 102
Muslim Brotherhood **1:**123
Pakistan **2:**183
Saudi Arabia **2:**123
Syria **2:**91, 92
Yemen **2:**133
Sunset Crater National Monument (Arizona)
illus. **5:**9
Sunshine State (nickname for Florida) **5:**237
Sun Valley (resort, Idaho) **5:**314
Sun Yat-sen (Chinese statesman) **2:**25, 396
Suomenlinna (Sveaborg) (Finnish fortress, Helsinki) **4:**63
Superga, Basilica of (Turin, Italy) **4:**145
Superior, Lake (Canada–U.S.) **5:**269, 270
table(s)
largest lakes **6:**347
Superior Upland (North America) *see* Canadian Shield
Supreme Headquarters Allied Powers Europe *see* SHAPE
Surabaya (Indonesia) **2:**323

Surami Range (republic of Georgia) **2:**80
Sûre River (Belgium–Luxembourg) **3:**208
Surin (Thailand) **2:**277
SURINAME 6:7, 153–59
illus.
　　bauxite processing **6:**159
　　flag **6:**vi
　　Paramaribo **6:**153, 156
　　rain forest **6:**157
map(s) **6:**154
Suriname River (Suriname) **6:**154
Surtsey (island south of Iceland) **4:**2
Suryavarman II (king of Cambodia) **2:**290
Susa (ancient city, Persia) **2:**160
Susquehanna River and Valley (U.S.) **5:**6, 212
Susquehannock (Indians of North America)
　　5:218
Susu (African people) **1:**167, 173
Sutherland Falls (New Zealand) **2:**539
illus. **2:**537
Sutlej River (central Asia) **2:**170, 183
Suva (capital, Fiji) **2:**597
illus. **2:**597
Suzerainty (type of government) **4:**121
Svealand (region, Sweden) **4:**38, 39
Svear (ancient tribe, Sweden) **4:**39, 48
Sverdrup, Otto (Norwegian explorer) **5:**62
Swabia (historic region, Germany) **3:**273
Swahili language 1:15, 36, 312, 334
Swains Island (American Samoa) **2:**603
Swakopmund (Namibia) **1:**348
Swamps *see also* Bogs; Marshes
　　Everglades **5:**240
　　Florida **5:**238
　　Great Cypress Swamp **5:**199, 215
　　Great Dismal Swamp **5:**223, 227
　　New Jersey Pine Barrens **5:**208
　　Okefenokee **5:**233–34
　　Sudd (Sudan) **1:**38, 125
Swan River (Australia) **2:**526
Swansea (Wales) **3:**124, 127
illus.
　　statue of Dylan Thomas **3:**126
**SWAPO (South-West African People's Organi-
　　zation) 1:**350
Swartberg (mountains, South Africa) **1:**395
Swazi (African people) **1:**47, 386, 398
SWAZILAND 1:47, **385–89**
illus.
　　farm **1:**387
　　flag **1:**xxiv
　　lumber industry **1:**389
　　people **1:**385
map(s) **1:**386
SWEDEN 4:38–50
　　automobiles **3:**41
　　Denmark, history of **4:**20
　　Estonia, relations with **4:**295
　　Finland, history of **4:**55–56
　　hydroelectricity **3:**37
　　Lapland **4:**35, 37
　　Norway **4:**26
　　women in society **3:**25–26
illus.
　　crystal **4:**43
　　farm **4:**42
　　flag **4:**v
　　Göteborg **4:**46
　　Gripsholm Castle **4:**49
　　sculptures in Millesgarden **4:**45
　　Stockholm **4:**38, 44
map(s) **4:**41

Swedes (people) **4:**40–41
　　in America **4:**46
　　Swedish Vikings **3:**51
Swedish language 4:40
Swift, Jonathan (Anglo-Irish writer) **3:**70
Swissair (airline) **3:**221, 289
Swiss Confederation 3:296–97
Swiss Guards (Vatican City) **3:**297; **4:**180
illus. **4:**180
SWITZERLAND 3:285–98
　　Alps **3:**299–304
　　climate **3:**30
　　highest standard of living in Europe **3:**25
　　languages **3:**20
　　Rhine River **3:**244–45
　　women get right to vote **3:**26
illus.
　　Alpine village **3:**285
　　flag **3:**vi
　　Geneva **3:**61, 294
　　Gstaad **3:**303
　　ice tunnel in Rhone Glacier **3:**303
　　Interlaken **3:**5
　　Jungfrau **3:**302
　　Lake of Lucerne and Mount Pilatus **3:**304
　　Lucerne **3:**296
　　Matterhorn **3:**300
　　Zermatt **3:**289
　　Zurich **3:**292
map(s) **3:**287
Sydney (capital, New South Wales, Australia)
　　2:485, 495, 500, 509, 511, 512
　　education **2:**497
　　sports **2:**519
illus.
　　Darling Harbor **2:**512
　　Olympic Games **2:**503
　　skyline **2:**511
Sydney (Nova Scotia) **5:**93
Symbolists poets 3:178
Synagogues
　　Prague (Czech Republic) **4:**227
Synge, John Millington (Irish playwright) **3:**67,
　　70
Syngman Rhee (Korean statesman) **2:**438
Syracuse (New York) **5:**46
Syracuse (Sicily) **4:**129
Syr Darya (river, Asia) **2:**347, 350, 353
SYRIA 2:90–96
　　Arab-Israeli wars **2:**114
　　archaeology **2:**51
　　cities **2:**47
　　Egypt **1:**122
　　Lebanon **2:**103
　　United Arab Republic **1:**35; **2:**55
illus.
　　clothing, Western and traditional **2:**92
　　Damascus **2:**90, 95
　　flag **2:**vii
　　Palmyra ruins **2:**96
　　village **2:**94
map(s) **2:**91
Syriac (Aramean dialect) **2:**93
Széchenyi, István (Hungarian statesman) **4:**245
Szechwan (province, China) *see* Sichuan
Szeged (Hungary) **4:**243
Szent-Györgyi, Albert (Hungarian-American
　　scientist) **4:**241
Szilard, Leo (Hungarian scientist) **4:**241
Szymborska, Wisława (Polish poet) **4:**215

• • • T • • •

Tabasca (Indians of North America) **5:**419
TABASCO (state, Mexico) **5:**375, **419**
Table Bay (Cape Town, South Africa) **1:**398, 403
Table Mountain (Cape Town, South Africa)
　　1:396, 398
　　illus. **1:**397
Tabriz (Iran) **2:**46, 159
Tacitus, Cornelius (Roman historian) **3:**33
Tacna-Arica dispute *see* Pacific, War of the
Tacoma (Washington) **5:**337
Taconic Mountains (Connecticut–
　　Massachusetts–New York) **5:**179–80, 189,
　　195, 201
Tadjoura (Djibouti) **1:**298
Tadzhikistan *see* Tajikistan
Tadzhiks (Asian people) *see* Tajiks
Taebaek Range (Korea) **2:**430, 435
Taegu (South Korea) **2:**436
Taft, William (27th president of U.S.) **5:**273
Tagalog dialect 2:334
Tagish (Indians of North America) **5:**146
Tagore, Rabindranath (Bengali poet) **2:**240
Tagus River (Spain–Portugal) **4:**66, 67, 71, 82
　　dams **4:**73
Tahiti (Pacific island, French Polynesia) **2:**558–
　　59, 601, 602
illus.
　　Papeete public transportation **2:**558
Tahlequah (capital of Cherokee Nation) **5:**306
Tahoe, Lake (California–Nevada) **5:**332, 342
　　illus. **5:**330, 332
Tahoua (Niger) **1:**145
Tai (people) **2:**283, 295
Taichung (Taiwan) **2:**424
Taif (Saudi Arabia) **2:**123
Taiga (woodland) **2:**342, 343; **3:**32
　　Russia **4:**307
　　map(s)
　　　world climate **6:**354
Tai language *see* Thai language
Taino (Indians of South America) **5:**456
Taipa (island, part of Macau) **2:**416
Taipei (capital, Taiwan) **2:**424, 425, 427
　　illus. **2:**423
Taiping Rebellion (1851–1864) **2:**421
Tairona (people of Colombia) **6:**126
**TAIWAN (Nationalist China; Republic of
　　China) 2:**375, 376, 380, 397, **423–28**
　　Japanese control **2:**446, 447
　　landforms **2:**368, 423
illus.
　　Confucianism **2:**373, 425
　　flag **2:**ix
　　painting vases **2:**426
　　people **2:**17
　　Taipei **2:**423
　　terraced rice paddies **2:**427
map(s) **2:**424
Taizz (Yemen) **2:**131
TAJIKISTAN 2:341, 342, 343, 344, **359–61**
　　illus. **2:**359
　　flag **2:**ix
　　map(s) **2:**360
Tajiks (Asian people) **2:**175, 344, 359
Taj Mahal (Agra, India) **2:**216
　　illus. **2:**195
Tajumulco (mountain, Guatemala) **6:**30

Takht-i-Sulaiman (mountain, Pakistan) **2:**182
Taki-Taki (language) *see* Sranang Tongo
Takkaze (Setit) River (Africa) **1:**283, 294
Takla Makan (desert, China) **2:**10
Talal (king of Jordan) **2:**121
Talamanca, Cordillera de (mountains, Costa Rica) **6:**63
Talas River (Kyrgyzstan–Kazakhstan) **2:**353
Taliban (militant Islamic fundamentalists) **2:**342
   Afghanistan **2:**174, 177–78, 179
   prisoners at Guantánamo Bay **5:**450
Tallahassee (capital, Florida) **5:**241
Tallahassee Hills (Florida) **5:**237
Tallinn (capital, Estonia) **4:**294–95, 296
   illus. **4:**293
Tamale (Ghana) **1:**198
Tamang (Asian people) **2:**231
Tamara (queen of Georgia) **2:**84
Tamar River (Australia) **2:**530
Tamatave (Madagascar) *see* Toamasina
Tamaulipan Indians 5:396
TAMAULIPAS (state, Mexico) **5:396**
Tamayo, Rufino (Mexican artist) **5:**372–73
Tambacounda (Senegal) **1:**153
Tamerlane (Timur the Lame) (Turkic conqueror) **2:**154, 162, 178
   Georgia (republic) **2:**84
   Turkmenistan **2:**358
   Uzbekistan **2:**350
Tamil language 2:248, 250, 310
   Hindus in Mauritius **1:**381
   Malaysia **2:**305
   motion pictures **2:**204
   southern India **2:**199
Tamil Nadu (Madras State) (India) **2:**247
   Madras (Chenai) **2:**207–8
Tamils (Asian people) **2:**30, 246, 247, 250
Tampa (Florida) **5:**49, 239, 241
Tampere (Finland) **4:**64
Tampico (Tamaulipas, Mexico) **5:**30, 389, 396
Tana, Lake (Ethiopia) **1:**39, 283
Tananarive (Madagascar) *see* Antananarivo
Tana River (east Africa) **1:**307
Tanga (Tanzania) **1:**334
Tanganyika (now part of Tanzania) **1:**40–41, 332, 337
Tanganyika, Lake (Africa) **1:**262, 328, 330
   Africa's rift valleys **1:**19
   table(s)
      largest lakes **6:**347
Tangaxoan Zincicha (Tarascan king) **5:**409
Tang dynasty (China) **2:**394, 420
Tangier (Morocco) **1:**67, 74; **4:**85
   illus. **1:**70
Tanglha Range (China) **2:**256
Tango (dance) **6:**275–76
   illus. **6:**277
Tanks (military vehicles)
   illus. **5:**171
Tanna (island, Vanuatu) **2:**594, 595, 596
Tannenberg, Battle of (1410) *see* Grünwald, Battle of
Tano River (Ghana) **1:**195
TANZANIA 1:3, 36, 40–41, **332–38**
   ancestors of early humans **1:**6
   Uganda, relations with **1:**323
   illus.
      adult education **1:**335
      agriculture **1:**337
      Arusha National Park **1:**338
      Dar es Salaam **1:**334

flag 1:xxiv
   Ngorongoro Crater **1:**332
   map(s) **1:**333
Taoudéni (Mali) **1:**140, 142
Tapioca 2:277
Tapiola (Finland) **4:**64
   illus. **4:**63
Tara (Ireland) **3:**74
Taranaki, Mount (New Zealand) *see* Egmont, Mount
Tarapacá (province, Chile) **6:**313
Tara River (Yugoslavia) **4:**275
Tarascan (Mexican Indian dialect) **5:**355
Tarascans (Indians of North America) **5:**409
Tarascos (Mexican people) **5:**376
Tarawa (atoll, Kiribati) **2:**580
Tarbela Dam (Indus River) **2:**183
Tárcoles River (Costa Rica) **6:**63
Tarik (Tariq) (Muslim warrior) **4:**123
Tarragona (Spain) **3:**46; **4:**111
Tar sands *see* Oil sands
Tartars *see* Tatars
Tartu (Estonia) **4:**295
Tashkent (capital, Uzbekistan) **2:**344, 350, 351
   illus. **2:**350
Tasman, Abel Janszoon (Dutch navigator) **2:**478, 499
   Fiji **2:**586, 599, 605
   New Zealand **2:**551
   Tasmania **2:**531
Tasman Glacier (New Zealand) **2:**539
TASMANIA (island state of Australia) **2:**484, 485, 486, 499, **528–31**
   illus. **2:**528
      coastline **2:**529
      Hobart **2:**530
      Port Arthur **2:**531
   map(s) **2:**529
   table(s)
      largest islands of the world **6:**346
Tasmanian devil 2:487, 529
   illus. **2:**529
Tasmanian tiger *see* Tasmanian wolf
Tasmanian wolf 2:487, 530
   illus. **2:**530
Tasman Sea 2:474
Tatars (Tartars) (nomads of central Asia) **3:**18; **4:**245 *see also* Mongols
   Crimean Tatars **4:**336
   Iran **2:**162
   Russia **4:**319–20, 328
Tatra (mountains, Europe) **3:**33; **4:**213, 232
Tattoos 2:444
Tau (island in American Samoa) **2:**603
Taufa'ahau Tupou IV (king of Tonga) **2:**606
Taupo, Lake (New Zealand) **2:**538
Taveuni (Fiji) **2:**597
Tavoy (Myanmar) **2:**269
Tawana (African people) **1:**351
Taxco (Guerrero, Mexico) **5:**416
Taxila (ancient city, Pakistan) **2:**191
Taya, Maaouya Ould Sid'Ahmed (president of Mauritania) **1:**139
Taygetus Mountains (Greece) **4:**189
Taylor, Charles (Liberian leader) **1:**183
Tay River (Scotland) **3:**132, 133, 138
Tazumal (Mayan ruins, El Salvador) **6:**43
Tbilisi (capital, republic of Georgia) **2:**47, 81, 84, 85
Tchaikovsky, Peter (Russian composer) **4:**314

Tea
   Georgia (republic) **2:**84
   Japanese tea ceremony **2:**461–62
   Sherpas drink with salt and butter **2:**232
   illus.
      Japanese ceremony **2:**461
      Moorish woman serving tea **1:**135
      Sri Lanka plantation **2:**248
Te Anau, Lake (New Zealand) **2:**539
Tear of the Clouds, Lake (New York) **5:**204
Teatro Angela Peralta (Mazatlán, Mexico) **5:**397
Tecun Umán (Quiché Indian chief) **6:**27
Teda (Tibbu) (African people) **1:**25
Tedzhen River (Turkmenistan) **2:**356
Tees River (England) **3:**83
Tegucigalpa (capital, Honduras) **6:**35–36, 38
   illus. **6:**34, 36
Teheran (capital, Iran) **2:**46, 159, 163
   illus. **2:**155
Tehuantepec, Isthmus of (Mexico) **5:**30, 357, 376, 417
Tehuelches (Indians of South America) **6:**269–70
Teide, Pico de (mountain, Canary Islands) **1:**32
Teixeira, Pedro (Portuguese explorer) **6:**169
Tekrur (early African kingdom) **1:**157–58
Tel Aviv-Jaffa (Israel) **2:**47, 108, 109
   illus. **2:**104
Television
   Asia **2:**40
   China **2:**405, 408
   France **3:**172
   Germany before reunification **3:**252
   Japan **2:**462
   Toronto **5:**108
Tell, The (region, north Africa) **1:**75, 89
Tell, William (legendary Swiss patriot) **3:**295, 297
Tell Abu Hureyra (archaeological site, Syria) **2:**51
Tell Atlas (mountains, Algeria) **1:**75
Tell el-Kebir (Egypt) **1:**121
Teller, Edward (Hungarian scientist) **4:**241
Tellier, Charles (French inventor) **6:**295
Telok Anson (Port Anson) (Malaysia) **2:**307
Telouet (Morocco)
   illus. **1:**65
Telugu language 2:199, 204
Tema (Ghana) **1:**197–98
Te Manga (mountain, Cook Islands) **2:**561
Temelin (Czech Republic) **3:**37, 319; **4:**229
Temne (African people) **1:**55, 173, 174
Tempe (Arizona) **5:**328
Temperature
   Antarctica **6:**324, 336
   Latin America **6:**3
   Sahara Desert **1:**25
   Saudi Arabia **2:**44
   table(s)
      extremes **6:**345
      measurement systems **6:**376
Temple, The (Jerusalem) **2:**46
Temple of the Holy Family (church, Barcelona, Spain) **4:**102–3
   illus. **4:**103
Temples
   Angkor Wat **2:**290
   cave temples of India **2:**214, 216
   cave temples of Xinjiang **2:**381
   Egypt **1:**111

Zimbabwe Ruins **1:**361
illus.
cave temples of India **2:**216
Ellora temples (India) **2:**215
Golden Temple at Amritsar **2:**218
Hindu **2:**247
Mayan **5:**374; **6:**29
Temptation of Saint Anthony (painting, Grünewald)
illus. **3:**254
Temuco (Chile) **6:**316
Tenasserim Mountains (Myanmar) **2:**267, 269
Tenekourou (mountain, Burkina Faso) **1:**190
Tenerife (island, Canary Islands) **1:**32, 33; **4:**84
Tenga (Mossi god) **1:**190
Teng Hsiao-ping (Chinese political leader) *see* Deng Xiaoping
Tengiz oil field (Kazakhstan) **2:**349
Ten Kingdoms (China) *see* Five Dynasties
Tenkodogo (early African kingdom) **1:**192
TENNESSEE 5:263–65
map(s) **5:**264
Tennessee River (U.S.) **5:**263
Tennessee Valley Authority (TVA) 5:263, 265
Tennis 3:24; **4:**226
illus. **3:**107
Tennis Court Oath (1789, France) **3:**184
Tenochtitlán (now **Mexico City**) (capital, Aztec empire) **5:**378, 410
Aztec ceremonials **5:**379
Cortés and Montezuma **5:**380
Teotihuacán (ancient city, Mexico) **5:**376, 413, 414
illus. **5:**377
Tepic (capital, Nayarit, Mexico) **5:**400
Tepic River (Mexico) **5:**400
Tequesta (Indians of North America) **5:**239
Tequila (alcoholic drink) **5:**359, 402
Terai (area, Nepal) **2:**230, 231
Teresa of Avila, Saint (Spanish nun) **4:**97, 98
Termez (Uzbekistan) **2:**350
Términos Lagoon (Campeche, Mexico) **5:**420
Ternate (island, Indonesia) **2:**315
Ter-Petrosyan, Levon Akopovich (president of Armenia) **2:**79
Terracing (in agriculture)
illus. **2:**382, 427
Terrorism *see also* September 11, 2001 terrorist attacks
Algeria **1:**78, 84
Asia, Central **2:**342
Bali **2:**326, 503
Colombia **6:**128, 129
Dar es Salaam (Tanzania), bombing of U.S. embassy **1:**333
Egypt **1:**116
Entebbe (Uganda) hostage rescue **1:**318
ETA (Basque organization) **4:**90
Georgia (republic) **2:**80, 85
German racial violence **3:**248–49
German troops sent to Afghanistan **3:**240
Guantánamo Bay prison facility **5:**450
Indian parliament building attacked **2:**194
Iron Guard of Romania **4:**256
Islamic view of U.S.-led global war **2:**40
Italy's Red Brigade **4:**162–63
Middle East conflicts fuel resurgence **2:**55
Moscow **4:**329
Nairobi (Kenya), bombing of U.S. embassy **1:**308
Northern Ireland's "Troubles" **3:**94, 149

Oklahoma City bombing **5:**307
Oman's support of U.S.-led war **2:**137
Shining Path of Peru **6:**226, 228
Somalia's alleged financial links to **1:**303
state-sponsored terrorism **1:**98
Uzbekistan's role against **2:**350, 352
illus.
Guantánamo Bay prison facility **5:**450
Tertullian (North African writer) **1:**91
Teso (African people) **1:**319
Tete (Mozambique) **1:**364
Teton Range (Wyoming) **5:**38, 315
Tetuán (Morocco) **1:**67
Tetum language 2:327
Teutoburg Forest, Battle of (Germany, A.D. 9) **3:**272
Teutonic Knights (military and religious order) **4:**296, 300, 304
Teutons (Germanic tribes) **3:**246, 321
Tewfik Pasha, Mohammed (khedive of Egypt) **1:**121
Texarkana (Arkansas–Texas) **5:**267
TEXAS 5:222, **250–55**, 383
illus.
Alamo, The **5:**252
Big Bend Nation Park **5:**250
canyons of the Rio Grande River **5:**255
Dallas **5:**254
Houston **5:**253
map(s) **5:**251
Texcoco, Lake (Mexico) **5:**378, 410
Textiles *see also* Weaving
batik **2:**307, 319
Belgian industry **3:**219
English industry **3:**108
France **3:**157
Italian industry **4:**152
Madras cloth **2:**207
Mexican industry **5:**363
New Hampshire **5:**185
Paraguayan lace **6:**248
Peru **6:**214
Rhode Island **5:**194
Venezuela **6:**142
illus.
batik **2:**320
Beninese craftsmen **1:**212
Chinese industry **2:**415
drying fabrics in sun in India **2:**224
Ghanaian artisan painting on cloth **1:**201
Italian industry **4:**152
Marimekko cottons **4:**61
Mexican factory **5:**363
Sierra Leone tie-dyed cloth **1:**177
South Carolina **5:**231
Thai industry **2:**277
Turkish factory **2:**64
Tezcatlipoca (Aztec god) **5:**378
TGV (French train) **3:**41
Thai (Asian people) **2:**254, 275, 279, 285
THAILAND 2:254, 259, **273–80**
energy needs **2:**37
industry **2:**258
Laos, history of **2:**285
Mekong River **2:**256–57
illus.
Bangkok **2:**273, 278, 279
Buddhist monks **2:**263
flag **2:**viii
rice growing **2:**276
textile industry **2:**277
map(s) **2:**274

Thailand, Gulf of 2:274, 277
Thai language 2:260, 275
Thal (desert, Pakistan) **2:**182
Thames River (Connecticut) **5:**195
Thames River (England) **3:**82, 83, 99–100
London Bridge **3:**110
illus. **3:**106
Thani family (rulers of Qatar) **2:**143
Thanksgiving Day 5:188
illus. **5:**45
Than Shwe (Myanmar political leader) **2:**272
Thar Desert (India–Pakistan) **2:**10, 166, 182
illus. **2:**198
Thassos (Greek island) **4:**199
Thatcher, Margaret (prime minister of United Kingdom) **3:**95
Thaw, The (period of lessened censorship in USSR) **4:**314
Theater
Asia, Southeast **2:**264
China **2:**406
Europe **3:**24
France **3:**172–73, 178, 197–98
Germany **3:**251, 281
Ireland **3:**70
Japan **2:**460
London (England) **3:**111
London (England): Shakespeare **3:**116
Oberammergau Passion Play **3:**273–74
United Kingdom **3:**89
illus.
Greek theater ruins **4:**209
Japanese *kabuki* **2:**459
Thebes (ancient city, Egypt) **1:**111, 117, 118
Thebes (Greek city-state) **4:**203
Theodosius (Roman emperor) **3:**48; **4:**111
Thera (Greek island) **4:**190
illus. **4:**200
Theravada Buddhism 2:247, 268, 288
Thermal springs
Aguascalientes **5:**404
Arkansas **5:**266, 267
Banff National Park **5:**126
Budapest (Hungary) **4:**242
California **5:**346
Iceland **3:**37; **4:**4
Idaho **5:**313
New Zealand **2:**537, 538
Theseus (Greek hero) **4:**190
Thessalonica (Greece) *see* Salonika
Thessaly (region, Greece) **4:**187, 188, 189
Thiès (Senegal) **1:**153
Thimphu (capital, Bhutan) **2:**236
Thingvellir (Plain of the Thing) (Iceland) **4:**5
illus.
church **4:**1
Third Reich (German history) **3:**276–77
Thirty-Three Immortals (Uruguayan patriots) **6:**263
Thirty Years' War (1618–1648) **3:**56, 280
Austria and Germany **3:**273, 322
Richelieu's policies in France **3:**183
Sweden **4:**49
White Mountain, Battle of the **4:**229
T'ho (ancient Mayan site) **5:**421
Thomas, Dylan (Welsh poet) **3:**126, 127
illus.
statue in Swansea **3:**126
Thompson (Manitoba) **5:**116
Thomson, Edgar (American businessman) **5:**214
Thonburi (Thailand) **2:**278

Thorbecke, Johan Rudolf (Dutch political leader) **3**:236
Thoreau, Henry David (American writer) **5**:189
Thorvaldsen, Bertel (Danish sculptor) **4**:19
Thousand Islands (Saint Lawrence River) **5**:105, 202
illus. **5**:95
Thrace (region, Greece–European Turkey) **2**:57; **4**:187, 188
Three Gorges Dam (China) **2**:369
Thunder Bay (Ontario) **5**:108
Thunderhead Mountain (South Dakota) **5**:300
Thuringian Forest (Germany) **3**:242
Thutmose I (Egyptian king) **1**:117
Thutmose III (Egyptian king) **1**:118
Thylacine *see* Tasmanian wolf
Thyra Danebod (Danish queen) **4**:20
Tiahuanaco (ancient empire, Bolivia) **6**:90, 239
illus. **6**:238
Tiananmen Square (Beijing, China) **2**:399–400
illus. **2**:418
Tianjin (Tientsin) (China) **2**:380
Tibban (waterway, Yemen) **2**:132
Tibbu (African people) *see* Teda
Tiberias, Lake *see* Galilee, Sea of
Tiberius (Roman emperor) **4**:130, 165
Tiber River (Italy) **4**:129, 164, 165, 167, 172
Tibesti Massif (mountain group, Chad–Libya) **1**:25, 95, 240
Tibet *see* Xizang (Tibet)
Tibetan Buddhism *see* Lamaism
Tibetan Highlands (Tsinghai, China) **2**:370
Tibetans (Asian people) **2**:385
Tibeto-Myanmar (people) **2**:269
Ticino (canton, Switzerland) **3**:286, 287, 288, 290
Ticino River (Switzerland–Italy) **3**:286
Tidal power **3**:157
Tides **5**:79, 84–85
Tidewater (region, U.S.) **5**:223, 227
Tidore (island, Indonesia) **2**:315
Tien Giang (Vietnamese name for Mekong River) **2**:256
Tien Shan (mountains, central Asia) **2**:10, 343
Kyrgyzstan **2**:353
Tajikistan **2**:359
Xinjiang **2**:380
illus. **2**:353, 359
Tientsin (China) *see* Tianjin
Tierra del Fuego (archipelago, South America) **6**:280, 316, 317
Andes **6**:100
Ona Indians **6**:270
Tiger Hills (Manitoba) **5**:115
Tigers
illus.
Russian circus **4**:315
Tignish (Prince Edward Island)
illus. **5**:89
Tigranes the Great (king of Armenia) **2**:50, 78
Tigrayan People's Front (TPLF) (Ethiopia) **1**:292
Tigre (region, Ethiopia) **1**:284, 285
Tigré (African people) **1**:36, 285
Tigré language **1**:295
Tigrinya language **1**:285, 295
Tigris River (Asia) **2**:11–12, 50–51, 147–48
table(s)
longest rivers of the world **6**:346
Tiguentourine (oil field, Algeria) **1**:76
Tihamah (coastal plain on the Red Sea) **2**:122, 131

Tijuana (Baja California, Mexico) **5**:390
illus.
border crossing to U.S. **5**:362
Tikal (ancient city, Guatemala) **6**:14, 28
illus.
step pyramid **6**:29
Tikar (African people) **1**:233
Tiko (Cameroon) **1**:232
Tikopia (Solomon Islands) **2**:591, 592
Till (soil) **5**:279, 290, 301
Till Plains (Illinois) **5**:281
Till Plains (Ohio) **5**:271, 272
illus. **5**:274
Timber *see* Lumber and lumbering
Timbuktu (Tombouctou) (Mali) **1**:6, 30, 50, 141, 142
Time **2**:153
Times Square (New York City)
illus. **5**:36
Time zones
map(s) **6**:356–57
Timișoara (Romania) **4**:254, 257
Timms Hill (Wisconsin) **5**:284
Timor (island, Malay Archipelago) **2**:315, 327, 328
Timor Sea (Pacific Ocean) **2**:524, 532, 534
Timsah, Lake (Egypt) **1**:120
Timucua (Indians of North America) **5**:238
Timur *see* Tamerlane
Tin **2**:304
illus.
Malaysian mine **2**:305
Tinakula (Solomon Islands) **2**:591
Tinneh (Indians of North America) **5**:349, 350
Tintagel Castle(Cornwall, England)
illus. **3**:115
Tipitapa River (Nicaragua) **6**:52
Tipperas (people) **2**:240
Tiradentes (Brazilian patriot) *see* Silva Xavier, Joaquim José da
Tiran, Strait of (off Sinai Peninsula) **2**:114
Tirana (capital, Albania) **4**:271
illus. **4**:268
Tiraspol (Moldova) **4**:346
Tirat Tsvi (Israel) **6**:345
Tirol *see* Tyrol
Tiryns (ancient city, Greece) **4**:198
Tisa River *see* Tisza (Tisa) River
Tisisat Falls *see* Blue Nile Falls
Tisza (Tisa) River (Europe) **4**:237, 275
Titano, Mount (San Marino) **4**:174
illus. **4**:174
Titicaca, Lake (Bolivia–Peru) **6**:3, 86, 210, 230–31
illus. **6**:210, 231
table(s)
largest lakes **6**:347
Titles (forms of address)
in England **3**:103, 118, 129, 130
Tito, Josip Broz (Yugoslav political leader) **4**:274, 280
Titograd (Yugoslavia) *see* Podgorica
Tiv (African people) **1**:219
Tivoli Gardens (Copenhagen, Denmark) **4**:17
illus. **4**:18
Tjapukai (aboriginal tribe, Australia)
illus. **2**:493
Tlalnepantla (Mexico) **5**:357
Tlaloc (rain god) **5**:376
Tlaxcala (capital, Tlaxcala state, Mexico) **5**:415
TLAXCALA (state, Mexico) **5**:415

Tlaxcalan (Indians of North America) **5**:380, 415
Tlemcen (Algeria) **1**:77
Tlingit (Indians of North America) **5**:146, 148, 164, 349, 350
Toa Falls (Cuba) **5**:442
Toamasina (Tamatave) (Madagascar) **1**:371, 373, 376
illus. **1**:372
Tobacco
American Indians **5**:24, 161
Brazil **6**:166, 175
British North America **5**:35
Caribbean islands **5**:430
Cuba **5**:451
international trade **5**:177
Kentucky **5**:261
Virginia **5**:226
illus.
Cuban farm **5**:442
Tobacco (Indians of North America) **5**:105
Tobago (Caribbean island) **5**:483 *see also* Trinidad and Tobago
map(s) **5**:429
Toba Kakar Range (Asia) **2**:167
Tobruk (Libya) **1**:96
Tofol (capital, Kosrae, Federated States of Micronesia) **2**:573
TOGO **1**:54, 205–9
illus.
bakery **1**:205
ferry on Mono River **1**:207
flag **1**:xxiii
Lomé **1**:209
phosphate mine **1**:208
map(s) **1**:206
Toiyabe Mountains (Nevada) **5**:331
Tokelau (island group, Pacific Ocean) **2**:601
Tokugawa family (Edo period) (in Japanese history) **2**:445, 452
Tokugawa Ieyasu (Japanese ruler) **2**:445
Tokyo (capital, Japan) **2**:440, 445, 457
illus. **2**:34, 445, 447
map(s) **2**:446
Tokyo Bay **2**:445
Tolbert, William R., Jr. (president of Liberia) **1**:183
Toledo (Ohio) **5**:273
Toledo (Spain) **4**:98, 113
illus. **4**:100
Toledo, Alejandro (president of Peru) **6**:228
Toledo, Montes de (mountains, Spain) **4**:82
Toliary (Tuléar) (Madagascar) **1**:371
Tollán (ancient Toltec city, Mexico) **5**:406
Tolosa, Juan de (founder of Zacatecas, Mexico) **5**:399
Tolstoi, Leo (Russian writer) **4**:313
Toltecs (Indians of North America) **5**:24, 376–77, 406
Toluca (capital, México State) **5**:413
Toma (African people) **1**:167
Toma, Lake (Switzerland) **3**:244
Tombalbaye, François (president of Chad) **1**:244
Tombigbee River (Alabama–Mississippi) **5**:242
Tombo (island, Guinea) **1**:167
Tombouctou *see* Timbuktu
Tomislav (Croatian ruler) **4**:287
TONGA **2**:601, 602, 603, **604–6**
Polynesian migrations **2**:600, 612
illus. **2**:604

flag **2**:x
map(s) **2**:606
Tonga (African people) **1**:273
Tongariro, Mount (volcano, New Zealand) **2**:538
Tongatapu (island group, Tonga) **2**:605, 606
illus. **2**:600
Tongoa (island, Vanuatu) **2**:594
Tongres (Belgium) **3**:214
Tongsa (Bhutan) **2**:236
Tonkawa (Indians of North America) **5**:253
Tonle Sap (lake, Cambodia) **2**:257, 287
Tonle Sap River (Cambodia) **2**:287
Tontons Macoute (Haitian secret police) **5**:470
Topeka (capital, Kansas) **5**:304
Top End (region, Northern Territory, Australia) **2**:532, 533
Tordesillas, Treaty of (1494) **4**:75; **6**:82, 187, 189
Tornadoes 5:159
illus. **5**:291
Torngat Mountains (Canada) **5**:77, 81
Toro (kingdom in Africa) **1**:38, 322
Toronto (capital, Ontario) **5**:41, 95, 106, 108; **5**:109
sports **5**:104
illus. **5**:37, 108
Ontario Science Center **5**:105
Torre Annunziata (Italy) **4**:138
Torremolinos (resort town, Spain) **4**:109
Torrens River (Australia) **2**:523
Torreón (Coahuila, Mexico) **5**:394
Torres Bodet, Jaime (Mexican government official) **5**:370
Torres García, Joaquín (Uruguayan painter) **6**:257
Torres Strait Islanders (Australian people) **2**:479, 495, 496, 498, 507, 508
illus. **2**:493, 507
Torrijos Herrera, Omar (Panamanian political leader) **6**:79, 80–81
Tortillas (Mexican food) **5**:368
Tortoises see Turtles and tortoises
Tortuga (Caribbean island) **5**:432, 467
Tosks (people) **4**:270
Totem poles (American Indian art objects) **5**:22, 132
illus. **5**:128
Totonac (Indians of North America) **5**:407
Toubkal, Djebel (Atlas Mountains, Morocco) **1**:66
Toubou (African people) **1**:239
Toucouleur (people) see Tukulor
Toulouse (France) **3**:152, 161–62
Toungoo (Burman dynasty, 15th–16th centuries) **2**:271
Touré, Amadou Toumani (president of Mali) **1**:143
Touré, Samory (Guinean hero) **1**:170
Touré, Sékou (Guinean political leader) **1**:170
illus. **1**:168
Tourism
Alps **3**:301–2
Arctic **5**:64
Bulgaria **4**:265
Costa Rica **6**:69
Cuba **5**:452
Czech Republic **4**:229
Easter Island **6**:322–23
Europe **3**:15–16, 24–25, 40–41
Florida **5**:239, 241

French vacationing **3**:175
Galápagos Islands **6**:203
German way of life **3**:249, 258, 262
Greece **4**:200
Italy **4**:168
Jamaica **5**:471
Japanese activities **2**:449
Las Vegas **5**:332
Malta **4**:184
Mexico **5**:364–65
Monaco **3**:206
Mountain States **5**:310
New Zealand **2**:545
Pacific states **5**:52
Prince Edward Island **5**:88, 89
Southern States **5**:222
Switzerland **3**:288–89
Thailand **2**:278
Uganda **1**:321
illus.
Antarctica **6**:338
cruise ship **5**:431; **6**:64
Cuba **5**:449
Paraguayan luxury hotel **6**:247
Tournai (Belgium) **3**:217, 219
Toussaint L'Ouverture (liberator of Haiti) **5**:468–69
Tovar y Tovar, Martín (Venezuelan painter) **6**:141–42
Town meeting (form of local government) **5**:181, 185
Townsville (Queensland, Australia) **2**:508
illus.
turtle sanctuary **2**:505
Toys 3:272
illus.
Egyptian men playing dominoes **1**:102
Tozeur (Tunisia) **1**:90
Trabant (East German automobile) **3**:259
Trabzon (Turkey) **2**:63
Tracy (cyclone, 1974) **2**:534, 535
Trade routes see also International trade
Asian history **2**:23–24
Cape Verde refueling stop **1**:150, 151
Danube River and the Amber Road **3**:320
Middle East **2**:43
Panama Canal **6**:78–79
Portuguese spice trade **4**:75
Sumerians **2**:48
trans-Sahara caravans **1**:218, 225
Viking route to Middle East **3**:51
Trade winds 2:561; **5**:478
Venezuela's mild climate **6**:132
Trafalgar, Battle of (1805) **4**:116
Trafalgar Square (Barbados) **5**:480
Trafalgar Square (London, England)
illus. **3**:97
Trail of Tears (Cherokee history) **5**:174, 222, 228, 236, 306
Trajan (Roman emperor) **4**:111
Trans-Alaska pipeline 5:64
illus. **5**:24, 350
Transcaucasia (region, Southwest Asia) **2**:50–51, 52, 53, 55
new countries **2**:27
Russia, history of **4**:309
way of life **2**:45–46
Transdanubia (region, Hungary) **4**:236–37
Trans-Dniester Republic 4:345, 347
Trans-Gabon Railroad 1:254
Transjordan (former name of Jordan) **2**:121

Transkei (black state in South African history) **1**:58–59, 404
Transoxania (region, Central Asia) **2**:352
Transportation see also Automobiles; Aviation; Boats; Railroads
Bangladesh's rivers **2**:242
Colombia's difficulties **6**:126
India's animal life **2**:201
Mercosur's planned waterway **6**:262
Mississippi River **5**:161
mules and llamas in Andes **6**:87
Nicaragua's difficulties **6**:57
North American inland navigation routes **5**:5
Rome (Italy) **4**:170
United States, history of **5**:43–44
U.S. trade and transportation **5**:177
illus.
Costa Rican oxcart **6**:67
Hungarian bus factory **4**:246
London traffic **3**:110
Myanmar pedicabs **2**:271
rickshaws **2**:237
sleighs and dogsleds in Russia **4**:308
snowmobiles **5**:141
Tahitian public transportation **2**:558
Trans-Siberian Railway 2:345
Transvaal (historic province, South Africa) **1**:404
Transylvania (province, Romania) **4**:248, 250, 255, 256, 257
Transylvania (region, Hungary) **4**:245
Transylvanian Alps (mountains, Europe) **4**:249
Traoré, Moussa (president of Mali) **1**:143
Trasimeno, Lake (Italy) **4**:128
Trastevere (district, Rome, Italy) **4**:170
Travel see Tourism
Travellers, Irish 3:144
Travemünde (Germany) **3**:250
Treblinka (Nazi concentration camp, Poland) **4**:221
Tree line 5:135, 141–42
Trees see Forests and Forestry
Trentino-Alto Adige (Italy) **4**:138, 154, 160
Trenton (capital, New Jersey) **5**:199, 210
illus. **5**:209
Trenton, Battle of (1776) **5**:210
Trent River (England) **3**:83
Tres Marías Islands (Mexico) **5**:400
Trevi Fountain (Rome, Italy) **4**:173
illus. **4**:173
Tribhuwan (king of Nepal) **2**:233
Trier (Germany)
illus. **3**:273
Triesen (Liechtenstein) **3**:305
Trieste (Italy–Yugoslavia) **4**:134, 160, 162
Triglav (mountain, Slovenia) **4**:282
Trimble, David (political leader in Northern Ireland) **3**:149
Trinidad (Cuba) **5**:444
TRINIDAD AND TOBAGO 5:427, 433, 438, **483–86**
English language **5**:435
illus.
Carnival **5**:483
flag **5**:vi
petroleum industry **5**:486
map(s) **5**:484
Trinity College (Dublin, Ireland) **3**:72
illus. **3**:69
Trio (Indians of South America) **6**:158
Tripartite Security Treaty (1951) see ANZUS Treaty

Triple Alliance (1882; Germany, Austria, Italy) **3:**187

Triple Alliance, War of the (1865–1870) **6:**190, 250, 264, 299

Triple Entente (1907) **3:**187

Tripoli (capital, Libya) **1:**95–96, 98
illus. **1:**95

Tripoli (territory, North Africa) **4:**160

Tripolitania (region, Libya) **1:**94–95, 97

Tripolitan War (1801–1805) **1:**97

Tristão, Nuno (Portuguese explorer) **1:**165

Trnava (Slovakia) **4:**234

Trobriand Islands (Papua New Guinea) **2:**585, 587

Trois-Rivières (Quebec) **5:**99

Trojan War (about 1194–1184 B.C.) **4:**202
Aeneas and the founding of Rome **4:**164
first recorded war in European history **3:**45–46

Tromso (Norway) **4:**33

Trondheim (Norway) **4:**33

Troodos Mountains (Cyprus) **2:**68, 69, 71

Tropical Atlantic air mass 5:15

Tropical continental air mass 5:15

Tropics 2:533; **6:**2–3, 329–30

Trotsky, Leon (Leib Davydovich Bronstein) (Russian revolutionist) **4:**322, 330

"Troubles" (fighting in Northern Ireland) **3:**149

Trovoada, Miguel (president of São Tomé and Príncipe) **1:**238

Troy (ancient city, Asia Minor) **2:**56; **4:**164, 201–2

Troy (New York) **5:**46

Trucial States see United Arab Emirates

Truckee River (Nevada) **5:**332

Trudeau, Pierre Elliott (prime minister of Canada) **5:**76, 97

Trujillo (Peru) **6:**216, 218

Trujillo Molina, Rafael (president of Dominican Republic) **5:**459–60

Truk (state, Federated States of Micronesia) see Chuuk

Truman, Harry S. (33rd president of U.S.)
Turkey, Truman Doctrine in **2:**67

Trust Territory of the Pacific Islands 2:570, 573, 574, 576
Palau **2:**572

Tsangpo (Tibetan name for Brahmaputra River) **2:**167

Tsar see Czar

Tsaratanana Massif (mountains, Madagascar) **1:**371

Tsaritsyn (Russia) see Volgograd

Tsavo National Game Park (Kenya) **1:**314

Tsetse fly 1:26, 41, 216, 248, 330, 332

Tsetserlik (Mongolia) **2:**366

Tshokwe (African people) **1:**266

Tshombe, Moïse (Congolese leader) **1:**269

Tsimihety (people) **1:**373

Tsimshian (Indians of North America) **5:**132

Tsinan (China) see Jinan

Tsinghai (province, China) see Qinghai

Tsiolkovski, Konstantin (Russian scientist) **4:**311–12

Tsiranana, Philibert (president of Madagascar) **1:**377

Tsiribihina River (Madagascar) **1:**371

Tsonga (African people) **1:**386

Tswana (African people) **1:**47, 351, 352, 354, 398

Tuamotu (island, Pacific Ocean) **2:**601

Tuareg (African people) **1:**86
Algeria **1:**78, 80, 83
Mali and the south Sahara **1:**25, 141, 142, 143
Niger and the Niger River area **1:**51, 146

Tuatara (lizard) **2:**477, 542
illus. **2:**542

Tubman, William V. S. (president of Liberia) **1:**183

Tuborg (Danish brewery) **4:**15–16

Tucson (Arizona) **5:**329
illus.
Mission San Xavier del Bac **5:**309

Tucumán (Argentina) **6:**293, 297

Tucumán (province, Argentina) **6:**270

Tucupita (Venezuela) **6:**147

Tudjman, Franco (president of Croatia) **4:**285, 287

Tudor, House of (English dynasty) **3:**119
rulers of England, list of **6:**361

Tuileries (park, Paris, France) **3:**195

Tu'i tongas (kings of Tonga) **2:**605

Tukulor (Toucouleur; Halphoolaren) (African people) **1:**135, 136, 154, 157

Tula de Allende (Mexico) **5:**406

Tulcea (Romania) **3:**329

Tuléar (Madagascar) see Toliary

Tulip Festival (Holland, Michigan)
illus. **5:**278

Tulsa (Oklahoma) **5:**306, 307
illus. **5:**305

Tulunid dynasty (Turkish rulers, Egypt) **1:**119

Tumbuka (African people) **1:**278

Tumen River (boundary, Manchuria–Korea) **2:**429–30

Tunal River (Mexico)
illus. **5:**398

Tunari (mountain, Bolivia) **6:**233

Tundra (Arctic and subarctic plains) **2:**341; **3:**31, 32; **4:**37; **5:**63, 73
Canada's Far North **5:**135
Europe, history of **3:**44–45
North America **5:**16
Northwest Territories **5:**142
Nunavut **5:**138
Russia **2:**343; **4:**307
Yukon Territory **5:**145
illus. **5:**6, 63
polygons **5:**142
special vehicles **5:**117
map(s)
world climate **6:**354
world vegetation **6:**353

Tung Chee-hwa (chief executive of Hong Kong) **2:**411

Tungsten 2:383

Tungurahua (province, Ecuador) **6:**196

Tungus (Asiatic people) **2:**363, 431

Tunica (Indians of North America) **5:**222

Tunis (capital, Tunisia) **1:**85–86, 88, 90, 92
illus. **1:**85

TUNISIA 1:24, 34, **85–92; 3:**187, 190
illus.
cattle **1:**89
flag **1:**xxii
Kairouan **1:**92
Roman ruins **1:**91
Tunis **1:**85
women in robes **1:**12
map(s) **1:**87

Tunnels
Alps **3:**289, 304
Europe **3:**41, 42
Suez Canal **1:**121
illus.
ice tunnel in Alps **3:**303

Tupac Amaru (Peruvian Indian chief) see Condorcanqui, José Gabriel

Tupamaros (political faction in Uruguay) **6:**265

Tupelo (Mississippi)
illus. **5:**246

Tupian Indians (South America) **6:**169

Tupolev TU-144 (supersonic airliner) **3:**42

Turajonzodah, Ali Akbar (Tajik Muslim leader) **2:**361

Turbo (Colombia) **6:**124

Turfan Depression (China) **2:**380

Turgenev, Ivan (Russian writer) **4:**313

Turin (Italy) **4:**141, 145
illus. **4:**145

Turkana, Lake (Kenya) **1:**308

Turkestan (region in Central Asia) **2:**345

TURKEY 2:56–67
Armenian border closed **2:**77
Bulgaria **4:**265
cities **2:**46
Cyprus **2:**68, 70
Greece **4:**191, 199, 205–8, 210–11
Hagia Sophia, church in Istanbul **2:**22
Italy, history of **4:**160
Kosovo Field, Battle of (1389) **4:**278, 279
Tigris and Euphrates rivers **2:**50
illus.
Ankara **2:**61, 62
Bodrum **2:**62
Cappadocia **2:**57
flag **2:**vii
Istanbul **2:**56, 61
people **2:**16
ruins at Ephesus **2:**66
shepherd with sheep and dog **2:**63
textile factory **2:**64
whirling dervishes **2:**59
wrestling **2:**60
map(s) **2:**58

Turki, Zoubeir (Tunisian artist) **1:**88

Turkic languages 2:44

Turkic peoples (Asia) **2:**91, 363, 365; **4:**345–46

Turkish language 2:44, 59
Azerbaijan **2:**87

Turkmen (Turkomans) (people) **2:**149, 175, 344, 357, 358
Kazakhstan **2:**347

Turkmenbashi see Niyazov, Saparmurad

TURKMENISTAN 2:341, 343, **356–58**
illus. **2:**356
flag **2:**ix
map(s) **2:**357

Turks (Asian people) **2:**57, 59
Armenian massacres **2:**78
Austria **3:**322–23
Bulgaria **4:**260, 261
Byzantine Empire threatened by **3:**53
Europe, movements of population **3:**18
India **2:**215
Muslim world **2:**51

Turks and Caicos Islands (Caribbean Sea) **3:**90

Turku (Finland) **4:**55, 59, 64

Turner, Ted (American businessman) **5:**222

Turner, Tina (American musician) **5:**263

Turov (Belarus) **4:**343

Turquino (mountain peak, Cuba) **5:**442

Turtle boats (first ironclad warships) **2:**432
Turtle Mountains (U.S.–Canada) **5:**297
Turtles and tortoises 5:422; **6:**203
illus. **2:**505; **5:**359, 436; **6:**203
Tuscaloosa (Alabama) **5:**243
Tuscany (region, Italy) **4:**129, 132, 133, 134, 154
Tutankhamen (Egyptian pharaoh) **1:**115
Tutchone (Indians of North America) **5:**146
Tutsi (African people) **1:**37
Burundi **1:**329–30, 331
Congo, Democratic Republic of **1:**270
Rwanda **1:**324, 325, 326, 327
Tutuila (island, American Samoa) **2:**602–3
TUVALU 2:582, 600, 601, 603, **610–12**
illus.
fishing **2:**610
flag **2:**x
map(s) **2:**611
Tuvinians (Turkic people) **2:**363
Tuxpan (Veracruz, Mexico) **5:**407
Tuxtla Gutiérrez (capital, Chiapas, Mexico) **5:**418
TVA *see* Tennessee Valley Authority
Twa (African people) **1:**325, 326, 329–30
Twain, Mark (American author) **5:**196
Twi language 1:199
Twin Cities (Minneapolis-St. Paul) (Minnesota) **5:**289
Two Sicilies, Kingdom of 4:129, 156
Tyne and Wear County (England) **3:**109
Tyne River (England) **3:**83
Tynwald (parliament of Isle of Man) **3:**84
Typhoons 2:380
Tyre (ancient Phoenician city) **2:**101
Tyrol (province, Austria) **3:**313
Tyrrhenian Sea 4:125, 129, 154
Tyumen province (Russia) **4:**309

Ubangi-Chari (region, Central African Republic) **1:**246, 247, 250
Ubangi River (central Africa) **1:**42
Central African Republic **1:**246, 247, 248
Congo **1:**257
Ucayali River (Peru) **6:**168, 209
Udaipur (India)
illus. **2:**203
UGANDA 1:36, 37–38, **316–23**
AIDS and Africa **1:**319
Amin, Idi **1:**323
Congo, Democratic Republic of **1:**270
regional cooperation **1:**3
illus.
fishing on Lake Victoria **1:**320
flag **1:**xxiv
Kampala **1:**316
Owen Falls Dam **1:**321
map(s) **1:**317
Uighurs (people) *see* Uygurs
Uinta Mountains (Utah) **5:**323, 325
Ujung Pandang (Macassar; Makassar) (Indonesia) **2:**315, 323
UKRAINE 3:2; **4:332–40**
Chernobyl **3:**37
Crimea **4:**336–37
food supply **3:**35
manufacturing **3:**40
mineral resources **3:**38

Poland, history of **4:**220
Russia, history of **4:**309
illus.
Crimean castle **4:**336
flag **4:**vi
Kiev **4:**332
woman on farm **4:**334
Yalta **4:**339
map(s) **4:**335
Ukrainian Catholic Church *see* Uniate Church
Ukrainian language 4:334, 335
Ukrainian Orthodox Church 4:334
Ukrainians (Slavic people) **4:**333, 334
Asia, Central **2:**344
Canada **5:**39
Moldova: Trans-Dniester population **4:**345
Ulaanbaatar (Urga) (capital, Mongolia) **2:**362, 364, 366
illus. **2:**362
Ulan-Ude (Russia) **2:**343
Ulbricht, Walter (East German political leader) **3:**279
Uliassutai (Mongolia) **2:**366
Uliga (Marshall Islands) **2:**575
Ulm (Germany) **3:**326
illus. **3:**327
Ulster (area, Ireland) **3:**76, 77, 142, 148
Ulster Cycle (in Irish literature) **3:**70, 145
Ulster Scots (Gaelic dialect) **3:**144
Ulúa River (Honduras) **6:**35
Ulugh-Beg (Uzbek prince) **2:**351
Uluru (Ayers Rock) (Australia) **2:**481, 483, 499, 532, 534
illus. **2:**481, 534
Ulyanov, Vladimir Ilich *see* Lenin, Vladimir Ilich
Umatilla (Indians of North America) **5:**339
Umbanda (African religion) **6:**188
Umbeluzi River (southeast Africa) **1:**385–86
Umberto I (king of Italy) **4:**159
Umm al Qaiwain (United Arab Emirates) **2:**138
Umm Said (Qatar) **2:**142
Umtali (Zimbabwe) *see* Mutare
Unalaska Island (Alaska)
illus. **5:**348
Underground Railroad (U.S. history) **5:**75, 274
Undset, Sigrid (Norwegian writer) **4:**28
Unemployment *see* Employment
UNESCO 3:202
Ungava Peninsula (Canada) **5:**40, 99
Uniate Church (Ukraine) **4:**334
Union, Acts of *see* Acts of Union
Union Islands *see* Tokelau
Unionists (Northern Ireland) *see* Loyalists
Union of South Africa 1:404
Union of Soviet Socialist Republics (1921–1991) *see also* Russia; names of republics
Afghanistan, intervention in **2:**174, 179
Albania, relations with **4:**271, 273
Bulgaria **4:**266
Chernobyl nuclear disaster **4:**332
China, ends aid to **2:**421
Cuba **5:**448, 449, 451
dissolution of union **3:**1, 64
East Germany, economy of **3:**259
Europe, history of **3:**60, 63
Finland, relations with **4:**58
former republics *see* Baltic States; Commonwealth of Independent States
Germany **3:**247, 277, 278
Hungary **4:**247

India, relations with **2:**229
Islam **2:**342
Korea **2:**438
leaders, list of **6:**364
Mongolia **2:**366
non-Slavic peoples **3:**19
Poland **4:**221–22
post-war Berlin **3:**280
supersonic aircraft **3:**42
Sweden, relations with **4:**50
Ukraine, history of **4:**339
United States, relations with **3:**61–62
Vietnam, relations with **2:**299
UNITA *see* National Union for the Total Independence of Angola
UNITED ARAB EMIRATES (Trucial States) 2:136, **138–39,** 143
illus.
flag **2:**vii
map(s) **2:**139
United Arab Republic (political union of Egypt and Syria) **1:**122; **2:**55, 96
United Empire Loyalists (Loyalists in Canada) **5:**38–39, 75, 97, 102, 109
UNITED KINGDOM *see also* Commonwealth of Nations; England; Northern Ireland; Scotland; Wales
Antarctic research **6:**334
China, trade with **2:**421
economy **3:**95
England **3:**79–120
Falkland Islands **6:**287, 300
Germany, military personnel in **3:**247
Gibraltar **4:**86, 123
Hong Kong **2:**411
Iraq, air strikes against **2:**154
Northern Ireland **3:**142–49
overseas territories **3:**90
Pakistan **2:**192
Pitcairn Island administered by **2:**562–63
Polynesia, history of **2:**602–3
population **3:**44
Scotland **3:**131–41
Sepoy Mutiny (1857), India **2:**216
Wales **3:**121–30
illus.
English country village **3:**85
flag **3:**vi
White Cliffs of Dover **3:**81
map(s) **3:**82
table(s)
British rulers and prime ministers **6:**360–62
United Kingdom Overseas Territories 3:90
Bermuda **5:**32–33
Falkland Islands **6:**286–87
Gibraltar **4:**86, 123
United Nations 3:3, 61
African peacekeepers **1:**3
Cambodia **2:**292
China and Taiwan **2:**428
Congo, Democratic Republic of **1:**269
Cyprus **2:**70, 73
East Timor administration **2:**328
El Salvador, civil war recovery plan for **6:**50
genocide, use of term **3:**278
Germany **3:**283
Haiti **5:**440, 467, 470
Iraq **2:**154
Iraq, sanctions against **2:**152
Ireland **3:**78

United Nations (cont.)
Israel and the Middle East **1:**122, 123; **2:**47, 52, 113, 114
Korea, South **2:**438
Kosovo **4:**278
Kuwait **2:**144, 146
Liberia, sanctions against **1:**183
Libya, sanctions against **1:**98
Marshall Islands **2:**576
member nations, list of **6:**358
Namibia mandate **1:**46, 350
Nauru **2:**579
Oceania, trust territories **2:**566
Palace of Nations, Geneva **3:**293
Palauan situation **2:**570
Palestine **2:**55
Rhodesia, sanctions against **1:**49
Santiago (Chile) office building **6:**310
six principal organs **6:**358
Somalia **1:**305
South Africa, disagreements with **1:**46, 402, 406
Swedish troops in the cause of world peace **4:**50
Swiss referendum on membership **3:**298
Western Sahara **1:**133
Western Samoa **2:**609
Yugoslavia **4:**279, 281
illus.
Geneva headquarters **3:**61
headquarters building (New York City) **5:**201
troops in Cyprus **2:**73
United Nations Economic Commission for Africa 1:282
United Provinces of Central America *see* Central America, United Provinces of
UNITED STATES 5:149–354
Antarctic research **6:**334
China, diplomatic relations reestablished **2:**421
economic development **5:**176–77
Europe, history of **3:**63
European culture influenced by **3:**26
glaciation and Ice Ages **5:**12–13
history *see* United States, history of the
Pacific Islands, Trust Territory of the **2:**569
population living abroad **5:**412
resources **5:**44–52
Rocky Mountains **5:**39
illus.
border with Canada **5:**71
flag **5:**vi
map(s) **5:**150–51
United States, history of the 5:173–77 *see also* articles on regions, such as New England
Afghanistan, intervention in **2:**174, 179
Boston's historical landmarks **5:**190
British North America **5:**35, 37, 43
Canada **5:**75
Canada: New Brunswick border dispute **5:**86
Caribbean Sea and islands **5:**438, 440
Civil War *see* Civil War, U.S.
Colombia, military aid to **6:**129
Cuba **5:**446–47, 448, 449, 450, 452
Dominican Republic **5:**460
Georgia (republic) **2:**80, 85
Germany, military personnel in **3:**247
Gulf War (1991) **2:**144
Haiti **5:**470
Hawaii **5:**354

Hungary: U.S. agencies in **4:**247
Iran **2:**163
Iraq **2:**154
Israel **2:**104, 114–15
Japan **2:**25, 445, 467
Kuwait **2:**146
Laos **2:**283
Latin America **6:**12–13, 17–18, 86, 113
Lebanon **2:**102
Liberia **1:**182–83
Libya **1:**98
Marshall Islands **2:**576
Mexican War **5:**383
Mexico, relations with **5:**364, 393
Middle Atlantic States **5:**200
Middle East policy **2:**55
New Zealand **2:**554
Nicaragua **6:**60
North Korea **2:**433
Palau **2:**571, 572
Panama **6:**80, 81
Panama Canal **6:**78–79
Philadelphia, the Cradle of Liberty **5:**213
Philippines **2:**331, 340
Polynesia **2:**602–3
slavery **5:**435
Somalia, troops in **1:**305
Soviet Union **3:**61–62
Taiwan **2:**428
United Kingdom, relations with **3:**95
Uzbekistan, anti-terrorism troops based in **2:**350, 352
Vietnam **2:**300
Vietnam War **2:**302
Wild West **5:**308
Yugoslavia, bombing of **4:**278, 281
table(s)
presidents and vice presidents **6:**359
United States Air Force 4:110; **5:**216, 298
Oklahoma City **5:**306
United States Air Force Academy (Colorado Springs, Colorado) **5:**320
illus.
Cadet Chapel **5:**319
United States Constitution 5:174
United States Marine Corps 6:12, 56
United States Military Academy (West Point, New York)
illus. **5:**206
United States Naval Academy (Annapolis, Maryland) **5:**218
illus. **5:**217
United States Navy 5:226, 344; **6:**12
United Tajik Opposition (UTO) (political party, Tajikistan) **2:**361
University City (Mexico) **5:**371
University Research Park (North Carolina) **5:**229
Unter den Linden (street, Berlin, Germany) **3:**280, 281
Unterwalden (canton, Switzerland) **3:**296, 297
Untouchables (social class) *see* Dalits
Upolu (island, Western Samoa) **2:**607, 608
Upper Austria (province of Austria) **3:**315, 318, 320
Upper Canada 5:97, 102, 109
Upper Volta *see* Burkina Faso
Uppsala (Sweden) **4:**40
Ur (ancient city in Mesopotamia) **2:**51
Ural-Altaic languages 3:20; **4:**240

Ural Mountains (Russia) **3:**30; **4:**306, 307
dividing line between Europe and Asia **3:**8, 28
division between Europe and Asia **2:**5
manufacturing center **3:**40
illus. **4:**307
Ural River (Russia–Kazakhstan) **3:**8
Uranium
Africa **1:**5, 148
Canada **5:**4
Tajikistan **2:**360–61
western U.S. **5:**9, 326
Urartu (ancient kingdom) **2:**50
Urban life *see* Cities and city life
Urdu language 2:187, 199, 243
Urga (Mongolia) *see* Ulaanbaatar
Urgel, Bishop of (prince of Andorra) **4:**119, 121
Uri (canton, Switzerland) **3:**296, 297
Uribe Vélez, Álvaro (president of Colombia) **6:**129
Urmia, Lake (Iran) **2:**156
Urquiza, Justo José (Argentine political leader) **6:**298–99
Uruapan (Michoacán, Mexico) **5:**409
URUGUAY 6:7, 114, **251–65**
economic problems **6:**265
education **6:**106
Euro-American culture **6:**95, 97
Mercosur **6:**262
Río de la Plata Basin **6:**284
illus.
antique automobiles **6:**257
Colonia **6:**264
flag **6:**vi
gaucho **6:**259
Montevideo **6:**251, 254, 255, 260
outdoor dining **6:**256
Punta del Este **6:**261
map(s) **6:**253
Uruguay River (South America) **6:**86, 173, 259, 261
Argentina **6:**280
Río de la Plata Basin **6:**284
Uruk (Sumeria) **2:**41
Ürümqi (capital, Xinjiang, China) **2:**380, 381
Ushuaia (Argentina) **6:**266, 345
illus. **6:**290
Usigli, Rodolfo (Mexican playwright) **5:**374
Usk River (Wales) **3:**127
Uskudar (sector of Istanbul, Turkey) **2:**62, 63
Usman dan Fodio (Fulani religious leader) **1:**226
USSR *see* Union of Soviet Socialist Republics
Ustaŝi Fascists (in Croatian history) **4:**280, 287
Ustica (island, Italy) **4:**130
Ust-Shchugor (Russia) **6:**345
Usumacinta River (Mexico) **5:**419
Usutu River (southeast Africa) **1:**385–86
UTAH 5:49, **323–26**
illus.
Great Salt Lake **5:**326
open-pit mine **5:**9
Zion National Park **5:**323
map(s) **5:**324
Ute (Indians of North America) **5:**309, 319, 320, 323, 324, 325
Utena (Lithuania) **4:**302
Uthoff, Ernst (Chilean dancer) **6:**310
Utrillo, Maurice (French artist) **3:**200
Uttaranchal (state, India) **2:**221
Utulei (American Samoa) **2:**602
Uygurs (Asian people) **2:**380–81, 385, 387

UZBEKISTAN 2:341, 342, 343, **350–52**
illus.
flag **2:**ix
Tashkent **2:**350
map(s) **2:**351
Uzbeks (people) **2:**175, 344, 347, 351, 355
Uzhgorod (Ukraine) **4:**338

• • • V • • •

Vaal River (South Africa) **1:**396
Vaduz (capital, Liechtenstein) **3:**305, 306, 307
illus. **3:**305
Váh River (Slovakia) **4:**232
Vahsel Bay (Weddell Sea, Antarctica) **6:**334
Vaisyas (caste, India) **2:**21, 210
Vaitupu (island, Tuvalu) **2:**610, 611
Vajpayee, Atal Behari (prime minister of India) **2:**218
Val d'Aosta (Italy) **4:**134, 154
Valdés Peninsula (South America) **6:**345
Valdez (Alaska) **5:**159
Valdivia (Chile) **6:**316
Valdivia, Pedro de (Spanish conquistador) **6:**316, 321
Valdivia River (Chile) **6:**316
Valencia (former kingdom, now province, Spain) **4:**88, 89–90, 94, 107
Valencia (Venezuela) **6:**132, 137
Valencia, Lake (Venezuela) **6:**137
Valentinian II (Roman emperor) **4:**242
Vale of Kashmir 2:173
Valladolid (Guanajuato, Mexico) **5:**405
Valle, Jose Cecilio del (Honduran political leader) **6:**38
Valle, Rafael Heliodoro (Honduran poet-historian) **6:**38
Valle Central (Chile) **6:**302, 305, 313–15, 319
Valle de los Caídos (monument, Spain) **4:**98
Valletta (capital, Malta) **4:**183
illus. **4:**182
Valle y Caviedes, Juan (Peruvian poet) **6:**214
Valley Forge (Pennsylvania)
illus. **5:**200
Valley Isle *see* Maui
Valley of Fire (Nevada) **5:**332
Valley of the Kings (Luxor, Egypt) **1:**111
Valois, House of (kings of France)
list of **6:**363
Valona (Albania) **4:**271
Valparaiso (Chile) **6:**314
illus. **6:**315
Van, Lake (Turkey) **2:**77
Van Allen, James (American scientist) **6:**333
Vancouver (British Columbia) **5:**42, 129, 130, 131, 132
illus. **5:**36–37, 130
Vancouver, George (English navigator) **5:**131, 338
Vancouver Island (Canada) **5:**8, 69, 129, 132
Vandals (Germanic tribe) **3:**18, 308
Africa **1:**83, 91, 99
Van Dieman's Land (former name of Tasmania) **2:**531
Vaner, Lake (Sweden) **4:**39
Vanua Levu (island, Fiji Islands) **2:**597
VANUATU 2:583, 586, **594–96; 3:**191
illus.
flag **2:**x

Port-Vila **2:**594
map(s) **2:**595
Varangians (Norsemen who settled in Russia) **4:**339
Vardar River (Macedonia–Greece) **3:**45; **4:**291
Vardzia (republic of Georgia)
illus. **2:**85
Vargas, Getúlio (Brazilian leader) **6:**114, 190
Vargas Llosa, Mario (Peruvian novelist) **6:**215
Varna (Bulgaria) **4:**264
Varzab River (Tajikistan)
illus. **2:**359
Vasco da Gama *see* Gama, Vasco da
Vásquez, Horacio (president of Dominican Republic) **5:**459
VATICAN CITY 4:125, 160, **177–81**
Hungary, relations with **4:**240
Italy **4:**135, 159, 167
popes, list of **6:**366–68
Swiss Guards, origin of **3:**297
illus. **3:**50
flag **4:**v
St. Peter's Basilica **4:**177, 178
St. Peter's Square **4:**177
Vatican Gardens **4:**179
map(s) **4:**179
Vatter, Lake (Sweden) **4:**39
Vava'u (island group, Tonga) **2:**605, 606
Vazov, Ivan (Bulgarian writer) **4:**261
Vedas (sacred books of Hinduism) **2:**19, 170, 211
Veddas (people) **2:**247
Vega Carpio, Lope Félix de (Spanish playwright) **4:**115
Velasco Ibarra, José María (Ecuadorian political leader) **6:**205
Velasco Maidana, José María (Bolivian composer) **6:**239
Velázquez, Diego Rodríguez de Silva y (Spanish painter) **4:**116
Velázquez de Cuéllar, Diego (Spanish soldier) **5:**444
Veld (Veldt) (African grassland) **1:**356, 385, 386, 395
Velvet Revolution (Czechoslovakia, 1989)
illus. **4:**231
Venda (African people) **1:**398
Venda (black state in South African history) **1:**58–59, 404
Venetian, Ronald (president of Suriname) **6:**159
Veneto (Venetia) (region, Italy) **4:**139, 158, 159
VENEZUELA 6:105, 115, **130–48**
Afro-American culture **6:**91
Amazon River **6:**168
Andes **6:**100–101
Angel Falls **6:**134
Columbus' third voyage **6:**82
economy **6:**88, 102, 103, 104
Guyana, territorial dispute with **6:**152
Maracaibo, Lake **6:**144
Mercosur **6:**262
Orinoco River **6:**146–47
Yanomamo Indians **6:**140
illus.
Angel Falls **6:**134
bullfight **6:**139
Caracas **6:**111, 130, 136, 137, 138, 145
cattle **6:**132
Colonia Tovar **6:**133
flag **6:**vi
iron mining **6:**143

Mérida's cable cars **6:**131
natural gas industry **6:**104
oil derricks **6:**2, 144
restaurant **6:**139
service industry **6:**143
Yanomamo Indians **6:**140
map(s) **6:**135
Orinoco River **6:**147
Venice (Italy) **4:**141, 147–48, 156
Greece, history of **4:**192, 196, 206
illus. **3:**43; **4:**147, 148
Venizelos, Eleutherios (Greek statesman) **4:**207–8, 209
Ventspils (Latvia) **4:**297
Ventuari River (South America) **6:**146
Venus (Romania) **4:**254
Veracruz (city, Veracruz, Mexico) **5:**358, 380, 389, 407
petrochemicals and the oil industry **5:**28, 30
VERACRUZ (state, Mexico) **5:**375, **407**
Veraguas (province, Panama) **6:**77
Verde, Cape (west Africa) **1:**153
Verdi, Giuseppe (Italian composer) **1:**121
Verdun (France) **3:**187
Verdun, Treaty of (843) **3:**272
Vereeniging (South Africa) **1:**402
VERMONT 5:186–87
illus. **5:**186
map(s) **5:**187
Verrazano, Giovanni da (Italian explorer) **5:**183, 192, 206, 210
Versailles, Palace of (near Paris, France) **3:**167, 276
illus. **3:**57, 166
Versailles, Treaty of (1783) **1:**163
Versailles, Treaty of (1919) **3:**188, 276; **4:**220
Verviers (Belgium) **3:**219
Verwoerd, Hendrik F. (prime minister of South Africa) **1:**404
Vesalius, Andreas (Belgian anatomist) **3:**293
Vespucci, Amerigo (Italian navigator) **6:**97, 153, 296
Vesuvius (volcano, Italy) **4:**128, 144
illus. **4:**144
Veto power (in government) **4:**220
Vevey (Switzerland) **3:**295
Vianden (Luxembourg)
illus. **3:**208
Vice-presidents of the U.S.
table(s) **6:**359
Viceroyalties (Spanish colonial government) **6:**90, 97, 224–25
Vichy Government (France, during World War II) **3:**188
presidents of France, list of **6:**364
Vicksburg (Mississippi) **5:**246
Vico (lake, Italy) **4:**128
Viçosa (Brazil) **6:**106
Victor Emmanuel II (king of Italy) **4:**158
illus. **4:**161
Victor Emmanuel III (king of Italy) **4:**159, 161
Victoria (British Columbia) **5:**129, 131
Victoria (Cameroon) **1:**232
Victoria (capital, British Columbia) **5:**42, 132, 133
illus. **5:**133
Victoria (capital, Seychelles) **1:**339
Victoria (queen of Great Britain) **3:**93
VICTORIA (state, Australia) **2:**492, **516–20**
illus.
Melbourne **2:**516

VICTORIA
illus. (cont.)
sheep ranching **2:**520
map(s) **2:**518
Victoria, Lake (Africa) **1:**39, 316, 317
Africa's rift valleys **1:**19
Kenya **1:**308, 309
Uganda **1:**38
White Nile, source of **1:**38
illus. **1:**320
table(s)
largest lakes **6:**347
Victoria Falls (Zambezi River) **1:**44, 276, 355
illus. **1:**48, 356
Victoria Island (Arctic Ocean) **5:**141
table(s)
largest islands of the world **6:**346
Victoria Nile (section of the Nile River) **1:**38, 317, 318, 320
illus.
Owen Falls Dam **1:**321
Victoria Peak (Belize) **6:**19–20
Vicuñas 6:87
Videla, Jorge (president of Argentina) **6:**301
Vieira, João Bernardo (president of Guinea-Bissau) **1:**165
Vienna (capital, Austria) **3:**315–18, 321, 322–23
Austrian German language **3:**310
Danube River **3:**327
tourism **3:**15
illus.
Burgtheater and St. Stephen's **3:**322
Donaupark Center **3:**328
public housing **3:**316
Schönbrunn **3:**323
Volksgarten and Hofburg **3:**309
Vienna, Congress of (1815) **3:**236, 324; **4:**158
Cape of Good Hope colony **1:**404
Rhineland given to Prussia **3:**274
Swiss neutrality recognized **3:**297
Vienna Woods (Wienerwald) (forest, Austria) **3:**315
Danube River **3:**327
Vientiane (administrative capital, Laos) **2:**257, 262, 282, 283, 285
Vietcong (Communist guerrillas) **2:**298, 302
Vietminh (Vietnamese Communist Organization) **2:**302
VIETNAM 2:27, **293–302**
Asia, Southeast **2:**254, 258, 259, 264
boat people **2:**31
border disputes **2:**31
Cambodia **2:**291, 292
economy **2:**35
Laos, ties with **2:**285
Mekong River **2:**256–57
religion **2:**260
illus.
Cao Dai sect **2:**296
fishing **2:**298
flag **2:**viii
flower vendors **2:**293
Hanoi **2:**297, 301
Ho Chi Minh City **2:**259
Hue **2:**300
rice growing **2:**299
map(s) **2:**294
Vietnamese (Asian people) **2:**254, 259, 293, 295, 301
Cambodia **2:**287
Vietnamese language 2:296

Vietnam Veterans Memorial
illus. **5:**171
Vietnam War 2:293, 298, 302
Cambodia **2:**290
Laos **2:**285
New Zealand **2:**554
United States **5:**176
illus.
Veterans Memorial **5:**171
View of Toledo (painting, El Greco)
illus. **4:**100
Vigeland, Gustav (Norwegian sculptor) **4:**28, 32
Viipuri (Russia) *see* Vyborg
Vike-Freiberga, Vaira (president of Latvia) **4:**300
Vikings *see also* Norsemen
Arctic exploration **5:**61
Denmark's Viking period **4:**20
England, history of **3:**115–16
Europe, history of **3:**51, 181
Greenland settlements **5:**14
Iceland **4:**1, 2, 4, 5
Ireland **3:**75
Newfoundland settlement **5:**78, 83
Northern Ireland **3:**147
Norway **4:**23, 25, 28
Scotland **3:**135, 138, 140
ship burial sites (Oland, Sweden) **4:**39
Spaniards in the north of Spain **4:**87
Swedish rock art **4:**43
Swedish Vikings **4:**48
Viking Ship Museum (Oslo, Norway) **4:**32
Vili (African people) **1:**258
Villa, Pancho (Mexican bandit and revolutionary) **5:**386, 387, 393
illus. **5:**383
Villa Constitución (Baja California Sur, Mexico) **5:**391
Villa de los Santos (Panama) **6:**75
Villahermosa (capital, Tabasco, Mexico) **5:**419
Villa-Lobos, Heitor (Brazilian composer) **6:**180–81
Villanueva, Carlos Raúl (Venezuelan architect) **6:**142
Villarrica (Paraguay) **6:**244
Villarroel, Gualberto (president of Bolivia) **6:**241
Villavicencio (Colombia) **6:**121
Vilnius (capital, Lithuania) **4:**302–3, 304
Viminal Hill (Rome, Italy) **4:**165
Viña del Mar (Chile) **6:**315
illus. **6:**315
Vincent, Saint 3:156
Vindhya Mountains (India) **2:**166, 198
Vindobona (Roman fortress, now Vienna, Austria) **3:**315, 321
Vineyards *see* Grapes; Wine
Vinland (Viking settlement in North America) **4:**25
Vinson Massif (Antarctica) **6:**345
Viola, Roberto (president of Argentina) **6:**301
Violence *see* Riots and demonstrations; Terrorism
Viollet-le-Duc, Eugène (French architect) **3:**163
VIRGINIA 5:35, 170, **223–26**
illus.
Colonial Williamsburg **5:**226
Shenandoah National Park **5:**223
map(s) **5:**224
Virginia Beach (Virginia) **5:**223, 225
Virginia City (Nevada) **5:**332

Virgin Islands, British (Caribbean islands) **3:**90
map(s) **5:**429
Virgin Islands, U.S. (Caribbean islands) **5:**172
map(s) **5:**429
Virgin Islands National Park (U.S. Virgin Islands) **5:**172
Virgin Lands program (Soviet history) **2:**346, 348
Virtual reality
illus. **5:**48
Virunga (mountains, central Africa) **1:**262, 317, 324, 325
Visayan Islands (Philippines) **2:**332
Visby (medieval city, Gotland, Sweden) **4:**39
Vishnu (Hindu god) **2:**201
Visigoths (West Goths) *see* Goths
Vistula River (central Europe) **4:**213, 216
Vitasha Mountains (Bulgaria) **4:**263
Viti Levu (island, Fiji Islands) **2:**583, 597
Vittorio Emanuele (kings of Italy) *see* Victor Emmanuel
Vittorio Veneto (Italy) **4:**160
Vizcaya (Basque province of Spain) **4:**88, 107–8
Vladikavkaz (Russia) **2:**81
Vladimir, Saint (Russian prince and ruler of Kiev) **4:**319, 336, 339
Vladivostok (Russia) **2:**343; **4:**307, 316
Vlorë (Albania) *see* Valona
Vltava River (Czech Republic) **4:**224, 229
Vojvodina (province, Serbia) **4:**275, 276, 278
Volcanic Plateau (region, New Zealand) **2:**537, 538
Volcanoes 5:335
California **5:**342
Cascade Range **5:**156, 339
Central America **6:**10
Costa Rica **6:**63
Ecuador **6:**193–94
El Salvador **6:**42–43
Europe **3:**28
Fujiyama (Japan) **2:**442
Guatemala **6:**30, 31
Hawaii **5:**157, 351
Iceland **4:**2–3
Indonesia **2:**313
Italy **4:**128, 129, 130
Latin America **6:**2, 101
Mexico **5:**357, 408, 414
Montserrat **5:**439
New Zealand **2:**537, 538
Nicaragua **6:**51, 52
Oceania **2:**558–59
Pacific States **5:**333, 334
volcanic rocks on Mauritius **1:**379
illus.
Guatemala **6:**32
Indonesia **2:**314
lava flows on Hawaii **5:**352
Momotombo and Momotombito **6:**52
Montserrat **5:**439
Mount St. Helens **5:**335
Popocatepetl **5:**357
Quilotoa Crater (Ecuador) **6:**192
Volcano National Park (Rwanda) **1:**324, 325
Volga River (Russia) **4:**306, 308, 317
European migrations **3:**19
hydroelectric dams **3:**37
waterways in Europe **3:**42, 44
map(s) **4:**317
table(s)
longest rivers of the world **6:**346

Volgograd (Russia) **4:**315
illus.
"Motherland" monument **4:**320
Volta, Lake (Ghana) **1:**195–96
Voltaic Plateau (Africa) **1:**192
Voltaire (French writer) **3:**266
Volta River (west Africa) **1:**189, 195
dam and man-made Lake Volta (Ghana) **1:**195–96, 200, 204
Volubilis (Roman ruins, Morocco) **1:**72–73
illus. **1:**73
Volunteer State (nickname for Tennessee) **5:**264
Vonjama (Liberia) **1:**180
Vonnegut, Kurt (American writer) **3:**268
Voodoo (folk religion) **5:**435, 464–65
Vorarlberg (province, Austria) **3:**310, 312–13
Voroneţ (Romania) **4:**252
Voronin, Vladimir (president of Moldova) **4:**347
Vosges (region, France) **3:**28
Vostok (Antarctica) **6:**324, 345
Voting *see* Elections; Suffrage
Voyageurs National Park (Minnesota) **5:**269
Voznesensky, Andrei (Soviet poet) **4:**314
Vulcano (island, Italy) **4:**130
Vumba (mountains, Zimbabwe) **1:**356
Vyborg (Viipuri) (Russia) **4:**52
Vytautas the Great (Lithuanian ruler) **4:**304
illus.
castle **4:**301

• • • W • • • •

Waal River (the Netherlands) *see* Rhine River
Wabash River (U.S.) **5:**44
Wachau (region, Austria) **3:**315, 326
Waco (Texas) **5:**255
Wadai (early African kingdom) **1:**244
Wade, Abdoulaye (president of Senegal) **1:**158
Wadi Halfa (former town, Sudan) **1:**129
Wadis (dry riverbeds) **1:**24, 25, 112; **2:**131
Wad Medani (Sudan) **1:**129
Wadsworth, Joseph (American colonist) **5:**197
Wages and salaries
French Guiana **6:**92
Haiti **5:**467
Italy **4:**162
Russia **4:**318
South American middle class **6:**109
Wagga Wagga (New South Wales, Australia) **2:**512
Wagner, Richard (German composer) **3:**257, 258–59
Wahhabism (Islamic reform movement) **2:**127
Wahid, Abdurrahman (president of Indonesia) **2:**326
Waialeale, Mount (Kauai, Hawaii) **5:**352; **6:**345
Waikato region (New Zealand) **2:**538
Waikato River (New Zealand) **2:**538
Waikiki Beach (Hawaii) **5:**353
Wailing Wall (Jerusalem) *see* Western Wall
Waipo Valley (Hawaii)
illus. **5:**351
Wairarapa (region, New Zealand) **2:**538
Waitangi, Treaty of 2:552, 554

Waitangi Day 2:552
illus. **2:**543
Waitomo Caves (New Zealand) **2:**538
illus. **2:**540
Wajda, Andrzej (Polish film director) **4:**215
Wakefield, Edward Gibbon (English colonizer) **2:**553
Wakefield, Edward Gibbon (English statesman) **2:**523
Wake Island (Pacific Ocean) **2:**569, 570
Wakhan Panhandle (region, Afghanistan) **2:**174
Walachia (province, Romania) **4:**248, 249, 256
Walcott, Derek (St. Lucian poet) **5:**440, 489
Walden Pond (Massachusetts) **5:**189
Waldheim, Kurt (president of Austria) **3:**325
WALES 3:81, 87, 114, **121–30** *see also* United Kingdom
England, history of **3:**117
first steam locomotive **3:**41
government **3:**96
language *see* Welsh language
Offa's Dyke **3:**128
United Kingdom and how it was created **3:**91
illus. **3:**121
Caerphilly Castle **3:**129
Cardiff Castle **3:**52, 126
dairy farm **3:**123
Eisteddfod **3:**125
hydroelectric dam **3:**122
traditional costumes **3:**124
map(s) **3:**123
Wales, University of 3:126
Wałęsa, Lech (president of Poland) **4:**222, 223
Walker, Thomas (American explorer) **5:**262
Walker, William (American adventurer) **6:**70
holiday celebrating his defeat **6:**67
Nicaragua **6:**58
Wallace, George (governor, Alabama) **5:**244
Wallace, Peter (British buccaneer) **6:**19
Wallace, Sir William (Scottish hero) **3:**140
Wallace Line (separating the animals and plants of Indonesia) **2:**315–17
Walla Walla (Indians of North America) **5:**337
Wallis and Futuna Islands (Pacific Ocean) **2:**601; **3:**191
Wallonia (region, Belgium) **3:**211, 213–15, 219, 220, 221, 224
Walloons (people) **3:**211, 212, 213–15, 221
Wallowa Mountains (Oregon) **5:**339
Walvis Bay (South African enclave within Namibia) **1:**348, 350
Wanganui River (New Zealand) **2:**538
Wangchuk, Jigme Dorji (king of Bhutan) **2:**236
Wangchuk, Jigme Singye (king of Bhutan) **2:**236
Wang River (Thailand) **2:**274
Wannsee (region in Berlin, Germany) **3:**281
Waqra (Qatar) **2:**142
Waratah (state flower of New South Wales) **2:**510
War crimes 3:272; **4:**275, 286
War of 1812 5:97, 219, 274
Warren (Michigan) **5:**278
Warsaw (capital, Poland) **4:**213, 215–16, 221, 222
illus. **4:**217
Warsaw Ghetto rising monument **4:**221
Warsaw Ghetto rising (1943) **4:**221

Warsaw Treaty Organization (Warsaw Pact) (1955) **3:**62; **4:**323
Czechoslovakia, 1968 invasion of **3:**63; **4:**230, 235
Wars of the Roses *see* Roses, Wars of the
Warwick (Rhode Island) **5:**194
Wasatch Range (Utah) **5:**323, 324
Wasco (Indians of North America) **5:**339
Wash, The (bay, England) **3:**82
WASHINGTON 5:50, 52, **336–38**
illus.
Olympic National Park **5:**336
map(s) **5:**337
Washington, D.C. (capital, U.S.) **5:**170, 199
megalopolis area **5:**46
metropolitan-area population **5:**200
Organization of American States headquarters **6:**110
illus. **5:**159
Washington, George (1st president of U.S.) **5:**201, 226
L'Enfant to design Washington, D.C. **5:**170
New Jersey campaigns **5:**210
illus. **5:**169
Washington, Lake (Washington) **5:**338
Washington, Mount (New Hampshire) **5:**184; **6:**345
Washoe (Indians of North America) **5:**164, 331, 332, 344
Wasmosy, Juan Carlos (president of Paraguay) **6:**250
Watchmaking 3:287–88, 295
Watchung Mountains (New Jersey) **5:**208
Water
Arizona's supply **5:**329
Australian supply **2:**483, 490–91
Continental Divide determines flow direction **5:**310
Dutch supply **3:**229
eastern United States' freshwater **5:**208
Egyptian villages **1:**104–5
Hong Kong water piped from mainland **2:**410
Lesotho Highlands Water Project **1:**392
Nauru's supply imported as ballast in ships **2:**558
Rocky Mountains: water rights **5:**38
Sahara's underground channels **1:**25
Saudi Arabia **2:**129
Virgin Islands import drinking water **5:**172
Wales supplies English cities **3:**124
Western Samoa's supply **2:**608
illus.
Ethiopian supply from irrigation **1:**287
water storage in India **2:**201
Water buffalo 1:103; **2:**276
Waterfalls
Angel Falls **6:**134
Congo River **1:**42
Cumberland Falls **5:**260
Iceland **4:**3
Iguaçú Falls **6:**280
Middle Atlantic States **5:**199
Niagara Falls **5:**105, 109, 202, 205, 270
Nile River **1:**39
Passaic River's Great Falls **5:**208
Rhine River **3:**244–45
Scotland **3:**132
Sutherland Falls **2:**539
Victoria Falls **1:**276
Yangtze River **2:**369

Waterfalls (cont.)
Yosemite Falls **5:**342
illus.
Angel Falls **6:**134
Bridal Veil Falls (Australia) **2:**509
Chilean Andes **6:**303
England **3:**98
Iguaçú Falls **6:**281
Kivu Falls **1:**261
Niagara Falls **5:**205
Sutherland Falls **2:**537
Victoria Falls **1:**48, 356
Waterford (Ireland) **3:**74, 75
Waterloo (Iowa) **5:**294
Waterloo, Battle of (1815) **3:**58
Duke of Wellington quotation **3:**104
France, history of **3:**185
illus.
memorial **3:**218
Watling Island *see* San Salvador
Wat Phra Keo (Temple of the Emerald Buddha) (Bangkok, Thailand) **2:**275
illus. **2:**279
Watson Lake (Yukon Territory) **5:**147
Watt, James (Scottish inventor) **3:**106, 141
Watts (district, Los Angeles, California) **5:**345
Watusi (Watutsi) (people) *see* Tutsi
Waukesha (Wisconsin) **5:**286
Wawel, castle of (Cracow, Poland) **4:**216
Wayana (Indians of South America) **6:**158
Wea (Indians of North America) **5:**280
Weaving 6:303
illus. **5:**328; **6:**245
Webi Shebeli (river, east Africa) **1:**283, 301
Weddell, James (Scottish navigator) **6:**332
Weddell Sea (Antarctica) **6:**332
Weddell seals 6:328
Weill, Kurt (German composer) **3:**280
Weimar (Germany) **3:**269
Weimar Republic (1919–1933) **3:**275–76
Wei River (China) **2:**371
Weiss, Peter (German dramatist) **3:**251
Welfare *see* Social welfare
Welkom (South Africa) **1:**402
Welland River (England) **3:**83
Wellesley, Arthur *see* Wellington, 1st duke of
Wellington (capital, New Zealand) **2:**546–48, 553
illus.
"Beehive" Parliament Building" **2:**546
Wellington, 1st duke of (Arthur Wellesley) (English general) **4:**116
Waterloo, Battle of **3:**104, 185
Wellington, Mount (Australia) **2:**530
Welsh (people)
Argentina **6:**271, 279, 282
United Kingdom **3:**86
Welsh Anglican Church 3:130
Welsh language (Cymraeg) 3:20, 87, 124, 125, 126, 130
illus.
signs in Welsh and English **3:**127
Wenceslaus, Saint 4:229
Weser River (Germany) **3:**243
West Africa 1:11, 50–58 *see also* names of countries
West Bank (Jordan River) **1:**123; **2:**105, 114–15, 116, 119, 121
Jordan's claim **2:**117, 120
Palestinian self-rule **2:**32, 55
illus. **2:**44
wall constructed by Israel **2:**33

West Bengal (state, India) **2:**205–6
West Berlin (Germany) *see* Berlin
West Country (England) **3:**100
WESTERN AUSTRALIA (state, Australia) **2:**490, 492, 493, **524–27**
illus.
Bungle Bungle Mountains **2:**524
friendly dolphins in Shark Bay **2:**525
Nambung National Park **2:**527
map(s) **2:**525
Western Cape Province (South Africa) **1:**395, 397
Western Cordillera (mountains, North America) **5:**7, 69
British Columbia **5:**128, 129
Canada's Far North **5:**135, 141, 145
Prairie Provinces **5:**111, 123
Western Ghats *see* Ghats, Eastern and Western
Western Highlands (Florida) **5:**237
Western New Guinea *see* Irian Jaya
Western Plateau (region, Australia) **2:**482–83
Western Provinces (Canada) *see* Prairie Provinces
WESTERN SAHARA 1:24, 55, 74, **132–33**
Spain **4:**86
map(s) **1:**132
Western Samoa *see* Samoa
Western Shield (Great Plateau) (Australia) **2:**521, 524
Western (Wailing) Wall (Jerusalem) **2:**46
West Falkland Island 6:286
West Germany (1949–1990) *see* Germany, Federal Republic of
West Indies (Caribbean islands) **5:**426–40 *see also* names of islands
West Indies, Federation of the 5:477, 486
West Indies Associated States *see* Organization of Eastern Caribbean States
West Irian (Indonesia) *see* Irian Jaya
Westland (region, Netherlands) **3:**231
Westman Islands (south of Iceland) **4:**2
Westminster Abbey (London)
illus. **3:**102
West Pakistan *see* Pakistan
Westphalia (historic region, Germany) **3:**250
Westphalia, Peace of (1648) **3:**236, 273
West Point (New York)
illus.
United States Military Academy **5:**206
West River (China) *see* Xijiang
West Side (area of Chicago, Illinois) **5:**283
West Timor (province, Indonesia) **2:**327
West Valley City (Utah) **5:**324
WEST VIRGINIA 5:226, **258–59**
illus. **5:**258
map(s) **5:**259
Westward movement (U.S. history) **5:**174, 295, 296, 302, 310
Appalachian Mountains, boundary to **5:**156, 199
Cumberland Gap **5:**257
Great Lakes transportation route **5:**270
Manifest Destiny **5:**169
Oklahoma **5:**306–7
West Yorkshire County (England) **3:**109
Weta (insects) **2:**542
Wetlands *see* Bogs; Marshes; Swamps
Wexford (Ireland) **3:**74
Whales, Bay of (Antarctic) **6:**332
Whale-watching tours 5:79
Whaling 4:28; **5:**62, 136; **6:**328, 334

Wheat
Argentina **6:**96, 294–95
Kansas **5:**304
Saskatchewan **5:**118, 121
United States **5:**298
illus. **5:**67; **6:**296
map(s)
world production **6:**355
Whirling dervishes
illus. **2:**59
White Armies (Russian Civil War) **4:**322
White Cliffs of Dover (England) **3:**83
illus. **3:**81
White Highlands (Kenya) **1:**39, 310
Whitehorse (capital, Yukon Territory) **5:**147, 148
White Island (New Hampshire) **5:**184
White Mountain, Battle of the (1620) **3:**322; **4:**229
White Mountain National Forest (New Hampshire) **5:**184
White Mountains (Arizona) **5:**327
White Mountains (Maine–New Hampshire) **5:**156, 180, 182, 184, 185
White Nile (river, Africa) **1:**38, 125
Victoria, Lake, source in Uganda **1:**316, 317
White Russians *see* Belorussians
White Sands National Monument (New Mexico)
illus. **5:**15
White South Africans 1:399–400, 401 *see also* Afrikaners
White Volta River *see* Volta River
Whitney, Eli (American inventor) **5:**196
Whitney, Mount (California) **5:**8, 156, 341, 342
Whooping crane (bird) **5:**252
Whyalla (South Australia, Australia) **2:**523
Whymper, Edward (English mountaineer) **3:**304
Wichita (Indians of North America) **5:**303
Wichita (Kansas) **5:**304
Wicklow (Ireland)
illus. **3:**75
Wicomico (Indians of North America) **5:**218
Wied, Wilhelm zu (German prince, king of Albania) **4:**272
Wienerwald *see* Vienna Woods
Wiesbaden (Germany) **3:**245
Wiesel, Elie (Romanian-American writer) **4:**252
Wight, Isle of (England) **3:**81, 100
Wigner, Eugene P. (Hungarian-American scientist) **4:**241
Wijdenbosh, Jules (president of Suriname) **6:**159
Wijetunge, Dingiri Banda (president of Sri Lanka) **2:**250
Wilde, Oscar (Irish author) **3:**105
Wilderness Road (American pioneer trail) **5:**224, 257
Wildlife *see* Animal life; Game reserves and parks
Wild West (U.S. history) **5:**308, 315, 316
Wilhelm I (emperor of Germany) *see* William I (emperor of Germany)
Wilhelm II (emperor of Germany) *see* William II (emperor of Germany)
Wilhelmina (queen of the Netherlands) **3:**237
Wilkes, Charles (American naval officer) **6:**332
Willamette River and Valley (Oregon) **5:**50–51, 157, 334, 339, 340
Willapa Hills (Washington) **5:**336
William (English prince)
illus. **3:**107, 118

William I (king of England) *see* William the Conqueror
William III (king of England) **3:**120, 141
Boyne, Battle of the (1690) **3:**76, 148
William I (emperor of Germany) **3:**275
illus. **3:**277
William II (emperor of Germany) **3:**275
William I (king of the Netherlands) **3:**223, 236
William II (king of the Netherlands) **3:**236
William I (prince of Orange; William the Silent; William of Orange) (founder of the Dutch republic) **3:**236
William and Mary (of England) *see* Mary II (queen of England); William III (king of England)
William of Orange *see* William I (prince of Orange)
Williams, Alberto (Argentine composer) **6:**276
Williams, Roger (American founder of Rhode Island) **5:**193, 194
William the Conqueror (William I) (king of England) **3:**54, 116, 117
France, history of **3:**182
Wales, history of **3:**129
William the Silent *see* William I (prince of Orange)
Willoughby, Francis (English colonist) **6:**154
Wilmington (Delaware) **5:**216
Wilson, Edward (British explorer) **6:**328
Wilson, J. Tuzo (Canadian geophysicist) **6:**333
Wimbledon tennis tournament
illus. **3:**107
Windhoek (capital, Namibia) **1:**348
illus. **1:**349
Wind River Canyon (Wyoming) **5:**316
Winds
Africa's *harmattan* **1:**172, 190, 196, 217
Alberta's chinook **5:**124, 125
Antarctica **6:**325
Croatia's *maestral* **4:**285
Egypt's *khamsin* **1:**114
France's *mistral* **3:**151
Italy's *sciròcco* **4:**134
Libya's *ghibli* **1:**97
New Zealand **2:**540
Oklahoma **5:**305, 307
Sudan's sandstorms **1:**124
Tasmania's "Roaring Forties" **2:**529
tornadoes **5:**291
Wyoming, the windiest state **5:**316
table(s)
strongest surface wind **6:**345
Windsor (Ontario) **5:**41, 107–8, 277
Windsor, House of **6:**361
Windsor Castle (England)
illus. **3:**43
Windsurfing
illus. **3:**251
Windward Islands (Caribbean Sea) **5:**426, 433, 481–82, 487, 489
Windward Passage (Caribbean Sea) **5:**441
Windy City (nickname for Chicago, Illinois) **5:**283
Wine
Aguascalientes **5:**404
Argentina **6:**280, 293
Australia **2:**491
California **5:**346
Chile **6:**309
Coahuila **5:**394
France **3:**156, 182

Georgia (republic) **2:**84
Germany **3:**262
Hungary **4:**244
Liechtenstein **3:**306–7
Moldova **4:**346
Portugal's port **4:**66–67
South Australia **2:**522, 523
illus.
Argentine vineyards **6:**282
Australian winery **2:**490
California wine country **5:**346
Chile **6:**304
French vineyard **3:**34
German vineyards **3:**262
Hungarian vineyards **4:**244
Italian vineyards **4:**150
New Zealand vineyard **2:**549
Portuguese vineyards **4:**65
South Australian vineyard **2:**522
Spanish sherry **4:**109
Wineland (Viking settlement in North America) *see* Vinland
Winnebago (Indians of North America) **5:**286
Winnipeg (capital, Manitoba) **5:**42, 112, 113, 116, 117
climate **5:**111, 115
illus. **5:**114
birthplace of Louis Riel **5:**112
Winnipeg, Lake (Canada) **5:**12
table(s)
largest lakes **6:**347
Winnipesaukee, Lake (New Hampshire) **5:**184
Winooski River (Vermont) **5:**187
Winter Carnival (festival, St. Paul, Minnesota)
illus. **5:**289
Winter Palace (St. Petersburg, Russia) **4:**330
Winterthur (Switzerland) **3:**295
WISCONSIN 5:284–86
map(s) **5:**285
Wisconsin River (Wisconsin) **5:**284
Witbank (South Africa) **1:**402
Witch doctors 5:435, 475
illus. **1:**13
Witwatersrand (Rand) (region, South Africa) **1:**395, 398, 400, 402
Władysław (king of Poland) **4:**304
Wobogo (king of Burkina Faso) **1:**192
Wojtyła, Karol *see* John Paul II
Wolfville (Nova Scotia, Canada) **5:**78
Wollongong (New South Wales, Australia) **2:**512
Wolof (African people) **1:**154, 155, 158, 160, 161–62
Wombats 2:505
illus. **2:**517
Women in society
Afghanistan **2:**177
Algeria **1:**79
Arab Muslim world **2:**45
Asia **2:**38–39
Asia, South **2:**171
Australia **2:**491, 492, 501
Bahrain **2:**141
Bangladesh **2:**240
Belgium suffrage **3:**224
Belize **6:**21
Bhutan **2:**236
Brazil **6:**163–64, 166
Canada suffrage **5:**117, 126
Chile **6:**308
China **2:**392–93, 395

Cyprus **2:**69–70
Europe **3:**25–26
Germany **3:**249
India **2:**213, 215, 221
Indonesia **2:**319
Iran **2:**158–59, 163
Iraq **2:**150–51
Japan **2:**450–51, 453–54, 456, 469
Japan's "education mamas" **2:**456–57
Korea, South **2:**436
Latin America **6:**109
Liechtenstein suffrage **3:**307
Melanesia **2:**585
Mexico **5:**369–70, 388
Montana voters **5:**312
Morocco **1:**68, 70
Myanmar **2:**269
New Zealand suffrage **2:**554
Nigeria **1:**220
Pakistan **2:**186, 192–93
Portugal suffrage **4:**77
Saudi Arabia **2:**125
Spain **4:**94–95
Sweden **4:**42
Switzerland suffrage **3:**298
Syria **2:**93
Tunisia **1:**88
Turkey: reforms of Kemal Atatürk **2:**66
United Arab Emirates **2:**138–39
United Kingdom **3:**90, 93
Uruguay **6:**252
U.S. struggle for equal rights **5:**175, 176
Wyoming **5:**315, 317
Yemen **2:**134
illus.
Algeria **1:**79
Asian universities **2:**39
Muslim women **1:**12; **2:**191
U.S. women march in capital **5:**173
Wonsan (North Korea) **2:**431
Woodland Indians 5:23–24 *see also* Algonquian; Dakota Sioux; Iroquois
Woodlark Island (Papua New Guinea) **2:**587
Woodroffe, Mount (Australia) **2:**483, 521
Wool 2:491, 500; **6:**87–88
Woolly daisies
illus. **5:**343
Worcester (Massachusetts) **5:**190
Worcester Music Festival 5:190
Work *see* Employment
World Court *see* International Court of Justice
World Financial Center (Shanghai, China) **2:**403
World Trade Center (New York City) **5:**203
World War I (1914–1918)
ANZAC troops **2:**554
Armenian massacres **2:**78
assassination of Franz Ferdinand **3:**317; **4:**280, 289
Australia **2:**501–2
Austria **3:**324–25
Belarus **4:**343
Belgium **3:**223–24
Brazil **6:**190
Egypt **1:**122
Europe **3:**19, 60
France **3:**187
Germany **3:**275
Greece **4:**207–8
Hungary **4:**246
Italy **4:**129, 160

World War II (cont.)
Japan **2:**446
Latvia **4:**300
Lithuania **4:**303
Ottoman Empire **2:**95
Poland **4:**220
Russian Revolution and Civil War **4:**321–22
Turkey **2:**65
United Kingdom **3:**93
illus. **5:**171
World War II (1939–1945)
Alaska **5:**350
Asia, East **2:**375
Asia, Southeast **2:**255, 264, 280
Australia **2:**502
Austria **3:**325
Belarus **4:**343
Belgium **3:**224
Brazil **6:**190
cargo cults **2:**595–96
Casablanca Conference (1943) **1:**74
Czechoslovakia and Sudetenland **4:**230
Denmark **4:**21–22
Egypt **1:**122
England: London, bombing of **3:**110
Europe **3:**19, 61
Finland **4:**58
France **3:**188
France: Paris and von Choltitz **3:**192–93
Germany **3:**277
Germany: Berlin **3:**280
Germany: Dresden **3:**268
Germany: Munich **3:**271
Germany: Nuremberg **3:**272
Greece **4:**209
Greenland: U.S. military bases **5:**11
Guam **2:**569
Hawaii **5:**354
Holocaust *see* Holocaust
Hungary **4:**246
Iceland **4:**6
Indonesia **2:**325
Italy **4:**161, 162
Japan **2:**439, 447
Japan: Koreans brought in as workers **2:**443
Japanese-Americans interned in California **5:**347
Korea, partition of **2:**438
Latvia **4:**300
Libya **1:**100
Lithuania **4:**303
Malta **4:**184
Marshall Islands **2:**575
Micronesia **2:**570
Nauru **2:**579
Netherlands **3:**233, 237
New Zealand **2:**554
Norway **4:**26
Oceania's strategic importance **2:**520, 558
Pearl Harbor **5:**353
Philippines **2:**340
Poland **4:**215, 220–22
Polynesia **2:**603
post-war economic recovery **5:**176
Romania **4:**254, 256
San Marino **4:**175
Solomon Islands **2:**592
Swedish neutrality **4:**49–50
Switzerland accused of arms sales **3:**298
Tuvalu **2:**612
Ukraine **4:**340
Ukraine: Uniate Church **4:**334
Union of Soviet Socialist Republics **4:**323, 331
United Kingdom **3:**94
Yugoslavia **4:**280
illus.
memorial in Hiroshima (Japan) **2:**448
U.S. forces **5:**171
war wreckage on Marshall Islands **2:**575
Worms, Diet of (1521) **3:**322
Worth, Charles Frederick (French couturier) **3:**196
Wounded Knee (South Dakota) **5:**299, 300
Wouri River (west Africa) **1:**234
Wren, Sir Christopher (English architect) **3:**110
Wrestling 2:463
illus. **2:**60, 463
Writing
Arabic scripts **1:**109
Armenian alphabet **2:**76
Asian languages **2:**372
Chinese system **2:**16, 402, 420
Cyrillic alphabet **4:**265
Georgian alphabet **2:**81
Hittites **2:**56
Incas used knotted strings **6:**223
Inuktitut language **5:**139
Japanese systems **2:**17, 443, 460–61
Khalkha Mongolian script **2:**365
Korean *hangul* alphabet **2:**437
Moldovan language **4:**345
Mongolian script **2:**364
Phoenician alphabet **2:**49, 94
Sumerian letter to enemy **2:**41
Sumerians developed **2:**11–12, 48, 152–53
Teotihuacán's hieroglyphics **5:**413
Thailand **2:**275
Turkish adopted Roman alphabet **2:**67
Vietnamese **2:**296
illus.
cuneiform **2:**12
Wrocław (Poland) **4:**221
Wuhan (China) **2:**369
Wuro (Bobo god) **1:**191
Wu Tai *see* Five Dynasties
Wyandot (Indians of North America) **5:**274
Wyandotte Cave (Indiana) **5:**279
Wye River (United Kingdom) **3:**122
Wye Valley (Wales) **3:**122
WYOMING 5:315–17
woman suffrage **5:**176
illus.
Grand Teton National Park **5:**315
Yellowstone National Park **5:**317
map(s) **5:**316

• • • X • • •

Xavier, Saint Francis (Spanish missionary) **4:**97
Xhosa (African people) **1:**398, 403, 404
Xia dynasty (China) **2:**420
Xian (Changan) (China) **2:**420
Xijiang (West River) (China) **2:**378
Xingu River (Brazil) **6:**168
Xinjiang-Uygur Autonomous Region (China) **2:**370, 378, 380–81, 385
Xizang (Tibet) **2:**378
Asia, landforms of **2:**10
China, autonomous region of **2:**421
climate **2:**370
Himalayas **2:**166–67
Lamaism **2:**169, 386–87
population **2:**383, 385
Yangtze River source **2:**368
Xochimilco, Lake (Mexico City) **5:**411
Xochitécatl (archaeologic site, Mexico) **5:**415
Xunantunich (Belize) **6:**14

• • • Y • • •

Yacine, Kateb (Algerian writer) **1:**80
Yaguarón (Paraguay) **6:**249
Yahya Khan, Agha Mohammed (Pakistani political leader) **2:**193–94
Yak (animal) **2:**167
Yakima (Indians of North America) **5:**337, 340
Yakoma (African people) **1:**247
Yakut (people) **5:**60
Yalla, Kumba (president of Guinea-Bissau) **1:**165
Yalta (Ukraine) **4:**337
illus. **4:**339
Yalta Conference (February 1945) **4:**337
Yalung River (China) **2:**368
Yalunka (African people) **1:**173, 174
Yalu River (Asia) **2:**429–30
Yamato Court (imperial line of Japan) **2:**443
Yamoussoukro (capital, Ivory Coast) **1:**185
Yanbu (Saudi Arabia) **2:**125
Yáñez, Agustín (Mexican author) **5:**373–74
Yangon (Rangoon) (Myanmar) **2:**262, 264, 270, 272
illus. **2:**265, 271
Yangon River (Myanmar) **2:**270
Yangtze Bridge (Wuhan, China) **2:**369
Yangtze River (Chang Jiang) (China) **2:**368–69, 378, 383, 401
Grand Canal **2:**371
map(s) **2:**368
table(s)
longest rivers of the world **6:**346
Yankees (nickname for New Englanders) **5:**178, 180, 186
Yankunytjatjara (aboriginal tribe, Australia) **2:**522
Yanomamo (Indians of South America) **6:**140
illus. **6:**140
Yaoundé (capital, Cameroon) **1:**230, 234
illus. **1:**232
Yap (state, Federated States of Micronesia) **2:**569, 570, 573
Yaqui Indians 5:392
Yarkon River (Israel) **2:**105
Yaroslav the Wise (ruler, Kievan Rus) **4:**339
Yarra River (Australia) **2:**519
Yasin, Abdallah ibn- (Muslim leader) **1:**139
Yatenga (early African kingdom) **1:**192
Yaviza (Panama) **6:**73
Ybbs-Persenbeug Dam (Danube River) **3:**326
Yeats, William Butler (Irish poet and dramatist) **3:**70
Yellow fever 6:78, 79
Yellowhead Pass (Alberta–British Columbia) **5:**8
Yellowknife (Northwest Territories, Canada) **5:**53, 64, 142, 143, 144
illus. **5:**144
Yellowknife Bay (Northwest Territories, Canada) **5:**144

Yellow River (Huang He; Hwang Ho) (China) **2:**1, 370–71, 378
  Yellow River civilization **2:**14–16
  map(s) **2:**370
  table(s)
    longest rivers of the world **6:**346
Yellow River civilization (Asia) **2:**14–16
Yellow Sea (Pacific Ocean) **2:**370
Yellowstone Lake (Wyoming) **5:**317
Yellowstone National Park (Wyoming–Montana–Idaho) **5:**311, 316, 317
  Rocky Mountains **5:**38, 39
  illus. **5:**317
Yellowstone River (Wyoming–Montana) **5:**8, 317
Yeltsin, Boris (president of Russia) **4:**318, 324, 325
  illus. **4:**325
YEMEN 2:130–35
  illus.
    Aden **2:**132
    flag **2:**vii
    khat plant **2:**133
    marketplace **2:**134
    Sana **2:**130
  map(s) **2:**131
Yeniçeri (Turkish soldiers) *see* Janissaries
Yenisei River (Russia) **4:**308; **5:**56
Yerba maté (beverage) **6:**95, 184, 246, 256, 274
Yerevan (Erivan) (capital, Armenia) **2:**47, 74, 76
  illus. **2:**74
Yevtushenko, Yevgeny (Soviet poet) **4:**314
Yialias River (Cyprus) **2:**69
Yibin (China) **2:**369
Yiddish language 3:20
Yi dynasty (Korea) **2:**433
Yi Sung-gy (Korean general) **2:**433
Yogyakarta (Indonesia) **2:**323
Yojoa (lake, Honduras) **6:**35
Yokohama (Japan) **2:**440
Yom Kippur (Day of Atonement) (Jewish religious holiday) **2:**108
Yom Kippur War (1973–1974) **2:**114
Yom River (Thailand) **2:**274
Yongle (emperor of China) **2:**421
Yoritomo, Minamoto (shogun) **2:**443–44
York, Cape (peninsula, Australia) **2:**504, 507
York, House of (English dynasty)
  rulers of England, list of **6:**360, 361
York Factory (trading post, Prairie Provinces, Canada) **5:**111, 117
York River (Virginia) **5:**223
Yorktown (Virginia) **5:**226
Yoruba (African people)
  Benin **1:**213, 214
  Nigeria **1:**58, 215, 217, 218, 219, 221, 223–24, 226
Yoruba language 1:213, 223
Yosemite Falls (California) **5:**342
Yosemite National Park (California) **5:**342
  illus. **5:**149
Yosemite Valley (California) **5:**342
  illus. **5:**341
Youlou, Fulbert (president of Congo) **1:**260
Young, Brigham (Mormon leader) **5:**324, 325
Young Drift Plains (North America) **5:**293
Young Pioneers (Communist organization)
  illus. **2:**399
Youngstown (Ohio) **5:**46, 273–74
Young Turks (reform movement in Turkey) **2:**65
Yüan dynasty (China) **2:**366, 394, 421
  illus. **2:**24

Yuan Shikai (Chinese military leader) **2:**396
YUCATÁN (state, Mexico) **5:421**
Yucatán Peninsula (Mexico) **5:**358, 422
  agriculture **5:**30
  Campeche **5:**420
  Cuba, proximity of **5:**442
  Mayan civilization **5:**25, 376
  North America, coastal plains of **5:**12
Yucca Mountain (Nevada) **5:**332
Yue language 2:372
YUGOSLAVIA (Serbia and Montenegro) 3:2, 9; **4:274–81**
  Albania, relations with **4:**273
  breakup of country **3:**64
  Danube River **3:**328
  Italy, history of **4:**160, 162
  NATO bombing **3:**95; **4:**163, 273, 292
  Sarajevo **3:**317
  Slovenia, history of **4:**284
  illus.
    Belgrade **4:**277
    flag **4:**vi
    Gulf of Kotor **4:**274
  map(s) **4:**276
Yukon Plateau (North America) **5:**7
Yukon River (North America) **5:**145, 334, 348
Yukon Sourdough Rendezvous 5:147
YUKON TERRITORY (Canada) **5:**42, 64, 136, **145–48**
  illus.
    Dawson City during the gold rush **5:**148
    St. Elias Mountains **5:**135
  map(s) **5:**146, 149
Yuma (Indians of North America) **5:**164, 344
Yunnan (province, China) **2:**368, 369
Yunque, El (mountain, Puerto Rico) **5:**166–67
Yuri Dolgorukii (prince of Suzdal) **4:**328
Yurts (Mongol tents) **2:**363

Zab Rivers (Great Zab and Little Zab) (Asia) **2:**50
Zacatecas (capital, Zacatecas state, Mexico) **5:**389, 399
ZACATECAS (state, Mexico) **5:**30–31, **399**
Zafy, Albert (president of Madagascar) **1:**377
Zaghawa (African people) **1:**244
Zaghlul Pasha, Saad (Egyptian leader) **1:**122
Zagreb (capital, Croatia) **4:**285, 286
Zagros (mountain system, Iran) **2:**156
Zahir, Mohammed *see* Mohammed Zahir Shah
Zaidi (sect of Islam) **2:**133
Zaïre *see* Congo, Democratic Republic of
Zaïre River (Africa) *see* Congo River
Zakynthos (Greek island) **4:**190
Zambezi River (Africa)
  Angola **1:**342
  Cabora Bassa Dam **1:**366
  Mozambique **1:**363, 364
  Namibia **1:**348
  Zambia **1:**44, 273, 275
  Zimbabwe **1:**355, 356
  table(s)
    longest rivers of the world **6:**346
ZAMBIA 1:44, **271–76**
  illus.
    farmer at well **1:**271
    flag **1:**xxiii

  Kariba Dam **1:**275
  loading copper ingots **1:**274
  Lusaka **1:**272
  Victoria Falls **1:**48
  map(s) **1:**273
Zamboanga (Philippines) **2:**336
Zamora (Michoacán, Mexico) **5:**409
Zanaga (Congo) **1:**259
Zante (Greek island) *see* Zakynthos
Zanzibar (island, Tanzania) **1:**40–41, 332, 336, 337
  government **1:**338
Zanzibar Town (Tanzania) **1:**334
  illus. **1:**336
Zapata, Emiliano (Mexican Indian leader) **5:**386, 387, 393, 412, 418
Zapatista National Liberation Army 5:418
  illus. **5:**387
Zapotec (Mexican Indian dialect) **5:**355
Zapotecas (Mexican people) **5:**375, 376, 417
  illus. **5:**368
  ancient sculpture **5:**375
Za Qu (Tibetan name for Mekong River) **2:**256
Zaragoza (Spain) **4:**111
Zarathustra *see* Zoroaster
Zaria (Nigeria) **1:**219
Zarzaïtine (oil field, Algeria) **1:**76
Zauditu (empress of Ethiopia) **1:**289
Zealand (Sjaelland) (island, Denmark) **4:**8, 17
Zebras
  illus. **1:**40
Zedillo Ponce de León, Ernesto (president of Mexico) **5:**386, 388
Zeebrugge (Belgium) **3:**221
Zeeland (province, Netherlands) **3:**228
Zempléni (mountains, Hungary) **4:**237
Zen Buddhism 2:420
Zengzhou (Ao) (China) **2:**420
Zerhoun (massif in Morocco) **1:**72
Zermatt (Switzerland) **3:**288
  illus. **3:**289
Zeroual, Lamine (president of Algeria) **1:**84
Zhao Ziyang (Chinese pol. leader) **2:**421
Zhelev, Zhelyu (president of Bulgaria) **4:**267
Zhengzhou (Chengchow) (China) **2:**370
Zhivkov, Todor (Bulgarian leader) **4:**266
Zhou (Chou) dynasty (China) **2:**15, 406, 420
Zhou Enlai (Chou En-lai) (Chinese political leader) **2:**412, 421
Zhuang (Chuang) (Asian people) **2:**385
Zhuangzi (Daoist teacher) **2:**420
Zhu Rongji (premier of China) **2:**421, 422
Zia, Begum Khalida (prime minister of Bangladesh) **2:**244
Zia ul-Haq, Mohammed (Pakistani political leader) **2:**193, 194
Ziaur Rahman (Zia) (president of Bangladesh) **2:**244
Ziel, Mount (Australia) **2:**483
Ziguinchor (Senegal) **1:**153
ZIMBABWE 1:49–50, **355–62**
  Congo, Democratic Republic of **1:**270
  Zimbabwe Ruins **1:**361
  illus.
    Christian congregation **1:**359
    flag **1:**xxiv
    Harare **1:**355, 357
    ruins of Monomotapa **1:**10
    soccer game **1:**360
    Victoria Falls **1:**48, 356
    young men **1:**49
  map(s) **1:**358

Zimbabwe Ruins (temple-fort complex) **1:**361

Zinder (Niger) **1:**145

Zinjanthropus (early human) **1:**336

Zionism (movement to regain a Jewish homeland) **2:**112–13

Zion National Park (Utah) **5:**323

illus. **5:**323

Živa (Slavic goddess of love and life) **4:**282

Žižka, Jan (Czech hero) **4:**229

Ziz River (Morocco) **1:**66

Zlín (Czech Republic) **4:**228

Zócalo (Plaza de la Constitución) (Mexico
City) **5:**411

Zog I (Ahmet Zogu) (Albanian king) **4:**272

Zola, Émile (French novelist) **3:**178, 187, 198,
199

Zomba (Malawi) **1:**278

Zonguldak (Turkey) **2:**63

Zorbing (sport) **2:**545

illus. **2:**545

Zorilla de San Martín, Juan (Uruguayan poet)
6:256

Zoroaster (Zarathustra) (founder of religion of
ancient Persia) **2:**176

Zoroastrianism (religion) **2:**157, 162, 209

Zoser (king of ancient Egypt) **1:**110

Zugspitze (mountain, Germany) **3:**242

illus. **3:**243

Zuider Zee (the Netherlands) **3:**228

Zulu (African people) **1:**388, 398

South Africa, history of **1:**404, 405

Swaziland **1:**386

illus. **1:**405

Zumbi (warrior-king of Palmares) **6:**188

Zurbarán, Francisco de (Spanish artist) **4:**115

Zurich (Switzerland) **3:**292–93, 295, 297

illus. **3:**292

Zurich, Lake (Switzerland) **3:**286, 292

Zwelithini, Goodwill (Zulu king) **1:**405

Zwinger (museum, Dresden, Germany) **3:**268

Zwingli, Ulrich (Swiss religious reformer) **3:**297